JavaScript

Annotated Archives

ABOUT THE AUTHORS

Jeff Frentzen is an online producer at ZDNet and author of *PC Week*'s column "Jeff's Internet Adventures."

Henry Sobotka is a veteran journalist and an expert multi-platform programmer in a variety of languages, including JavaScript, Java, HTML, and C/C++.

Dewayne McNair is a JavaScript programmer and consultant based in Texas.

JavaScript

Annotated Archives

Jeff Frentzen and Henry Sobotka
with additional material from Dewayne McNair

Osborne/**McGraw-Hill**

Berkeley   New York   St. Louis   San Francisco   Auckland   Bogotá
Hamburg   London   Madrid   Mexico City   Milan   Montreal   New Delhi
Panama City   Paris   São Paulo   Singapore   Sydney   Tokyo   Toronto

Osborne/**McGraw-Hill**
2600 Tenth Street
Berkeley, California 94710
U.S.A.

For information on translations or book distributors outside the U.S.A., or to arrange
bulk purchase discounts for sales promotions, premiums, or fund-raisers, please
contact Osborne/**McGraw-Hill** at the above address.

JavaScript Annotated Archives

1234567890 AGM AGM 901987654321098

ISBN 0-07-882364-1

Publisher	**Proofreader**
Brandon A. Nordin	Stefany Otis
Editor-in-Chief	**Indexer**
Scott Rogers	Valerie Robbins
Acquisitions Editor	**Computer Designer**
Wendy Rinaldi	Roberta Steele
Project Editors	**Illustrator**
Claire Splan and Madhu Prasher	Brian Wells
Editorial Assistant	**Series Design**
Ann Sellers	Roberta Steele and Peter Hancik
Copy Editor	**Cover Design**
Jan Jue	Regan Honda

To Speet

Contents at a Glance

PART 1
Web Page Enhancements

PART 2
Web Creation Utilities

PART 3
Appendixes

Contents

PART 2
Web Creation Utilities

PART 3
Appendixes

Acknowledgments

Thanks to Lila S. French, who co-authored the JavaScript tools section. It would have been good to have worked more closely. Also, thanks to Dewayne McNair for composing the chapter about server-side JavaScript. You really pulled this one out of the fire. Additional hiyas go to Wendy Rinaldi, Ann Sellers, Claire Splan, Lisa Lucas, Madhu Prasher, Roberta Steele, Stefany Otis, and other trusty people at Osborne McGraw-Hill who did their utmost to make this book read well. To Scott Rogers, for initiating the Annotated Archives series and trusting in us to write the first one. Others we must not forget: Elizabeth From, Derek and Christian Frentzen, Kurt Anderson, John Long, Angus Davis, Willie Meier, David Cossette, the helpful people on the Netscape JavaScript discussion forum, Jonathan Hawke, D. Mark Newman, and other valued script writers; Eric Lundquist, Sam Whitmore, and Eamonn Sullivan at *PC Week*.

Introduction

The hope of many professional and amateur World Wide Web developers is to quickly and inexpensively add interactive features to their pages. By virtue of its suitability for use on the web, the JavaScript programming language has eclipsed other popular Internet languages—such as Java, ActiveX, and even Common Gateway Interface (CGI)—in popularity. Next to basic Hypertext Markup Language (HTML), JavaScript is found on more web pages than any other scripting or programming language.

If you pulled this book from a shelf of JavaScript books that on the surface all look alike, you probably turned to this page to find out what makes this book different from the others. Here's a quick way to find out. Are you looking for:

◆ A basic introduction to the JavaScript scripting language?

◆ A massive collection of scripts that you can "plug into" your web pages?

◆ A complete JavaScript programmer's reference book?

If you answered no to any of those questions, this book might be just right for you.

Audience

This is not a book about authoring on the web or how to maintain web servers. This book is for intermediate or experienced programmers who are interested in understanding how to make JavaScript work on their web site.

You already understand how JavaScript is written, you will buy a true programmer's reference book with this one, and should you want hundreds of scripts to add to your web pages, you will know how to access the Internet and find them. (There is a brief listing of good web resources for JavaScript in Appendix B.)

The format for the book is simple. Each chapter covers a genre of JavaScript examples progressing from simple to more complex. For example, many people use JavaScript to create interactive menus on their web sites. They also use the language to create useful effects such as exploding windows, rotating graphical banners, and the like. Take a quick tour of our table of contents to get a sense of the JavaScript genres that we think are important and that are frequently used.

However, if you are a beginner, you may still get a lot out of this book. The reason? The JavaScript examples in this book are fully functional, and with very little modification, beginners can use them in their web pages quickly and easily. Moreover, the building blocks of the language—objects, methods, properties, statements, and so on—and their syntax are explained, but on the fly, meaning as they occur in our selection of scripts.

We did not set out to write all new JavaScript examples from scratch. After scouring the Internet and collecting some commonly used JavaScript examples, we show you how you can use them on your web pages. In addition, we show you how they work and how you can modify them to suit your needs.

Annotations

Within the context of these genres, we touch on programming style and good ways of using JavaScript, strictly from a programmer's point of view. We also touch on the use and value of the JavaScript examples and genres, taken from a webmaster or web designer's point of view. We do not, however, offer every script example we've come across or could write. And we believe that, after reading this book, you should have enough information to carry on and find your own JavaScript examples to work with or create from scratch.

This book will be useful for those who have a rudimentary understanding of JavaScript principles, and perhaps a bit of scripting experience. Although JavaScript has a reputation for being somehow object-oriented and esoteric, it really isn't much different than other interpreted scripting languages.

JavaScript Circa Late 1997

JavaScript shares a similar name with Java; the latter is a true object-oriented programming language that was developed by Sun Microsystems. JavaScript was created by Netscape Communications, makers of the Navigator web browser, currently the most popular web browser. Soon after Sun's announcement of Java, Netscape introduced JavaScript with the release of Navigator version 2.0, in 1995.

Netscape developed JavaScript under the name Mocha; when it first appeared in early versions of Navigator 2.0, it was called LiveScript. It was eventually renamed

JavaScript to piggyback on the media and computer industry attention that swelled around Java.

The two languages couldn't be more far apart. Java is an object-oriented programming (OOP) language similar to C++. It has strong typing (variable data types must be declared), static binding (object references must exist at compile time), and is compiled. In contrast, JavaScript is object-based with loose typing and dynamic binding. Moreover, it is interpreted by the client's browser, although the term "JavaScript compiler" is commonly used to refer to the browser's built-in mechanism that reads the code and either executes it or spits out error messages.

Netscape intended LiveScript/JavaScript to be an easy-to-use scripting language that anyone with a programmer's itch could write. Two years after JavaScript was introduced, it has become one of the most commonly used tools for web developers. JavaScript is used more frequently than Java, ActiveX, browser plug-ins, and other gizmos you might find attached to web documents.

For the most part, JavaScripts reside within the <SCRIPT>...</SCRIPT> tags in ordinary HTML documents. (If you don't know what an HTML document is, put this book down and get yourself a primer on the Internet and authoring for the World Wide Web.)

For those who want to go on, JavaScript offers web page authors and Internet and intranet programmers the ability to write scripts that will interact with objects within a web page, such as forms, frames, background color, and much more. One of its most useful applications is validating form input before it is submitted to a CGI script on the server.

If Java and JavaScript share one thing, it is that both JavaScript and web-based Java applications run within the client's browser. Some JavaScript is intended to run on a web server. We have included an example of this brand of JavaScript, which is called LiveWire.

At this time, Navigator and Microsoft's Internet Explorer offer the best support for JavaScript. Some JavaScript functions are not available in Internet Explorer. As companies, Microsoft and Netscape are mean-spirited competitors. Shortly after Netscape released JavaScript, Microsoft released a port called JScript. From the web user's perspective, this was an inconsiderate move. Since then, both companies have made conciliatory efforts to bring the two JavaScript types in line.

In mid-1997, Netscape upgraded JavaScript from the widely used version 1.1 to version 1.2. Version 1.2 introduced several new JavaScript components, many of which we cover in Chapter 2.

Unfortunately, version 1.2 only works in the latest Netscape web browser, Netscape Communicator. On the other hand, JavaScript 1.2 introduces several innovative features and functions, such as script-based animation and multi-window menus.

Currently, JavaScript 1.2 has proven less successful than the previous version. It has not quite caught on with the majority of JavaScript programmers because so many users continue to surf the Web with Netscape Navigator 3.0 or the Microsoft browser, which does not support JavaScript 1.2. However, it includes several improvements over 1.1, and new features that programmers will hopefully embrace over time. The trouble is, Communicator, the only web browser that supports these new features, has not caught on yet with the Internet user community.

If you have read through this brief introduction and still feel this book is for you, please consider buying it. We have taken pains to offer you what we believe to be the best JavaScript examples available, from which you can study to learn more about the scripting language, plug into your web pages, and modify to your heart's content.

What Is Here?

This book is organized by parts and chapters.

Part 1: Web Page Enhancements offers JavaScript examples that are typically added to web pages as pop-up windows, status bar messages, and other small enhancements that add functionality and even humor to a page.

Part 2: Web Creation Utilities covers HTML frames, menu systems, and server-side JavaScript. Dewayne McNair has contributed a server-side JavaScript application—a company phone book—that you may find very useful if you run a corporate intranet.

Appendix A provides a review of four currently available Javascript programming tools, namely Netscape's Visual Javascript, Borland's Intrabuilder, Acadia Software's Infuse, and Sausage Software's Hot Dog Professional.

Appendix B includes a guide to our favorite web sites devoted to JavaScript. Author Lila S. French contributed to the testing and writing of this appendix.

You can find this index on the CD-ROM, in the GUIDE folder.

Conventions Used in This Book

Until the Web is integrated with television or some other medium, its primary use for many users is as a research tool. People want to find information, and no matter how many multimedia doodads and how much fancy page formatting you add to your web pages, your readers still just want to find information.

All standard exposition and all script annotations are rendered in readable typeface and in the type style of this sentence.

The scripts are presented in the typeface used in the following example, so you can keep the various code fragments separate from the annotations and other information.

```
1   function qOver(imgname, n){
2     if ((navigator.userAgent.indexOf("Mozilla/3.0") != -1) ||
3         (navigator.userAgent.indexOf("Mozilla/4.0") != -1))
4     {
5         imgname.src = pic[n-1]+'u.gif'
```

You should also watch for the following special notes, tips, and cautions throughout the book:

PROGRAMMER'S NOTE   *Programmer's notes sit apart from the bulk of the text, and are intended to highlight something special about a script or programming action.*

PROGRAMMER'S TIP   *Programmer's tips point out facts to remember within the context of whatever scripting we are discussing.*

CAUTION   *Used sparingly, Cautions indicate that the nearby topic or JavaScript code comes with caveats or warnings for use.*

The CD-ROM

The CD-ROM that accompanies this book includes all of the JavaScript examples, which you can use, modify, or study to help you learn and understand the language.

To access the CD-ROM, make sure you have inserted it properly into your computer's CD-ROM caddy or carriage. Using a JavaScript-aware web browser, namely Netscape Navigator 3.*x* or 4.*x* or Microsoft Internet Explorer 3.*x* or 4.*x*, locate the CD-ROM drive using the Open File command.

Locate the HOME.HTM file in the CD-ROM's root directory. This file contains an index of the JavaScript examples on the disc, arranged according to their location in the printed book. For example, to find all of the JavaScript examples in Chapter 2, locate the folder called CHAP2 on the CD-ROM. To find the script examples in Chapter 3, locate the CHAP3 folder, and so on.

To guarantee maximum platform compatibility, we have used DOS 8.3 filename conventions on the CD-ROM. This will make the disc's file and folder names accessible to those with Windows 3.1 and (if there are any of you out there) DOS web browsers.

Web Page Enhancements

External Windows
Alerts, Prompts, and Confirms
Status Bar Enhancements

Banners and Tickers
Cookies
Search Engines

External Windows

One of the most popular and easiest web page enhancements to produce is the external JavaScript window. The window object represents a web browser window or a frame that exists on the client's machine. It can be used to control the screen "real estate" for your web documents. An external window makes use of properties in the window object to launch one or more instances of the browser.

For user interface developers, the pop-up window has many uses, including overlapping "slide show" pages, remote windows that help users navigate through a web site, and even alerts that warn or confirm that some action has been initiated or completed. Keep in mind, though, that the external window object opens a complete instance of the web browser; it does not open small alert dialog boxes (see Chapter 2 for more about alerts).

External windows can be designed to appear when the user first loads a web page, during a mouse-over event, or after a button is clicked. You can launch multiple windows from the same web page, although it is very easy to overdo this effect. Most web designers want to keep the number of external windows open at one time to a minimum.

Here is an example of basic external window syntax:

```
msgWindow=window.open("test.html",
                      "NameofWindow",
                      "width=350,
                       height=400,
                       resizable=no,
                       menubar=no,
                       toolbar=no,
                       directories=no,
                       location=no,
                       scrollbars=yes,
                       status=no")
```

The **window.open** method looks up an existing window or opens a new window. In this case, you want a 350×400-pixel window to open on top of the existing browser window. It is another instance of the browser, with properties that include a name (**NameofWindow**) and scroll bars, but no menu bar, toolbar, directory buttons, or status bar.

Notice that **window.open( )** is the command to open a new window. Within the "( )" are the three arguments that define the content and look of the window.

The first two arguments are:

◆ **test.html**   The name of the actual HTML file that displays in the external window.

◆ **NameofWindow**   Any unique name you choose.

The third argument specifies the features of the new window:

◆ **width** and **height**   Given in pixels.

◆ **resizable**   Will you allow the user to manually resize your window?

◆ **toolbar**   Do you want the browser toolbar to be visible?

◆ **menubar**, **directories**, **location**, and **status**   Navigational features of the browser are either visible or not available.

◆ **scrollbars**   You can designate yes or no.

As the default value of all these options is no, you can keep your code simple by only including those set to yes.

With Internet Explorer, **directories** and **location** are not separate options, but rather function as a unit with **toolbar**. They appear automatically when you set **toolbar** to yes, even if you specify no for **directories** and **location**. Set them to yes and opt for no toolbar, and you won't see any of the three. Also, scroll bars appear immediately in a new Explorer window if you specify yes; with Navigator they only show up if the content of the window exceeds its size.

Notice there are no spaces between options in the third argument listing the features. This is an *extremely* important detail, because a single space is all it takes to keep any options after the blank from taking effect when the window is created. As an alternative to specifying yes and no, you can use "1" for yes and "0" for no. For example, the preceding script snippet could be rendered as

```
msgWindow=window.open("test.html",
                      "NameofWindow",
                      "width=350,
                       height=400,
                       resizable=0,
                       menubar=0,
                       toolbar=0,
                       directories=0,
                       location=0,
                       scrollbars=1,
                       status=0")
```

A third and simpler (but less commonly seen) method is just to list the features you want. This automatically gives them a default value of yes or 1. For example, writing

```
msgWindow=window.open("test.html", "NameofWindow",
            "width=350,height=400,resizable,menubar,status")
```

creates a resizable 350×400-pixel window with a menu bar and status bar.

Opening a new window from JavaScript is a bit trickier than it looks. Security issues have dictated that the newly opened window contents (first document only) cannot be printed or saved to disk by the user. However, if a link to another location is provided in that new window, a subsequent download will permit saving and/or printing in the usual fashion.

You can control the window size and attributes to fit the desired application. However, closing the window (aside from doing so from a menu or close box) is still a bit buggy. If a new window has opened on your computer's display, clicking on it again will send the desired data to the end of the file display, but the window will not be brought to the front by that action. The user must select the Window menu at the top of the screen and manually bring the window to the front.

PROGRAMMER'S NOTE   *External window functions were not properly implemented in Netscape Navigator 2.0, but this was fixed in version 2.01.*

New in JavaScript 1.2 for Navigator 4.0

JavaScript 1.2 adds twelve new options to the list of properties you can specify when creating a window:

- ◆ innerWidth=[pixels]
- ◆ innerHeight=[pixels]
- ◆ outerWidth=[pixels]
- ◆ outerHeight=[pixels]
- ◆ screenX=[pixels]
- ◆ screenY=[pixels]
- ◆ alwaysRaised=[yes/no or 1/0] (**S**)
- ◆ alwaysLowered=[yes/no or 1/0] (**S**)
- ◆ z-lock=[yes/no or 1/0] (**S**)
- ◆ titlebar=[yes/no or 1/0] (**S**)
- ◆ hotkeys=[yes/no or 1/0]
- ◆ dependent=[yes/no or 1/0]

The four features marked with an "**S**" are secure features that can only be implemented in a signed script. The signed-script process is relatively complex and beyond the scope of this chapter. For complete information, go to **http://developer.netscape.com/library/documentation/communicator/jssec/index.htm**.

New in JavaScript 1.2 for Navigator 4.0 (continued)

Some of the other new features require signed scripts under certain circumstances which are indicated next.

The first two, **innerWidth** and **innerHeight**, replace **height** and **width**. They specify the dimensions of the document area, whereas **outerWidth** and **outerHeight** control the size of the entire browser window. Both inner and outer width and height settings resulting in a window smaller than 100×100 require a signed script.

If you assign values to both pairs of settings, those for **outerWidth** and **outerHeight** will prevail, regardless of whether they are larger or smaller than the specified height and width. There may seem to be no point in using both sets of options; however, if you skip the height and width settings, your new window will only be the right size for Netscape 4 users.

If you create a fully loaded window—with several or all the options such as **menubar**, **toolbar**, **directories**, **location**, **scrollbars**, and **status bar**—**outerWidth** and **outerHeight** will give you better control of its overall size. But should you decide you want a plain window with none of the extras, or just one or two of the narrower options (for example, **menubar**, **status bar**), you're probably better off just using the height and width settings to size the document area.

Next, **screenX** and **screenY** allow you to control exactly where your new window will appear, in terms of distance in pixels from the window's top-left corner to the top-left corner of the screen. If you do not assign any values to **screenX** and **screenY**, the default location of your new window will be 0,0—the top-left corner of the screen. Similarly, if you only specify one, the other will be 0. To specify an offscreen position, a signed script is required.

When deciding on values for window size and location, you should always bear in mind that people use different screen resolutions. A 500×500-pixel window at

```
screenX=500,
screenY=200
```

will fit nicely into the lower-right corner of a monitor set at 1024×768, but run off the right edge of a 640×480 screen. Think small.

The **alwaysRaised, alwaysLowered** and **z-lock** properties control the "float" status of your window—if you specify yes or 1 for **alwaysRaised**, the new window will always appear in front or on top of the browser window; conversely, **alwaysLowered** when true keeps a window below or behind the browser window. With **z-lock** activated, as soon as a new window loses focus and disappears behind the browser, it remains locked there even if it regains focus. Again, these three features require signed scripts.

New in JavaScript 1.2 for Navigator 4.0 (continued)

The **titlebar** property allows you to create a window without a titlebar in a signed script. **hotkeys**, when set to true, disables most hotkeys (except for the security and quit keys) in a window without a menu bar. Finally, making **dependent** true results in a window that automatically closes with its parent window.

The following code, for example, shows the option settings for a dependent window with outer dimensions of 500×450 pixels that opens 150 pixels from the left and 100 pixels from the top of the screen:

```
("","windowName",
 "outerWidth=500,
 outerHeight=450,
 screenX=150,
 screenY=100,
 dependent=yes")
```

function

Window Function

N2   N2.01   N2.02+   N3   N4   E3   E4

This simple external window script opens a new instance of the browser when the user clicks on a button; in this case, the button is a standard HTML form button. Figure 1-1 shows the new external window opened above the parent browser window.

```
1  <SCRIPT LANGUAGE="JavaScript">
2   function newWin() {
3      msgWindow=window.open("js_pwin.htm","OpenWindow",
4                     "width=450,height=400,scrollbars=yes");
5   }
6  </SCRIPT>
7  <FORM>
8  <INPUT TYPE=BUTTON NAME="button2" VALUE="Box Score"
                                    ONCLICK="newWin()">
9  </FORM>
```

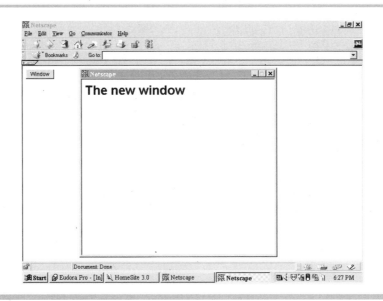

FIGURE 1-1. Window function output

ANNOTATIONS

1   `<SCRIPT LANGUAGE="JavaScript">`

Although a simple <SCRIPT> tag is all it takes to make JavaScript work with Netscape browsers, specifying the language is essential for ensuring that your script works with Microsoft's Internet Explorer. Otherwise, it'll just be ignored.

You can also specify the JavaScript version with the following tags:

```
<SCRIPT LANGUAGE='JavaScript1.1'>
<SCRIPT LANGUAGE='JavaScript1.2'>
```

Note that there is no blank space between the word "JavaScript" and the version number. If you put one in, the version number is ignored.

The main reason for specifying version number is to stave off the error messages that will inevitably appear when an older version of Netscape encounters a script that uses the features of a newer version of JavaScript. Netscape 2.x, for example, will simply ignore any script introduced with either of the preceding tags. Similarly, Netscape 3.x will skip over scripts whose language is defined as "JavaScript1.2," yet read those specified as "JavaScript1.1" or "JavaScript." In other words, a higher version browser can read all the lower versions of the language, but a lower version stops at its own level of JavaScript. Specifying the language version enables you to create scripts with different levels of functionality that kick in depending on what version of Netscape or Explorer your site visitor is using.

```
2   function newWin() {
3       msgWindow=window.open("js_pwin.htm","OpenWindow",
4                       "width=450,height=400,scrollbars=yes");
5   }
6   </SCRIPT>
```

This script uses a function named **newWin** to create a new window. A function in JavaScript must always be declared with the keyword **function**. Simply writing
`newWin() {... }`
provokes an error message saying that "newWin is not defined." The absence of the word "function" causes JavaScript to interpret it as a call to **newWin( )** rather than as the definition of the function.

The basic formula for creating a function in JavaScript is

```
function nameofFunction([optional argument1, arg2, arg3, etc.]){
                statement1           // what the function does
            [statement2; statement3
            statement4...]
}
```

The opening bracket for arguments does not necessarily have to be glued to the function's name. It is simply a matter of observing good programming style. Arguments are one or more comma-separated items passed to a function that does something to or with them. For example,

```
function addUp(a, b) {
                    c = a + b
                    return c
                }
```

would add whatever numbers you passed to it with calls such as
```
            addUp(3, 4)
            addUp(512, 364)
```
so that **c** would become 7 in the first case and 876 in the second. And because JavaScript has no data typing,
```
            addUp(523, 'amber')
```
would return "523amber" and
```
            addUp('rem', 'ember')
```

would produce "remember."

Arguments can be a number, string, object, or even another function. For example, you could create

```
function hodgePodge(number, string, someObject, doit)
```

and call it with

```
function hodgePodge(733, "gumbo", blackBox, mixup())
```

This assumes the object **blackBox** and function **mixup( )** are defined elsewhere in your script.

A function's arguments constitute an array indexed beginning at zero, so that in the preceding example, **number** is **hodgePodge.arguments[0]**, **string** is **hodgePodge.arguments[1]**, and so on, and **hodgePodge.arguments.length** is 4. This array is particularly useful for functions that take a variable number of arguments.

For a function that does not take any arguments, simply follow its name with a pair of empty parentheses as in

```
function noArgument()
```

The closing parenthesis for any argument is followed by a pair of curly braces containing the statements that define what your function does. Each statement must be on a separate line or, if you put more than one on a line, each must be separated by a semicolon. For instance, **addUp** could have been written as

```
c = a + b; return c
```

PROGRAMMER'S NOTE   *If you're a longtime C programmer accustomed to separating all statements with semicolons, you can calmly continue doing so in JavaScript. Aside from their use in multiple in-line statements, they are optional. Adding them is probably a good idea to avoid developing new habits that will produce compile-time errors in other languages.*

Also, if you write

```
function noArgument(void)
```

out of sheer habit, you'll get a "missing formal parameter" JavaScript error message. And if you instinctively define the type of data your function returns, as in

```
function int addUp(a, b)
```

the result will be a "missing function name" complaint.

Returning to our **newWin** function, it opens a new 450×400-pixel window into which it loads JS_PWIN.HTM. This new window has none of the browser's built-in navigational buttons or location entry field at the top, no status bar at the bottom, and cannot be resized by the user. It simply has the standard titlebar with a control-menu box at left and minimize/maximize buttons at right. To close this window, the user must either open the control-menu box and select <u>C</u>lose, or press ALT-F4.

The specified dimensions (450×400 pixels in this case) control the size of the *document area* of the window when it is first opened, and when it is restored after having been maximized to full screen. In other words, if you add the menu bar, navigational and directory buttons, location entry field, scroll bars, and status bar, the overall size of your window will be larger. Also, when specifying size, you have to assign values to both **width** and **height**. If you omit either dimension, the new window will simply default to the screen size of the user's browser.

The **scrollbars=yes** option gives our example window scroll bars, but they only appear when the content of the window exceeds its size; in other words, if all JS_PWIN.HTM contains is the word "Hi!", you won't see any scroll bars.

One way to become familiar with these options is to start out with a snippet of code such as

```
testWindow=window.open("test.html", "MyWindow",
    "toolbar=no,width=450,height=400,location=no,
     directories=no,status=no,scrollbars=no,resizable=no,
     menubar=no")
```

and then set the options to yes (or 1 if you prefer) one at a time and observe what happens. This can help you decide exactly what style of window you want to create.

A much easier way to explore the properties of a new window is to open the file WNDWOPTS.HTM on the accompanying CD. This script can be found in the CHAP1/SCRIPTS/WINOPTS directory. It not only allows you to see immediately what your new window will look like, but also generates the required code, which you can then cut and paste into your script or web page. The annotated script for this device can be found at the end of this chapter.

CAUTION   *Make sure that there are no blank spaces in the features argument. As a general rule, JavaScript is a relatively free-form language in terms of spacing, but this is one place where the requirements are strict. Put or leave a single blank space in the features argument, and all the options following it will be ignored.*

The **name** argument in **window.open( )** is not the name you use when referring to the new window in JavaScript, but rather the name for referring to it when using the <TARGET=...> attribute of an HTML tag, or the **target** property of a form or link. Do not confuse the two names!

Taking the preceding code as an example, writing

```
                    MyWindow.document.write("Hi!<BR>")
```

will produce a JavaScript error message saying "MyWindow is not defined." The correct way to do it is

```
                    testWindow.document.write("Hi!<BR>")
```

In selecting the dimensions for your window, bear in mind that there is no way of predicting what screen resolution the visitor to your site is using. A 450×400 window, for example, will fill most of a 640×480 screen, but look quite small in a 1280×1024 high-resolution setting.

Finally, in the body of this page, an HTML form displays a button that the user clicks on to load the new window. The sample code for this last touch is

```
7   <FORM>
8   <INPUT TYPE=BUTTON NAME="button2" VALUE="Box Score"
                                      ONCLICK="newWin()">
9   </FORM>
```

Simple Pop-up Window 1

simp1

N2 N2.01 N2.02+ N3 N4 E3 E4

```
1   <script>
2   <!--
3   var popup = null;
4     popup = window.open('', 'popupnav',
            'width=200,height=170,resizable=1,scrollbars=1');
6     if (popup != null) {
7       if (popup.opener == null) {
8         popup.opener = self;
9       }
10    popup.location.href = 'j20a.htm';
11    }
12  // -->
13  </script>
```

ANNOTATIONS

```
1   <script>
2   <!--
```

"<!--" is the opening HTML tag for a comment; the closing tag is "-->" several lines later. The purpose of enclosing the script in comment tags is simply to hide it from browsers incapable of executing JavaScript.

```
3   var popup = null;
```

Ignore this line for a moment. It is basically a setup for what comes later.

```
4   popup = window.open('', 'popupnav',
        'width=200,height=170,resizable=1,scrollbars=1');
```

This line creates a 200×170-pixel window. As the options indicate, it can be resized by the user and scroll bars will automatically appear if the new window's contents exceed its dimensions. Its name for JavaScript references is **popup**, and **popupnav** for HTML <TARGET=...> attributes or the **target** property of links and forms. Again, notice there are no spaces between options in the features argument.

This script is placed in the <HEAD> section of the HTML code, and the window pops open automatically when the page is loaded. Alternatively, the script could have been put between the <BODY> tags. The main advantage of putting it in the <HEAD> is to keep it separate from the page content in the <BODY>.

Another way to achieve the same effect is to make the window-creation a function:

```
function popOpen() {
    popup = window.open('', 'popupnav',
        'width=200,height=170,resizable=1,scrollbars=1');
}
```

which can then be called with

```
<SCRIPT>
popOpen()
</SCRIPT>
```

between the <BODY> tags, which forces it to execute when the page is loaded. Or you can simply add the line

```
popOpen()
```

below the function in the <HEAD> section. A third way is to use the **onLoad** event handler in the <BODY> tag as follows:

```
<BODY onLoad="popOpen()">
```

Again, the advantage of the latter method from a programming and page-maintenance standpoint is that it keeps your script separate from the body content. Otherwise, the main difference between the three techniques is essentially a matter of timing. For instance, putting the function call in the <HEAD> section results in immediate execution; placing it between the <BODY> tags calls it as the body content is being loaded (with the exact timing dependent on whether you place the script at the beginning, middle, or end of the <BODY> section); using **onLoad** pops open the window after the page has been loaded.

```
6     if (popup != null) {
7       if (popup.opener == null) {
8         popup.opener = self;
9       }
10      popup.location.href = 'j20a.htm';
11    }
```

This fragment of code, combined with the setup line

```
3   var popup = null;
```

is a little routine often found on web pages that contain a window-opening script. At first glance, it appears as a top contender in an Obfuscated JavaScript competition. However, it serves a useful purpose, defining the **opener** property (which is new with Netscape 3.0) as **self**, a built-in term that Netscape 2.x can understand.

Essentially, it's an error handler. The setup line assigns the built-in property **null** to **popup**. Next, **window.open( )**, creating the new window, is assigned to **popup**. Then the error handler kicks in with

```
if (popup != null)
```

which tests whether the new window has been opened. If it is open, the statement on line 10 takes effect and the document FILENAME.HTM is loaded into the pop-up window. Line 10 can be written without specifying the **href** property, that is,

```
popup.location = 'filename.htm'
```

because, unless specified otherwise, the location object defaults to its **href** property.

A second **if** statement within the first tests for the nonexistence of the **opener** property:

```
if (popup.opener == null)
```

If it does not exist, the **opener** property is created by the statement on line 8 and assigned **self**. This prevents Netscape 2.x users from getting a "Javascript error: opener not defined" message. The **opener** property is commonly used to refer to objects, functions, or variables defined on the new window's parent page. For example, if you had a function **mailForm( )** as a part of a script on the parent page, you could call it from the pop-up window with

```
opener.mailForm()
```

Similarly, you could assign a new value to a variable defined in the parent page with, for instance:

```
opener.x = 16
```

Or, assuming the parent page creates a vehicle object with a **wheels** property, you could alter its value with

```
opener.vehicle.wheels = 2
```

The **opener** property also lets you change the properties of the parent window if you want—for example:

```
opener.document.bgColor="red"
```

or

```
opener.document.write("Hi!"<BR>)
```

In brief, it gives the child window access to the content of its parent's scripts. If your script doesn't use your new window's **opener** property, you can safely omit this snippet. But if it does, including it ensures that your page is user friendly for all the people still surfing with older browsers. Check out Figure 1-2 for an illustration of the final external window created by this code.

```
12   // -->
13   </script>
```

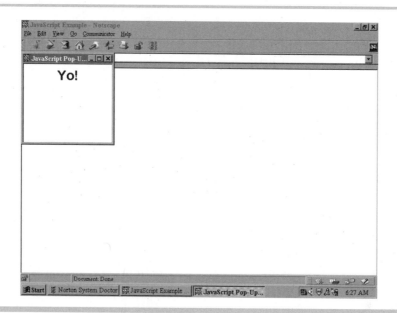

FIGURE 1-2. Simple pop-up window 1 output

Note the double forward slashes (//) in front of the comment-closing tag. This ensures that the script itself doesn't try to process the tag, but instead skips it as a comment.

JavaScript allows the two basic types of comments familiar to C++ and Java programmers:

```
//  Single-line with everything right of double slash ignored,
/* And block comments
enclosed by single slashes and asterisks */
```

You can vary both types as much as you want within a script:

```
/* and starting out with a block comment,
// then inserting a single one like this,
is perfectly acceptable, albeit redundant */

/* but if you have a block comment
/* and within it add a second one like this
you'll get a Javascript error message */
complaining about a nested comment. */
```

This error is most likely to occur when you decide to comment-out a block of script for debugging purposes, and forget to "uncomment" multiline comments within it.

Simple Pop-up Window 2

Simp2

N2 N2.01 N2.02+ N3 N4 E3 **E4**

```
1   <HTML>
2   <HEAD>
3   <TITLE></TITLE>
4
5   <SCRIPT LANGUAGE="JavaScript">
6
7   <!--Hide from JavaScript-Impaired Browsers
8   function WinOpen() {
9
10  msg=open("","DisplayWindow","HEIGHT=200,WIDTH=496,
                      status=yes,toolbar=yes,directories=no,
                               menubar=yes,location=yes");
11  msg.document.write("<HTML><TITLE>A New Window</TITLE>");
12  msg.document.write("<IMG SRC='hello.gif'><P><FORM>
                        <INPUT TYPE='BUTTON'VALUE='Close'" +
13              "onClick='self.close()'>"  +
14    "</FORM></BODY></HTML><P>")
15    }
16  // END HIDING CONTENTS -->
17  </SCRIPT>
18  </HEAD>
19  <BODY BGCOLOR="blue">
20  <P>
21  <FORM>
22  <INPUT TYPE="button" NAME="Button1"
                      VALUE="Click Here to Open New Window"
      onclick="WinOpen()">
23  </FORM>
24  <P>
25  </BODY>
26  </HTML>
```

ANNOTATIONS

```
1    <HTML>
2    <HEAD>
3    <TITLE></TITLE>
4
5    <SCRIPT LANGUAGE="JavaScript">
6
7    <!--Hide from JavaScript-Impaired Browsers
8    function WinOpen() {
9
10    msg=open("","DisplayWindow","HEIGHT=200,WIDTH=496,
                         status=yes,toolbar=yes,directories=no,
                                 menubar=yes,location=yes");
```

The **WinOpen** function first creates a 150×496-pixel window named
DisplayWindow with the standard browser status bar, toolbar, menu bar, and
location field, but without the directories buttons (that is, the "What's New," "What's
Cool" icons in the case of Netscape Navigator). Adding all these options makes the
new window look like a minibrowser. Any of the options can be turned off simply
by replacing yes with either no or 0 (or turned on by using 1 instead of yes). Figure
1-3 shows the external window output, which resembles a second instance of the
Navigator browser.

```
11    msg.document.write("<HTML><TITLE>A New Window</TITLE>");
```

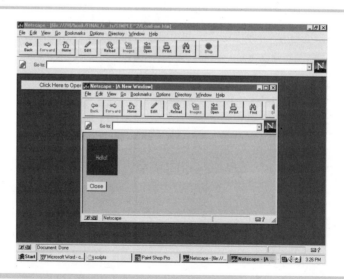

FIGURE 1-3.   Simple pop-up window 2 output

Next, **document.write( )** uses standard HTML code to give the new window a title. Otherwise, only the browser's name will appear by default in the titlebar. Notice that the new window is referred to as "msg" and not as "DisplayWindow" to invoke its properties. The name assigned in the open statement is used solely with the <TARGET=...> attribute of HTML tags, or the target property of the corresponding JavaScript link and form objects.

```
12   msg.document.write("<IMG SRC='hello.gif'><P><FORM>
                         <INPUT TYPE='BUTTON' VALUE='Close'" +
13                       "onClick='self.close()'>" +
14       "</FORM></BODY></HTML><P>")
15   }
```

Document.write( ) then goes on to add an image and a form to the page with normal HTML tags. The form contains a button labeled "Close." When clicked, it calls **self.close( )**, a built-in JavaScript function that shuts the pop-up window. In this case, the author could also have written

```
window.close()
```

or

```
msg.close()
```

to achieve the same result. Although which method you use is a question of personal preference or style, here **self.close( )** is the best choice from the standpoint of writing clear code. It tells you immediately which window is closing without your having to remember that **msg** is the child's name.

Finally, check out the <P> that ends the **document.write( )** statement on line 14. Its purpose is to force a screen write. Otherwise, the output of **document.write( )** won't appear on the page except in a last-second flash when a new page is loaded. Adding a <BR> tag serves the same purpose. You don't have to put a <BR> or <P> kicker at the end of each **document.write( )** statement in your script, but simply at the end of the last one in a set.

Both these **document.write( )** calls could easily have been combined into one long stretch from the opening <HTML> in the first to the <P> that closes the second. The main reason for breaking them up, as this author has done, is to make your code more readable and easier to maintain. Similarly, use of the plus signs on both sides of the **onClick** event handler isolates the function, thereby making it easier to find than if it were buried in a long string of HTML code.

*If you use a **document.write( )** for multiple lines of HTML code, make sure the code is uninterrupted. A single carriage return will produce an "unterminated string literal" JavaScript error message.*

In the preceding code, the quotation marks alternate between single and double. This is very important and can often get dizzying when you're dealing with strings of HTML. Whether you start out with single or double quotation marks doesn't really matter—the important thing is to switch to the opposite kind inside of your initial choice.

If you have to use quotation marks or an apostrophe within quotation marks within quotation marks, your best bet is to escape them by preceding each occurrence with a backslash. You can then even nest apostrophes inside of single quotation marks as the following (extreme) example shows:

```
document.write('Melissa said, "Then Jason says to me, \'Haven\'t
you heard the one about the waiter who replied to the programmer
who asked, \"What\'s this instance of an object doing in
my wife\'s soup?\"\ \"OOPS!\"\'"')
```

Many web page authors do not understand when to enclose the attributes of an HTML tag in quotation marks. In early forms of HTML, all attributes apparently had to be quoted. As of at least HTML 2.0, however, quotation marks are only necessary if the attribute contains any white space, or any character other than the letters (upper- or lowercase) A to Z, numbers, a period (.), or a hyphen (-) .

For instance, in the preceding code, writing

```
<IMG SRC=hello.gif>
<INPUT TYPE=BUTTON VALUE=CLOSE>
```

would have been perfectly correct. But

```
onClick='self.close()'
```

needs to be quoted because of the parentheses in the function call. Bearing this in mind when you're using **document.write( )** for HTML code can save you a lot of headaches in trying to nest single and double quotation marks properly.

The preceding rule applies exclusively to HTML but not to JavaScript, in which periods serve to delimit objects, methods, and properties, as in

```
top.frame1.window1.document.bgColor = "blue"
top.frame2.window2.dataGrabber.processForm()
```

This means to avoid an error message, you must always use quotation marks (either single or double) to denote string values in JavaScript statements. For example:

```
window.location="mypage.htm"
pix.src='sky.gif'
message="Hello world!"
```

The script ends with the commented-out closing tag to hide the script from JavaScript-impaired browsers, and here includes a comment clearly indicating the purpose of the line:

```
16  // END HIDING CONTENTS -->
17  </SCRIPT>
18  </HEAD>
19  <BODY BGCOLOR="blue">
```

At this point in the HTML code, you can insert your own page, as well as change the BGCOLOR value in the <BODY> tag preceding to suit your own needs.

```
20   <P>
21   <FORM>
22   <INPUT TYPE="button" NAME="Button1"
                     VALUE="Click Here to Open New Window"
```

Simply modify the button's VALUE to obtain a label that fits the content of your page. You can also change the button's NAME, if you wish, to something more suggestive of its function—for example, **Opener**. Also, this name can be used to refer to the button in a script. For example, assuming you gave the preceding form a name with

```
                     <FORM NAME=Switcher>
```

you could then write a function such as

```
function changeButtonLabel() {
     self.document.Switcher.button1.value="New label"
}
```

and assign it to the **onClick** event handler of a second button to change the label of the first. In this case, **onClick** calls the **WinOpen** function to create the new window described earlier, and the page ends with the conventional closing tags:

```
     onclick="WinOpen()")>
23   </FORM>
24   <P>
25   </BODY>
26   </HTML>
```

Remember that although HTML is case insensitive, JavaScript is always case sensitive. You can write "onclick," "onClick," "oNcLiCk," or "ONCLICK" if it is an HTML attribute, but in JavaScript the function has to be called with "WinOpen( )," not "winOpen( )," "Winopen," "winopen," or "WINOPEN" (or any other combination of upper- and lowercase letters). All of these case-sensitive variations would be considered separate functions by JavaScript and would produce an error message unless they existed.

simp3

Simple Pop-up Window 3

N2 N2.01 **N2.02+** N3 N4 E3 **E4**

It is not necessary to call a separate HTML file into an external window. You can create the contents of that window directly with JavaScript. In Figure 1-4, you see the output of this code.

```
1    <SCRIPT Language='JavaScript'>
2    <!-- JavaScript Follows
3    function winopen () {
4    msg=open("","NewWindow","toolbar=no,location=no,
               directories=no,status=no,menubar=no,scrollbars=no,
            resizable=no,copyhistory=yes,width=400,height=260");
5    msg.document.write("<HEAD><TITLE>Welcome.</TITLE></HEAD>");
6    msg.document.write("<CENTER><h1><B>This is your new
                            window.</B></h1></CENTER><BR>");
7    }
8    //JavaScript Ends -->
9    </SCRIPT>
```

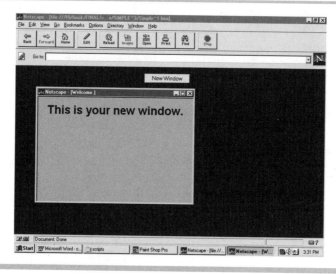

FIGURE 1-4.   Simple pop-up window 3 output

ANNOTATIONS

```
1    <SCRIPT Language='JavaScript'>
2    <!-- JavaScript Follows
3    function winopen () {
```

```
4   msg=open("","NewWindow","toolbar=no,location=no,
              directories=no,status=no,menubar=no,scrollbars=no,
              resizable=no,copyhistory=yes,width=400,height=260");
5   msg.document.write("<HEAD><TITLE>Welcome.</TITLE></HEAD>");
```

This script uses the function **winopen** to open a no-frills 400×260-pixel window and to call **document.write( )** to set the title to "Welcome."

PROGRAMMER'S NOTE *Introduced with the beta version of Navigator 2.0, the **copyhistory=yes** window feature copied a parent window's history to a child created with this option specified. For security reasons, however, **copyhistory** was abandoned in the official release and no longer works. Nonetheless, due to the common practice of cutting and pasting or copying code, it continues to appear in countless scripts. To avoid propagating what could now well be considered a "Web legend," it has simply been deleted from any other scripts in this book that still used it.*

With Internet Explorer, however, the parent's history is automatically copied to the child window regardless of a yes or no **copyhistory** setting. It can then be accessed by selecting G̲o and Open H̲istory Window from the menu—assuming, of course, that the new window is given a menu bar. Moreover, any history the child develops is added to the parent's history. In other words, both share a common history.

In the case of Navigator, a new window starts out with a blank past and can develop its own history if used to access various pages. But that record of locations is not added to its parent's history and vanishes the instant the new window is closed.

```
6   msg.document.write("<CENTER><h1><B>This is your new
                        window.</B></h1></CENTER><BR>");
7   }
8   //JavaScript Ends -->
9   </SCRIPT>
```

The **winopen( )** function then displays a message in the new window. Notice that with **document.write( )** you don't have to use the full formal array of HTML tags. For instance, line 5 produces exactly the same effect with the <HEAD> tags dropped:

```
    msg.document.write("<TITLE>Welcome.</TITLE>");
```

Similarly, there is no need to specify <HTML> or, with line 6, to add <BODY> before and after the message. JavaScript will automatically put things in their place. Even if you insert a <BODY> tag in front of <TITLE> in the preceding line, "Welcome" ends up in the titlebar, where it belongs. Although this means you can create a document with minimal tags, you still have to use them properly in pairs. Leave out the closing </TITLE> tag in the preceding script, and no message will appear in either the new window's titlebar or body, except as a last-second flash when the window is closed.

more

More Complex Pop-up Window

N2 N2.01 N2.02+ N3 N4 E3 E4

```
1   <HTML><HEAD>
2   <SCRIPT LANGUAGE="JavaScript"><!-- hide from old browsers
3   function PopIt(label, msg)
4   {
5    var s1 =
6      "<TITLE>Information!</TITLE>" +
7      "<BODY BGCOLOR='#ffffff'><TABLE BORDER=0><TR>" +
8      "<TD WIDTH='90%' HEIGHT='90%' VALIGN=TOP ALIGN=LEFT>"+
9      "<FONT SIZE=4>"
10
11   var s2 = "<FONT COLOR='#FF0000'><B>"+label+"</B></FONT><P>"
12
13   var s3 =
14     "</TD><TD WIDTH='10%'></TD></TR><TR><TD></TD>"+
15     "<TD VALIGN=TOP ALIGN=RIGHT>"+
16     "<FORM><INPUT TYPE='BUTTON' VALUE='Okay'" +
17                  "onClick='self.close()'>"  +
18     "</FORM></TD></TR></TABLE></BODY>"
19     popup = window.open("","popDialog","height=160,width=300,
                                               scrollbars=no")
20     popup.document.write(s1+s2+msg+s3)
21     popup.document.close()
22   }
23
24   function popHelp()
25   {
26     PopIt('PopIt', 'This function allows you to '  +
27                    'create a popup window.')
28   }
29   <!-- done hiding -->
30
31   </SCRIPT><title>Pop-Up Window</title></HEAD>
32   <BODY bgcolor="#ffffff">
33   Push the <i>Pop-Up</i> button to create a popup window
                                       in your browser.<p>
34
```

```
35   <CENTER><FORM><INPUT TYPE="BUTTON" VALUE="Pop-Up"
                       onClick="popHelp()"></FORM></CENTER><p>
36   </BODY></HTML>
```

ANNOTATIONS

```
1   <HTML><HEAD>
2   <SCRIPT LANGUAGE="JavaScript"><!-- hide from old browsers
3   function PopIt(label, msg)
```

This script creates the function **PopIt**, which takes two arguments: **label** and **msg**. Though both arguments are passed strings when the function is called on line 26, the quotation marks associated with strings are not used in the arguments. If you wrote

```
function PopIt('label', 'msg')
```

you would get a "missing formal parameter" JavaScript error message. On the other hand, if you called **PopIt** with

```
PopIt(label, msg)
```

you would see error messages saying that **label** and **msg** are not defined.

Be sure *not* to use quotation marks in the arguments when defining a function, but only when calling the function and passing strings to its arguments. You can use single or double quotes for the strings; it doesn't matter as long as you either alternate or escape any apostrophes or quotation marks within the string. The final look and feel of this example can be seen in Figure 1-5.

```
4    {
5      var s1 =
6        "<TITLE>Information!</TITLE>" +
7        "<BODY BGCOLOR='#ffffff'><TABLE BORDER=0><TR>" +
8        "<TD WIDTH='90%' HEIGHT='90%' VALIGN=TOP ALIGN=LEFT>"+
9        "<FONT SIZE=4>"
10
11     var s2 = "<FONT COLOR='FF0000'><B>"+label+"</B></FONT><P>"
12
13     var s3 =
14       "</TD><TD WIDTH=10%></TD></TR><TR><TD></TD>"+
15       "<TD VALIGN=TOP ALIGN=RIGHT>"+
16       "<FORM><INPUT TYPE='BUTTON' VALUE='Okay'" +
17                   "onClick='self.close()'>"  +
18       "</FORM></TD></TR></TABLE></BODY>"
```

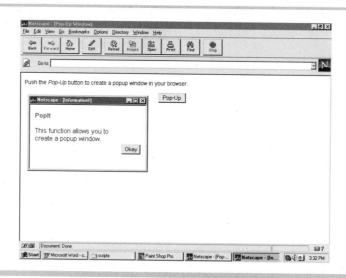

FIGURE 1-5. More complex pop-up window output

The next 15 lines set up three variables—**s1**, **s2**, and **s3**—each of which is assigned concatenated strings of HTML code. Notice that the keyword **var** appears in front of each one. This makes the three variables *local* in scope, meaning that they can only be used within the **PopIt** function. For example, if the **popHelp** function on line 24 had a second line consisting of

```
document.write(s1)
```

the result would be an error message saying that "s1 is not defined." Remove "var" from in front of "s1," and the variable immediately becomes *global* in scope, meaning that it can be used anywhere within the script, or by other scripts on the same page, or by any other script on a page within the same frameset while this page remains loaded.

Variables declared outside of functions are automatically global. They do not have to be preceded by the keyword **var** if you immediately assign them a value. Doing so is considered good style. If you simply declare them, failure to add **var** will cause JavaScript to read them as a call and produce an "x is undefined" message. For example:

```
x = 1000;            // okay
var x = "Hello";     // okay
var x;               // okay
var x, y, z;         // okay
x;                   // error
```

If you define a global variable and then overload it by creating a local variable with the same name in a function, any assignments to it will only affect the local and leave the global unaltered. This also applies if the global is simply declared without being defined. For example:

```
var cat = "purr";                      // global
  function tangle() {
      var cat = "meow";                // local
      document.write(cat);             // output:   meow
      cat = "woof";                    // local
      untangle(cat);
  }


  function untangle(dog) {
      document.write(dog);             // output:   woof
      document.write(cat);             // output:   purr
  }
```

If the global declaration is left undefined, for example:

```
      var cat;
```

tangle( ) produces exactly the same output, and **untangle( )** yields:

```
      document.write(cat);             // output:   undefined
```

Moreover, the scope of an overloaded local variable in JavaScript encompasses the entire function, including apparent assignments to the global that precede the declaration of the local. For instance:

```
var cat = "purr";                      // global
  function tangle() {
      cat = "meow";                    // local (!)
      document.write(cat);             // output:   meow
      var cat = "woof";                // local
      document.write(cat);             // output:   woof
      untangle();
  }


  function untangle() {
      document.write(cat);             // output:   purr (!)
      }
```

In this case, you might expect the first assignment in **tangle( )** to alter the global, but the surprising output of **untangle( )** shows that it does not. Remove **var** from **tangle( )** and the output of **untangle( )** becomes "woof" as expected, because now there is only a single global variable. As this indicates, the scoping of variables in

JavaScript is very clean and, if you absolutely must, you can confidently overload a variable without worrying about unpredictable behavior.

The author of this script has also wisely chosen to break up what would otherwise be long strings of HTML code and chain them together with plus (+) signs. This not only makes the script easier to read and simplifies page maintenance, but it also reduces the likelihood of the "unterminated string literal" error message that can easily occur for seemingly trivial reasons when you're working with long strings—an accidental carriage return or a misnested quotation mark is all it takes.

Turning long strings of redundant HTML code into variables for use by **document.write( )** is also an excellent way to separate the content of your page from the code, which makes both much easier to work with and maintain, and often results in a substantially lighter and faster page. If you're using long redundant strings of HTML code for consistent formatting or a complex table, you should seriously consider using JavaScript variables to handle them.

The three variables in this script constitute the HTML code for the new window. The first sets up the titlebar and starts building a table. Then **s2** fills a cell with a large red heading, whose content is whatever gets passed to **PopIt( )** as its first argument when the function is called. In this case, as line 26 later indicates, **label** becomes the word "PopIt" that appears in the new window. Lastly, **s3** contains the code that closes the table and also creates a form with a button reading "Okay," with which the user can easily close the pop-up window.

```
19     popup = window.open("","popDialog","height=160,width=300,
                                                   scrollbars=no")
20     popup.document.write(s1+s2+msg+s3)
21     popup.document.close()
22   }
```

PopIt( ) creates a simple 160×300 window as an object named **popup**, then uses **document.write( )** to display the three variables plus **msg** (its second argument) in the new window. The function ends with a call to **document.close( )**, which serves the same purpose as ending a **document.write( )** call with a <BR> or <P> tag. In other words, it ends the **document.write( )** stream and displays it.

There is an important difference between the two basic techniques of making **document.write( )** content visible. When you use <BR> or <P>, subsequent calls to **document.write( )** append their content to that of the preceding call and continue doing so until the document is closed or a new page loaded into its place. On the other hand, if you use **document.close( )**, a subsequent **document.write( )** automatically opens a new document that erases or overwrites the previous stream. This is true regardless of whether you precede the call with **document.open( )**.

```
24   function popHelp()
25   {
```

```
26      PopIt('PopIt', 'This function allows you to ' +
27                     'create a popup window.')
28   }
```

The second function in this script, **popHelp**, calls **PopIt( )** when the button labeled "Pop-Up" is clicked. The main value of calling **PopIt( )** from a separate function lies in avoiding what would otherwise be a very long **onClick( )** call in line 35 later. Another way of getting around that would be to make the content of the **PopIt** function's second argument a variable, for example:

```
s4 = 'This function allows you to create a popup window.'
```

and call it directly from line 35 with

```
onClick="PopIt('PopIt', s4)"
```

Notice that there are no quotation marks around **s4** in the argument, because it is already defined as a string. Were you to write

```
onClick="PopIt('PopIt', 's4')"
```

the message appearing in the pop-up window would be "s4." Both techniques share the advantage of isolating the content (message) from HTML code so that it can easily be located and changed.

```
29   <!-- done hiding -->
30
31   </SCRIPT><title>Pop-Up Window</title></HEAD>
32   <BODY bgcolor="ffffff">
33   Push the <i>Pop-Up</i> button to create a popup window
                                         in your browser.<p>
34
35   <CENTER><FORM><INPUT TYPE="BUTTON" VALUE="Pop-Up"
                     onClick="popHelp()"></FORM></CENTER><p>
36   </BODY></HTML>
```

With that the script ends, and the body of the page contains an instruction followed by a form. The form consists solely of the button that calls **popHelp( )** as the first step in the sequence of creating the pop-up window. All this JavaScript code may seem like a roundabout and twisted way to perform a simple task. But that's not really the point of this example. Rather, it is meant to show how you can take advantage of JavaScript's tremendous flexibility to separate HTML code from content with both a parent and a child window. By using this technique, or your own variation of it, you can create complex pages that are much easier to tinker with and modify over time, and avoid a spaghetti-tangle of HTML tags and text.

Pop-up on Mouse-over 1

pop1   N2 N2.01 N2.02+ N3 N4 E3 E4

You don't have to create a form button to launch an external window. This JavaScript
example makes use of **onMouseOver**, an event handler that executes JavaScript
code whenever the mouse is moved over a designated hypertext link. The user
moves the mouse across the Click Here link, and an external window pops up.
Move the mouse away from the link and the window closes. The latter event is
called **onMouseOut**.

```
1   <html><body><center><font size=4 color=darkgreen>
2
3   An external window will appear when the mouse is moved over
                        the plain HTML text link below:<BR><BR>
4   <A HREF="javascript:"onMouseOver=
            "m=window.open('pop.htm','','width=150,height=150');
                return true;"
                        onMouseOut="m.close();   return true;">
5   Click here</A>
6
7   <font size=3><BR>
8   If you are using Netscape 3,
                    the window will close automatically.<BR>
9   If you are using Microsoft Explorer or Netscape 2,<BR>
                        you will have to close it manually.<BR>
10  <BR><font size=4>
11  It also works with images:<P>
12  <A HREF="javascript:"onMouseOver="m =
                window.open('pop.htm','','width=200,height=130');
            return true;"onMouseOut=" m.close();   return true;">
                    <IMG SRC="1.gif" ALIGN=MIDDLE BORDER=2></A>
13  </center></body>
14  </html>
```

The external window will automatically close in Netscape Navigator 3.x and
above. If this script runs in any other JavaScript-capable browser, the user has to
close the window manually (see Figure 1-6).

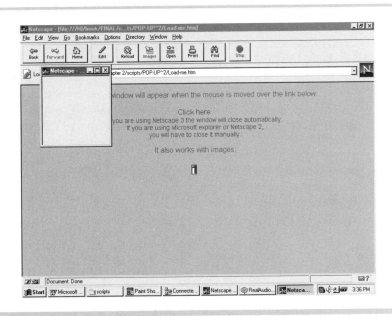

FIGURE 1-6.   Pop-up on mouse-over 1 output

The **onMouseOver** event is not limited to user interaction with text-based hyperlinks. This example also includes code that opens a window when the mouse is passed over a graphic.

ANNOTATIONS

```
1   <html><body><center><font size=4 color=darkgreen>

2

3   An external window will appear when the mouse is moved over
                        the plain HTML text link below:<BR><BR>

4   <A HREF="javascript:"onMouseOver=
            "m=window.open('pop.htm','','width=150,height=150');
                return true;"
```

Here the entire script is embedded in an HREF tag. Take a close look at how the quotation marks are used, because they are key to making this function work. The first pair of double quotes encloses "javascript:", which in this case is a URL

(Uniform Resource Locator). As the URL contains a character (the colon) other than a letter from A to Z, a number, a period, or a hyphen, it has to be wrapped in quotes. The second pair encases the code executed by the **onMouseOver** event handler and, nested within them, single quotation marks are used for the new window's properties.

The event handler opens a plain 150×150-pixel window named **m** that loads the file POP.HTM. The window-creation statement is followed by a second one: **return true**. This statement is not necessary for the window to open. What it does is prevent the URL "javascript:" from appearing in the browser's status bar. And because the two JavaScript statements are on the same line, they must be separated by a semicolon. Though a carriage return could be used in place of the semicolon, this type of event-handler script is a form of in-line code—a semicolon is always the smarter and safer choice. Finally, the semicolon after "true" is optional, but good style.

```
4        onMouseOut="m.close(); return true;">
```

The HREF tag also includes an **onMouseOut** event handler that closes the window when the cursor moves off the link. The most important thing to notice here is the use of the window's name (**m**) in the **close( )** statement. Were you to write

```
         self.close()
```

or

```
         window.close()
```

the statement would be interpreted as referring to the parent window. In that case, the **onMouseOut** event would trigger a JavaScript confirm message: "Close window?". Responding "OK" would close the main browser window while leaving the pop-up child open.

As only Netscape 3.x and 4.x recognize the **onMouseOut** event, Microsoft Explorer or Netscape 2.x users have to close the pop-up window manually. As you can see from lines 8 and 9 later, the author has wisely added a message to that effect.

When you're enhancing a page with JavaScript, always bear in mind that the fantastic effects you spend hours creating may not work with browsers other than the version you're using. Failure to accommodate people with other browsers can cause frustration and annoyance to the extent that a visitor may simply decide never to return to your site again. If you want your pages to be as user friendly and as accessible to as wide an audience as possible, take the extra time to provide for all the dinosaurs still roaming the Web.

```
5   Click here</A>

6

7   <font size=3><BR>
8   If you are using Netscape 3,
                      the window will close automatically.<BR>
9   If you are using Microsoft Explorer or Netscape 2,<BR>
                      you will have to close it manually.<BR>
```

```
10   <BR><font size=4>
11   It also works with images:<P>
12   <A HREF="javascript:"onMouseOver="m =
                window.open('pop.htm','','width=200,height=130');
             return true;"onMouseOut=" m.close();  return true;">
                   <IMG SRC="1.gif" ALIGN=MIDDLE BORDER=2></A>
13   </center></body>
14   </html>
```

This page goes on to demonstrate how exactly the same technique can be used with a graphic as opposed to a text link. The code is identical except for the size of the pop-up window and replacement of the "Click here" instruction with an image tag.

pop2

Pop-up on Mouse-over 2

N2 N2.01 N2.02+ N3 N4 E3 **E4**

The **onMouseOver** event can be simplified to launch an external window that stays open until the user decides to close it. This approach is compatible with more browsers than the one used in the previous example. The script also assigns a separate function to the event handler instead of using in-line code. See Figure 1-7 to see how the pop-up window will look.

```
1    <HTML>
2    <HEAD>
3
4    <TITLE></TITLE><SCRIPT Language='JavaScript'>
5    function winopen () {
6    msg=open("","NewWindow","toolbar=no,location=no,
               directories=no,status=no,menubar=no,scrollbars=no,
                            resizable=no,width=400,height=260");
7    msg.document.write("<HEAD><TITLE>Hello</TITLE></HEAD>");
8    msg.document.write("<CENTER><h2><B>
                This window will stay open</B></h2></CENTER>");
9    }
10   //JavaScript Ends -->
11   </SCRIPT>
12   </HEAD>
13   <BODY BGCOLOR="ffffff">
14
```

```
15   Move mouse over <a href="" onMouseOver="winopen();
                         return true;">THIS</a> without clicking
16   </BODY>
17   </HTML>
```

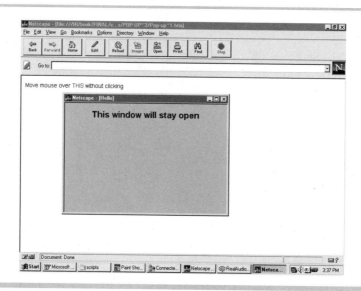

FIGURE 1-7.   Pop-up on mouse-over 2 output

ANNOTATIONS

```
1    <HTML>
2    <HEAD>
3
4    <TITLE></TITLE><SCRIPT Language='JavaScript'>
5    function winopen () {
6    msg=open("","NewWindow","toolbar=no,location=no,
                 directories=no,status=no,menubar=no,scrollbars=no,
                       resizable=no,width=400,height=260");
7    msg.document.write("<HEAD><TITLE>Hello</TITLE></HEAD>");
8    msg.document.write("<CENTER><h2><B>
                 This window will stay open</B></h2></CENTER>");
9    }
10   //JavaScript Ends -->
11   </SCRIPT>
```

The entire script consists of a single function, **winopen**, which begins by creating a no-frills 400×260-pixel window named **msg** for JavaScript purposes and **NewWindow** for <TARGET> tags or the **target** property of links and forms. Because the default value of new window options is no, writing

```
msg=open("","NewWindow","width=400,height=260");
```

produces exactly the same result. Preserving the full array of optional features, however, makes it easier for you to adapt the properties of the new window to your own preferences should you decide to use this script for your site.

Notice that the call to **open( )** does not specify "window.open( )." Within a script or function, the **open( )** method belongs to the window object by default. In an event handler, however, **open( )** is interpreted as **document.open( )**. In other words,

```
onMouseOver=open()
```

instantly replaces the current page with a blank document when the cursor touches the link.

Finally, **winopen( )** uses **document.write( )** to put "Hello" in the new window's titlebar and to display a message in the document area.

```
12   </HEAD>
13   <BODY BGCOLOR="ffffff">
14
15   Move mouse over <a href="" onMouseOver="winopen();
                            return true;">THIS</a> without clicking
16   </BODY>
17   </HTML>
```

The body of the page consists of a single sentence with the word "THIS" tagged as a link with **winopen( )** assigned to its **onMouseOver** event handler. Notice the empty HREF attribute. Omit it and the anchor tags no longer create a link. Again, **return true** is used to prevent the status bar display from changing to the address of the new window.

Window with User-Input Message

window

N2 N2.01 N2.02+ N3 N4 E3 **E4**

This script takes whatever you type in the HTML form text field on the page and displays it in a new window. As shown in Figure 1-8, it's a neat little example of how to transfer user input from parent to child.

```
1   <HTML>
2   <HEAD>
3   <TITLE></TITLE>
4   <SCRIPT Language='JavaScript'>
5   <!-- JavaScript Follows
```

```
6    function winmsg() {
7    var Message=document.message.txt.value;
8    msg=open("","NewWindow","toolbar=no,location=no,
               directories=no,status=no,menubar=no,scrollbars=no,
                           resizable=no,width=400,height=260");
9    msg.document.write("<HEAD><TITLE>Hello</TITLE></HEAD>");
10   msg.document.write("<center><B>This is what you were saying:
                           </B><p>", Message, "</center>");
11   msg.document.write("<CENTER><FORM><INPUT TYPE='BUTTON'
                                           VALUE='Okay'" +
12       "onClick='self.close()'></FORM><CENTER>");
13   }
14   //JavaScript Ends -->
15   </SCRIPT>
16   </HEAD>
17   <BODY BGCOLOR="FF0000">
18   <form name="message">
19   <input type="text" name="txt" size="30">
20   <input type="button" value="open" onClick="winmsg()">
21   <input type="reset" value="reset">
22   </form>
23   </BODY>
24   </HTML>
```

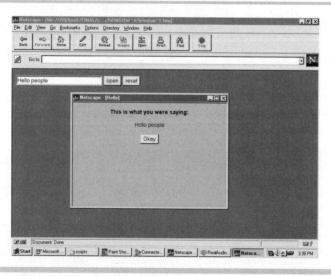

FIGURE 1-8.   Window with user-input message

ANNOTATIONS

```
1    <HTML>
2    <HEAD>
3    <TITLE></TITLE>
4    <SCRIPT Language='JavaScript'>
5    <!-- JavaScript Follows
6    function winmsg() {
7    var Message=document.message.txt.value
```

The core of this script is the function **winmsg**, which starts by creating the variable **Message** and assigns it the value of the text field in the form on the page. The keyword **var** makes this a local variable that can only be used by **winmsg( )**. If you change the event-handler code for the button created in the new window with line 12 to

```
onClick="document.write(opener.Message)"
```

JavaScript simply writes "undefined." Omitting **var** makes **Message** a global variable accessible to the child window, so that now the preceding change would cause a click to rewrite whatever you enter in the text field.

The other important thing to notice here is the proper way of referring to the text field so that the function can read its value:

```
document.formName.elementName.value
```

Leave out the word "document," for instance, and you'll get an error message saying that "message" (the name of the form in this script) is undefined. Another option is to give **winmsg( )** an argument, for example:

```
function winmsg(userform) { ... }
```

and change the button's event handler on line 20 to

```
onClick="winmsg(this.form)"
```

In that case, you would not have to specify **document** in line 7 and could create the variable simply with

```
var Message=userform.txt.value;
```

Moreover, instead of using the text field's name (**txt** in this case), you can also refer to it by means of the form elements array which, like all JavaScript arrays, is indexed beginning at zero. Since the text field is the first element, the preceding line could be changed to

```
var Message=userform.elements[0].value
```

JavaScript also has a built-in forms array that indexes the forms in each document. To use it, you have to specify **document** or risk a "forms is undefined" error message. Here the form is the first on the page, so line 7 can be changed to

```
              var Message=document.forms[0].elements[0].value;
```

This type of abstract reference can come in handy; for example, in a function that uses a **for** loop to read or write to forms.

```
8    msg=open("","NewWindow","toolbar=no,location=no,
                  directories=no,status=no,menubar=no,scrollbars=no,
                              resizable=no,width=400,height=260");
9    msg.document.write("<HEAD><TITLE>Hello</TITLE></HEAD>");
10   msg.document.write("<center><B>This is what you were saying:
                              </B><p>", Message, "</center>");
```

Our **winmsg( )** function next goes on to open a no-frills 400×260-pixel window, put "Hello again" in the titlebar, and display the content of the text field through use of the variable **Message** in line 10. Line 10 also shows how you can use commas instead of plus signs to concatenate strings with **document.write( )**. For example, assuming three variables called **cat**, **dog**, and **bird**, you could display their values with either

```
              document.write(cat, ' ', dog, ' ', bird)
```

or

```
              document.write(cat + ' ' + dog + ' ' + bird)
```

If you try to use commas to concatenate strings in the definition of a variable, for example:

```
              var hybrid = "cat", "dog", "bird";
```

you can expect a "missing variable name" JavaScript error message. On the other hand, writing

```
              var hybrid = "cat" + "dog" + "bird"
```

makes **hybrid** a concatenated string with the value "catdogbird."

```
11   msg.document.write("<CENTER><FORM><INPUT TYPE='BUTTON'
                                            VALUE='Okay'" +
12       "onClick='self.close()'></FORM><CENTER>");
13   }
14   //JavaScript Ends -->
15   </SCRIPT>
```

The **winmsg( )** function ends by creating a form in the new window. The form consists of a button labeled "Okay" which, when clicked, closes the child window. If you wanted to use the pop-up window's name to close it, you would have to write

```
              onClick = opener.msg.close()
```

because within the context of the child window, **msg** is undefined. In this case, **self.close( )** is clearly the simplest and best choice.

```
16   </HEAD>
17   <BODY BGCOLOR="FF0000">
```

```
18   <form name="message">
19   <input type="text" name="txt" size="30">
20   <input type="button" value="open" onClick="winmsg()">
21   <input type="reset" value="reset">
22   </form>
23   </BODY>
24   </HTML>
```

The body of this page consists of a form named **message** containing a text field named **txt** and two buttons: one labeled "open" that calls **winmsg( )** when clicked, and the other a standard reset button that clears the form—that is, erases the text field.

A fairly common mistake is to write

```
<INPUT TYPE=BUTTON VALUE=RESET>
```

and then get thoroughly frustrated because it doesn't work. Remember that **reset** is a separate input type just like **button**, **radio**, **checkbox**, and **text**. Its value is simply the label that appears on the button. This means that, to create a reset button labeled "CLEAR FORM," write

```
<INPUT TYPE=RESET VALUE="CLEAR FORM">
```

select

Select a Window to Open

N2   N2.01   N2.02+   N3   N4   E3   **E4**

This script shows you how to use a selection list in an HTML form to give a visitor to your page a choice of windows to open. After the user selects one of the three windows, clicking on the open button makes it appear. Figure 1-9 shows the drop-down menu form.

```
1    <HTML>
2    <HEAD>
3    <TITLE></TITLE>
4    <SCRIPT Language='JavaScript'>
5    <!-- JavaScript Follows
6    function newwin(windower) {
7       var myindex=windower.selector.selectedIndex;
8       var place=windower.selector.options[myindex].value;
9       msg=open(place,"","location=yes");
10   }
11   //JavaScript Ends -->
12   </SCRIPT>
13   </HEAD>
```

```
14  <BODY>
15
16  <form name="windower">
17  <select name="selector">
18  <option value="1.html">First window
19  <option value="2.html">Second window
20  <option value="3.html">Third window
21  </select>
22  <INPUT TYPE="button" value="open"
                                  onClick="newwin(this.form);">
23  </FORM>
24  </BODY>
25  </HTML>
```

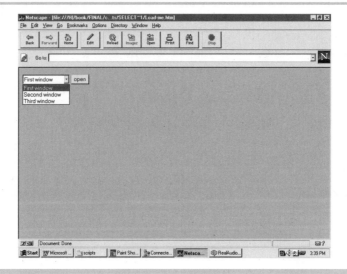

FIGURE 1-9.   Select a window to open output

ANNOTATIONS

```
1   <HTML>
2   <HEAD>
3   <TITLE></TITLE>
4   <SCRIPT Language='JavaScript'>
5   <!-- JavaScript Follows
```

```
6   function newwin(windower) {
7       var myindex=windower.selector.selectedIndex;
8       var place=windower.selector.options[myindex].value;
9       msg=open(place,"","location=yes");
10  }
11  //JavaScript Ends -->
12  </SCRIPT>
```

The entire script consists of a three-line function **newwin** with one argument, **windower**. The **onClick** call in line 22 passes the object **this.form** to **newwin( )** as its argument.

First **newwin( )** establishes two variables specified as local through use of the keyword **var**. The first, **myindex**, is assigned the value of the **selectedIndex** property of the **select** form. This property is an integer specifying the index of the user's choice from the array of options. As there are three choices, the array consists of **options[0]**, **options[1]**, and **options[2]**, and **myindex** will have the value 0, 1, or 2.

Note that **windower** in the two variables refers to **newwin( )**'s argument, and not to the form itself, which happens to have the same name. You could just as well write

```
function newwin(monkey) {
    var myindex=monkey.selector.selectedIndex;
    var place=monkey.selector.options[myindex].value
    ... }
```

which would turn **monkey** into **this.form** from the call in line 22. In other words, the argument and the form do not have to have the same name. Also, instead of using **this.form**, you could call the function with a full reference to the form by name, for example:

```
onClick = "newwin(document.windower)"
```

The second variable, **place**, is assigned the value of the selected option as determined by the value of the first, **myindex**. A glance at lines 18 to 20 reveals that its possible values are three filenames.

Then **newwin( )** creates a new window named **msg** which loads the file that has the name passed to **place** by means of the selection index. As no dimensions are specified for the new window, it will be the same size as the browser. Its sole feature is a location entry field.

Viewed with Microsoft's Internet Explorer, this new window will not have an address field, because the **directories**, **location**, and **toolbar** window features constitute a single unit for that browser. It's all or none, and **toolbar** is the option on which the other two depend.

```
13  </HEAD>
14  <BODY>
15
16  <form name="windower">
```

```
17  <select name="selector">
18  <option value="1.html">First window
19  <option value="2.html">Second window
20  <option value="3.html">Third window
21  </select>
22  <INPUT TYPE="button" value="open"
                                onClick="newwin(this.form);">
23  </FORM>
24  </BODY>
25  </HTML>
```

The visible portion of the page contains a form consisting of two elements: a select list and a button. The list is **elements[0]** and the button is **elements[1]**. Unlike buttons in which VALUE simply means the label, with a select list VALUE is the data passed to your script or returned to the server when a particular option is selected and the form is submitted. A select list option's label is its **text** property. Thus, if you wanted to use pure array indexing to change the text of the third list option to "Neat window," for example, you would write

```
document.forms[0].elements[0].options[2].text = "Neat window"
```

You can also combine use of the object names with array references. Thus,

```
document.windower.elements[1].value = "Yo!"
```

would change the button's label to "Yo!". Of course, you could give the button a name in its HTML tag and then replace "elements[1]" in the preceding reference with its name. A prime advantage of using names is that it can spare you the tedium of element counting, especially if you have a complex form.

Lastly, forms are updated instantly without a page reload. Combined with JavaScript's ability to modify them on-the-fly, this makes them a very valuable device in creating a dynamic interactive web site.

Replace Buttons with Graphics

replace

N2 N2.01 N2.02+ N3 N4 E3 E4

Ever created a web page that you think would be a totally stunning visual master-piece if you could just get rid of or do something about those invariable dull gray form buttons you absolutely need? This script shows how you can easily replace them with the image of your choice by using a link to trigger a JavaScript function.

All the button does is open a window (see Figure 1-10), but you can use exactly the same technique to run any other script.

```
1   <HTML>
2   <HEAD>
3   <TITLE></TITLE><script>
4   <!--
5   function launch() {
6       var newWin = window.open("file1.html", "", "toolbar=1,
                    location=1,directories=0,status=1,menubar=1,
                                    scrollbar=1,resizable=1");

7
8       if (navigator.appVersion.indexOf("(X11") != -1 ||
9           navigator.appVersion.indexOf("(Mac") != -1)
10        newWin = window.open("file1.html", "",
11              "toolbar=1,location=1,directories=0,status=1,
                        menubar=1,scrollbar=1,resizable=1");
12  }
13
14  document.bgColor="black"
15  document.fgColor="yellow"
16  document.linkColor="blue"
17  document.vlinkColor="black"
18
19  //-->
20  </script>
21  </HEAD>
22
23  <BODY bgcolor="#000000">
24  <H4>This example replaces those ugly gray HTML form buttons
                                with a graphic link!</H4>
25  <P>
26  <table border=3><tr><td>
27  <center><A HREF="javascript: launch()">
                        <img src="click.gif" border=0></a>
28  </td></tr></table>
29  </center>
30  </BODY>
31  </HTML>
```

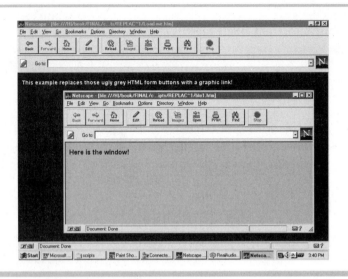

FIGURE 1-10. Replace buttons with graphics output

ANNOTATIONS

```
1    <HTML>
2    <HEAD>
3    <TITLE></TITLE><script>
4    <!--
5    function launch() {
6        var newWin = window.open("file1.html", "", "toolbar=1,
                    location=1,directories=0,status=1,menubar=1,
                                    scrollbar=1,resizable=1");
```

The **launch** function begins by opening a full-size resizable new window with all the standard browser bars and buttons except for directories. The window has no name for <TARGET> tags, but is named **newWin** for JavaScript purposes. Upon opening, it loads FILE1.HTML.

```
8        if (navigator.appVersion.indexOf("(X11") != -1 ||
9            navigator.appVersion.indexOf("(Mac") != -1)
10         newWin = window.open("file1.html", "",
11                 "toolbar=1,location=1,directories=0,status=1,
                         menubar=1,scrollbar=1,resizable=1");
12    }
```

The function checks the user's browser version to accommodate users running X-Windows or Macintosh versions of Navigator. Due to a bug, the two versions ignore the first argument of **window.open( )** and fail to load the specified file.

There are two work-arounds for this. One approach is to repeat the **window.open( )** command as in the preceding script, and the other is to specify the location of the new window in a separate line. Using the preceding example, that would mean adding the line

```
newWin.location = "file1.html"
```

To check for version, the script obtains the value of **navigator.appVersion**, a built-in JavaScript read-only property consisting of a string in the format *releaseNumber* (*version*; *country*). For example, for someone running the international version of Navigator 3.01 in Windows 95,

```
document.write(navigator.appVersion)
```

would produce "3.01 (Win95; I)." At the same time, our sample script uses the **indexOf** method to analyze that string. This method returns the first occurrence of a search value within the calling string starting at an optional **fromIndex** which, if not specified, is 0 by default. If the search string is not found, **indexOf** returns –1. For example:

```
msg = "Hello new world!";
msg.indexOf("n", 0);
```

returns 6 because "n" is the sixth letter (count starting from 0) in **msg**. The value it returns is relative to the start of the string and not to the starting point of the search. Thus,

```
msg.indexOf("n", 4);
```

also returns 6 but shortens the search by starting it at the first "o."

```
msg.indexOf("z");
```

returns –1 because there is no "z" in our string. Looking back at lines 8 and 9 of the script, you should now be able to see how they check for the strings "(X11" and "(Mac" and, if either is found—that is, one of the two searches does not return –1—the window is created a second time and forces FILE1.HTML to load.

```
14    document.bgColor="black"
15    document.fgColor="yellow"
16    document.linkColor="blue"
17    document.vlinkColor="black"
18
19    //-->
20    </script>
```

The remainder of this script shows how you can use JavaScript to set a document's colors. The background color (**bgColor**) is set to black; foreground (**fgColor**) or text, to yellow; links (**linkColor**), to blue; and visited links (**vlinkColor**), to black. You can also use the red-green-blue (RGB) hexadecimal values for this. For example:

```
document.bgColor="FF0000"
```

creates a red background. These values will override the browser's color settings unless the user specifies otherwise by selecting Options/General Preferences/ Colors from the Navigator menu bar, or View/Options/General with Explorer.

Setting the background color in a new window is not as simple as you might expect. You would think that adding the following line to our **launch** function would be enough to change the background of FILE1.HTML to red:

```
newWin.document.bgColor = "red"
```

However, this only works with Internet Explorer 3.x and Navigator 4.0. With older versions of Navigator, the background color will only change if the preceding is a separate function assigned to a button or link's event handler.

Moreover, if you use **document.write( )** to create the content of your new window, a line such as

```
newWin.document.bgColor = "green"
```

will only work if preceded by **document.open( )**, or if placed after **document.write( )**, which automatically opens the document.

If you use color names instead of RGB values, watch your spelling. Writing "grey" instead of "gray" will give you "green," because JavaScript doesn't know what "grey" is, interpreting it as the first three letters of "green."

Also, if you use **document.bgColor** in a script and forget to remove the BGCOLOR attribute from your page's <BODY> tag, Navigator will use the JavaScript value, but Explorer will set the tag value.

```
21   </HEAD>
22
23   <BODY bgcolor="#000000">
24   <H4>This example replaces those ugly gray HTML form buttons
                                       with a graphic link!</H4>
25   <P>
26   <table border=3><tr><td>
27   <center><A HREF="javascript: launch()">
                             <img src="click.gif" border=0></a>
28   </td></tr></table>
29   </center>
30   </BODY>
31   </HTML>
```

As line 27 shows, the technique for creating a virtual form button is simple: a standard HTML anchor with "javascript:" followed by the name of your function assigned to the HREF. A simple table with a raised border is all it takes to create a 3-D effect. In fact, with a table you don't even need an image to produce what looks like a button—just make the text link the button label. If you use a 3-D image, you can eliminate the table altogether.

If you're looking for neat buttons and bars to dress up your web page, probably the best starting point is the "Images and Icons" section of the Web Developer's Virtual Library at **http://WWW.Stars.com/Vlib/Providers/Images_and_Icons.html**. You will find dozens of links to source sites along with a detailed description of each one.

riddle

Custom Dialog

N2 **N2.01** **N2.02+** **N3** **N4** **E3** **E4**

This script shows how to open a window that obtains information with a form, then incorporates the user input into the page it writes when the new window is closed. Although the content of this page—"Riddle of the Day"—is trivial, the technique it deploys can readily be applied in more serious contexts.

```
1   <html>
2   <head>
3   <title>Riddle</title>
4   <script language="JavaScript">
5   // Copyright 1997, Henry Sobotka; released to public domain
6   var wDays = new Array("Sunday", "Monday", "Tuesday",
7               "Wednesday", "Thursday", "Friday", "Saturday");
8   var today = new Date();
9   var Rtitl = "<title>" + wDays[today.getDay()] +
                                        "'s Riddle</title>";
10  var Rhead = "<center><font size=+4>" +
11              "Riddle of the Day</font></center>";
12  var Rform1 =
                "<br><form name=Rform>Please enter your name: " +
13               "<input type=text name=Gname size=29>";
14  var Rque =
                "<p><b>Why did the rabbit cross the road?</b><p>";
15  var Rans = "Because it was stapled to the chicken!";
16  var key1 = "stapled";
17  var key2 = "chicken";
18  var key3 = "staple";
19  var Rform2 = "<input type=text name=Gans size=50>" +
20          "<p><center><input type=button value='   OK   '" +
21                  "onClick='opener.CheckAns(this.form)'>" +
22                      "<spacer type=horizontal size=25>" +
```

```
23                     "<input type=button value='    Hint    ' " +
24                        "onClick='opener.Hint(this.form)'>" +
25                        "<spacer type=horizontal size=25>" +
26                     "<input type=button value=Cancel
                            onClick='opener.NoAns()'>" +
27                     "</center></form>";
28  var Rpage = Rtitl + Rhead.fontcolor("blanchedAlmond") +
                            Rform1 + Rque + Rform2;
29  var NewTry = "<center><form>" +
30            "<input type=button value='Try again?' " +
31            "onClick=\"self.location='riddle.htm'\">";
32  var showA = "<spacer type=horizontal size=50>" +
33          "<input type=button value='Show answer' " +
34          "onClick=
        \"document.write('<body bgColor=peachpuff><center>" +
35          "<font size=+4 color=crimson>" +
36          "Because it was stapled to the chicken!</font>
                            </center><p>')\">";
37  var fEnd = "</form></center>";
38  var hintCount = 0;
39
40  function openRbox() {
41     Rbox = window.open("","","width=500,height=300");
42     Rbox.document.open();
43     Rbox.document.write(Rpage);
44     if (document.cookie) {
45         Rbox.document.Rform.Gname.value = document.cookie;
46         Rbox.document.Rform.Gans.focus();
47     }
48     else Rbox.document.Rform.Gname.focus();
49     Rbox.document.bgColor = "lightcoral";
50     Rbox.document.close();
51  }
52
53  function CheckAns(form) {
54     var Gname = form.Gname.value;
55     var Gans = form.Gans.value.toLowerCase();
56     document.cookie = Gname;
57     Rbox.close();
58     if (Gans.indexOf(key1) != -1 && Gans.indexOf(key2) != -1
59         && Gans.indexOf(key2) > Gans.indexOf(key1)
60         && (Gans.indexOf(key2) - Gans.indexOf(key1)) > 10
61         && (Gans.length <
```

```
                         (Gans.indexOf(key2) + key2.length + 3)
62        || Gans.indexOf(key2 + "'s") != -1))
63        document.write("<title>Ding!</title>" +
                              Rhead.fontcolor("crimson") +
64              "<center><h2>Right, " + Gname + "!<p>" +
65          Gans.fontcolor("crimson") + "!</h2></center>");
66     else if (Gans.indexOf(key3) != -1
                              || Gans.indexOf(key2) != -1)
67        document.write("<title>Bzzzt!</title>" +
                              Rhead.fontcolor("crimson") +
68              "<center><h2>Wrong, " + Gname + "!<p>" +
69     "You answered: " + Gans.fontcolor("crimson") + "!<p>" +
70                  "<b>Warm! But no banana...</b><p>" +
71            NewTry + showA + fEnd + "</h2></center>");
72     else
73        document.write("<title>Bzzzt!</title>" +
                              Rhead.fontcolor("crimson") +
74              "<center><h2>Wrong, " + Gname + "!<p>" +
75       "You answered: " + Gans.fontcolor("crimson") + "!" +
76            NewTry + showA + fEnd + "</h2></center>");
77     document.bgColor = "peachpuff";
78     document.close();
79  }
80
81  function Hint(form) {
82     var hintStr = Rans.split(' ');
83     if (hintCount == hintStr.length) {
84        hintCount = 0;
85        form.Gans.value = hintStr[hintCount];
86        hintCount++;
87     }
88     else form.Gans.value += ' ' + hintStr[hintCount++];
89  }
90
91  function NoAns(){
92     Rbox.close();
93     document.write("<title>Main Page</title>" +
94                 Rhead + NewTry + showA + fEnd);
95     document.bgColor = "peachpuff";
96     document.close();
97  }
98  </script>
99  </head>
```

```
100  <body onLoad='openRbox()' bgColor=peachpuff>
101  </body>
102  </html>
```

ANNOTATIONS

This page opens a window for user input when it loads. Depending on the user's answer to the riddle, the script then writes one of three pages—wrong, close, and right—in response. It also demonstrates how to use a simple form of fuzzy logic to test the user's answer.

```
1   <html>
2   <head>
3   <title>Riddle</title>
4   <script language="JavaScript">
5   // Copyright 1997, Henry Sobotka; released to public domain
6   var wDays = new Array("Sunday", "Monday", "Tuesday",
7                   "Wednesday", "Thursday", "Friday", "Saturday");
8   var today = new Date();
9   var Rtitl = "<title>" + wDays[today.getDay()] +
                                      "'s Riddle</title>";
```

The script first creates an array of the names of the days of the week and **today** as a new Date object, then uses **today**'s built-in **getDay( )** method to index the **wDays** array for the name of the week to display in the new window's titlebar. The array itself is designed to be aligned with the value returned by **getDay( )**, namely an integer from 0 (Sunday) to 6 (Saturday).

This indexing also makes it easy to have a full week's riddles and answers set up as arrays so that you wouldn't have to update a page such as this every day. You could even use **today**'s **getDate( )** function, which returns an integer from 1 to 31, to reference a month-long array.

```
10  var Rhead = "<center><font size=+4>" +
11              "Riddle of the Day</font></center>";
12  var Rform1 =
                "<br><form name=Rform>Please enter your name: " +
13                "<input type=text name=Gname size=29>";
14  var Rque =
                "<p><b>Why did the rabbit cross the road?</b><p>";
```

The next three variables, like **Rtitle**, are strings of HTML code used to write the content of the window that pops open when the page is loaded. They and the variables from lines 19 through 37 constitute modular components that can be used at multiple points in the script.

```
15   var Rans = "Because it was stapled to the chicken!";
16   var key1 = "stapled";
17   var key2 = "chicken";
18   var key3 = "staple";
```

The next four variables consist of the answer to the riddle along with three keywords used in the fuzzy-logic routine to assess the user's response. They are placed immediately after the question itself to simplify page maintenance.

```
19   var Rform2 = "<input type=text name=Gans size=50>" +
20          "<p><center><input type=button value='    OK    '" +
21                  "onClick='opener.CheckAns(this.form)'>" +
22                      "<spacer type=horizontal size=25>" +
23              "<input type=button value='    Hint    '" +
24                  "onClick='opener.Hint(this.form)'>" +
25                      "<spacer type=horizontal size=25>" +
26              "<input type=button value=Cancel
                                onClick='opener.NoAns()'>" +
27              "</center></form>";
28   var Rpage = Rtitl + Rhead.fontcolor("blanchedAlmond") +
                                Rform1 + Rque + Rform2;
```

Next the variable **Rform2** contains the HTML code for the three buttons (OK, Hint, and Cancel) that appear in the pop-up window. Notice that the assignments to their **onClick** event handlers all specify **opener** because the functions they call are found in the script loaded into the parent window. **Rpage** is then assigned a concatenation of the page-component variables while at the same time setting **Rhead**'s **fontcolor** property, which is equivalent to writing a

```
<font color=blanchedAlmond>
```

HTML tag. **Rpage** is used as the argument for the **document.write( )** call in line 43.

```
29   var NewTry = "<center><form>" +
30              "<input type=button value='Try again?' " +
31              "onClick=\"self.location='riddle.htm'\">";
32   var showA = "<spacer type=horizontal size=50>" +
33              "<input type=button value='Show answer' " +
34              "onClick=
              \"document.write('<body bgColor=peachpuff><center>" +
35              "<font size=+4 color=crimson>" +
36              "Because it was stapled to the chicken!</font>
                                </center><p>')\">";
37   var fEnd = "</form></center>";
38   var hintCount = 0;
```

The **NewTry, showA** and **fEnd** variables hold the HTML code written in response to a wrong answer to the riddle. They are used by **CheckAns( )** in lines 71 and 76.

The assignment to the "Show answer" button's **onClick** handler contains the HTML code that displays the answer to the riddle. It *cannot* make use of the **Rans** variable in line 36 because the **document.write( )** call that creates the page with the "Show answer" button wipes out the script containing **Rans**. An alternative would be to use frames and put this script in the head of the main frameset page where it would remain loaded so that all its variables and functions would be accessible from any documents it wrote.

The other button, "Try again?", reloads the page with the script when clicked. Lastly, the **hintCount** variable serves as a counter in the **Hint( )** function (line 81).

```
40   function openRbox() {
41       Rbox = window.open("","","width=500,height=300");
42       Rbox.document.open();
43       Rbox.document.write(Rpage);
44       if (document.cookie) {
45           Rbox.document.Rform.Gname.value = document.cookie;
46           Rbox.document.Rform.Gans.focus();
47       }
48       else Rbox.document.Rform.Gname.focus();
49       Rbox.document.bgColor = "lightcoral";
50       Rbox.document.close();
51   }
```

openRbox( ), assigned to the page's **onLoad** event handler in the <BODY> tag on line 100, opens a 300×500-pixel window named **Rbox** and fills it with the **Rpage** concatenation. It then looks for the cookie created in line 56 to store the user's name so that it only has to be entered once. If the cookie exists, its content is loaded into the name text field and the answer field is given focus by line 46. Otherwise, the name field gets the focus. Finally, line 49 colors the document and 50 closes it.

```
53   function CheckAns(form) {
54       var Gname = form.Gname.value;
55       var Gans = form.Gans.value.toLowerCase();
56       document.cookie = Gname;
57       Rbox.close();
```

CheckAns( ), called by the OK button in the pop-up window, first assigns two variables, **Gname** and **Gans**, the contents of the name and answer text fields respectively. In the latter case, the built-in JavaScript **toLowerCase( )** method is called to convert the user's response to a lowercase string for comparison purposes.

Line 56 then creates an temporary cookie to store the user's name. This cookie is not written to the COOKIES.TXT file; it crumbles when the browser session ends. Then line 57 closes the pop-up window.

```
58       if (Gans.indexOf(key1) != -1 && Gans.indexOf(key2) != -1
59           && Gans.indexOf(key2) > Gans.indexOf(key1)
```

```
60        && (Gans.indexOf(key2) - Gans.indexOf(key1)) > 10
61        && (Gans.length <
                      (Gans.indexOf(key2) + key2.length + 3)
62        || Gans.indexOf(key2 + "'s") != -1))
```

Lines 58 to 62 contain some simple fuzzy logic to evaluate the user's answer. While it would obviously be much easier to test for an exact match between the user's response (**Gans**) and the right answer (**Rans**), chances are that a user-entered right answer will not match the variable string word for word. Using an exact match as criterion would only breed irritation and anger in users who got the answer right, but in their own words. Hence this routine uses four criteria to consider an answer correct:

1. It must contain the words "stapled" and "chicken";

2. The word "chicken" must come after "stapled" to rule out a response such as "It was chicken of getting stapled to the punk";

3. There must be at least a two-letter word between "stapled" and "chicken"; and

4. The last word must be "chicken" (to rule out "chicken sandwich", for example), or the answer must contain the possessive "chicken's" (to allow for "chicken's wing", for instance).

All of these criteria are tested for by deploying the JavaScript **indexOf( )** method, which returns -1 if the string used as its argument is not found in the search target, or the zero-based index of the first occurrence of the string if it is found. Each of the *if* conditions in lines 58 to 62 corresponds to one of these four criteria. The "+ 3" in line 61 makes allowance for the user typing a blank space or entering a question or exclamation mark after "chicken".

```
63    document.write("<title>Ding!</title>" +
                              Rhead.fontcolor("crimson") +
64              "<center><h2>Right, " + Gname + "!<p>" +
65        Gans.fontcolor("crimson") + "!</h2></center>");
```

If all four tests are passed, a page entitled "Ding!" appears and displays a message incorporating the user's name and response.

```
66    else if (Gans.indexOf(key3) != -1
                          || Gans.indexOf(key2) != -1)
67    document.write("<title>Bzzzt!</title>" +
                              Rhead.fontcolor("crimson") +
68              "<center><h2>Wrong, " + Gname + "!<p>" +
69    "You answered: " + Gans.fontcolor("crimson") + "!<p>" +
70                  "<b>Warm! But no banana...</b><p>" +
71              NewTry + showA + fEnd + "</h2></center>");
```

Otherwise, if either the word "staple" or "chicken" are found in the user's answer, it writes a "wrong-but-close" page with the global **Rhead**, **NewTry**, **showA**, and **fEnd** variables, as well as the user's name and answer.

```
72    else
73        document.write("<title>Bzzzt!</title>" +
                                    Rhead.fontcolor("crimson") +
74                "<center><h2>Wrong, " + Gname + "!<p>" +
75        "You answered: " + Gans.fontcolor("crimson") + "!" +
76                NewTry + showA + fEnd + "</h2></center>");
77    document.bgColor = "peachpuff";
78    document.close();
79  }
```

Any other responses are handled by the *else* routine which writes a "wrong answer" page identical to the one for a "warm" answer with the exception of line 70.

```
81  function Hint(form) {
82      var hintStr = Rans.split(' ');
83      if (hintCount == hintStr.length) {
84          hintCount = 0;
85          form.Gans.value = hintStr[hintCount];
86          hintCount++;
87      }
88      else form.Gans.value += ' ' + hintStr[hintCount++];
89  }
```

The **Hint( )** function displays one word of the correct answer in the pop-up window's text field with each click on the "Hint" button. First, it uses JavaScript's **split( )** method to divide the **Rans** string at each blank space; this produces an array comprised of its member words. Then, if the values of **hintCount** and **length** of the **hintStr** array are identical, meaning that the end of the array has been reached, **hintCount** is reset to zero and the first word of the answer (**hintStr[0]**) is displayed. This loops the display; otherwise once the end of the **hintStr** array has been reached, each subsequent click on the "Hint" button appends the word "null" in the text field.

If **hintCount** does not equal the **length** of **hintStr**, line 88 appends a blank space followed by the next member of the array while simultaneously incrementing the index.

```
91  function NoAns(){
92      Rbox.close();
93      document.write("<title>Main Page</title>" +
94                Rhead + NewTry + showA + fEnd);
95      document.bgColor = "peachpuff";
```

```
96    document.close();
97  }
```

The **NoAns( )** function assigned to the pop-up window's "Cancel" button closes the riddle window and uses the script's global string variables to write a page containing the "Try again?" and "Show answer" buttons. An alternative would be to have it load another page into the parent window with

```
self.location = "mainpage.htm"
```

Or this function could be eliminated altogether by assigning

```
opener.location="mainpage.htm";self.close()
```

directly to the "Cancel" button's event handler up in line 26.

```
98  </script>
99  </head>
100 <body onLoad='openRbox()' bgColor=peachpuff>
101 </body>
102 </html>
```

When you have a single page like this that writes various subpages without using frames or layers, the most important thing to remember is that **document.write( )** instantly wipes out your script so that its variables and functions can no longer be accessed from the subpage. Forgetting this simple fact is the origin of many "*x* is undefined" or "*x* has no property named *y*" JavaScript error messages and the ensuing frustration.

While a "Riddle of the Day" may be the last thing you want on your web site, you can use the techniques demonstrated in this script to create pages that incorporate serious user input. For software downloads, for example, the pop-up window might get information about the visitor's computer and operating system, then write a link to the appropriate file in the main window. Particularly in the case of sprawling sites, using a dialog window to profile your visitor and steer them in the right direction with a page tailored to their interests may not only make it easier for them to find what they want, but also lighten the load on your server by staving off needless downloads of information they don't want.

parent

Parent-Child Windows

| N2 | N2.01 | N2.02+ | N3 | N4 | E3 | E4 |

This script opens a pop-up window with a list of links that is loaded into the parent window (see Figure 1-11). It comes in two flavors. One opens the pop-up child when the main window is loaded, the other does it when you click a button.

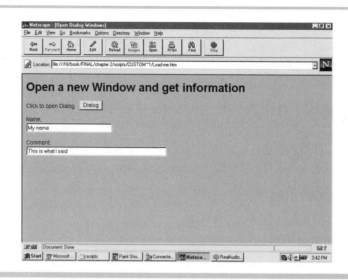

FIGURE 1-11.   Parent window

PARENT WINDOW

```
1    <html>
2    <head>
3    <title>Window Opener</title>
4    </head>
5    <SCRIPT LANGUAGE="JavaScript">
6
7    function windowOpener() {
8      controlWindow=window.open("window.htm","","toolbar=no,
            location=no,directories=no,status=yes,menubar=no,
            scrollbars=yes,resizable=no,width=220,height=265");
9    }
10
11   </SCRIPT>
12   <BODY bgcolor="#FFF000"
                    onLoad="setTimeout('windowOpener()',1000)">
13   <font face="Arial,Helvetica">
14   <center>
15   <h1>Open It!</h1>
16   </center>
17   </font>
```

```
18   </body>
19   </html>
```

BUTTON VARIATION FOR MAIN WINDOW

```
12   <BODY bgcolor="#FFF000">
13   <font face="Arial,Helvetica">
14   <center>
15   <form><INPUT type="button" Value="Open It!"
16       onClick="windowOpener()">
17   </form>
18   </center>
19   </font>
20   </body>
21   </html>
```

CHILD WINDOW

```
1    <HTML>
2    <HEAD>
3    <TITLE>Open Window</TITLE>
4    <SCRIPT LANGUAGE = "JavaScript">
5    <!--
6        function get(url) {
7            opener.location = url;
8        }
9
10   //-->
11   </SCRIPT>
12   </HEAD>
13   <BODY>
14   <h2>This child window can load pages
                              into the parent window</h2><p>
15   JavaScript:<Br>
16   <UL><A HREF="JavaScript:get(
         'http://www.javascripts.com/jsguildsite/jsguild.html')">
                               Javascript Writers Guild</A>
             One of the coolest html layouts I've seen</UL>
17   <UL><A HREF="JavaScript:get(
         'http://www.tradepub.com/javascript/m_main2_0.htm')">
```

```
                     JS Resources A2Z</A> Yellow Pages of JavaScript</UL>
18   <UL><A HREF="JavaScript:get(
                   'http://www.geocities.com/SiliconValley/9000')">
        Javascript Book</A> Two individuals writing a JavaScript
            book.  Lots of kewl scripts and tons of links.</UL>
19   <UL><A HREF="JavaScript:get(
                'http://www.geocities.com/SiliconValley/Park/2328')">
                TazzMania HomePage--Java</A> A few scripts with
                                          cut and paste</UL>
20   <UL><A HREF="JavaScript:get(
            'http://www.javascripts.com')">Wizards Walk Among Us</A>
                                    Another JavaScript resource</UL>
21   <UL><A HREF="JavaScript:get(
                    'http://www.sapien.net/demo/javascript/')">
                        Poland's Javascript Examples</A>
                        Small collection of scripts.</UL>
22   <UL><A HREF="JavaScript:get(
                    'http://w3.one.net/~ronlwzz/JavaScript.htm')">
                Kentucky Dudes JavaScript Resources</A></UL>
23   <UL><A HREF="JavaScript:get(
                            'http://www.ios.com/~jas/')">
            JAS's International JavaScript Resources</A>
                        JavaScript Resources galore.</UL>
24   <UL><A HREF="JavaScript:get(
                        'http://www.microsoft.com/jscript/')">
                            MicroSoft JScript</A>
                    Microsoft's version of JavaScript</UL>
25   <UL><A HREF="JavaScript:get(
                'http://www.essex1.com/people/timothy/js-index.htm')">
                        Timothy's JavaScript Examples</A>
                        Small collection of scripts.</UL>
26   </BODY>
27   </HTML>
```

ANNOTATIONS

```
1    <html>
2    <head>
3    <title>Window Opener</title>
4    </head>
5    <SCRIPT LANGUAGE="JavaScript">
6
```

```
7   function windowOpener() {
8     controlWindow=window.open("window.htm","","toolbar=no,
              location=no,directories=no,status=yes,menubar=no,
              scrollbars=yes,resizable=no,width=220,height=265");
9   }
```

This function opens a 220×265-pixel window named **controlWindow**, which loads the file WINDOW.HTM containing the index of links. The child window cannot be resized, and its only features are a status bar and scroll bars. The scroll bars are essential because the list of URLs extends well beyond the small document area.

```
11  </SCRIPT>
12  <BODY bgcolor="#FFF000"
              onLoad="setTimeout('windowOpener()',1000)">
```

The **onLoad** event handler calls **windowOpener( )** one second (1,000 milliseconds) after this page has been loaded. The **setTimeout** method is a built-in JavaScript feature that enables you to time events. It takes two comma-separated arguments: the called function as a string, and the number of milliseconds for which the function is delayed.

```
13  <font face="Arial,Helvetica">
14  <center>
15  <h1>Open It!</h1>
16  </center>
17  </font>
18  </body>
19  </html>
```

If you don't want the main window to launch the pop-up index automatically, you can add a user-controlled button as shown next. All this involves is removing the **onLoad** event handler from the <BODY> tag, creating a form consisting of one button, and having it call **windowOpener( )** with its **onClick** event handler.

```
12  <BODY bgcolor="#FFF000">
13  <font face="Arial,Helvetica">
14  <center>
15  <form><INPUT type="button" Value="Open It!"
16     onClick="windowOpener()">
17  </form>
```

Figures 1-12 and 1-13 shows the parent and child windows that can be called by this script.

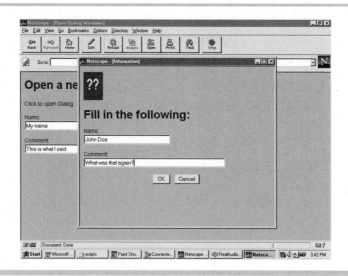

FIGURE 1-12. Button variation for main window

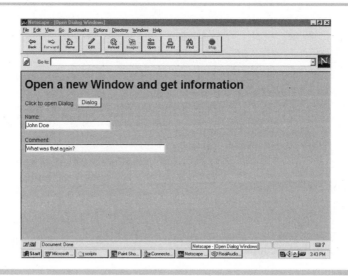

FIGURE 1-13. Child window

```
1   <HTML>
2   <HEAD>
3   <TITLE>Open Window</TITLE>
4   <SCRIPT LANGUAGE = "JavaScript">
5   <!--
6       function get(url) {
7           opener.location = url;
8       }
```

This one-line function is all it takes to load the links into the parent window. It takes one argument, **url**, whose value is assigned to **opener.location**, or the parent window's location. This simple assignment loads the linked page into the main window.

```
10  //-->
11  </SCRIPT>
12  </HEAD>
13  <BODY>
14  <h2>This child window can load pages
                            into the parent window</h2><p>
15  JavaScript:<Br>
16  <UL><A HREF="JavaScript:get(
        'http://www.javascripts.com/jsguildsite/jsguild.html')">
                            Javascript Writers Guild</A>
                One of the coolest html layouts I've seen</UL>
17  <UL><A HREF="JavaScript:get(
        'http://www.tradepub.com/javascript/m_main2_0.htm')">
        JS Resources A2Z</A> Yellow Pages of JavaScript</UL>
```

. . .

The body of the child window consists of an unordered list of links (HTML bullets rather than numbers). The **href** for each one is a JavaScript call that passes the full URL string to the **get( )** function as its argument. If you do not designate the URL as a string by enclosing it in quotation marks when passing it to **get( )**, you will produce an "http://... undefined" error message. Single quotes have to be used here, because they are nested within doubles.

By replacing the preceding list of URLs with links to pages within your site, you could use this approach as an interesting alternative to a frames setup.

winopts

Web Designer's Guide to Window Options

N2 **N2.01** N2.02+ **N3** **N4** **E3** **E4**

This device allows you to both explore and test different kinds of windows, including the new features and methods introduced with JavaScript 1.2 for Navigator 4.0. In addition, it can generate the code for the window you like.

Though this script appears very complicated, it really isn't. Aside from demonstrating the new window methods, there is little in it that hasn't been discussed earlier in this chapter. Yet it serves as an example of how you can combine those simple techniques to build something useful.

```
1   <HTML>
2   <HEAD>
3   <TITLE>New Window Options Viewer</TITLE>
4   <SCRIPT LANGUAGE="JavaScript">
5   // Copyright 1997, Henry Sobotka; released to public domain
6   x = navigator.appVersion.charAt(0);
7   varN = '';
8   fileName = '';
9   winName = '';
10  newCode = '';
11  codeLine = '';
12  msgWindow = null;
13  boogWin = null;
14  var a, b, c, d, e, f, g, h, i, j, k, l, m, n, o;
15  var q = '"';
16
17  function newWin() {
18  with (document.Switcher) {
19  fileName = fileN.value;
20  winName = winN.value;
21  if (eval(WinH.value) > 0 ) a = 'height=' +  WinH.value + ',';
22  else a = '';
23  if (eval(WinW.value) > 0 ) b = 'width=' +  WinW.value + ',';
24  else b = '';
25  if (MenuB[0].checked == true) c = "menubar,";
26  else c = '';
27  if (ToolB[0].checked == true) d = "toolbar,";
28  else d = '';
29  if (DirB[0].checked == true) e = "directories,";
30  else e = '';
```

```
31   if (LocF[0].checked == true) f = "location,";
32   else f = '';
33   if (ScrollB[0].checked == true) g = "scrollbars,";
34   else g = '';
35   if (StatusB[0].checked == true) h = "status,";
36   else h = '';
37   if (rSize[0].checked == true) i = "resizable,";
38   else i = '';
39   if (eval(innerW.value) > 0 || recChng[0].checked == true )
                        j = 'innerWidth=' + innerW.value + ',';
40   else j = '';
41   if ( eval(innerH.value) > 0 || recChng[0].checked == true )
                        k = 'innerHeight=' + innerH.value + ',';
42   else k = '';
43   if (eval(outerW.value) > 0 || recChng[0].checked == true )
                        l = 'outerWidth=' + outerW.value + ',';
44   else l = '';
45   if ( eval(outerH.value) > 0 || recChng[0].checked == true )
                        m = 'outerHeight=' + outerH.value + ',';
46   else m = '';
47   if ( eval(scrX.value) > 0 || recChng[0].checked == true )
                        n = 'screenX=' + scrX.value + ',';
48   else n = '';
49   if ( eval(scrY.value) > 0 || recChng[0].checked == true )
                        o = 'screenY=' + scrY.value + ',';
50   else o = '';
51      }
52   }
53
54   function showWin() {
55   msgWindow = window.open(fileName, winName, a + b + c + d + e
                   + f + g + h + i + j + k + l + m + n + o + q);
56   msgWindow.focus();
57   }
58
59   function genCode() {
60   if (varN == "") { varN = 'newWin'; }
61   else { varN = document.Switcher.vName.value; }
62   codeLine = '<SCRI' + 'PT>' + varN + '=window.open("' +
                   fileName + '", "' + winName + '", "' + a + b + c
                                   + d + e + f + g + h + i;
63   if (eval(x) > 3) { codeLine += j + k + l + m + n + o; }
64   if ( codeLine.charAt(codeLine.length - 1) == ',') {
```

```
         newCode = codeLine.substring(0, codeLine.length - 1) }
65    else { newCode = codeLine }
66  newCode += '")</SCRI' + 'PT>';
67  document.Switcher.codeOut.value = newCode;
68  }
69
70  function gNav4(){
71    alert("This function requires Navigator 4.x!");
72  }
73  </SCRIPT>
74  <SCRIPT LANGUAGE="JavaScript1.2">
75
76  function makeWin() {
77      if(confirm('Create a child window?') )
78         msgWindow = window.open("","",
                              "width=300,height=300,resizable");
79      msgWindow.focus();
80  }
81
82  function moveWinBy() {
83   with (document.Switcher) {
84   LR =   eval(moveLR.value)
85   UD =   eval(moveUD.value)
86   if (winMeth[0].checked == true) {
87     if (msgWindow == null) { makeWin(); }
88         msgWindow.focus()
89         msgWindow.moveBy(LR, UD);
90         if (recChng[0].checked == true) {
91             cnt1 = eval(leftV.value); cnt1 += eval(LR);
                                          leftV.value = cnt1;
92             cnt2 = eval(topV.value); cnt2 += eval(UD);
                                          topV.value = cnt2; }
93       }
94     else self.moveBy(LR, UD);
95     }
96  }
97
98  function moveWinTo() {
99  with (document.Switcher) {
100  HA =   eval(hAxis.value)
101  VA =   eval(vAxis.value)
102   if (winMeth[0].checked == true) {
103      if (msgWindow == null ) { makeWin(); }
```

```
104     msgWindow.focus()
105     msgWindow.moveTo(HA, VA)
106        if (recChng[0].checked == true ) {
107                     scrX.value = eval(HA);
108                     scrY.value = eval(VA); }
109     }
110     else self.moveTo(HA, VA);
111    }
112 }
113
114 function sizeWinBy() {
115 with (document.Switcher) {
116 if (rSize[1].checked == true)
117     { alert('You have to set resizable to "yes" before you
                                    can resize a window.') }
118  rbh =   eval(rsizbH.value)
119  rbv =   eval(rsizbV.value)
120 if(winMeth[0].checked == true) {
121    if( msgWindow == null ) { makeWin(); }
122    msgWindow.focus()
123    msgWindow.resizeBy(rbh, rbv)
124   if ( recChng[0].checked == true ) {
125                     cnt3 = eval(outerW.value);
                         cnt3 += eval(rbh); outerW.value = cnt3;
126                     cnt4 = eval(outerH.value);
                        cnt4 += eval(rbv); outerH.value = cnt4; }
127    }
128 else self.resizeBy(rbh, rbv)
129    }
130 }
131
132 function sizeWinTo() {
133 with (document.Switcher) {
134 if (rSize[1].checked == true)
135     { alert('You have to set resizable to "yes" before you
                                    can resize a window.') }
136  rth =   eval(rsiztH.value)
137  rtv =   eval(rsiztV.value)
138 if(winMeth[0].checked == true) {
139    if( msgWindow == null ) { makeWin(); }
140    msgWindow.focus()
141    msgWindow.resizeTo(rth, rtv)
142   if ( recChng[0].checked == true ) {
```

```
143                         outerW.value = eval(rth);
144                         outerH.value = eval(rtv); }
145       }
146  else self.resizeTo(rth, rtv)
147     }
148 }
149
150  function armWnd(){
151     window.captureEvents(Event.CLICK);
152     window.onClick = setWnd;
153  }
154
155  var clickCount = 0;
156
157  function setWnd(e){
158     var x = e.screenX;
159     var y = e.screenY;
160     if( msgWindow == null ) { makeWin(); }
161     msgWindow.focus();
162     msgWindow.moveTo(x,y);
163     clickCount++;
164     if (clickCount==5) {
165         clickCount = 0;
166         window.releaseEvents(Event.CLICK);
167     }
168     return false;
169  }
170
171  function winDance() {
172     boogWin = window.open("", "", "outerWidth=150,
        outerHeight=150,screenX=50,screenY=50,resizable");
173     with (boogWin) {
174     for (var i = 0; i < 400; i++) {
175         if ( i % 5 == 0 ) { resizeBy( 5, 5); }
176         if ( i % 10 == 0 ) { resizeBy( -15, -15); }
177         if ( i < 100 )  moveBy(4, 0);
178         if ( i > 100 && i < 200 ) moveBy(0, 4);
179         if ( i > 200 && i < 300 ) moveBy(-4, 0);
180         if ( i > 300 && i < 400 ) moveBy(0, -4);
181     }
182     }
183  }
```

```
184  </SCRIPT>
185  </HEAD>
186  <BODY BGCOLOR="#87cefa">
187  <SCRIPT>
188  with (document) {
189
190  ht1 = '<FORM NAME=Switcher><TABLE WIDTH="100%"
                                          CELLPADDING=15><TR><TD>';
191  ht2 = '</TD><TD BGCOLOR=blue><FONT SIZE=+3 COLOR=gold>';
192  ht3 = '<B>Window<BR>Creation<BR>Options';
193  ht4 = '</B></FONT></TD></TR>';
194  ht5 = '</TABLE><BR><CENTER>';
195  tx1 = 'This page allows you to explore and test the various
            options available when creating a new window, as well
            as the <I>moveBy</I>, <I>moveTo</I>, <I>resizeBy</I>,
            and <I>resizeTo</I> methods introduced with
            JavaScript 1.2 for Navigator 4.0.<BR>It can also
            generate the JavaScript code for creating your
            window.';
196
197  write(ht1 + tx1 + ht2 + ht3 + ht4 + ht5);
198
199  mt1= '<TABLE BORDER=0 WIDTH="95%" CELLSPACING=3
                                      CELLPADDING=7><TR>';
200  trs = '<TD ROWSPAN=';
201  th1 = ' BGCOLOR=blue ALIGN=RIGHT>
                            <FONT COLOR=gold SIZE=+1><B>';
202  th2 = '</B></FONT></TD>';
203  tf1 = '<TD ALIGN=CENTER COLSPAN=2><INPUT TYPE=TEXT NAME=';
204  tf2 = ' SIZE=30></TD><TD COLSPAN=2><I>';
205  tf3 = '</I></TD></TR><TR>';
206
207  write(mt1 + trs + 3 + th1 + 'NAMES' + th2 + tf1
                                      + 'vName' + tf2);
208  write('Window object name for JavaScript references.');
209  write(tf3 + tf1 + 'fileN' + tf2);
210  write('Name of file to load.');
211  write(tf3 + tf1 + 'winN' + tf2);
212  write('Window name for &lt;TARGET=...&gt;
                            in tags and target property.');
213  write(tf3 + trs + 2 + th1 + 'SIZING' + th2);
214
```

```
215  tf4 = '<TD ALIGN=RIGHT WIDTH=125>';
216  tf5 = '<INPUT TYPE=TEXT NAME=';
217  tf6 = ' SIZE=5 VALUE=0></TD>';
218  tc1 = ' COLSPAN=2 VALIGN=TOP><I>';
219  tx2 = 'Both height and width values must be set for either
             to work. These dimensions apply solely to the
                            document area of the new window.';
220
221  write(tf4 + 'Height:' + tf5 + 'WinH' + tf6 + tf4 + 'Width:'
                                    + tf5 + 'WinW' + tf6);
222  write(trs + 2 + tc1 + tx2 + tf3 + tf4 + 'Resizable?');
223
224  rb1 = '</TD><TD ALIGN=CENTER WIDTH=125>Yes
                            <INPUT TYPE=RADIO NAME=';
225  rb2 = '> No<INPUT TYPE=RADIO NAME=';
226  rb3 = ' CHECKED></TD>';
227  rc1 = '</TR><TR>';
228  tc2 = '<TD ROWSPAN=2 VALIGN=TOP>';
229  th3 = '<TD ALIGN=CENTER BGCOLOR=blue>
                            <FONT SIZE=+2 COLOR=gold><B>';
230  th4 = '<TD ROWSPAN=3 ALIGN=CENTER>';
231  ta1 = '<TEXTAREA COLS=45 ROWS=6 NAME=';
232  ta2 = ' VALUE="" WRAP=physical></TEXTAREA></TD>';
233  te1 = '</TR></TABLE>';
234  tx3 = '<I>With Microsoft\'s Internet Explorer, the toolbar,
             location and directories options function as a unit.
             Select "toolbar" for all three; the other two cannot
             be selected separately.';
235
236  write(rb1 + 'rSize' + rb2 + 'rSize' + rb3 + rc1);
237  write(trs + 6 + th1 + 'APPEARANCE' + th2 + tf4);
238  write('Menubar?' + rb1 + 'MenuB' + rb2 + 'MenuB' + rb3);
239  write(tc2 + tx3 + tf3 + tf4);
240  write('Toolbar?' + rb1 + 'ToolB' + rb2 + 'ToolB' + rb3);
241  write(rc1 + tf4);
242  write('Location field?' + rb1 + 'LocF'
                                    + rb2 + 'LocF' + rb3);
243  write(th3 + 'Code Viewer' + th2 + rc1 + tf4);
244  write('Directories?' + rb1 + 'DirB' + rb2 + 'DirB' + rb3);
245  write(th4 + ta1 + 'codeOut' + ta2 + rc1 + tf4);
246  write('Scrollbars?' + rb1 + 'ScrollB'
                                    + rb2 + 'ScrollB' + rb3);
247  write(rc1 + tf4);
```

```
248 write('Statusbar?' + rb1 + 'StatusB'
                                        + rb2 + 'StatusB' + rb3);
249 write(te1+ '<BR>');
250
251 fb1 = '<INPUT TYPE=BUTTON  VALUE="';
252 fb2 = '" ONCLICK="';
253 sp1 = '<SPACER TYPE=HORIZONTAL SIZE=15>';
254
255 write(fb1 + 'Show Window' + fb2 +
                            'newWin();showWin()' + '">' + sp1);
256 write(fb1 + 'Close Window' + fb2 +
                            'msgWindow.close()' + '">' + sp1);
257 write(fb1 + 'Generate Code' + fb2 +
                            'newWin();genCode()' + '"><BR><BR>');
258
259 th5 = '<TD COLSPAN=4 ALIGN=CENTER BGCOLOR=blue>
                                    <FONT SIZE=+2 COLOR=gold><B>';
260 th6 = '<TR><TD ROWSPAN=2 ALIGN=RIGHT BGCOLOR=blue>
                                    <FONT COLOR=gold SIZE=+1><B>';
261 tw1 = '<TD WIDTH=125 ALIGN=LEFT>';
262 tv1 = '<TD VALIGN=TOP ALIGN=LEFT>';
263 tv2 = '<TD ALIGN=RIGHT>';
264 rb4 = '<INPUT TYPE=RADIO NAME=';
265 rb5 = ' ONCLICK="';
266 rb6 = ' CHECKED ONCLICK="';
267 rb7 = '</TD><TD ALIGN=CENTER><NOBR>Yes ';
268 tn1 = '</NOBR></TD>';
269
270 write(mt1 + th5);
271 write('New in JavaScript 1.2 / Navigator 4.0');
272 write(ht4 + th6 + 'SIZE' + th2 + tf4);
273 write('innerWidth<BR>' + tf5 + 'innerW' + tf6 + tw1);
274 write('innerHeight<BR>' + tf5 + 'innerH' + tf6 + tv1);
275 write('Sets the dimensions of the document area of the
            window (same as <i>width</i> and <i>height</i>.
                                    </TD></TR>' + tf4);
276 write('outerWidth<BR>' + tf5 + 'outerW' + tf6 + tw1);
277 write('outerHeight<BR>' + tf5 + 'outerH' + tf6 + tv1);
278 write('Sets the dimensions of the full size of the window.
                                    </TD></TR>');
279 write(th6 + 'LOCATION' + th2 + tv2);
280 write('screenX<BR>' + tf5 + 'scrX' + tf6 + '<TD>');
281 write('screenY<BR>' + tf5 + 'scrY' + tf6 + tv1);
```

```
282  write('Determines where the window will open, measured in
              pixels from the top left corner of the screen.</TD>');
283  write(te1+ '<BR>');
284
285  tr2 = '<TR><TD COLSPAN=8>';
286  wh1 = 'Width:<BR>Height:</TD><TD>';
287  tv3 = '<TR ALIGN=CENTER>';
288  th7 = '<TD COLSPAN=2>';
289  th8 = '<TD COLSPAN=4>';
290  th9 = '<TD COLSPAN=8 ALIGN=CENTER BGCOLOR=blue>
                                   <FONT SIZE=+2 COLOR=gold><B>';
291  tf7= ' SIZE=5 VALUE=0><BR>';
292  tx5 = 'These buttons allow you to see how the new resize and
              move methods work with either your browser or a new
              window by selecting either the parent or child radio
              button below.  By setting "Record size / position
              changes?" to yes, adjustments you make to a child
              window\'s size and position with these buttons will
              be reflected in the script produced by pressing
              "Generate Code".<BR><B>NOTE:</B> For resize to work,
              the resizable option for your new window must be set
              to "yes".</TD>';
293  hr1 = tr2 + '<HR>' + rc1;
294
295  write(mt1 + th9);
296  write('New JavaScript 1.2 Window Methods');
297  write(ht4 + tr2 + tx5 + rc1);
298  write(tv2 + '+ right, - left:<BR>- up, + down:</TD><TD>');
299  write(tf5 + 'moveLR' + tf7);
300  write(tf5 + 'moveUD' + tf6);
301  write(tv2 + 'From left:<BR>From top:</TD><TD>');
302  write(tf5 + 'hAxis' + tf7);
303  write(tf5 + 'vAxis' + tf6);
304  write(tv2 + wh1);
305  write(tf5 + 'rsizbH' + tf7);
306  write(tf5 + 'rsizbV' + tf6);
307  write(tv2 + wh1);
308  write(tf5 + 'rsiztH' + tf7);
309  write(tf5 + 'rsiztV' + tf6 + '</TR>' + tv3);
310  write(th7 + fb1 + 'moveBy' + fb2 +
              'if( eval(x) > 3) moveWinBy();else gNav4()"></TD>');
311  write(th7 + fb1 + 'moveTo' + fb2 +
```

```
              'if( eval(x) > 3) moveWinTo();else gNav4()"></TD>');
312  write(th7 + fb1 + 'resizeBy' + fb2 +
              'if( eval(x) > 3) sizeWinBy();else gNav4()"></TD>');
313  write(th7 + fb1 + 'resizeTo' + fb2 +
          'if( eval(x) > 3) sizeWinTo();else gNav4()"></TD></TR>');
314  write(tv3 + th8 + 'Child: ' + rb4 +
                                'winMeth CHECKED>Parent: ');
315  write(rb4 + 'winMeth><BR></TD>');
316  write(th8 + 'Record size / position changes?  Yes ');
317  write(rb4 + 'recChng> No ' + rb4 + 'recChng' + rb3 + rc1
                                      + hr1 + th8);
318
319  tx6 = 'The "Arm 5 clicks" button makes the main browser
          window capture clicks and move the child window to
          the location pointed at by the tip of your cursor.
          After five clicks, the window will automatically
          become disarmed. Otherwise the onClick event handlers
          of the buttons on the page would remain
                                shortcircuited.</TD>';
320  tx7 = 'If a click doesn\'t move the child window, it
          doesn\'t count. After the fifth click, the child
          window vanishes behind the browser.<BR><BR><CENTER>';
321  tx8= 'And for a bit of fun, here\'s a very primitive version
          of a dancing window made by combining <I>moveBy</I>
          and <I>resizeBy</I> with "for" and "if" statements.
          The trail it leaves on the screen will vanish when it
                                stops.<BR><BR><CENTER>';
322
323  write(tx6 + th8 + tx7);
324  write(fb1 + 'Arm 5 clicks' + fb2 + 'if( eval(x) > 3)
          armWnd();else gNav4()"></CENTER></TD></TR>' + hr1);
325  write(th6 + 'WINDOW<BR> BOOGIE</B></FONT>
                                </TD><TD COLSPAN=7>');
326  write(tx8 + fb1 + 'Boogie!' + fb2 + 'if( eval(x) > 3)
                        winDance();else gNav4()">' + sp1);
327  write(fb1 + '  Close  ' + fb2 + 'if( eval(x) > 3 &&
          boogWin != null) boogWin.close();else gNav4()">');
328  write('</CENTER></TD>' + te1 +'</FORM></CENTER>');
329  }
330  </SCRIPT>
331  </BODY>
332  </HTML>
```

ANNOTATIONS

```
1    <HTML>
2    <HEAD>
3    <TITLE>New Window Options Viewer</TITLE>
4    <SCRIPT LANGUAGE="JavaScript">
5    // Copyright 1997, Henry Sobotka; released to public domain
6    x = navigator.appVersion.charAt(0);
7    varN = '';
8    fileName = '';
9    winName = '';
10   newCode = '';
11   codeLine = '';
12   msgWindow = null;
13   boogWin = null;
14   var a, b, c, d, e, f, g, h, i, j, k, l, m, n, o;
15   var q = '"';
```

The script reads the user's version of Navigator using the string method **charAt( )** with **navigator.appVersion**. This returns the first character (0, as in all arrays) in the string or version number (2, 3, or 4) and assigns it to **x**. The value of **x** is used in functions, as on line 62, or with buttons, as on lines 277 and 278, to determine behavior.

Next comes a series of global variables consisting of empty strings, two windows initialized as **null**, and finally the variables for the window-creation functions. The purpose of declaring them here is to make them available to all the functions on the page.

```
17   function newWin() {
18   with (document.Switcher) {
```

The statements within this function are encased in a **with** clause. This saves having to spell out "document.Switcher" for every reference to an element of the form. An alternative would be to give the function an argument, for example:

```
                         newWin(form)
```

and call it with

```
                         newWin(this.form)
```

in which case the elements could be referred to as

```
                         form.fileN.value
```

Or you could even combine the two:

```
                         with (form)
```

This function then assigns the values, if any, entered in the text fields for the name of the file to be loaded by the new window—and its target name—to two of the global variables.

```
19  fileName = fileN.value;
20  winName = winN.value;
```

The remainder of this function reads the text fields for height and width, along with the radio buttons for various window features. If values are found in the former, or if a button is set to yes, one of the alphabetical variables (**a** to **o**) is assigned the appropriate string for the code that creates the new window.

```
21  if (eval(WinH.value) > 0 ) a = 'height=' +  WinH.value + ',';
22  else a = '';
23  if (eval(WinW.value) > 0 ) b = 'width=' +  WinW.value + ',';
24  else b = '';
25  if (MenuB[0].checked == true) c = "menubar,";
26  else c = '';
27  if (ToolB[0].checked == true) d = "toolbar,";
28  else d = '';
29  if (DirB[0].checked == true) e = "directories,";
30  else e = '';
31  if (LocF[0].checked == true) f = "location,";
32  else f = '';
33  if (ScrollB[0].checked == true) g = "scrollbars,";
34  else g = '';
35  if (StatusB[0].checked == true) h = "status,";
36  else h = '';
37  if (rSize[0].checked == true) i = "resizable,";
38  else i = '';
39  if (eval(innerW.value) > 0 || recChng[0].checked == true )
                     j = 'innerWidth=' +  innerW.value + ',';
40  else j = '';
41  if ( eval(innerH.value) > 0 || recChng[0].checked == true )
                    k = 'innerHeight=' +  innerH.value + ',';
42  else k = '';
43  if (eval(outerW.value) > 0 || recChng[0].checked == true )
                     l = 'outerWidth=' +  outerW.value + ',';
44  else l = '';
45  if ( eval(outerH.value) > 0 || recChng[0].checked == true )
                    m = 'outerHeight=' +  outerH.value + ',';
46  else m = '';
47  if ( eval(scrX.value) > 0 || recChng[0].checked == true )
```

```
                                   n = 'screenX=' +  scrX.value + ',';
48   else n = '';
49   if ( eval(scrY.value) > 0 || recChng[0].checked == true )
                                   o = 'screenY=' +  scrY.value + ',';
50   else o = '';
51      }
52   }
```

In lines 39 to 50, which involve JavaScript 1.2 features, **newWin( )** also checks to see if the "Record changes?" radio button is set to yes. If it is, the resize and move values are monitored and reflected in the script produced with the "Generate code" button.

```
54   function showWin() {
55   msgWindow = window.open(fileName, winName, a + b + c + d + e
                      + f + g + h + i + j + k + l + m + n + o + q);
56   msgWindow.focus();
```

The preceding function uses the list of values read by **newWin( )** to create the new window.

```
59   function genCode() {
60   if (varN == "") { varN = 'newWin'; }
61   else { varN = document.Switcher.vName.value; }
62   codeLine = '<SCRI' + 'PT>' + varN + '=window.open("' +
                   fileName + '", "' + winName + '", "' + a + b + c
                                     + d + e + f + g + h + i;
63   if (eval(x) > 3) { codeLine += j + k + l + m + n + o; }
64   if ( codeLine.charAt(codeLine.length - 1) == ',') {
              newCode = codeLine.substring(0, codeLine.length - 1) }
65      else { newCode = codeLine }
66   newCode += '")</SCRI' + 'PT>';
67   document.Switcher.codeOut.value = newCode;
68   }
```

The **genCode** function generates the code that appears in the text area on the page. First it checks whether a name for the window object has been entered into the text field. If not, it names the new window **newWin**. Line 62 assembles the code for pre-Navigator 4.0 browsers, and line 63 adds the string for JavaScript 1.2 if **x** (our version-detector) is greater than 3. Line 64 looks for a comma at the end of the code string; if it finds one, the comma gets stripped off.

Notice how the <SCRIPT> tags on lines 62 and 66 are broken up. This is to prevent what is between them from being interpreted as a script. You have to use this same technique when using **document.write( )** to create scripts; otherwise, you can expect an error message.

```
70   function gNav4(){
71       alert("This function requires Navigator 4.x!");
72   }
73   </SCRIPT>
74   <SCRIPT LANGUAGE="JavaScript1.2">
```

The **gNav4** function, attached to the buttons on the page and called if the user's browser is not Navigator 4.0, simply launches an alert. The JavaScript 1.2 features on this page are covered by a separate script. Specifying the language version ensures that only Navigator 4.0 will read it.

```
76   function makeWin() {
77       if(confirm('Create a child window?') )
78           msgWindow = window.open("","",
                                  "width=300,height=300,resizable");
79       msgWindow.focus();
80   }
```

Here is another simple window-creation function called to make a window automatically if the user presses one of the resize or move buttons without having defined a window:

```
82   function moveWinBy() {
83    with (document.Switcher) {
84    LR =   eval(moveLR.value)
85    UD =   eval(moveUD.value)
86    if (winMeth[0].checked == true) {
87      if (msgWindow == null) { makeWin(); }
88          msgWindow.focus()
89          msgWindow.moveBy(LR, UD);
90          if (recChng[0].checked == true) {
91              cnt1 = eval(leftV.value); cnt1 += eval(LR);
                                          leftV.value = cnt1;
92              cnt2 = eval(topV.value); cnt2 += eval(UD);
                                          topV.value = cnt2; }
93          }
94      else self.moveBy(LR, UD);
95      }
96   }
```

The preceding function and the following one are virtually identical. The former moves a window *by* a certain number of pixels, whereas the latter moves it *to* a specified position on the screen. They begin by reading the move values from the text fields in the **Switcher** form. Next they ascertain if the "child" or "parent" radio button is set. If the former, the functions check if a child window exists and, if not, call **makeWin( )** to create one and then move it by the specified number of pixels or to the desired position. If "Record changes?" is set to yes, then lines 91 and 92 add the amounts to the values used by the code generator.

The new methods, **moveBy( )** and **moveTo( )**, each take a pair of arguments consisting of positive or negative numbers, specifying the distance by which or location to which the window is to be moved. In the case of **moveBy**, positive numbers mean to the right or down, while negative numbers indicate left or up. To move a window offscreen, you must use a signed script. Otherwise, values that would move the window offscreen are ignored: the window stops at the edge of the screen.

```
98   function moveWinTo() {
99   with (document.Switcher) {
100  HA =   eval(hAxis.value)
101  VA =   eval(vAxis.value)
102    if (winMeth[0].checked == true) {
103       if (msgWindow == null ) { makeWin(); }
104      msgWindow.focus()
105      msgWindow.moveTo(HA, VA)
106         if (recChng[0].checked == true ) {
107                     scrX.value = eval(HA);
108                     scrY.value = eval(VA); }
109      }
110      else self.moveTo(HA, VA);
111    }
112  }
113
114  function sizeWinBy() {
115  with (document.Switcher) {
116  if (rSize[1].checked == true)
117      { alert('You have to set resizable to "yes" before you
                                      can resize a window.') }
118    rbh =   eval(rsizbH.value)
119    rbv =   eval(rsizbV.value)
120  if(winMeth[0].checked == true) {
121     if( msgWindow == null ) { makeWin(); }
122     msgWindow.focus()
123     msgWindow.resizeBy(rbh, rbv)
124     if ( recChng[0].checked == true ) {
125                     cnt3 = eval(outerW.value);
                        cnt3 += eval(rbh); outerW.value = cnt3;
126                     cnt4 = eval(outerH.value);
                        cnt4 += eval(rbv); outerH.value = cnt4; }
127      }
```

```
128 else self.resizeBy(rbh, rbv)
129   }
130 }
```

The **sizeWinBy** and **sizeWinTo** functions resemble not only each other, but also the preceding pair. The main difference is that they also make sure, if a new window has been created, that it is **resizable**. Otherwise, the resize functions obviously won't work.

The new **resizeBy( )** and **resizeTo( )** windows also take a pair of numbers as their arguments, the first designating width and the second, height. In the case of **resizeBy**, positive numbers expand the browser's size and negative numbers shrink it. To reduce a window to a size smaller than 100×100 pixels, you must use a signed script.

```
132 function sizeWinTo() {
133 with (document.Switcher) {
134 if (rSize[1].checked == true)
135     { alert('You have to set resizable to "yes" before you
                                   can resize a window.') }
136  rth = eval(rsiztH.value)
137  rtv = eval(rsiztV.value)
138 if(winMeth[0].checked == true) {
139    if( msgWindow == null ) { makeWin(); }
140    msgWindow.focus()
141    msgWindow.resizeTo(rth, rtv)
142   if ( recChng[0].checked == true ) {
143                    outerW.value = eval(rth);
144                    outerH.value = eval(rtv); }
145    }
146 else self.resizeTo(rth, rtv)
147   }
148 }
```

The next function, **armWnd**, is assigned to the "Arm 5 clicks" button on the page. It sets up the window to capture click events.

```
150 function armWnd(){
151    window.captureEvents(Event.CLICK);
152    window.onClick = setWnd;
153 }
```

Whether capturing events in a window or document, there are two basic steps involved: specify the event (line 151) and assign it a handler (line 152). Similarly, to capture either a keydown or mousedown event in a document, you would go:

```
document.captureEvents(Event.KEYDOWN | Event.MOUSEDOWN)
```

Notice the use of the bitwise ('|') as opposed to the logical ('||') OR operator. There are two other important details to note here: the event must be specified in UPPERCASE letters, and the handler function assignment omits the parentheses. In other words:

```
window.captureEvents(Event.dblclick);    // WRONG!
document.onClick=foobar();               // WRONG!
```

You can also use the **which** property of most event types to capture specific events. Thus

```
if(String.fromCharCode(KeyPress.which) == 'y')
```

uses the **String** object's **fromCharCode** method to convert the ASCII value of the pressed key, stored in the **which** property of a **KeyPress** event, to a string to test for the letter 'y'.

```
155 var clickCount = 0;
156
157 function setWnd(e){
158    var x = e.screenX;
159    var y = e.screenY;
160    if( msgWindow == null ) { makeWin(); }
161    msgWindow.focus();
162    msgWindow.moveTo(x,y);
163    clickCount++;
164    if (clickCount==5) {
165        clickCount = 0;
166        window.releaseEvents(Event.CLICK);
167    }
168    return false;
169 }
```

The **clickCount** variable declared and defined in line 155 is used by **setWnd** to keep track of the number of clicks. **setWnd**'s sole argument, **e**, is the event itself. The function assigns the screen coordinates of the event to the local variables **x** and **y**, tests for a window and creates one if there is none (line 160), then moves the window to the location of the click with line 162. Line 163 increments the click counter and the routine in 164 through 167 turns the event-capturing off after five clicks. The counter is used here instead of a button to turn off the clicks because the window would capture the click before the button.

```
171 function winDance() {
172    boogWin = window.open("", "", "outerWidth=150,
       outerHeight=150,screenX=50,screenY=50,resizable");
173    with (boogWin) {
174    for (var i = 0; i < 400; i++) {
175        if ( i % 5 == 0 ) { resizeBy( 5, 5); }
```

```
176           if ( i % 10 == 0 ) { resizeBy( -15, -15); }
177           if ( i < 100 )  moveBy(4, 0);
178           if ( i > 100 && i < 200 ) moveBy(0, 4);
179           if ( i > 200 && i < 300 ) moveBy(-4, 0);
180           if ( i > 300 && i < 400 ) moveBy(0, -4);
181       }
182     }
183 }
184 </SCRIPT>
185 </HEAD>
186 <BODY BGCOLOR="#87cefa">
187 <SCRIPT>
```

Next, the **winDance** function combines a simple **for** loop with **if** tests with the preceding new methods to create a primitive dancing window. After creating a small 150×150 resizable window—50 pixels to the right and down from the top left corner of the screen—it increases its size by 5 pixels on every fifth count, then reduces it by 15 every tenth beat. Meanwhile, the window takes 100 four-pixel steps first to the right, then down, next left, and finally up.

The second script on the page shows how you can convert the HTML code for a redundant table layout into variables used by **document.write( )**.

```
188 with (document) {
189
190 ht1 = '<FORM NAME=Switcher><TABLE WIDTH="100%"
                          CELLPADDING=15><TR><TD>';
191 ht2 = '</TD><TD BGCOLOR=blue><FONT SIZE=+3 COLOR=gold>';
192 ht3 = '<B>Window<BR>Creation<BR>Options';
193 ht4 = '</B></FONT></TD></TR>';
194 ht5 = '</TABLE><BR><CENTER>';
195 tx1 = 'This page allows you to explore and test the various
          options available when creating a new window, as well
          as the <I>moveBy</I>, <I>moveTo</I>, <I>resizeBy</I>,
          and <I>resizeTo</I> methods introduced with
          JavaScript 1.2 for Navigator 4.0.<BR>It can also
          generate the JavaScript code for creating your
          window.';
```

One of the advantages of this method is that it isolates the code from the content, making the latter much easier to find and edit.

```
197 write(ht1 + tx1 + ht2 + ht3 + ht4 + ht5);
```

Although the script could be organized with all the string variables together at the top followed by all the **write( )** statements, an advantage of the alternating system used here is that the variables are kept closer to the point of use. This can make them easier to find.

```
199 mt1= '<TABLE BORDER=0 WIDTH="95%" CELLSPACING=3
                                        CELLPADDING=7><TR>';
200 trs = '<TD ROWSPAN=';
201 th1 = ' BGCOLOR=blue ALIGN=RIGHT>
                                <FONT COLOR=gold SIZE=+1><B>';
202 th2 = '</B></FONT></TD>';
203 tf1 = '<TD ALIGN=CENTER COLSPAN=2><INPUT TYPE=TEXT NAME=';
204 tf2 = ' SIZE=30></TD><TD COLSPAN=2><I>';
205 tf3 = '</I></TD></TR><TR>';
206
207 write(mt1 + trs + 3 + th1 + 'NAMES' + th2 + tf1
                                        + 'vName' + tf2);
208 write('Window object name for JavaScript references.');
209 write(tf3 + tf1 + 'fileN' + tf2);
210 write('Name of file to load.');
211 write(tf3 + tf1 + 'winN' + tf2);
212 write('Window name for &lt;TARGET=...&gt;
                                in tags and target property.');
213 write(tf3 + trs + 2 + th1 + 'SIZING' + th2);
```

   Notice how in the preceding sequence, the table headings, text content, and names of the text fields are very easy to spot within the code.

```
215 tf4 = '<TD ALIGN=RIGHT WIDTH=125>';
216 tf5 = '<INPUT TYPE=TEXT NAME=';
217 tf6= ' SIZE=5 VALUE=0></TD>';
218 tc1 = ' COLSPAN=2 VALIGN=TOP><I>';
219 tx2 = 'Both height and width values must be set for either
            to work. These dimensions apply solely to the
                                document area of the new window.';
220
221 write(tf4 + 'Height:' + tf5 + 'WinH' + tf6 + tf4 + 'Width:'
                                + tf5 + 'WinW' + tf6);
222 write(trs + 2 + tc1 + tx2 + tf3 + tf4 + 'Resizable?');
223
224 rb1 = '</TD><TD ALIGN=CENTER WIDTH=125>Yes
                                <INPUT TYPE=RADIO NAME=';
225 rb2 = '> No<INPUT TYPE=RADIO NAME=';
226 rb3 = ' CHECKED></TD>';
227 rc1 = '</TR><TR>';
228 tc2= '<TD ROWSPAN=2 VALIGN=TOP>';
229 th3 = '<TD ALIGN=CENTER BGCOLOR=blue>';
```

```
                                   <FONT SIZE=+2 COLOR=gold><B>';
230 th4 = '<TD ROWSPAN=3 ALIGN=CENTER>';
231 ta1 = '<TEXTAREA COLS=45 ROWS=6 NAME=';
232 ta2 = ' VALUE="" WRAP=physical></TEXTAREA></TD>';
233 te1 = '</TR></TABLE>';
234 tx3 = '<I>With Microsoft\'s Internet Explorer, the toolbar,
            location and directories options function as a unit.
            Select "toolbar" for all three; the other two cannot
            be selected separately.';
235
236 write(rb1 + 'rSize' + rb2 + 'rSize' + rb3 + rc1);
237 write(trs + 6 + th1 + 'APPEARANCE' + th2 + tf4);
238 write('Menubar?' + rb1 + 'MenuB' + rb2 + 'MenuB' + rb3);
239 write(tc2 + tx3 + tf3 + tf4);
240 write('Toolbar?' + rb1 + 'ToolB' + rb2 + 'ToolB' + rb3);
241 write(rc1 + tf4);
242 write('Location field?' + rb1 + 'LocF'
                                    + rb2 + 'LocF' + rb3);
243 write(th3 + 'Code Viewer' + th2 + rc1 + tf4);
244 write('Directories?' + rb1 + 'DirB' + rb2 + 'DirB' + rb3);
245 write(th4 + ta1 + 'codeOut' + ta2 + rc1 + tf4);
246 write('Scrollbars?' + rb1 + 'ScrollB'
                                    + rb2 + 'ScrollB' + rb3);
247 write(rc1 + tf4);
248 write('Statusbar?' + rb1 + 'StatusB'
                                    + rb2 + 'StatusB' + rb3);
249 write(te1+ '<BR>');
```

The preceding section creates the radio buttons. Again, see how much easier it is to spot the text, as well as the names of each pair.

```
251 fb1 = '<INPUT TYPE=BUTTON  VALUE="';
252 fb2 = '" ONCLICK="';
253 sp1 = '<SPACER TYPE=HORIZONTAL SIZE=15>';
254
255 write(fb1 + 'Show Window' + fb2 +
                          'newWin();showWin()' + '">' + sp1);
256 write(fb1 + 'Close Window' + fb2 +
                          'msgWindow.close()' + '">' + sp1);
257 write(fb1 + 'Generate Code' + fb2 +
                          'newWin();genCode()' + '"><BR><BR>');
```

The preceding three lines create the main buttons. Their assigned labels and the functions clearly stand out. Next come the variables for the JavaScript 1.2 table and its creation:

```
259 th5 = '<TD COLSPAN=4 ALIGN=CENTER BGCOLOR=blue>
                               <FONT SIZE=+2 COLOR=gold><B>';
260 th6 = '<TR><TD ROWSPAN=2 ALIGN=RIGHT BGCOLOR=blue>
                               <FONT COLOR=gold SIZE=+1><B>';
261 tw1 = '<TD WIDTH=125 ALIGN=LEFT>';
262 tv1 = '<TD VALIGN=TOP ALIGN=LEFT>';
263 tv2 = '<TD ALIGN=RIGHT>';
264 rb4 = '<INPUT TYPE=RADIO NAME=';
265 rb5 = ' ONCLICK="';
266 rb6 = ' CHECKED ONCLICK="';
267 rb7 = '</TD><TD ALIGN=CENTER><NOBR>Yes ';
268 tn1 = '</NOBR></TD>';
269
270 write(mt1 + th5);
271 write('New in JavaScript 1.2 / Navigator 4.0');
272 write(ht4 + th6 + 'SIZE' + th2 + tf4);
273 write('innerWidth<BR>' + tf5 + 'innerW' + tf6 + tw1);
274 write('innerHeight<BR>' + tf5 + 'innerH' + tf6 + tv1);
275 write('Sets the dimensions of the document area of the
               window (same as <i>width</i> and <i>height</i>.
                                     </TD></TR>' + tf4);
276 write('outerWidth<BR>' + tf5 + 'outerW' + tf6 + tw1);
277 write('outerHeight<BR>' + tf5 + 'outerH' + tf6 + tv1);
278 write('Sets the dimensions of the full size of the window.
                                     </TD></TR>');
279 write(th6 + 'LOCATION' + th2 + tv2);
280 write('screenX<BR>' + tf5 + 'scrX' + tf6 + '<TD>');
281 write('screenY<BR>' + tf5 + 'scrY' + tf6 + tv1);
282 write('Determines where the window will open, measured in
               pixels from the top left corner of the screen.</TD>');
283 write(te1+ '<BR>');
```

Next we find the variables for the new methods section of the page, followed by the **write( )** cluster which produces the table.

In lines 310 through 313, the **onClick** event handlers test for the browser version number. The **eval( )** method is used to ensure that **x** is treated as a number and not a character.

```
285 tr2 = '<TR><TD COLSPAN=8>';
286 wh1 = 'Width:<BR>Height:</TD><TD>';
287 tv3 = '<TR ALIGN=CENTER>';
288 th7 = '<TD COLSPAN=2>';
289 th8 = '<TD COLSPAN=4>';
290 th9 = '<TD COLSPAN=8 ALIGN=CENTER BGCOLOR=blue>
```

```
                              <FONT SIZE=+2 COLOR=gold><B>';
291 tf7= ' SIZE=5 VALUE=0><BR>';
292 tx5 = 'These buttons allow you to see how the new resize and
          move methods work with either your browser or a new
          window by selecting either the parent or child radio
          button below.  By setting "Record size / position
          changes?" to yes, adjustments you make to a child
          window\'s size and position with these buttons will
          be reflected in the script produced by pressing
          "Generate Code".<BR><B>NOTE:</B> For resize to work,
          the resizable option for your new window must be set
          to "yes".</TD>';
293 hr1 = tr2 + '<HR>' + rc1;
294
295 write(mt1 + th9);
296 write('New JavaScript 1.2 Window Methods');
297 write(ht4 + tr2 + tx5 + rc1);
298 write(tv2 + '+ right, - left:<BR>- up, + down:</TD><TD>');
299 write(tf5 + 'moveLR' + tf7);
300 write(tf5 + 'moveUD' + tf6);
301 write(tv2 + 'From left:<BR>From top:</TD><TD>');
302 write(tf5 + 'hAxis' + tf7);
303 write(tf5 + 'vAxis' + tf6);
304 write(tv2 + wh1);
305 write(tf5 + 'rsizbH' + tf7);
306 write(tf5 + 'rsizbV' + tf6);
307 write(tv2 + wh1);
308 write(tf5 + 'rsiztH' + tf7);
309 write(tf5 + 'rsiztV' + tf6 + '</TR>' + tv3);
310 write(th7 + fb1 + 'moveBy' + fb2 +
            'if( eval(x) > 3) moveWinBy();else gNav4()"></TD>');
311 write(th7 + fb1 + 'moveTo' + fb2 +
            'if( eval(x) > 3) moveWinTo();else gNav4()"></TD>');
312 write(th7 + fb1 + 'resizeBy' + fb2 +
            'if( eval(x) > 3) sizeWinBy();else gNav4()"></TD>');
313 write(th7 + fb1 + 'resizeTo' + fb2 +
        'if( eval(x) > 3) sizeWinTo();else gNav4()"></TD></TR>');
314 write(tv3 + th8 + 'Child: ' + rb4 +
                                'winMeth CHECKED>Parent: ');
315 write(rb4 + 'winMeth><BR></TD>');
316 write(th8 + 'Record size / position changes?  Yes ');
317 write(rb4 + 'recChng> No ' + rb4 + 'recChng' + rb3 + rc1
                                          + hr1 + th8);
```

The page ends with the last three segments of text isolated as variables, and a sequence of **write**s for the remainder of the body, again with all three buttons testing for browser version.

```
319 tx6 = 'The "Arm 5 clicks" button makes the main browser
            window capture clicks and move the child window to
            the location pointed at by the tip of your cursor.
            After five clicks, the window will automatically
            become disarmed. Otherwise the onClick event handlers
            of the buttons on the page would remain
                                        shortcircuited.</TD>';
320 tx7 = 'If a click doesn\'t move the child window, it
            doesn\'t count. After the fifth click, the child
            window vanishes behind the browser.<BR><BR><CENTER>';
321 tx8 = 'And for a bit of fun, here\'s a very primitive version
            of a dancing window made by combining <I>moveBy</I>
            and <I>resizeBy</I> with "for" and "if" statements.
            The trail it leaves on the screen will vanish when it
                                        stops.<BR><BR><CENTER>';
322
323 write(tx6 + th8 + tx7);
324 write(fb1 + 'Arm 5 clicks' + fb2 + 'if( eval(x) > 3)
            armWnd();else gNav4()"></CENTER></TD></TR>' + hr1);
325 write(th6 + 'WINDOW<BR> BOOGIE</B></FONT>
                                        </TD><TD COLSPAN=7>');
326 write(tx8 + fb1 + 'Boogie!' + fb2 + 'if( eval(x) > 3)
                            winDance();else gNav4()">' + sp1);
327 write(fb1 + '  Close  ' + fb2 + 'if( eval(x) > 3 &&
            boogWin != null) boogWin.close();else gNav4()">');
328 write('</CENTER></TD>' + te1 +'</FORM></CENTER>');
329 }
330 </SCRIPT>
331 </BODY>
332 </HTML>
```

Though this approach is often more time-consuming to set up, the investment can pay off in terms of making it easier to maintain and update. Also, depending on how redundant the HTML code is, your page can end up substantially smaller in byte size and, as a result, faster.

You could even build your own library of HTML code strings and simply copy them from one page to another. Or, if the same code can be applied to a number of pages, you can put the script with the variables in the head of a main frame where they can be accessed from anywhere within the frameset.

Alerts, Prompts, and Confirms

O f all the JavaScript examples in this book, nonprogrammers will have the least trouble creating and using simple interactive dialog boxes, which are divided into three categories:

◆ Alert

◆ Confirm

◆ Prompt

All three are methods of the **window** object that were first implemented in Navigator 2.0. Each opens a dialog box that requires a response before anything else can be done at your site. It freezes the action, so to speak, until closed.

For example, say you access a web page with a button that reads, "Time on this page." When you click on that button, a dialog box opens showing the number of minutes and seconds you have been on that page. If the **alert** method is used, the box will contain an OK button which, when clicked, closes the dialog box. You can't do anything else within that page until you click on OK.

The features of these three methods can be summarized as follows:

◆ **alert**   Exclamation mark (!) warning icon and message with an OK button

◆ **confirm**   Question mark (?) query icon and message with OK and Cancel buttons

◆ **prompt**   Message and text field for user input with OK and Cancel buttons

The shape and color of these icons are system specific. The **alert** icon, for example, is a black exclamation mark in a yellow triangle in Windows 95 and Macintosh systems; black, in a yellow circle in Windows 3.x; and white, in a green triangle in OS/2. Similarly, **confirm** icons appear as a blue question mark in a white cartoon-style balloon in Windows 95; black, in a yellow triangle in Macintosh; and white, in a green circle in both Windows 3.x and OS/2.

The operating system also determines other properties of these dialog boxes. All open at the middle of the screen except **prompt**s in Windows 3.x, which appear in the upper-left corner of the browser window. In OS/2 the **prompt** OK button is grayed out and ineffective unless the text field has a default value or the user inputs data. With Windows 95 and 3.x there is no such event-related connection. Finally, OS/2 and Macintosh automatically add system sound effects to **alert**s and **confirm**s, which the other operating systems do not.

The size of all three types of dialog box is determined by the length of your message. If you have an extremely long message, you are better off creating a new window. These dialog boxes do not inherit scroll bars, and part of your message, along with the OK and Cancel buttons, may end up as invisible beyond the bottom edge of the screen.

You should use **alert**s for messages that do not require a user decision. The code syntax is very simple:

```
alert("message")
```

The message argument can be a string passed directly, for example:

```
alert("You forgot to fill in your e-mail address.")
```

or indirectly through a variable:

```
var x = "You forgot to fill in your e-mail address."
alert(x)
```

The latter approach is particularly useful for longer messages or those with dynamic components. You can also combine the two. For example:

```
var creditLimit = 1000;
var order = 1200;
alert('Your $' + order + ' order is $' + eval(order - creditLimit) +
        ' over your $' + creditLimit + ' credit limit.')
```

produces the message "Your $1200 order is $200 over your $1000 credit limit." If you assign the variables values based on user input instead of the magic numbers in our example, you can easily create a dynamic, interactive **alert**.

The message can also be an integer or a property of an existing object. Suppose you created a **game** object with

```
function game(cards) {
    this.cards = cards
}
```

Writing

```
game.cards = "poker";
alert(game.cards)
```

would produce the word "poker" in the dialog box. Obviously, though, there are likely very few situations in which an integer or property would make an appropriate **alert** message without some form of string attached.

The messages rely on a default system font for displaying text in the dialog box, and you cannot designate a title for the titlebar or change the default icons. Their content cannot be formatted apart from using the escape sequence \n for line breaks or \t for tabs. If you try adding HTML formatting tags, for example:

```
alert("You <I>must</I> enter your zip code")
```

the message will appear with the code visible: "You <I>must</I> enter your zip code." Exactly the same thing happens if you try using JavaScript formatting methods:

```
var x = "must";
var y = x.italics();
alert("You " + y + " enter your zip code")
```

results in "You <I>must</I> enter your zip code."

Finally, you can also use the **open** method to create an **alert** dialog box, for example:

```
open=alert('Your browser does not support Java!')
```
but this is rarely necessary.

The basic syntax for a **confirm** dialog box is identical to that for an **alert**:

```
confirm("message")
```

However, because it forces a user choice between OK or Cancel, this method normally appears in an **if** condition with a statement defining what happens upon confirmation. For example:

```
var x = document.orderForm.quantityField.value;
if (confirm('You are ordering ' + x + ' cases of frozen burritos')) {
    processOrder()
}
```

In this instance, the function **processOrder( )** is called when the user selects OK, or the **confirm** dialog box closes and nothing else happens when the user clicks on Cancel. Add an **else** statement to the preceding code, for example:

```
else { document.orderForm.quantityField.focus();
    document.orderForm.quantityField.select();
}
```

and it will be executed if the user selects Cancel.

As with **alert**s, the message argument for **confirm** can be either a string or a property of an existing object.

Prompt boxes, on the other hand, contain a text field for user input, so their syntax differs slightly. The format is

```
prompt("message", [inputDefault])
```

The square brackets simply mean that specifying a default value for the input field is optional. If you do not specify a value, the word "undefined" appears in the field. To produce a blank input field, use an empty pair of single or double quotation marks:

```
prompt("Enter your occupation:", "")
```

Otherwise the default value can be any string, integer, or property of an existing object. The most common method of accessing the user input is to assign the **prompt** to a variable:

```
var address = prompt("Enter your address:","")
```

With a **prompt**, JavaScript will automatically distinguish numeric from string values. Even though a street address usually begins with a number, it will be treated as a string. But write

```
var groupSize = prompt("How many persons are in your group?", "")
var registrationFee = '$' + groupSize * 200
```

and if the user enters "12," **registrationFee** becomes $2400.

By default, these **alert**, **confirm**, and **prompt** dialog boxes are all methods of the **window** object, so you do not have to specify, for example:

```
window.alert("You must register before entering this site!")
```

On the other hand, if you create a child window with

```
newWin = open("","", "width=350,height=350")
```

you can then write

```
newWin.alert("You must log out before leaving!")
```

to have the **alert** come from the child. The same applies to **prompt**s and **confirm**s.

    Alerts are particularly useful in combination with a function that determines the type or version or plug-in capability of a user's web browser, or one that error-traps user input such as the data entered or not entered into a form before allowing the user to proceed. You can then use the **alert** to prompt the user to fill in valid information (for example, an eight-digit code number) or the required field that was overlooked.

    Confirms, on the other hand, fit best wherever user yes-no confirmation might be appropriate, such as before billing $5,000 to their credit card or downloading a 20MB file. With **confirm**s you can launch a process if the user selects OK, and either have nothing happen or trigger an alternative function if the choice is Cancel.

    Finally, a **prompt** box is really a miniform with one text field for user input. Although you can even create a series of **prompt**s instead of a multifield form to obtain data from a visitor, a standard HTML form has two advantages: it gives users an immediate overview of all the requested information, and it allows them to move back and forth among the different fields before submitting it. Because a **prompt** vanishes the instant the user clicks on OK, there is no way to review or change the input data unless you provide a separate means of doing so.

    The following sample scripts show how these basic principles can be applied in a variety of ways to create different effects.

PROGRAMMER'S NOTE   *You can control the width of these dialog boxes by using the newline character \n to force line breaks. Otherwise the wrap point for each line will be determined by the browser. The box's height will adjust to the length of the message. Two newline characters (\n\n) start a new paragraph, and the tab escape sequence \t can be used to indent text.*

alert1

Alert on Click 1

N2 | N2.01 | N2.02+ | N3 | N4 | E3 | **E4**

You should use the **alert** method sparingly. Designing your web page with more than a couple of **alert**s can defeat the purpose of using them in the first place. You can employ them as a replacement for bubble help, or to let users know about a feature or page at your site that is not yet functional. Other uses include creating interactive one-liners and warnings.

    The first **alert** example can be used for any of the previously mentioned purposes and illustrates that you can be fairly creative with little more than a simple form button and some choice text. Almost all **alert** scripts are easy to create; the real challenge lies in writing clever, simple, and informative text to appear in the dialog box (see Figure 2-1).

```
1    <HTML>
2    <HEAD>
3    <TITLE>JavaScript Example</TITLE>
4    </HEAD>
5    <BODY>
6    <CENTER><FORM><INPUT TYPE="button" Value="CLICK HERE"
7        onClick="alert(' Wouldn\'t one of these be cool on your
                    page? You can say whatever you want here! ')">
                                        </FORM></CENTER>
8    </BODY>
9    </HTML>
```

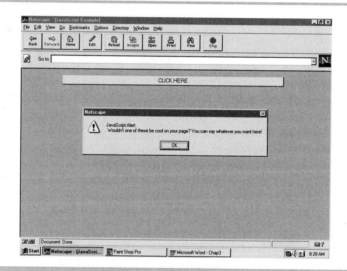

FIGURE 2-1.   You can be fairly creative with little more than a simple form button

ANNOTATIONS

```
1    <HTML>
2    <HEAD>
```

```
3   <TITLE>JavaScript Example</TITLE>
4   </HEAD>
5   <BODY>
6   <CENTER><FORM><INPUT TYPE="button" Value="CLICK HERE"
7       onClick="alert(' Wouldn\'t one of these be cool on your
                    page? You can say whatever you want here! ')">
                                            </FORM></CENTER>
8   </BODY>
9   </HTML>
```

This script shows how to assign an **alert** to the **onClick** event handler of a standard HTML form button. As you can see, it simply involves putting the message of your choice in quotation marks between the opening and closing brackets that follow "alert." The important thing is to exercise care in nesting the quotation marks and to escape any that appear within the inner pair by preceding them with a backslash, as in "wouldn't" in line 7.

alert2

Alert on Click 2

N2 N2.01 N2.02+ N3 N4 E3 **E4**

In this example, an **alert** pops up when the user clicks on a radio button as opposed to a submit-type button. The real-world application of this **alert** variation follows the guidelines set down in the previous example—in other words, use it sparingly.

A good use of this **alert** type might be as bubble help for users choosing options from a list. By adding an **alert** dialog box feature, you can have users click on a radio button to get information about a link or other aspects of your site (see Figure 2-2).

```
1   <HTML>
2   <HEAD>
3   <TITLE>JavaScript Example</TITLE>
4   </HEAD>
5   <BODY>
6   <CENTER><FORM METHOD="post" NAME="message">Click in circle
                                    below </CENTER>
7   <CENTER><INPUT type="radio" name="message"
            onClick="alert('See, you can make this come up by
                    clicking on anything ')"></FORM></CENTER>
8   </BODY>
9   </HTML>
```

FIGURE 2-2.   This alert type might be useful as instant bubble help

ANNOTATIONS

```
1    <HTML>
2    <HEAD>
3    <TITLE>JavaScript Example</TITLE>
4    </HEAD>
5    <BODY>
6    <CENTER><FORM METHOD="post" NAME="message">Click in circle
                                           below </CENTER>
7    <CENTER><INPUT type="radio" name="message"
             onClick="alert('See, you can make this come up by
                       clicking on anything ')"></FORM></CENTER>
8    </BODY>
9    </HTML>
```

Apart from the **alert** message, there is really only one difference between this and the preceding script: the form input type has been changed to **radio**. You can also have a **checkbox** do exactly the same thing by modifying the prior script to read

```
7              type=checkbox
```

In our sample, the radio button remains checked once clicked. You can very easily add the following code to clear the button when the user closes the **alert**:

```
7    onClick="alert('...');this.form.message.checked=false"
```

Here **message** is the name of the radio button, and any valid reference to it would do the job just as well, for example:

```
document.formName.buttonName.checked=false
```

or, using the built-in JavaScript arrays:

```
document.forms[0].elements[0].checked=false
```

or, any of various possible combinations such as

```
this.form.elements[0].checked=false
```

Exactly the same technique will clear a **checkbox**. The kind of reference you use to access form elements is essentially a question of personal programming style and script function. Array references are valuable in a function that uses a **for** loop to run through and process a form. Well-chosen element names make a script more readable and eliminate the need for comments because they speak for themselves. For instance, with

```
document.bulbOrder.wattButtons
```

three months later you won't be scratching your head trying to remember what's what and what does what in your script. Ditto for anyone else who might be asked to modify it or who wants to adapt it to his or her own purposes.

Alert on Click 3

alert3

N2 N2.01 N2.02+ N3 N4 E3 **E4**

Although this script appears identical in many respects to the Alert on Click 1 example, it contains important differences in behavior. It offers the user a submit-type button which, if pressed, delivers more than one **alert** message. This example is more complicated to write, but provides additional sets of dialog boxes that could be employed to warn users, make them laugh, or provide some other form of simple interactivity (see Figure 2-3).

```
1  <HTML>
2  <HEAD>
3  <TITLE>JavaScript Example</TITLE>
4  </HEAD>
5  <BODY>
6  <CENTER><FORM><INPUT TYPE="button" Value="CLICK HERE"
        onClick="alert('Don\'t be fooled. This is different.');
      alert('See, you can have more than one alert in a row.');
   alert('You can have as many as you want!')"></FORM></CENTER>
7  </BODY>
8  </HTML>
```

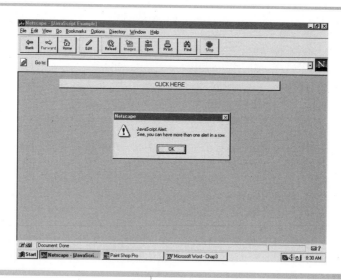

FIGURE 2-3.   The art of delivering more than one alert message

ANNOTATIONS

```
1    <HTML>
2    <HEAD>
3    <TITLE>JavaScript Example</TITLE>
4    </HEAD>
5    <BODY>
6    <CENTER><FORM><INPUT TYPE="button" Value="CLICK HERE"
         onClick="alert('Don\'t be fooled. This is different.');
      alert('See, you can have more than one alert in a row.');
   alert('You can have as many as you want!')"></FORM></CENTER>
7    </BODY>
8    </HTML>
```

With this script, each click on the OK button in the **alert** dialog box displays the next **alert** with its message. As it shows, you can assign any number of calls to a JavaScript event handler by separating them with semicolons. Whenever you have more than one, however, you should consider creating a separate function. The preceding code, for example, can be converted into

```
function stringAlerts() {
    alert("Don't be fooled. This is different.");
    alert("See, you can have more than one alert in a row.");
```

```
    alert("You can have as many as you want!");
}
```

and called with

```
        ONCLICK="stringAlerts()"
```

This approach has several advantages: it makes for easier maintenance, results in more readable code, and eliminates the hassles of working inside the quotation marks required by the event handler. As you can see, with the function you no longer need to escape the apostrophe in "Don't."

Another option for creating the same effect is to construct an array of messages accompanied by a very simple function. For example:

```
        alertMsg = new Array();
        alertMsg[0] = "Hi!";
        alertMsg[1] = "Ho!";
        alertMsg[2] = "Hee!";
        alertMsg[3] = "Hah!";
        alertMsg[4] = "Huh!";
        alertMsg[5] = "Duh!";
```

sets up a series of messages for the **alert** boxes which obviously can be as long as you want. Then

```
function showMsg() {
    for (var counter = 0; i < alertMsg.length; counter++) {
    alert(alertMsg[counter]);
    }
}
```

displays the next message with each click on the **alert** OK button just like our sample script. With this approach, the code for the HTML form button would be

```
        onClick="showMsg()"
```

Or, to have the next message in your array displayed with each click of the form button, you can have

```
        onClick="nextMsg()"
```

call the following simple function in which the counter keeps track of the number of clicks, then recycles back to zero when the end of the array is reached:

```
var counter = 0;
function nextMsg() {
    alert(alertMsg[counter]);
    counter++;
    if (counter == alertMsg.length) { counter = 0 }
}
```

Yet another variation on this type of device would be to combine it with a process that generates a pseudorandom number within range of the length of your array.

For instance, the following function gets the current time in the form of a 12-digit number, converts it to a string, and simply reads the tenth digit to obtain a random number between 0 and 9:

```
function randMsg() {
    now = new Date;
    seed = now.getTime();
    nStr = seed.toString();
    randN = nStr.substring(9,10);
    alert(alertMsg[randN])
}
```

It is not difficult to manipulate **alert**s and create various effects with them. Here the onus is not really on the code writing, but rather on your imagination and creativity.

Alert on Mouse-over

mouseovr

[N2] [N2.01] [N2.02+] [N3] [N4] [E3] [E4]

An **alert** dialog box does not have to be controlled by a user clicking on a button. In this example, an **alert** pops up when the user moves his or her mouse over a hypertext link or a graphic.

As in earlier examples, this application of an **alert** allows the web developer to program simple interactive bubble help or other instructions and information into a web page (see Figure 2-4).

```
1   <HTML>
2   <HEAD>
3   <TITLE>JavaScript Example</TITLE>
4   </HEAD>
5   <BODY>
6   <CENTER><TABLE WIDTH="40%">
7   <TR>
8   <TD><A HREF="http://www.bodo.com/" ONMOUSEOVER="alert
                      ('And it doesn\'t need to be text!')">
       <IMG SRC="3dhomer1.gif" BORDER=0 HEIGHT=117 WIDTH=89></A>
9   </TD>
10  <TD align=right><A HREF="http://www.bodo.com/" ONMOUSEOVER=
                  "alert('Yet another cool way to put a message
                      on your page')">Put your cursor here</A>
11  </TD>
12  </TR>
13  </TABLE></CENTER>
```

```
14   <BR>
15   </BODY>
16   </HTML>
```

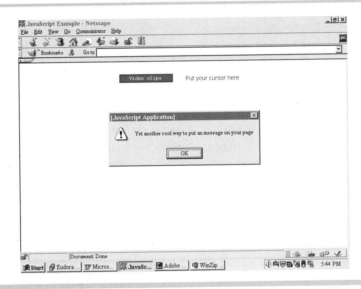

FIGURE 2-4.   An alert appears when the user moves the mouse over a link

ANNOTATIONS

```
1    <HTML>
2    <HEAD>
3    <TITLE>JavaScript Example</TITLE>
4    </HEAD>
5    <BODY>
6    <CENTER><TABLE WIDTH="40%">
7    <TR>
8    <TD><A HREF="http://www.bodo.com/" ONMOUSEOVER="alert
                        ('And it doesn\'t need to be text!')">
       <IMG SRC="3dhomer1.gif" BORDER=0 HEIGHT=117 WIDTH=89></A>
9    </TD>
10   <TD align=right><A HREF="http://www.bodo.com/" ONMOUSEOVER=
                "alert('Yet another cool way to put a message
                        on your page')">Put your cursor here</A>
11   </TD>
```

```
12   </TR>
13   </TABLE></CENTER>
14   <BR>
15   </BODY>
16   </HTML>
```

This code shows how you can assign an **alert** to the **onMouseOver** event handler of an HTML link. The **alert** syntax is exactly the same as for the **onClick** event of form elements, and the link itself can be either an image (line 8) or text (line 10).

The one major drawback of this technique is that the **onMouseOver** handler disables the link itself. The instant the mouse pointer comes within range, the **alert** box pops open and makes clicking on the link impossible.

You can also assign an **alert** directly to either a text or graphic anchor with

```
HREF="javascript:alert('Hidee-o-diddly-o!')"
```

in which case a click on the link opens the dialog box. This approach allows you to use more visually attractive components than standard HTML form buttons for **alert**s.

To combine an **alert** with an active link, you have to create a separate function. You *cannot* do it in-line with

```
HREF="javascript:alert('Go!');self.location='nextPage.htm'"
```

But convert code similar to the above into a JavaScript function, for example:

```
function warnPlayer() {
    alert("You are about to enter the Depths of Doom!");
    self.location = "doomdpth.htm"
}
```

assign it to the anchor with

```
HREF="javascript:warnPlayer()"
```

and you've created an **alert** buffer for your link. This function, however, automatically opens the link when the **alert** box closes. To give the user a choice, you have to use a **confirm** dialog box:

```
function warnPlayer() {
    if (confirm("Are you ready to enter the Depths of Doom?"))
        self.location = "doomdpth.htm"
}
```

Now selecting OK in the **confirm** dialog box opens the link, whereas clicking on Cancel closes the dialog window and nothing further happens unless you create an alternative event with an **else** statement. For example, making

```
else self.location = "chicken.htm"
```

the last line of **warnPlayer( )** opens DOOMDPTH.HTM with a click on OK, and CHICKEN.HTM if the user opts for Cancel. With simple **if-else** routines such as this involving single statements for both the conditional test (**if**) and its failure (**else**), you do not need to enclose the instructions in curly braces, for example:

```
if (x == 10) { x = 0 }
else { x++ }
```

It's not a bad idea, however, to get into the habit of using them even with the simplest of conditions. That way, when you get to writing more complex scripts, you may avoid the unwanted behavior that can result from ambiguities. For example:

```
if (x == 10) x = 0;
  else  x++;
  y = x * 5;          // y always gets x times 5
```

is quite different from

```
if (x == 10) x = 0;
  else { x++;
  y = x * 5 }         // y only gets x times 5 when x is not 10
```

In some situations, a misplaced curly brace can make the difference between a function that freezes or crashes your browser with a General Protection Fault (the JavaScript equivalent of a core dump), and one that does exactly what you want.

onload1

onLoad Alert

| N2 | N2.01 | N2.02+ | N3 | N4 | E3 | E4 |

Relying on web surfers to move their mouse over a graphic or click on a link is all well and good, but there will be times when you want to warn or instruct them about the content of a page before it can load. The **onLoad alert** fills that need quite nicely.

Perhaps you would like a real-world scenario in which this script would be useful? Not all of the web pages you see are, shall we say, family oriented. Some are downright adult in nature. With the **onLoad** script, you can program any page with possibly objectionable material to warn users to stay away unless they have no qualms about the nature of your web content. This approach will not replace a sitewide or webwide content rating system—several of those exist—but may be a good alternative in a pinch.

A less cautionary application of the **onLoad** script might be a case where you simply wish to greet your users with a friendly message (see Figure 2-5).

```
1   <HTML>
2   <HEAD>
3   <TITLE></TITLE>
4   </HEAD>
5   <BODY onLoad="loadalert()">
6   <P><SCRIPT language="JavaScript"><!-- Hide the script
                               from old browsers --
```

```
7    // Michael P. Scholtis (mpscho@planetx.bloomu.edu)
8    // All rights reserved.  January 9, 1996
9    // You may use this JavaScript example as you see fit,
                                              as long as the
10   // information within this comment above is included
                                              in your script.
11   function loadalert ()
12        {alert("THIS IS WHERE YOUR MESSAGE GOES!")
13   }
14   // --End Hiding Here --></SCRIPT>
15   </P>
16   </BODY>
17   </HTML>
```

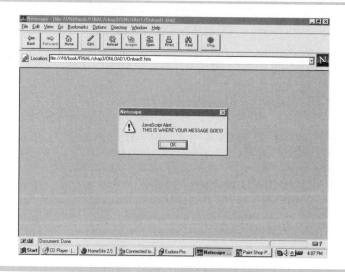

FIGURE 2-5.   Warn users before they view possibly objectionable material

ANNOTATIONS

```
1    <HTML>
2    <HEAD>
3    <TITLE></TITLE>
4    </HEAD>
5    <BODY onLoad="loadalert()">
```

```
6    <P><SCRIPT language="JavaScript"><!-- Hide the script
                                      from old browsers --
7    // Michael P. Scholtis (mpscho@planetx.bloomu.edu)
8    // All rights reserved.  January 9, 1996
9    // You may use this JavaScript example as you see fit,
                                      as long as the
10   // information within this comment above is included
                                      in your script.
11   function loadalert ()
12         {alert("THIS IS WHERE YOUR MESSAGE GOES!")
13   }
14   // --End Hiding Here --></SCRIPT>
15   </P>
16   </BODY>
17   </HTML>
```

Here the **alert** is made the sole statement of the **loadalert( )** function, which is called from the HTML <BODY> tag on line 5. Although Scholtis has chosen to put the script in the body of the page, exactly the same effect would be produced by putting it between the <HEAD> tags. While here the location is immaterial because the body has no real content, in the case of a full page it's smarter to put it in the head to keep the script separate from the content. The location has no effect on the timing here because the **onLoad** event handler always executes *after* the page has been laid out.

On the other hand, if you want your **alert** to appear the instant the page is loaded, just make it the first line of a script in the head. In that case, you shouldn't use a function, but rather a straightforward **alert**. Bear in mind, however, that the page-loading process will grind to a halt and only resume once the user has responded to the **alert**.

Yet another possibility is to assign the **alert** directly to **onLoad**, for example:

```
<BODY ONLOAD="alert('Yo, stranger!')">
```

As you may have noticed, the style of Scholtis' **loadalert( )** function differs slightly from the others we've seen so far in that the opening curly brace is not on the first line. The JavaScript compiler doesn't really care where that brace is, as long as it's the first nonwhite space encountered after the closing bracket of the function argument. Although most JavaScript programmers use the so-called UNIX style of putting the opening brace on the same line as the function declaration and the closing brace on a separate line at the end, for example:

```
function writeBanana() {
    document.write("Banana!<BR>")
    }
```

you can just as readily use the classic C/C++ style of aligning both braces at the left margin:

```
function stroustrupIt(c)
{
        c++;
}
```

As in the other languages that favor this approach, the prime advantage lies in making it much easier to keep track of opening and closing braces, especially if you have a heavily nesting function that for some reason or other can't be broken down into smaller units.

On the other hand, feel free to go the utter stylistic slob route and risk a ballistic flaming with

```
function cramp(x,y){if(x!=y||x<y&&!z){x+=y;++y}else{x++;--y}}
```

Hey, it works, don't it?!

ysjs

You Support JavaScript

N2 N2.01 N2.02+ N3 N4 E3 **E4**

This little script demonstrates how to use **onLoad** to check the user's browser for JavaScript compatibility. A JavaScript-enabled browser will launch the **alert**; other browsers will just display the content of the page. As a practical matter, this device is of little value other than to remind visitors that they can view all of the cool script-based features you've programmed into your pages (see Figure 2-6).

```
1   <HTML>
2   <HEAD>
3   <TITLE>Kurt's JavaScript Archive
4   </TITLE>
5   <script>
6     function loadalert () {
7        alert("Your browser supports JavaScript!")
8   }
9   </script>
10  </HEAD>
11  <BODY>
12  <body onLoad="loadalert()">
13  </BODY>
14  </HTML>
```

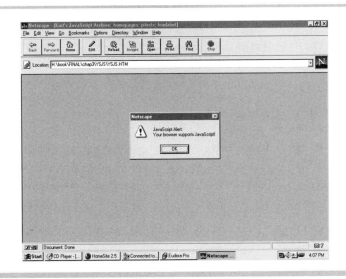

FIGURE 2-6. Check the user's browser for JavaScript compatibility

ANNOTATIONS

```
1    <HTML>
2    <HEAD>
3    <TITLE>Kurt's JavaScript Archive
4    </TITLE>
5    <script>
6    function loadalert () {
7        alert("Your browser supports JavaScript!")
8    }
9    </script>
10   </HEAD>
11   <BODY>
12   <body onLoad="loadalert()">
13   </BODY>
14   </HTML>
```

The only difference between this and the previous sample is the message and the
fact that here the script is placed in the head instead of the body. Even the function

names are identical. The point of including it here is to show that what really makes an **alert** is the message, and that what is essentially the same code can be used for entirely different purposes.

status

Status Bar Alert

N2 N2.01 N2.02+ N3 N4 E3 **E4**

Before you complain that this script belongs in the chapter on status bar messages, we will admit that it probably does, but is also relevant here.

This **alert** combines the mouse-over event with a status bar message. It really doesn't work off the **alert** method at all, but contextually fits in with the other scripts in this chapter. If you want to impart some information to your users and already employ some form of mouse-over event, this script may be used in conjunction with those effects.

For example, say you use the Alert on Mouse-over script (shown earlier) and have three or four text links or graphics that launch **alert** dialog boxes. On the same page, you may wish to invoke a similar effect—send the user a message or display important information outside of the browser's display window. The Status Bar Alert script could be a good way to maintain some user interface conventions without having too many **alert** dialog boxes popping up.

A basic rule of thumb to follow when adapting this script for use in parallel with other **alert** scripts: don't overdo things. The Status Bar Alert imparts a secondary, less critical message to the user. The **alert** dialog box sends a warning or otherwise "sharp" message (see Figure 2-7).

```
1   <HTML>
2   <HEAD>
3   <TITLE>
4   </TITLE>
5   </HEAD>
6   <BODY>
7   <A HREF="status.htm" onMouseOver="self.status='A is
                              for Apple';return true">A</A>
8   <A HREF="status.htm" onMouseOver="self.status='B is
                              for Boy';return true">B</A>
9   <A HREF="status.htm" onMouseOver="self.status='C is
                              for Cool';return true">C</A>
10  <A HREF="status.htm" onMouseOver="self.status='D is
                              for Dog';return true">D</A>
11  <A HREF="status.htm" onMouseOver="self.status='E is
                        for Elephant';return true">E</A><BR><BR>
```

```
12   </body>
13   </html>
```

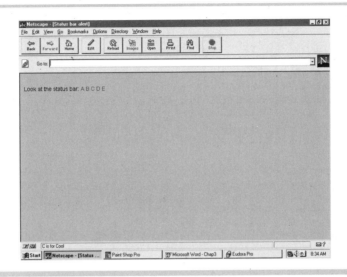

FIGURE 2-7. This alert dialog box sends a warning or otherwise "sharp" message

ANNOTATIONS

```
1    <HTML>
2    <HEAD>
3    <TITLE>
4    </TITLE>
5    </HEAD>
6    <BODY>
7    <A HREF="status.htm" onMouseOver="self.status='A is
                      for Apple';return true">A</A>
8    <A HREF="status.htm" onMouseOver="self.status='B is
                      for Boy';return true">B</A>
9    <A HREF="status.htm" onMouseOver="self.status='C is
                      for Cool';return true">C</A>
10   <A HREF="status.htm" onMouseOver="self.status='D is
                      for Dog';return true">D</A>
11   <A HREF="status.htm" onMouseOver="self.status='E is
                      for Elephant';return true">E</A><BR><BR>
```

```
12   </body>
13   </html>
```

Lines 7 to 11 in the preceding code demonstrate the basic syntax for putting a message in the browser's status bar:

```
window.status='Message'; return true
```

You don't have to specify **window** or **self**; by default the message will appear in the same window as the link. On the other hand, you can also put a message in another window's status bar by specifying the name. Assuming you had created a new window named **childWin**,

```
onMouseOver="childWin.status='Need help?'; return true"
```

would display that message in the child window's status bar when the mouse pointer comes within range of the link in the parent.

> **CAUTION** *If you omit **return true**, the link's HREF will appear in the status bar when the mouse pointer is over the text or image anchor—your message will only be displayed when the pointer moves off the link. In effect, the omission turns your message into an **onMouseOut** event.*

On a page that uses graphic links, status bar messages are a good way to tell visitors exactly where each link leads. With the messages, you can provide the kind of help found in many desktop applications—and do so in a more user-friendly way than by use of a barrage of **alert** boxes, each one of which has to be closed before the visitor can do anything else at your site.

reverse

Text Reversal Alert

[N2] [N2.01] [N2.02+] [N3] [N4] [E3] [E4]

If an **alert** dialog box can be considered fun—and a few of these scripts can be used for humorous effects—this script provides a good demonstration. It is not particularly useful outside of the fact that it can be done relatively easily.

The Text Reversal Alert features a text area in which users can type any text message they want, press a button, and see their message displayed in an **alert** dialog box. However, the funny part is the letters and/or numbers in the message are reversed when they appear in the **alert** (see Figure 2-8).

```
1   <HTML>
2   <HEAD>
3   </HEAD>
4   <BODY>
5   <FORM name=mangler><INPUT type=text name=text
                                     value='reverse text'>
```

```
6   <BR><INPUT type=button value='Reverse Text' onclick=rev()>
                    </FORM><SCRIPT><!-- Copyright 1996 -
                 Jon Eyrick - scripter@actionaccess.com
7   // this script will reverse your text.
8   function rev(){
9   var text=document.mangler.text.value;
10  var backwards="";
11  for(count=text.length; count >= 0; count--)
12  backwards+=text.substring(count,count-1);
13  alert(backwards);}
14  //--></SCRIPT>
15  <BR>
16  </BODY>
17  </HTML>
```

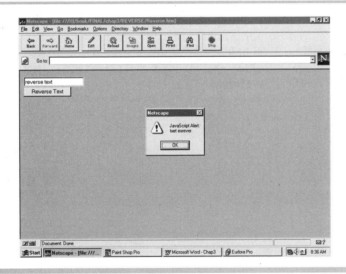

FIGURE 2-8.   A "fun" alert box example

ANNOTATIONS

```
1   <HTML60>
2   <HEAD>
3   </HEAD>
4   <BODY>
```

```
5    <FORM name=mangler><INPUT type=text name=text
                                    value='reverse text'>
6    <BR><INPUT type=button value='Reverse Text' onclick=rev()>
                 </FORM><SCRIPT><!-- Copyright 1996 -
                 Jon Eyrick - scripter@actionaccess.com
7    // this script will reverse your text.
8    function rev(){
9    var text=document.mangler.text.value;
10   var backwards="";
```

The function **rev( )** begins by getting the content of the text field named **text** found in the form named **mangler** and assigning it to the **text** variable. Then line 10 declares **backwards** as a variable and assigns it the value of an empty string with the two quotation marks. Omitting this line would produce a "backwards is undefined" error message when the JavaScript compiler reaches the increment on line 12 later.

```
11   for(count=text.length; count >= 0; count--)
12   backwards+=text.substring(count,count-1);
```

Next **rev( )** sets up a **for** loop, which in JavaScript (as in most programming languages) consists of three semicolon-separated expressions—**initialization**, **condition**, and **increment**—followed by the statement(s) that are executed as long as the condition remains true. In other words, the syntax is

```
for (initialization; condition; increment) {
      statement(s);
}
```

Although the three expressions are optional, as in C,

```
for ( ; ; )
```

creates an "infinite" loop which, in the case of JavaScript, is guaranteed to freeze your browser unless terminated by a **break** or **return** statement.

In this script, the **for** loop is controlled by the new variable **count**, which is declared and at the same time assigned the length of whatever text is entered into the form's text field. The **length** property gives you access to the number of elements that make up JavaScript objects such as strings and arrays. For example, if

```
message = "This is a test"
```

message.length is 14. In our Text Reversal script, the increment is actually a decrement that starts with the length of the user input and counts backwards as long as **count** is greater than or equal to zero, at which point it stops. With each count, the statement on line 12 is executed.

Although **for** loop statements are normally enclosed in curly braces, if you omit them as this author has done, JavaScript will only treat the first statement immediately following the **for** expression as part of the loop. For instance, write

```
var k = 0;
for ( var i = 0; i < 10; i++)
k += i;
if (k == 5) document.mangler.text.value = k
```

and "5" will never appear in the text field, because the **if** test is only applied after the **for** loop has ended. Add a pair of curly braces, however, with

```
for ( var i = 0; i < 10; i++) {
    k += i;
    if (k == 5) document.mangler.text.value = k }
```

and "5" will appear in the text field the instant **k** reaches that value. The indentation, incidentally, has nothing to do with the loop's behavior; it's merely a matter of code writing style.

To get back to our Text Reversal script, with each pass through the loop, line 12 adds another letter to the **backwards** string. The individual letters are obtained with JavaScript's built-in **substring( )** method, whose syntax is

```
stringName.substring(index1, index2)
```

The index arguments may be any two integers from 0 to **length** – 1, counting from left to right. If **index2** is greater than **index1**, the returned substring extends from the character at the first index to the character in the position immediately before the second index. Thus,

```
hamString = "To be, or not to be"
hamString.substring(7,9)
```

returns "or," the parameters (12,15) return "t t," and so on. If **index1** is greater than **index2**, as it is in our Text Reversal script, the **substring( )** method returns the characters from the one at **index2** to the one in the position before **index1**. What this possibly confusing description boils down to is that

```
hamString.substring(7,9)
```

and

```
hamString.substring(9,7)
```

both return exactly the same substring, that is, "or."

```
13   alert(backwards);}
14   //--></SCRIPT>
15   <BR>
16   </BODY>
17   </HTML>
```

Finally, on line 13 our **rev( )** function ends by passing the entire **backwards** string to the **alert( )** method, which displays it in an **alert** dialog box. You could also display the result of the text reversal in the input field by replacing line 13 with

```
document.mangler.text.value = backwards
```

While there are not many real-world situations in which you're likely to use a function such as **rev( )** other than for amusement, you can sometimes learn quite a bit about JavaScript just by taking a close look at a trivial function.

Timerless Timer Alert

timer

N2 N2.01 N2.02+ N3 N4 E3 E4

This page features a button which, when clicked, opens an **alert** that displays the amount of time you have spent at the site. It's a web page enhancement you might use to cater to time-tracking visitors whose Internet service provider charges by the hour, or to remind shoppers that there are only *x* number of days left until your superspecial sale ends. Perhaps more important, the code—which is also displayed on the page—serves as a good introduction to the JavaScript **Date** object by demonstrating how to get the time at two different moments (logon and **alert** button click), then format and display the resulting data. With a solid grasp of these basic functions and a little imagination, you can create a variety of original time-related devices for your site—anything from a student exam timer to the virtual cuckoo clock you've been contemplating (see Figure 2-9).

```
1    <HTML>
2    <HEAD>
3    <SCRIPT>
4    <!--  Activate Cloaking Device
5     var onHours = " ";
6     var onMinutes = " ";
7     var onSeconds = " ";
8     var offHours = 0;
9     var offMinutes = 0;
10    var offSeconds = 0;
11    var logSeconds = 0;
12    var logMinutes = 0;
13    var logHours = 0;
14    var OnTimeValue = " ";
15    var OffTimeValue = " ";
16    var PageTimeValue = " ";
17    // Captures logon time.
18    function getLogonTime()
19       {
20       var now = new Date();
21       // Used to display logon time.
22       var ampm = (now.getHours() >= 12) ? " P.M." : " A.M."
```

```
23      var Hours = now.getHours();
24          Hours = ((Hours > 12) ? Hours - 12 : Hours);
25      var Minutes = ((now.getMinutes() < 10) ? ":
                            0" : ":") + now.getMinutes();
26      var Seconds = ((now.getSeconds() < 10) ? ":
                            0" : ":") + now.getSeconds();
27      // String to display logon time.
28      OnTimeValue =(" "
29          + Hours
30          + Minutes
31          + Seconds
32          + " "
33          + ampm);
34      // Capture logon time for use in timer().
35      onHours = now.getHours();
36      onMinutes = now.getMinutes();
37      onSeconds = now.getSeconds();
38      }
39  function getLogoffTime()
40      {
41      var now = new Date();
42      // Used to display logoff time.
43      var ampm = (now.getHours() >= 12) ? " P.M." : " A.M."
44      var Hours = now.getHours();
45          Hours = ((Hours > 12) ? Hours - 12 : Hours);
46      var Minutes = ((now.getMinutes() < 10) ?
                            ":0" : ":") + now.getMinutes();
47      var Seconds = ((now.getSeconds() < 10) ?
                            ": 0" : ":") + now.getSeconds();
48      // String to display logoff time.
49      OffTimeValue =(" "
50          + Hours
51          + Minutes
52          + Seconds
53          + " "
54          + ampm);
55      // Capture logoff time for use in timer().
56      offHours = now.getHours();
57      offMinutes = now.getMinutes();
58      offSeconds = now.getSeconds();
59      timer();
60      }
61  // Compute difference between logoff time and logon time.
```

```
62   function timer()
63      {
64      if (offSeconds >= onSeconds)
65         { logSeconds = offSeconds - onSeconds; }
66      else
67         {
68         offMinutes -= 1;
69         logSeconds = (offSeconds + 60) - onSeconds;
70         }
71      if (offMinutes >= onMinutes)
72         { logMinutes = offMinutes - onMinutes; }
73      else
74         {
75         offHours -= 1;
76         logMinutes = (offMinutes + 60) - onMinutes;
77         }
78      logHours = offHours - onHours;
79      // Used to display time on page.
80      logHours =  ((logHours < 10) ? "0" : ":") + logHours;
81      logMinutes = ((logMinutes < 10) ?
                                    ": 0" : ":") + logMinutes;
82      logSeconds = ((logSeconds < 10) ?
                                    ": 0" : ":") +logSeconds;
83      // String to display time on page.
84      PageTimeValue =(" "
85         + logHours
86         + logMinutes
87         + logSeconds);
88      displayTimes();
89      }
90   function displayTimes()
91      {
92      alert("\nLOG ON TIME   : "
                          +OnTimeValue+"\n\nLOG OFF TIME  : "
            +OffTimeValue+"\n\nTIME ON PAGE : " + PageTimeValue);
93      }
94   // Deactivate Cloaking -->
95   </SCRIPT>
96   </HEAD>
97   <BODY BGCOLOR="FFFFFF" TEXT=000000 onLoad="getLogonTime();">
98   <CENTER><STRONG><EM>
99   <FORM>
100  <INPUT TYPE="button" value="Time on Page"
```

```
                                          onClick="getLogoffTime()">
101  </FORM>
102  </CENTER>
103  <BR>
104  </BODY>
105  </HTML>
```

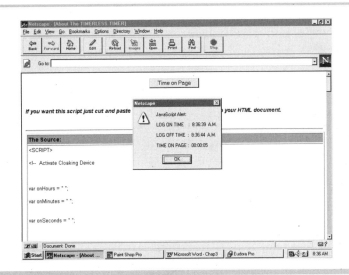

FIGURE 2-9. Help users keep track on their time online

ANNOTATIONS

If you're a JavaScript newbie, you shouldn't feel intimidated by the length and apparent complexity of this script. Its two basic functions, **getLogonTime( )** and **getLogoffTime( )**, are essentially identical. The third, **timer( )**, calculates the difference between the two times and formats the strings displayed in the **alert**.

The script is also well commented, with comments preceding not only the various functions, but also their components. This is a good habit to develop. Your comments will serve as reminders six months down the road of what does what in your script. They can also help visitors who might take a look at your code with their browser's view-source function.

Incidentally, the "Cloaking Device" on line 4 is just the standard HTML comment tag closed on line 94 to prevent JavaScript-incapable browsers from displaying the script as page content.

```
1    <HTML>
2    <HEAD>
3    <SCRIPT>
4    <!-- Activate Cloaking Device
5     var onHours = " ";
6     var onMinutes = " ";
7     var onSeconds = " ";
8     var offHours = 0;
9     var offMinutes = 0;
10    var offSeconds = 0;
11    var logSeconds = 0;
12    var logMinutes = 0;
13    var logHours = 0;
14    var OnTimeValue = " ";
15    var OffTimeValue = " ";
16    var PageTimeValue = " ";
```

Our author begins by declaring a dozen global variables. The first six are assigned their respective time-component values by the logon/logoff functions and then read by **timer( )** to calculate the difference. The remaining six are used by **timer( )** to calculate and format the display string for the **alert**.

Although the first three (**onHours, onMinutes, onSeconds**) are declared as strings, they could equally well have been initialized with 0, because the values assigned to them in **getLogonTime** are integers. This shows how, unlike C languages, for example, JavaScript does not require datatyping—the same variables can freely be assigned strings and numbers without provoking the least squawk from the compiler. For instance:

```
function showVars() {
    var horse = "Giddyap!";
    document.testform.output.
    value = horse;      // output: "Giddyap!"
    horse = 9 + 6;
    document.testform.output.
    value = horse;      // output: "15"
}
```

Now let's take a look at the pair of time-capturing functions that come next in our script. The first, **getLogonTime( )**, runs automatically when the page loads because it is called by the **onLoad** event handler in the <BODY> tag on line 97.

```
17    // Captures logon time.
18    function getLogonTime()
19        {
20        var now = new Date();
```

```
21      // Used to display logon time.
22      var ampm = (now.getHours() >= 12) ? " P.M." : " A.M."
23      var Hours = now.getHours();
24          Hours = ((Hours > 12) ? Hours - 12 : Hours);
25      var Minutes = ((now.getMinutes() < 10) ? ":
                                0" : ":") + now.getMinutes();
26      var Seconds = ((now.getSeconds() < 10) ? ":
                                0" : ":") + now.getSeconds();
```

getLogonTime( ) begins by creating a **Date** object on line 20. The syntax is simple:

```
variableName = new Date()
```

Invoking this constructor is always the first step to using JavaScript's built-in time-related features. Skip it and you're asking for error messages.

With the **Date** object created (in our script as the variable **now**), its **getHours( )**, **getMinutes( )**, and **getSeconds( )** methods can be used. The first call is to **getHours( )** on line 22 in a conditional expression that determines whether the current time is A.M. or P.M. **getHours( )** returns an integer between 0 and 23. The conditional expression is a shorthand version of **if-else** that takes the following form:

```
(testCondition) ? doifTrue : doifFalse
```

Thus, line 22 tests if the current time is equal to or greater than 12. If it is, the local variable **ampm** is assigned the string "P.M."; if false, **ampm** gets "A.M.".

Next the value of **now.getHours( )** is assigned to a new variable, **Hours**, which on line 24 turns the 24-hour-clock into a 12-hour one by subtracting 12 if the method returns an integer greater than 12. Lines 25 and 26 apply similar tests to **getMinutes( )** and **getSeconds( )** while at the same time formatting the time strings and assigning the resulting strings to two new variables, **Minutes** and **Seconds**. Both these methods return an integer between 0 and 59. If the number is less than 10, our script prepends ":0"—otherwise a colon alone.

```
27      // String to display logon time.
28      OnTimeValue =(" "
29          + Hours
30          + Minutes
31          + Seconds
32          + " "
33          + ampm);
34      // Capture logon time for use in timer().
35      onHours = now.getHours();
36      onMinutes = now.getMinutes();
37      onSeconds = now.getSeconds();
38      }
```

getLogonTime( ) then assembles the time string by concatenating the variables in lines 28 to 33 while inserting a blank space at the start of the string and before

ampm. This could have been written as a single line, but a vertical such as the one used here makes the code more readable.

Finally, the function ends by again using the three **Date** object methods to assign the current time to the three global variables declared in the opening lines of this script. It is worth noting that these second calls may produce different integers from those returned in lines 22 through 26. While the values differ only by the number of milliseconds between the two calls, the difference becomes apparent whenever that time span straddles the top of the hour.

```
39   function getLogoffTime()
40      {
41      var now = new Date();
42      // Used to display logoff time.
43      var ampm = (now.getHours() >= 12) ? " P.M." : " A.M."
44      var Hours = now.getHours();
45           Hours = ((Hours > 12) ? Hours - 12 : Hours);
46      var Minutes = ((now.getMinutes() < 10) ?
                               ":0" : ":") + now.getMinutes();
47      var Seconds = ((now.getSeconds() < 10) ?
                               ": 0" : ":") + now.getSeconds();
48      // String to display logoff time.
49      OffTimeValue =(" "
50           + Hours
51           + Minutes
52           + Seconds
53           + " "
54           + ampm);
55      // Capture logoff time for use in timer().
56      offHours = now.getHours();
57      offMinutes = now.getMinutes();
58      offSeconds = now.getSeconds();
59      timer();
60      }
```

The **getLogoffTime( )** function is virtually identical to **getLogonTime( )**. The only differences are that it creates a separate time string in lines 49 to 54, uses the "off" set of global variables in 56 through 58, and ends by calling **timer( )**. It is also the function called by the **onClick** event handler attached to the button on line 100.

When you have parallel functions such as these, often you can combine them into one by adding an argument that serves as a switch for handling the differences. Here, for example, it could have been done with

```
function getUserTimes(switch) {
    var now = new Date();                    // common components
       . . .
```

```
if (switch == "on")
 {OnTimeValue = ...; onHours = ...;} // differences
if (switch == "off")
 {OffTimeValue = ...; offHours = ...;}
}
```

and assigning **getUserTimes("on")** to **onLoad** and **getUserTimes("off")** to **onClick**. Better yet, separate functions could be created for the differences and passed the results of **getUserTimes( )**, for example:

```
if (switch == "on")
        {setOnTime(Hours, Minutes, Seconds, ampm)}
    if (switch == "off")
        {setOffTime(Hours, Minutes, Seconds, ampm)}
```

While at times it may be undesirable to merge parallel functions, you should always at least consider whether it would be worth the effort. All the variables, functions, and objects in your scripts consume memory space and processor time, and compact code is more likely than not to outperform a sprawling script littered with redundancies.

Returning to our script, the **timer( )** function called at the end of **getLogoffTime( )** calculates the difference between the instant the page finished loading and the moment the user clicks on the "Time on Page" button.

```
61   // Compute difference between logoff time and logon time.
62   function timer()
63      {
64      if (offSeconds >= onSeconds)
65          { logSeconds = offSeconds - onSeconds; }
66      else
67          {
68          offMinutes -= 1;
69          logSeconds = (offSeconds + 60) - onSeconds;
70          }
71      if (offMinutes >= onMinutes)
72          { logMinutes = offMinutes - onMinutes; }
73      else
74          {
75          offHours -= 1;
76          logMinutes = (offMinutes + 60) - onMinutes;
77          }
78      logHours = offHours - onHours;
```

timer( ) starts out by doing the math on the minutes and seconds. If an "off" value is greater than the "on," a simple subtraction is performed. Otherwise it is incremented by "60," and "1" is subtracted from the next higher unit (minutes or hours).

Obviously, omitting this step could result in confusing negative time values being displayed.

A similar test should also be applied to **logHours**. Without it, if a user logs in at 11 P.M. and out after midnight, **logHours** is assigned –23 (that is, 0 minus 23), which then gets prefixed by a 0 (line 80) because the negative number is less than 10. As a result, the hour value displayed in the **alert** becomes the string "0-23." A good exercise might be for you to enhance this script by eliminating that little bug.

```
79      // Used to display time on page.
80      logHours =  ((logHours < 10) ? "0" : ":") + logHours;
81      logMinutes = ((logMinutes < 10) ?
                                        ": 0" : ":") + logMinutes;
82      logSeconds = ((logSeconds < 10) ?
                                        ": 0" : ":") +logSeconds;
83      // String to display time on page.
84      PageTimeValue =(" "
85          + logHours
86          + logMinutes
87          + logSeconds);
88      displayTimes();
89          }
```

Lines 80 to 82 create the display strings for the three time values by adding colons and prefixing 0 to single digits. Their concatenation in lines 84 through 87 is assigned to **PageTimeValue**, the last of the three strings displayed in the **alert**. The **timer( )** ends with a call to **displayTimes( )**, which creates the **alert** and fills it with the three time values (logon time, logoff time, and the difference between them) accompanied by explanatory text.

```
90      function displayTimes()
91          {
92      alert("\nLOG ON TIME      : "
                            +OnTimeValue+"\n\nLOG OFF TIME   : "
            +OffTimeValue+"\n\nTIME ON PAGE : " + PageTimeValue);
93          }
```

Finally, following is the HTML code with the two event handlers that make this page work: the first is in the <BODY> tag, and the second, attached to the standard form button.

```
94      // Deactivate Cloaking -->
95      </SCRIPT>
96      </HEAD>
97      <BODY BGCOLOR="FFFFFF" TEXT=000000 onLoad="getLogonTime()";>
98      <CENTER><STRONG><EM>
99      <FORM>
```

```
100   <INPUT TYPE="button" value="Time on Page"
                               onClick="getLogoffTime()">
101   </FORM>
102   </CENTER>
103   <BR>
104   </BODY>
105   </HTML>
```

Although this script directs its output to an **alert** box, you can easily make it display the time elsewhere (such as in a separate frame, new window, or form text field) by modifying **displayTimes( )** to suit your needs. Its functions represent the basic components of a timer that gets and computes the difference between two moments, **onLoad** and **onClick**.

You might even try an opposite approach by simply creating two **Date** objects—say, **now1** and **now2**—and calculating the difference with

```
diff = now2 - now1
```

in which case **diff** will be the number of milliseconds elapsed between the two times. Then dividing by 1,000 yields the number of seconds, which can be divided by 60 to get a minutes value, 60 for hours, 24 for days, and so on. Use ordinary string functions to format the output, and you'll have built another version of our timer.

confirm

Confirm 1

N2 N2.01 N2.02+ N3 N4 E3 E4

This page is an example of a web site gatekeeper. Upon loading, it pops open a **confirm** dialog box that asks, "Are you sure you want to enter?" Clicking on OK gives you access to the page; selecting Cancel returns visitors to the page they came from.

The script can easily be adapted for a variety of purposes, such as displaying a warning that a site contains adult material, waiving legal liability, or even seeing if you can get rich with

```
confirm("By clicking on 'OK', you grant me full,
         clear, irrevocable title to all your
     tangible and intangible property and possessions.")
```

These dialog boxes are a cinch to create. The hard part is using them well (see Figure 2-10).

```
1   <HTML>
2   <HEAD>
3   <TITLE></TITLE><script>
4   function checkAGE(){if (!confirm
```

```
5    ("Are you sure you want to enter?
                          (--You can say whatever you want.)"))
6    history.go(-1);return " "}
7    document.writeln(checkAGE())
8    </script>
9    </HEAD>
10   <BODY BGCOLOR="ffffff">
11   </BODY>
12   </HTML>
```

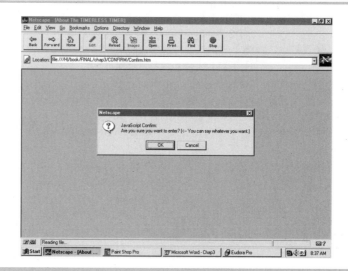

FIGURE 2-10. An example of a web site gatekeeper

ANNOTATIONS

This script consists of two functions: **checkAGE( )**, which launches the **confirm** box and responds to the user input, and **document.writeln( )**, which calls **checkAGE( )**.

```
1    <HTML>
2    <HEAD>
3    <TITLE></TITLE><script>
4    function checkAGE(){if (!confirm
5    ("Are you sure you want to enter?
                          (< --You can say whatever you want.)"))
6    history.go(-1);return " "}
```

With the negation **!confirm**, the **if** condition beginning on line 4 tests for a user click on Cancel while creating the **confirm** box with its message. If the user decides to not go on and clicks on "Cancel," **history.go(-1)** turns the browser back one page and the function returns an empty string to its caller, **document.writeln( )**.

history.go( ) is a built-in JavaScript object-method whose argument can be either a negative or positive integer that takes the user back or forth that number of pages in the user's history list, or a specific URL. As a feature of the language, it should be used with discretion, especially at the front of a site. When you don't know where your visitor's coming from, you don't know where **history.go(-1)** might send them. Several links deep into a site, however, it can become a useful navigation tool.

```
7    document.writeln(checkAGE())
8    </script>
9    </HEAD>
10   <BODY BGCOLOR="ffffff">
11   </BODY>
12   </HTML>
```

checkAGE( ) can be called in any number of ways: directly from the script with

```
checkAGE()
```

on line 7, or by adding an event handler to the <BODY> tag on line 10, that is,

```
onLoad="checkAGE()"
```

or from a second script between the <BODY> tags. The difference is essentially one of timing. A call placed in the head, as in our sample script, executes before the page is displayed. You can see the difference in timing by changing your browser's default background color to anything but white: the body will then only be loaded (page turns white) with a click on OK. Use the **onLoad** event handler, however, which executes after the page has been laid out, and the page will turn white before the **confirm** pops open. Ditto for a call from a body script.

usermsgs

Validation Demo

N2 N2.01 N2.02+ N3 N4 E3 **E4**

Our next script shows how you can easily combine **alert**s with **confirm**s. It contains a text anchor where a click launches a **confirm**. Selecting OK displays an **alert** with one message, and selecting Cancel displays another **alert** with a different message.

Combine this technique with arrays of messages, and you could create a maze of dialog boxes. Do it inadvertently and you're liable to annoy visitors to your site. Apply some imagination and ingenuity, however, and you could come up with a fun labyrinth-style game made entirely of **alert**s, **confirm**s, and **prompt**s (see Figure 2-11).

```
1   <HTML>
2   <HEAD>
3   <TITLE>
4   </TITLE>
5   </HEAD>
6   <BODY>
7   <SCRIPT>
8           // JavaScript Form Validation Demo
9           // by Paul Colton
10  </SCRIPT>
11  <A HREF="usermsgs.htm" onClick="if(confirm
                            ('Are you sure about this?'))
                    alert('Confidence is a great thing!');
                else alert('Maybe next time, hang in there.');">
                    Click me for a confirmation.</A><BR><BR>
12  </BODY>
13  </HTML>
```

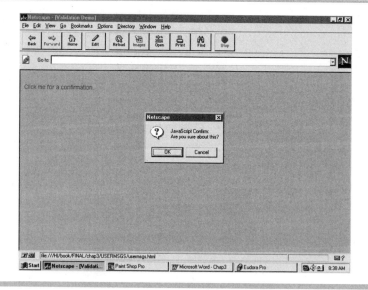

FIGURE 2-11.   You can easily combine alerts with confirms

ANNOTATIONS

The formal script that follows consists of the author's identifying comments. The real action lies in the link on line 11.

```
1    <HTML>
2    <HEAD>
3    <TITLE>
4    </TITLE>
5    </HEAD>
6    <BODY>
7    <SCRIPT>
8            // JavaScript Form Validation Demo
9            // by Paul Colton
10   </SCRIPT>
11   <A HREF="usermsgs.htm" onClick="if(confirm
                            ('Are you sure about this?'))
                  alert('Confidence is a great thing!');
            else alert('Maybe next time, hang in there.');">
                  Click me for a confirmation.</A><BR><BR>
12   </BODY>
13   </HTML>
```

The **onClick**-called script uses an **if** test for the confirm and launches the "Confidence is a great thing!" **alert** if the user clicks OK. Otherwise Cancel displays the second **alert**. This sample again shows how you can write an entire function in the string assigned to **onClick**. Usually, for reasons such as readability, easier maintenance, and even writability (because you're not coding between a pair of quotation marks), it's wiser to create a separate function and call it with the event handler.

Also, if you have a number of functions assigned to an event handler, for example:

```
onClick="addupBill();calcTax();setTotal();displayPaymentForm()"
```

you're probably better off writing

```
                function getPayment() {
                    addupBill();
                    calcTax();
                    setTotal();
                    displayPaymentForm();
                }
```

and calling it with

```
onClick="getPayment()"
```

The result code is not only neater and more reader friendly than a one-liner, it's also less likely to lead to errors should you decide to add, remove, or change a function. Also, since JavaScript runs a single thread, you don't have to worry about the sequence getting screwed up. The component functions will execute one after another as called.

name

Name Prompt

[N2] [N2.01] [N2.02+] [N3] [N4] [E3] [E4]

Our first example of a **prompt** shows how to get user input with a dialog box and incorporate it into your page. This is a device you can use to personalize visits to your site. Assign the visitor's name to a variable, use a frameset to pass it from page to page, and you can add a personal touch to all of the content. The human ego being what it is, just as our ears invariably perk up whenever we hear our name spoken, our eyes immediately gravitate to the sight of our name. You can use this as a conscious sales tactic, or to give an institutional site a friendly feel, or even for a "Personal Insults" page. One thing is certain: using a person's name is a powerful hook (see Figure 2-12).

```
1   <HTML>
2   <HEAD>
3   <TITLE></TITLE>
4   </HEAD>
5   <BODY>
6   <P><SCRIPT language="JavaScript">
7   <!-- Hide the script from old browsers --
8   // Michael P. Scholtis (mpscho@planetx.bloomu.edu)
9   // All rights reserved.  July 28, 1996
10  // You may use this JavaScript example as you
                                    see fit, as long as the
11  // information within this comment above is
                                    included in your script.
12  var namePrompt = prompt("Please enter your name.)","");
13  function dispname (namePrompt){
14          document.write(" "+namePrompt+" ");
15  }
16  // --End Hiding Here -->
17  </SCRIPT>
18  <FONT COLOR="#FF0000">
```

```
19   <FONT SIZE=+1>Welcome to my home page </FONT>
20   </FONT>
21   <SCRIPT LANGUAGE="JavaScript">
22   <!--
23       {dispname(namePrompt);}
24   //-->
25   </SCRIPT>
26   </P>
27   </BODY>
28   </HTML>
```

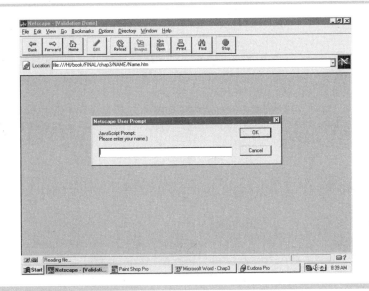

FIGURE 2-12. You can personalize your site for users

ANNOTATIONS

Here Michael Scholtis' script consists of a single function, **dispname( )**, which
is called from the body of the page and takes one argument—the variable
namePrompt to which the content of the **prompt** text field is assigned.

```
1    <HTML>
2    <HEAD>
3    <TITLE></TITLE>
4    </HEAD>
```

```
5    <BODY>
6    <P><SCRIPT language="JavaScript">
7    <!-- Hide the script from old browsers --
8    // Michael P. Scholtis (mpscho@planetx.bloomu.edu)
9    // All rights reserved.  July 28, 1996
10   // You may use this JavaScript example as you
                                     see fit, as long as the
11   // information within this comment above is
                                     included in your script.
12   var namePrompt = prompt("Please enter your name.)","");
13   function dispname (namePrompt){
14          document.write(" "+namePrompt+" ");
15   }
16   // --End Hiding Here -->
17   </SCRIPT>
```

The script begins on line 12 by declaring the variable **namePrompt**, and assigning it the **prompt( )** method, whose first argument is the message to be displayed, and whose second is the default content of the text field. Here the latter is an empty string. If you omit this second argument, the word "undefined" will appear in the text field. This argument can be a string, integer, variable, or even a function. For example:

```
prompt("The number is:", addUp())
```

calling

```
function addUp() {
     x = 5 + 7;
     return x;
         }
```

displays "12" in the **prompt** text field. In other words, you can make the default value of the text field static or dynamic, depending on the nature and purpose of your **prompt**. You could even have a function select the appropriate message from an array. Simple as these dialog boxes may be, you can do a lot of neat little things with them.

Getting back to our sample script, **dispname( )** then takes the user's input from the **prompt** and passes it to **document.write( )**, which adds a blank space before and after the string when displaying it on the page.

```
18   <FONT COLOR="#FF0000">
19   <FONT SIZE=+1>Welcome to my home page </FONT>
20   </FONT>
21   <SCRIPT LANGUAGE="JavaScript">
22   <!--
23      {dispname(namePrompt);}
24   //-->
```

```
25  </SCRIPT>
26  </P>
27  </BODY>
28  </HTML>
```

Here **dispname( )** is placed so that its output—that is, whatever the user writes in the **prompt** text field—is displayed right next to the "Welcome to my home page" message. A simple enhancement to this script would be to use JavaScript string methods to format **namePrompt**. For instance, modify the **document.write( )** variable in line 14 to read

```
namePrompt.fontcolor("red")
```

to match the color with the welcome message, or

```
namePrompt.fontsize(4)
```

to make the font size identical. Other formatting methods available include **bold( )**, **italics( )**, **strike( )**, and everyone's favorite, **blink( )**. For multiple formatting, just apply the methods in sequence, for example:

```
namePrompt = namePrompt.bold();
namePrompt = namePrompt.italics();
namePrompt = namePrompt.strike();
namePrompt = namePrompt.blink();
document.write(namePrompt);
```

displays **namePrompt** in blinking, crossed-out bold italics. Now for a really flashy effect, you could figure out some way to make your visitor's name blink through an array of colors. If that doesn't turn him or her on...

various

Page of Prompts and Confirms

N2 N2.01 N2.02+ N3 N4 E3 **E4**

This section closes with a page that displays all three types of dialog box: **alert**, **confirm**, and **prompt**. The script shows how to use an **alert** in connection with testing user input from a form. Although here the data is drawn from a text field, you can readily derive it from any other form elements such as radio buttons, checkboxes, text areas, or selection lists.

As this file also demonstrates, there's nothing to stop you from adding a batch of all three types of dialog box to your page. Again, unless you want to annoy visitors or make them feel overwhelmed, be sparing in your use of fly-open components. There may be other ways to provide bubble help or to create your effect without using a device that jumps into the user's face with a message and demands a response before anything else can happen on your page.

If you really want to go overboard, be smart about it. Have fun by constructing a series of interactive "overlays" or **onMouseOverquilt** of graphic links that open dialog boxes to tell jokes or involve the user in rapid-fire gags. Or build a dialog box-based educational game. Make these dialog boxes part of the process, and rather than an annoyance, they become objects that actively engage users and enable your site to interact with them (see Figure 2-13).

```
1   <HTML>
2   <HEAD>
3   <TITLE>Your Web Page Title
4   </TITLE>
5   <SCRIPT LANGUAGE="JavaScript">
6   <!--Hide JavaScript from Java-Impaired Browsers
7   function test_it() {
8      ent1 = document.isnform.question1.value
9      if (ent1 != null && ent1.length != 0) {
10        ent1 = "" + eval(ent1);
11     }
12  }
13  function alertBox() {
14     if (ent1 < 10) {
15        alert("I'm sorry. The number you entered: "+ ent1
16        + ", must be more than 9");
17     }
18  }
19  function confirmBox() {
20     if (confirm("Are you sure you REALLY want to
                    go to our Home Page?"))
21     {
22        location.href = "index.htm";
23     }
24  }
25  function promptBox() {
26     entry = "";
27     if (prompt("I'm Sorry. I forgot to ask.  How many shirts "
28        + "do you wish to order?",entry)) {
29        // process here
30        }
31  }
32  // -->
33  </SCRIPT>
34  </HEAD>
35  <BODY BGCOLOR="white">
```

```
36  <!--Your page goes here -->
37  <P><FORM NAME="isnform">Type a number less than 10 here:
38  <INPUT TYPE="text" NAME="question1" SIZE=2 VALUE=""
                                      onChange="test_it(this)">
39  <INPUT TYPE ="button" VALUE = "Then Click Here"
                        onClick="alertBox(this.form)"></FORM>
40  <P><FORM>I'm ready to transfer you to our Home Page.
41  <INPUT TYPE ="button" VALUE = "Just Click Here"
                                      onClick="confirmBox()">
42  </FORM>
43  <P><FORM NAME="isnform1">I'm ready to process your order:
44  <INPUT TYPE ="button" VALUE = "Just Click Here"
                                      onClick="promptBox()">
45  </FORM>
46  <P>
47  </BODY>
48  </HTML>
```

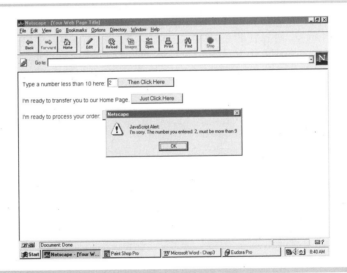

FIGURE 2-13. An alert that tests user input from a form

ANNOTATIONS

Apart from **test_it( )**, which is used by the **alertBox( )** function, the other two are entirely separate. This script is also yet another example of good naming practice.

Each of the three dialog-box function names clearly indicates what it does: **alertBox( )**, **confirmBox( )**, and **promptBox( )**. At that degree of clarity, programmer's comments become superfluous. Your code explains itself.

```
1    <HTML>
2    <HEAD>
3    <TITLE>Your Web Page Title
4    </TITLE>
5    <SCRIPT LANGUAGE="JavaScript">
6    <!--Hide JavaScript from Java-Impaired Browsers
7    function test_it() {
8      ent1 = document.isnform.question1.value
9      if (ent1 != null && ent1.length != 0) {
10       ent1 = "" + eval(ent1);
11     }
12   }
```

Although capitalization has emerged as the preferred style of indicating word breaks in names, the older technique of using underlines is perfectly acceptable in JavaScript, as line 7 shows. An underline is treated as just another ordinary character.

Our **test_it( )** function is called by the **onChange** event handler for the **question1** text field on line 38. This handler takes effect when the field loses focus, and only if the text input has changed. It changes with the user input and invariably loses focus with a click on the "Then Click Here" button (line 39), if not earlier.

test_it( ) first gets the value entered into the text field and assigns it to the variable **ent1**. Line 9 then tests that value for emptiness (**null**) and zero length. If it passes both tests and has substance at least the length of one character, it is forced to a number by the built-in JavaScript **eval( )** method. The empty string first assigned to **ent1** in line 10 is not really necessary, but it's rather a smart precaution that clears any value that may still be assigned to the variable before adding to it the integer returned by **eval( )**.

PROGRAMMER'S TIP   *When you're working with form input and getting mangled results because "6 + 8" becomes "68" instead of the "14" you want, use **eval( )** to force conversion of the value from string to number.*

```
13   function alertBox() {
14     if (ent1 < 10) {
15       alert("I'm sorry. The number you entered: "+ ent1
16       + ", must be more than 9");
17     }
18   }
```

A user click on the "Then Click Here" button calls **alertBox( )**. It tests whether the value of **ent1** is less than 10 and if it is, displays the **alert** specified on lines 15 and 16. The message that appears in the dialog box includes the number entered by the user (**ent1**). On the other hand, if the number is 10 or more, nothing happens when you click on the button.

```
19  function confirmBox() {
20     if (confirm("Are you sure you REALLY want to
                       go to our Home Page?"))
21     {
22        location.href = "index.htm";
23     }
24  }
```

confirmBox( ), called by the next button on the page (line 41), displays a navigation-oriented message. A click on OK then loads the page INDEX.HTM or whatever file you substitute. Selecting Cancel simply closes the **confirm** box.

```
25  function promptBox() {
26     entry = "";
27     if (prompt("I'm Sorry. I forgot to ask.  How many shirts "
28        + "do you wish to order?",entry)) {
29        // process here
30        }
31  }
```

Finally, the **promptBox( )** function assigned to the last button on the page begins by declaring the variable **entry** as an empty string, then using it as the second argument of the **prompt** constructor in line 28. The function here does nothing but serve as a demo; line 29 shows where to insert whatever you want to do with the user input.

For instance, the **if** clause in our sample script could be made operative with code such as

```
if (prompt('Enter quantity:','') > 50 ) { applyVolumeDiscount() }
```

which would test the user-input number against 50 and, if greater, call the assumed **applyVolumeDiscount( )** function.

To get the value entered into the **prompt** text field, assign the **prompt** method to a variable:

```
var userAge = prompt("Enter your age, please:", "")
```

After that you can test or process the input, make it the property of an object, or format, convert, or display it—essentially do anything possible with a Java string variable of that type. With data readily convertible back and forth between numeric and string values, that means just about anything.

```
32    // -->
33    </SCRIPT>
34    </HEAD>
35    <BODY BGCOLOR="white">
36    <!--Your page goes here -->
37    <P><FORM NAME="isnform">Type a number less than 10 here:
38    <INPUT TYPE="text" NAME="question1" SIZE=2 VALUE=""
                                       onChange="test_it(this)">
39    <INPUT TYPE ="button" VALUE = "Then Click Here"
                            onClick="alertBox(this.form)"></FORM>
40    <P><FORM>I'm ready to transfer you to our Home Page.
41    <INPUT TYPE ="button" VALUE = "Just Click Here"
                                       onClick="confirmBox()">
42    </FORM>
43    <P><FORM NAME="isnform1">I'm ready to process your order:
44    <INPUT TYPE ="button" VALUE = "Just Click Here"
                                       onClick="promptBox()">
45    </FORM>
46    <P>
47    </BODY>
48    </HTML>
```

The remainder of this page contains the HTML code for the standard form that displays the text field and three buttons to whose event handlers the script's functions are assigned. Like the other sample scripts in this section, this one suggests some of the ways in which you can use these dialog boxes.

While it's pretty easy to cut and paste code (unless you belong to the class of TotalNerd whose members use the dabWithWhiteOut( ) method to erase onscreen errors), a good way to start learning from the snip process is to rename all the user-created elements. Tracking down the names will give you insight into what happens and where. Plus, chances are you can come up with names more in line with your own purposes. The result will be not only a more solid grasp of the code, but a stronger sense that it's your own—which in turn can spark the confidence you need to start playing with it freely, and to gradually build it into an application that does exactly what you want.

PROGRAMMER'S NOTE   *You can use **alert**s, **confirm**s, and **prompt**s as a debugging tool to pass or check variables, and format the output as error messages. Insert **alert**s at key places in your code to display the values of variables at that point, or **prompt**s to assign test values to your variables. While you can also use **document.write**( ) in a separate frame to gain a clear view of what's happening in your script, these dialog boxes have the advantage of behaving like breakpoints, that is, they halt the thread. Assigning a break or escape-type function to the Cancel button of a **confirm** called by a **showValue** alert could spare you many a browser or system crash.*

Status Bar Enhancements

A web browser's status bar area—visible along the bottom of Netscape Navigator and Microsoft Internet Explorer's display window—is widely considered sacred ground by users and web developers.

This is where the browser displays the current status of document transfers and connections to remote sites. As users pass their mouse over a hypertext link in the main browser window, the corresponding URL displays in the status bar. For many users, this is a preferred convenience, and they do not appreciate seeing anything other than URL information in that space.

For web developers, the situation is not as clear. The status bar space remains open territory, ripe for customization through JavaScript. Unlike the toolbar, location, and other display areas on the browser, the status bar cannot be removed or customized by users. But web developers can have a field day down there.

Take it easy, though. A number of users truly dislike a lot of status bar messages. From a user-interface design point of view, apply a "less is more" philosophy to pages when you contemplate loading them with status bar enhancements. In addition, consider how difficult or easy it is to update those scripts on a regular basis.

Programming JavaScript for the status bar is subject to some serious limitations. For example, you cannot place an actual hypertext link in the status bar. This space is able to display text-based messages, period. Try formatting a string for the status bar with

```
msg = "Hot java!"
status = msg.italics()
```

and the result displayed will be "<I>Hot java!</I>." The same applies to the HTML ampersand entities in either standard or numeric form.

```
status = "caf&eacute;"
```

and

```
status = "caf&#233;"
```

will show exactly that (literally) in the status bar. To display accented and other special characters in the status bar, you have to use either hexadecimal or octal escape sequences. For hexadecimal values, the formula is a backslash followed by a lower-case "x," then the character number (same as the ones used for the numeric ampersand entities) in hexadecimal form; only the "x" is case sensitive, not the hexadecimal letters. For octals, use a backslash followed immediately by the octal. Thus, either

```
status = "caf\xE9"        // or '\xe9' but not '\Xe9'
```

or

```
status = "caf\351"
```

will produce the word "café." Two-byte or wide (Chinese, Japanese, and Korean) characters will display automatically if the code is sent as a string and the appropriate viewer (GB, Big5, and so forth) is turned on.

Beyond that, the good news is you can make the text scroll to the left, to the right, bounce around, and otherwise act in ways that will either delight or repulse users.

The most popular JavaScript-based customizations of the status bar include displaying

◆ A continuously updated, real-time clock

◆ Special descriptions of hypertext links

◆ Scrolling text messages

Working with the status bar is primarily done by use of the **onMouseOver** event handler, which is invoked when the user points at a hypertext link. By setting the value of **self.status** to a string, you can assign a value to the status bar (you could also use **window.status** or **status** here).

For example, the following HTML code:

```
<HTML>
<HEAD>
<TITLE>Status Bar Example</TITLE>
</HEAD>
<BODY>
<A HREF="home.html" onMouseOver="self.status=
                    'Time to go home'; return true;">Home</A>
<A HREF="next.html" onMouseOver="self.status=
                    'Go to the next page'; return true;">Next</A>
</BODY>
</HTML>
```

attaches a different message to each link. This can be more informative than the URLs that Navigator normally displays when a user points at a link.

Notice that both of the **onMouseOver** event handlers in the script **return true** after setting the status bar to a new value. This is necessary to display a new value in the status bar with the **onMouseOver** event handler.

All of this customization is well and good, and in terms of a web site's user interface, modifying the status bar can be very helpful for visitors. However, many users dislike seeing a customized status bar area. As soon as you implement any of the script examples provided in this chapter, expect to hear from people who do not appreciate anything other than URL-related information on the status bar. It does not matter how politely you respond that the information you are providing is useful.

On the other hand, this should not deter your efforts. The status bar area *is* up for grabs, in a sense. You can use this space to provide a wealth of information about your site and the links you have carefully placed on your pages, and even though some users will resent those efforts, others will be glad you did it.

Barclock

N2 N2.01 N2.02+ N3 N4 E3 E4

Placing a simple time clock in the status bar is a fairly unobtrusive way of changing the makeup of your web page, adding a useful bit of information for which the user may be grateful. If there are hypertext links on the same page as the script, the clock will disappear when the user moves the mouse over the link and be replaced by the document URL specified in the link (see Figure 3-1).

```
1   <html>
2   <head>
3   <title>JavaScript Warehouse - Status Clock</title>
4   </head>
5   <body bgcolor="White" text="Black" link=
        "Blue" vlink="Purple" alink="Red" onLoad="startclock()">
6   <center><h2>Status Clock</h2></center>
7   <hr align="center" size="3">
8   <script Language="JavaScript">
9   / Navigation - Stop
10  // Netscape's Clock - Start
11  // this code was taken from
                        Netscape's JavaScript documentation at
12  // www.netscape.com on Jan.25.96
13  var timerID = null;
14  var timerRunning = false;
15  function stopclock (){
16      if(timerRunning)
17          clearTimeout(timerID);
18          timerRunning = false;
19  }
20
21  function showtime () {
22      var now = new Date();
23      var hours = now.getHours();
24      var minutes = now.getMinutes();
25      var seconds = now.getSeconds()
26      var timeValue = "" + ((hours > 12) ? hours - 12 : hours)
27      timeValue += ((minutes < 10) ? ":0" : ":") + minutes
28      timeValue += ((seconds < 10) ? ":0" : ":") + seconds
29      timeValue += (hours >= 12) ? " P.M." : " A.M."
30      window.status = timeValue;
```

```
31      timerID = setTimeout("showtime()",1000);
32      timerRunning = true;
33  }
34
35  function startclock () {
36  // Make sure the clock is stopped
37  stopclock();
38  showtime();
39  }
40  </script>
41  <center>Look in your status bar!</center>
42  </body>
43  </html>
```

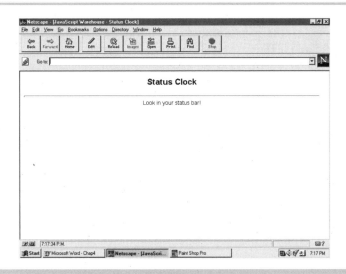

FIGURE 3-1.   Users may appreciate seeing a real-time clock on your web page

ANNOTATIONS

This script displays the current local time in the status bar. An adaptation of Example 2 of the **setTimeout( )** method in Netscape's *JavaScript Authoring Guide,* it shows you how to extract and format time values with the **Date** object. It differs from the original model only in directing the output to the status bar instead of to a form text field.

```
1    <html>
2    <head>
3    <title>JavaScript Warehouse - Status Clock</title>
4    </head>
5    <body bgcolor="White" text="Black" link=
         "Blue" vlink="Purple" alink="Red" onLoad="startclock()">
```

The status bar clock starts ticking as soon as this page has been loaded through assignment of the main function, **startclock( )**, on line 35, to the **onLoad** event handler in the <BODY> tag. It could equally well be launched by placing the same function call within a script in the head or body of the page. Or, to make your clock user-controllable, you could assign it to another event handler such as a button's **onClick** or an image's **onMouseOver**.

```
6    <center><h2>Status Clock</h2></center>
7    <hr align="center" size="3">
8    <script Language="JavaScript">
9    / Navigation - Stop
10   // Netscape's Clock - Start
11   // this code was taken from Netscape's
                                    JavaScript documentation at
12   // www.netscape.com on Jan.25.96
13   var timerID = null;
14   var timerRunning = false;
```

The script itself begins by declaring and initializing two variables, **timerID** and **timerRunning**. Neither is essential for building the clock. Rather, they fall into the category of good programming practice. **timerID**, an identifier created solely for use by the **clearTimeout( )** method on line 17, is assigned the **setTimeout( )** on line 31. **timerRunning**, on the other hand, is a Boolean flag that keeps track of whether the clock is running by being set to **true** or **false**. Because in JavaScript, as in most programming languages that use a Boolean data type, **true** is 1 and **false** is 0, you could achieve the same results by initializing the variable with

<code>var timerRunning = 0</code>

on line 14 earlier, and setting it to **true** with

<code>var timerRunning = 1</code>

on line 32 later. The advantage of using **true** and **false** lies in making it crystal-clear that the variable is a Boolean value. Initialization by use of "0" is ambiguous because the value could also be an integer. This ambiguity is no problem in a language such as C++ with a Boolean data type, where

<code>bool timerRunning = 0</code>

immediately indicates the variable is some sort of flag. But JavaScript's lack of explicit data typing makes it wiser to use the Boolean literals **true** and **false**:

```
15   function stopclock (){
16      if(timerRunning)
17          clearTimeout(timerID);
18          timerRunning = false;
19   }
```

The **stopclock** function, which is the first called by **startclock( )** on line 37, stops the clock—if it happens to be running—by canceling the time-out assigned to **timerID** and resetting **timerRunning** to **false**. Note that

```
                    if (timerRunning)
```

is simply shorthand for

```
          if (timerRunning == true)
```

or

```
          if (timerRunning == 1)
```

Like **setTimeout( )**, its opposite, **clearTimeout( )** is a built-in frame or window method. It takes a single argument: the identifier to which the **setTimeout( )** to be canceled has been assigned. Canceling the time-out is what actually stops the clock. Assign the **stopclock( )** function in this script to one HTML form button and **startclock( )** to another, and you can stop and start the clock at will.

```
21   function showtime () {
22      var now = new Date();    // = Mon May 12 15:03:32 EDT 1997
23      var hours = now.getHours();      // = 15
24      var minutes = now.getMinutes();  // = 3
25      var seconds = now.getSeconds()   // = 32
```

The **showtime** function is what makes this script tick. The preceding comments show the values of each variable at the particular moment indicated in line 22. They represent the output of, for example:

```
          status = now ; status = hours ; status = minutes...
```

Similarly, the **Date** object's other methods would yield the following values:

```
          status = now.getDay()              // = 1
          status = now.getDate()             // = 12
          status = now.getMonth()            // = 4
          status = now getYear()             // = 97
          status = now getTimezoneOffset()/60    // = 4
          status = now.getTime()             // = 863463814630
```

Day and month are counted starting from zero (Sunday and January), the time zone offset returns the number of minutes behind or ahead of Greenwich Mean Time (GMT)—which here is converted into hours through division by 60—and **getTime( )** yields the number of milliseconds since 00:00:00 hours on January 1, 1970.

PROGRAMMER'S NOTE   *All of these methods have their "set" counterparts, that is,* **setHours( )**, **setDay( )**, *setYear( ), and so on. What they set, however, are the properties of your* **Date** *object—not the user's system clock.*

In programming the **Date** object, it's important to remember that the values it returns are relative to the user. In other words, they display whatever local values they get from your visitor's system. If your visitor has a computer that boots every day with the clock set at 00:00:00 on January 1, 1980, the date and time values your JavaScript application displays will be just as skewed.

This raises a fundamental issue that every web designer must face when adding a clock to a page: whose time will it display—the server's or the client's? As local time is usually readily accessible from a variety of sources such as computer and real desktop clocks, application status bars, a wall clock, watch, and so on, it's often more interesting to display the current time at your site. This creates a much stronger sense of time and place, especially if your visitor is on the other side of the planet.

You can use the following code as a model to display your local time:

```
var now = new Date();
difhrs = now.getTimezoneOffset()/60;
lochrs = now.getHours();
GMThours = (difhrs < 0 ) ? lochrs - difhrs : lochrs + difhrs;
now.setHours(GMThours - 4);      // adapt with your GMT offset
status = now.toLocaleString();
```

This creates a new **Date** object, gets your visitor's time zone offset and local time, calculates GMT, sets the **now** object to your local time, and displays it in the status bar in a format familiar to the visitor. Just change the number in the fifth line to your local time zone offset. You can easily take this a step further to construct a world clock, for example:

```
var LA = new Date();
LA.setHours(GMThours - 8);
var NZ = new Date();
NZ.setHours(GMThours + 12);
var PAR = new Date();
PAR.setHours(GMThours + 1);
status = "The time is now " +
    LA.toLocaleString() + " in Los Angeles, " +
    NZ.toLocaleString() + " in New Zealand, and " +
    PAR.toLocaleString() + " in Paris."
```

displays the current time in those locations in the status bar. Grab any phone book, almanac, or similar reference source listing the time zones for various cities and countries around the world and you're in business.

For this to work properly, however, your visitor's operating system must have the time zone (**TZ**) parameter configured and, of course, the computer clock set at the right time. But these are factors over which you have absolutely no control, so they're not worth worrying about. Similarly, the formatting displayed by **toLocaleString( )** depends on your visitor's system. It might separate the date components by slashes or hyphens, display them as month-day-year, day-month-year, year-month-day, and so on—whatever the local preference happens to be.

```
26    var timeValue = "" + ((hours > 12) ? hours - 12 : hours)
27    timeValue += ((minutes < 10) ? ":0" : ":") + minutes
28    timeValue += ((seconds < 10) ? ":0" : ":") + seconds
29    timeValue += (hours >= 12) ? " P.M." : " A.M."
```

The next four lines of our sample script format the **hours**, **minutes**, and **seconds** values to display the time in 12-hour A.M./P.M. format. Line 26 converts the 24-hour clock value returned by **getHours( )** into a 12-hour value, lines 27 and 28 add colons plus a leading zero if the number of minutes or seconds is less than ten, and line 29 tacks on either "A.M." or "P.M." by testing the value of **hours**.

To display a 24-hour clock, change line 26 to

```
var timeValue = "" + ((hours < 10) ? "0" + hours : hours)
```

if you also want a leading zero for hours less than ten, or to

```
var timeValue = "" + hours
```

if you don't, and omit line 29.

```
30    window.status = timeValue;
31    timerID = setTimeout("showtime()",1000);
32    timerRunning = true;
33 }
```

This brings us to the core of this script: line 30, which displays the time in the status bar, and line 31, which makes the clock tick by calling **showtime( )** again after one second (1000 milliseconds) has elapsed. If you're new to programming, this is a prime example of what is known as a *recursive function*, that is, one that calls itself.

The JavaScript **setTimeout( )** method takes two arguments: an expression and the number of milliseconds to wait before evaluating it. This is a one-time method, meaning it executes *once* after the specified time has elapsed and *not every 1000 milliseconds*, to use our example. The repetition here that makes the clock tick comes from the recursive function call. Also, if the expression is a function call, it must be quoted, or else it will be called immediately instead of after the specified number of milliseconds.

JavaScript 1.2 introduces a new method, **setInterval( )**, which does just that— calls a function repeatedly at a specified time interval—and has a corresponding **clearInterval( )** method to stop the process. Their basic syntax is the same as for **set/clearTimeout( )**, that is:

```
timerID = setInterval(expression, msecs)
clearInterval(timerID)
```

At the same time, JavaScript 1.2 provides a new syntax for function calls for both **setTimeout( )** and **setInterval( )**:

```
setTimeout(function, msecs, [arg1, ..., argn])
setInterval(function, msecs, [arg1, ..., argn])
```

Thus, to execute the function **pickWear** with the arguments **shirt**, **blouse**, and **vest** every three seconds, you could write

```
setInterval("pickWear('shirt', 'blouse', 'vest')", 3000)
```

or

```
setInterval(pickWear, 3000, 'shirt', 'blouse', 'vest')
```

Notice that in the latter case the function is called by name alone, with no quotes or brackets.

```
35   function startclock () {
36   // Make sure the clock is stopped
37   stopclock();
38   showtime();
39   }
```

Finally, lines 35 to 39 contain the main function called when the page is loaded. First it stops the clock if the latter happens to be running, and then it launches **showtime( )** with its recursive loop that updates and displays the time.

```
40   </script>
41   <center>Look in your status bar!</center>
42   </body>
43   </html>
```

If you find the time displayed by this script a bit jerky, skipping a second every now and then, you can smoothen the clock display by speeding up the recursive call with

```
timerID = setTimeout("showtime()",100)
```

Bear in mind, however, that this increases the load on your user's processor.

JavaScript clock mechanics, as shown in this script, remain essentially the same no matter where you display the output: in the status bar, in a form element such as a text field or button face, or in a specific frame, layer, or window—any instantly refreshable component of your page. Just don't write

```
document.write(timeValue)
```

because that instantly wipes out your script and leaves you with a dead clock. To use **document.write( )**, make sure your clock display is in a different frame, layer, or window from your script.

You can also easily tinker with the mechanics to create a gag barclock that runs backwards. Add

```
var t = 0
```

to the top of our script (outside of the functions), and after line 25 insert

```
now.setSeconds(seconds - t);
seconds = now.getSeconds();
t++;
```

to make the seconds run backwards. Then use similar routines to perform the subtraction on minutes and hours and call them into play at the top of the clock with

```
if (seconds == 59)
```

and

```
if (minutes == 59)
```

and you can credit yourself with having created a totally useless but nonetheless entertaining little device. Do it as an exercise, and you'll likely emerge with a solid grasp of JavaScript's time-related functions and how to manipulate them.

timer

Visit Timer

 N2 N2.01 N2.02+ N3 N4 E3 E4

As with the previous example, the Visit Timer script displays useful information in the status bar area, in this case a running total of the hours, minutes, and seconds a visitor has been at your web page.

Admittedly, the Visit Timer and Barclock scripts provide only the most bare enhancement to a web page, but they are subtle and useful enough that the user will more likely thank you than send you a nasty note (see Figure 3-2).

```
1   <HTML>
2   <HEAD>
3   <TITLE>Timer</TITLE>   <SCRIPT LANGUAGE="JavaScript">
4   <!--                           -->
5   <!-- Timer taken from Tomer and
                    Yehuda Shiran. Altered for purposes -->
6   <!-- to keep the timer showing in
                        the status bar, by Richard Dows.   -->
7   <!--                           -->
8   <!-- Copyright(c) 1996, Random Access, Inc.            -->
9   <!--                         -->
10  <!-- Hide from Old Browsers
11  var Temp;
12  var TimerId = null;
```

```
13   var TimerRunning = false;
14   Seconds = 0
15   Minutes = 0
16   Hours = 0
17
18   function showtime()
19   {
20     if(Seconds >= 59)
21     {
22       Seconds = 0
23       if(Minutes >= 59)
24       {
25         Minutes = 0
26         if(Hours >= 23)
27         {
28           Seconds = 0
29           Minutes = 0
30           Hours = 0
31         }
32         else {
33           ++Hours
34         }
35       }
36       else {
37         ++Minutes
38       }
39     }
40     else {
41       ++Seconds
42     }
43
44     if(Seconds != 1) { var ss="s" } else { var ss="" }
45     if(Minutes != 1) { var ms="s" } else { var ms="" }
46     if(Hours != 1) { var hs="s" } else { var hs="" }
47
48     Temp = 'You have been here '+Hours+' hour' +hs+',
              '+Minutes+' minute'+ms+', '+ Seconds+' second'+ss+''
49     window.status = Temp;
50     TimerId = setTimeout("showtime()", 1000);
51     TimerRunning = true;
52   }
53
```

```
54  function stopClock() {
55     if(TimerRunning)
56        clearTimeout(TimerId);
57        TimerRunning = false;
58  }
59
60  function startClock() {
61    stopClock();
62    showtime();
63  }
64  //-->
65  </SCRIPT></HEAD>
66  <BODY onLoad="startClock()" BGCOLOR="#FFFFFF">
67  <TABLE CELLPADDING=0 CELLSPACING=0 WIDTH=100%>
68    <TR>
69       <TD ROWSPAN=1 COLSPAN=1 BGCOLOR="red">
70       <FONT COLOR="white"><B>Timer</B></FONT>
71       </TD>
72    </TR>
73  </TABLE>
74  </BODY>
75  </HTML>
```

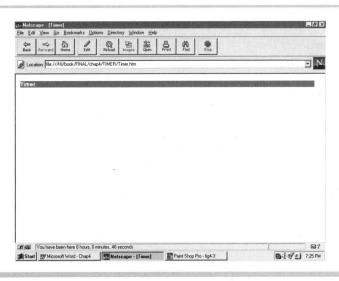

FIGURE 3-2. A clock that displays how long the user has visited a page

ANNOTATIONS

The main difference between this script and the preceding one is the difference between a stopwatch and a clock. In both cases, the main function **startClock** (on line 60) is called by the **onLoad** event handler in the <BODY> tag, and consists of a call to **stopClock( )** followed by **showtime( )**. This script, however, does not use the JavaScript **Date** object, but simply creates three variables—**Hours**, **Minutes**, and **Seconds**—which are initialized at zero and incremented every second like a clock.

```
1   <HTML>
2   <HEAD>
3   <TITLE>Timer</TITLE>   <SCRIPT LANGUAGE="JavaScript">
4   <!--                     -->
5   <!-- Timer taken from Tomer and
                    Yehuda Shiran. Altered for purposes -->
6   <!-- to keep the timer showing in
                        the status bar, by Richard Dows.  -->
7   <!--                     -->
8   <!-- Copyright(c) 1996, Random Access, Inc.            -->
9   <!--                  -->
10  <!-- Hide from Old Browsers
11  var Temp;
12  var TimerId = null;
13  var TimerRunning = false;
14  Seconds = 0
15  Minutes = 0
16  Hours = 0
```

The first variable, **Temp**, in line 11, is simply declared without being initialized. It comes into play on line 48, where it is assigned the string value displayed in the status bar. If you wish, you could also initialize it with

```
var Temp = ''
```

or you could omit the declaration altogether and let line 48 as is do the job. JavaScript allows you this kind of freedom. The approach you choose is essentially a reflection of your programming style.

The next two variables, **TimerID** and **TimerRunning**, are identical to those in the previous script, as is the **stopClock** function on line 54 in which they are used. The final three, **Hours**, **Minutes**, and **Seconds**, are what make this timer tick.

```
18  function showtime()
19  {
20    if(Seconds >= 59)
21    {
22      Seconds = 0
```

```
23      if(Minutes >= 59)
24      {
25        Minutes = 0
26        if(Hours >= 23)
27        {
28          Seconds = 0
29          Minutes = 0
30          Hours = 0
31        }
32        else {
33            ++Hours
34        }
35      }
36      else {
37          ++Minutes
38      }
39      }
40      else {
41        ++Seconds
42      }
```

The nested **if-else** conditions making up the first 24 lines of **showtime( )** do two things: they advance the time and, when necessary, make the top-of-the-clock adjustments. The **if** clauses on lines 20, 23, and 26 test the values of the three key variables and reset them to zero whenever they respectively hit 59, 59, or 23. Otherwise their values are incremented by lines 33, 37, and 41.

```
44    if(Seconds != 1) { var ss="s" } else { var ss="" }
45    if(Minutes != 1) { var ms="s" } else { var ms="" }
46    if(Hours != 1) { var hs="s" } else { var hs="" }
```

The next three lines represent the kind of little touch that often gets neglected but definitely enhances the quality of a page. They ensure that the sentence displayed in the status bar is grammatically correct by pluralizing where appropriate. For the visitor, the effect is much more attractive than stumbling across "You have been here 1 hours, 1 minutes, and 1 seconds" or "You have been here 3 hour, 5 minute, and 7 second."

▌PROGRAMMER'S NOTE   *This simple routine can readily be adapted to a variety of circumstances where whether the singular or plural should be employed depends on user input, such as in confirming an order.*

```
if (orderQty !=1 ) { var qt = 's' } else { var qt = '' }
confirm("You have ordered " + orderQty + " " + item + qt)
```

Visitors will invariably judge the quality of your business, products, services, organization, or institution by the quality of your web page. Omit the extra effort that this degree of attention to detail demands, and you may find yourself projecting a shoddy image.

```
48   Temp = 'You have been here '+Hours+' hour' +hs+',
              '+Minutes+' minute'+ms+', '+ Seconds+' second'+ss+''
49   window.status = Temp;
50   TimerId = setTimeout("showtime()", 1000);
51   TimerRunning = true;
52   }
```

Our **showtime** function ends by creating the string for the timer display in line 48 and assigning it to **Temp**, and then assigning **Temp** to the window's status property. You can create exactly the same effect by omitting the **Temp** variable altogether (that is, deleting lines 11 and 49) and changing 48 to read

```
     status = 'You have been here ' ...  // remainder as is
```

This approach is more computer efficient in that it doesn't occupy memory with a variable not used elsewhere, as well as a shade faster, because it's two fewer instructions to process. While here the difference is trivial, highly streamlined code can make as much difference in the performance of a larger application as aerodynamic body design can with an automobile. Get into the habit of finding ways to tighten up your code, and you'll soon be writing trim code with the first draft.

Finally, **showtime( )** calls itself recursively and sets **TimerRunning** to **true** just like the Barclock script earlier.

```
54   function stopClock() {
55      if(TimerRunning)
56        clearTimeout(TimerId);
57        TimerRunning = false;
58   }
```

stopClock( ) is identical to the function of the same name in the preceding script and serves to stop the timer if it is running.

```
60   function startClock() {
61     stopClock();
62     showtime();
63   }
```

Similarly, as in the previous script, **startClock( )** first calls **stopClock( )** and then **showtime( )** to start the timer ticking.

```
64   //-->
65   </SCRIPT></HEAD>
66   <BODY onLoad="startClock()" BGCOLOR="#FFFFFF">
```

```
67   <TABLE CELLPADDING=0 CELLSPACING=0 WIDTH=100%>
68     <TR>
69       <TD ROWSPAN=1 COLSPAN=1 BGCOLOR="red">
70       <FONT COLOR="white"><B>Timer</B></FONT>
71       </TD>
72     </TR>
73   </TABLE>
74   </BODY>
75   </HTML>
```

Unless you're running a cyberpeep show and charging by the minute, there aren't all that many situations in which displaying how long a user has been at a page is worthwhile. But think of the preceding as a stopwatch, and there are a variety of circumstances where it can come in handy. If you're using JavaScript combined with an HTML form to administer a test, for example, you could display elapsed time or adapt our script to make it show the remaining time by initializing **Hours** with, for example:

```
              Hours = 3           // allotted time for test
```

reversing the conditional tests with

```
       if (Seconds == 0)  { Seconds = 59
          if (Minutes == 0) { Minutes = 59
              if (Hours == 0) ...                // remainder as is
```

and decrementing the **Hours**, **Minutes**, and **Seconds** in lines 33, 37, and 41 with

```
                --Hours
                --Minutes
                --Seconds
```

This type of countdown timer can also come in handy in a game or quiz setting; to add a dramatic touch to an upcoming special event, for example, "Our annual giant clearance sale begins in exactly 3 days, 14 hours and 7 seconds!"; or to keep track of an impending deadline for entering a contest, completing a project, submitting applications or bids, filing tax returns, and so on—not to mention rocket launches, New Year's Eve, and the Turn of the Millennium.

banner

Unfurling Banner

[N2] [N2.01] [N2.02+] [N3] [N4] [E3] [E4]

One of the most common uses of the status bar area—aside from built-in browser functionality for indicating document URLs—is to display a custom, text-based message. Such a message could announce what is new on a web page or just say hello to web surfers.

This effect should be used sparingly, perhaps just on a home page, as any special status bar message will wear out its welcome after a few scrollbys. JavaScript's status bar techniques are fairly limited and can only perform a couple of tasks.

In this example, the script displays a series of one-line messages in the status bar area. Each letter in each word displays one at a time and erases itself once the entire line is displayed (see Figure 3-3).

```
1   <HTML>
2   <HEAD>
3   <TITLE>Banner</TITLE>
4   <SCRIPT LANGUAGE="JavaScript">
5   <!--
6   var speed = 100
7   var pause = 1000
8   var timerID = null
9   var bannerRunning = false
10
11  var ar = new Array()
12  ar[0] = "Welcome to our JavaScript book"
13  ar[1] = "The Banner script works in the status bar area"
14  ar[2] = "It is a very stable banner"
15  ar[3] = "It is only one of many such examples"
16
17  var currentMessage = 0
18  var offset = 0
19
20  function stopBanner() {
21      if (bannerRunning)
22              clearTimeout(timerID)
23      bannerRunning = false
24  }
25
26  function startBanner() {
27      stopBanner()
28      showBanner()
29  }
30
31  function showBanner() {
32      var text = ar[currentMessage]
33      if (offset < text.length) {
34          if (text.charAt(offset) == " ")
35                  offset++
36          var partialMessage = text.substring(0, offset + 1)
```

```
37          window.status = partialMessage
38          offset++ // Internet Explorer sometimes
                               has trouble with "++offset"
39          timerID = setTimeout("showBanner()", speed)
40          bannerRunning = true
41      } else {
42              offset = 0
43              currentMessage++
44              if (currentMessage == ar.length)
45                      currentMessage = 0
46              timerID = setTimeout("showBanner()", pause)
47              bannerRunning = true
48      }
49  }
50  // -->
51  </SCRIPT>
52  </HEAD>
53  <BODY onLoad="startBanner()">
54  </BODY>
55  </HTML>
```

FIGURE 3-3.   An elegant way to display a custom, text-based message

ANNOTATIONS

This script is a variation of the two preceding ones in that the **onLoad** event handler in the <BODY> tag calls the main function, here **startBanner( )** on line 26. This in turn first stops, then starts and recursively calls **showBanner( )**, which displays the message in the status bar. Although a clock or timer may seem very different from a scrolling message, within the context of the status bar they have one very important characteristic in common: both are strings. The difference lies in the content of the strings and how you manipulate them with the various functions that JavaScript provides.

```
1    <HTML>
2    <HEAD>
3    <TITLE>Banner</TITLE>
4    <SCRIPT LANGUAGE="JavaScript">
5    <!--
6    var speed = 100
7    var pause = 1000
8    var timerID = null
9    var bannerRunning = false
```

The first two variables, **speed** and **pause**, are declared and initialized for use as the millisecond arguments in the **setTimeout( )** calls on lines 39 and 46 later. Use of this approach, as opposed to entering the numbers directly in each call, has a number of advantages that fall into the realm of good programming practice. First and foremost, it converts what might otherwise be perceived as magic numbers into variables whose name reflects their purpose. On a more practical level, putting the two key values that determine the timing of the display next to each other at the top makes them easier to tinker with and adjust. Moreover, the names alone tell you exactly what you're doing if you change the values.

As in the two previous scripts, the **timerID** and **bannerRunning** variables are established solely for use by the **stopBanner** function on line 20.

```
11   var ar = new Array()
12   ar[0] = "Welcome to our JavaScript book"
13   ar[1] = "The Banner script works in the status bar area"
14   ar[2] = "It is a very stable banner"
15   ar[3] = "It is only one of many such examples"
```

Next, the script creates **ar** as a new **Array** in line 11, then fills four of its elements with the string messages which will be displayed, one after another, in the status bar. You could also construct the same array with

```
var ar = new Array('Welcome...', 'The Banner...',
                   'It is a very...', 'It is only one...')
```

and the same indexing would work. This approach, however, is more suitable for arrays whose elements consist of a series of integers or single words. For messages and the like, indexed listing as in lines 12 to 15 makes for easier maintenance and more readable code.

Array members can be more than string literals. They can also include variables and function calls. For example, you could combine this script with the Barclock one we saw earlier in this chapter. This could be done by adapting the **showtime( )** function in Barclock to return **timeValue**, replacing lines 30 to 32 with

```
return timeValue
```

you could then write

```
ar[4] = "The time is now " + showtime()
```

If you make this line 16 of this script, however, **showtime( )** will only be called once when the page is loaded and the array created, and the time displayed will be frozen at that moment. To update the time on each pass, you have to constantly re-create **ar[4]** in the **showBanner( )** function by inserting, after line 43,

```
if (currentMessage == 3)
    ar[4] = "The time is now " + showtime()
```

The same applies if a variable is part of the array string. Unless you refresh the variable each time the array member passes through the loop, its value will remain at the initial setting. Obviously, you don't have to do this if the variable only has to be set once, for example:

```
ar[4] = "Welcome to J-World, " + guestName + "!"
```

would work fine as line 16, providing you used a prompt dialog box or some other means to get and assign your visitor's name to **guestName** before the array is created, that is, before the page is loaded. Or you could have a separate function do the job with something like

```
function setGreeting() {
        guestName = document.guestForm.nameField.value
        ar[4] = "Welcome to J-World, " + guestName + "!"

    }
```

and call it from an event handler such as **onBlur, onChange,** or **onClick.**

```
17   var currentMessage = 0
18   var offset = 0
```

The next two variables, **currentMessage** and **offset**, come into play in **showBanner( )**. The first is the array index whose value determines which message is displayed, and the second is used as the second argument in the **substring** method on line 36 that fixes the length of the string shown.

```
20   function stopBanner() {
21       if (bannerRunning)
22               clearTimeout(timerID)
23       bannerRunning = false
24   }
```

As in the clock and timer scripts, **stopBanner( )** serves to stop the banner from running if it happens to be when the page is loaded, for example, if the user decides to reload the page.

```
26   function startBanner() {
27       stopBanner()
28       showBanner()
29   }
```

Similarly, the main function here, **startBanner( )**, is identical to the **startClock** functions we saw earlier in consisting solely of two calls that stop and show the banner.

```
31   function showBanner() {
32       var text = ar[currentMessage]
33       if (offset < text.length) {
34           if (text.charAt(offset) == " ")
35                     offset++
36           var partialMessage = text.substring(0, offset + 1)
37           window.status = partialMessage
38           offset++ // Internet Explorer sometimes
                                 has trouble with "++offset"
39           timerID = setTimeout("showBanner()", speed)
40           bannerRunning = true
```

This function begins by assigning **ar[0]**, **ar[1]**, **ar[2]**, or **ar[3]**—depending on the current value of the array index, **currentMessage**—to a new local variable, **text**. Next the first **if** makes sure that the value of **offset**, used in line 36 to determine the length of the displayed text, is less than the length of the message. The second **if** increments **offset** if the next character happens to be a blank space. This creates a smoother typing effect by keeping the rhythm of the letters appearing one after another from being broken by the blanks between words.

charAt( ) is a built-in JavaScript string method that returns the character at a specified position, starting at zero and counting from left to right. Its syntax is very simple:

```
stringname.charAt(index)
```

where **index** is any integer from 0 to the length of the string minus 1. If **index** is out of range, **charAt( )** returns an empty string.

Next, the portion of the message or substring extending from the first letter (0) to the letter before **offset** + 1 is assigned to another new local variable, **partialMessage**, which is displayed in the status bar by the assignment in line 37. Finally, **showBanner( )** increments **offset** before calling itself with the **setTimeout( )** in line 39 and setting **bannerRunning** to **true**.

```
41       } else {
42               offset = 0
43               currentMessage++
44               if (currentMessage == ar.length)
45                       currentMessage = 0
46               timerID = setTimeout("showBanner()", pause)
47               bannerRunning = true
48       }
49   }
```

If the end of the message string has been reached, the **else** instructions kick in either to reset **offset** to zero and increment the array index, or if the end of the array has been reached, to recycle back to the beginning by resetting the index to zero in line 45 before issuing the recursive call in line 46, which starts displaying the next message after a second's pause.

```
50  // -->
51  </SCRIPT>
52  </HEAD>
53  <BODY onLoad="startBanner()">
54  </BODY>
55  </HTML>
```

While watching a message unfurl letter by letter can be fun, it can easily provoke impatience and annoyance. Use it with the utmost discretion, meaning where appropriate, such as when suspense enhances the effect. Otherwise, visitors are more likely than not to tune out by following a link elsewhere before reading any of the dozen messages you spent hours perfecting. To make **showBanner( )** display the full messages instead of scrolling, cut or comment-out everything except

```
31  function showBanner() {
32      var text = ar[currentMessage]
43          currentMessage++
44          if (currentMessage == ar.length)
45              currentMessage = 0
46          timerID = setTimeout("showBanner()", pause)
47          bannerRunning = true
48      }
```

and assign **pause** in line 7 a higher value, such as "2000" or "3000," to give the user a few seconds to read each message before the next one appears.

If you have an important message to convey, the place to do it is in the body of your page, not in the status bar. On the other hand, the status bar is the ideal location for a series of kicker- or teaser-type messages such as promos or announcements ("Chicken on special this week at 55¢ a pound," "Have you checked out our new Free Downloads page?", "This week's winner is..."), reminders ("The registration deadline is 5 P.M. Monday," "This is United Way Month. Give generously!", "If personal problems are interfering with your work, our Employee Assistance Program is there to help you"), and the like. A zen-minded visitor might be thoroughly delighted to see your favorite koans flash by in the status bar while poking around your site. On the other hand, if you're designing an intranet that will also serve as a PA system, writing

```
        if (alarm)
            status = slowLetterUnfurl("THE BUILDING IS ON FIRE. " +
```

```
            "LEAVE THE PREMISES IMMEDIATELY. THIS IS NOT A DRILL. " +
                       "PLEASE REMAIN CALM! ")
```

may likely have you seeking new challenges from the ranks of the formerly employed. Some messages ought to be screamed, others belong in the status bar, and still others are best left unspoken.

controls

Scroll Controls

N2 N2.01 N2.02+ N3 N4 E3 E4

A status bar control, represented by an HTML forms button and designed to stop, start, or slow down a status bar message, can be very effective if used infrequently.

For example, allowing users to turn on a status bar message has potential as an interactive device. The web is designed as an environment in which users wield an enormous amount of control over their browser's features. Users may respect the integrity of your page if you offer them choices on how and where to proceed.

In practice, this script example may not be useful, but it should give you a good idea of how to create functions that let users manipulate status bar messages (see Figure 3-4).

```
1   <HTML>
2   <HEAD>
3   <TITLE>JavaScript Warehouse - Status Bar Controls</TITLE>
4   <SCRIPT LANGUAGE="JavaScript">
5   var b_speed=8;    //defines banner speed
6   var banner_id=10;
7   var b_pause=0;    //to pause the banner
8   var b_pos=0;
9   function stop() {
10     if(!b_pause) {
11        clearTimeout(banner_id);
12        b_pause=1;
13     }
14     else {
15        banner_main();
16        b_pause=0;
17     }
18  }
19  function banner_main() {
20     msg="Welcome to JavaScript Warehouse!"
21        +"  JavaScript can do some really"
22        +" Cool stuff.  Keep coming back to http:
```

```
                                    //www.ezl.com/~mlile/javascript/"
23        +"  for more examples..."
24     var k=(40/msg.length)+1;
25     for(var j=0;j<=k;j++) msg+="      "+msg;
26     window.status=msg.substring(b_pos,b_pos+120);
27     if(b_pos++==msg.length){
28         b_pos=0;
28     }
29     banner_id=setTimeout("banner_main()",1000/b_speed);
30 }
31 </script>
32 </HEAD>
33 <BODY BGCOLOR="White" TEXT="Black" LINK="Blue"
                                    VLINK="Purple" ALINK="Red">
34 <CENTER><H2>Status Bar Controls</H2></CENTER>
35 <HR ALIGN="CENTER" SIZE="3">
36 <P ALIGN=Center>
37 <FORM name="form1" action="">
38 <P ALIGN=Center>
39 <input type="button" value="Start"
40 onclick='{
41     clearTimeout(banner_id);
42     b_pos=0;
43     banner_main()
44     }'>
45 <input type="button" value="Slower" onclick='
46 {
47     if (b_speed<3){
48         alert("Does not get any slower!");
49     }
50     else b_speed=b_speed-1;
51 }'>
52 <input type="button" value="Faster" onclick='
53 {
54     if (b_speed>18){
55         alert("Does not get any faster!");
56     }
57     else b_speed=b_speed+2;
58 }'>
59 <input type="button" value="Pause" onclick='stop()'>
60 <input type="button" value="Reset" onclick='b_speed=8;'>
61 </FORM>
62 <HR ALIGN="CENTER" SIZE="3">
```

```
63    </BODY>
64    </HTML>
```

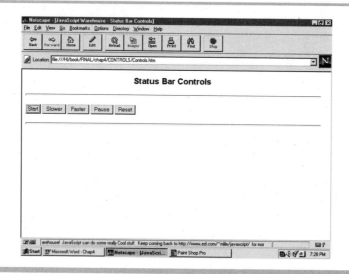

FIGURE 3-4.   This banner scroller is effective if used sparingly

ANNOTATIONS

This script is interesting not only because it shows you how to stop, start, and control the speed of a status bar banner, but also because of how it does those things and how the overall application is designed. Moreover, although it works as is, it's not really an off-the-rack script, but requires a few adjustments.

```
1    <HTML>
2    <HEAD>
3    <TITLE>JavaScript Warehouse - Status Bar Controls</TITLE>
4    <SCRIPT LANGUAGE="JavaScript">
5    var b_speed=8;              //defines banner speed
```

The first variable, **b_speed**, serves as a divisor in the millisecond argument to the **setTimeout( )** call on line 29 that makes the banner scroll along the status bar; in other words, the time-out interval is 1000 divided by **b_speed**. A glance at lines 50, 57 and 60 shows that clicking the "Faster" button increases the value of **b_speed** by 2 while "Slower" decreases it by 1, and "Reset" restores the default value of 8. This produces the following scale of rounded millisecond (msec) values for the time-outs:

b_speed	2	3	4	5	6	7	8	10	12	14	16	18	20
msecs	500	333	250	200	167	143	125	100	83	71	62	56	50

This divisor approach is well worth learning, because it's a technique that can be applied in various circumstances involving a user-controlled scale. It produces an entirely different range of values than if you were to make **b_speed** itself the second argument for **setTimeout( )**, initialize it with say, 500, and then have the "Faster" or "Slower" button, respectively, increase or decrease its value by 100.

When you run this script, however, you'll likely notice that the speed differences are not always perceptible. This is because **setTimeout( )** appears to have a core granularity of 280 milliseconds, meaning any settings below that figure are, for all intents and purposes, useless. To see the effect firsthand, create a function that gets and displays the time, then after a time-out calls a second function that also reads and shows the time. For example:

```
function milSec1() {
    now1 = new Date;
    document.testform.output1.value = now1.getTime();
    setTimeout("milSec2()", testspeed);
}
function milSec2() {
    now2 = new Date;
    document.testform.output2.value = now2.getTime();
}
```

Attach **milSec1( )** to a form button, assign different values to **testspeed**, and compare the difference between the two times to the value of **testspeed**. The results of running this test on two Pentiums were similar: at very low values of **testspeed** (1 to 100), the smallest time difference was 250 milliseconds, whereas readings of 280 to 310 were more common; at 500, the range extended from 530 to 780; and at 1000, from 1030 to 1280.

Yet when the **setTimeout** was removed so that **milSec1( )** called **milSec(2)** directly, the difference between the two output times was usually 0 and occasionally 30 milliseconds, which means the script was executing in less than a millisecond while now and then bumping into a 30-msec process. In other words, there is a lag coming from **setTimeout( )**.

What this means is that you shouldn't rely on **setTimeout( )** for split-second timing and expect to get precise results. It also points to a problem with the **b_speed** scale in our script: most of the resulting millisecond values fall into the makes-no-difference range, which is why the speed changes tend to be inconsistent and often imperceptible. While lower millisecond values definitely speed things up, the inconsistencies at those high-speed settings account for the jerkiness of the motion.

To use a higher range of millisecond values, all you have to do is change the "1000" on line 29 to a higher number, for example, 2000 produces a scale from 100 to 1000; 4000, from 200 to 2000; and so on.

```
6   var banner_id=10;
7   var b_pause=0;              //to pause the banner
8   var b_pos=0;
```

The second variable, **banner_id**, is the identifier used for the **clearTimeout( )** that stops the banner; it is the same as the **TimerID** we saw in earlier scripts in this chapter. Assigning it a value of 10 serves no other purpose than to initialize it. The real function of this variable becomes apparent on line 29, where it is assigned the **setTimeout( )**. You could just as well write

```
                    var banner_id = 'kitchen sink'
```

or simply declare it with

```
                        var banner_id;
```

Declaring it as a global variable, however, is essential so that the script attached to the "Start" button can access it.

b_pause is a Boolean variable—the counterpart of **TimerRunning** in the Barclock and Visit Timer scripts earlier—that comes into play in the **stop( )** function next, whereas **b_pos** is used by **banner_main( )** to establish the length of the displayed text.

```
9   function stop() {
10      if(!b_pause) {
11          clearTimeout(banner_id);
12          b_pause=1;
13      }
14      else {
15          banner_main();
16          b_pause=0;
17      }
18  }
```

The preceding **stop( )** function, which is assigned to the "Pause" button's event handler on line 59, is very similar to the **stopClock( )** seen previously in this chapter with one important difference: the additional **else** clause restarts the banner with a second click. First it tests the value of **b_pause** to check whether the banner is running; if it is, **clearTimeout( )** stops it and **b_pause** is set to 1 or **true**; if not, it calls **banner_main( )** and sets **b_pause** to 0 or **false**.

You might want to make this dual function clear to the user by naming the "Pause" button (for example, "pauseButton") and adding

```
                    document.form1.pauseButton.value = "Restart"
```
after line 12 and
```
                    document.form1.pauseButton.value = "Pause"
```
after line 16. This appropriately changes the button's label with each click.

```
19  function banner_main() {
20     msg="Welcome to JavaScript Warehouse!"
21        +"  JavaScript can do some really"
22        +" Cool stuff.  Keep coming back to http:
                          //www.ezl.com/~mlile/javascript/"
23        +"  for more examples..."
```

As its name implies, **banner_main( )** is the function that runs the show here. First it declares a variable, **msg**, and assigns it the string that will scroll through the status bar.

```
24     var k=(40/msg.length)+1;
25     for(var j=0;j<=k;j++) msg+="      "+msg;
```

Next comes a **for** loop that loops the message. The variable **k** on line 24 may seem cryptic at first glance, but all it does is create a number between 1 and 2 for use as the stopper in the **for** loop. You could easily omit it altogether and change line 25 to read either
```
              for (var j = 0; j < 2; j++)
```
or
```
              for (var j = 0; j <=1; j++)
```
and achieve exactly the same effect. The **for** loop then increments **msg** with a few blank spaces followed by **msg** to loop the text in the status bar.

```
26     window.status=msg.substring(b_pos,b_pos+120);
27     if(b_pos++==msg.length){
28         b_pos=0;
28     }
29     banner_id=setTimeout("banner_main()",1000/b_speed);
30  }
```

These next few lines show you how to create the scroll effect. Line 26 assigns a 120-character-long substring of **msg** to the status bar. Then on the next line, the **if** test increments **b_pos** by 1 so that, on the next pass through **banner_main( )**, **substring(1,121)** appears in the status bar, then **substring(2, 122)**, and so on, until the value of **b_pos** attains the length of the message and gets reset back to zero. These multiple passes through the function derive from the by-now familiar recursive call in the **setTimeout( )** on line 29.

```
31  </script>
32  </HEAD>
```

```
33  <BODY BGCOLOR="White" TEXT="Black" LINK="Blue"
                                    VLINK="Purple" ALINK="Red">
34  <CENTER><H2>Status Bar Controls</H2></CENTER>
35  <HR ALIGN="CENTER" SIZE="3">
36  <P ALIGN=Center>
37  <FORM name="form1" action="">
38  <P ALIGN=Center>
39  <input type="button" value="Start"
40  onclick='{
41      clearTimeout(banner_id);
42      b_pos=0;
43      banner_main()
44      }'>
```

Clicking on the "Start" button stops the banner, if it is running, with the **clearTimeout( )**, sets **b_pos** to zero to ensure that the message starts scrolling from the beginning, then calls **banner_main( )** to display it. This event handler, as well as those assigned to the "Slower" and "Faster" buttons later, could equally well have been made separate functions in the main script. The approach used here demonstrates that you can write entire functions within the HTML tag for the button. You can also declare and initialize variables there, and the same rules as elsewhere apply: declare the variable with the keyword **var** and it becomes local, meaning it can only be used within the event handler. Omit **var** and it becomes accessible to other functions on the page, but only after the button has been clicked.

```
45  <input type="button" value="Slower" onclick='
46  {
47      if (b_speed<3){
48          alert("Does not get any slower!");
49      }
50      else b_speed=b_speed-1;
51  }'>
52  <input type="button" value="Faster" onclick='
53  {
54      if (b_speed>18){
55          alert("Does not get any faster!");
56      }
57      else b_speed=b_speed+2;
58  }'>
```

The speed controls for the banner are a pair of parallel functions that increase and decrease the value of **b_speed**, and that issue alerts at either end of the scale that at the same time prevent any further increments or decrements.

The problem with using "–1" and "+2," however, is that you can only increase the value of **b_speed** two steps at a time in the range from 2 to 8 (where the differences between steps are the greatest), and only decrease it one at a time from 20 to 8 (where the differences are minimal). The simplest way around this is to change "+2" to "+1." Or you could construct a more elaborate **else** with

```
else {
    if (b_speed > 8) b_speed -= 2;
    else b_speed -= 1
}
```

for **Slower**, then do the equivalent for **Faster**. The result will be buttons that produce the same behavior in both directions.

```
59  <input type="button" value="Pause" onclick='stop()'>
60  <input type="button" value="Reset" onclick='b_speed=8;'>
61  </FORM>
62  <HR ALIGN="CENTER" SIZE="3">
63  </BODY>
64  </HTML>
```

Finally, the "Pause" button calls **stop( )**, which we looked at earlier, while "Reset" directly reassigns **b_speed** its initial default value of 8.

This type of status-bar message setup with speed controls and a pause button might seldom be used, but it can be quite useful as a designer tool in helping you to work out just the right speed for your scrolling status-bar message.

statusbt

On/Off Button

|N2 |N2.01 |N2.02+ |N3 |N4 |E3 |E4

Once you have determined that your web page readers should decide when and how to view your status bar message, then what? Here is a working example of a status bar enhancement that gives users the option of not reading it.

In practice, you can have some fun with this script. For instance, rather than design and create a separate page describing "what's new" on your site, run the news on the status bar. It can be activated only if the user wants to read it, and those who don't want to see the status bar become a clutter of small type can ignore it.

To add a more interesting interactivity to this script, tell your readers that a special or secret message will appear in the status bar when they select the button that starts your message. Just make sure that message really is special (see Figure 3-5).

```
1   <HTML>
2   <HEAD>
3   <TITLE>JavaScript Warehouse -
                        Status Bar Message Button</TITLE>
```

```
4    <SCRIPT LANGUAGE="JavaScript"><!-- hide from old browsers
5      function setMessage()
6      {
7          var msg="JavaScript Warehouse - http:
                                //www.ezl.com/~mlile/javascript/"
8          window.status = msg
9      }
10   <!-- done hiding -->
11   </SCRIPT>
12   </HEAD>
13   <BODY BGCOLOR="White" TEXT="Black" LINK="Blue"
                                VLINK="Purple" ALINK="Red">
14   <CENTER><H2>Status Bar Message Button</H2></CENTER>
15   <HR ALIGN="CENTER" SIZE="3">
16   <CENTER><FORM>
17   <INPUT TYPE="button" VALUE="Status Bar"
                                onClick="setMessage()">
18   </FORM></CENTER>
19   <HR ALIGN="CENTER" SIZE="3">
20   </BODY>
21   </HTML>
```

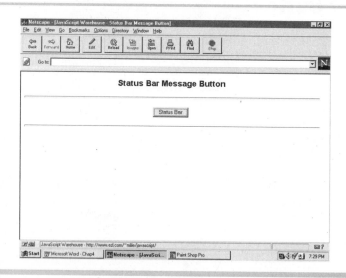

FIGURE 3-5.   Let your readers decide: "Shall I view the status-bar message, or not?"

ANNOTATIONS

This simple script demonstrates how you can use a button to display a status bar message. Its core function, **setMessage( )**, can easily be adapted to show and erase the message on alternate clicks, display a different text with each click, or echo user input in the status bar.

```
1   <HTML>
2   <HEAD>
3   <TITLE>JavaScript Warehouse -
                            Status Bar Message Button</TITLE>
4   <SCRIPT LANGUAGE="JavaScript"><!-- hide from old browsers
5    function setMessage()
6   {
7       var msg="JavaScript Warehouse - http:
                            //www.ezl.com/~mlile/javascript/"
8       window.status = msg
9   }
```

setMessage( ) creates and initializes a local variable, **msg**, then assigns it to the status bar. The entire function could be reduced to a single line, for example:

```
            status = "Welcome to Widget World!"
```

and you could even assign it directly to the button's event handler with

```
        onClick = "status = 'Home of the Web's wackiest widgets!'"
```

To display user input from a text field in the status bar, all it takes is

```
            status = document.formName.textfieldName.value
```

For alternate clicks to show and hide the message, write

```
        var offOn = false;
         function showHideMsg() {
             offOn =! offOn
             if (offOn) status = "Looking for widgets?";
             else status = '';
         }
```

Here the first line of the function reverses the Boolean variable **offOn** each time it is called, then tests its value and displays either the message or an empty string. Finally, if you construct an array of messages, you could display one after another with each click by writing

```
            var idx = 0;
            msgArray = new Array('do', 're', 'me', 'fa', 'sol');
            function showNote() {
                status = msgArray[idx];
                idx++;
```

```
                    if (idx == msgArray.length) idx = 0;
              }
```

And as an alternative to the button, you could use

```
              setTimeout("showNote()", 3000)
```

to make your array of messages appear in sequence automatically.

```
10    <!-- done hiding -->
11    </SCRIPT>
12    </HEAD>
13    <BODY BGCOLOR="White" TEXT="Black" LINK="Blue"
                                   VLINK="Purple" ALINK="Red">
14    <CENTER><H2>Status Bar Message Button</H2></CENTER>
15    <HR ALIGN="CENTER" SIZE="3">
16    <CENTER><FORM>
17    <INPUT TYPE="button" VALUE="Status Bar"
                                   onClick="setMessage()">
18    </FORM></CENTER>
19    <HR ALIGN="CENTER" SIZE="3">
20    </BODY>
21    </HTML>
```

As you must realize by now, there's nothing complicated or mysterious about putting messages into the status bar. Essentially, all it takes is a single line of code. The tough part is coming up with a use of the status bar that enhances your web site without annoying visitors—and at the same time gets your message across, whether it's the soup of the day, a teaser for your latest product, or the local time and weather.

typewrit

Typewriter

N2 N2.01 N2.02+ N3 N4 E3 E4

This example is similar to the Unfurling Banner script, but more closely emulates the activity of a person pounding out lines of text on a typewriter.

With minor alterations, this script could be set up to start running automatically when the page loads (see Figure 3-6).

```
1    <HTML>
2    <HEAD>
3    <TITLE>Typewriter style status bar message</TITLE>
4    <SCRIPT LANGUAGE="JavaScript">
5    var i = 0;
6    var TextNumber = 0;
```

```
7   var TextInput = new Object();
8   var HelpText="";
9   var Text = "";
10  var Speed=300
11  var WaitSpace="        "
12
13  TextInput[0] = 'This new banner is called a "T-banner!"';
14  TextInput[1] = "This banner displays slowly.";
15  TextInput[2] = 'It types one letter at a time, like a typewriter'
16  TextInput[3] = "This line can say whatever you like"
17  TextInput[4] = "This one can say it, too!"
18
19  TotalTextInput = 4; // (0, 1, 2, 3, 4)
20
21  for (var Typewrit = 0; Typewrit <= TotalTextInput; Typewrit++) {
22      TextInput[Typewrit]+=WaitSpace
23  }
24
25  var TimerId
26  var TimerSet=false;
27
28  function startBanner ()  {
29          TimerSet=!TimerSet
30          if (TimerSet)
31                  banner();
32          else
33                  kill();
34  }
35
36  function banner() {
37     Text=rollMessage();
38     TimerId = setTimeout("banner()", Speed)
39     window.status=Text;
40  }
41
42  function rollMessage () {
43     i++;
44     var CheckSpace = HelpText.substring(i-1, i);
45     CheckSpace = "" + CheckSpace;
46     if (CheckSpace == " ") {i++;}
47     if (i >= HelpText.length+1) {i=0;
                                if (TextNumber < TotalTextInput)
48     {TextNumber++;} else {TextNumber = 0;} init();}
```

```
49          Text = HelpText.substring(0, i);
50       return (Text);
51    }
52
53    function init () {
54       Text = TextInput[TextNumber]
55       HelpText = Text;
56    }
57
58    function kill () {
59       clearTimeout (TimerId)
60    }
61    </SCRIPT>
62    </HEAD>
63    <BODY BGCOLOR="White" >
64    <CENTER><H3>Typewriter style Banner</H3></CENTER>
65    <CENTER><FORM>
66    <INPUT TYPE="button" NAME="button2" VALUE="Start/Stop"
                              onClick="startBanner(this.form)">
67    </FORM></CENTER>
68    </BODY>
69    </HTML>
```

FIGURE 3-6.   Your message can emulate the action of a typewriter

ANNOTATIONS

The typewriter effect created by this script is really an illusion. What you are seeing when you run it is not one letter after another being added to the status bar, but rather the message continuously being rewritten one letter longer in each pass. It just happens so fast that, to the human eye, it ends up looking like someone's typing. As you'll discover next, there's a very simple way to really add the letters one by one without rewriting the whole message up to that point each time around.

```
1   <HTML>
2   <HEAD>
3   <TITLE>Typewriter style status bar message</TITLE>
4   <SCRIPT LANGUAGE="JavaScript">
6   var TextNumber = 0;
7   var TextInput = new Object();
8   var HelpText="";
9   var Text = "";
10  var Speed=300
11  var WaitSpace="        "
```

Our script begins with the customary declaration of variables. The first two serve as indices for the substring and array of messages respectively, whereas **Speed** is the millisecond value for the **setTimeout** on line 38. **HelpText** and **Text** are used in processing the message and sending it to the status bar. Lastly, **WaitSpace** is a string of blank spaces that provides invisible padding at the end of each message to keep it displayed briefly before being replaced by the next one.

Amid them all, **TextInput** is declared as a **new Object**. A glance at lines 13 to 17 that follow indicates that **TextInput** gets to hold the messages that will be displayed. Why not use an array? Because this script predates the introduction of the **Array** object with Navigator 3.0 and this was the work-around for constructing arrays back in the old days. You created indexed multiple instances of an object. Today, of course, you would normally write

```
TextInput = new Array()
```

and line 19 would be unnecessary, because an **Array** has a built-in **length** property whose value you can access directly.

```
13  TextInput[0] = 'This new banner is called a "T-banner!"';
14  TextInput[1] = "This banner displays slowly."
15  TextInput[2] = 'It types one letter at a time, like a typewriter'
16  TextInput[3] = "This line can say whatever you like"
17  TextInput[4] = "This one can say it, too!"
18
19  TotalTextInput = 4; // (0, 1, 2, 3, 4)
```

Next comes the list of messages followed by a variable consisting of the array's ceiling index. This could also have been done by giving the new object **TextInput** a property called **limit** and assigning "4" to it with

```
TextInput.limit = 4;
```

In this case you would have to replace the two references to **TotalTextInput** on lines 21 and 47 next with **TextInput.limit**.

```
21  for (var Typewrit = 0; Typewrit <= TotalTextInput; Typewrit++) {
22      TextInput[Typewrit]+=WaitSpace
23  }
```

This **for** loop, which runs automatically when the page is loaded as the script is read by the compiler, adds the string of blank spaces assigned to **WaitSpace** to the end of each message. It's certainly more efficient and elegant than having a string of blank spaces dangling at the end of each message. And the name the blank string is given immediately tells you what it's for.

On the other hand, you could achieve a similar effect by modifying the value of the **Speed** variable, which controls the timeout interval, whenever the end of each string is reached. Insert

```
if (i == HelpText.length) Speed = 3000
else Speed = 300
```

just before line 38, and you can eliminate the **WaitSpace** variable as well as the **for** routine in lines 21 to 23. Obviously, you can set both speeds at the millisecond values of your choice. This approach has the advantage of using a timer instead of a mechanical routine ("typing" invisible blank spaces) to control the duration of the full-message display before it gets replaced by the next.

```
25  var TimerId
26  var TimerSet=false;
27
28  function startBanner ()  {
29          TimerSet=!TimerSet
30          if (TimerSet)
31                  banner();
32          else
33                  kill();
34  }
```

Lines 25 to 34 represent yet another variation of all the stop-and-start clock and banner functions that accompany the use of **setTimeout( )**. **startBanner( )** is the main function called by clicking on the button in line 66. It resets the Boolean variable **TimerSet** to its opposite, tests its value, and either starts or stops the message display.

```
36   function banner() {
37      Text=rollMessage();
38      TimerId = setTimeout("banner()", Speed)
39      window.status=Text;
40   }
```

Next comes **banner( )**, which processes the message with a call to **rollMessage( )**, sets the time-out for the recursive call, and displays the string of letters. Incidentally, if you want to dress up the string of characters, line 39 is the place to do it. For example:

```
                  window.status = Text + '<<<'
```

adds a set of "arrowheads" to the end of each substring as it goes into the status bar.

```
42   function rollMessage () {
43      i++;
44      var CheckSpace = HelpText.substring(i-1, i);
45      CheckSpace = "" + CheckSpace;
46      if (CheckSpace == " ") {i++;}
47      if (i >= HelpText.length+1) {i=0;
                            if (TextNumber < TotalTextInput)
48        {TextNumber++;} else {TextNumber = 0;} init();}
49          Text = HelpText.substring(0, i);
50      return (Text);
51   }
```

rollMessage( ) is the function that simulates the typing. First it increments the **i** variable used in line 44 in the index arguments of the substring method. Thus, each time the function runs, **CheckSpace** gets the next character in the message. Line 45 ensures that **CheckSpace** is treated as a string. Then **CheckSpace** is tested to see if it's a blank, in which case **i** is immediately incremented. This reduces the pause that would otherwise occur between words due to "typing" a blank space.

Lines 47 and 48 serve to reset **i** to zero when the end of each displayed string is reached, and **TextNumber** to zero at the last message in the array. Then **Text** is assigned the substring extending from zero to the current value of **i**, which is next returned to **banner( )** for display.

This section of the script has a little bug in it: the increment of **TextNumber** on line 48 prevents the first array message from displaying the first time around because its initial value of zero is immediately upped to 1 on the first pass. To get around it without rewriting the entire function, just call **init( )** first with the **onClick** in line 66, that is:

```
          onClick = "init(); startBanner(this.form)"
```

```
53   function init () {
54      Text = TextInput[TextNumber]
```

```
55      HelpText = Text;
56   }
```

This function assigns the message indexed by **TextNumber** to **Text** and the latter to **HelpText**, which is used by **rollMessage( )** earlier.

```
58   function kill () {
59      clearTimeout (TimerId)
60   }
```

Finally, **kill( )** stops the virtual typewriter with a simple **clearTimeout( )** call.

```
61   </SCRIPT>
62   </HEAD>
63   <BODY BGCOLOR="White" >
64   <CENTER><H3>Typewriter style Banner</H3></CENTER>
65   <CENTER><FORM>
66   <INPUT TYPE="button" NAME="button2" VALUE="Start/Stop"
                              onClick="startBanner(this.form)">
67   </FORM></CENTER>
68   </BODY>
69   </HTML>
```

If all that leaves you feeling slightly bewildered and overwhelmed—relax! There's a somewhat easier way of creating exactly the same typewriter effect. Instead of rewriting the status bar in each pass, you can just increment its value. For instance:

```
status = ''
function typeMsg() {
    ltr = msg[idx].substring(i,i++);
    if (ltr != ' ') { status += ltr;
                      setTimeout("typeMsg()", 300) }
    else {status += ' '; typeMsg() }
    if (i > msg[idx].length) {
            i = 0; idx++; status='' }
    if (idx == msg.length) idx = 0;
}
```

which assumes an **Array** named **msg**, and two global variables, **i** and **idx**, initialized at zero. Initialization of the status bar with an empty string is essential to prevent "null" from displaying before the first letter. Otherwise, **typeMsg( )** is pretty straightforward. It assigns each subsequent character in the message to **ltr**, and if it is not a blank space, adds it to the status bar and sets the timeout. Otherwise a blank gets added to the status bar and the recursive function call is issued immediately. The second-to-the-last **if** resets **i**, increments **idx**, and clears the status bar at the end of each message, whereas the last one resets the array index to zero when the final message is reached.

banner2

Tape Scroll

N2 N2.01 N2.02+ N3 N4 E3 E4

You do not have to appeal to the conventional left-to-right reading habits of your users. A different approach can go a long way to adding surprise and entertainment to something as simple as a status bar message.

This script uses standard status bar message syntax, but the result is somewhat different. The message starts its movement from the right-hand side of the status bar (see Figure 3-7).

```
1   <HTML>
2   <HEAD>
3   <TITLE>N-Banner</TITLE>
4   <SCRIPT LANGUAGE="JavaScript">
5   <!--
6   // Copyright (c) 1996-97 Tomer Shiran. All rights reserved.
7   // Permission given to use the
                script provided that this notice remains as is.
8   // Additional scripts can be found at
                            http://www.geocities.com/~yehuda/
9   function scrollBanner(seed) {
10    var speed = 10
11    var str = " "
12    var ar = new Array()
13    ar[0] = "Welcome to our JavaScript page. "
14    ar[1] = "We hope you enjoy the N-Banner script. "
15    ar[2] = "It is designed to be more
                            stable than regular banners. "
16    ar[3] = "Don't forget to check out our other scripts. "
17    var total = ar.join("")
18    if (seed > 0) {
19       for (var i = 0; i < seed; ++i) {
20          str += " "
21       }
22       str += total
23       seed--
24       var cmd = "scrollBanner(" + seed + ")"
25       window.status = str
```

```
26        timerID = setTimeout(cmd, speed)
27    } else
28      if (-seed < total.length) {
29          str += total.substring(-seed, total.length)
30          seed--
31          var cmd = "scrollBanner(" + seed + ")"
32          window.status = str
33          timerID = setTimeout(cmd, speed)
34      } else {
35          window.status = str
36          timerID = setTimeout("scrollBanner(100)", speed)
37      }
38 }
39 // -->
40 </SCRIPT>
41 </HEAD>
42 <BODY onLoad="scrollBanner(100)">
43 </BODY>
44 </HTML>
```

FIGURE 3-7. A right-to-left scroller adds a little surprise to your page

ANNOTATIONS

This script consists of a single function, **scrollBanner( )**, called by the **onLoad** event handler in the <BODY> tag so that it starts running as soon as the page has been written to screen by the browser. The right-to-left scroll is created by adding a diminishing number of leading blank spaces to the message with each recursive pass.

```
1  <HTML>
2  <HEAD>
3  <TITLE>N-Banner</TITLE>
4  <SCRIPT LANGUAGE="JavaScript">
5  <!--
6  // Copyright (c) 1996-97 Tomer Shiran. All rights reserved.
7  // Permission given to use the
              script provided that this notice remains as is.
```

```
8    // Additional scripts can be found at
                         http://www.geocities.com/~yehuda/
9    function scrollBanner(seed) {
10     var speed = 10
11     var str = " "
12     var ar = new Array()
13     ar[0] = "Welcome to our JavaScript page. "
14     ar[1] = "We hope you enjoy the N-Banner script. "
15     ar[2] = "It is designed to be more
                         stable than regular banners. "
16     ar[3] = "Don't forget to check out our other scripts."
17     var total = ar.join("")
```

The **seed** argument to **scrollBanner** is an integer that determines the message's initial distance in number of blank spaces from the left edge of the status bar. Here it's initialized at 100 when called (line 42). You can easily increase or decrease its value to set a different starting-point for your scrolling message.

scrollBanner( ) begins by declaring and initializing two variables: **speed**, which is the millisecond argument to **setTimeout( )**, and **str**, which will be assigned the message. It then constructs an array of messages. If you neglect to add the blank to the end of each message, the sentences will be glued head-to-tail.

Finally, in line 17, **ar** uses the built-in **join( )** method to assemble the array into a single string. The argument to **join( )** is the character that separates joined elements. For example:

```
ar.join('/')
```

would produce "...page. /We hope...script. /It is...banners. /Don't forget...". In this case the argument is a blank string. A simple alternative to adding a blank space to the end of each member of the array would be

```
ar.join(' ')
```

The **join( )** method has a counterpart, **split( )**, which can be used to split strings into an array. It, too, takes a single argument—the character at which the string is split. Thus,

```
ar.split('/')
```

would restore the string created in our **join( )** example back to the original array. Although JavaScript 1.2 introduces three new string methods, **match( )**, **replace( )**, and **split( )**, which can be used with regular expressions to find and replace a member of a string, you can also use the **split( )** and **join( )** methods to do a global search-and-replace. If you wanted to replace every occurrence of the word "coffee" with "tea" in a string named **msg**, for instance, writing

```
msg.split('coffee')
msg.join('tea')
```

would do the trick. To switch words, that is, replace each occurrence of "coffee" with "tea" and vice versa, just use any arbitrary set of characters that does not occur in your string as a temporary intermediary:

```
msg.split('coffee')
msg.join('*!!!*')         // 'coffee' now replaced by '*!!!*'
msg.split('tea')
msg.join('coffee')        // 'tea' replaced by 'coffee'
msg.split('*!!!')
msg.join('tea')           // '*!!!*' replaced by 'tea'
```

In a page created by **document.write( )** that incorporates a visitor's name into the text, for example, you could process your message string with this split-join technique instead of assigning the user's name to a variable.

```
18    if (seed > 0) {
19        for (var i = 0; i < seed; ++i) {
20            str += " "
21        }
22        str += total
23        seed--
24        var cmd = "scrollBanner(" + seed + ")"
25        window.status = str
26        timerID = setTimeout(cmd, speed)
```

scrollBanner( ) next checks whether **seed** is greater than zero, and if it is, adds **seed** (number of) blanks to our global variable **str** with the **for** loop, tags on the joined array in line 22, then decrements **seed**. Line 24 declares a local variable, **cmd**, which is used as the first argument to **setTimeout( )** in line 26, and assigns it an appropriate string for the function call including the current value of **seed**. The assembled string, **str**, is then displayed in the status bar, and the by-now old-hat recursive function call is issued by **setTimeout( )**.

```
27    } else
28        if (-seed < total.length) {
29            str += total.substring(-seed, total.length)
30            seed--
31            var cmd = "scrollBanner(" + seed + ")"
32            window.status = str
33            timerID = setTimeout(cmd, speed)
```

Once **seed** reaches zero, this **else if** routine kicks in to display a substring extending from the value of **seed** to the last character of **total**, the joined array of messages. The minus sign in front of **seed**, now an "increasing" negative number, converts it into a positive integer. The remainder of this routine is the same as in the first **if** clause.

```
34          } else {
35              window.status = str
36              timerID = setTimeout("scrollBanner(100)", speed)
37          }
38  }
39  // -->
40  </SCRIPT>
41  </HEAD>
42  <BODY onLoad="scrollBanner(100)">
43  </BODY>
44  </HTML>
```

Finally, when the end of the message is reached, both **if** tests fail and the blank space assigned to **str** in line 11 clears the status bar before **setTimeout( )** calls **scrollBanner( )** with **seed** restored to its initial value of 100.

You can easily adapt this script to scroll the messages in an array one after another, rather than as a single string. First create a global variable for use as an index by adding, for example:

```
var idx = 0
```

outside of the **scrollBanner( )** function. Then comment-out or delete line 17, which joins the array, and replace **total** in lines 22, 28 and 29 with **ar[idx]**. Finally, add the following two lines to the **else** instructions that begin on line 35:

```
if (idx < ar.length - 1) idx++
    else idx = 0
```

to loop the array. That's all there is to it!

1letter

Slip 'n' Slide

[N2] [N2.01] [N2.02+] [N3] [N4] [E3] [E4]

When you have a very short message to display, perhaps the name of the current web site or page, this script example offers some entertainment value. We say "some" because it is one of those scripts that can provoke readers to send you nasty comments.

When the script loads, it displays your status bar message one letter at a time; each letter slides across from right to left. When the entire message has displayed, the process loops around and starts again.

If you view this script on the accompanying CD-ROM, note that the message used is three words long. It was taken from a web site that used the same three-word title in other areas of the same HTML page. A user does not have to look at the status bar to read new or critical information (see Figure 3-8).

If you choose to place critical information in your page using this script, we recommend that you place the same information elsewhere on your web page, in a format that is more or less static (that is, don't use the <BLINK> tag).

```
1    <html>
2    <!-- homepages/banners/one-letter.html -->
3    <head>
4    <script language="JavaScript">
5    <!-- Hide the script from old browsers --
6    /*  This code is compliments of Kurt's JavaScript Archive.
7        It can be found at
                        http://www.andersonhouse.com/jsarchive/.
8        For more info e-mail jsarchive@andersonhouse.com.
9                       ---------
10       This JavaScript may be used and modified freely,
     so long as this message and the comments above remain intact.
11       And of course, a return link wouldn't hurt either!
12   */
13
14   var init_msg = "Kurt's JavaScript Archive!"
15   var str = ""
16   var msg = ""
17   var leftmsg = ""
18
19   function setMessage() {
20      if (msg == "") {
21         str = " "
22         msg = init_msg
23         leftmsg = ""
24      }
25      if (str.length == 1) {
26         while (msg.substring(0, 1) == " ") {
27                 leftmsg = leftmsg + str
28                 str = msg.substring(0, 1)
29                 msg = msg.substring(1, msg.length)
30         }
31         leftmsg = leftmsg + str
32         str = msg.substring(0, 1)
33         msg = msg.substring(1, msg.length)
34
35         for (var ii = 0; ii < 120; ii++) {
36                 str = " " + str
37         }
```

```
38       }
39       else {
40           str = str.substring(10, str.length)
41       }
42       window.status = leftmsg + str
43           setTimeout('setMessage()',100)
44   }
45   // --End Hiding Here -->
46   </script>
47   <title>
48   Kurt's JSArchive: homepages: banners: one-letter.html
49   </title>
50   </head>
51   <body onload="setTimeout('setMessage()',100)"
                   background="/images/bg/softgrey.gif">
52   </body>
53   </html>
```

| Kurt's JavaSc | | | | ✉ ? |
| Start | Microsoft Word - Chap4 | Netscape - [Kurt's JS... | Paint Shop Pro | | 7:32 PM |

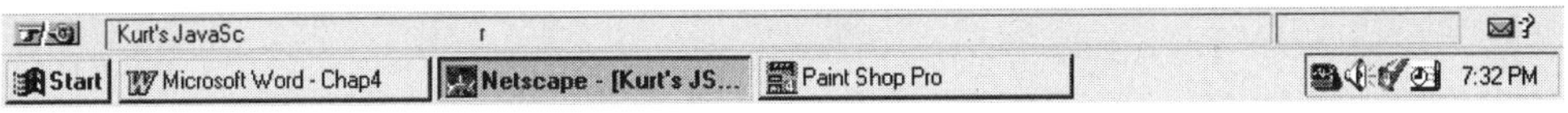

FIGURE 3-8. This script displays your status bar message one letter at a time

ANNOTATIONS

Like the scroll in the preceding script, the sliding-letter effect here is created by a string with a diminishing number of leading blank spaces. Only instead of slipping out of sight when it reaches the left edge of the status-bar display area, the letter is added to a separate string that accumulates the letters as they arrive one by one. Also like the scrolling-message script, this one consists of a single function assigned to **onLoad**.

```
1   <html>
2   <!-- homepages/banners/one-letter.html -->
3   <head>
4   <script language="JavaScript">
5   <!-- Hide the script from old browsers --
6   /*    This code is compliments of Kurt's JavaScript Archive.
7         It can be found at
```

```
                          http://www.andersonhouse.com/jsarchive/.
 8           For more info e-mail jsarchive@andersonhouse.com.
 9                             ---------
10        This JavaScript may be used and modified freely,
       so long as this message and the comments above remain intact.
11           And of course, a return link wouldn't hurt either!
12    */
13
14    var init_msg = "Kurt's JavaScript Archive!"
15    var str = ""
16    var msg = ""
17    var leftmsg = ""
```

The script begins by declaring four string variables: the message displayed in the status bar followed by **str**, which will be used to move each letter from right to left; **msg**, for holding what remains of the initial message whenever a letter is chopped off and sent to the left; and **leftmsg**, which collects the letters that have slid across the status bar.

```
19    function setMessage() {
20        if (msg == "") {
21            str = " "
22            msg = init_msg
23            leftmsg = ""
24        }
```

The first **if** sequence operates the first time the **setMessage( )** function is called when the page is loaded, and subsequently whenever all the letters have slid from right to left and the remaining string, **msg**, is empty. **str** is assigned a blank space, **msg** is initialized or reinitialized with the full message, and the string of accumulated letters on the left, **leftmsg**, is cleared (except, obviously, the first time around, when it's empty to begin with).

```
25        if (str.length == 1) {
26            while (msg.substring(0, 1) == " ") {
27                    leftmsg = leftmsg + str
28                    str = msg.substring(0, 1)
29                    msg = msg.substring(1, msg.length)
30            }
```

This second **if** test is invariably **true** whenever the first **if** is **true** because the latter assigns **str** a blank space in line 21, which makes its length equal to 1; it is also **true** whenever each letter has completed its slide. The **while** routine manages the blank spaces between words. **while** checks for a blank and immediately adds it to **leftmsg**, for the obvious reason that you cannot see a blank space sliding across the status bar. It then gets the next letter of **msg** with the **substring( )** method and assigns the remaining substring back to **msg**. In effect, this clips off the first letter.

```
31          leftmsg = leftmsg + str
32          str = msg.substring(0, 1)
33          msg = msg.substring(1, msg.length)
34
35          for (var ii = 0; ii < 120; ii++) {
36              str = " " + str
37          }
38      }
```

Lines 31 to 33, which are identical to lines 27 to 29, use the same technique to clip each letter and build up **leftmsg**. Then the **for** loop starting on line 35 adds 120 leading blank spaces to the letter. The "120" is the number to adjust upwards or downwards if you want the letters to start their slide farther to the right or left. The unit of measurement, of course, is blank spaces.

```
39      else {
40          str = str.substring(10, str.length)
41      }
42      window.status = leftmsg + str
43          setTimeout('setMessage()',100)
44  }
```

The **else** instruction on line 40 is what slides the letters across the status bar by trimming the first 10 blanks off **str** with each pass through the recursive function. Change the "10" to "1," and each letter will slide across one space at a time. Conversely, the higher the value, the longer the skid.

Then **leftmsg** and **str** are assigned to the status bar, and finally, **setTimeout( )** issues the recursive call.

```
45  // --End Hiding Here -->
46  </script>
47  <title>
48  Kurt's JSArchive: homepages: banners: one-letter.html
49  </title>
50  </head>
51  <body onload="setTimeout('setMessage()',100)"
                    background="/images/bg/softgrey.gif">
52  </body>
53  </html>
```

While animated letters are undoubtedly fun, bear in mind that your visitor isn't a captive audience in a movie theater sitting through the opening credits, but rather is only a click away from another page. If you intend to use this type of device on your page, you really have to ask yourself two basic questions:

◆   Is the effect strong or impressive enough that users will watch it to the end without losing patience?

And, equally if not more important:

◆   Will it be an irritant for visitors to your page after they've seen it once or twice?

barfill

Scrambled Slide

N2 N2.01 N2.02+ N3 N4 E3 E4

You can make your message appear one letter at a time, or you can use this script to make all of the letters slide across the status bar, at different speeds, and eventually form each line of message text.

As with the previous script, take care not to overuse this technique nor to present a message that is not represented on the HTML page display proper (see Figure 3-9).

```
1    <HTML>
2    <HEAD>
3    <TITLE>Barfill</TITLE>
4    <SCRIPT LANGUAGE="JavaScript">
5    <!--
6    var speed = 10
7    var pause = 1500
8    var timerID = null
9    var bannerRunning = false
10
11   var ar = new Array()
12   ar[0] = "Welcome to our JavaScript book"
13   ar[1] = "The Banner script works in the status bar area"
14   ar[2] = "It is a very stable banner"
15   ar[3] = "It is only one of many such examples"
16
17   var message = 0
18   var state = ""
19
20   clearState()
21
```

```
22   function stopBanner() {
23      if (bannerRunning)
24           clearTimeout(timerID)
25           bannerRunning = false
26   }
27
28   function startBanner() {
29      stopBanner()
30      showBanner()
31   }
32
33   function clearState() {
34      state = ""
35      for (var i = 0; i < ar[message].length; ++i) {
36           state += "0"
37      }
38   }
39
40   function showBanner() {
41      if (getString()) {
42           message++
43           if (ar.length <= message)
44               message = 0
45           clearState()
46           timerID = setTimeout("showBanner()", pause)
47           bannerRunning = true
48      } else {
49           var str = ""
50           for (var j = 0; j < state.length; ++j) {
51               str += (state.charAt(j) == "1") ?
                             ar[message].charAt(j) : "      "
52           }
53           window.status = str
54           timerID = setTimeout("showBanner()", speed)
55           bannerRunning = true
56      }
57   }
58
59   function getString() {
60      var full = true
61      for var j = 0; j < state.length; ++j) {
62           if (state.charAt(j) == 0)
63               full = false
```

```
64        }
65        if (full)
66            return true
67        while (1) {
68            var num = getRandom(ar[message].length)
69            if (state.charAt(num) == "0")
70                break
71        }
72        state = state.substring(0, num) + "1"
                            + state.substring(num + 1, state.length)
73        return false
74   }
75
76   function getRandom(max) {
77        return Math.round((max - 1) * Math.random())
78   }
79   // -->
80   </SCRIPT>
81   </HEAD>
82   <BODY onLoad="startBanner()">
83   </BODY>
84   </HTML>
```

FIGURE 3-9.   You can adjust the speed of each letter as it moves across the status
bar area

ANNOTATIONS

The scrambled-letters effect is achieved by creating a string of zeros—**state**—the
same length as each message and randomly switching each 0 to 1. This determines
which letter of the message gets sent next and keeps track of those that have been
sent. You can watch the **state** string at work by adding a text field to the page with

```
<form name=output><input type=text size=50 name=display></form>
```
and then inserting

```
document.output.display.value = state
```

between lines 53 and 54. To view it in slow motion, just set **speed** in line 6 to a
higher value such as 500 or 1000 (milliseconds).

```
1    <HTML>
2    <HEAD>
3    <TITLE>Barfill</TITLE>
4    <SCRIPT LANGUAGE="JavaScript">
5    <!--
6    var speed = 10
7    var pause = 1500
8    var timerID = null
9    var bannerRunning = false
10
11   var ar = new Array()
12   ar[0] = "Welcome to our JavaScript book"
13   ar[1] = "The Banner script works in the status bar area"
14   ar[2] = "It is a very stable banner"
15   ar[3] = "It is only one of many such examples"
```

These first few lines are the standard opening routine we've seen throughout this
chapter that lays the groundwork for **setTimeout( )** and creates a message array.
The one difference is that this script creates two variables to control the duration of
the timeout: **speed**, for the recursive calls that select and move the letters across one
at a time, and **pause**, which keeps each full message displayed for 1.5 seconds before
the next member of the array takes its turn.

```
17   var message = 0
18   var state = ""
19
20   clearState()
```

The next variable, **message**, is used to index the array, whereas **state** will get to
hold the string of flags that controls the process. This string is created by **clearState( )**,
which automatically runs when the page is loaded because of the call on line 20.

```
22   function stopBanner() {
23       if (bannerRunning)
24           clearTimeout(timerID)
25           bannerRunning = false
26   }
27
28   function startBanner() {
29       stopBanner()
30       showBanner()
31   }
```

Here we have the standard stop/start routine seen so often in this chapter. **startBanner( )** is the main function called from the **onLoad** event handler in line 82. It stops the banner if running, then calls **showBanner( )** to start the show.

```
33   function clearState() {
34       state = ""
35       for (var i = 0; i < ar[message].length; ++i) {
36           state += "0"
37       }
38   }
```

As mentioned, **clearState( )** creates a control string of zeros exactly the same length as each message. First it clears **state** with the empty string assignment, and then it tags on the appropriate number of zeros with the **for** loop.

```
40   function showBanner() {
41       if (getString()) {
42           message++
43           if (ar.length <= message)
44               message = 0
45           clearState()
46           timerID = setTimeout("showBanner()", pause)
47           bannerRunning = true
```

The first **if** in **showBanner( )** serves to cycle and recycle the messages. **getString( )** returns **true** whenever there are no more zeros left in **state**. In that case **message** is incremented to access the next member of the array or, if the end of the array has been reached, **message** is reset to zero. Then **clearState( )** assigns a new set of zeros to **state**, and **setTimeout( )** creates a brief pause between messages.

```
48       } else {
49           var str = ""
50           for (var j = 0; j < state.length; ++j) {
51               str += (state.charAt(j) == "1") ?
                                  ar[message].charAt(j) : "       "
52           }
```

Otherwise, that is, if there are any zeros in **state**, the new local variable **str** is initialized as an empty string and assigned either the character in the same position in the message as a "1" in **state**, or a string of blank spaces. For example:

message: jasmine
state: 0011010
str: blanks + blanks + 's' + 'm' + blanks + 'n' + blanks

```
53           window.status = str
54           timerID = setTimeout("showBanner()", speed)
```

```
55              bannerRunning = true
56      }
57  }
```

The resulting value of **str** is then displayed in the status bar, and **setTimeout( )** loops the process with its recursive function call after a 10-millisecond delay.

```
59  function getString() {
60      var full = true
61      for var j = 0; j < state.length; ++j) {
62          if (state.charAt(j) == 0)
63              full = false
64      }
```

getString( ) begins by declaring a local variable, **full**, and assigning it the Boolean literal, **true**. Its **for** loop then inspects **state** and, if it finds any zeros, sets **full** to **false**.

```
65      if (full)
66          return true
```

At the end of the inspection, if **full** is still **true**, then all the letters have been displayed and **getString( )** returns **true** to its caller, **showBanner( )**, which then pulls the next message from the array.

```
67      while (1) {
68          var num = getRandom(ar[message].length)
69          if (state.charAt(num) == "0")
70              break
71      }
```

This **while** routine assigns a random number to another new local variable, **num**, then checks if the character at that position in **state** is a 0 or 1. If it's a 1, the process gets another random number and checks that character, and keeps doing that until it eventually hits a 0 and breaks.

```
72      state = state.substring(0, num) + "1"
                    + state.substring(num + 1, state.length)
73      return false
74  }
```

Then line 72 converts the randomly selected zero to a "1" by reassembling the **state** string. This cut-and-reassemble is necessary because the **charAt( )** method is read-only. Write

```
            state.charAt(num) = '1'
```

and you'll get a JavaScript error message saying "0 can't be set by assignment."

```
76   function getRandom(max) {
77       return Math.round((max - 1) * Math.random())
78   }
79   // -->
80   </SCRIPT>
81   </HEAD>
82   <BODY onLoad="startBanner()">
83   </BODY>
84   </HTML>
```

Lastly, the **getRandom( )** function determines which zero in **state** will next be switched to a one. The JavaScript **Math.random( )** method returns a pseudorandom number between 0 and 1, which here is multiplied by **max** – 1, where **max** is the length of the current message being displayed. At the same time, **Math.round( )** rounds the resulting number up or down to the nearest integer, depending on whether the fractional portion is greater or less than 5. Hence this function returns a series of integers between zero and the length of the message.

This use of "random" numbers also ensures that each time the same message reappears, more likely than not the individual letters will be displayed in a different order, because the odds are against the same sequence of "random" numbers turning up twice in a row.

While this device is undeniably captivating and fun, there are definitely times *not* to use it, such as to display a help message. The last thing a user looking to the status bar for help wants is a little song and dance. Just think how you would react if, for example, you clicked the Help button in a Microsoft application and had to sit through a minivideo of Bill Gates leading a cavalry charge to the rescue before getting the help you want.

On the other hand, in circumstances that inherently involve an element of suspense or surprise, such as announcing the winner of a contest or award, a special event, shopper's bonus, and the like, a scrambled-letter routine might well enhance the overall impact.

flash

Flashbar

N2　N2.01　N2.02+　N3　N4　E3　E4

If you want to design a page that will absolutely grab your readers and hit them over the head with a message in the status bar, this is the script for you. It is such a simple script to set up, the temptation to use it will probably be great.

One legitimate application of this script would keep its use to a minimum. For example, you might want to tell users that your web site has moved, or you are having a fire sale at your online store. In those cases, the urgency of your message will be understandable (see Figure 3-10).

```
1   <HTML>
2   <HEAD>
3   <TITLE>Titlebar Flash</TITLE>
4   <script language="JavaScript">
5   <!--
6   /* MjM'S JAVA CODENAME = FLASH
7      This JavaScript Code was written by MjM for Hyperchat UK
8      I am not responsible for any damage caused by my code.
9      This code can be modified as long as
                           the Author's Name is still attached.
10     Email : MjM@hyperchat.co.uk
11     © Copyright 1996
12  */
13
14  var yourwords = "MjM's HTML & JavaScript Guide -
                       http://hyperchat.co.uk/u/mjm/guide.htm";
15  var speed = 150;
16  var control = 1;
17
18  function flash()
19  {
20    if (control == 1)
21      {
22        window.status=yourwords;
23        control=0;
24      }
25    else
26      {
27        window.status="";
28        control=1;
29      }
30    setTimeout("flash();",speed);
31  }
32  // -->
33  </script>
34  </HEAD>
35  <BODY BGCOLOR="#FFFFFF" onload="flash();">
36  </BODY>
37  </HTML>
```

FIGURE 3-10. A flashing scroller will grab your readers' attention

ANNOTATIONS

As you may suspect, this script creates the flashing effect by repeatedly turning the status bar display on and off. It's a technique that can also easily be applied to any component of the string assigned to the status bar.

```
1   <HTML>
2   <HEAD>
3   <TITLE>Titlebar Flash</TITLE>
4   <script language="JavaScript">
5   <!--
6   /* MjM'S JAVA CODENAME = FLASH
7      This JavaScript Code was written by MjM for Hyperchat UK
8      I am not responsible for any damage caused by my code.
9      This code can be modified as long as
                             the Author's Name is still attached.
10     Email : MjM@hyperchat.co.uk
11     © Copyright 1996
12  */
13
14  var yourwords = "MjM's HTML & JavaScript Guide -
                        http://hyperchat.co.uk/u/mjm/guide.htm";
15  var speed = 150;
16  var control = 1;
```

First come two variables: **speed** for the **setTimeout( )**, and **control**, a Boolean value that controls the alternation between off and on.

```
18  function flash()
19  {
20    if (control == 1)
21      {
22        window.status=yourwords;
23        control=0;
24      }
25    else
26      {
```

```
27          window.status="";
28          control=1;
29        }
30      setTimeout("flash();",speed);
31    }
32    // -->
33    </script>
34    </HEAD>
35    <BODY BGCOLOR="#FFFFFF" onload="flash();">
36    </BODY>
37    </HTML>
```

flash( ) tests the value of **control** and displays either the message or a blank string, then sets **control** to its "opposite" value. You could also streamline the process by assigning **control** a Boolean literal as in

```
var control = false;
function flash() {
    control =! control;
    if (control) status = yourwords;
    else status = "";
    setTimeout("flash()", speed);
}
```

To display a different message from an array with each flash, create a global array index with, for example:

```
var idx = 0
```

and change the **if** statement to read

```
if (control) status = msg[idx]
```

where **msg** is the name of the array, and add

```
if (idx < msg.length) idx = 0
```

either before or after the **setTimeout( )** line to loop the array. Needless to say, the array doesn't have to consist of a series of messages; you could make each member one word of a sentence and flash the message one word at a time.

Similarly, you can make a single word in your message blink with

```
var blinker = ''
```

followed by

```
if (control) blinker = 'flashing'
else blinker = '              '
var yourwords = 'This message has a ' + blinker + ' word."
```

As letters and blank spaces do not occupy the same amount of space on a line, you'll have to adjust the length of the blank string assigned to **blinker** in the **else** instruction by trial and error.

You could even use this technique to create neon-sign style effects such as displaying one letter or word at a time, and maybe flashing once or twice before recycling. But all this knowledge can be a dangerous thing, so unless your mind is bent on creating "The Status Bar from Hell," you would be well-advised to use it sparingly.

bounce

Bouncer

N2   N2.01   N2.02+   N3   N4   E3   E4

The status bar message on this page bounces back and forth from left to right. While it certainly ranks as a "neat" effect, like any motion in the status bar, it's likely to draw the user's eye away from the real content. Whether you're using a web site to sell a product or service, or to convey knowledge or information, you want the attention focused on the main stage and not on a sideshow that turns out to be such a distraction it ultimately defeats the purpose of what you're trying to achieve (see Figure 3-11).

```
1   <!DOCTYPE HTML PUBLIC "-//W3C//DTD HTML 3.2//EN"><html>
2   <head>
3   <script language="JavaScript">
4   <!-- Hide the script from old browsers --
5   /*   This code is compliments of Kurt's JavaScript Archive.
6        It can be found at http://
                             www.andersonhouse.com/jsarchive/.
7        For more info e-mail jsarchive@andersonhouse.com.
8                       ---------
9        This JavaScript may be used and modified
                                        freely, so long
10       as this message and the comments above remain intact.
11       And of course, a return link wouldn't hurt either!
12   */
13
14   /* MjM'S JAVA CODENAME = PINGPONG
15      This JavaScript Code was written by MjM for Hyperchat UK
16      I am not responsible for any damage caused by my code.
17      This code can be modified as long as
                       the Author's Name is still attached.
18      Email : MjM@hyperchat.co.uk
```

```
19      © Copyright 1996
20   */
21
22   var yourwords = "* This is a bouncing banner! *";
23   var buffer1="                          ";
24   var buffer2="                          ";
25   var message1=buffer1+yourwords+buffer2;
26   var dir = "left";
27   var speed = 75;
28
29   function pingpong() {
30
31      if (dir == "left") {
32          message2=message1.substring(2,message1.length)+"  ";
33          window.status=message2;
34          setTimeout("pingpong();",speed);
35          message1=message2;
36          if (message1.substring(0,1) == "*") {
37              dir="right";
38          }
39      }
40      else {
41          message2="  "+message1.substring(0,message1.length-2);
42          window.status=message2;
43          setTimeout("pingpong();",speed);
44          message1=message2;
45          if (message1.substring(message1.length-1,
                                     message1.length) == "*") {
46              dir="left";
47          }
48      }
49   }
50   // --End Hiding Here -->
51   </script>
52   </head>
53   <body onLoad="pingpong()" background="/images/
                                     bg/softgrey.gif">
54   </body>
55   </html>
```

FIGURE 3-11. This status bar message bounces back and forth from left to right

ANNOTATIONS

Like the other status-bar motion effects covered in this chapter, the bouncing banner uses blank spaces to do the job. Adding spaces to the beginning of the displayed string moves it to the right; clipping them off moves it left. Loop the routine and you've got a banner that bounces back and forth.

```
1   <!DOCTYPE HTML PUBLIC "-//W3C//DTD HTML 3.2//EN"><html>
2   <head>
3   <script language="JavaScript">
4   <!-- Hide the script from old browsers --
5   /*    This code is compliments of Kurt's JavaScript Archive.
6         It can be found at http://
                              www.andersonhouse.com/jsarchive/.
7         For more info e-mail jsarchive@andersonhouse.com.
8                    ---------
9         This JavaScript may be used and modified
                                          freely, so long
10        as this message and the comments above remain intact.
11        And of course, a return link wouldn't hurt either!
12  */
13
14  /* MjM'S JAVA CODENAME = PINGPONG
15     This JavaScript Code was written by MjM for Hyperchat UK
16     I am not responsible for any damage caused by my code.
17     This code can be modified as long as
                         the Author's Name is still attached.
18     Email : MjM@hyperchat.co.uk
19     © Copyright 1996
20  */
21
22  var yourwords = "* This is a bouncing banner! *";
23  var buffer1="                    ";
24  var buffer2="                    ";
25  var message1=buffer1+yourwords+buffer2;
```

```
26  var dir = "left";
27  var speed = 75;
```

This script's global variables consist of the message, two strings of blank spaces, and then **message1**, which chains the first three together. Next **dir** keeps track of the direction of the motion, while **speed** provides the millisecond setting for **setTimeout( )**.

Although you could easily make **dir** a zero-one control switch or use a Boolean literal as in the preceding script, "left" and "right" immediately make clear what is happening in each of **pingpong( )**'s two main sections next. Otherwise you would have to add a comment to remind yourself or anyone who reads your code that "0" is the setting for leftward and "1" for rightward motion, or vice versa. Better to let the code speak for itself as it does here:

```
29  function pingpong() {
30
31      if (dir == "left") {
32          message2=message1.substring(2,message1.length)+"  ";
33          window.status=message2;
34          setTimeout("pingpong();",speed);
35          message1=message2;
36          if (message1.substring(0,1) == "*") {
37              dir="right";
38          }
39      }
```

To create leftward motion, **pingpong( )** assigns a new variable, **message2**, a substring consisting of **message1** minus its first two characters plus a few trailing blanks. **message2** displays itself in the status bar, and after setting the time-out, assigns the clipped version to **message1**. This clipping continues until all the padding has been removed and the first character in **message1** is the asterisk that begins the message string. That's the signal to reverse direction.

The asterisk itself is simply a convenient decoration. You could equally test for the first letter of your message in line 36 or any other decorative typographic symbol of your choice.

```
40      else {
41          message2="  "+message1.substring(0,message1.length-2);
42          window.status=message2;
43          setTimeout("pingpong();",speed);
44          message1=message2;
45          if (message1.substring(message1.length-1,
                                   message1.length) == "*") {
46              dir="left";
```

```
47                }
48           }
49      }
```

The move-right routine is essentially the same except that **message2** gets a little padding first, then **message1** minus its last two characters. And the **if** test on line 45 looks for the asterisk at the end of the message string as the signal to start moving left again.

```
50   // --End Hiding Here -->
51   </script>
52   </head>
53   <body onLoad="pingpong()" background="/images/
                                       bg/softgrey.gif">
54   </body>
55   </html>
```

As you must realize by now, the key to creating visual effects in the status bar is string manipulation. If you wanted, you could use the techniques covered in this chapter, add music, and make a bunch of letters do a waltz, polka, or cancan in the status bar. But unless the main attraction of your page is a status bar flea circus, you should always remember that any movement down there is a distraction, and continuous distractions can become an annoyance or worse.

Another important factor to consider is that JavaScript is single threaded. As you may have noticed, all the scripts in this chapter do nothing but create and continuously update various forms of status bar displays. If you have any other script functions on your page, any one that takes longer than the specified timeout to execute will stall the motion in the status bar until it finishes carrying out its responsibilities. In other words, you run into timing and interference problems.

Before doing anything fancy or eye-catching with the status bar, it's a good idea to think about what the word "status" means and how that relates to what you are thinking of doing in that little strip at the bottom of the browser window. Also, look at how professional (commercial) applications use the status bar and what they put down there. Finally, ask yourself the basic question: "Does it really enhance my page, or is it a distraction?" After all, the last thing you want to do is spend hours or weeks designing a phenomenal web site only to have a trivial status bar gimmick steal the show.

Banners and Tickers

I f you want to quickly add some interactivity to a web page, with little programming, a JavaScript banner (or a ticker) is ideal. Typically, a banner announces some important feature or function of your web site—a new page or news that will be of interest to any visitors.

As with the status bar enhancement, a banner is most effective when used sparingly. A good rule of thumb is to place no more than one banner or ticker on a page. Of course, there are exceptions to this rule, but a user interface design on the Web must be balanced, and too many scrolling text messages will clutter your page.

On the other hand, we have seen some creative web developers place multiple banners on a web page for comic effect, or as part of an interactive scheme that relies on the user following the contents of a banner (or banners) from page to page. This approach, however, must be executed with skill to be successful.

The types of JavaScript banners and tickers covered here—moving text in an HTML form text area or as part of a submit button, and so on—are derived from the **Form** object. Each of the following scripts creates a **Form** object. As a document can contain more than one form, **Form** objects are stored in an array called **forms**.

Chew on that last statement for a minute, and don't get overly concerned about its seeming redundancy. If you want to create more than one form object on a page, the topmost form on the page is **form[0]**, the second is **form[1]**, and so on. In addition to referring to each form by name, you can refer to the first form in a document as **document.form[0]**, the next as **document.form[1]**, and so on.

The elements in a form, such as text fields, radio buttons, and so on, concern us the most when creating a JavaScript banner. These are stored in an *elements array*. You could refer to the first element (regardless of what it is) in the first form as

```
document.form[0].element[0]
```

These array references are particularly useful when you're using a loop to process a number of forms or form elements. For single references, however, naming the elements spares you not only the tedium of counting forms and elements, but also the necessity of adjusting references whenever the addition of another element or form modifies the array index.

Using form elements for a banner has the same drawback as using the status bar: you cannot format the text or background of the field in any way. Beyond using a table to give the field a 3-D frame or surrounding it with its own color, you're stuck with the fixed properties and aesthetics of form elements, whose appearance varies slightly from platform to platform because they are system-dependent GUI (graphic user interface) components.

On the other hand, with form elements you have to use the standard or numeric ampersand entities to display special characters, that is, "caf´" or "café" to spell "café." Unlike the status bar, in forms the corresponding hexadecimal and octal escape sequences ("caf\xe9" and "caf\351") are displayed literally. Two-byte or wide (Chinese, Japanese, Korean) characters can be used freely anywhere in forms—text fields or areas, button labels, select options—and will display properly if the appropriate viewer for the code (GB, Big5, and so on) is active.

banner1

Scrolling Marquee

| N2 | N2.01 | N2.02+ | N3 | N4 | E3 | E4 |

One of the most used and imitated (and therefore most popular) web page enhancements is the Java ticker applet. It is about as utilitarian an enhancement as one can find and is usually seen scrolling a simple text description at the top or bottom of a web page (see Figure 4-1).

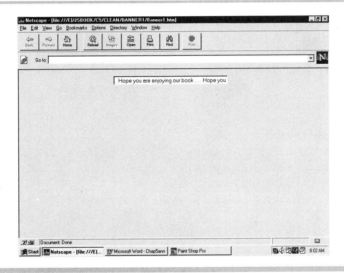

FIGURE 4-1. Scrolling Marquee output

Since JavaScript is more popular than Java on the Web—by a long shot—why not take that same ticker concept and use JavaScript instead? The results may not be as attractive, as you cannot specify a particular font or font color for the scrolling text. The text message may not scroll as evenly as it would in the equivalent Java-based applet, but this and other trade-offs are the price you pay for not learning to program in Java. On the plus side, you can easily copy this script off of the CD-ROM, follow our instructions for use, and have a functional scrolling banner with a minimum of fuss.

Perhaps now you understand why JavaScript is such a popular alternative to more complex languages.

```
1    <HTML>
2    <HEAD>
```

```
3    </HEAD>
4    <BODY onload="banner()">
5    <SCRIPT LANGUAGE="JavaScript1.1">
6    <!-- hide from old browsers
7    var id,position=0;
8    function banner() {
9        var i,k,msg=document.form.message.value;
10       k=(66/msg.length)+1;
11       for(i=0;i<=k;i++) msg+=" "+msg;
12       document.form.banner.value =
                          msg.substring(position,position+50);
13       if(position++==document.form.message.value.length)
                                             position=0;
14       id=setTimeout("banner()",
                          1000/document.form.speed.value); }
15   // End -->
16   </SCRIPT>
17   <CENTER><FORM NAME="form">
18   <INPUT TYPE=hidden NAME=message
            value="Hope you are enjoying our book . . . ">
19   <INPUT TYPE=hidden NAME=speed value=80>
20   <INPUT TYPE=text NAME=banner size=40></CENTER>
21   </BODY>
22   </HTML>
```

ANNOTATIONS

As in the status bar scripts covered in the preceding chapter, the scroll effect is achieved by repeatedly displaying an advancing substring of the looped message. The only difference is that the output is directed to an HTML form field. Although this script is located in the body of the page, it works equally well if moved up into the head. It also shows how you can use and reference hidden form elements for values assigned to variables.

```
1    <HTML>
2    <HEAD>
3    </HEAD>
4    <BODY onload="banner()">
5    <SCRIPT LANGUAGE="JavaScript1.1">
6    <!-- hide from old browsers
7    var id,position=0;
```

The first global variable this script declares is the identifier used with **setTimeout( )** on line 14. The second is used by the **substring( )** method to display a shifting segment of the looped message. Note that in JavaScript you can declare a batch of comma-separated variables on the same line, and they need not be of the same type. Line 9 provides another example of this technique. You can also create a chain such as

```
var id = position = i = x = anyOtherVariables = 0
```

to assign a number of variables the same value. In our script, **id** remains undefined at this stage; only **position** is initialized.

```
8    function banner() {
9        var i,k,msg=document.form.message.value;
10       k=(66/msg.length)+1;
11       for(i=0;i<=k;i++) msg+=" "+msg;
12       document.form.banner.value =
                    msg.substring(position,position+50);
```

banner( ), which starts running as soon as the page has been laid out because of the **onLoad** assignment in the <BODY> tag on line 4, sets out by declaring two local variables used as controls by the **for** loop on line 11, and a third, **msg**, which is assigned the string that will be displayed. In this case its value comes from the hidden form element named **message** on line 18.

As you may surmise, there is no need to use a hidden input for the message. You could assign the text directly to **msg** in line 9, or pull its value from an array if you wanted to run a series of messages. Although, as their name implies, hidden form elements do not appear in the browser window, View Document Source can easily be used to see them. So don't think of them as a place where you can safely stash a secret formula.

Line 10 assigns **k** a value based on the length of the message, which in this case works out to 2.3469387755102042. Because **k** serves no other purpose than to loop the message, you could freely delete its declaration as well as line 10 and change line 11 to read

```
for (i = 0; i < 2; i++)
```

The value to use as the ceiling in this **for** loop really depends on a combination of three factors: the length of the message, the width of the text field, and the length of the substring displayed. Reduce the message to a single word such as "Hope," widen the text field to 100, and change the 50 in line 12 to 100, and you have to increase the loop ceiling to 5 to fill the display area. Raise that ceiling too high (for example, to 15) under the same conditions, and you'll get a General Protection Fault (don't ask why!).

The loop in line 11 increments **msg** by a blank space plus itself, and the 50-character substring extending from **position** to **position** + 50 is displayed in the text field named **banner**.

```
13        if(position++==document.form.message.value.length)
                                              position=0;
14        id=setTimeout("banner()",
                         1000/document.form.speed.value); }
```

Next, the **if** test in line 13 increments **position** and measures that value against the length of the message. If the end of the message has been reached, **position** is reset to zero. The function ends with a recursive **setTimeout( )**. Because there is no **clearTimeout( )** in this script that uses the identifier **id**, you can safely remove its declaration from line 7 as well as the assignment in line 14. That is, simply write

```
setTimeout(...)
```

The millisecond argument to **setTimeout** provides an example of how to reference a value in a form field—whether hidden or not. In this case the actual setting for the timeout is 12.5 milliseconds.

```
15  // End -->
16  </SCRIPT>
17  <CENTER><FORM NAME="form">
18  <INPUT TYPE=hidden NAME=message
               value="Hope you are enjoying our book . . . ">
19  <INPUT TYPE=hidden NAME=speed value=80>
20  <INPUT TYPE=text NAME=banner size=40></CENTER>
21  </BODY>
22  </HTML>
```

As you can see, creating a marquee in a text field involves exactly the same string-manipulation techniques as scrolling a message in the status bar. Moreover, you can easily create slip-and-slide and scrambled-letter effects in a text field by adapting the status bar scripts in Chapter 3. All you have to do is create the text field and make it the target of the output instead of the status bar. Of course, the same precautions apply. Overdo it and your message will likely be bypassed by visitors with little patience for circus antics.

banner2

Textfield Typewriter

N2 N2.01 N2.02+ N3 N4 E3 E4

Here we come a little closer to emulating a news ticker, with functions that let you add multiple lines of scrolling text that run one after another, displayed in a one-letter-at-a-time, typewriter-style format that suggests immediacy and importance (see Figure 4-2).

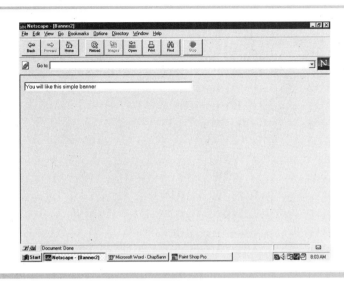

FIGURE 4-2. Textfield Typewriter output

For those who want to spice up their page with several bits of information—a "what's new" announcement or series of declarations that make a strong statement—Banner2 might be preferred over the more simple scroll effect of Banner1.

```
1    <HTML>
2    <HEAD>
3    <TITLE>Banner2</TITLE>
4    <SCRIPT LANGUAGE="JavaScript1.1">
5    <!--
6    var speed = 50
7    var pause = 500
8    var timerID = null
9    var bannerRunning = false
10
11   var ar = new Array()
12   ar[0] = "Welcome to our JavaScript book"
13   ar[1] = "You will like this simple banner"
14   ar[2] = "It is a little more complicated than Banner1"
15
16   var currentMessage = 0
17   var offset = 0
18
```

```
19   function stopBanner() {
20       if (bannerRunning)
21               clearTimeout(timerID)
22       bannerRunning = false
23   }
24
25   function startBanner() {
26       stopBanner()
27       showBanner()
28   }
29
30   function showBanner() {
31       var text = ar[currentMessage]
32       if (offset < text.length) {
33           if (text.charAt(offset) == " ")
34               offset++
35           var partialMessage = text.substring(0, offset + 1)
36           document.bannerForm.bannerField.value =
                                                    partialMessage
37           offset++ // IE sometimes has trouble with "++offset"
38           timerID = setTimeout("showBanner()", speed)
39           bannerRunning = true
40       } else {
41           offset = 0
42           currentMessage++
43           if (currentMessage == ar.length)
44               currentMessage = 0
45           timerID = setTimeout("showBanner()", pause)
46           bannerRunning = true
47       }
48   }
49   // -->
50   </SCRIPT>
51   </HEAD>
52   <BODY>
53   <FORM NAME="bannerForm">
54   <INPUT TYPE="text" NAME="bannerField"
                       VALUE="Click here..." SIZE=60
           onFocus="if (!bannerRunning) { startBanner()}">
55   </FORM>
56   </BODY>
57   </HTML>
```

ANNOTATIONS

Like the status bar typewriter, this script creates its effect by means of an illusion, that is, repeatedly unfurling a substring of each message one character longer than the one before. The only differences are that a text field displays the output, and the script uses a click in the text field instead of a button or **onLoad** to call the main function.

```
1   <HTML>
2   <HEAD>
3   <TITLE>Banner2</TITLE>
4   <SCRIPT LANGUAGE="JavaScript1.1">
5   <!--
6   var speed = 50
7   var pause = 500
8   var timerID = null
9   var bannerRunning = false
```

This script first declares four global variables used by the **setTimeout( )** routine: **speed**, the millisecond value of the timeout before "typing" the next letter; the longer **pause** for a timeout between messages; **timerID**, the identifier used by **clearTimeout( )**; and lastly, **bannerRunning**, a Boolean value that keeps track of whether the banner is running.

```
11  var ar = new Array()
12  ar[0] = "Welcome to our JavaScript book"
13  ar[1] = "You will like this simple banner"
14  ar[2] = "It is a little more complicated than Banner1"
15
16  var currentMessage = 0
17  var offset = 0
```

Next comes the array of messages followed by two more global variables—**currentMessage**, which becomes the index used to access the array, and **offset**, whose increments increase the length of the displayed string one character at a time to create the typewriter effect.

```
19  function stopBanner() {
20      if (bannerRunning)
21              clearTimeout(timerID)
22      bannerRunning = false
23  }
24
25  function startBanner() {
26      stopBanner()
```

```
27        showBanner()
28    }
```

startBanner( ), the main function assigned to the text field's **onFocus** event handler in line 54, first calls **stopBanner( )**—which stops the banner with a **clearTimeout( )** call if it is running and sets **bannerRunning** to **false**. Then **startBanner( )** calls **showBanner( )**, this script's workhorse. As the **onFocus** handler will not call **startBanner( )** unless the banner is not running, the **stopBanner( )** call can be considered redundant; at best it provides dual protection.

```
30    function showBanner() {
31        var text = ar[currentMessage]
32        if (offset < text.length) {
33            if (text.charAt(offset) == " ")
34                offset++
```

After assigning the message indexed by **currentMessage** to a new local variable, **text**, and making sure the end of the message has not been reached by comparing its length with **offset** with the first **if** test, **showBanner( )** checks for a blank space. If the next character is a blank, **offset** is immediately incremented so as not to break the rhythm of the letters appearing one after another.

```
35        var partialMessage = text.substring(0, offset + 1)
36        document.bannerForm.bannerField.value =
                                                 partialMessage
37        offset++ // IE sometimes has trouble with "++offset"
38        timerID = setTimeout("showBanner()", speed)
39        bannerRunning = true
```

Next, **partialMessage**, another new local variable, gets the substring of **text** extending from the beginning of the message to the letter immediately before **offset** + 1. The assignment in line 36 then displays the substring in the form's text field. Finally, **offset** is incremented so that the next substring displayed will be one character longer, **setTimeout( )** with its recursive function call is assigned to the identifier, and the Boolean flag **bannerRunning** is set to **true**.

```
40        } else {
41            offset = 0
42            currentMessage++
43            if (currentMessage == ar.length)
44                currentMessage = 0
45            timerID = setTimeout("showBanner()", pause)
46            bannerRunning = true
47        }
48    }
```

Otherwise, if the end of the message has been reached, **offset** is reset to zero, the array index is incremented, and if it has reached the end of the array, is also switched back to zero. Then the recursive call to **showBanner( )** is issued after a longer 500-millisecond timeout (the value assigned to **pause** in line 7) while **bannerRunning** again gets **true**.

```
49  // -->
50  </SCRIPT>
51  </HEAD>
52  <BODY>
53  <FORM NAME="bannerForm">
54  <INPUT TYPE="text" NAME="bannerField"
                        VALUE="Click here..." SIZE=60
          onFocus="if (!bannerRunning) { startBanner()}">
55  </FORM>
56  </BODY>
57  </HTML>
```

Finally, the text field's **onFocus** event handler is used to call **startBanner( )**. Clicking in the field starts the banner if it is not already running. Incidentally, the curly braces around **startBanner( )** are not really necessary, as it is the only statement attached to the **if** test.

You can achieve the same typewriter effect as the preceding script does by incrementing the value assigned to the text field directly to display the lengthening string. Combine and modify lines 35 and 36 to read

```
document.bannerForm.bannerField.value +=
                    text.substring(offset, offset + 1)
```

Insert

```
document.bannerForm.bannerField.value += ' '
```

before or after line 34 to handle the blank spaces between words, and be sure to enclose the now two **if** statements in curly brackets so that both get executed. Next add

```
document.bannerForm.bannerField.value = ''
```

to the **else** statements to clear the display for the next message, and finally make

```
this.value=''
```

the first of the **onFocus** statements in line 54 to erase "Click here..." before the first message displays.

While cut-and-paste JavaScript certainly makes it much easier to enhance a web page than hacking out the code, you'll be able to do much more if you start mastering the language by playing with the scripts. Especially if you're a beginner, it's tempting to think of scripts as something not to be tampered with unless you know exactly what you're doing. Wrong! A script is not a toaster or a Porsche. You can make a backup copy of the original and tinker all you want. In fact, you can start out with the JavaScript equivalent of a toaster and emerge from the jungle of browser crashes, system locks, and programmer's frustration with a Porsche!

advanced

Advanced Scrolling Text

| N2 | N2.01 | N2.02+ | N3 | N4 | E3 | E4 |

This page contains a form input field with scrolling text (see Figure 4-3). You can insert any text, of any length, and place the banner anywhere on the page. Other features include the ability to set the scrolling speed, width of the scroll box, and number of scroll iterations ("out of the box," the value is 10). Also, you can stop and restart scrolling at any time.

FIGURE 4-3.   Advanced Scrolling Text output

```
1   <HTML>
2   <HEAD>
3   <TITLE>Advanced Scrolling </TITLE>
4   </HEAD>
5   <BODY BGCOLOR="#FFFFFF" onLoad="startscrl()">
6   <SCRIPT LANGUAGE="JavaScript1.1">
7   <!— start javascript ---
8   /*
9   Feel free to use this script in your own page,
```

```
                                         making changes where
10   necessary, but do leave the following line in the code.
                              Thanks
11
12   Copyright 1996, E.T. Smith Associates Brogue,
                                        Pennsylvania, USA
13
14   Special thanks to Andy Augustine for helping me rewrite the
15   script to be more readable and object oriented. Check out
16   http://www.freqgrafx.com/411/ for javascript info and codes.
17   */
18   function scrl_param(){
19      this.bgn_ln = "About to start to scroll";
20      this.txt_ln = "Scrolling Text Box...   "
21               + "A number of features...   "
22               + "simple set up...    "
23               + "user stop/restart...    "
24               + "place anywhere on page...    "
25               + "set length of box...    "
26               + "any number of scroll iterations...    ";
27      this.end_ln = "All Done Scrolling";
28      this.speed = 100;
29      this.box_lg = 70;
30      this.max = 10;
31      this.count = 0;
32      this.pos = 0;
33      this.stop = 0;
34      this.box_ln = " ";
35      if( this.txt_ln.length < this.box_lg ){
36         this.msg_ln = this.txt_ln;
37         for( var i = 0 ;
                   i < (this.box_lg - this.txt_ln.length) ; i++ )
38            this.msg_ln += " ";
39      }
40      else{
41        this.msg_ln = this.txt_ln;
42        this.msg_ln += "              ";
43      }
44   }
45
46   var scrl = new scrl_param();
47
48   function scrlbox()
```

```
49  {
50    if( scrl.pos > scrl.msg_ln.length ){
51        scrl.pos = 1;
52        scrl.count++;
53    }
54    scrl.box_ln = " ";
55    scrl.box_ln +=
              scrl.msg_ln.substring(scrl.pos,scrl.msg_ln.length);
56    scrl.box_ln += scrl.msg_ln.substring(0,scrl.pos);
57    if( scrl.stop == 0 ){
58        document.scrlform.scrlbox.focus();
59        if( scrl.count < scrl.max ){
60            scrl.pos++;
61            document.scrlform.scrlbox.value = scrl.box_ln;
62            time3 = window.setTimeout('scrlbox()',scrl.speed);
63        }
64        else {
65            if ( scrl.end_ln.length > 2 ){
66                time2 =
                      window.setTimeout(
                              "document.scrlform.scrlbox.value ="
67                          + 'scrl.end_ln',scrl.speed);
68            }
69            document.scrlform.scrlbox.blur();
70        }
71    }
72  }
73
74  function startscrl()
75  {
76    scrl.stop = 0;
77    scrl.pos = 0;
78    scrlbox();
79  }
80
81  function stopscrl()
82  {
83    scrl.stop = 1;
84  }
85  // --- end javascript -->
86  </SCRIPT>
87  <SCRIPT LANGUAGE="JavaScript1.1">
88  <!-- start javascript ---
```

```
89   document.write("<DIV ALIGN=CENTER><FORM NAME='scrlform'>");
90   document.write("<INPUT NAME='scrlbox' SIZE=" + scrl.box_lg
91       + " onFocus='startscrl();' onBlur='stopscrl();' VALUE='"
92       + scrl.bgn_ln + "'><BR>");
93   document.write("<SMALL><EM>To stop scrolling, select
             anywhere on page except the scrolling text field. ");
94   document.write("To restart scrolling text,
             select the text field<BR></EM>");
95   time1 = window.setTimeout('scrlbox()',2000);
96   document.write("<P></FORM></DIV>");
97   // --- end javascript -->
98   </SCRIPT>
99   </body>
100  </HTML>
```

ANNOTATIONS

This script starts its banner scrolling when the page is loaded with the call to **startscrl( )** in line 5. It allows the user to stop the scroll by clicking anywhere on the page, then restart it with a click in the text field where the message appears. After the message has scrolled by ten times, it comes to a halt and displays "All Done Scrolling." At that point, the page has to be reloaded to start the scrolling again.

From a programming standpoint, this script is particularly interesting because of its object-oriented approach. It creates *object* **scrl_param( )** in lines 18 through 44, then instantiates it as **scrl** in line 46 for use in the subsequent functions. While clearly there are other JavaScript techniques for producing exactly the same effect without formally creating an object, the advantages of doing so are all those of object-oriented programming in general.

Although this script—which actually consists of two scripts, with the second beginning on line 87—appears in the body of the page, it could just as well be moved up between the <HEAD> tags. Similarly, merging the two scripts by deleting lines 85 to 88 makes no difference in terms of functionality.

```
1    <HTML>
2    <HEAD>
3    <TITLE>Advanced Scrolling </TITLE>
4    </HEAD>
5    <BODY BGCOLOR="#FFFFFF" onLoad="startscrl()">
6    <SCRIPT LANGUAGE="JavaScript1.1">
7    <!-- start javascript ---
8    /*
9    Feel free to use this script in your own page,
```

```
                                                    making changes where
10  necessary, but do leave the following line in the code.
                                    Thanks

11

12  Copyright 1996, E.T. Smith Associates Brogue,
                                                    Pennsylvania, USA

13

14  Special thanks to Andy Augustine for helping me rewrite the
15  script to be more readable and object oriented. Check out
16  http://www.freqgrafx.com/411/ for javascript info and codes.
17  */
18  function scrl_param(){
19      this.bgn_ln = "About to start to scroll";
20      this.txt_ln = "Scrolling Text Box...   "
21              + "A number of features...   "
22              + "simple set up...       "
23              + "user stop/restart...    "
24              + "place anywhere on page...   "
25              + "set length of box...    "
26              + "any number of scroll iterations...    ";
27      this.end_ln = "All Done Scrolling";
```

The **scrl_param( )** object is first given three properties consisting of the messages that will be displayed in the text field. The first, **bgn_ln**, is the initial value assigned to the text field in line 92; but because **startscrl( )** is called as soon as the page is loaded, the message immediately disappears, making it invisible for all practical purposes except perhaps on a very slow machine. You can easily make it appear by removing the **onLoad** event handler from the <BODY> tag on line 5. The **setTimeout( )** in line 95 will then automatically start the scrolling 2 seconds later. You can also control the duration of the initial message display by adjusting that **setTimeout( )**'s millisecond argument.

The second property is a concatenated string that is the actual scrolling message. The third, **end_ln**, only appears after the maximum number of scrollbys specified by **this.max** in line 30. Each time you stop the banner by clicking on the page, however, it restarts the same iteration; so unless you curb the impulse to click, or assign **max** a lower value, it could be some time before you ever get to see "All Done Scrolling."

```
28      this.speed = 100;
29      this.box_lg = 70;
30      this.max = 10;
31      this.count = 0;
32      this.pos = 0;
33      this.stop = 0;
34      this.box_ln = " ";
```

Next comes a batch of seven control properties: **speed** is the **setTimeout( )** millisecond argument for the scrolling, **box_lg** is the width of the text field used for the display, **max** is the maximum number of iterations before the scrolling stops, **count** is the scrollby counter, **pos** is the substring position marker, **stop** is a Boolean value that keeps track of whether the banner is scrolling, and finally, **box_ln** is the string assigned to the text field for display.

```
35      if( this.txt_ln.length < this.box_lg ){
36          this.msg_ln = this.txt_ln;
37          for( var i = 0 ;
                    i < (this.box_lg - this.txt_ln.length) ; i++ )
38          this.msg_ln += " ";
39      }
40      else{
41        this.msg_ln = this.txt_ln;
42        this.msg_ln += "              ";
43      }
44  }
```

Lastly, **scrl_param( )** is given a property, **msg_ln**, whose value depends on whether the concatenated message, **txt_ln**, is shorter than the size of the text box as specified by **box_lg**. If it is shorter, **txt_ln** is assigned to **msg_ln** and the **for** loop in lines 37 and 38 tags on a string of blanks equivalent to the difference in lengths. On the other hand, if the message is longer than the box, the **else** clause makes the same assignment, then tags on a string of blanks of arbitrary length to create a space between the end of one scrollby and the start of the next.

```
46  var scrl = new scrl_param();
```

Now that the object **scrl_param( )** has been created, **scrl** is defined as an instance of it by means of the **new** keyword. This means that **scrl** now has all the properties of **scrl_param( )**, for example, **scrl.pos**, **scrl.msg_ln**, **scrl.count**, and so on, as you can see in the next three functions.

```
48  function scrlbox()
49  {
50    if( scrl.pos > scrl.msg_ln.length ){
51        scrl.pos = 1;
52        scrl.count++;
53    }
```

As its name implies, **scrlbox( )** does the actual scrolling. This function first checks whether the end of the message has been reached by testing the position marker, **scrl.pos**, against the length of **scrl.msg_ln**. If its value is greater, **scrl.pos** is reset to one and **scr.count**, which keeps track of the number of scrollbys, is incremented.

```
54    scrl.box_ln = " ";
55    scrl.box_ln +=
            scrl.msg_ln.substring(scrl.pos,scrl.msg_ln.length);
56    scrl.box_ln += scrl.msg_ln.substring(0,scrl.pos);
```

Next the message string is assembled and assigned to **scrl.box_ln**. This string consists of an initial blank followed by two substrings: the first extending from the position marker to the end of the message, and the second, from the beginning of the message to the position marker—thereby looping it.

```
57    if( scrl.stop == 0 ){
58        document.scrlform.scrlbox.focus();
59        if( scrl.count < scrl.max ){
60            scrl.pos++;
61            document.scrlform.scrlbox.value = scrl.box_ln;
62            time3 = window.setTimeout('scrlbox()',scrl.speed);
63        }
```

Now comes the routine that displays the message. It begins by testing the value of **scrl.stop** to make sure the scrolling has not been stopped by the user. If **stop** is zero or **false**, the text field is given the focus with line 58, and if the **scrl.max** ceiling has not been reached, **scrl.pos** is incremented; the text field is assigned **scrl.box_ln**, assembled in lines 54 to 56; and a **setTimeout** issues a recursive call to create the scroll effect.

As this script does not use the **clearTimeout( )** method, assignment of the **setTimeout( )** to **time3** is really unnecessary. Line 62 can be shortened to

```
            setTimeout('scrlbox()',scrl.speed);
```

without affecting performance. The same applies to **time1** in line 95 and **time2** in line 66.

```
64        else {
65            if ( scrl.end_ln.length > 2 ){
66                time2 =
                    window.setTimeout(
                            "document.scrlform.scrlbox.value ="
67                            + 'scrl.end_ln',scrl.speed);
68            }
69            document.scrlform.scrlbox.blur();
70        }
71    }
72 }
```

This **else** clause, which goes with the **if** in line 59, kicks in when **scrl.count** reaches **scrl.max**. If the **end_ln** message (line 27) is more than two characters long, it is displayed by the **setTimeout( )** in line 66. The value of 2 for length is arbitrary;

you can modify line 65 to test for a line of any length (including one or two characters) with

```
if (scrl.end_ln.length > 0)
```

You can also skip the **setTimeout( )** and assign **scrl.end_ln** directly to the text field by replacing lines 66 and 67 with

```
document.scrlform.scrlbox.value = scrl.end_ln;
```

The only difference is that the **scrl.end_ln** message will then appear one-tenth of a second sooner, that is, the value of **scrl.speed** which is set to 100 by line 28.

```
74   function startscrl()
75   {
76      scrl.stop = 0;
77      scrl.pos = 0;
78      scrlbox();
79   }
80
81   function stopscrl()
82   {
83      scrl.stop = 1;
84   }
```

The start and stop functions in lines 74 through 84 are assigned to the text field's **onFocus** and **onBlur** event handlers in line 91. **startscrl( )** sets the Boolean value of **scrl.stop** to zero or **false**, resets the scroll position marker **scrl.pos** to zero, and calls **scrlbox( )**. **stopscrl( )** assigns a Boolean one or **true** to **scrl.stop**, which stops the scrolling by causing any calls to **scrlbox( )** to fail the **if** test in line 57; in that case nothing happens.

```
85   // --- end javascript -->
86   </SCRIPT>
87   <SCRIPT LANGUAGE="JavaScript1.1">
88   <!-- start javascript ---
89   document.write("<DIV ALIGN=CENTER><FORM NAME='scrlform'>");
90   document.write("<INPUT NAME='scrlbox' SIZE=" + scrl.box_lg
91      + " onFocus='startscrl();' onBlur='stopscrl();' VALUE='"
92      + scrl.bgn_ln + "'><BR>");
93   document.write("<SMALL><EM>To stop scrolling, select
             anywhere on page except the scrolling text field. ");
94   document.write("To restart scrolling text,
             select the text field<BR></EM>");
95   time1 = window.setTimeout('scrlbox()',2000);
96   document.write("<P></FORM></DIV>");
97   // --- end javascript -->
```

```
98   </SCRIPT>
99   </body>
100  </HTML>
```

The second script beginning on line 87 constructs the page with a series of **document.write( )** statements and also calls **scrlbox( )** after a 2-second delay with the **setTimeout( )** assignment in line 95. As mentioned, though, this call is overridden by the **onLoad** call in the <BODY> tag on line 5, which starts the scrolling as soon as the page has been laid out.

Notice that the <INPUT> tag in lines 90 to 92 omits specifying

```
TYPE=text
```

yet a text field nonetheless appears. While such omissions are scarcely to be encouraged, it makes no difference here, because a text field is the default HTML form input device. In other words, writing

```
<FORM><INPUT><INPUT><INPUT VALUE=Click></FORM>
```

produces three text fields, with the word "Click" in the third.

Although this second script can easily be merged with the first, there is certainly something to be said for maintaining the logical division between the scrolling banner functions and the **document.write( )** page-layout mechanism. Moreover, the second script *must* come after the first, because it uses objects, properties, and functions defined in the first. Switch their order and you'll end up with JavaScript error messages culminating in a blank page.

Finally, this script contains a little bug that only crops up if, instead of clicking on the page to stop the banner, you click elsewhere on the screen so as to remove the focus from the Netscape window—or, with a virtual desktop setup, if you click on any other "screen." In that case, when **scrl.count** reaches **scrl.max**, Netscape 3.01 either crashes immediately, or sometimes displays an "Insufficient memory to perform operation" message before succumbing to a GPF. A smarter and sturdier Netscape 4.0 flickers for a few seconds, informs you of a "JavaScript error: too many timeouts and intervals," but hangs in there.

The bug comes from the **setTimeout( )** in lines 66 and 67. Attaching a counter variable to it reveals that Netscape 4.0 processes it 1,002 times before launching the alert messages and keeps recycling it that many times before redisplaying the error messages until you succeed in leaving the page. Changing those two lines to read

```
document.scrlform.scrlbox.value = scrl.end_ln;
```

as suggested earlier completely eliminates the rampant loop and crashes.

You can also easily adapt this script to make use of button controls by inserting the following code between lines 89 and 96; where you insert it determines where the buttons appear on the page.

```
document.write("<INPUT TYPE=button
                        onClick='startscrl()' VALUE=START>");
   document.write("<INPUT TYPE=button
                        onClick='stopscrl()' VALUE=STOP>");
```

Similarly, you can add buttons that allow the user to speed up or slow down the scrolling with a function such as

```
function speedUp() {
        scrl.speed -= 20;
        startscrl();
    }
```

and **slowDown( )** in which

```
        scrl.speed += 20
```

or any other number of your choice. Bear in mind, however, that the starting **scrl.speed** in this script is 100, as well as the inaccuracy of timeout settings below 250 discussed in the previous chapter.

messages

Messages

| N2 | N2.01 | N2.02+ | N3 | N4 | E3 | E4 |

Subtlety is often a virtue on the Web. This script is decidedly more artistic in execution than its predecessors in this chapter. Each line of text appears in its entirety, then disappears, and there is a beat before the next line displays. A simple idea, but very nicely done (see Figure 4-4).

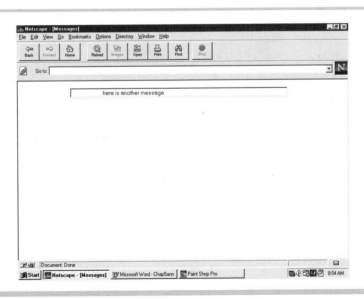

FIGURE 4-4. Messages output

Displaying a message as a series of phrases instead of scrolling it is also less likely to test a user's patience, because each phrase can be absorbed in an eyeful, as opposed to having to wait for it letter by letter.

In addition, you can adjust the display speed of the messages. To do this, change the number in line 20,

```
timer = setTimeout("idleMsg()",1500)
```

from 1500 to the speed you want. Finding just the right speed is really a matter of trial and error plus judgment. Each phrase should be displayed long enough for a slower reader to absorb it word by word, yet not so long as to make a faster reader feel frustrated. Bear in mind too that, in the world of the Internet, slower readers are not necessarily semiliterate yokels; they could very well be highly educated persons whose first language is not English.

```
1    <HTML>
2    <TITLE>Messages</TITLE>
3    <HEAD>
4    <BODY BGCOLOR="#FFFFFF">
5    <script language="JavaScript">
6    <!--- hide script from old browsers
7    var CurrentMsg = 'hello ';
8    function update(msg) {
9       var pad_str="";
10      n = msg.length;
11      if(n<72) {
12         pad = (73-n)/2;
13         for(var i=0; i<pad; i++) {
14            pad_str+=" ";
15         }
16      }
17      CurrentMsg = pad_str + msg;
18      document.messages.field.value = CurrentMsg;
19      clearTimeout(timer);
20      timer = setTimeout("idleMsg()",1500);
21   }
22
23   function MakeArray(n) {
24      this.length=n;
25      for(var i = 1; i<= n; i++) {
26         this[i] = "";
27      }
28   return(this);
```

```
29   }
30
31
32   var index = 1;
33   var notice_num = 9;
34   var notices = new MakeArray(notice_num);
35   notices[1] = "Put you first message here";
36   notices[2] = "Put your second message here";
37   notices[3] = "You can adjust the speed too";
38   notices[4] = "where it says (\"idleMsg()\",1500)
                                             is the speed";
39   notices[5] = "make the number higher for faster";
40   notices[6] = "make it lower for slower";
41   notices[7] = "here is another message ";
42   notices[8] = "Bye";
43   var timer = setTimeout('idleMsg()',1500);
44
45   function nochange() {
46       document.messages.field.value = CurrentMsg;
47   }
48
49   function idleMsg() {
50       update(notices[index++]);
51       if(index>notice_num) {
52           index=1;
53       }
54   }
55   // end hiding from old browsers-->
56   </script>
57   </HEAD>
58   <CENTER>
59   <form name="messages" onSubmit="return false">
60   <input type="text" name="field" size=73
         value="                         Hi"
         onFocus="self.status='This is a JavaScript information
                 data field'; return true" onChange="nochange()">
61   </form>
62   </CENTER>
63   </body>
64   </HTML>
```

ANNOTATIONS

This script constructs an array of messages, displays them one by one in a text field, then blanks out the display area for a moment before starting over. The **setTimeout( )** on line 43 starts the process 1.5 seconds after the page is loaded.

```
1    <HTML>
2    <TITLE>Messages</TITLE>
3    <HEAD>
4    <BODY BGCOLOR="#FFFFFF">
5    <script language="JavaScript">
6    <!--- hide script from old browsers
7    var CurrentMsg = 'hello ';
```

This global variable, **CurrentMsg**, gets assigned the display message in line 17. As its original value of "hello" never appears, initializing it as an empty string might be more appropriate.

```
8    function update(msg) {
9        var pad_str="";
10       n = msg.length;
11       if(n<72) {
12           pad = (73-n)/2;
13           for(var i=0; i<pad; i++) {
14                   pad_str+=" ";
15           }
16       }
```

update( ), which is called in line 50 by this script's main function, **idleMsg( )**, formats each message for display. It assigns the length of the current message to **n** and then measures **n** in relation to 72, a number based on the size of the text field specified in line 60. If the current message is shorter than the text field, the **if** clause calculates the value of half the difference in length between the text field and the message. This value, **pad**, is then used to control the **for** loop, which creates a string of blank spaces prepended to the message by line 17. This theoretically centers the text in the display area, but because a blank is not the same width as a character, ends up shifted to the left.

```
17       CurrentMsg = pad_str + msg;
18       document.messages.field.value = CurrentMsg;
19       clearTimeout(timer);
20       timer = setTimeout("idleMsg()",1500);
21   }
```

Here the padding and message are assigned to **CurrentMsg** and displayed in the text field, then a recursive call to **idleMsg( )** is issued after a 1.5-second timeout. The

clearTimeout( ) in line 19 is not necessary in terms of functionality—meaning that the script will work equally well without it—but falls into the "good housekeeping" category.

```
23   function MakeArray(n) {
24       this.length=n;
25       for(var i = 1; i<= n; i++) {
26           this[i] = "";
27       }
28   return(this);
29   }
```

The **MakeArray( )** function suggests that this script predates the introduction of the JavaScript **Array** object. It creates an object that has a **length** property and consists of **n** empty strings. This object is then instantiated as the **notices** array in line 34. If you prefer to use the language's built-in **Array** object, you can delete lines 23 through 29, and modify line 34 to read

```
var notices = new Array(notice_num)
```

or just

```
var notices = new Array()
```

Either way, you have to reduce the value of **notice_num** to 8 or add a ninth **Array** member, for example:

```
notices[9] = ""
```

to stave off a "**msg** has no property named 'length'" JavaScript error message when the loop reaches the now nonexistent ninth member, which **MakeArray( )** creates in the original version as an empty string. This "hidden" ninth member is what causes the text field to go blank for a moment before redisplaying the sequence of messages. Hence, if you simply shorten the length of the array to 8, you lose the blank pause between cycles.

```
32   var index = 1;
33   var notice_num = 9;
34   var notices = new MakeArray(notice_num);
35   notices[1] = "Put you first message here";
36   notices[2] = "Put your second message here";
37   notices[3] = "You can adjust the speed too";
38   notices[4] = "where it says (\"idleMsg()\",1500)
                                          is the speed";
39   notices[5] = "make the number higher for faster";
40   notices[6] = "make it lower for slower";
41   notices[7] = "here is another message ";
42   notices[8] = "Bye";
43   var timer = setTimeout('idleMsg()',1500);
```

The next 12 lines first declare and assign values to the global variable **index**, used to index the array, and **notice_num**, the length of the **notices** array created by **MakeArray( )**. Then comes the list of array members, each of which is assigned a component of the overall message. As mentioned, the invisible **notices[9]** is an empty string that blanks out the text field between the "Bye" of **notices[8]** and the return of **notices[1]**.

The array indexing here is designed to be user friendly by starting at 1. If you're a seasoned programmer, however, you might feel more comfortable rewriting it in standard form, that is, with the index beginning at zero.

```
45  function nochange() {
46      document.messages.field.value = CurrentMsg;
47  }
```

nochange( ) is a function that protects the display area from user tampering. Assigned to the text field's **onChange** event handler, it redisplays the current message whenever the text field loses focus and its value has changed. As the display field is updated every 1.5 seconds and the text field has to lose focus for the **onChange** handler to be called, this protection is not all that essential or effective here. In a static form, however, this type of function can be very useful for giving certain fields a rough equivalent of read-only protection.

```
49  function idleMsg() {
50      update(notices[index++]);
51      if(index>notice_num) {
52          index=1;
53      }
54  }
```

Finally, we come to **idleMsg( )**, which is this script's main function. Initially called by the **setTimeout** in line 43 and subsequently by the recursive call in line 20, it runs **update( )** with the current array member as its sole argument, while at the same time incrementing the array index. Then if the end of the array has been reached, the index is reset to one.

```
55  // end hiding from old browsers-->
56  </script>
57  </HEAD>
58  <CENTER>
59  <form name="messages" onSubmit="return false">
60  <input type="text" name="field" size=73
        value="                              Hi"
        onFocus="self.status='This is a JavaScript information
                data field'; return true" onChange="nochange()">
61  </form>
```

```
62    </CENTER>
63    </body>
64    </HTML>
```

The remainder of the page consists of standard HTML code that creates the form. Note that the text input also has an **onFocus** event handler that displays a message in the status bar when the user clicks in the field.

To gain greater control over the appearance of either a scrolling message or a cue card-type sequence such as the one in this script, you need only direct the output to a separate frame. Assuming a frameset with a frame named **banner**, you would then change line 18 to

```
top.banner.document.write(CurrentMsg)
```

followed by

```
top.banner.document.close()
```

to have each phrase erase the previous one. The same applies to the use of layers with JavaScript 1.2, which gives you much more freedom in terms of the size and position of the message-display area on your page. In that case, you also have the option of putting each component of the message in a separate layer and using the built-in layers array to cycle through the stack, turning each layer's visibility property on and off, for example:

```
function showLayer(index) {
    for (i = 0; i < 9; i++) document.layers[i].visibility='hide';
    document.layers[index].visibility='show';
}
```

This function first hides all the layers (here nine are assumed), then displays the current one as specified by the value of **index**.

Nor do you necessarily have to stack the layers. You could spread them out over the page and have each component of your message appear at a different spot. But like all flashing-sign techniques, discretion is the key unless you're designing Cyber Sid's Used Car Emporium.

teletype

Automatic TeleType

‹N2 ‹N2.01 ‹N2.02+ ‹N3 ‹N4 ‹E3 ‹E4

So far, these banner scripts have been limited to one line of text scrolling in an HTML form box. The Automatic TeleType script provides a larger text area in which your message can automatically "tap" itself out in typewriter style, but with some additional controls and functions to make it more aesthetically pleasing (see Figure 4-5).

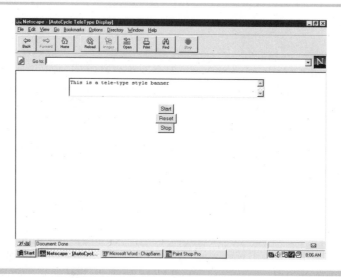

FIGURE 4-5.   Automatic TeleType output

For example, the larger text box creates more white space around your message and the border of the box. White space, when used wisely, is one of the web designer's most formidable tools. If your web page suffers from having too many textual and graphical elements, a little bit of white space will give your users a visual break—an ideal situation where you can use this script for dramatic effect.

As with previous banner scripts, you can add as many lines of message text as you want. Each line can be defined to automatically start as soon as your page loads into the browser, or you can add handy, user-friendly Start and Stop buttons. Although you think you have control over the appearance and behavior of your web page, the users have a modicum of control because their browser can be configured to display your page according to their preferences. If you provide a manual Start button, they may appreciate your respect for giving them a choice.

```
1   <HTML>
2   <HEAD>
3   <TITLE>Automatic TeleType Display</TITLE>
4   <SCRIPT>
5   <!--  Activate Cloaking Device
6   var i = 0;
7   var TextNumber = 0;
8   var TextInput = new Object();
9   var HelpText="";
10  var Text = "";
```

```
11   var Speed=60;
12   var WaitSpace="              ";
13   var addPadding="\r\n";
14   TextInput[0] = "This is a tele-type style banner";
15   TextInput[1] = "This is a tele-type style banner";
16   TextInput[2] = "The TextArea utilizes
                                        a wrap-around feature.";
17   TextInput[3] = "The messages can be made to cycle manually";
18   TextInput[4] = "You can stop or start the banner manually";
19   TotalTextInput = 5;
20   var Version =  navigator.appVersion;
21   if (Version.substring(0, 1)==3)
22   {
23     Speed=300;
24     addPadding="";
25   }
26   for (var addPause = 0;
                          addPause <= TotalTextInput; addPause++)
27     {TextInput[addPause]=addPadding
                          +TextInput[addPause]+WaitSpace;}
28   var TimerId
29   var TimerSet=false;
30
31   function startMessage()
32   {
33     if (!TimerSet)
34       {
35         TimerSet=true;
36         teletype();
37       }
38   }
39
40   function teletype()
41   {
42     Text=rollMessage();
43     TimerId = setTimeout("teletype()", Speed)
44     document.forms[0].elements[0].value=Text;
45   }
46
47   function rollMessage ()
48   {
49     i++;
50     var CheckSpace = HelpText.substring(i-1, i);
```

```
51    CheckSpace = "" + CheckSpace;
52    if (CheckSpace == " ")
53         {i++;}
54    if (i >= HelpText.length+1)
55    {
56      i=0;
57      if (TextNumber < TotalTextInput)
58           {TextNumber++;}
59      else {TextNumber = 0;}
60      initMessage();
61    }
62    Text = HelpText.substring(0, i);
63    return (Text);
64 }
65
66 function titleDisplay()
67 {
68    document.forms[0].elements[0].value=
                    "\r\n            Automatic Tele-type display";
69    initMessage();
70 }
71
72 function initMessage()
73 {
74    Text = TextInput[TextNumber]
75    HelpText = Text;
76 }
77
78 function stopMessage()
79 {
80    TimerSet=false;
81    clearTimeout (TimerId);
82 }
83
84 function resetDisplay()
85 {
86    TimerSet=false;
87    clearTimeout (TimerId);
88    TextNumber=0;
89    i=0;
90    titleDisplay();
91 }
92 // Deactivate Cloaking -->
```

```
93   </SCRIPT>
94   </HEAD>
95   <BODY onLoad="titleDisplay()" BGCOLOR="FFFFFF">
96   <CENTER><FORM>
97   <TEXTAREA ROWS=2 COLS=60 wrap=yes></TEXTAREA>
98   <p>
99   <INPUT TYPE="button" VALUE="Start" onClick="startMessage()">
100  <br>
101  <INPUT TYPE="button" VALUE="Reset" onClick="resetDisplay()">
102  <br>
103  <INPUT TYPE="button" VALUE="Stop" onClick="stopMessage()">
104  <p>
105  </FORM></CENTER>
106  </BODY>
107  </HTML>
```

ANNOTATIONS

Like the status bar typewriter seen in the preceding chapter, this script "types out" an array of messages letter-by-letter by displaying a continuously lengthening substring of each member. Its main function, **teletype( )**, is launched via **startMessage( )**, which is assigned to the Start button.

```
1    <HTML>
2    <HEAD>
3    <TITLE>Automatic TeleType Display</TITLE>
4    <SCRIPT>
5    <!-- Activate Cloaking Device
6    var i = 0;
7    var TextNumber = 0;
8    var TextInput = new Object();
9    var HelpText="";
10   var Text = "";
11   var Speed=60;
12   var WaitSpace="                    "
13   var addPadding="\r\n";
```

The opening cluster of global variable declarations and definitions begins with **i**, the end-of-substring marker for the displayed text, and **TextNumber**, the array index. Next the **Object( )** constructor is used to create **TextInput**, which in lines 14 through 18 is assigned the array of messages. You can also construct the array directly with

```
                               var TextInput = new Array()
```

in which case line 19 becomes unnecessary because you can then use
TextInput.length instead of **TotalTextInput** to control the loop in line 26 and
TextInput.length - 1 for the recycling in line 57.

Next come two empty strings, **HelpText** and **Text**, used as carriers in processing
the message; **Speed**, which is the millisecond value of the timeout; **WaitSpace**,
which is a string of blanks tagged on to each message so that it remains displayed
for a moment before being replaced by its successor; and finally **addPadding**,
assigned the escape sequences for a carriage return and newline character.

```
14   TextInput[0] = "This is a tele-type style banner";
15   TextInput[1] = "This is a tele-type style banner";
16   TextInput[2] = "The TextArea utilizes
                                         a wrap-around feature.";
17   TextInput[3] = "The messages can be made to cycle manually";
18   TextInput[4] = "You can stop or start the banner manually";
19   TotalTextInput = 5;
20   var Version =  navigator.appVersion;
21   if (Version.substring(0, 1)==3)
22   {
23     Speed=300;
24     addPadding="";
25   }
```

After creating the array of messages and the **TotalTextInput** variable
representing its length, our script checks the user's version of Navigator. If it's 3.*x*,
Speed is set at 300 and **addPadding** gets an empty string to compensate for version
variances in speed and position.

```
26   for (var addPause = 0;
                        addPause <= TotalTextInput; addPause++)
27     {TextInput[addPause]=addPadding
                            +TextInput[addPause]+WaitSpace;}
28   var TimerId
29   var TimerSet=false;
```

The **for** loop in lines 26 and 27 then formats the array by prepending **addPadding**
and appending **WaitSpace** to each member. **TimerId** is declared for use by the
clearTimeout( ) in **stopMessage( )** on line 81, and **TimerSet** is a Boolean literal that
keeps track of whether the "teletype" is running.

```
31   function startMessage()
32   {
33     if (!TimerSet)
34       {
```

```
35        TimerSet=true;
36        teletype();
37     }
38  }
```

startMessage( ), assigned to the Start button, checks whether **TimerSet** is **false** and, if it is, sets it to **true** and calls **teletype( )**.

```
40  function teletype()
41  {
42    Text=rollMessage();
43    TimerId = setTimeout("teletype()", Speed)
44    document.forms[0].elements[0].value=Text;
45  }
```

teletype( ) assigns **Text** the **rollMessage( )** function, which pulls the substring of the array message, then issues a recursive call in line 43 and displays the value of **Text** in the text area. You can streamline this function by merging line 44 with 42 into

```
document.forms[0].element[0].value = rollMessage()
```

Here there is no perceptible difference in effect in putting the combined line before or after line 43, because the timeout is long enough for the next instruction to be executed before the recursive call kicks in. In general, however, it's a good idea to keep a **setTimeout( )** for last to avoid any possible timing conflicts between the recursive call and any instructions between the timeout statement and the end of the function.

```
47  function rollMessage ()
48  {
49    i++;
50    var CheckSpace = HelpText.substring(i-1, i);
51    CheckSpace = "" + CheckSpace;
52    if (CheckSpace == " ")
53         {i++;}
```

After incrementing **i**, the end-of-display-text position marker, **rollMessage( )** pulls the next character of the message, assigns it to the local variable **CheckSpace** in line 50, and then prepends an empty string to force **CheckSpace** to be treated as a string. The **if** clause then peeks ahead to see whether the next character is a blank space and, if it is, increments **i** again. As in this script's status-bar counterpart, this keeps blanks from occupying a full beat in the letter-by-letter rhythm of the display.

```
54    if (i >= HelpText.length+1)
55    {
```

```
56      i=0;
57      if (TextNumber < TotalTextInput)
58            {TextNumber++;}
59      else {TextNumber = 0;}
60      initMessage();
61    }
```

The next **if** tests **i** against the length of the message, and if the end of the message has been reached, resets **i** to zero. It then either increments the array index **TextNumber**, or recycles the messages by setting the index to zero again. Finally, **initMessage( )** is called to get the next message.

```
62    Text = HelpText.substring(0, i);
63    return (Text);
64  }
```

rollMessage( ) ends by assigning the substring extending from position 0 to **i** to **Text** and returns it to **teletype( )** for display in the text field.

```
66  function titleDisplay()
67  {
68    document.forms[0].elements[0].value=
                    "\r\n            Automatic Tele-type display";
69    initMessage();
70  }
```

The **titleDisplay( )** function called by the **onLoad** event handler in the <BODY> tag on line 95 determines the content of the text area when the page is first loaded and also calls **initMessage( )** to get the first member of the array. The **titleDisplay( )** function is also called in line 90 by **resetDisplay( )**, which is assigned to the Reset button on the page.

```
72  function initMessage()
73  {
74    Text = TextInput[TextNumber]
75    HelpText = Text;
76  }
```

The **initMessage( )** function pulls the next message from the array, assigns it to **Text**, and then, **Text** to **HelpText**. Condensing the process to

```
            HelpText = TextInput[TextNumber]
```

has no impact on performance and makes for tighter code. You can tighten it even further by eliminating the **Text** and **HelpText** variables altogether, and referencing the array strings and substrings directly in **rollMessage( )** with **TextInput[Text-Number]**.

```
78   function stopMessage()
79   {
80     TimerSet=false;
81     clearTimeout (TimerId);
82   }
83
84   function resetDisplay()
85   {
86     TimerSet=false;
87     clearTimeout (TimerId);
88     TextNumber=0;
89     i=0;
90     titleDisplay();
91   }
```

Both these stop and reset functions set to **false** the Boolean flag that keeps track of whether the teletype is running, then clear the **TimerId** timeout. **resetDisplay( )** goes on to reset both the array index and substring position marker to zero before restoring the text area's original value with the call to **titleDisplay( )**.

```
92   // Deactivate Cloaking -->
93   </SCRIPT>
94   </HEAD>
95   <BODY onLoad="titleDisplay()" BGCOLOR="FFFFFF">
96   <CENTER><FORM>
97   <TEXTAREA ROWS=2 COLS=60 wrap=yes></TEXTAREA>
98   <p>
99   <INPUT TYPE="button" VALUE="Start" onClick="startMessage()">
100  <br>
101  <INPUT TYPE="button" VALUE="Reset" onClick="resetDisplay()">
102  <br>
103  <INPUT TYPE="button" VALUE="Stop" onClick="stopMessage()">
104  <p>
105  </FORM></CENTER>
106  </BODY>
107  </HTML>
```

The body of the page consists of the text area used for display and the three control buttons—Start, Reset, and Stop—each with its own event handler.

Although you may have absolutely no use for a teletype simulator on your page, you can learn a lot about how to construct, access, and display an array and its members and substrings from a script such as the foregoing—not to mention the use of buttons to give users one of their most cherished values: control.

The **CheckSpace** routine in lines 50 to 52, for instance, can serve as the basis for writing a function that parses a user input field into first, middle (if any), and last name by testing for blank spaces. Or you can use the substring functions illustrated to pull the first name for incorporation into the text to personalize the content.

In assessing what value a script might have for your own purposes, the important question is not "What does this script do?" but rather "What can I do with this script?"

feeder

News Feeder

N2 N2.01 N2.02+ N3 N4 E3 E4

Attractive and not overwhelming, the News Feeder is an effective replacement for those tricky CGI- (Common Gateway Interface) or Java-based news ticker applications that can fill a variety of needs. For example, you can use as

◆ An excellent vehicle for carrying breaking news items

◆ A "what's new" section on your home page

◆ Any other type of special announcement

Unlike the more sophisticated CGI tickers, you cannot associate lines of text with URLs or expect any other kinds of special effects. Though News Feeder is well designed and quite useful, it does only one thing—display text (see Figure 4-6). It just does so in a manner that will please your web readers and can spin many lines of text in a small corner of your page.

```
1    <HTML>
2    <HEAD>
3    <TITLE>News Feeder
4    </TITLE>
5    <script language="JavaScript1.1">
6    function makeArray() {
7       this.length = makeArray.arguments.length
8       for (var i = 0; i < this.length; i++)
```

```
9        this[i+1] = makeArray.arguments[i]
10  }
11  var fArray = new makeArray;
12  fArray[0]="Message 1 goes here. ";
13  fArray[1]="Message 2 goes here. "
14  fArray[2]="Message 3 goes here. "
15  fArray[3]="Message 4 goes here. "
16
17  var x = 1;
18  var y = 0;
19  var msg1 = fArray[y];
20
21  function newsFeed() {
22     if (x==msg1.length+1) {
23         for (var z=0; z < 70000; z++);
24         y+=1;
25         if (y > 3) y=0;
26         document.form1.news2.value=' ';
27         msg1 = fArray[y];
28         x=0;
29     }
30     document.form1.news2.value=msg1.substring(0,x);
31     x+=1;
32     setTimeout("newsFeed() ",100);
33  }
34  </script>
35  <body bgcolor=teal link=goldenrod onLoad="newsFeed()">
36  <form name="form1">
37  <textarea wrap=physical rows=10 cols=25 name="news2">
38  </textarea>
39  </form>
40  </HEAD>
41  <BODY BGCOLOR="ffffff">
42  </BODY>
43  </HTML>
```

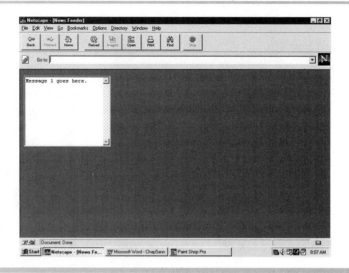

FIGURE 4-6. News Feeder output

ANNOTATIONS

This device resembles the teletype in the preceding script, except that it does not have any control buttons and does not test for blank spaces. It also provides a prime example of how valid JavaScript routines can sometimes be mangled by cutting and pasting.

```
1    <HTML>
2    <HEAD>
3    <TITLE>News Feeder
4    </TITLE>
5    <script language="JavaScript1.1">
6    function makeArray() {
7        this.length = makeArray.arguments.length
8        for (var i = 0; i < this.length; i++)
9        this[i+1] = makeArray.arguments[i]
10   }
```

This standard array-construction routine creates an object with a **length** property assigned the number of arguments passed to the function, then assigns each argument to an indexed replicate.

In this script, however, it does absolutely nothing, because when **makeArray( )** is called in line 11 to instantiate **fArray**, it doesn't even have the brackets to hold an argument. Hence the value of **makeArray.arguments.length** is zero, and the **for** loop counts from zero to zero. You could, in fact, comment-out lines 7 through 9, reducing the function to

```
function makeArray() { }
```

and the teletype would still work, because that's all it takes to construct the **fArray** object so that the array of string assignments in lines 12 through 15 doesn't provoke an "**fArray** is undefined" JavaScript error message.

```
11   var fArray = new makeArray;
12   fArray[0]="Message 1 goes here. ";
13   fArray[1]="Message 2 goes here. "
14   fArray[2]="Message 3 goes here. "
15   fArray[3]="Message 4 goes here. "
17   var x = 1;
18   var y = 0;
19   var msg1 = fArray[y];
```

To get **makeArray( )** to work properly, you have to give it arguments in lines 11 through 15 by modifying them to read

```
var fArray = new makeArray(
                "Message 1 goes here. ",
                "Message 2 goes here. ",
                "Message 3 goes here. ",
                "Message 4 goes here. "
                );
```

Now **fArray[1]** becomes "Message 1...," **fArray[2]** becomes "Message 2...," and so on. Passed these four arguments, **makeArray( )** does its job. But because line 9 makes **this[1]** the first array member, you have to change both the initial value of the array index **y** in line 18 and its reset value in line 25 to 1 for this adaptation to function smoothly.

Or you can delete **makeArray( )** altogether and use

```
fArray = new Array();
```

in line 11 to construct the array, while leaving lines 12 through 15 as is. What creates the array in this script as it stands is not the **makeArray( )** function but rather the assignments to **fArray[0]**, **[1]**, **[2]**, and **[3]** combined with the fact that **makeArray( )** creates an empty object so that the instantiation and replication work. It also gives **fArray** a **length** property with line 7, but its value remains zero, even though the array has four members, because **makeArray( )** is passed zero arguments in line 11.

Next this script establishes two control variables—**x**, the substring position marker, and **y**, the message index—before assigning **fArray[0]** to **msg1**, the variable used to feed the display.

```
21   function newsFeed() {
22       if (x==msg1.length+1) {
```

```
23          for (var z=0; z < 70000; z++);
24          y+=1;
25          if (y > 3) y=0;
26          document.form1.news2.value=' ';
27          msg1 = fArray[y];
28          x=0;
29      }
```

The **onLoad**-called main function, **newsFeed( )**, opens with an array recycling routine. The **if** tests for the end of the message string. If it has been reached, a pause is created by counting to 70,000, following which the array index **y** is incremented, or if it has reached the end of the array, reset to zero. Whether you adapt this script by having **makeArray( )** work properly or by using the JavaScript **Array** object, **fArray** will have a **length** property so that you can replace the 3 in line 25 with **fArray.length**.

Note that the semicolon at the end of line 23 makes the **for** loop do nothing else except count to 70,000. This puts a system-locking load on the processor for a few seconds, which users may find annoying to say the least. To eliminate it, make lines 24 through 28 of **newsFeed( )** a separate function, for example:

```
function nextMsg() {
    y+=1;
    if (y > 3) y=0;
    document.form1.news2.value=' ';
    msg1 = fArray[y];
    x=0;
}
```

and replace the **for** counter in line 23 with

```
setTimeout("nextMsg()", 3000)
```

for a 3-second delay between messages. If you do, you might also want to set the timeout in line 32 to a higher value, such as 250, to compensate for the gain in speed obtained from the compiler not having to read through the entire **if** statement to find the closing brace and next instruction.

```
30      document.form1.news2.value=msg1.substring(0,x);
31      x+=1;
32      setTimeout("newsFeed() ",100);
33  }
```

Finally, **newsFeed( )** assigns the substring of **msg1** extending from zero to **x** to the display text area, increments **x**, and calls itself after one-tenth of a second.

```
34  </script>
35  <body bgcolor=teal link=goldenrod onLoad="newsFeed()">
36  <form name="form1">
37  <textarea wrap=physical rows=10 cols=25 name="news2">
38  </textarea>
```

```
39  </form>
40  </HEAD>
41  <BODY BGCOLOR="ffffff">
42  </BODY>
43  </HTML>
```

This script points to one of the dangers of blind cut-and-paste. While it's relatively easy to grab a snippet of code from here and another from there to assemble the effects you want, if you don't understand what you're copying, you may very well be propagating gibberish. And the way the Web works, before long, thousands of pages worldwide could be sporting the same sort of zero-counting **makeArray( )** function—wasting valuable bandwidth and computer time.

One of the first things you should do in adopting a script is to make sure every variable has a purpose and every function does something. Programmers experiment and may often leave behind the results of fiddling around in a script, where it ends up as excess baggage. Copy code—copiously if copasetic with the copyright—but keep your eyes peeled!

Button Banner

button

| N2 | N2.01 | N2.02+ | N3 | N4 | E3 | E4 |

If you are looking for a way to dress up an HTML form's Submit button, this script offers an eye-catching variation on the scrolling banner (see Figure 4-7).

FIGURE 4-7.   Button Banner output

It places the banner—a very short one—inside a Submit button. You will not be able to get much mileage out of this cutesy effect, although if used prudently you may catch your web users off guard. It is rather amusing to see this effect at first and may even encourage users to fill out a survey form, or a questionnaire, just so they can push this button. Unfortunately, if users expect something spectacular to happen when this button is pushed, they will be disappointed. An **Alert** window simply pops open as the text continues scrolling.

```
1    <HTML>
2    <HEAD>
3    <TITLE>Button Banner</TITLE>
4    </HEAD>
5    <BODY BGCOLOR="#FFFFFF">
6    <form name="form2" onSubmit=null>
7    <!--Replace the 'onSubmit=null' with 'action=[blah.html]'-->
8    <input type="submit"
             name="banner" VALUE=".......Submit......."
             onClick="alert('You have to put an \'action=[url]\'
                          on the form tag!!')">
9    <br>
10   </form>
11   <script language="JavaScript1.1">
12   <!-- Jon Eyrick - scripts@actionaccess.com
13   // I do not take full credit for this script,
                                  I only made half of this.

15   var id,position=0;
16   function banner() {
17      var i,k,msg="  Submit   Submit   Submit   Submit   Submit";
18      k=(60/msg.length)+1;
19      for(i=0;i<=k;i++) msg+=" "+msg;
20      document.form2.banner.value=
                          msg.substring(position,position+60);
21      if(position++==msg.length) position=0;
22      id=setTimeout("banner()",150); }
23   // end -->
24   banner();
25   </script>
26   </body>
27   </HTML>
```

ANNOTATIONS

This script uses the same substring technique as some of the status bar scripts to
display a scrolling message in an HTML form button. While here it appears in the
body of the page, you might wish to move it up into the head. In that case, however,
you should move the **banner( )** call from line 24 to an **onLoad** event handler in the
<BODY> tag, so that the browser can lay out the form required by the function
before attempting to use it.

```
1   <HTML>
2   <HEAD>
3   <TITLE>Button Banner</TITLE>
4   </HEAD>
5   <BODY BGCOLOR="#FFFFFF">
6   <form name="form2" onSubmit=null>
7   <!--Replace the 'onSubmit=null' with 'action=[blah.html]'-->
8   <input type="submit"
            name="banner" VALUE=".......Submit......."
            onClick="alert('You have to put an \'action=[url]\'
                    on the form tag!!')">
9   <br>
10  </form>
```

The value initially assigned to the button in the <INPUT> tag is immediately
replaced by the scrolling that starts with the call to **banner( )** in line 24, so it appears
in an imperceptible flash. Nonetheless, it serves an important purpose in
determining the width of the button where the message will scroll. Also, while
clicking on the button here launches an **Alert**, you can readily assign the button
some other function and adapt the scrolling message to whatever your button does.

```
11  <script language="JavaScript1.1">
12  <!-- Jon Eyrick - scripts@actionaccess.com
13  // I do not take full credit for this script,
                                I only made half of this.
14
15  var id,position=0;
16  function banner() {
17     var i,k,msg="  Submit   Submit   Submit   Submit   Submit";
18     k=(60/msg.length)+1;
19     for(i=0;i<=k;i++) msg+=" "+msg;
20     document.form2.banner.value=
                        msg.substring(position,position+60);
```

The script first declares two global variables: **id**, which gets the **setTimeout( )** in line 22 and is not really necessary because there is no **clearTimeout( )**, and **position**, which marks the front end of the scrolling message.

The main **banner( )** function called from the body of the page then sets up three local variables: **i**, used as the counter by the **for** loop in line 19; **k**, which controls the loop; and **msg**, which is the string displayed on the button. Line 18 then gives **k** a value that here, because **msg.length** is 40, amounts to 2.5. As with the previous occurrence of this routine, you can drop line 18 and replace the **k** in line 19 with 2 or 3. The **for** loop in line 19 appends a blank space and **msg** to **msg** that number of times to loop the text. The substring extending from **position** to **position+60** is then displayed on the button named "banner" by line 20. As the button itself is only 20 characters wide, you can calmly change **position+60** to **position+20** without affecting the appearance of the scrolling.

```
21      if(position++==msg.length) position=0;
22      id=setTimeout("banner()",150); }
23  // end -->
24  banner();
25  </script>
26  </body>
27  </HTML>
```

Next, **banner( )** checks for the end of the **msg** string with an **if** test that at the same time increments **position**, and if the scrolling has reached the end of the message, resets the position-marker to zero before finally calling itself after a 150-millisecond timeout.

In addition to attracting attention to an otherwise static button, scrolling can also come in handy if the message you want to put on a button is longer than its best width from the standpoint of layout. Whatever the message, however, make sure the click lives up to the promise, or your visitor may take off feeling disappointed, or worse yet, cheated.

Rotating Button Banner

button2

| N2 | N2.01 | N2.02+ | N3 | N4 | E3 | E4 |

Compared with the previous "scrolling text in button" example, this one is far more interesting and can be reused frequently. In this case, the user is confronted with an HTML form button that acts as a URL launching tool.

The titles of web sites automatically rotate on the button's face, and after a few seconds the users see they can wait for the titles to cycle once or twice before deciding which site they would like to visit (see Figure 4-8). They click on the button, and they jump to the site. As a user-interface device, the Rotating Button

Banner is robust enough for you to employ it on numerous pages on your site, without your users growing tired of it. This is a high compliment to pay to the script's author.

FIGURE 4-8.   Rotating Button Banner output

The rotating menu can be easily configured to point to many URLs. You can also change the speed at which it turns.

```
1   <HTML>
2   <HEAD>
3   <TITLE>Rotating Button Banner</TITLE>
4   <BASE TARGET="welcome">
5   <SCRIPT LANGUAGE="JavaScript1.1">
6   <!-- begin
7   var timerID     =null;
8   var pos         =0;
9   var menuItem    =null;
10
11  function initArray() {
12      this.length = initArray.arguments.length
13      for (var i = 0; i < this.length; i++) {
14          this[i+1] = initArray.arguments[i]
15      }
```

```
16  }
17  function parsemenuItem(data,num) {
18      for(var i=0;i<data.length;i++)  {
19          if(data.substring(i,i+1)=="|")  break;
20      }
21      if (num==0) return(data.substring(0,i));
22      else  return(data.substring(i+1,data.length));
23  }
24  function startTimer() {
25      stopTimer();
26      menuItem = new initArray(
            "Netscape|http://www.netscape.com",
27          "Microsoft|http://www.microsoft.com",
28          "IBM|http://www.ibm.com",
29          "Yahoo|http://www.yahoo.com",
30          "Excite|http://www.excite.com",
31          "Hotbot|http://www.hotbot.com",
32          "GrapeJam|http://www.grapejam.com",
33          "Email|mailto:rzeitel@mars.superlink.net"
34          );
35      showTimer();
36  }
37  function stopTimer() {
38      timerID=null;
39      menuItem=null;
40  }
41  function showTimer() {
42      pos= (pos == menuItem.length) ? 1 : pos + 1;
43      document.forms[0].elements[0].value=
                                    parsemenuItem(menuItem[pos],0);
44      timerID=window.setTimeout('showTimer()',1000);
45  }
46  function goToUrl()  {
47      this.location=parsemenuItem(menuItem[pos],1);
48      return (false);
49  }
50  // end -->
51  </SCRIPT>
52  </HEAD>
53  <BODY onLoad="window.startTimer()" BGCOLOR="#FFFFFF">
54  <CENTER><FORM>
55  <INPUT TYPE="button" VALUE="  WHERE TO?  "   NAME="goTo"
```

```
            onClick="window.goToUrl()">
56   </FORM></CENTER>
57   </body>
58   </HTML>
```

ANNOTATIONS

This script essentially creates an array of two-part strings: the first is the name of the web site displayed on the HTML button, and the second is the site's URL, which is assigned to the browser window's **location** property when the button is clicked.

```
1    <HTML>
2    <HEAD>
3    <TITLE>Rotating Button Banner</TITLE>
4    <BASE TARGET="welcome">
5    <SCRIPT LANGUAGE="JavaScript1.1">
6    <!-- begin
7    var timerID      =null;
8    var pos          =0;
9    var menuItem     =null;
```

The script begins by declaring three global variables: the by-now familiar **timerID**, for timeout purposes; **pos**, used as the array index; and **menuItem**, which will be assigned the array. The first and third are initialized with **null**, while **pos** is set to zero.

```
11   function initArray() {
12       this.length = initArray.arguments.length
13       for (var i = 0; i < this.length; i++) {
14           this[i+1] = initArray.arguments[i]
15       }
16   }
```

initArray( ) is the same as the **makeArray( )** function seen earlier in this chapter's "feeder" script. Here, however, it does what it was designed to do because of array-creation arguments passed to it in lines 26 through 34. Thus, when called by those lines, it gives **menuItem** a **length** property whose value is 5, that is, the number of arguments, and assigns **menuItem[0]** the string "Netscape | http://..."; **menuItem[2]**, "Microsoft | http://..."; and so on.

```
17   function parsemenuItem(data,num) {
18       for(var i=0;i<data.length;i++)  {
19           if(data.substring(i,i+1)=="|")  break;
20       }
```

```
21      if (num==0) return(data.substring(0,i));
22      else   return(data.substring(i+1,data.length));
23   }
```

The **parsemenuItem( )** function, which is used by both **showTimer( )** and **goToUrl( )** later, parses each member of the **menuItem** array listed in lines 26 through 32 by calculating **i**, the position of the vertical bar (|) dividing each member of **menuItem** into the name that appears on the button and the full URL. The value passed to **parsemenuItem( )**'s **data** argument is the **menuItem** string. **num** is a binary flag. Set to "0" or **false** in the call on line 43, it returns the front end of the message preceding the "|" to **showTimer( )** for display. Set to "1" or **true** in the call on line 47, it returns the HTTP address after the "|" to **goToUrl( )** in response to the button's **onClick** event handler, which opens the link.

You can elegantly reduce this function to two lines with the JavaScript string **split( )** method:

```
function parsemenuItem(data,num) {
    menuParts = data.split('|');
    return(menuParts[num]);
}
```

This divides the **data** string into a two-member array named **menuParts** accessed by use of the binary flag **num** as index.

```
24   function startTimer() {
25      stopTimer();
26      menuItem = new initArray(
            "Netscape|http://www.netscape.com",
27          "Microsoft|http://www.microsoft.com",
28          "IBM|http://www.ibm.com",
29          "Yahoo|http://www.yahoo.com",
30          "Excite|http://www.excite.com",
31          "Hotbot|http://www.hotbot.com",
32          "GrapeJam|http://www.grapejam.com",
33          "Email|mailto:rzeitel@mars.superlink.net"
34          );
35      showTimer();
36   }
```

startTimer( ), called by the **onLoad** event handler in the <BODY> tag, first goes through a "clean slate" routine by calling **stopTimer( )**, which resets **TimerID** and **menuItem** to **null** value, instantiates the array with the call to **initArray( )**, and finally calls **showTimer( )**, which displays the rotating list on the button.

Here again you have the option of creating the array with

```
menuItem = new Array();
```

in which case you can calmly delete **initArray( )**. But because the array indexing will then start at zero instead of one, you also have to change the end of line 42 to

```
                    ? 0 : pos + 1;
```

as well as reverse lines 42 and 43 to ensure that **menuItem[0]** displays before **pos** is incremented on the first pass.

```
37   function stopTimer() {
38       timerID=null;
39       menuItem=null;
40   }
```

This routine function clears the **setTimeout( )** and destroys the **menuItem** object and array with its **null** assignments. As the same job is done automatically by lines 7 and 9 when the page is loaded, this function is redundant, and there's no harm in dropping it.

```
41   function showTimer() {
42       pos= (pos == menuItem.length) ? 1 : pos + 1;
43       document.forms[0].elements[0].value=
                                     parsemenuItem(menuItem[pos],0);
44       timerID=window.setTimeout('showTimer()',1000);
45   }
```

showTimer( ), which creates the rotating button-label effect, tests the value of **pos** against the **length** of **menuItem**; if the end of the array has been reached, **pos** gets 1, otherwise its value is simply incremented. Then the call to **parsemenuItem( )** in line 43 returns the name portion of the current **menuItem** member and displays it on the button face. Finally, line 44 issues the recursive function call that loops the process at 1-second intervals.

```
46   function goToUrl()   {
47       this.location=parsemenuItem(menuItem[pos],1);
48       return (false);
49   }
```

The last function in this script, **goToUrl( )**, is assigned to the button's **onClick** event handler. Here, with **parsemenuItem( )**'s **num** argument set at 1, the latter function returns the address portion of the **menuItem** string, which is assigned to the browser window's **location** property. Note that line 55 inherently makes **goToUrl( )** a new method of the **window** object, so that the **this** in line 47 refers to **window**.

```
50   // end -->
51   </SCRIPT>
52   </HEAD>
53   <BODY onLoad="window.startTimer()" BGCOLOR="#FFFFFF">
```

```
54  <CENTER><FORM>
55  <INPUT TYPE="button" VALUE="  WHERE TO? "  NAME="goTo"
        onClick="window.goToUrl()">
56  </FORM></CENTER>
57  </body>
58  </HTML>
```

Another approach to the combination name-address array is to construct a **siteArray** object with two basic properties, **name** and **address**, by writing

```
function webSite(name, address) {
    this.name = name;
    this.address = address;
}
```

and then to create an array of **webSite** objects with

```
menuItem = new Array();
menuItem[0] = new webSite("Netscape", "http://...")
menuItem[1] = new webSite("Microsoft", "http://...")
// etc.
```

You can then access the site names with **menuItem[i].name** and addresses with **menuItem[i].address** where **i** is the array index.

When confronted with a choice of different ways to produce the same effect on a page, your best option is probably to go with the approach you understand the most and feel comfortable using. At least then you won't feel intimidated by the script to the extent of not daring to touch it, because you're not really sure what you're doing.

Another important consideration is expandability. The bar-split string array in this script works very nicely, because each member simply has two components: name and address. But if you intend later to associate other elements such as a message, site description, or graphic with each array member, creating an object with those properties and then an array of those objects is the route to go. A good example of such a complex array can be found in the "random" script later in this chapter.

rotate

Rotating Banners

N2 N2.01 N2.02+ N3 N4 E3 E4

If you run your business on the Web, you may already buy or sell advertising banners or have been tempted to use them. Currently, they are a big part of the Web's business model—in some web-based businesses, it is the only model available. As such, you may want to employ advertising banners on your pages, and this script helps deploy this often-critical aspect of your web presence (see Figure 4-9).

FIGURE 4-9. Rotating Banners output

The script loads GIF files one at a time, as the script cycles through each one at a speed that you configure. The Rotating Banners script is, in addition, extremely easy to use. Each graphic can have one associated hypertext link. Even if you don't want to cycle through a series of GIF files that display banner ads, you can attach any graphics you want. For example, you may want to use graphics from other parts of your web site, offering your users a glimpse of what lies beneath your home page.

```
1   <HTML>
2   <HEAD>
3   <TITLE>Rotating Advertisements</TITLE>
4   </HEAD>
5   <SCRIPT LANGUAGE="JavaScript1.1">
6   var sponsor = 1;
7
8   function GoSponsor() {
9       if (sponsor==1)
10          window.location.href=
                "http://www.starwave.com/sponsor/adcouncil/stop";
11      if (sponsor==2)
12          window.location.href="http://www.academic.org/";
13      if (sponsor==3)
14          window.location.href=
                    "http://www.pacificcoast.com/entry/benny3";
```

```
15  }
16
17  function rotate() {
18      if (++sponsor > 3)  sponsor = 1;
19      document.images[0].src = "banner" + sponsor + ".gif";
20      window.setTimeout('rotate();',8000);
21  }
22  </SCRIPT>
23  <BODY onLoad="window.setTimeout('rotate();',8000);">
24  <body bgcolor="ffffff">
25  <center>
26  <h1>Rotating Advertisement Banners</h1>
27  <hr>
28  <A HREF="javascript:GoSponsor();">
29  <IMG NAME="banner" SRC="banner1.gif">
30  </A>
31  </body>
32  </html>
```

ANNOTATIONS

Instead of names rotating on a button, this script makes GIF images revolve within an HTML anchor tag. Each image has the advertiser's URL associated with it through the **GoSponsor( )** function. A click on the link loads the page referenced by the sponsor's web address.

```
1   <HTML>
2   <HEAD>
3   <TITLE>Rotating Advertisements</TITLE>
4   </HEAD>
5   <SCRIPT LANGUAGE="JavaScript1.1">
6   var sponsor = 1;
```

sponsor is a numeric global variable used by **GoSponsor( )** to assign the right URL to the window's location by means of the **if** test in line 9, as well as by **rotate( )** in concatenating the GIF filename string assigned to the **Image** object's **src** property in line 19.

```
8   function GoSponsor() {
9       if (sponsor==1)
10          window.location.href=
                "http://www.starwave.com/sponsor/adcouncil/stop";
11      if (sponsor==2)
```

```
12              window.location.href="http://www.academic.org/";
13      if (sponsor==3)
14              window.location.href=
                        "http://www.pacificcoast.com/entry/benny3";
15  }
```

The **GoSponsor** function assigned to the link as a JavaScript URL assigns the window location object a different **href** property based on the value of **sponsor**.

This type of setup is perfect for the **switch** statement introduced with JavaScript 1.2. You could easily convert the **if** tests to

```
        function GoSponsor() {
            switch(sponsor) {
                case 1 :
                    window.location = "http://...";
                    break;
                case 2 :
                    window.location = "http://...";
                    break;
                case 3 :
                    //etc.
            }
        }
```

Although the use of **break** is optional, it ensures that processing jumps out of the **switch** statement when the specified **case** is encountered. Otherwise, any statements following that **case** will be executed. While pointless in this example where the **case**-test variable (that is, **sponsor**) is program controlled, **switch** statements normally end with a **default** statement that takes effect when no **case** matches the argument. For example, a **switch(occupation)** statement listing four cases—"banker," "electrician," "lawyer," "programmer"—might end with

```
        default :
                document.write("Sorry, we are not hiring any "
                                + occupation + "s this month.")
```

which would execute if the string passed to **switch** were "shepherd" or any other unlisted occupation.

```
17  function rotate() {
18      if (++sponsor > 3)   sponsor = 1;
19      document.images[0].src = "banner" + sponsor + ".gif";
20      window.setTimeout('rotate();',8000);
21  }
```

This script's main function, **rotate( )**, is called by the **setTimeout( )** assigned to the <BODY> tag's **onLoad** event handler 8 seconds after the page is loaded. It first tests the value of **sponsor** against 3, the total number of sponsors, while incrementing the value and, if greater than 3, resets it to 1. Then line 19 assigns the **src** property of the first image on the page a concatenated string that evaluates to a filename, that is, BANNER1.GIF, BANNER2.GIF, or BANNER3.GIF. Finally, after an 8-second timeout, the function issues the recursive call that loops the process.

```
22   </SCRIPT>
23   <BODY onLoad="window.setTimeout('rotate();',8000);">
24   <body bgcolor="ffffff">
25   <center>
26   <h1>Rotating Advertisement Banners</h1>
27   <hr>
28   <A HREF="javascript:GoSponsor();">
29   <IMG NAME="banner" SRC="banner1.gif">
30   </A>
31   </body>
32   </html>
```

While this type of revolving billboard has become a popular advertising format on the Web, the code behind it can readily be adapted to just about any combination of image and **onClick** action. Moreover, if automatic rotation is inappropriate, you can easily provide user control by attaching the index increment and image selection to button clicks, or even a <SELECT> list of options.

Ultimately, this is a fine example of an essentially simple script with tremendous potential for enhancement and adaptation. You could even use it as the foundation for a jukebox by changing the images to song titles and having a click load the desired MIDI file.

random

Random Banner

N2   N2.01   N2.02+   N3   N4   E3   E4

As with the Rotating Banners script, this script displays GIF files on your page and allows you to associate each graphic with a hypertext link (see Figure 4-10). The difference here, though, is that the script randomly picks and displays the banner GIFs. In addition, the banners can be in different sizes and shapes. This example picks from five different banners:

◆ JavaScript World Banner (400×40)

◆ The Internet Link Exchange (440×40)

◆ AAA WebSite Promotions (468×60)

◆ Pacific Coast Comforters (468×60)

◆ JavaScript World Mini-Logo (100×40)

```
1    <html>
2    <head>
3    <title>Random Ad Banner</title>
4    <script language="JavaScript1.1">
5    function create() {
6        this.width = ''
7        this.height = ''
8        this.src = ''
9        this.href = ''
10       this.border = ''
11       this.mouseover = ''
12       this.sponsor = ''
13   }
14   ads = new Array()
15   for(var i=1; i<=5; i++) { ads[i] = new create() }
16   ads[1].width = "400"
17   ads[1].height = "40"
18   ads[1].src = "banner.gif"
19   //This URL might be a complete path name, e.g.
            'http://chelsea.ios.com/~benny3/javascript/banner.gif'
20   //In this example, the images are in the same path
             as the accompanying CD-ROM
21   ads[1].href = "http://www.andersonhouse.com/jsarchive/"
22   ads[1].border = "0"
23   ads[1].mouseover = "Click For JavaScript World"
24   ads[1].sponsor = "JavaScript World Banner"
25   ads[2].width = "100"
26   ads[2].height = "40"
27   ads[2].src = "logo.jpg"
28   ads[2].href = "http://chelsea.ios.com/~benny3/javascript/"
29   ads[2].border = "0"
30   ads[2].mouseover = "JavaScript World!"
31   ads[2].sponsor = "JavaScript World Mini-Logo"
32   ads[3].width = "468"
33   ads[3].height = "60"
34   ads[3].src = "sponsor1.gif"
35   ads[3].href = "http://www.pacificcoast.com/entry/benny3/"
36   ads[3].border = "0"
37   ads[3].mouseover = "Pacific Coast Down Comforters Ad"
38   ads[3].sponsor = "Pacific Coast Comforters"
39   ads[4].width = "468"
40   ads[4].height = "60"
41   ads[4].src = "sponsor2.gif"
```

```
42  ads[4].href =
        "http://websitepromote.com/aaa-bin/partner/
                                gpo?partno=p388&fn=ip"
43  ads[4].border = "0"
44  ads[4].mouseover = "Submit to
                        over 100 directories with AAA Promotions"
45  ads[4].sponsor = "AAA WebSite Promotions"
46  ads[5].width = "440"
47  ads[5].height = "40"
48  ads[5].src = "logoshow.jpg"
49  ads[5].href =
                "http://ad.linkexchange.com/X075202/gotoad.map"
50  ads[5].border = "0 ismap"
51  ads[5].mouseover =
                        "Click Here To Visit This ILE Member Site"
52  ads[5].sponsor = "The Internet Link Exchange"
53  var n = Math.random() + ''
54  n = parseInt(n.charAt(5))
55  if(n > 5) {
56      n = n - 5
57  }
58  else if(n==0) {
59      n = n + 5
60  }
61  n += ""
62  var image = ads[n]
63  var ad = ""
64  ad += '<a href="' + image.href + '" \n'
65  ad += 'onMouseOver="self.status=\'' + image.mouseover
                                + '\'\;return true" \n'
66  ad += 'onMouseOut="self.status=\'\'"> \n'
67  ad += '<img src="' + image.src + '" width=' + image.width
68  ad += '\n height=' + image.height
                        + ' border=' + image.border
69  ad += '\n><br>Please visit our sponsor: '
                        + image.sponsor + '</a>'
70  </script>
71  </head>
72  <body bgcolor="ffffff">
73  <h3 align=center>Simple Ad Rotator</h3>
74  <hr align=center width=50%>
75  <center>
76  <p>
```

```
77  <script language="JavaScript1.1">
78  <!-- hiding this script
79  document.write(ad)
80  // -->
81  </script>
82  </p>
83  </center>
84  </body>
85  </html>
```

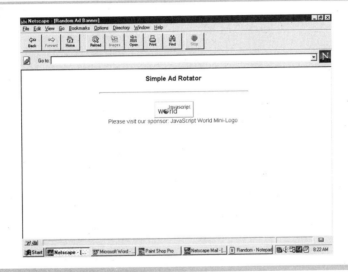

FIGURE 4-10. Random Banner output

ANNOTATIONS

This script creates an array of **ads**, each with a set of seven properties; randomly picks one; and displays it on the page. To view the different ads, you have to reload the page. Yet you can easily combine it with the preceding script to create "random" automatic rotation, or you could attach the show-another process to a manual control button.

```
1  <html>
2  <head>
3  <title>Random Ad Banner</title>
4  <script language="JavaScript1.1">
```

```
5   function create() {
6       this.width = ''
7       this.height = ''
8       this.src = ''
9       this.href = ''
10      this.border = ''
11      this.mouseover = ''
12      this.sponsor = ''
13  }
```

The script begins by constructing an empty object with seven properties: **width**, **height**, **src**, **href**, **border**, **mouseover**, and **sponsor**, each of which is initially assigned an empty string. You could also construct the object by making these properties arguments, for example:

```
function create(width, height, src, href,
                                border, mouseover, sponsor) {
             this.width = width;
             this.height = height;
             this.src = src;
             // etc.
   }
```

Either way, the basic object gets constructed.

```
14  ads = new Array()
15  for(var i=1; i<=5; i++) { ads[i] = new create() }
```

Next **ads** is created as an array, and the **for** loop in line 15 gives each member the properties specified in **create( )**, thereby instantiating the objects. If you opt to give **create( )** arguments, you have to forego this loop and instantiate each member separately with, for example:

```
ads[1] = new create(400,
             40,
             "banner.gif",
             "http: //www.andersonhouse.com/jsarchive/",
             0,
             "Click For JavaScript World",
             "JavaScript World Banner"
             )
```

This makes the code more readable, but less easily maintainable in that it's not immediately clear what property some arguments represent. Specifying each property separately as our script does in lines 16 through 52 may be a more tedious approach, but it certainly leaves no doubt as to what's what.

```
16   ads[1].width = "400"
17   ads[1].height = "40"
18   ads[1].src = "banner.gif"
19   //This URL might be a complete path name, e.g.
             'http://chelsea.ios.com/~benny3/javascript/banner.gif'
20   //In this example, the images are in the same path
                as the accompanying CD-ROM
21   ads[1].href = "http://www.andersonhouse.com/jsarchive/"
22   ads[1].border = "0"
23   ads[1].mouseover = "Click For JavaScript World"
24   ads[1].sponsor = "JavaScript World Banner"
```

The **width** and **height** properties determine the size of the image; **src**, the graphics filename; and **border**, the size of the image border. **href** stores the link; **mouseover**, a status-bar help message; and **sponsor**, the name used in a promotional message that appears below the image.

```
53   var n = Math.random() + ''
54   n = parseInt(n.charAt(5))
55   if(n > 5) {
56        n = n - 5
57   }
58   else if(n==0) {
59        n = n + 5
60   }
61   n += ""
62   var image = ads[n]
```

Lines 53 through 60 then generate a pseudorandom number between one and five based on the sixth character in the float between zero and one returned by the built-in JavaScript **Math.random( )** method. This sixth character is either the fourth or fifth digit, depending on whether the decimal point—the first character—is preceded by a zero. The selection of that particular character is an arbitrary choice.

As the digit can be any number from zero to nine, the **if** routine in lines 55 through 60 subtracts five from numbers greater than five, or boosts zero to five to generate a value of **n**, the array index, between one and five. Needless to say, if you have ten images, you can eliminate this adjustment altogether. On the other hand, with six to nine images or 11 and up, you'll have to do a bit of mathematical acrobatics to end up with a number between zero and the length of your array.

Then in line 62, the **ads[n]** object is assigned to a new variable, **image**.

```
63   var ad = ""
64   ad += '<a href="' + image.href + '" \n'
65   ad += 'onMouseOver="self.status=\'' + image.mouseover
                          + '\'\;return true" \n'
```

```
66  ad += 'onMouseOut="self.status=\'\'"> \n'
67  ad += '<img src="' + image.src + '" width=' + image.width
68  ad += '\n height=' + image.height
                        + ' border=' + image.border
69  ad += '\n><br>Please visit our sponsor: '
                        + image.sponsor + '</a>'
```

Finally, lines 63 to 69 use **image** in assembling a new string variable, **ad**, consisting of the HTML code fed to **document.write( )** in line 79. As you can see, the simple assignment in line 62 gives **image** all the specific properties of **ads[n]** so they can now be referenced directly.

```
70  </script>
71  </head>
72  <body bgcolor="ffffff">
73  <h3 align=center>Simple Ad Rotator</h3>
74  <hr align=center width=50%>
75  <center>
76  <p>
77  <script language="JavaScript1.1">
78  <!-- hiding this script
79  document.write(ad)
80  // -->
81  </script>
82  </p>
83  </center>
84  </body>
85  </html>
```

Finally, line 79—which is really the only line in a separate script—displays the randomly selected ad when this page is loaded by writing the string of HTML code assigned to **ad** in lines 63 to 69.

In using this script, bear in mind that a sponsor may not be happy about having their ad displayed randomly. While the chances of a coin toss resulting in "heads" are exactly 50-50, that does not preclude the possibility of throwing 5, 10, 50, or 15 zillion "heads" in a row, although the odds of the latter happening must approximate one out of the number of angels that can dance on the head of a pin. Sponsors normally want some sort of guarantee for their cash, and few are likely to put their money on a form of advertising roulette.

On the other hand, there are all kinds of other situations—including promotional—to which this script can be adapted. The ads, for example, could be an array of your company's main products, or those it wants to push in any given time frame. Or they could be employees featured at random, your production plants, or the high-tech equipment that gives you a competitive edge. Or just a random picture or message of the day. If the array consists entirely of "your stuff," you don't really have to worry about the randomness.

LED Banner

led

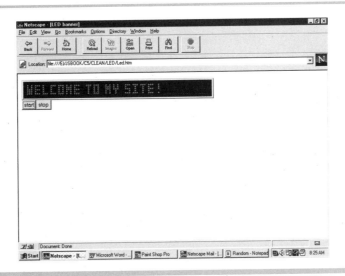

| N2 | N2.01 | N2.02+ | N3 | N4 | E3 | E4 |

If you're unhappy with form fields, frames, or layers as the display area for your banner and want something that looks more like the real thing—an electronic display panel—then this is the script for you. Although this banner comes with user-controlled start and stop buttons, you can easily automate the process by starting it with a page **onLoad** handler (see Figure 4-11).

FIGURE 4-11. LED Banner output

Check out the two versions of this script on the accompanying CD-ROM. The first one, LED.HTM, is an exact transcription of the annotated script (next). The second version, LED2.HTM, is a simplified version of the same thing.

This script is probably not the best choice for use on a corporate web site, with its strong "viva Las Vegas" feel. Rather, you may want to consider including it on a games-related or otherwise fun site, given the script's colorful arcade quality.

While close to 500 lines long, due mainly to the array of display characters extending from lines 37 to 389, there's a simple way to reduce it to less than half that size without sacrificing any functionality. And while it may seem intimidatingly complex at first sight, after walking through it step by step, you'll realize that most of it is familiar ground by now. It's also an excellent example of how you can make a script self-explanatory by giving its components names that accurately reflect what they are or do.

```
1    <HTML>
2    <HEAD>
3    <TITLE>LED banner</TITLE>
4    </HEAD>
5    <BODY BGCOLOR="#FFFFFF">
6    <SCRIPT LANGUAGE="JavaScript1.1">
7    <!--// Copyright 1996 - Tomer and Yehuda Shiran
8    var messages = new Array()
9    messages[0] = "the javascript planet"
10   messages[1] = "welcome to my site!"
11   messages[2] = "232 scripts available!"
12   messages[3] = "this site is updated..."
13   messages[4] = "several times a week."
14   messages[5] = "new:scripts by request"
15   messages[6] = "this script was requested"
16   var space = 1
17   var height = 5
18   var width = 3
19   var letters = new letterArray()
20   var on = new Image(5, 5)
21   var off = new Image(5, 5)
22   on.src = "ledon.gif"
23   off.src = "ledoff.gif"
24   var imageNum = document.images.length
25   var boardWidth = 0
26
27   for (var i = 0; i < messages.length; ++i) {
28       var lengthWithNoSpaces =
                     messages[i].split(" ").join("").length
29       var numberOfSpaces =
                     messages[i].length - lengthWithNoSpaces
30       var currentBoardWidth = lengthWithNoSpaces
                 * (width + space)
                 - space + numberOfSpaces * space * 2
31       if (boardWidth < currentBoardWidth)
32           boardWidth = currentBoardWidth
33   }
34   var running = false
35   var timerID = null
```

```
36
37   function letterArray() {
38      this.a = new Array(height)
39      this.a[0] = " * "
40      this.a[1] = "* *"
41      this.a[2] = "***"
42      this.a[3] = "* *"
43      this.a[4] = "* *"
44
45      this.b = new Array(height)
46      this.b[0] = "** "
47      this.b[1] = "* *"
48      this.b[2] = "**"
49      this.b[3] = "* *"
50      this.b[4] = "**"
51
52      this.c = new Array(height)
53      this.c[0] = "***"
54      this.c[1] = "*   "
55      this.c[2] = "*   "
56      this.c[3] = "*   "
57      this.c[4] = "***"
```

Please see the accompanying CD-ROM for the code from lines 58 through 390, which creates similar arrays for the remainder of the alphabet, common punctuation signs and the numbers from 0 to 9.

```
391  function drawBlank() {
392     var gt = unescape("%3e")
393     document.write('<TABLE BORDER=2 CELLPADDING=8'
                        + gt + '<TR' + gt +
394        '<TD WIDTH=468 ALIGN="center" VALIGN="center"' + gt)
395     for (var y = 0; y < height; ++y) {
396         for (var x = 0; x < boardWidth; ++x) {
397             document.write('<IMG SRC="' + off.src +
398                            '" HEIGHT=5 WIDTH=5' + gt)
399         }
400         document.write('<BR' + gt)
401     }
402     document.write('</TD' + gt + '</TR' + gt + '</TABLE' + gt)
403  }
```

```
404
405 function setLight(state, x, y) {
406    if (state)
407        document.images[computeIndex(x, y)].src = on.src
408    else
409        document.images[computeIndex(x, y)].src = off.src
410 }
411
412 function drawLetter(letter, startX) {
413    for (var x = 0; x < width; ++x) {
414        for (var y = 0; y < height; ++y) {
415            setLight(letters[letter][y].charAt(x) ==
                                        "*", startX + x, y)
416        }
417    }
418 }
419
420 function drawSpace(startX) {
421    for (var x = 0; x < space; ++x) {
422        for (var y = 0; y < height; ++y) {
423            setLight(false, startX + x, y)
424        }
425    }
426 }
427
428 function computeIndex(x, y) {
429    return (y * boardWidth + x) + imageNum
430 }
431
432 function floodBoard(startX) {
433    for (var x = startX; x < boardWidth; ++x) {
434        for (var y = 0; y < height; ++y) {
435            setLight(false, x, y)
436        }
437    }
438 }
439
440 function drawMessage(num) {
441    var text = messages[num]
442    var i = 0
443    var j = 0
444    while (1) {
445        if (text.charAt(j) != " ") {
```

```
446            drawLetter(text.charAt(j), i)
447            i += width
448        }
449        else {
450            drawSpace(i)
451            i += space
452        }
453        if (j < text.length - 1) {
454            drawSpace(i)
455            i += space
456        }
457        else
458            break
459        ++j
460    }
461    floodBoard(i)
462    if (num < messages.length - 1)
463        val = ++num
464    else
465        val = 0
466    timerID = setTimeout("drawMessage(val)", 3000)
467 }
468
469 document.write('<FORM>')
470 drawBlank()
471
472 function startSign() {
473    drawMessage(0)
474    running = true
475 }
476
477 function stopSign() {
478    if(running)
479        clearTimeout(timerID)
480        running = false
481 }
482
483 document.write('<INPUT TYPE="button" VALUE="start"
                         onClick="startSign()">')
484 document.write('<INPUT TYPE="button" VALUE="stop"
                         onClick="stopSign(); floodBoard(0)">')
485 document.write('</FORM>')
486 // -->
```

```
487  </SCRIPT>
488  </body>
489  </HTML>
```

ANNOTATIONS

Essentially, this script fills a standard HTML table cell with rows and columns of the same tiny 5×5-pixel pure black image, LEDOFF.GIF. It then displays the message by means of an array of characters constructed of blanks and asterisks. Whenever the process encounters an asterisk, the corresponding image is switched to LEDON.GIF, in this case bright green, thereby shaping each character as it scans across the board. If you don't like the green-on-black combination, all you have to do is replace the two little GIF files with the colors of your choice.

Notice that the script is located in the body, with the simple layout produced by the **document.write( )** on line 469 followed by the call to **drawBlank( )** on line 470, which draws the display panel, and then lines 483 to 485, which add the control buttons.

```
1   <HTML>
2   <HEAD>
3   <TITLE>LED banner</TITLE>
4   </HEAD>
5   <BODY BGCOLOR="#FFFFFF">
6   <SCRIPT LANGUAGE="JavaScript1.1">
7   <!--// Copyright 1996 - Tomer and Yehuda Shiran
8   var messages = new Array()
9   messages[0] = "the javascript planet"
10  messages[1] = "welcome to my site!"
11  messages[2] = "232 scripts available!"
12  messages[3] = "this site is updated..."
13  messages[4] = "several times a week."
14  messages[5] = "new:scripts by request"
15  messages[6] = "this script was requested"
16  var space = 1
17  var height = 5
18  var width = 3
```

The script starts by constructing an array of six messages, then declares and defines three global variables: **space**, which is used to create the spaces between letters and words in the display, and **height** and **width**, which specify the

dimensions of the displayed letters—three characters wide by five high, as you
can also see from the letters themselves in **letterArray( )** beginning on line 37.

```
19    var letters = new letterArray()
20    var on = new Image(5, 5)
21    var off = new Image(5, 5)
22    on.src = "ledon.gif"
23    off.src = "ledoff.gif"
24    var imageNum = document.images.length
25    var boardWidth = 0
```

The script then sets up **letters** as an instance of **letterArray( )** and goes on to
create two **Image** objects, **on** and **off**, specifying their 5×5-pixel size as arguments
and the source GIF files in lines 22 and 23. This is followed by two more variables,
imageNum, assigned the number of images on the page (that is, the length of the
built-in **images** array), and **boardWidth**, used in the **for** loop next as well as later by
the **drawBlank( )**, **computeIndex( )**, and **floodBoard( )** functions.

```
27    for (var i = 0; i < messages.length; ++i) {
28        var lengthWithNoSpaces =
                        messages[i].split(" ").join("").length
29        var numberOfSpaces =
                        messages[i].length - lengthWithNoSpaces
30        var currentBoardWidth = lengthWithNoSpaces
                    * (width + space)
                    - space + numberOfSpaces * space * 2
31        if (boardWidth < currentBoardWidth)
32            boardWidth = currentBoardWidth
33    }
```

This **for** loop, which runs when the page is loaded, sets the width of the display
panel based on the length of the longest string in the **messages** array. First, line 28,
in a single swoop, splits each message into separate words by specifying a blank
space as the separator, joins the string back together again with the blanks replaced
by an empty string, that is, no space, and assigns the length of the condensed string
to **lengthWithNoSpaces**. The **numberOfSpaces** is then calculated by subtracting
the length of the spaceless string from the length of the original message. Next,
currentBoardWidth is defined as the number of letters (**lengthWithNoSpaces**)
multiplied by their **width** plus a **space** (for the space between letters) minus one
space (last letter) plus **numberOfSpaces** times **space** times two (two spaces between
words). If the resulting value is greater than **boardWidth**, it gets assigned to the
latter by the **if** statement. Thus, **boardWidth** ends up getting the highest value of
currentBoardWidth, so that the longest message fits neatly into the display panel.

```
34   var running = false
35   var timerID = null
```

Lines 34 and 35 introduce the familiar timeout variables—**running**, a Boolean value that keeps track of whether the banner is running, and **timerID**, the identifier for the **clearTimeout( )** in **stopSign( )** on line 479.

```
37   function letterArray() {
38      this.a = new Array(height)
39      this.a[0] = " * "
40      this.a[1] = "* *"
41      this.a[2] = "***"
42      this.a[3] = "* *"
43      this.a[4] = "* *"
```

letterArray( ) then methodically constructs each of the 50 letters of the alphabet, numbers, and punctuation signs available for display out of five three-character strings of asterisks and blanks. Notice how the array referencing changes to a string in square brackets for the punctuation signs and numbers starting on line 220. This effectively makes each sign or number the name of that array.

```
220     this['!'] = new Array(height)
221     this['!'][0] = " * "
222     this['!'][1] = " * "
223     this['!'][2] = " * "
224     this['!'][3] = "   "
225     this['!'][4] = " * "
```

There's another far shorter and less painstaking way to create a font such as this. Begin by constructing an array of the eight possible asterisk/space combinations:

```
astArray = new Array()
astArray[0] = '*  '
astArray[1] = ' * '
astArray[2] = '  *'
astArray[3] = '** '
astArray[4] = '* *'
astArray[5] = ' **'
astArray[6] = '***'
astArray[7] = '   '
```

Then add a function to read the asterisk array from a code composed of the indices for the five lines of **astArray** required for each character, for example:

```
function makeLetter(code) {
    letstr = ''
    for (var y = 0; y < code.length; y++)
        letstr += astArray[code.charAt(y)]
```

```
    return letstr
}
```

Each pass through the **for** loop increments **letstr** by the string assigned to the **astArray** member whose index corresponds to the **code** digit at position **y**. This gets the appropriate string of blanks and asterisks for each member of the array constructed with

```
letters = new Array()
letters['a'] = makeLetter('14644')
letters['b'] = makeLetter('34343')
letters['c'] = makeLetter('60006')
letters['d'] = makeLetter('34443')
letters['e'] = makeLetter('60606')
```

and so on. Then change the **charAt( )** argument in line 415 to

```
setLight(letters[letter].charAt((y * width) + x) == "*", startX + x, y)
```

so that it accesses the **letters** array and reads the right character of **letstr**. Finally, delete line 19 as well as the complete array of characters extending from lines 37 to 389. The file LED2.HTM, found in the same directory as this script on the accompanying CD-ROM, is the full shorter version.

The result of these little adjustments is a script that runs about 200 instead of almost 500 lines, and shrinks the file from roughly 12K to 7K, and 5K after deleting comments.

PROGRAMMER'S TIP *You can lighten and speed up scripted web pages by saving a commented copy separately while publishing a version stripped of comments. Think of the former as the source and the latter as the executable. Use search-and-replace to condense all those long names of functions, variables, objects, properties, and so on, to two or three letters, as well as to close all but essential blank spaces, and you can probably lop off another substantial chunk. It won't be readable (you have your source file for that), but it sure will be a lot trimmer and faster as well as more computer-, user-, and web-friendly. Hug—don't hog—bandwidth!*

The shorter version of our LED script (LED2.HTM on the CD-ROM) is also much easier to maintain and play around with. For instance, you can reshape or adjust the letters simply by modifying the digits in each one's **makeLetter( )** argument. Plus it only takes one line of code to add a new character or letter to the array.

This also makes it much easier to expand the display matrix from 3×5 to say, 5×7. Think of the asterisks and blanks in **astArray** as ones and zeros, and you'll see that the array is the equivalent of the eight binary numbers from 0 to 111. This immediately tells you that the length of a 5-asterisk-wide array will be 11111 plus one, or 32. Because the array index can now be either one or two digits, a code string argument is no longer practical for **makeLetter( )**. Instead, make each array index a separate argument. The number of arguments then corresponds to the height of the characters, and you can use the function's **arguments** property to index the array. Thus, for a height of 7, modify **makeLetter( )** to read

```
function makeLetter(a, b, c, d, e, f, g) {
    letstr = ''
    for (var y = 0; y < makeLetter.arguments.length; y++)
        letstr += astArray[makeLetter.arguments[y]]
    return letstr
}
```

Beyond that, all you have to do is create the expanded **astArray**, adjust the global **height** and **width** variables in lines 17 and 18 accordingly, and of course, assign the appropriate sequence of **astArray** members to each character. While this requires some effort, unless you have an insatiable passion for drawing with asterisks, it certainly beats bashing out every single character individually.

```
391  function drawBlank() {
392      var gt = unescape("%3e")
393      document.write('<TABLE BORDER=2 CELLPADDING=8'
                            + gt + '<TR' + gt +
394          '<TD WIDTH=468 ALIGN="center" VALIGN="center"' + gt)
395      for (var y = 0; y < height; ++y) {
396          for (var x = 0; x < boardWidth; ++x) {
397                  document.write('<IMG SRC="' + off.src +
398                                      '" HEIGHT=5 WIDTH=5' + gt)
399          }
400          document.write('<BR' + gt)
401      }
402      document.write('</TD' + gt + '</TR' + gt + '</TABLE' + gt)
403  }
```

drawBlank( ), run when the page load reaches line 470, creates the display panel with **document.write( )** statements and a standard HTML table. Making the greater-than sign (>) a variable named **gt** is not necessary. Note too that the fixed table cell width in line 394 has to be adjusted for longer messages to avoid the vertical stretch that occurs when **boardWidth** exceeds cell width. You can easily assign it a value based on **boardWidth** and 5 pixels per character by modifying the beginning of line 394 to read

```
'<TD WIDTH =' + (boardWidth * 5)  + ' BGCOLOR...   // etc.
```

With this, the display panel will automatically stretch to fit your longest message. The short version of this script, LED2.HTM, incorporates this feature.

```
405  function setLight(state, x, y) {
406      if (state)
407          document.images[computeIndex(x, y)].src = on.src
408      else
409          document.images[computeIndex(x, y)].src = off.src
410  }
```

setLight( ), which is called by **drawLetter( )**, **drawSpace( )**, and **floodBoard( )**, switches the image at the array position calculated by **computeIndex( )** between LEDON.GIF or LEDOFF.GIF. This turns the display panel's cells on and off. The **state** argument is a Boolean value that conveys on or off. In **drawSpace( )** and **floodBoard( )** it is simply set to **false**; in **drawLetter( )** its value depends on whether an asterisk or blank space is encountered in reading the letter.

```
412 function drawLetter(letter, startX) {
413    for (var x = 0; x < width; ++x) {
414        for (var y = 0; y < height; ++y) {
415            setLight(letters[letter][y].charAt(x) ==
                                         "*", startX + x, y)
416        }
417    }
418 }
```

This function, called by **drawMessage( )** next, uses a nested **for** loop to scan each letter in the message. If it encounters an asterisk, **setLight( )**'s **state** argument is **true** and the corresponding image switches from LEDOFF.GIF to LEDON.GIF. The **startX** argument in this function, as well as in **drawSpace( )** and **floodBoard( )** next, is a coordinate marking the top left corner of each character or space.

```
420 function drawSpace(startX) {
421    for (var x = 0; x < space; ++x) {
422        for (var y = 0; y < height; ++y) {
423            setLight(false, startX + x, y)
424        }
425    }
426 }
```

Similarly, **drawSpace( )** draws the spaces between letters and words by passing **setLight( )** a **state** argument of **false**.

```
428 function computeIndex(x, y) {
429    return (y * boardWidth + x) + imageNum
430 }
```

This function computes the **images** array index of the GIF at the position represented by **x** and **y** (height and width coordinates). **imageNum** (declared on line 24) is the length of the **images** array when the page loads. While intended to compensate for graphics on the page above the display panel, this variable could skew the function if you have any images below the banner. In that case, you'll have to adjust line 429 by subtracting the number of images that come after the display panel on the page; or you could simply set its value in line 24 to the actual number of images preceding the banner that you have on your page. If you have no images above the banner and some after, another option is to delete both the declaration on line 24 and "+ **imageNum**" on line 429.

```
432  function floodBoard(startX) {
433     for (var x = startX; x < boardWidth; ++x) {
434        for (var y = 0; y < height; ++y) {
435           setLight(false, x, y)
436        }
437     }
438  }
```

floodBoard( ) uses a similar nested **for** loop to turn all the images off between messages when called by **drawMessage( )** in line 461, or when a user click on the stop button triggers the event handler in line 484.

```
440  function drawMessage(num) {
441     var text = messages[num]
442     var i = 0
443     var j = 0
444     while (1) {
445        if (text.charAt(j) != " ") {
446           drawLetter(text.charAt(j), i)
447           i += width
448        }
449        else {
450           drawSpace(i)
451           i += space
452        }
```

We now arrive at this script's main function, **drawMessage( )**, which is assigned to the start button's event handler. It first declares three local variables: **text**, which is assigned the message from the array indexed by **num**; **i**, which marks horizontal position in the display and whose value is passed to the **startX** argument; and **j**, which tracks the "read" position in the message.

The first **if** test in the **while** loop checks whether the next message character is a space; if it is not, it draws the character in that position and, if it is, draws a space instead. In the former case, the position index **i** is incremented by **width** (3), in the latter by **space** (1).

```
453        if (j < text.length - 1) {
454           drawSpace(i)
455           i += space
456        }
457        else
458           break
```

```
459        ++j
460     }
```

The next **if** tests the value of the character index **j** against the length of the message. If the end of the message has not been reached, it draws the space between letters and increments **i** accordingly, and **j** is incremented by line 459. Otherwise, it breaks out of the **while** loop.

```
461     floodBoard(i)
462     if (num < messages.length - 1)
463         val = ++num
464     else
465         val = 0
466     timerID = setTimeout("drawMessage(val)", 3000)
467 }
```

Then **floodBoard( )** is called with **i** as the value of its **startX** argument and sweeps across the rest of the panel between the end of the message and right border of the table cell, turning all the images "off" (which they already are by default).

Finally, the **if/else** routine in lines 462 through 465 either increments the **messages** array index or resets it to zero to recycle the messages following the last one in the sequence. After a 3-second timeout the next message is drawn by the recursive call in line 466.

```
469 document.write('<FORM>')
470 drawBlank()
```

These next two lines start laying out the page by creating an HTML form and calling **drawBlank( )**, which, as we saw earlier, creates the display panel.

```
472 function startSign() {
473     drawMessage(0)
474     running = true
475 }
476
477 function stopSign() {
478     if(running)
479         clearTimeout(timerID)
480         running = false
481 }
```

Next come the two functions assigned respectively to the panel's start and stop buttons. The first calls **drawMessage( )** with a 0 argument, which represents the starting index of the array, and then sets the Boolean value of the **running** variable to **true**.

stopSign( ) tests whether the banner is running, and if it is, stops it by clearing the **timerID** timeout before setting **running** to **false**.

```
483 document.write('<INPUT TYPE="button" VALUE="start"
                                 onClick="startSign()">')
484 document.write('<INPUT TYPE="button" VALUE="stop"
                                 onClick="stopSign(); floodBoard(0)">')
485 document.write('</FORM>')
486 // -->
487 </SCRIPT>
488 </body>
489 </HTML>
```

Lastly, our script uses **document.write( )** statements to create the start and stop buttons with their event handlers and closes the form.

As you must realize by now, there are all kinds of ways in which you can use JavaScript to display moving messages. They can scroll by or unfold letter-by-letter in a form field, separate frame or layer, or image panel, and either run automatically or come equipped with user controls. Their potential uses are virtually boundless.

Yet while motion on a screen is invariably eye-catching, it can also be distracting and, at worst, annoying. Moreover, a web audience is not captive: another site is only a click away. This means giving some thought to the speed and timing of your banner script. There's no point in highlighting a message by putting it in a banner if it makes a visitor lose patience during the process.

With the exception of news and stock tickers and the like, which are updated continuously, there's another inherent problem in the use of banners. A fixed array of messages is likely to be read the first or second time a visitor loads your page, but after that may be automatically ignored, so that even a new set of messages will go unnoticed. As there's no simple, clear-cut way to work around this psychological factor, you might well want to stop and think twice before jumping on the banner wagon.

Cookies

Maintaining state—in other words, recording the state of a user's interaction with an application at exit so as to restore it upon the next use—can be valuable to web developers who want to implement interactive online applications. A currently popular method of maintaining state is the use of *cookies,* also known as "persistent cookies" and "magic cookies."

In many cases, developers deploy cookie functions in the context of server-end CGI programs. Beginning with Navigator 2.0, though, Netscape addressed the problem of state with cookies. Since then, Microsoft's Internet Explorer adopted cookies, and we imagine within a short time all web browsers will be cookie enabled.

Cookies consist of specific data that is transferred between web servers and a user's browser. When a cookie is left with your browser, it means that the server has left some record of your visit. This information can be used later, when you visit the server (or site) again.

To illustrate, say a user sends a request to a server, and a web page is sent by the server to a user's browser. The server immediately forgets about the user and the page it just sent. When a user clicks on a link on that page, the server has not kept a record of what page the user is coming from. In addition, it does not record other important information. This data includes what browser the user has, other pages (on the server and on other servers) the user has downloaded, and, if the user returns to the page, the user's previous actions on the page.

Cookie information, which is maintained by the browser, can be read and updated by a server and makes it possible to identify browsers that have visited a site before.

JavaScript provides the **Navigator** object, which keeps track of information about the user's browser version. The **Navigator** object can be used in conjunction with cookies, allowing the developer to create easy-to-implement code to maintain state on a web site.

JavaScript can work with client-side state information stored as cookies, making the cookie property of the document object available for processing. A JavaScript containing cookie functions makes all attributes of cookies for the page available to the script and enables the script to set new cookies. Much of the server-end processing needed for cookies can be handled by use of JavaScript.

Unlike CGI cookies, which involve a client-server dialog, a JavaScript cookie is created directly on the client's machine by the script running within the browser. The core recipe for making a JavaScript cookie is quite simple:

```
document.cookie = "NAME=VALUE"
```

For instance:

```
document.cookie = "yourName=Coyote"
```

creates a cookie called **yourName** whose value is "Coyote." Add an expiry date with

```
+ "; expires=Friday, 31-Dec-99, 23:59:59 GMT"
```

to the preceding line of code, and **yourName** with its assigned string will remain stored in the client's machine until the expiry date—or more specifically, as long as the file COOKIES.TXT, where Navigator stashes its cookies (or the corresponding file in the case of other browsers), remains intact and in use. Omit the expiry date and it crumbles when the browser session ends.

As with the term "Java," the name "cookie" was invented anonymously. It probably stems from hacker jargon such as "magic cookie" to refer to small data objects passed between routines or programs that enable the receiver to perform some action, or the "fortune cookie" returned by the UNIX program "fortune"—a random quote, joke or bit of trivia taken from a collection stored in a file (the cookie jar) and displayed when the user logs in or out.

There are numerous reasons for deploying cookie-aware web pages. They add a level of interactivity to web sites that includes the server's ability to "remember" user preferences and the user's previous behavior at a site.

Sites use cookies in web-based interactive tours in which the server recalls where a user left off when he or she last visited. Some sites use cookies to implement online shopping services. Nearly all of the more sophisticated cookie-enabled sites require CGI scripts to work successfully, in addition to JavaScript, Java, or built-in web server extensions.

Many sites now rely on cookies, and by refusing them, users can disrupt their operation. A cookie is limited to 4,096 text characters, and its contents are not accessible from other pages or to other web users. As web server administrators or developers, we have no idea what cookies are set in a user's browser unless the user sends his or her cookie file to us. There are other limitations, as well. Navigator can store 300 cookies. Within that 300, each is limited to 4K in length, including all the optional attributes, and only 20 cookies can be stored for each domain. When the number of cookies is exceeded, the browser will delete the least recently used. If the length of a cookie exceeds the limit, it is trimmed to fit.

Compared with Netscape's browser, Microsoft Internet Explorer 3.*x* uses cookies in a slightly different way. If you develop a JavaScript with cookie functions, **document.cookie** will not work if you access the HTML file from your local hard disk; it only works over an Internet connection. Also, Explorer limits you to one cookie NAME=VALUE pair per domain, whereas Netscape allows up to 20 pairs per domain.

User Paranoia

There is a bit of paranoia in the user community regarding cookies. For example, one marketing-related method of tracking users' movements is via banner advertising graphics that appear on many pages. Companies can do this because the banner graphics are actually stored on their servers. Some of these servers will place, or attempt to place, several cookies on your system. Some users react negatively to this activity and justifiably wonder "who's watching" and why all these cookies (which are ASCII-readable) are being left on their local system.

Users who object to this can refuse the cookie. In Netscape Communicator 4.0—and, we hope, in the next iteration of Microsoft's browser—you can set a user preference that refuses all cookies. In earlier browsers, you can set the browser to notify you when a server tries to leave a cookie on your system. In either case, the user has some control over the situation.

At any time, users can view the cookies being set by the currently visited site by typing the following line in the browser's location bar:

```
JavaScript:alert(document.cookie);
```

Cookies cannot store any information that you have not given, cannot contain active code, and cannot be read from any site other than the one leaving the cookie. Ignore the paranoia and let these snippets of text do their work, which is to make the Web more interactive and user configurable.

As a side note, some enterprising Internet companies are figuring out ways to leave cookies in your browser's cache. This may successfully circumvent the browser's ability to delete cookies when the cookie file reaches its size limit. For more information about this and other cookie developments, visit the Cookie Central web site at **http://www.cookiecentral.com**.

The Compleat Cookie takes six ingredients: NAME, VALUE, EXPIRES, PATH, DOMAIN, and SECURE. If you open COOKIES.TXT, you'll see them laid out in what appears to be logical processing order:

DOMAIN   PATH   SECURE   EXPIRES   NAME   VALUE

with the six components separated by tabs, and the cookies themselves, by newline characters. To find the right cookie for your page on the client machine, the browser scans COOKIE.TXT for matching DOMAIN and PATH values, which by default are set to those of the page that created the cookie. Next the security flag and expiry date are read; assuming the cookie is not stale, the browser returns its NAME and VALUE. In the case of JavaScript cookies, the SECURE status would appear to be irrelevant for cookies that are simply read from the client's hard drive into their browser's memory space, or that are written by the script to memory and then by Navigator to COOKIES.TXT. Here security depends primarily on the channel over which the page containing the cookie-making script is originally transmitted, as well as the connection used for sending any information derived from or related to the cookie back to the server.

In the construction of a JavaScript cookie, these six ingredients are all semicolon-separated components of a single string, best concatenated for the sake of readability:

```
document.cookie="victim=Roadrunner; " +
            "expires=Friday, 13-Aug-99 13:13:13 GMT; " +
            "domain=wcoy.beepbeepbird.paradise.com; " +
            "path=/canyon/gulch/cave/cauldron/gulp; " +
            "secure"
```

A NAME=VALUE string is the only mandatory requirement for creating a cookie; the others are optional. Moreover, this item *must* come first in the string assigned to **document.cookie**. Put "expires=" up front and your cookie will be named "expires," with its value set to whatever expiry date you specify. The name can be whatever you choose, and VALUE is simply any string of characters to carry the data. According to Netscape specifications, this string may not contain semicolons, commas, or spaces. Hence the scripts in this chapter all use the JavaScript **escape( )** and **unescape( )** methods to convert the VALUE strings into acceptable form, or in the case of older scripts, into elaborate encode-decode functions. Yet write

```
document.cookie=
        "Bad cookie=This is, supposedly, an invalid cookie"
```

and then output the value of **document.cookie** with **document.write( )**, or by assignment to the status bar or to a form field, and you'll see exactly that cookie with commas and blanks—no escaping and unescaping necessary. Only the characters used as separators—semicolons and "equal signs" (=) in the cookie-making string assigned to **document.cookie**, and the tabs and newline characters in COOKIES.TXT—would seem to be absolutely taboo. Presumably, Navigator just treats everything before "=" as the name, and the string up to the first semicolon or actual end as the value, and splits the two with a tab. The EXPIRES, DOMAIN, PATH, and SECURE strings can all be identified by those words, and the end of each assigned value, by a semicolon or the end of the string. The identifiers along with "=" are dropped and replaced by tabs, the order is shuffled, and the result is the entry format you see in COOKIES.TXT.

Similarly, you'll discover that not one of the scripts in this chapter complies with the specifications for the EXPIRES attribute. Netscape documentation clearly states that a cookie's expiry date must be expressed in the form WDY, DD-MON-YY HH:MM:SS GMT, where WDY is the fully spelled-out name of the weekday, the date elements are separated by hyphens, and the year is reduced to two digits, for example:

Sunday, 03-Aug-97 17:55:26 GMT

Yet most of the scripts in this chapter that set an **expires** value simply use the **toGMTString( )** method, which returns dates in a slightly different format:

Sun, 03 Aug 1997 17:55:26 GMT

(that varies slightly from platform to platform), and their cookies nonetheless expire on time. One doesn't even bother with the conversion to GMT and gets away with it. The **DATE** value is stored in COOKIES.TXT as the number of seconds since January 1, 1970, 00:00:00 GMT, or "870630926" in the case of our example. Presumably, with JavaScript cookies, as long as the date is in a format that Navigator can recognize and convert to a GMT-based millisecond value, it's valid.

The DOMAIN, PATH, and SECURE attributes are generally not specified in creating a cookie. By default, the cookie will get the DOMAIN and PATH of the document that created it. As for SECURE, a JavaScript cookie created and stored on the client machine doesn't travel anywhere except back and forth between memory and hard drive, so security can scarcely be considered vital—unless, of course, you're convinced that "They" have tapped into your microprocessor... Moreover, JavaScript offers no means of sending cookie data to the server—a cookie has no **send( )** method; it has to use a submit-form or e-mail process whose security is entirely contingent upon the blanket provided by the browser's mechanisms.

A cookie with the same path and name as an existing cookie will overwrite the latter. Hence the standard technique of deleting a cookie is simply to create a new one with the same name but an expiry date in the past.

Most scripts in this chapter use a set of basic cookie functions originally created and subsequently revised by Bill Dortch of hIdaho Design. This standard library includes

- ◆ **getCookieVal( )**, a subroutine of **GetCookie** which returns a cookie's **value** string

- ◆ **GetCookie( )**, which fetches a cookie stored in COOKIES.TXT

- ◆ **SetCookie( )**, which creates a cookie

- ◆ **DeleteCookie( )**, which destroys a cookie

The original versions can all be found in the file DORTCH.HTM on the accompanying CD-ROM. They are also annotated in this chapter where they occur in the various scripts. The only one that does not appear in our selection, **FixCookieDate( )**, compensates for a Mac 2.*x* date bug. It and the others are thoroughly commented by the author in DORTCH.HTM, which is well worth reading if you plan to use these functions.

PROGRAMMER'S TIP   *When developing cookies, you can easily see how your code turns up in COOKIES.TXT by giving that file another name such as COOKIES.BAK. Navigator will then create a new COOKIES.TXT file that will only contain your cookie. This spares you sifting through all the other cookies you may have accumulated while web surfing. Note that you must exit Navigator to make it write or to update COOKIES.TXT.*

Also, a simple way to monitor cookies while developing them is to display them in the status bar by adding

```
self.status = document.cookie; return true
```

to your cookie maker function or, in the case of long cookies, direct the output to a form text area. You can do the same thing with the scripts in this chapter to view the cookies they create.

duncooky

Duncan Crombie's Cookie Extender

N2 N2.01 N2.02+ N3 N4 E3 E4

This page creates a form with three fields where you can enter a background color of your choice as either a string literal ("dodgerblue") or hexadecimal RGB value ("1E90FF"), your name, and "Head Count" or the number of asterisks strung across the top of the page. When you press the Set Multi-Cookie button, nothing visible happens, but a cookie containing the three values you entered is created. Next click on the "reload this page" link to have the browser read the cookie and rewrite the page based on your input (see Figure 5-1).

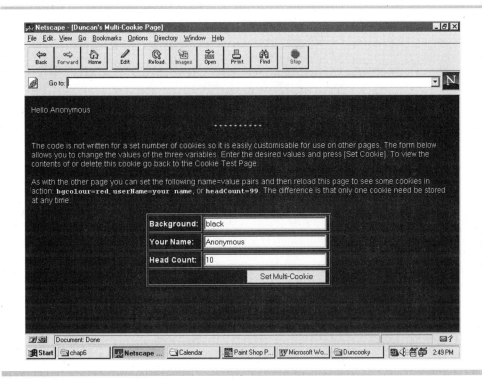

FIGURE 5-1.   This script uses a cookie to store and retrieve user input that personalizes a web page

The code, a compact variation on the Dortch cookie functions, shows how you can use a cookie to store and retrieve user input that personalizes a web page.

```
1    <HTML>
2    <HEAD>
3    <TITLE>Duncan's Multi-Cookie Page</TITLE>
4    <SCRIPT language="JavaScript">
5    <!-- Hide from older browsers
6    // Original JavaScript code by Duncan Crombie:
                                    dcrombie@ozemail.com.au
7    // Please acknowledge use of this code
                                    by including this header.
8    var bikky = document.cookie;
9    function getCookie(name) {
10       var index = bikky.indexOf(name + "=");
11       if (index == -1) return null;
12       index = bikky.indexOf("=", index) + 1;
13       var endstr = bikky.indexOf(";", index);
14       if (endstr == -1) endstr = bikky.length;
15       return unescape(bikky.substring(index, endstr));
16   }
17   var today = new Date();
18   var expiry = new Date(today.getTime()
                                    + 28 * 24 * 60 * 60 * 1000);
19   function setCookie(name) {
20       document.cookie = eval('"' + name + '="
                                    + escape(' + name + ') + "; expires='
                                    + expiry.toGMTString() + '"');
21       bikky = document.cookie;
22   }
23   function blankArray(arrayLength) {
24       this.length = arrayLength;
25       for (var i=0; i < this.length; i++)
26           this[i] = "";
27   }
28   function defineCookie(newData) {
29       userData = newData[0];
30       for (var i=1; i < newData.length; i++)
31           userData += "!" + newData[i];
32       setCookie("userData");
33   }
34
35   var userData = getCookie("userData");
```

```
36  if (userData == null)
37      userData = "black!Anonymous!0";
38  var numVars = 1;
39  var start = userData.indexOf("!") + 1;
40  while (start != 0) {
41     numVars++;
42     start = userData.indexOf("!", start) + 1;
43  }
44  var data = new blankArray(numVars);
45  for (var i=0; i < data.length; i++) {
46      var end = userData.indexOf("!", start);
47      if (end == -1) end = userData.length;
48      data[i] = userData.substring(start, end);
49      start = end + 1;
50  }
51  // Stop hiding -->
52  </SCRIPT>
53  </HEAD>
54  <BODY bgcolor="black" text="white" link="yellow"
                                 alink="lime" vlink="skyblue"
                            onLoad="document.bgColor=data[0];">
55  <SCRIPT language="JavaScript">
56  <!-- Hide from older browsers
57  userName = data[1];
58  if (userName != null) document.write("Hello "
                                      + userName + " ");
59  document.writeln("<p>");
60  // Stop hiding -->
61  </SCRIPT>
62  <SCRIPT language="JavaScript">
63  <!-- Hide from older browsers
64  headCount = data[2];
65  if (headCount != null) {
66      document.writeln("<DIV align='center'>");
67      for (var i=0; i < headCount && i != null; i++)
68          document.write("* ");
69  }
70  document.writeln("</DIV><p>");
71  // Stop hiding -->
72  </SCRIPT>
73  <FORM name="cookieTest" method="post">
74  <DIV align="center"><TABLE border>
75  <TR><TD><strong>Background: </strong>
```

```
76   <TD><INPUT name="data0" type="text" value="black" size="30">
77   <TR><TD><strong>Your Name: </strong>
78   <TD><INPUT name="data1" type="text" value="Anonymous"
                                               size="30">
79   <TR><TD><strong>Head Count: </strong>
80   <TD><INPUT name="data2" type="text" value="10" size="30">
81   <TR><TD align="right" colspan="2"><INPUT type="button"
                              value="Set Multi-Cookie" onClick="
82   with (this.form) {
83      data[0] = data0.value;
84      data[1] = data1.value;
85      data[2] = data2.value;
86   }
87   defineCookie(data);
88   ">
89   </TABLE></DIV></FORM><p>
90   </BODY>
91   </HTML>
```

ANNOTATIONS

A click on the Set Multi-Cookie button assigns the user input to an array named **data**, then calls **defineCookie( )** with **data** as its sole argument. This converts the user input into a **value** string for the cookie with the three user-entered preferences separated by exclamation marks. The result is a cookie in the following raw form:

userData=purple!Wanda!25

though with the exclamation marks escaped, it becomes

userData=purple%21Wanda%2125

for COOKIE.TXT. The cookie is timed to crumble four weeks after its creation.

```
1   <HTML>
2   <HEAD>
3   <TITLE>Duncan's Multi-Cookie Page</TITLE>
4   <SCRIPT language="JavaScript">
5   <!-- Hide from older browsers
6   // Original JavaScript code by Duncan Crombie:
                                    dcrombie@ozemail.com.au
7   // Please acknowledge use of this code
                              by including this header.
8   var bikky = document.cookie;
```

This script begins by declaring a global variable, **bikky**, and assigning it the built-in JavaScript **document.cookie** property, a string that holds a cookie's NAME and VALUE joined by "=". Thus

```
document.write(document.cookie)
```

or

```
document.write(bikky)
```

will in this case produce

```
userData=salmon%21Jason%2117
```

assuming those three values have been entered into the form on DUNCOOKY.HTM. The word "bikky," incidentally, is an Anglo-Australian diminutive form of "biscuit."

```
9   function getCookie(name) {
10      var index = bikky.indexOf(name + "=");
11      if (index == -1) return null;
12      index = bikky.indexOf("=", index) + 1;
13      var endstr = bikky.indexOf(";", index);
14      if (endstr == -1) endstr = bikky.length;
15      return unescape(bikky.substring(index, endstr));
16   }
```

Fed the name of a cookie as its argument, **getCookie( )** first assigns the local variable **index** the index of the "**userData=**" string in **bikky**. If the **indexOf( )** method returns –1 because that string is not found, our function returns **null**. Otherwise, it increments **index** by one and looks for the index of the next semicolon starting at the position specified by **index** as the optional offset argument to **indexOf( )**.

Thus, if you write

```
teststring = "Yabadabadoo!"
pos = teststring.indexOf("ba")
```

pos gets 2 (as usual, the count starts with 0). But if you specify an offset with

```
pos = teststring.indexOf("ba", 3)
```

pos becomes 6 because the search now starts from the second "a" in position 3.

Although the scan for a semicolon is unnecessary on this page, which creates a single cookie named **userData**, it makes this function usable on pages that turn out a batch of cookies. For example, if this script were rewritten to produce three cookies named **userColor**, **userName**, and **userHeadCount**, **bikky** would become a string of semicolon-separated NAME=VALUE pairs such as

```
userColor=salmon;userName=Jason;userHeadCount=17
```

getCookie("userColor") would then return "salmon"; **getCookie("userName")**, "Jason"; and **getCookie("userHeadCount")**, "17."

The integer indicating the position of the semicolon that marks the end of the NAME=VALUE pair is assigned to the local variable **endstr** or, if no semicolon is found, **endstr** gets the value of **bikky.length** or the last position in the string. Finally, **getCookie( )** returns the substring extending from **index** to **endstr** in unescaped form, in other words with the "%21" separators converted back to exclamation marks.

    getCookie( ) is called from line 35 whenever DUNCOOKY.HTM is loaded.

```
17  var today = new Date();
18  var expiry = new Date(today.getTime()
                          + 28 * 24 * 60 * 60 * 1000);
```

Next a global variable **today** is created as a new **Date** object, and its **getTime( )** method is called upon to set the cookie's expiration date at 28 days from the value of **today**. To give **bikky** a longer life, you can change the number "28" in line 18 to a higher value; for a shorter span, you can decrease the "28" or tinker with the values in the day-length formula (24 hours times 60 minutes times 60 seconds times 1000 milliseconds).

```
19  function setCookie(name) {
20     document.cookie = eval('"' + name + '="
                           + escape(' + name + ') + "; expires='
                           + expiry.toGMTString() + '"');
21     bikky = document.cookie;
22  }
```

This function, called by **defineCookie( )** in line 32 with **userData** as its **name** argument, uses the JavaScript **eval( )** method to produce a NAME=VALUE pair and **expires** setting for the cookie and assigns it to **bikky**. Omit **eval( )** and **bikky** becomes

```
"userData=" + escape(userData) + "
```

The JavaScript **escape( )** function converts nonalphanumeric characters to "%xx" strings where **xx** is the ASCII code for the character. This hides any forbidden characters (commas, semicolons, or spaces) in the cookie's **value** string. Thus, you can enter a string such as

```
;;; Tyler, Sr.
```

as "Your Name" in the form on this page, and **escape( )** will turn it into an acceptable

```
%3B%3B%3BTyler%2C%20Sr.
```

Furthermore, **unescape( )** will restore the original characters to greet you with "Hello ;;; Tyler, Sr." when you reload the page.

```
23  function blankArray(arrayLength) {
24     this.length = arrayLength;
25     for (var i=0; i < this.length; i++)
```

```
26          this[i] = "";
27  }
```

The next function, **blankArray( )**, creates an empty **Array** object that is instantiated as **data** on line 44. This is exactly the same array constructor we saw in earlier chapters. It creates a **blankArray** object with a **length** property assigned the value of **arrayLength**, then replicates it **arrayLength** times while assigning an empty string to each copy. With JavaScript now providing a built-in **Array** object, this routine is outdated. You can easily upgrade this script by deleting lines 23 through 27, and modifying 44 to read

```
var data = new Array(numVars)
```

without affecting its functionality.

```
28  function defineCookie(newData) {
29      userData = newData[0];
30      for (var i=1; i < newData.length; i++)
31          userData += "!" + newData[i];
32      setCookie("userData");
33  }
```

defineCookie( ) is the function called when you click on the Set Multi-Cookie button. Its argument is the **data** array, which is filled with the user's input by the assignments on lines 83 to 85. Its **for** loop creates a string consisting of the three array values separated by exclamation marks. Here you can eliminate the **for** loop by using the built-in JavaScript **join( )** method, which converts the elements of an array into a string separated by the character used as its argument (or commas if no separator is specified). Thus, you can change line 29 to

```
userData = newData.join('!');
```

and delete lines 30 and 31.

```
35  var userData = getCookie("userData");
36  if (userData == null)
37      userData = "black!Anonymous!0";
38  var numVars = 1;
39  var start = userData.indexOf("!") + 1;
40  while (start != 0) {
41      numVars++;
42      start = userData.indexOf("!", start) + 1;
43  }
```

The sequence of lines extending from lines 35 to 50 runs when the page is loaded. Line 35 looks for the **userData** cookie, and if none is found, assigns it the default string indicated on line 37. Next comes a global variable, **numVars**, which the **while** loop in lines 40 to 43 increments for each exclamation mark found in the **userData** string. When no more exclamation marks are found beyond the starting position of the search indicated by **start**, **indexOf( )** returns –1 and **start** becomes zero (–1 + 1) to terminate the routine.

```
44   var data = new blankArray(numVars);
45   for (var i=0; i < data.length; i++) {
46       var end = userData.indexOf("!", start);
47       if (end == -1) end = userData.length;
48       data[i] = userData.substring(start, end);
49       start = end + 1;
50   }
```

The resulting value of **numVars** then specifies the length of the **data** array created on line 44, which the **for** loop in lines 45 to 50 fills with the three strings separated by exclamation marks. Here, as an alternative, you can eliminate the **for** routine entirely by using the JavaScript counterpart of **join( )**, namely **split( )**. Deleting lines 45 to 50 and replacing line 44 with

```
var data = userData.split('!')
```

will automatically create an array populated with the three substrings in **userData** that are separated by exclamation marks.

```
51   // Stop hiding -->
52   </SCRIPT>
53   </HEAD>
54   <BODY bgcolor="black" text="white" link="yellow"
                              alink="lime" vlink="skyblue"
                      onLoad="document.bgColor=data[0];">
55   <SCRIPT language="JavaScript">
56   <!-- Hide from older browsers
57   userName = data[1];
58   if (userName != null) document.write("Hello "
                                    + userName + " ");
59   document.writeln("<p>");
```

The **onLoad** assignment in line 54 sets the document's background color to the value stored in **data[0]**, which is black by default (line 37). Subsequently it becomes whatever the user specifies in the form's first text field. Line 57 assigns **data[1]** to **userName**, and if its value is not **null**, writes a personal greeting; here the default value is "Anonymous."

```
60   // Stop hiding -->
61   </SCRIPT>
62   <SCRIPT language="JavaScript">
63   <!-- Hide from older browsers
64   headCount = data[2];
65   if (headCount != null) {
```

```
66    document.writeln("<DIV align='center'>");
67    for (var i=0; i < headCount && i != null; i++)
68        document.write("* ");
69  }
70  document.writeln("</DIV><p>");
```

The third member of the array is assigned to **headCount**, whose initial value is 0 because of line 37. After making sure **headCount** exists, line 68 writes the number of asterisks (plus blank space) indicated by the value of **headCount**. The row is put between HTML <DIV> tags and centered by lines 66 and 70.

```
71  // Stop hiding -->
72  </SCRIPT>
73  <FORM name="cookieTest" method="post">
74  <DIV align="center"><TABLE border>
75  <TR><TD><strong>Background: </strong>
76  <TD><INPUT name="data0" type="text" value="black" size="30">
77  <TR><TD><strong>Your Name: </strong>
78  <TD><INPUT name="data1" type="text" value="Anonymous"
                                            size="30">
79  <TR><TD><strong>Head Count: </strong>
80  <TD><INPUT name="data2" type="text" value="10" size="30">
81  <TR><TD align="right" colspan="2"><INPUT type="button"
                            value="Set Multi-Cookie" onClick="
82  with (this.form) {
83    data[0] = data0.value;
84    data[1] = data1.value;
85    data[2] = data2.value;
86  }
87  defineCookie(data);
88  ">
```

Next comes the HTML code that creates the form with its three input areas and button. The **onClick** assignment fills the **data** array with the values entered into the text fields named **data0**, **data1**, and **data2**, then calls **defineCookie( )** with the ensuing array as its argument.

```
89  </TABLE></DIV></FORM><p>
90  </BODY>
91  </HTML>
```

As you may have noticed, there's a great deal of similarity between the cookie-processing functions and those we saw in the preceding chapters on status-bar messages and scrolling banners. Both essentially involve manipulating strings and arrays by assembling and parsing them. The main difference is that, instead of displaying the output, the cookie functions let the browser stash it in COOKIES.TXT. Until the expiry date is reached, the browser can read the output from that file whenever the page is loaded.

counter

Cookie Counter

N2   N2.01   N2.02+   N3   N4   E3   E4

When users revisit a web page, you want their experience to seem as personalized and interactive as possible. That may entice them to come back again and again. With this script, you tell users how many times they have visited the site. This feedback, accomplished by use of cookies, tells the user, "You have been to my site X times before," as soon as the page loads. It is best to place this feedback somewhere in the top section of the web page, where the user is sure to see it.

The number of times your browser has been to this page is stored as a cookie in your browser. The code that puts the cookie there and updates it is embedded right in this page's HTML (see Figure 5-2).

```
1   <html>
2   <head>
3   <title>Cookie counter</title>
4   <script>
5   cookie_name = "Counter_Cookie";
6   function doCookie() {
7     if(document.cookie) {
8         index = document.cookie.indexOf(cookie_name);
9     } else {
10        index = -1;
11    }
12    if (index == -1) {
13        document.cookie=cookie_name+"=1;
                 expires=Tuesday, 01-Apr-1999 08:00:00 GMT";
14    } else {
15        countbegin =
                 (document.cookie.indexOf("=", index) + 1);
16        countend = document.cookie.indexOf(";", index);
17        if (countend == -1) {
18            countend = document.cookie.length;
19        }
20        count = eval(document.cookie.substring(countbegin,
```

```
                                                    countend)) + 1;
21          document.cookie=cookie_name+"="+count+";
                    expires=Tuesday, 01-Apr-1999 08:00:00 GMT";
22      }
23  }
24  function gettimes() {
25      if(document.cookie) {
26          index = document.cookie.indexOf(cookie_name);
27          if (index != -1) {
28              countbegin =
                        (document.cookie.indexOf("=", index) + 1);
29              countend = document.cookie.indexOf(";", index);
30              if (countend == -1) {
31                  countend = document.cookie.length;
32              }
33              count = document.cookie.substring(countbegin,
                                                    countend);
34              if (count == 1) {
35                  return (count+" time");
36              } else {
37                  return (count+" times");
38              }
39          }
40      }
41      return ("0 times");
42  }
43  </script>
44  </head>
45  <body bgcolor="#BCBCBC" onLoad="doCookie()">
46  <h3>Here is a cookie:</h3>
47  <center>
48  <script>
49      document.write("<b>You have been to this page "
                                    +gettimes()+" before.</b>");
50  </script>
51  </center>
52  <p>
53    Go ahead and re-load this page...
                        see how the counter above updates.
54  </body>
55  </html>
```

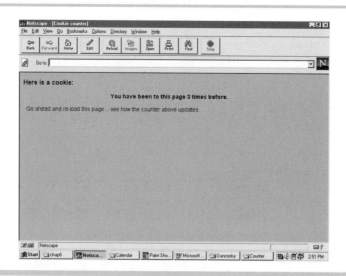

FIGURE 5-2.   Cookie Counter tells users how many times they have visited your site

ANNOTATIONS

This two-function script creates a cookie named **Counter_Cookie** whose value is an integer that keeps track of the number of times you have visited or loaded the page. The cookie is created by the assignment of **doCookie( )** to the **onLoad** event handler in the <BODY> tag, and its value displayed by the call to **gettimes( )** in **document.write( )** on line 49. As functions assigned to **onLoad** only execute after the page has been laid out, no cookie exists the first time that **gettimes( )** is called.

```
1    <html>
2    <head>
3    <title>Cookie counter</title>
4    <script>
5    cookie_name = "Counter_Cookie";
6    function doCookie() {
7        if(document.cookie) {
8            index = document.cookie.indexOf(cookie_name);
9        } else {
10            index = -1;
11        }
```

This script begins by declaring **cookie_name** as a global variable and assigning it the string "**Counter_Cookie**." The first function, which runs when the page is loaded, starts by checking for the existence of a cookie; if it finds one, the new variable **index** is assigned the value of **indexOf(cookie_name)** or zero, because a cookie's name is its first component with the name's first letter at position zero in the **document.cookie** string. If no cookie exists, **index** gets –1.

```
12    if (index == -1) {
13        document.cookie=cookie_name+"=1;
                    expires=Tuesday, 01-Apr-1999 08:00:00 GMT";
14    } else {
15        countbegin =
                    (document.cookie.indexOf("=", index) + 1);
16        countend = document.cookie.indexOf(";", index);
17        if (countend == -1) {
18            countend = document.cookie.length;
19        }
```

In that case, line 13 then creates **Counter_Cookie** with a value of 1 and the specified expiry date. Otherwise, it gets the index of the "=" sign in the cookie and assigns its value plus one to a new variable **countbegin**. In other words, **countbegin** gets the value 15. Next, **countend** is assigned the index of the first semicolon, but because this is not a multiple cookie, it has no semicolon (the semicolon separating the NAME=VALUE pair from **expires** does not count because it is not part of the **document.cookie** property). Therefore **indexOf( )** here returns –1, and line 18 assigns **countend** the **length** of the cookie which ranges from 16 up (depending on the number of digits in the number of times you loaded the page).

```
20        count = eval(document.cookie.substring(countbegin,
                                        countend)) + 1;
21        document.cookie=cookie_name+"="+count+";
                    expires=Tuesday, 01-Apr-1999 08:00:00 GMT";
22    }
23  }
```

Next, line 20 applies **eval( )** to the cookie substring extending from **countbegin** to **countend**, which records the number of times you have visited this page, increments it by one, and assigns the result to the new variable **count**. Here **eval( )** prevents JavaScript from doing string addition of the "1 + 2 = 12" variety. Finally, **doCookie( )** creates an updated cookie with the latest value of **count** and the same expiry date with line 21.

```
24  function gettimes() {
25    if(document.cookie) {
26        index = document.cookie.indexOf(cookie_name);
27        if (index != -1) {
28            countbegin =
                    (document.cookie.indexOf("=", index) + 1);
```

```
29        countend = document.cookie.indexOf(";", index);
30        if (countend == -1) {
31            countend = document.cookie.length;
32        }
33        count = document.cookie.substring(countbegin,
                                            countend);
```

The start of the **gettimes( )** function, which is used to display the cookie's value when the page is written, is identical to portions of **doCookie( )**. The **if** test on lines 25 and 26 is the same as the one on lines 7 and 8, and the routine from lines 28 to 31 mirrors the earlier one in lines 15 to 18. The only difference between line 33 and line 20 is that **eval( )** is unnecessary here, because **count** is simply read and not incremented.

```
34        if (count == 1) {
35            return (count+" time");
36        } else {
37            return (count+" times");
38        }
39    }
40  }
41  return ("0 times");
42 }
```

Finally, the **if/else** routine from lines 34 through 38 returns the value of **count** to **document.write( )** on line 49 along with the appropriate singular or plural string, "time" or "times." On the other hand, if no cookie exists, as is the case the first time the page is loaded, line 41 takes effect and returns "0 times."

```
43 </script>
44 </head>
45 <body bgcolor="#BCBCBC" onLoad="doCookie()">
46 <h3>Here is a cookie:</h3>
47 <center>
48 <script>
49   document.write("<b>You have been to this page "
                                    +gettimes()+" before.</b>");
50 </script>
51 </center>
52 <p>
53   Go ahead and re-load this page...
                                see how the counter above updates.
54 </body>
55 </html>
```

The remainder of the page consists of standard HTML code along with the **onLoad** and **document.write( )** calls to the script's two functions. In view of their similarity, a good exercise would be to try to streamline this script by eliminating the duplicate routines. One approach might be to write a single function that both makes and reads the cookie; another might be to split the common portions into a separate third function. After you have your new **Counter_Cookie=count** cookie working properly, expand it to hold a set of values; then cut those into a batch of separate cookies. If you don't blow a fuse out of frustration, you're likely to emerge from the process with a solid grasp of how to create and parse cookie strings—a thoroughly baked CookieMaster!

Count+

Count+

N2   N2.01   N2.02+   N3   N4   E3   E4

Although we don't want to overdo the visit-count script, this script type is one of the more common and useful examples of JavaScript working with cookies. There are a few more examples worth describing.

A simple "you've been here before" message is nice, but you can take that sort of personal touch a little further. In this example, the script displays some additional information about the user's past activity on the site and personalizes the message (see Figure 5-3).

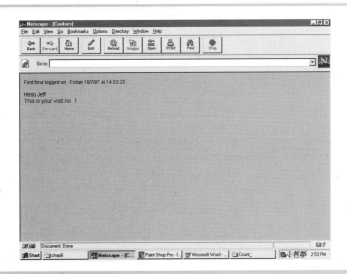

FIGURE 5-3. This script personalizes a message for returning users

The script uses cookies and **document.write( )** to display its message; in this form, you can easily place the entire "hello user" feedback in a separate external window if you like.

The first piece of information about users remembers the first time they logged on to the web page. As the script runs, it pops up a display prompt window asking for the users' name. The users do not have to enter anything, but if they do, the script finishes inserting the text they entered in an onscreen message ("Hello _____, This is your visit no. X").

```
1   <title>Cookies</title>
2   <script language="JavaScript">
3   var lastlogout;
4
5   var now=new Date()
6   var day=now.getDay()
7   if (day==0) day="Sunday   ";
8   else if (day==1) day="Monday   ";
9   else if (day==2) day="Tuesday   ";
10  else if (day==3) day="Wednesday   ";
11  else if (day==4) day="Thursday   ";
12  else if (day==5) day="Friday   ";
13  else if (day==6) day="Saturday ";
14  now=" "+day+" "+now.getDate()+"/"+(now.getMonth()+1)+"/"
        +now.getYear()+" at "+now.getHours()+":"+now.getMinutes()
                                +":"+now.getSeconds()+"</font>"
15  var lastvisit;
16  var username;
17  var guest = "Guest";
18  var expdate = new Date();
19  var visits;
20  pathname = location.pathname;
21  var myDomain =
            pathname.substring(0,pathname.lastIndexOf('/')) +'/';
22  var largeExpDate = new Date();
23  largeExpDate.setTime(largeExpDate.getTime()
                                + (60 * 24 * 3600 * 1000));
24  expdate.setTime(expdate.getTime()
                                +  (24 * 60 * 60 * 1000 * 365));
25
26  function writename() {
27    username = prompt('Please enter your name:',"");
28    if (username == "" )
29    {
```

```
30      alert('It is ok if you want to remain anonymous!');
31       username = guest;
32     }
33     if (username == null )
34     {
35     alert('Oi!');
36     }
37     else
38     {
39     pathname = location.pathname;
40     myDomain =
            pathname.substring(0,pathname.lastIndexOf('/')) +'/';
41     var largeExpDate = new Date ();
42     largeExpDate.setTime(largeExpDate.getTime()
                                    + (60 * 24 * 3600 * 1000));
43     SetCookie('username',username,largeExpDate,myDomain);
44     }
45 }
46
47 function DeleteCookie ()
48 {
49  pathname = location.pathname;
50  myDomain =
            pathname.substring(0,pathname.lastIndexOf('/'))+'/';
51  var largeExpDate = new Date();
52  largeExpDate.setTime(largeExpDate.getTime()
                                   + (60 * 24 * 3600 * -1000));
53  SetCookie('username',"unknown",largeExpDate,myDomain);
54  SetCookie("visits",0, expdate, "/", null, false);
55  SetCookie('last',"none",expdate,myDomain);
56  alert("\nThe Cookie has been deleted.");
57 }
58
59 function getCookieVal (offset)
60 {
61  var endstr = document.cookie.indexOf (";", offset);
62  if (endstr == -1)
63      endstr = document.cookie.length;
64  return unescape(document.cookie.substring(offset, endstr));
65 }
66
67 function GetCookie (name)
```

```
68  {
69   var arg = name + "=";
70   var alen = arg.length;
71   var clen = document.cookie.length;
72   var i = 0;
73   while (i < clen)
74   {
75     var j = i + alen;
76     if (document.cookie.substring(i, j) == arg)
77         return getCookieVal (j);
78     i = document.cookie.indexOf(" ", i) + 1;
79     if (i == 0)
80         break;
81   }
82   return null;
83  }
84
85  function SetCookie (name, value)
86  {
87   var argv = SetCookie.arguments;
88   var argc = SetCookie.arguments.length;
89   var expires = (2 < argc) ? argv[2] : null;
90   var path = (3 < argc) ? argv[3] : null;
91   var domain = (4 < argc) ? argv[4] : null;
92   var secure = (5 < argc) ? argv[5] : false;
93   document.cookie = name + "=" + escape (value) +
94       ((expires == null) ? "" : ("; expires=" + expires)) +
95       ((path == null) ? "" : ("; path=" + path)) +
96       ((domain == null) ? "" : ("; domain=" + domain)) +
97       ((secure == true) ? "; secure" : "");
98  }
99
100 function logoff()
101 {
102  var logofftime= new Date();
103  logofftime="<font color=green>"+logofftime.getHours()+
                           ":"+logofftime.getMinutes()+
                     ":"+logofftime.getSeconds()+"</font>";
104  SetCookie("lastoff",logofftime,largeExpDate,myDomain);
105 }
106
107 if(!(visits = GetCookie("visits")))
```

```
108 visits = 0; visits++;
109 SetCookie("visits", visits, expdate, "/", null, false);
110 if (visits ==1){ var time=" time."}
111 else {var time=" times."}
112 </script>
113 <script language="JavaScript">
114 username = GetCookie('username');
115 if(!(username =  GetCookie('username'))) {writename()}
116 if (username == "" ||username == "unknown") { writename() }
117 if (GetCookie('last')=="none" || GetCookie('last')==null )
118 {
119   newcomer()
120 }
121 else
122 {
123  lastvisit=GetCookie('last')
124  regular()
125 }
126
127 function newcomer()
128 {
129  document.write("<font size=-1>First time logged on  
                                        "+now+"</font><br>");
130  SetCookie("last",now,largeExpDate,myDomain);
131  SetCookie("first",now,largeExpDate,myDomain);
132 }
133 function regular()
134 {
135  var firstvisit=GetCookie('first');
136  lastlogout=GetCookie('lastoff')
137  document.write("User logged in on "+now+"<br>");
138  document.write("Last logged in on  "+ lastvisit);
139  document.write(" until "+lastlogout+" .<br>");
140  document.write("Your first time login on this page was on "
                                    + firstvisit+"</font>");
141  SetCookie("last",now,largeExpDate,myDomain);
142 }
143
144 document.write("<br>Hello "+username+"<BR>");
145 document.write("This is your visit no.
                      "+visits+" </strong></font><br>");
146 </script>
```

ANNOTATIONS

This script uses five cookies—**username**, **last**, **first**, **lastoff**, and **visits**—to store its information. It has a little bug in failing to call the **logoff( )** function that creates the **lastoff** cookie. Hence when you reload the page, the second line reads "Last logged in on [date] at [time] until null." To make the missing cookie, which then replaces "null" with the last logout time, just add

```
onUnload="logoff()"
```

to the page's <BODY> tag.

```
1    <title>Cookies</title>
2    <script language="JavaScript">
3    var lastlogout;
```

The first global variable, **lastlogout**, is used by **regular( )** in lines 136 and 139. Its value is determined by **logoff( )**, so unless the latter function is called as suggested, **lastlogout** retains and displays its initial value of **null**.

```
5    var now=new Date()
6    var day=now.getDay()
7    if (day==0) day="Sunday   ";
8    else if (day==1) day="Monday   ";
9    else if (day==2) day="Tuesday   ";
10   else if (day==3) day="Wednesday   ";
11   else if (day==4) day="Thursday   ";
12   else if (day==5) day="Friday   ";
13   else if (day==6) day="Saturday ";
14   now=" "+day+" "+now.getDate()+"/"+(now.getMonth()+1)+"/"
        +now.getYear()+" at "+now.getHours()+":"+now.getMinutes()
                                +":"+now.getSeconds()+"</font>"
```

The sequence from line 5 to line 14 begins by creating a **Date** object, **now**, which ends up becoming a string used as the value of the **first** and **last** cookies, as well as by the **newcomer( )** and **regular( )** functions to display visit dates and times. The **if** routine in lines 7 through 13 tests the integer returned by **getDay( )** and assigns **day** a string consisting of the corresponding weekday with trailing blanks for spacing purposes. Line 14 then assembles the **now** string, made up of the weekday followed by the date formatted with slash separators, then the time with hours, minutes, and seconds separated by colons. Note the "+1" added to the value of the month; this is essential because the integer returned by **getMonth( )** is based on a count starting from January=0.

When you run this script, you may notice that the minute and second values under ten appear as a single digit. To add a leading zero, insert the following code before line 14:

```
      nowMin = now.getMinutes() < 10  ?
                       '0' + now.getMinutes() : now.getMinutes();
      nowSec = now.getSeconds() < 10  ?
                       '0' + now.getSeconds() : now.getSeconds();
```

Then replace the calls to **getMinutes( )** and **getSeconds( )** in line 14 with these variables:

```
      ... ":" + nowMin + ":" + nowSec + ...
```

If you do this, you might also want to add a similar formatting routine to this script's **logoff( )** function.

```
15  var lastvisit;
16  var username;
17  var guest = "Guest";
18  var expdate = new Date();
19  var visits;
20  pathname = location.pathname;
21  var myDomain =
            pathname.substring(0,pathname.lastIndexOf('/')) +'/';
22  var largeExpDate = new Date();
23  largeExpDate.setTime(largeExpDate.getTime()
                                + (60 * 24 * 3600 * 1000));
24  expdate.setTime(expdate.getTime()
                             +  (24 * 60 * 60 * 1000 * 365));
```

This next batch of code declares several global variables and also creates two **Date** objects before calling their **setTime( )** methods. All these variables and values will eventually serve to provide the NAME=VALUE, PATH, and EXPIRES components when this script creates its cookies.

lastvisit, for instance, is assigned the **last** cookie in line 123 before serving in **regular( )** on line 138 to display the date and time of the last visit. **username** and **guest** are used by **writename( )** later, while **visits** ends up keeping track of the number of your visits to this page.

location.pathname in line 20 is a built-in JavaScript property that returns the current page's URL string. Next, **myDomain** gets the substring ending at the character preceding the last slash in **pathname** plus an appended slash. Instead of appending a final slash, you can grab the one in the original URL string by assigning **myDomain** a substring that is one character longer with

```
      pathname.substring(0,pathname.lastIndexOf('/') + 1);
```

The two **Date** objects, **expdate** and **largeExpDate**, are misnamed in that line 23 assigns the latter a date 60 days after the value returned by **getTime( )**, whereas **expdate** gets a date 365 days away. You might want to reverse either the names or values to avoid confusion.

Note that the values assigned to both these variables end up formatted as local time, and not GMT as specified—yet the cookies nonetheless work. Display the value of **expdate** and you'll see something like "Tue Jul 14 14:00:18 EDT 1998." This also explains why this script displays local time even though it has no GMT-conversion function.

```
26   function writename() {
27     username = prompt('Please enter your name:',"");
28     if (username == "" )
29     {
30       alert('It is ok if you want to remain anonymous!');
31       username = guest;
32     }
33     if (username == null )
34     {
35     alert('Oi!');
36     }
```

Our script's first function, **writename( )**, runs when this page is loaded because of the calls on lines 115 and 116. It begins by prompting for your name. If you enter a name in the prompt's text field, the string you enter is assigned to **username**. But if you click on OK without entering a name, **username** gets "Guest," the string assigned to **guest** in line 17. Click on the prompt box's CANCEL button, however, and you'll see the 'Oi!' alert and be greeted with "Hello null." In this case no **username** cookie is created, so the next time you reload the page, the prompt box will reappear.

```
37     else
38     {
39     pathname = location.pathname;
40     myDomain =
               pathname.substring(0,pathname.lastIndexOf('/')) +'/';
41     var largeExpDate = new Date ();
42     largeExpDate.setTime(largeExpDate.getTime()
                                     + (60 * 24 * 3600 * 1000));
43     SetCookie('username',username,largeExpDate,myDomain);
44     }
45   }
```

The **else** routine then creates the **username** cookie in line 43 with the call to **SetCookie( )**, whose arguments represent the NAME, VALUE, EXPIRES, and PATH attributes attached to the cookie. Lines 39 to 42 are nearly identical to lines 20 to 23. As the scope of the latter is global, you can safely delete these four lines from this function.

```
47  function DeleteCookie ()
48  {
49   pathname = location.pathname;
50   myDomain =
              pathname.substring(0,pathname.lastIndexOf('/'))+'/';
51   var largeExpDate = new Date();
52   largeExpDate.setTime(largeExpDate.getTime()
                                   + (60 * 24 * 3600 * -1000));
53   SetCookie('username',"unknown",largeExpDate,myDomain);
54   SetCookie("visits",0, expdate, "/", null, false);
55   SetCookie('last',"none",expdate,myDomain);
56   alert("\nThe Cookie has been deleted.");
57  }
```

The next function, **DeleteCookie( )**, is not used by this script, but serves as an example of how to delete a cookie. You can easily put it to work by adding a button to the page and attaching this function to its event handler. As you may suspect from a close look at the code, however, it does not delete all the cookies.

Here again lines 49 to 51 are unnecessary as they merely echo the global lines 20 to 22. Yet while line 52 closely resembles line 23, it is vital to this function because it assigns **largeExpDate** a date 60 days in the past. Attaching the resulting value to the EXPIRES attribute of the **username** cookie through **SetCookie( )**'s third argument in line 53 effectively destroys that cookie by creating an "anticookie," which overwrites the original. For this to happen, however, the anticookie's PATH specification must be exactly the same as in the original cookie. Set a different path and all you do is create an instantly vanishing second cookie instead of one that destroys the original by overwriting it.

Although lines 54 and 55 set the value of **visits** to 0 and **last** to "none," these two cookies are not deleted, because **expdate** retains its original global value of 365 days from the moment **getTime( )** is called in line 24. To have this function also destroy the **visits** and **last** cookies, just replace both **expdate** arguments with the now negative **largeExpDate**.

In using this technique for destroying a cookie, what you use as the second (VALUE) argument is really irrelevant because the expired EXPIRES date makes the cookie crumble immediately upon creation. For good measure, however, you can use **null** or an empty string ("") as the second argument.

An easy way to monitor the current values of the cookies and their destruction is to add a text area to this page to serve as an output field along with a button to display the cookies. Assuming the form is named **outform** and the text area **output**, the code for the button's event handler would be

```
onClick="document.outform.output.value = document.cookie"
```

This will display the **username**, **last**, **first**, and **visits** cookies when clicked after loading the page for the first time. Then if you've assigned the **logoff( )** function to this page's **onUnload** event handler as suggested earlier, the **lastoff** cookie will also appear when you click the button after reloading the page.

If you've also added a button to use **DeleteCookie( )**, click on it and then on your display-cookie button to see which ones remain. Unless you've already done so, you'll have to add two more **SetCookie( )** lines with negative expiry dates to **DeleteCookie( )** to get rid of **first** and **lastoff**.

Here you'll also run into a minor snag. Although **lastoff** will effectively be deleted, the **onUnload** call will re-create it when the page is unloaded. To stop this from happening, you can create a Boolean flag by declaring, for example,

```
var delCookie = false;
```

as a global variable, and having **DeleteCookie( )** set it to **true** by adding

```
delCookie = true;
```

as the last line to the function. Then just make **logoff( )** subject to the value of **delCookie** being false by inserting

```
if (!delCookie) {
```

after line 101 and adding a closing brace after line 104. This stops **logoff( )** from running if the delete-cookie function has been run.

```
59    function getCookieVal (offset)
60    {
61     var endstr = document.cookie.indexOf (";", offset);
62     if (endstr == -1)
63         endstr = document.cookie.length;
64     return unescape(document.cookie.substring(offset, endstr));
65    }
```

getCookieVal( ) is an original Dortch function called by **GetCookie( )** in line 77 to read a cookie's VALUE attribute. It assigns **endstr** the integer indicating the position of the first semicolon to the right of the position specified by **offset**. If the resulting value of **endstr** is –1 because no semicolon is found, **endstr** gets the length of the cookie string and **getCookieVal** returns the unescaped substring extending from **offset** to the end of the string. As **GetCookie( )** in line 75 makes **offset** the first position after the "=" following the cookie's name, **getCookieVal( )** returns the value segment of the cookie string. In other words, with a cookie such as **username=Coyote**, the call to **getCookieVal( )** in **GetCookie("username")** will return "Coyote."

```
67    function GetCookie (name)
68    {
69     var arg = name + "=";
70     var alen = arg.length;
71     var clen = document.cookie.length;
72     var i = 0;
```

GetCookie( ) is another original Dortch function that does exactly what its name implies—it gets the cookie specified by its sole argument, **name**, and returns either the value portion of the string or **null** if no cookie with that name exists. First a local variable, **arg**, is assigned a string consisting of the cookie's name with "=" appended. A second local variable, **alen**, gets the length of the resulting string, and a third, **clen**, the length of the cookie string to be used as a control. The final local variable, **i**, serves as a control in the subsequent **while** routine.

```
73   while (i < clen)
74   {
75     var j = i + alen;
76     if (document.cookie.substring(i, j) == arg)
77         return getCookieVal (j);
78     i = document.cookie.indexOf(" ", i) + 1;
79     if (i == 0)
80         break;
81   }
82   return null;
83   }
```

The **while** first makes sure that **clen** is greater than **i**, which has been assigned 0—in other words, that the cookie's length is greater than zero. It then assigns a new local variable, **j**, the value of **i** plus **alen**. If the cookie substring extending from position 0 to **j** matches the **arg** string (cookie's name with "=" appended), it calls **getCookieVal( )** with **j** as its **offset** argument.

It then assigns **i** the value of the index of a blank space in the cookie string. As (unescaped) blanks in cookies are prohibited, **indexOf(' ')** will here return −1. Adding +1 to it makes **i**'s value 0, so that the next **if** test succeeds, and the **break** instruction terminates the **while** loop.

```
85   function SetCookie (name, value)
86   {
87     var argv = SetCookie.arguments;
88     var argc = SetCookie.arguments.length;
89     var expires = (2 < argc) ? argv[2] : null;
90     var path = (3 < argc) ? argv[3] : null;
91     var domain = (4 < argc) ? argv[4] : null;
92     var secure = (5 < argc) ? argv[5] : false;
```

This **SetCookie( )** is a variation of the original Dortch function. Whereas the latter is written with all six cookie attributes as arguments, this version only takes two, but can accommodate the other four.

The assignment in line 87 effectively converts the arguments passed to **SetCookie( )** into an array named **argv**, whose length is next assigned to **argc**. Line 88 is equivalent to writing

```
        var argc = argv.length
```

Lines 89 to 92 then test whether more arguments than **name** and **value** have been passed to **SetCookie( )** and create a set of local variables representing cookie attributes which are assigned either the value specified by the argument or **null** (**false** in the case of **secure**).

```
93   document.cookie = name + "=" + escape (value) +
94       ((expires == null) ? "" : ("; expires=" + expires)) +
95       ((path == null) ? "" : ("; path=" + path)) +
96       ((domain == null) ? "" : ("; domain=" + domain)) +
97       ((secure == true) ? "; secure" : "");
98   }
```

Lines 93 to 97 then create the cookie by assembling a string consisting of the specified **name** followed by "=" and the escaped **value**, plus the appropriate strings for the EXPIRES, PATH, DOMAIN, and SECURE attributes if any values for them have been passed as arguments to **SetCookie( )**.

```
100  function logoff()
101  {
102   var logofftime= new Date();
103   logofftime="<font color=green>"+logofftime.getHours()+
                          ":"+logofftime.getMinutes()+
                     ":"+logofftime.getSeconds()+"</font>";
104   SetCookie("lastoff",logofftime,largeExpDate,myDomain);
105  }
```

This **logoff( )** function, as mentioned, is not called anywhere in this script, and the best way to make it operative is to assign it to an **onUnload** event handler in the <BODY> tag. It creates a new **Date** object named **logofftime** and assigns it a string consisting of the hours, minutes, and seconds values separated by colons and displayed in green. Here again you might wish to insert the formatting routine described earlier to add leading zeros to minute and second values under ten. **logoff( )** ends with a call to **SetCookie( )** that creates the **lastoff** cookie, which records the time you log off this page.

```
107  if(!(visits = GetCookie("visits")))
108  visits = 0; visits++;
109  SetCookie("visits", visits, expdate, "/", null, false);
110  if (visits ==1){ var time=" time."}
111  else {var time=" times."}
112  </script>
```

Lines 107 to 109 automatically create and update the **visits** cookie whenever this page is loaded. The **if** first tests for the presence of a **visits** cookie. If none is found, the variable **visits** is set to 0 and immediately incremented to 1. This integer then becomes the second (**value**) argument in the call to **SetCookie( )**. Otherwise, if the **visits** cookie is found, its value as obtained by the call to **GetCookie( )** in line 107 is incremented by the second statement in line 108, and an updated **visits** cookie is created. Finally, lines 110 and 111 declare a new variable, **time**, which is assigned the appropriate grammatical string for the value of **visits**. Although this **time** variable is not used by any of the **document.write( )** calls that create the text on this page, with it you can easily change the message displayed by line 145 to

```
"You have visited this site " + visits + time
```

It is important to note that using "/" as the PATH setting for the **visits** cookie makes it ubiquitous. As a result, it can sometimes interfere with other scripts, as you'll see in the annotations to the next script. It becomes a sort of free-floating barnacle clinging to every other cookie. To observe this **visits** cookie popping up elsewhere, create a page containing just a text field, and with a <BODY> tag along the lines of

```
onLoad="document.outform.output.value=unescape(document.cookie)"
```

where **outform** and **output** represent whatever names you give your form and text field. Then save the page in any directory other than the one containing COUNT_.HTM. When you load it, the text field should display "visits=x" where "x" is the number of times you loaded COUNT_.HTM. Even if you give your new page its own cookie with, for example,

```
document.cookie="newcookie=" + escape("This is my cookie!")
```

and reload the result, you'll see

```
newcookie=This is my cookie!; visits=x
```

in the text field. On the other hand, put this new page in the same directory as COUNT_.HTM, and its text field will display all of the latter's cookies, because now both pages lie in exactly the same path.

```
113 <script language="JavaScript">
114 username = GetCookie('username');
115 if(!(username =  GetCookie('username'))) {writename()}
116 if (username == "" ||username == "unknown") { writename() }
117 if (GetCookie('last')=="none" || GetCookie('last')==null )
118 {
119   newcomer()
120 }
121 else
```

```
122 {
123   lastvisit=GetCookie('last')
124   regular()
125 }
```

Lines 114 to 125 contain the remainder of the process that runs when this page is loaded. There is no need to embed these lines in a separate script as they are here. First the **username** variable is assigned the **username** cookie's value through the call to **GetCookie( )**. If no **username** cookie is found, or if its value is an empty string or "unknown," the call to **writename( )** launches the dialog box that prompts for a name.

Next the script looks for the **last** cookie, which records the date and time of your last visit to this page. If its value is **null** or "none," the **newcomer( )** function next is run; otherwise, the value of the **last** cookie is assigned to the **lastvisit** variable and **regular( )** is called.

```
127 function newcomer()
128 {
129   document.write("<font size=-1>First time logged on  
                                  "+now+"</font><br>");
130   SetCookie("last",now,largeExpDate,myDomain);
131   SetCookie("first",now,largeExpDate,myDomain);
132 }
```

newcomer( ) writes the message that appears the first time you load this page and displays the **now** string assembled back in line 14. It then creates the **last** and **first** cookies with **now** as their values, **largeExpDate** as the EXPIRES setting, and **myDomain** as PATH.

```
133 function regular()
134 {
135   var firstvisit=GetCookie('first');
136   lastlogout=GetCookie('lastoff')
137   document.write("User logged in on "+now+"<br>");
138   document.write("Last logged in on  "+ lastvisit);
139   document.write(" until "+lastlogout+" .<br>");
140   document.write("Your first time login on this page was on "
                                  + firstvisit+"</font>");
141   SetCookie("last",now,largeExpDate,myDomain);
142 }
```

On your second and subsequent visits to this page, **regular( )** first assigns the values of the **first** and **lastoff** cookies to the **firstvisit** and **lastlogout** variables. It then uses those two variables along with the **now** string and **lastvisit**, which on line 123 got the value of the **last** cookie, to write its message. Finally, it creates a new **last** cookie with the current value of **now** to store the date and time of your visit.

As mentioned earlier, line 136 will not do anything, and line 139 will produce "until null" unless you modify this script so that it calls **logoff( )**, which creates the **lastoff** cookie.

```
144 document.write("<br>Hello "+username+"<BR>");
145 document.write("This is your visit no.
                       "+visits+" </strong></font><br>");
146 </script>
```

The last two **document.write( )**s create the page run whether you're a first-time or repeat visitor to the page. The first uses the value of **username** for a personal greeting, and the second displays how often you have loaded the page as recorded by the value of the **visits** cookie.

Separate cookies are undoubtedly the easiest way to store different items of information for use by your page. All you need is a script capable of setting and reading the various NAME=VALUE pairs, and of adding expiry dates if you want the cookies to last beyond a single browser session. The main drawback of this approach is that you may soon run into the 20-cookie ceiling. The solution then is to pack more data into each cookie. The Personal Information Form script later in this chapter demonstrates precisely how to do that.

visit

Visit Record

N2 N2.01 N2.02+ N3 N4 E3 E4

Both Windows versions (and possibly others) freeze the first time this page is loaded if the preceding script, COUNT_.HTM, has been run and has written its ubiquitous cookie, or if any other cookie lies in its path. For a detailed explanation, see the annotation to line 87 (the culprit) next.

This script works with cookies to remember the last time you visited (see Figure 5-4). Reload the page to see the time of this visit. This idea could be extended to loading only material new to this user, as well as loading or not loading parts of a page based on preferences set by users on a previous visit.

FIGURE 5-4. This script works with cookies to keep track of the last time
you visited

A cookie is used to record the time of a visit. The record of the user's last visit
disappears in about 30 days, so you don't get stale cookies. JavaScript **Date**
functions act up in weird ways on various platforms, and the author developed this
script on the Macintosh.

```
1   <HTML>
2   <HEAD>
3   <SCRIPT LANGUAGE="JavaScript">
4   <!-- to hide script contents from old browsers
5   //
6   //Cookie Functions
7   //Written by:  Bill Dortch, hIdaho Design
8   //The following functions are released to the public domain.
9
10  function encode (str) {
11    var dest = "";
12    var len = str.length;
13    var index = 0;
14    var code = null;
15    for (var i = 0; i < len; i++) {
16      var ch = str.charAt(i);
17      if (ch == " ") code = "%20";
```

```
18      else if (ch == "%") code = "%25";
19      else if (ch == ",") code = "%2C";
20      else if (ch == ";") code = "%3B";
21      else if (ch == "\b") code = "%08";
22      else if (ch == "\t") code = "%09";
23      else if (ch == "\n") code = "%0A";
24      else if (ch == "\f") code = "%0C";
25      else if (ch == "\r") code = "%0D";
26      if (code != null) {
27        dest += str.substring(index,i) + code;
28        index = i + 1;
29        code = null;
30      }
31    }
32    if (index < len)
33      dest += str.substring(index, len);
34    return dest;
35  }
36
37  function decode (str) {
38    var dest = "";
39    var len = str.length;
40    var index = 0;
41    var code = null;
42    var i = 0;
43    while (i < len) {
44      i = str.indexOf ("%", i);
45      if (i == -1)
46        break;
47      if (index < i)
48        dest += str.substring(index, i);
49      code = str.substring (i+1,i+3);
50      i += 3;
51      index = i;
52      if (code == "20") dest += " ";
53      else if (code == "25") dest += "%";
54      else if (code == "2C") dest += ",";
55      else if (code == "3B") dest += ";";
56      else if (code == "08") dest += "\b";
57      else if (code == "09") dest += "\t";
58      else if (code == "0A") dest += "\n";
59      else if (code == "0C") dest += "\f";
60      else if (code == "0D") dest += "\r";
```

```
61      else {
62        i -= 2;
63        index -= 3;
64      }
65    }
66    if (index < len)
67      dest += str.substring(index, len);
68    return dest;
69  }
70
71  function getCookieVal (offset) {
72    var endstr = document.cookie.indexOf (";", offset);
73    if (endstr == -1)
74      endstr = document.cookie.length;
75    return decode(document.cookie.substring(offset, endstr));
76  }
77
78  function GetCookie (name) {
79    var arg = name + "=";
80    var alen = arg.length;
81    var clen = document.cookie.length;
82    var i = 0;
83    while (i < clen) {
84      var j = i + alen;
85      if (document.cookie.substring(i, j) == arg)
86        return getCookieVal (j);
87      i = document.cookie.indexOf(" ", i) + 2;
88      if (i == 0) break;
89    }
90    return null;
91  }
92
93  function SetCookie (name, value, expires) {
94    document.cookie = name + "=" + encode(value)
            + ((expires == null) ?
                    "" : ("; expires=" + expires.toString()));
95  }
96
97  function setLastVisitCookie()
98  {
99  var nowDate = new Date()
100 var expdate = new Date()
101 expdate.setTime (expdate.getTime()
```

```
                                    + 30*(24 * 60 * 60 * 1000))
102  SetCookie ("Last_Visit", nowDate.toGMTString(), expdate)
103  }
104  // --> <!-- end hiding contents from old browsers  -->
105  </SCRIPT>
106  <TITLE>Your Last Visit
107  </TITLE>
108  </HEAD>
109  <BODY onLoad="setLastVisitCookie()">
110  <CENTER>
111  <H1>Your Last Visit</H1>
112  <HR>
113  <SCRIPT LANGUAGE="JavaScript">
114  <!--  to hide script contents from old browsers
115  var lastVisit = GetCookie("Last_Visit")
116  var htmlOut = ""
117  if (lastVisit == null) {
118      htmlOut += "No record of you visiting in last 30 days."
119  } else {
120    htmlOut += "Your last visit was " +
                                    lastVisit.substring(0,25)
121  }
122  document.write("<H3>")
123  document.write(htmlOut.bold().fontcolor("red"))
124  document.write("</H3>")
125  // --> <!-- end hiding contents from old browsers  -->
126  </SCRIPT>
127  </CENTER>
128  <p>
129  </BODY>
130  </HTML>
```

ANNOTATIONS

This script creates a 30-day **Last_Visit** cookie to store the date and time whenever you load this page and displays its value or, if no cookie is found, a "No record of your visit" message. Although the display is formatted as GMT, a couple extra lines of code are all it takes to convert the value to local time.

Much of the script consists of Dortch functions, two of which, **encode( )** and **decode( )**, have become obsolete with the addition of **escape( )** and **unescape( )** to JavaScript methods. Although superseded in this context, the pair of coding functions serves as a neat model of how to encode and decode a string that can be applied in a variety of circumstances.

```
1   <HTML>
2   <HEAD>
3   <SCRIPT LANGUAGE="JavaScript">
4   <!-- to hide script contents from old browsers
5   //
6   //Cookie Functions
7   //Written by:  Bill Dortch, hIdaho Design
8   //The following functions are released to the public domain.
9
10  function encode (str) {
11     var dest = "";
12     var len = str.length;
13     var index = 0;
14     var code = null;
```

encode( ), called by **SetCookie( )** in line 94, takes a single argument, namely the string to be encoded. The function begins by declaring a set of local variables: **dest**, which will hold the encoded version of the string; **len**, the length of the input string; **index**, which serves as a position marker within the string; and **code**, which carries the code string for each character converted to "%xx" format. The encoded characters are those prohibited by cookie specifications—commas, semicolons, and blank spaces, including all the standard escape sequences (backspace, tab, newline, formfeed, and return) considered white space—plus the percentage sign, because it serves as the signal that a hexadecimal code follows.

```
15    for (var i = 0; i < len; i++) {
16      var ch = str.charAt(i);
17      if (ch == " ") code = "%20";
18      else if (ch == "%") code = "%25";
19      else if (ch == ",") code = "%2C";
20      else if (ch == ";") code = "%3B";
21      else if (ch == "\b") code = "%08";
22      else if (ch == "\t") code = "%09";
23      else if (ch == "\n") code = "%0A";
24      else if (ch == "\f") code = "%0C";
25      else if (ch == "\r") code = "%0D";
```

The **for** loop uses a new local variable, **ch**, to read the character at the position of the **index** specified by i. Then the **if/else if** sequence tests for the specified values of **ch** and assigns the corresponding code string to **code**.

```
26      if (code != null) {
27        dest += str.substring(index,i) + code;
```

```
28          index = i + 1;
29          code = null;
30       }
31    }
```

Whenever a character has been encoded, the **dest** string is incremented by the **substring** leading up to the encoded character plus the **code** string. Then the value of **index** is advanced to the position of the next character following the one that has just been encoded, and **code** is reinitialized to **null**.

```
32    if (index < len)
33       dest += str.substring(index, len);
34    return dest;
35 }
```

The final **if** routine serves to tag on any characters between the final encoded character and the end of the input string by testing the value of **index** against **len** and attaching the remaining substring to **dest**, then returning the latter to **SetCookie( )**.

```
37 function decode (str) {
38    var dest = "";
39    var len = str.length;
40    var index = 0;
41    var code = null;
42    var i = 0;
43    while (i < len) {
44       i = str.indexOf ("%", i);
45       if (i == -1)
46          break;
47       if (index < i)
48          dest += str.substring(index, i);
49       code = str.substring (i+1,i+3);
50       i += 3;
51       index = i;
```

Like its counterpart, **decode( )** takes the string to be processed as its sole argument. The function is called by **getCookieVal( )** and sets out declaring the same first four local variables as **encode( )**. The fifth, **i**, is used to find the percentage signs that indicate a two-digit hexadecimal code follows. In line 44, **i** gets the index of the next "%" in **str** after the position marked by the value of **i**. If **indexOf( )** returns –1 because no "%" is found, the **while** loop terminates. Otherwise **dest**, the output string, gets the substring leading up to the code marker, and **code** is assigned the three-character "%xx" string. Finally, lines 50 and 51 advance the values of **index** and **i** to the first position beyond the code sequence.

```
52    if (code == "20") dest += " ";
53    else if (code == "25") dest += "%";
54    else if (code == "2C") dest += ",";
55    else if (code == "3B") dest += ";";
56    else if (code == "08") dest += "\b";
57    else if (code == "09") dest += "\t";
58    else if (code == "0A") dest += "\n";
59    else if (code == "0C") dest += "\f";
60    else if (code == "0D") dest += "\r";
61    else {
62      i -= 2;
63      index -= 3;
64    }
65  }
```

Next the **if** tests convert any of the nine specified characters encountered back into their original form by appending the appropriate character or escape sequence to **dest**. Otherwise the catchall **else** instruction rolls back the values of **i** and **index**, which were incremented in lines 50 and 51, so that **index** is one less than **i**.

```
66  if (index < len)
67    dest += str.substring(index, len);
68  return dest;
69 }
```

decode( ) ends in exactly the same way as **encode( )**, with a routine that tags on any characters between the last decoded one and the end of **str** before returning **dest**.

If you wish, you can do away with the preceding **encode( )** and **decode( )** functions just by changing the word "decode" in line 75 to "unescape" and "encode" in line 94 to "escape." The more recent version of the Dortch functions included on the accompanying CD-ROM does just that.

```
71 function getCookieVal (offset) {
72   var endstr = document.cookie.indexOf (";", offset);
73   if (endstr == -1)
74     endstr = document.cookie.length;
75   return decode(document.cookie.substring(offset, endstr));
76 }
```

getCookieVal( ), also a Dortch function, is identical to the version we saw in the preceding script, COUNT_.HTM, apart from its use of "decode" instead of "unescape" in line 75. Its sole argument, **offset**, marks the start of the cookie's VALUE string, which it returns in decoded form.

```
78 function GetCookie (name) {
79   var arg = name + "=";
80   var alen = arg.length;
```

```
81    var clen = document.cookie.length;
82    var i = 0;
83    while (i < clen) {
84      var j = i + alen;
85      if (document.cookie.substring(i, j) == arg)
86        return getCookieVal (j);
87      i = document.cookie.indexOf(" ", i) + 2;
88      if (i == 0) break;
89    }
90    return null;
91  }
```

This too is the same Dortch function we saw in COUNT_.HTM with one exception: line 87, where we now have "+ 2" instead of "+ 1." This modification causes Navigator 3 in Windows (both 95 and 3.*x*), and possibly on other platforms, to freeze the first time this page is loaded if any other cookie (such as the ubiquitous **visits** created by COUNT_.HTM) lies in its path.

This happens because **clen** is expected to have a value of zero the first time this page is loaded, so the **while** routine is bypassed and **GetCookie( )** returns **null**. But if there's a ubiquitous cookie lying around, **clen** will get the value of its length—for example, 9 if the cookie reads "visits=23." This traps Navigator 3 in an infinite **while** loop because line 87 sets the value of **i** to 1 and the **break** instruction in line 88 never takes effect. Change the "+ 2" back to "+ 1," however, and you eliminate the bug completely. Now line 87 will do exactly what it was intended to, namely set **i** to 0 because **indexOf( )** is expected to return –1, as a cookie should not contain the blank space it looks for.

Other Navigator versions don't grab the foreign cookie, so **clen** is zero the first time around and the **while** routine is skipped.

```
93  function SetCookie (name, value, expires) {
94    document.cookie = name + "=" + encode(value)
           + ((expires == null) ?
                    "" : ("; expires=" + expires.toString())));
95  }
```

Next, **SetCookie( )** is an abbreviated Dortch function in that it only accommodates three arguments instead of the six in the original version. It assembles the cookie as a string consisting of its **name**, encoded **value**, and expiry attribute if any. The function also differs from the Dortch version at the end of line 94, where it applies the **toString( )** instead of the original **toGMTString( )** method to **expires**. Again, this violates the specifications but still produces a functioning cookie.

```
97  function setLastVisitCookie()
98  {
```

```
99   var nowDate = new Date()
100  var expdate = new Date()
101  expdate.setTime (expdate.getTime()
                                    + 30*(24 * 60 * 60 * 1000))
102  SetCookie ("Last_Visit", nowDate.toGMTString(), expdate)
103  }
```

This script's main function, **setLastVisitCookie( )**, is called by the **onLoad** event handler in the <BODY> tag. It creates two **Date** objects as local variables: **nowDate**, which becomes the cookie's value string when passed to **SetCookie( )** in the format returned by **toGMTString( )**, and **expdate**, which in line 101 gets a value 30 days from the time the page is loaded and then serves as **SetCookie**'s **expires** argument.

```
104  // --> <!-- end hiding contents from old browsers  -->
105  </SCRIPT>
106  <TITLE>Your Last Visit
107  </TITLE>
108  </HEAD>
109  <BODY onLoad="setLastVisitCookie()">
110  <CENTER>
111  <H1>Your Last Visit</H1>
112  <HR>
113  <SCRIPT LANGUAGE="JavaScript">
114  <!--  to hide script contents from old browsers
115  var lastVisit = GetCookie("Last_Visit")
116  var htmlOut = ""
117  if (lastVisit == null) {
118       htmlOut += "No record of you visiting in last 30 days."
119  } else {
120     htmlOut += "Your last visit was " +
                                       lastVisit.substring(0,25)
121  }
122  document.write("<H3>")
123  document.write(htmlOut.bold().fontcolor("red"))
124  document.write("</H3>")
```

This script runs and writes the page as it is loaded; it executes before the call to **setLastVisitCookie( )** in the <BODY> tag. It assigns a new global variable, **lastVisit**, the cookie value string returned by **GetCookie( )** and initializes **htmlOut**, another new global that serves as the carrier for the displayed text, as an empty string.

If **GetCookie( )** returns **null** because no **Last_Visit** cookie is found, **htmlOut** gets the "No record" message. Otherwise, it is assigned the "Your last visit" message plus the first 25 characters of **Last_Visit**'s value string—the **substring( )** method here cuts off the final "GMT."

Perhaps the easiest way to make this script display local time instead of GMT is to insert

`lv = new Date(lastVisit);`

between lines 119 and 120, then change the end of 120 to read

`+ lv.toLocaleString()`

For fancier formatting, you could adapt the date-formatting routine at the beginning of COUNT_.HTM while using the JavaScript **getTimezoneOffset( )** method and some simple math for the conversion to local time.

```
125 // --> <!-- end hiding contents from old browsers  -->
126 </SCRIPT>
127 </CENTER>
128 <p>
129 </BODY>
130 </HTML>
```

With a relatively simple script such as this, don't let what it actually does limit your perception of its potential for adaptation. Its simplicity, in fact, makes it more readily adaptable. Although the cookie's value here is a date, it could easily become any other item of visitor-related information you might want to display on your page for a personal touch. Nor does the value have to be incorporated into the text. It can be used behind the scenes, such as in a function that takes a visitor immediately to a specific page within your site, or one that sets the background and foreground colors to their preferences. As we'll see in the next script, you can fill a cookie with all kinds of data.

Personal Information Form

persform

[N2] [N2.01] [N2.02+] [N3] [N4] [E3] [E4]

When it comes to ordering products or providing web sites with personal information, most web surfers can recall a negative experience: they filled out a form to order pizza, or requested a librar_y book, only to have all their personal data—name, phone number, address, and e-mail—blank the next time they needed to use the form.

On a web site, maintaining state means your users can be considered unique or special. You can program your pages to load certain features based on user preference, or present them with a form (such as an order form) that will keep track of what they want to buy.

This script uses a form that remembers all fields marked with a "*" for six months from the time users submit the form (see Figure 5-5). You may leave the "*" in most of the text fields or edit it out, it doesn't matter. The e-mail field must be exact, though.

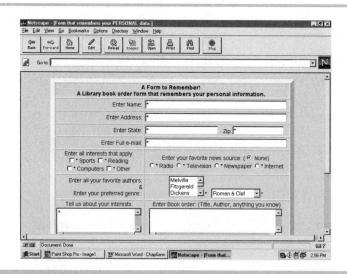

FIGURE 5-5. A sample form that "remembers" information about your users

Edit out the "*" and enter your exact e-mail address so this form can send you a copy. You may extend the expiration six months from the current date, and save any changes to the "*" fields by pressing the "Save Changes and Set New Expiration" button. It only sends a request to a dummy test account and a copy to you (if you filled in your e-mail correctly).

```
1   <html><head>
2   <title>Form that remembers your PERSONAL data.</title>
3   <script language="javascript">
4   <!-- begin script
5   // JavaScript to save Personal Form data for recall on next
6   // use. 3-Mar-1996 Copyright (C) 1996 by Geoff Inglis.
7   //  You may use these routines in your pages (commercial or
8   //  noncommercial) as long as you include these four lines.
9   //  You may not Re-sell this code. Questions
10  //  (or if you use this code) email: inglis@axsnet.com
11  //\/\/\/\/\/\/\/\/\   ** Here is the CookieName */\/\/\/\/\/\/\
12  TheCookieName = 'BigCookieinthesky';
```

```
13  numDays      = 183;
14
15  function WriteOneBigCookie () {
16     var expire = new Date ();
17     expire.setTime (expire.getTime()
                                + (numDays * 24 * 3600000));
18     var WholeCookie = expire ;
19     WholeCookie = WholeCookie + '`' +
                  checknull(document.TestForm.Entry1.value);
21     WholeCookie = WholeCookie + '`' +
                  checknull(document.TestForm.Entry2.value);
22     WholeCookie = WholeCookie + '`' +
                  checknull(document.TestForm.Entry2b.value);
23     WholeCookie = WholeCookie + '`' +
                  checknull(document.TestForm.Entry2c.value);
24     WholeCookie = WholeCookie + '`' +
                  checknull(document.TestForm.Emailadd.value);
25     WholeCookie = WholeCookie + '`' +
                     document.TestForm.Entry4.checked;
26     WholeCookie = WholeCookie + '`' +
                     document.TestForm.Entry5.checked;
27     WholeCookie = WholeCookie + '`' +
                     document.TestForm.Entry6.checked;
28     WholeCookie = WholeCookie + '`' +
                     document.TestForm.Entry7.checked;
29     WholeCookie = WholeCookie + '`' +
                     setChkIndx(document.TestForm.Entry8);
30     WholeCookie = WholeCookie + '`' +
                     document.TestForm.Entry9.selectedIndex;
31     WholeCookie = WholeCookie + '`' +
                     findChkIndx_MS(document.TestForm.Entry10);
32     WholeCookie = WholeCookie + '`' +
                  checknull(document.TestForm.Entry11.value);
33     document.cookie = TheCookieName +"=" +
                     escape (WholeCookie) +
                        "; expires=" + expire.toGMTString();
34  }
35  function UpdateForm () {
36     TheCookieValue =  GetCookie(TheCookieName);
37     document.TestForm.action =
38        'mailto:test@envmed.rochester.edu,'
39        + document.TestForm.Emailadd.value
40        + '?Subject=JavaScript Cookie Form';
```

```
41      document.TestForm.ExpDate.value  =
                                parseCookie(TheCookieValue,0);
42      document.TestForm.Entry1.value   =
                                parseCookie(TheCookieValue,1);
43      document.TestForm.Entry2.value   =
                                parseCookie(TheCookieValue,2);
44      document.TestForm.Entry2b.value  =
                                parseCookie(TheCookieValue,3);
45      document.TestForm.Entry2c.value  =
                                parseCookie(TheCookieValue,4);
46      document.TestForm.Emailadd.value =
                                parseCookie(TheCookieValue,5);
47      document.TestForm.Entry4.checked =
            (parseCookie(TheCookieValue,6)=='true')? true:false ;
48      document.TestForm.Entry5.checked =
            (parseCookie(TheCookieValue,7)=='true')? true:false ;
49      document.TestForm.Entry6.checked =
            (parseCookie(TheCookieValue,8)=='true')? true:false ;
50      document.TestForm.Entry7.checked =
            (parseCookie(TheCookieValue,9)=='true')? true:false ;
51      if (parseCookie(TheCookieValue,10) != "*" )
52          document.TestForm.Entry8[parseCookie(TheCookieValue,
                                    10)].checked = true;
53      if (parseCookie(TheCookieValue,11) != "*" )
54          document.TestForm.Entry9.selectedIndex =
                                parseCookie(TheCookieValue,11);
55      setChkIndx_MS(document.TestForm.Entry10,
                                parseCookie(TheCookieValue,12));
56      document.TestForm.Entry11.value =
                                parseCookie(TheCookieValue,13);
57  }
58
59  function checknull(theEntry) {
60      if (theEntry == "") return "*";
61      return theEntry;
62  }
63
64  function setChkIndx(theName) {
65      for (var i=0; i < theName.length; i++ ) {
66          if (theName[i].checked == true) return i;
67      }
68      return "*";
69  }
```

```
70
71  function findChkIndx_MS(theName) {
72     var indxlist = "";
73     for (var i=0; i < theName.options.length; i++ ) {
74         if (theName.options[i].selected == true)
75             indxlist = indxlist + "," + i;
76     }
77     return (indxlist == "")?indxlist = "*":indxlist;
78  }
79
80  function setChkIndx_MS(formObj,theList) {
81     for (var i=0; i < formObj.options.length; i++) {
82         formObj.options[i].selected = false;}
83     var ilen = 0;
84     while ( ilen < theList.length-1 ) {
85         var indxstart = theList.indexOf(',',ilen);
86         if (indxstart == -1) return;
87         ilen = theList.indexOf(',',indxstart+1);
88         if (ilen == -1) ilen = theList.length;
89         var indx = parseInt(theList.substring(indxstart + 1,
                                                 ilen) ,10);
90         formObj.options[indx].selected = true;
91     }
92  }
93
94  function GetCookie (CookieName) {
95     var cname = CookieName + "=";
96     var i = 0;
97     while (i < document.cookie.length) {
98        var j = i + cname.length;
99        if (document.cookie.substring(i, j) == cname){
100           var leng = document.cookie.indexOf (";", j);
101           if (leng == -1) leng = document.cookie.length;
102           return unescape(document.cookie.substring(j, leng));
103        }
104        i = document.cookie.indexOf(" ", i) + 1;
105        if (i == 0) break;
106     }
107     return "*";
108  }
109
110  function DelEatCookie (name) {
111     var expire = new Date();
```

```
112    expire.setTime (expire.getTime() - 2 * 86400001);
113    document.cookie = name + "=*; expires=" +
                                            expire.toGMTString();
114  }
115
116  function parseCookie(cookieValue, citem) {
117     var indx = 0, citemlen =0;
118     if ( cookieValue == null ) return "*"
119     if ( cookieValue == "*"  ) return "*"
120     for(var i=0; i < citem; i++) {
121         indx = ( citem==0 )?0:cookieValue.indexOf("`",
                                            indx + 1)+1;}
122     citemlen=(cookieValue.indexOf("`",indx)>0) ?
                cookieValue.indexOf("`", indx+1):cookieValue.length;
123     return cookieValue.substring(indx, citemlen);
124  }
125  // end script -->
126  </script>
127  </head>
128  <body bgcolor="b9edff" onLoad="UpdateForm()">
129  <CENTER>
130  <!-- <FORM METHOD="post" ACTION=" " NAME="TestForm"
                                            ENCTYPE="text/plain" >
131  Above line with ENCTYPE does NOT work
                                    on any Mac version. Sigh. -->
132  <FORM METHOD="post" ACTION=" " NAME="TestForm" >
133  <TABLE Border="10">
134  <TR><TH colspan="2" align="center">
135  A Form to Remember! <BR>
136  A Library book order form that remembers
                                    your personal information.
137  </TH></TR>
138  <TR><TD align="right" >Enter Name:</TD>
139  <TD> <input type="text" name="Entry1" size="50" >
140  </TD></TR>
141  <TR><TD align="right" >Enter Address:</TD>
142  <TD><input type="text" name="Entry2" size="50" >
143  </TD></TR>
144  <TR><TD align="right" >Enter State:</TD>
145  <TD><input type="text" name="Entry2b" size="25" >
146      Zip:<input type="text" name="Entry2c" size="17" >
147  </TD></TR>
148  <TR><TD align="right">Enter Full e-mail:</TD>
```

```
149 <TD align="center"><input type="text"
                                      name="Emailadd" size="50">
150 </TD></TR>
151 <TR><TD align="center">Enter all interests that apply:<BR>
152 <input type="checkbox" name="Entry4" value="sports">* Sports
153 <input type="checkbox" name="Entry6" value="books">
                                              * Reading<BR>
154 <input type="checkbox" name="Entry5" value="computers">
                                              * Computers
155 <input type="checkbox" name="Entry7" value="other">
                                              * Other </TD>
156 <TD align="center">Enter your favorite news source:
157 (<input type="radio" name="Entry8" value="None" CHECKED
                                  onClick=0> None)   <BR>
158  <input type="radio" name="Entry8" value="Radio" onClick=0>
                                              * Radio
159  <input type="radio" name="Entry8" value="Television"
                                  onClick=0>* Television
160  <input type="radio" name="Entry8" value="Newspaper"
                                  onClick=0>* Newspaper
161  <input type="radio" name="Entry8" value="Internet"
                                  onClick=0>* Internet
162 </TD></TR>
163 <TR><TD align="right">
164 Enter all your favorite authors:<BR>
165 &<BR>
166 Enter your preferred genre:
167 </TD>
168 <TD align="center"><SELECT name="Entry10" Size="3" MULTIPLE>
169 <OPTION>Melville
170 <OPTION>Fitzgerald
171 <OPTION>Dickens
172 <OPTION>Wells
173 <OPTION>Tolstoy
174 <OPTION>Cooper
175 <OPTION>McCarthy
176 <OPTION>Vonnegurt
177 <OPTION>Updike
178 <OPTION>Smiley
179 <OPTION>Chekhov
180 <OPTION>Oates
181 </SELECT>*  
182 <SELECT name="Entry9">
```

```
183  <OPTION>Roman á Clef
184  <OPTION>Anti-novel
185  <OPTION>Science Fiction
186  <OPTION>Mystery
187  <OPTION>Historical Novel
188  <OPTION>Saga
189  <OPTION>Short Story
190  <OPTION>Fable
191  <OPTION>Biography
192  </SELECT>*
193  </TD></TR>
194  <TR><TD align="center">Tell us about your interests:<BR>
195  <TEXTAREA name="Entry11" ROWS=3 COLS=25>
196  </TEXTAREA></TD>
197  <TD align="center">Enter Book order: (Title, Author,
                                        anything you know)<BR>
198  <TEXTAREA name="Entry11a" ROWS=3 COLS=40>
199  </TEXTAREA>
200  </TD></TR>
201  <TR><TD align="left">Settings will expire on: <BR>
202  <input type="text" name="ExpDate" size="28" >
203  <BR>(Do NOT edit.) Field set by Form.</TD>
204  <TD align="center">
205  Submit this form. (Save fields & E-mail to address above):
206  <BR><input type="submit"
207     value=" PRESS HERE to Order Book NOW. "
208     onClick="
209     document.TestForm.action =
210     'mailto:test@envmed.rochester.edu,'
211     + document.TestForm.Emailadd.value
212     + '?Subject=JavaScript Cookie Form';
213     WriteOneBigCookie();
214     UpdateForm();
215     // This doesn't work with a mailto ACTION
216     document.TestForm.submit();
217     ">
218  </TD></TR>
219  </TABLE><BR>
220  <TABLE BORDER="10">
221  <TR><TH align="center" colspan="2" > Maintenance Functions
222  (Not all needed for most forms).<BR>
223  Provided for instruction and playing.</TH></TR>
224  <TR><TD align="center">
```

```
225 <input type="button" value="SAVE Changes and/or
                                        Set New Expiration"
226    onClick="
227    WriteOneBigCookie();
228    UpdateForm();
229    ">
230 </TD><TD align="center">
231 <input type="button" value="DELETE ALL stored values,
                                        & Clear form"
232    onClick="
233    if (confirm('Do you REALLY want to Delete
                                all your saved Fields?')) {
234    DelEatCookie(TheCookieName);
235    document.TestForm.EntryReset.click();
236    UpdateForm();}
237    ">
238 </TD></TR>
239 <TR><TD align="center">
240 <input type="reset" name="EntryReset"
241    value="CLEAR current form, but NOT stored Values"></TD>
242 <TD align="center">
243 <input type="button" value="RECALL stored values"
244    onClick="
245    UpdateForm();
246    ">
247 </TD></TR>
248 </TABLE></FORM>
249 </CENTER>
250 </body>
251 </html>
```

ANNOTATIONS

This script, which concocts a giant cookie named **BigCookieinthesky** with a lifespan of 183 days, demonstrates how to transfer data back and forth between a complex form and a JavaScript cookie. While at first glance the page may strike you as requesting an odd clutter of information, bear in mind that it is intended to be a demo and, as such, systematically covers all of the presently available HTML form elements.

```
1   <html><head>
2   <title>Form that remembers your PERSONAL data.</title>
```

```
3    <script language="javascript">
4    <!-- begin script
5    // JavaScript to save Personal Form data for recall on next
6    // use. 3-Mar-1996 Copyright (C) 1996 by Geoff Inglis.
7    //   You may use these routines in your pages (commercial or
8    //   noncommercial) as long as you include these four lines.
9    //   You may not Re-sell this code. Questions
10   //   (or if you use this code) email: inglis@axsnet.com
11   //\/\/\/\/\/\/\/\   ** Here is the CookieName */\/\/\/\/\/\/\
12   TheCookieName = 'BigCookieinthesky';
13   numDays       = 183;
```

The script begins by declaring two global variables: the name of the cookie and its lifespan in days. Putting these two key cookie components right at the top makes them very easy to change without having to pore over all the code in search of the locations that have to be revised.

```
15   function WriteOneBigCookie () {
16      var expire = new Date ();
17      expire.setTime (expire.getTime()
                                       + (numDays * 24 * 3600000));
18      var WholeCookie = expire ;
```

The first function—the cookie-maker—is assigned to the PRESS HERE and SAVE buttons in the HTML form on this page. It begins by creating **expire** as a new **Date** object, setting it at **numDays** days from the millisecond value returned by **getTime( )**, and assigning the result to a new local variable, **WholeCookie**, which represents the cookie's VALUE string. **expire** is also used in line 33 to set **BigCookieinthesky**'s expiry date. Here it is included in the cookie string so that its value can be displayed in a form text field because the date attached to "EXPIRES=" is inaccessible to JavaScript.

The next sequence from lines 19 to 32 gradually adds the data from each element of the form to the **WholeCookie** string, while using a grave accent (`` ` ``) to separate the items. The start of all these lines is equivalent to writing

```
                    WholeCookie += '`' + ...
```

which produces tighter and more readable code.

```
19   WholeCookie = WholeCookie + '`' +
                       checknull(document.TestForm.Entry1.value);
21   WholeCookie = WholeCookie + '`' +
                       checknull(document.TestForm.Entry2.value);
22   WholeCookie = WholeCookie + '`' +
                       checknull(document.TestForm.Entry2b.value);
23   WholeCookie = WholeCookie + '`' +
                       checknull(document.TestForm.Entry2c.value);
```

```
24      WholeCookie = WholeCookie + '`' +
                    checknull(document.TestForm.Emailadd.value);
```

WriteOneBigCookie( ) first runs the values of the five text fields in the form through **checknull( )**, a function (line 59) that tests for an empty string and returns an asterisk (*) if one is found, or otherwise returns exactly the same value it received as its argument. These asterisks essentially serve as placeholders for blank fields.

```
25      WholeCookie = WholeCookie + '`' +
                    document.TestForm.Entry4.checked;
26      WholeCookie = WholeCookie + '`' +
                    document.TestForm.Entry5.checked;
27      WholeCookie = WholeCookie + '`' +
                    document.TestForm.Entry6.checked;
28      WholeCookie = WholeCookie + '`' +
                    document.TestForm.Entry7.checked;
```

Next, **WholeCookie** gets the Boolean literals (**true** or **false**) reflecting the status of the **checked** property of the four check boxes.

```
29      WholeCookie = WholeCookie + '`' +
                    setChkIndx(document.TestForm.Entry8);
30      WholeCookie = WholeCookie + '`' +
                    document.TestForm.Entry9.selectedIndex;
31      WholeCookie = WholeCookie + '`' +
                    findChkIndx_MS(document.TestForm.Entry10);
32      WholeCookie = WholeCookie + '`' +
                    checknull(document.TestForm.Entry11.value);
```

Then the call to **setChkIndx( )** determines which radio button is checked, line 30 records the selected favorite genre, line 31 runs **findChkIndx_MS( )** to process the multiple-selection list choices, and the now familiar **checknull( )** tests the text area for an empty string. As you may notice, the "Enter book order" text area named **Entry11a** does not become a part of the **WholeCookie** string, but could easily be added by duplicating line 32, then changing the "11" to "11a."

```
33      document.cookie = TheCookieName +"=" +
                    escape (WholeCookie) +
                    "; expires=" + expire.toGMTString();
34      }
```

Finally, **WriteOneBigCookie( )** creates its cookie by assembling the assigned NAME, escaped VALUE, and EXPIRES components into the proper string. If you don't touch the form, but simply click on the SAVE button, the cookie ends up looking like "BigCookieinthesky=Mon Jan 12 18:15:31 EST 1998 `*`*`*`*`*`false`false`false`false`0`0`*`*." Fill it in and the value string is more likely to resemble "BigCookieinthesky=Mon Jan 12 18:16:56 EST 1998` Wile E. Coyote`1313 Roadrunner Trail, Backfire Gulley`Frustration`Whazzata-roadrunner?!!?` wcoy@desertlore.edu`false`false`true`true`4`1`,0,4,5,7,8`Snare CAD-CAM, virtual roadrunning, alt.roadrunner.beep-beep.beep-beep.beep-beep."

```
35    function UpdateForm () {
36       TheCookieValue =  GetCookie(TheCookieName);
37       document.TestForm.action =
38          'mailto:test@envmed.rochester.edu,'
39          + document.TestForm.Emailadd.value
40          + '?Subject=JavaScript Cookie Form';
```

This next function, which transfers the data from the cookie to the form, is attached to all except the RESET button on this page, as well as to the **onLoad** event handler, so that the form is automatically filled out with the information in the cookie when the page is loaded. First it assigns a new variable, **TheCookieValue**, the cookie's value string returned by **GetCookie( )**. It then sets the form's **action** property to a "mailto" URL plus the e-mail address the user may have entered into the form, and specifies the subject of the mailing.

The sequence from lines 41 to 46 then systematically calls on **parseCookie( )** to retrieve the data stored in the cookie and restores the saved form entries and settings.

```
41    document.TestForm.ExpDate.value  =
                                parseCookie(TheCookieValue,0);
42    document.TestForm.Entry1.value   =
                                parseCookie(TheCookieValue,1);
43    document.TestForm.Entry2.value   =
                                parseCookie(TheCookieValue,2);
44    document.TestForm.Entry2b.value  =
                                parseCookie(TheCookieValue,3);
45    document.TestForm.Entry2c.value  =
                                parseCookie(TheCookieValue,4);
46    document.TestForm.Emailadd.value =
                                parseCookie(TheCookieValue,5);
```

First the expiry date field followed by the five name-and-address text fields are processed.

```
47    document.TestForm.Entry4.checked =
          (parseCookie(TheCookieValue,6)=='true')? true:false ;
48    document.TestForm.Entry5.checked =
          (parseCookie(TheCookieValue,7)=='true')? true:false ;
49    document.TestForm.Entry6.checked =
          (parseCookie(TheCookieValue,8)=='true')? true:false ;
```

```
50      document.TestForm.Entry7.checked =
            (parseCookie(TheCookieValue,9)=='true')? true:false ;
```

Then the Boolean values recording the check box settings are read and restored.

```
51      if (parseCookie(TheCookieValue,10) != "*" )
52          document.TestForm.Entry8[parseCookie(TheCookieValue,
                                        10)].checked = true;
53      if (parseCookie(TheCookieValue,11) != "*" )
54          document.TestForm.Entry9.selectedIndex =
                                    parseCookie(TheCookieValue,11);
55      setChkIndx_MS(document.TestForm.Entry10,
                            parseCookie(TheCookieValue,12));
56      document.TestForm.Entry11.value =
                            parseCookie(TheCookieValue,13);
57  }
```

Finally, lines 51 to 56 process the radio button group, two selection lists, and the "interests" text area.

```
59  function checknull(theEntry) {
60      if (theEntry == "") return "*";
61      return theEntry;
62  }
```

As we have seen, this subroutine is used by **WriteOneBigCookie( )** to check the text fields for empty strings, which it replaces with an asterisk. Otherwise, it returns exactly the same string it received.

```
64  function setChkIndx(theName) {
65      for (var i=0; i < theName.length; i++ ) {
66          if (theName[i].checked == true) return i;
67      }
68      return "*";
69  }
```

This next function called by **WriteOneBigCookie( )** in line 29 uses a **for** loop to run through the group of radio buttons and determine which one in the array is checked. If none is checked, which is unlikely to occur as the None button is checked by default (line 157), **setChkIndx( )** returns an asterisk.

```
71  function findChkIndx_MS(theName) {
72      var indxlist = "";
73      for (var i=0; i < theName.options.length; i++ ) {
74          if (theName.options[i].selected == true)
75              indxlist = indxlist + "," + i;
76      }
```

```
77      return (indxlist == "")?indxlist = "*":indxlist;
78  }
```

findChkIndx_MS( ) processes the multiple-selection list of authors for
WriteOneBigCookie( ) by declaring a local variable, indxlist, and initializing it as
an empty string, then using a for loop to identify the selected options and assemble
indxlist into a comma-separated string of the index values of the selections. If
indxlist emerges as an empty string, the function returns an asterisk, otherwise it
returns the value of indxlist.

```
80  function setChkIndx_MS(formObj,theList) {
81      for (var i=0; i < formObj.options.length; i++) {
82          formObj.options[i].selected = false;}
83      var ilen = 0;
84      while ( ilen < theList.length-1 ) {
85          var indxstart = theList.indexOf(',',ilen);
86          if (indxstart == -1) return;
87          ilen = theList.indexOf(',',indxstart+1);
88          if (ilen == -1) ilen = theList.length;
89          var indx = parseInt(theList.substring(indxstart + 1,
                                                  ilen) ,10);
90          formObj.options[indx].selected = true;
91      }
92  }
```

The preceding function's counterpart, setChkIndx_MS( ), is called by
UpdateForm( ) in line 55 and restores the user-entered choices in the multiple-
selection field. Its initial for loop in lines 81 and 82 deselects all the options to ensure
a clean read. It then uses two local variables, indxstart and indx, to access the
comma-separated integers recording the indices of the user's selections. The first
if ends the routine, and the second sets ilen at the last position in the string when
no more commas are found. The JavaScript parseInt( ) method used in line 89
effectively casts the substring as an integer for use as the options in line 90. Its
first argument is the string to be converted. Its second is the numerical base or
radix—here "10" for decimal. Specifying "8" as the second argument returns an
octal and specifying "16" returns a hexadecimal number.

```
94  function GetCookie (CookieName) {
95      var cname = CookieName + "=";
96      var i = 0;
97      while (i < document.cookie.length) {
98          var j = i + cname.length;
99          if (document.cookie.substring(i, j) == cname){
100             var leng = document.cookie.indexOf (";", j);
101             if (leng == -1) leng = document.cookie.length;
```

```
102          return unescape(document.cookie.substring(j, leng));
103      }
104      i = document.cookie.indexOf(" ", i) + 1;
105      if (i == 0) break;
106  }
107  return "*";
108 }
```

This **GetCookie( )** function is a variation of the Dortch original. Although the variable names and routine differ slightly, it essentially does exactly the same thing: return the unescaped string extending from the first position after the "=" following the cookie's name to the end of the VALUE string, which is marked by either a semicolon or the end of the cookie string. This version also varies in that, if the cookie is not found, instead of **null** it returns an asterisk.

```
110 function DelEatCookie (name) {
111     var expire = new Date();
112     expire.setTime (expire.getTime() - 2 * 86400001);
113     document.cookie = name + "=*; expires=" +
                                         expire.toGMTString();
114 }
```

The main differences between this cookie-crumbler and Dortch's **DeleteCookie( )** are a punnier name and less distant-past expiry date. Whereas Dortch uses the dawn of computer time, namely "Thu, 01-Jan-70 00:00:01 GMT," our script sets **expire** at two days ago—86,400,000 being the number of milliseconds in a day (24 x 60 x 60 x 1,000) with an extra one added for good measure. The Dortch function also accommodates **path** and **domain** arguments, which can help in targeting the right cookie.

```
116 function parseCookie(cookieValue, citem) {
117     var indx = 0, citemlen =0;
118     if ( cookieValue == null ) return "*"
119     if ( cookieValue == "*"  ) return "*"
120     for(var i=0; i < citem; i++) {
121         indx = ( citem==0 )?0:cookieValue.indexOf("`",
                                               indx + 1)+1;}
122     citemlen=(cookieValue.indexOf("`",indx)>0)  ?
              cookieValue.indexOf("`", indx+1):cookieValue.length;
123     return cookieValue.substring(indx, citemlen);
124 }
```

Our script ends with **parseCookie( )**, which reads the cookie's VALUE string and returns the appropriate substrings recording the setting of each form element to

UpdateForm( ). Its first argument, **cookieValue**, is passed the entire VALUE string; its second, **citem**, represents an index to the form elements.

First line 117 declares two local variables, **indx** and **citemlen**, which will be used to extract the substring, and sets both to 0. The **if** statements on the next two lines are essentially error handlers that return an asterisk if the value of **cookieValue** is **null** or "*." Then the **for** loop boosts **indx** to the correct current value for form element indexed by **citem**, in other words aligns it with the grave-accent (`) separator preceding the item's stored value. Next, line 122 gives **citemlen** the integer representing either the position of the next separator or, if none is found, the end of the string. Finally, **parseCookie( )** returns to **UpdateForm( )** the substring of **cookieValue** extending from **indx** to **citemlen**.

A far simpler approach to the entire parse/update process—one that was probably impossible when this script was written due to the less-developed state of the language at the time—would be to use

```
cArray = cookieValue.split('`')
```

to create an array of the cookie string's items, and to align it with the built-in array of form elements so that you could essentially write

```
document.TestForm.elements[i].value = cArray[i]
```

with appropriate adjustments for handling the checkbox, radio button, and selection list values. Similarly, to construct the cookie string, you could assign the value of each form element to a member of an array and assemble the **WholeCookie** string with, for example,

```
WholeCookie = vArray.join('`')
```

You might combine this with, as the author suggests in the comments found in EXTRANOT.TXT on the accompanying CD-ROM, a test for the **type** property of the form elements. For example:

```
if (document.TestForm.elements[i].type == "checkbox")
     { ... }              // set checked value from cArray[i]
if (document.TestForm.elements[i].type == "select-multiple")
     { ... }              // set selected options from cArray[i]
```

and so on. The appropriate code for each type of form element can easily be derived from **UpdateForm( )** and its subroutine. With JavaScript 1.2, you could even deploy a **switch** structure to handle the cases represented by different types of form element:

```
switch (document.TestForm.elements[i].type) {
        case "text" :
                [...];       // assign cArray[i] string value
                break;
        case "radio" :
                [...];       // assign cArray[i] Boolean value
                break;
```

and so on. Upgrading code in this way by taking advantage of improvements to the language will not only result in a tighter, faster, more efficient script, but also deepen your understanding and appreciation of JavaScript and its potential.

```
125 // end script -->
126 </script>
127 </head>
128 <body bgcolor="b9edff" onLoad="UpdateForm()">
129 <CENTER>
```

Lines 128 to 250 consist mainly of standard HTML code to create the form, buttons, and text that appear on the page. The assignment of **UpdateForm( )** to **onLoad** in line 128 automatically loads the data from the cookie into the form once the page has been laid out or, if the cookie has not yet been created, sets the elements to their default values.

```
130 <!-- <FORM METHOD="post" ACTION=" " NAME="TestForm"
                                      ENCTYPE="text/plain" >
131 Above line with ENCTYPE does NOT work
                                  on any Mac version. Sigh. -->
132 <FORM METHOD="post" ACTION=" " NAME="TestForm" >
133 <TABLE Border="10">
134 <TR><TH colspan="2" align="center">
135 A Form to Remember! <BR>
136 A Library book order form that remembers
                                  your personal information.
137 </TH></TR>
138 <TR><TD align="right" >Enter Name:</TD>
139 <TD> <input type="text" name="Entry1" size="50" >
140 </TD></TR>
141 <TR><TD align="right" >Enter Address:</TD>
142 <TD><input type="text" name="Entry2" size="50" >
143 </TD></TR>
144 <TR><TD align="right" >Enter State:</TD>
145 <TD><input type="text" name="Entry2b" size="25" >
146     Zip:<input type="text" name="Entry2c" size="17" >
147 </TD></TR>
148 <TR><TD align="right">Enter Full e-mail:</TD>
149 <TD align="center"><input type="text"
                                  name="Emailadd" size="50">
150 </TD></TR>
```

First come the text fields for your name, address, and other personal information.

```
151 <TR><TD align="center">Enter all interests that apply:<BR>
152 <input type="checkbox" name="Entry4" value="sports">* Sports
153 <input type="checkbox" name="Entry6" value="books">
                                                    * Reading<BR>
154 <input type="checkbox" name="Entry5" value="computers">
                                                    * Computers
155 <input type="checkbox" name="Entry7" value="other">
                                                    * Other </TD>
```

Then the four checkboxes whose value attribute, like that of the radio buttons next, represents the string sent along when the form is submitted.

```
156 <TD align="center">Enter your favorite news source:
157 (<input type="radio" name="Entry8" value="None" CHECKED
                                        onClick=0> None)   <BR>
158  <input type="radio" name="Entry8" value="Radio" onClick=0>
                                                    * Radio
159  <input type="radio" name="Entry8" value="Television"
                                        onClick=0>* Television
160  <input type="radio" name="Entry8" value="Newspaper"
                                        onClick=0>* Newspaper
161  <input type="radio" name="Entry8" value="Internet"
                                        onClick=0>* Internet
162 </TD></TR>
```

Next come the radio buttons, which all have the same **name**. This identifies them as members of the same group in which only one button can be checked at a time.

```
163 <TR><TD align="right">
164 Enter all your favorite authors:<BR>
165 &<BR>
166 Enter your preferred genre:
167 </TD>
168 <TD align="center"><SELECT name="Entry10" Size="3" MULTIPLE>
169 <OPTION>Melville
170 <OPTION>Fitzgerald
171 <OPTION>Dickens
172 <OPTION>Wells
173 <OPTION>Tolstoy
174 <OPTION>Cooper
175 <OPTION>McCarthy
176 <OPTION>Vonnegurt
177 <OPTION>Updike
178 <OPTION>Smiley
179 <OPTION>Chekhov
```

```
180  <OPTION>Oates
181  </SELECT>*  
182  <SELECT name="Entry9">
183  <OPTION>Roman á Clef
184  <OPTION>Anti-novel
185  <OPTION>Science Fiction
186  <OPTION>Mystery
187  <OPTION>Historical Novel
188  <OPTION>Saga
189  <OPTION>Short Story
190  <OPTION>Fable
191  <OPTION>Biography
192  </SELECT>*
193  </TD></TR>
```

Then we have the two selection lists. As you can see, adding the word "multiple" to the <SELECT> tag is all it takes to create a multiple-selection list. The size attribute refers to the number of choices visible in the list window.

```
194  <TR><TD align="center">Tell us about your interests:<BR>
195  <TEXTAREA name="Entry11" ROWS=3 COLS=25>
196  </TEXTAREA></TD>
197  <TD align="center">Enter Book order: (Title, Author,
                                             anything you know)<BR>
198  <TEXTAREA name="Entry11a" ROWS=3 COLS=40>
199  </TEXTAREA>
200  </TD></TR>
201  <TR><TD align="left">Settings will expire on: <BR>
202  <input type="text" name="ExpDate" size="28" >
203  <BR>(Do NOT edit.) Field set by Form.</TD>
```

The final entry fields are the two text areas and the expiry-date text field, whose value is automatically filled in by the **UpdateForm( )** function (line 41).

```
204  <TD align="center">
205  Submit this form. (Save fields & E-mail to address above):
206  <BR><input type="submit"
207      value=" PRESS HERE to Order Book NOW. "
208·     onClick="
209      document.TestForm.action =
210      'mailto:test@envmed.rochester.edu,'
211      + document.TestForm.Emailadd.value
212      + '?Subject=JavaScript Cookie Form';
213      WriteOneBigCookie();
214      UpdateForm();
```

```
215      // This doesn't work with a mailto ACTION
216      document.TestForm.submit();
217      ">
218  </TD></TR>
219  </TABLE><BR>
```

The first button's **onClick** event handler assigns the form's **action** property the same **mailto** URL that we saw in lines 37 to 40, and then it calls **WriteOneBigCookie( )** followed by **UpdateForm( )**.

```
220  <TABLE BORDER="10">
221  <TR><TH align="center" colspan="2" > Maintenance Functions
222  (Not all needed for most forms).<BR>
223  Provided for instruction and playing.</TH></TR>
224  <TR><TD align="center">
225  <input type="button" value="SAVE Changes and/or
                                           Set New Expiration"
226      onClick="
227      WriteOneBigCookie();
228      UpdateForm();
229      ">
```

The first of the four maintenance buttons on this page calls the script's two main functions to create the cookie and update the form.

```
230  </TD><TD align="center">
231  <input type="button" value="DELETE ALL stored values,
                                           & Clear form"
232      onClick="
233      if (confirm('Do you REALLY want to Delete
                                  all your saved Fields?')) {
234      DelEatCookie(TheCookieName);
235      document.TestForm.EntryReset.click();
236      UpdateForm();}
237      ">
```

The second maintenance button calls **DelEatCookie( )** after asking the user to confirm the deletion. Line 235 simulates a click on the CLEAR button by giving it focus for a moment before the call to **UpdateForm( )**.

```
238  </TD></TR>
239  <TR><TD align="center">
240  <input type="reset" name="EntryReset"
241      value="CLEAR current form, but NOT stored Values"></TD>
```

```
242 <TD align="center">
243 <input type="button" value="RECALL stored values"
244     onClick="
245     UpdateForm();
246     ">
247 </TD></TR>
248 </TABLE></FORM>
249 </CENTER>
250 </body>
251 </html>
```

The third button is a standard HTML RESET button that restores the form's original settings, whereas the fourth uses **UpdateForm( )** to retrieve the user's entries from **BigCookieinthesky**'s value string.

While cookies are commonly used to store information about users between visits to a site, they can also serve as a handy means of transferring data between separate pages without using frames or layers. Cookies with the same DOMAIN and PATH attributes essentially belong to all the pages located in the same directory. For example, if one page creates a "name=Jorge" cookie and a second an "age=36" cookie, put

```
document.write(document.cookie)
```

on a third page and the result will be "name=Jorge; age=36" if all three pages lie in exactly the same path. Thus, you can store the output of one process in a cookie for use as the input for another process on a separate page.

In fact, you can even stash a JavaScript function in a cookie with, for instance,

```
document.cookie = "jsf=" +
                escape("function multip(a,b){return a * b}")
```

and retrieve it from another page in the same path with

```
var i = document.cookie.indexOf("jsf=") + 4;
var scr = unescape(document.cookie.substring(i,
                              document.cookie.length));
document.write("<SCR" + "IPT>" + scr + "</SCR" + "IPT>")
```

Assign **multip(9,12)** to a button on this page, and your output field will display "108." In case you're wondering, the "4" added to the value of **i** represents the length of "jsf=". Also, the use of **document.cookie.length** as the second substring index assumes that the **jsf** cookie is the last in the string.

This does not mean that you should put all your scripts into cookies. Rather, the point is that a cookie can carry any kind of data capable of conversion into a string. Moreover, when using cookies in this way as part of a script's internal processes, you're probably best off deploying ephemeral cookies that have no expiry date and vanish at the end of the browser session. Don't forget too that, even though you're working under a 20-cookie ceiling, the fact that you can easily delete cookies when they are no longer needed by the process and replace them with new ones gives you theoretically infinite room to play around in.

calendar

Reminder Calendar

⎣N2⎦ ⎣N2.01⎦ ⎣N2.02+⎦ ⎣N3⎦ ⎣N4⎦ ⎣E3⎦ ⎣E4⎦

In this handy script—good for both personal and business use—you can add items to an HTML-based monthly calendar. To use it, click on a date to add a reminder, click on that date again to see the reminder, and then reload the page to see dates with reminders in different colors (see Figure 5-6).

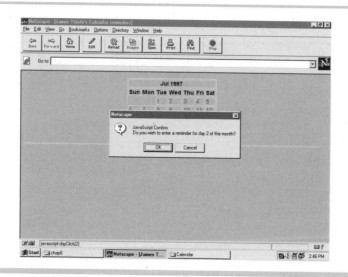

FIGURE 5-6. Use this to add items to a to-do list

The user interface is a bit lame, and you cannot delete a reminder. This version does not keep reminders for more than 24 hours, but it can be modified to keep the reminders intact for a longer period by setting a later expiry date for its cookies.

```
1   <HTML>
2   <HEAD>
3   <SCRIPT LANGUAGE="JavaScript">
4   <!-- to hide script contents from old browsers
5   //
6   //Cookie Functions
```

```
7    //Written by:  Bill Dortch, hIdaho Design
8    //The following functions are released to the public domain.
9
10   function encode (str) {
11      var dest = "";
12      var len = str.length;
13      var index = 0;
14      var code = null;
15      for (var i = 0; i < len; i++) {
16          var ch = str.charAt(i);
17          if (ch == " ") code = "%20";
18          else if (ch == "%") code = "%25";
19          else if (ch == ",") code = "%2C";
20          else if (ch == ";") code = "%3B";
21          else if (ch == "\b") code = "%08";
22          else if (ch == "\t") code = "%09";
23          else if (ch == "\n") code = "%0A";
24          else if (ch == "\f") code = "%0C";
25          else if (ch == "\r") code = "%0D";
26          if (code != null) {
27              dest += str.substring(index,i) + code;
28              index = i + 1;
29              code = null;
30          }
31      }
32      if (index < len)
33      dest += str.substring(index, len);
34      return dest;
35   }
36
37   function decode (str) {
38      var dest = "";
39      var len = str.length;
40      var index = 0;
41      var code = null;
42      var i = 0;
43      while (i < len) {
44          i = str.indexOf ("%", i);
45          if (i == -1)
46              break;
47          if (index < i)
48              dest += str.substring(index, i);
49          code = str.substring (i+1,i+3);
```

```
50          i += 3;
51          index = i;
52          if (code == "20") dest += " ";
53          else if (code == "25") dest += "%";
54          else if (code == "2C") dest += ",";
55          else if (code == "3B") dest += ";";
56          else if (code == "08") dest += "\b";
57          else if (code == "09") dest += "\t";
58          else if (code == "0A") dest += "\n";
59          else if (code == "0C") dest += "\f";
60          else if (code == "0D") dest += "\r";
61          else {
62                i -= 2;
63                index -= 3;
64          }
65      }
66      if (index < len)
67      dest += str.substring(index, len);
68      return dest;
69  }
70
71  function getCookieVal (offset) {
72      var endstr = document.cookie.indexOf (";", offset);
73      if (endstr == -1)
74          endstr = document.cookie.length;
75      return decode(document.cookie.substring(offset, endstr));
76  }
77
78  function GetCookie (name) {
79      var arg = name + "=";
80      var alen = arg.length;
81      var clen = document.cookie.length;
82      var i = 0;
83      while (i < clen) {
84          var j = i + alen;
85          if (document.cookie.substring(i, j) == arg)
86              return getCookieVal (j);
87          i = document.cookie.indexOf(" ", i) + 1;
88          if (i == 0) break;
89      }
90      return null;
91  }
92
```

```
93  function SetCookie (name, value, expires) {
94     document.cookie = name + "=" + encode(value) +
                       ((expires == null) ? "" : ("; expires=" +
                                              expires.toGMTString()));
95  }
96
97  //
98  // Reminder calendar
99  // Written by James Thiele
100 // jet@eskimo.com
101 // http://www.eskimo.com/~jet/javascript/
102 function arrayOfDaysInMonths(isLeapYear)
103 {
104   this[0] = 31;
105   this[1] = 28;
106   if (isLeapYear)
107       this[1] = 29;
108   this[2] = 31;
109   this[3] = 30;
110   this[4] = 31;
111   this[5] = 30;
112   this[6] = 31;
113   this[7] = 31;
114   this[8] = 30;
115   this[9] = 31;
116   this[10] = 30;
117   this[11] = 31;
118 }
119 function daysInMonth(month, year)
120 {
121     var isLeapYear = (((year % 4 == 0) && (year % 100 != 0))
                                    || (year % 400 == 0));
122     var monthDays  = new arrayOfDaysInMonths(isLeapYear);
123     return monthDays[month];
124 }
125 function calendar()
126 {
127     var monthNames = "JanFebMarAprMayJunJulAugSepOctNovDec";
128     var today      = new Date();
129     var day        = today.getDate();
130     var month      = today.getMonth();
131     var year       = today.getYear() + 1900;
132     var numDays    = daysInMonth(month, year);
```

```
133    var firstDay   = today;
134    firstDay.setDate(1);
135    var startDay = firstDay.getDay();
136    var column = 0;
137
138    document.write("<CENTER>");
139    document.write("<TABLE BORDER>");
140    document.write("<TR><TH COLSPAN=7>");
141    document.write(monthNames.substring(3*month,
                                3*(month + 1)) + " " + year);
142    document.write("<TR><TH>Sun<TH>Mon<TH>Tue<TH>Wed<TH>Thu
                                <TH>Fri<TH>Sat");
143    document.write("<TR>");
144    for (i = 0; i < startDay; i++)
145    {
146      document.write("<TD>");
147      column++;
148    }
149    for (i=1; i <= numDays; i++)
150    {
151      var s = "" + i;
152      if ((GetCookie("d"+i) != null))
153          s = s.fontcolor("#FF0000");
154      s = s.link("javascript:dayClick(" + i + ")")
155      document.write("<TD>" + s);
156
157       if (++column == 7)
158       {
159         document.write("<TR>");
160         column = 0;
161       }
162    }
163    document.write("</TABLE>");
164    document.writeln("</CENTER>");
165 }
166
167 function dayClick(day)
168 {
169    var expdate = new Date ();
170    expdate.setTime(expdate.getTime()+(24 * 60 * 60 * 1000));
171    var prefix              = "d";
172    var theCookieName         = prefix + day;
```

```
173    var theDayclickedReminder = GetCookie(theCookieName);
174    if (theDayclickedReminder != null) {
175        alert("The reminder for day " + day + " is:" +
                                        theDayclickedReminder);
176    }
177    if (confirm("Do you wish to enter a reminder for day " +
                                day + " of this month?"))
178    {
179        x = prompt("Enter a reminder for day "+ day +
                    " of this month", theDayclickedReminder);
180        SetCookie (theCookieName, x, expdate);
181    }
182 }
183 // --> <!-- end hiding contents from old browsers  -->
184 </SCRIPT>
185 <TITLE>James Thiele's Calendar reminders
186 </TITLE>
187 </HEAD>
188 <BODY>
189 <SCRIPT LANGUAGE="JavaScript">
190 <!--  to hide script contents from old browsers
191 calendar();
192 document.write("<HR>");
193 // --> <!-- end hiding contents from old browsers  -->
194 </SCRIPT>
195 </BODY>
196 </HTML>
```

⌐ANNOTATIONS

This script creates cookies in the form "dx=reminder" where x is the date of the month. Thus, after several entries, the value of **unescape(document.cookie)** will look something like this: "d6=Dentist appointment; d11=Kids back from camp; d23=Gobles' barbecue." Although it uses a **Prompt** dialog box to get the reminders and an **Alert** to display them, one possible adaptation would be to use a text field or text area for both input and output, combined with an **onMouseOver** instead of **onClick** event handler for the calendar dates, so that simply positioning the cursor over a date would display that day's reminders.

```
1    <HTML>
2    <HEAD>
3    <SCRIPT LANGUAGE="JavaScript">
```

```
4    <!--  to hide script contents from old browsers
5    //
6    //Cookie Functions
7    //Written by:  Bill Dortch, hIdaho Design
8    //The following functions are released to the public domain.
9
10   function encode (str) {
11       var dest = "";
12       var len = str.length;
13       var index = 0;
14       var code = null;
15       for (var i = 0; i < len; i++) {
16           var ch = str.charAt(i);
17           if (ch == " ") code = "%20";
18           else if (ch == "%") code = "%25";
19           else if (ch == ",") code = "%2C";
20           else if (ch == ";") code = "%3B";
21           else if (ch == "\b") code = "%08";
22           else if (ch == "\t") code = "%09";
23           else if (ch == "\n") code = "%0A";
24           else if (ch == "\f") code = "%0C";
25           else if (ch == "\r") code = "%0D";
26           if (code != null) {
27               dest += str.substring(index,i) + code;
28               index = i + 1;
29               code = null;
30           }
31       }
32       if (index < len)
33       dest += str.substring(index, len);
34       return dest;
35   }
36
37   function decode (str) {
38       var dest = "";
39       var len = str.length;
40       var index = 0;
41       var code = null;
42       var i = 0;
43       while (i < len) {
44           i = str.indexOf ("%", i);
45           if (i == -1)
46               break;
47           if (index < i)
```

```
48          dest += str.substring(index, i);
49      code = str.substring (i+1,i+3);
50      i += 3;
51      index = i;
52      if (code == "20") dest += " ";
53      else if (code == "25") dest += "%";
54      else if (code == "2C") dest += ",";
55      else if (code == "3B") dest += ";";
56      else if (code == "08") dest += "\b";
57      else if (code == "09") dest += "\t";
58      else if (code == "0A") dest += "\n";
59      else if (code == "0C") dest += "\f";
60      else if (code == "0D") dest += "\r";
61      else {
62              i -= 2;
63              index -= 3;
64      }
65   }
66   if (index < len)
67   dest += str.substring(index, len);
68   return dest;
69 }
70
71 function getCookieVal (offset) {
72   var endstr = document.cookie.indexOf (";", offset);
73   if (endstr == -1)
74       endstr = document.cookie.length;
75   return decode(document.cookie.substring(offset, endstr));
76 }
77
78 function GetCookie (name) {
79   var arg = name + "=";
80   var alen = arg.length;
81   var clen = document.cookie.length;
82   var i = 0;
83   while (i < clen) {
84     var j = i + alen;
85     if (document.cookie.substring(i, j) == arg)
86         return getCookieVal (j);
87     i = document.cookie.indexOf(" ", i) + 1;
88     if (i == 0) break;
89   }
90   return null;
91 }
```

```
92
93  function SetCookie (name, value, expires) {
94      document.cookie = name + "=" + encode(value) +
                          ((expires == null) ? "" : ("; expires=" +
                                          expires.toGMTString()));
95  }
```

Lines 10 to 95 should look very familiar by now—they're exactly the same Dortch functions that we saw earlier in this chapter, including the original homemade encode/decode routine, which has since been replaced by the use of JavaScript's **escape( )/unescape( )** methods. The real action in this script begins in line 102.

```
98   // Reminder calendar
99   // Written by James Thiele
100  // jet@eskimo.com
101  // http://www.eskimo.com/~jet/javascript/
102  function arrayOfDaysInMonths(isLeapYear)
103  {
104    this[0] = 31;
105    this[1] = 28;
106    if (isLeapYear)
107        this[1] = 29;
108    this[2] = 31;
109    this[3] = 30;
110    this[4] = 31;
111    this[5] = 30;
112    this[6] = 31;
113    this[7] = 31;
114    this[8] = 30;
115    this[9] = 31;
116    this[10] = 30;
117    this[11] = 31;
118  }
```

The first calendar function creates an array of the number of days in each month, with the Boolean **isLeapYear** argument and **if** test in line 106 designed to accommodate leap years.

```
119  function daysInMonth(month, year)
120  {
121      var isLeapYear = (((year % 4 == 0) && (year % 100 != 0))
                                      || (year % 400 == 0));
122      var monthDays  = new arrayOfDaysInMonths(isLeapYear);
123      return monthDays[month];
124  }
```

daysInMonth( ) is the function that reads the array to return the number of days in the month of the year specified as its arguments. **isLeapYear** is a local Boolean variable whose value becomes either **true** or **false** depending on the outcome of the standard leap-year math applied to **year**.

```
125  function calendar()
126  {
127      var monthNames = "JanFebMarAprMayJunJulAugSepOctNovDec";
```

This script's main function, **calendar( )**, is called from line 191 when the page is loaded and writes the calendar in which each date is a link with a JavaScript URL that calls the **dayClick( )** function on line 167. It sets out declaring a local variable, **monthNames**, and assigns it a long string of abbreviated three-letter month names from which the name of the current month is extracted by line 141 for display at the top of the calendar.

To display the full names of the month, you could convert **monthNames** into an array with

```
monthNames = new Array("January", "February", "March" ... )
```

and access it in line 141 with

```
document.write(monthNames[month] + " " + year)
```

As the integer returned by **getMonth( )** and assigned to **month** in line 130 is based on a count starting from January=0, no adjustment is necessary to align the index with the **monthNames** array.

```
128      var today      = new Date();
129      var day        = today.getDate();
130      var month      = today.getMonth();
131      var year       = today.getYear() + 1900;
132      var numDays    = daysInMonth(month, year);
133      var firstDay   = today;
134      firstDay.setDate(1);
135      var startDay = firstDay.getDay();
136      var column = 0;
```

Next **calendar( )** creates **today** as a **Date** object and assigns the values returned by its **getDate( )**, **getMonth( )**, and **getYear( )** methods to the new local variables **day**, **month**, and **year**. The last is incremented because **getYear( )** returns the year of the specified date minus 1900. Then **numDays** gets the number of days in the current month returned by **daysInMonth( )**.

The assignments and calls in lines 133 to 135 essentially determine the day of the week of the first of the month. This is done by assigning the **today Date** object to a new variable **firstDay**—making it a new **Date** object—then setting the date of **firstDay** to 1 and calling its **getDay( )** method, which returns an integer representing the day of the week starting from Sunday=0.

The last variable, **column**, will serve as a control in creating the calendar table.

```
138    document.write("<CENTER>");
139    document.write("<TABLE BORDER>");
140    document.write("<TR><TH COLSPAN=7>");
141    document.write(monthNames.substring(3*month,
                                3*(month + 1)) + " " + year);
142    document.write("<TR><TH>Sun<TH>Mon<TH>Tue<TH>Wed<TH>Thu
                                        <TH>Fri<TH>Sat");
```

Lines 138 to 142 then construct the heading for the calendar. The **month** value is multiplied by three in line 141 because the name of each month in the **monthNames** string is three letters long.

```
143    document.write("<TR>");
144    for (i = 0; i < startDay; i++)
145    {
146       document.write("<TD>");
147       column++;
148    }
```

Next a **for** loop uses **startDay** as a control to create empty cells for any days preceding the first of the month.

```
149    for (i=1; i <= numDays; i++)
150    {
151       var s = "" + i;
152       if ((GetCookie("d"+i) != null))
153            s = s.fontcolor("#FF0000");
154       s = s.link("javascript:dayClick(" + i + ")")
155       document.write("<TD>" + s);
```

The second **for** loop, which extends to line 162, writes the rows of dates until the value of i equals **numDays**, or number of days in the month. First it declares **s** as a new variable assigned an empty string followed by **i**. The empty string ensures that **s** is treated as a string despite the assignment of **i**, an integer.

Line 152 then looks for a cookie for the date represented by the value of i and, if it finds one, sets the **fontcolor** for **s** to red so that any days with reminders are highlighted. Next, line 154 gives **s** a link property with a JavaScript URL that calls **dayClick()** with i as its sole argument, and finally line 155 writes the actual cell containing **s**, the anchored date.

Here you could insert

```
if (i == day) s = s.fontcolor("green")
```

after line 153 to have the calendar automatically highlight the current date of the month in green. To highlight the current date by means of a gold cell background color, just put

```
        if (i == day) document.write("<TD bgColor=gold>" + s)
```

after line 154 and add the word "else" at the beginning of line 155. Obviously, in both cases you can use any color you choose. To color in all the cells, simply set a **bgColor** attribute in the <TD> tag on line 155.

You might also want to do the same for any cells preceding the first of the month by modifying the <TD> tag in line 146, but the **bgColor** won't show up because the cells are empty. A simple work-around is to make the dummy content invisible by giving it the same **fgColor** as the cell's **bgColor**. For example:

```
        var dummy = '*';
```

followed by

```
        document.write("<TD bgColor=white>" + dummy.fontcolor("white");
```

in line 146 will do the trick.

To do the same with the cells following the last of the month, add

```
        while (++column <= 7) {
                document.write("<TD bgColor=white>" +
                                        star.fontcolor("white"));
        }
```

after line 162. Right now the scripted cell-writing stops at month's end and lets the browser's table-layout process fill in the rest of the row if necessary.

```
157     if (++column == 7)
158     {
159        document.write("<TR>");
160        column = 0;
161     }
162     }
163     document.write("</TABLE>");
164     document.writeln("</CENTER>");
165 }
```

The **if** sequence in lines 156 to 161 starts a new row whenever the incremented value of **column** equals 7 and resets the control variable to 0.

```
167 function dayClick(day)
168 {
169     var expdate = new Date ();
170     expdate.setTime(expdate.getTime()+(24 * 60 * 60 * 1000));
171     var prefix             = "d";
172     var theCookieName      = prefix + day;
173     var theDayclickedReminder = GetCookie(theCookieName);
174     if (theDayclickedReminder != null) {
175        alert("The reminder for day " + day + " is:"  +
                                        theDayclickedReminder);
176     }
```

The **dayClick( )** function sets and gets any reminder cookies for each day of the month. It is called by the JavaScript link attached to each date; position your mouse cursor over the eighth of the month, for instance, and you'll see the potential call in the status bar as "javascript:dayClick(8)."

dayClick( ) first creates **expDate** as a new **Date** object and sets its time to 24 hours in the future. As the value of **expDate** becomes the expiry date of these cookies, you can easily extend their lifespan by adding "* x" to the now-familiar milliseconds-per-day multiplication where **x** represents the number of days you want your cookies to survive. Bear in mind, however, that if you give them a 30-day lifespan, you'll start seeing this month's reminders popping up among next month's!

Next, line 171 assigns the letter "d" to a new variable, **prefix**, which is prepended to **day** in 172 to name the cookie. Line 173 then reaches for the cookie with that name and, if it finds one, launches an **Alert** that displays a message along with **theDayclickedReminder**, or value of the string for that particular cookie returned by **GetCookie( )**.

```
177    if (confirm("Do you wish to enter a reminder for day " +
                                        day + " of this month?"))
178    {
179        x = prompt("Enter a reminder for day "+ day +
                        " of this month", theDayclickedReminder);
180        SetCookie (theCookieName, x, expdate);
181    }
182 }
```

dayClick( ) then opens a Confirm dialog box with line 177. If the user clicks on OK, a **Prompt** opens displaying the value of **theDayclickedReminder** or **null** if there is no cookie for that date. Whatever the user enters into the **Prompt**'s input field is assigned to **x**, which becomes the value argument in the subsequent call to **SetCookie( )**.

To make this calendar capable of deleting reminders, just insert

```
        if (x == '') DeleteCookie(theCookieName);
```

after line 179 and add the word "else" to the beginning of line 180. The original CALENDAR.HTM file on the accompanying CD-ROM includes the Dortch **DeleteCookie( )** function; it was cut from this annotated version because the script does not use it.

```
183 // --> <!-- end hiding contents from old browsers   -->
184 </SCRIPT>
185 <TITLE>James Thiele's Calendar reminders
186 </TITLE>
187 </HEAD>
188 <BODY>
189 <SCRIPT LANGUAGE="JavaScript">
190 <!--  to hide script contents from old browsers
```

```
191 calendar();
192 document.write("<HR>");
193 // --> <!-- end hiding contents from old browsers  -->
194 </SCRIPT>
195 </BODY>
196 </HTML>
```

Finally, we have the body of the page containing a separate script that calls **calendar( )** and writes a horizontal rule.

An interesting exercise would be to enhance this calendar so that you could flip ahead a month or more to enter reminders, or even look back at past months. That would involve making the value of **month** user adjustable, instead of being set to the current month (as is now the case), and ensuring that **startDay** in line 135 gets the right value for writing the calendar. You'd also have to adjust the cookie-naming process in lines 171 and 172 to accommodate different months. Finally, to avoid running up against the 20-cookie limit, you might consider having one cookie for each month with a separator to distinguish days—in other words, a cookie that looks something like

March=| |Garage sale| | | | | | |Bernie's birthday| | | | | | | | | | |First day of spring!| | | | | | | | | | |

Use an array combined with the **join( )** method to create the cookie string and **split( )** to load it back into an array, and accessing individual days becomes a simple matter of indexing—you don't have to worry about counting separators. Of course, if you get that far, you'll soon be adding all of kinds of bells and whistles—why not? It's *your* SuperCalendar!

Validate

validate

| N2 | N2.01 | N2.02+ | N3 | N4 | E3 | E4 |

Password protection is arguably impossible by use of JavaScript. That is, you can set up a method in JavaScript for allowing only certain users into your site, and then watch any technically savvy user maneuver around it and onto your pages. No matter what brilliant method you use to encode the correct password, the encoding algorithms and the result have to be in the script, which is readily accessible to anyone.

On the other hand, JavaScript can temporarily halt users surfing your site, to give you a chance to let them know something, or to ask them to give you information.

This script does just that. In a two-step process, your site identifies the users— during their first visit, it drops a cookie in your browser—and gives them some information about your site, page, or whatever comes next after the halt page on your site (see Figure 5-7). The example contains the *halt page,* which holds the cookie code and the HTML form to give to or take information from the user. If the user responds agreeably to the form, the script sends them forward to the next page, which is nominally coded and included here just so the example will work properly. You can, of course, do anything you wish on this page.

```
1   <HTML>
2   <HEAD>
3   <TITLE>JavaScript Example</TITLE>
4   <SCRIPT>
5
6   function getCookieVal (offset) {
7       var endstr = document.cookie.indexOf (";", offset);
8       if (endstr == -1)
9           endstr = document.cookie.length;
10      return unescape(document.cookie.substring(offset,
                                                    endstr));
11  }
12  function GetCookie (name) {
13      var arg = name + "=";
14      var alen = arg.length;
15      var clen = document.cookie.length;
16      var i = 0;
17      while (i < clen) {
18          var j = i + alen;
19          if (document.cookie.substring(i, j) == arg)
20              return getCookieVal (j);
21          i = document.cookie.indexOf(" ", i) + 1;
22          if (i == 0) break;
23      }
24      return null;
25  }
26
27  function SetCookie (name, value) {
28      var argv = SetCookie.arguments;
29      var argc = SetCookie.arguments.length;
30      var expires = (argc > 2) ? argv[2] : null;
31      var path = (argc > 3) ? argv[3] : null;
32      var domain = (argc > 4) ? argv[4] : null;
33      var secure = (argc > 5) ? argv[5] : false;
34      document.cookie = name + "=" + escape (value) +
35          ((expires == null) ? "" : ("; expires=" +
```

```
                                            expires.toGMTString())) +
36      ((path == null) ? "" : ("; path=" + path)) +
37      ((domain == null) ? "" : ("; domain=" + domain)) +
38      ((secure == true) ? "; secure" : "");
39  }
40
41  <SCRIPT>
42  </HEAD>
43  <BODY>
44  <CENTER></CENTER>
45  <CENTER>Fill your name in the space provided. </CENTER>
46  <CENTER>Press &quot;Submit Request&quot; </CENTER>
47  <CENTER>Press &quot;Enter&quot; 
48  <FORM NAME="demoForm" onSubmit="
49      if(demoForm.UserName.value.length != 0) {
50          var expdate = new Date ();
51          expdate.setTime(expdate.getTime() +
                                    (24 * 60 * 60 * 1000));
52          SetCookie('DemoName', demoForm.UserName.value,
                                            expdate);
53          alert('Hey ' + demoForm.UserName.value + ',
                how is it going? Now all you have to do
                                    is click Enter');
54          return false;
55      } else {
56          alert('You left the Name field blank.');
57          return false;
58      }"></CENTER>
59  <CENTER></CENTER>
60  <CENTER><FONT SIZE=+1>
            Enter Your Name Here To Request Access: </FONT>
61  <INPUT TYPE="text" NAME="UserName" SIZE=40></CENTER>
62  <CENTER></CENTER>
63  <CENTER><INPUT TYPE="submit" VALUE="Submit Request">
64  <INPUT TYPE="button" VALUE="Enter"
65      onClick="
66          if(GetCookie('DemoName') == null)
67              alert('Did you submit request?')
68          else
69              window.open('open.htm', '_top')"></FORM></CENTER>
70  </BODY>
71  </HTML>
```

Here is the code for OPEN.HTM:

```
1    <HTML>
2    <HEAD>
3    <TITLE></TITLE>
4    </HEAD>
5    <BODY BGCOLOR="ffffff">
6    <H3>Hey ho daddy-o</H3>
7    </BODY>
8    </HTML>
```

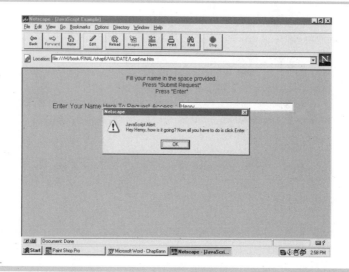

FIGURE 5-7.   Validate can be used as a personalized warning or greeting

ANNOTATIONS

The script between the <HEAD> tags on this page consists solely of three basic Dortch functions we've seen repeatedly in this chapter: **getCookieVal( )**, **GetCookie( )**, and **SetCookie( )**. The process of not loading the OPEN.HTM page until the user enters a name into the text field is controlled entirely by the event handlers attached to the two buttons. Once a name has been entered, a click on the Submit Request button creates **DemoName**, a cookie that stores the name for 24 hours. If you reload this page within that period, you can access the second page immediately, without having to reenter your name.

```
1   <HTML>
2   <HEAD>
3   <TITLE>JavaScript Example</TITLE>
4   <SCRIPT>
5
6   function getCookieVal (offset) {
7       var endstr = document.cookie.indexOf (";", offset);
8       if (endstr == -1)
9           endstr = document.cookie.length;
10      return unescape(document.cookie.substring(offset,
                                                  endstr));
11  }
12  function GetCookie (name) {
13      var arg = name + "=";
14      var alen = arg.length;
15      var clen = document.cookie.length;
16      var i = 0;
17      while (i < clen) {
18          var j = i + alen;
19          if (document.cookie.substring(i, j) == arg)
20              return getCookieVal (j);
21          i = document.cookie.indexOf(" ", i) + 1;
22          if (i == 0) break;
23      }
24      return null;
25  }
26
27  function SetCookie (name, value) {
28      var argv = SetCookie.arguments;
29      var argc = SetCookie.arguments.length;
30      var expires = (argc > 2) ? argv[2] : null;
31      var path = (argc > 3) ? argv[3] : null;
32      var domain = (argc > 4) ? argv[4] : null;
33      var secure = (argc > 5) ? argv[5] : false;
34      document.cookie = name + "=" + escape (value) +
35          ((expires == null) ? "" : ("; expires=" +
                                        expires.toGMTString())) +
36          ((path == null) ? "" : ("; path=" + path)) +
37          ((domain == null) ? "" : ("; domain=" + domain)) +
38          ((secure == true) ? "; secure" : "");
39  }
```

Notice that here we have the more recent version of the Dortch functions, in which **escape( )** and **unescape( )** replace the homemade encode-decode routine used in the two preceding scripts.

```
41   <SCRIPT>
42   </HEAD>
43   <BODY>
44   <CENTER></CENTER>
45   <CENTER>Fill your name in the space provided. </CENTER>
46   <CENTER>Press &quot;Submit Request&quot; </CENTER>
47   <CENTER>Press &quot;Enter&quot; 
48   <FORM NAME="demoForm" onSubmit="
49       if(demoForm.UserName.value.length != 0) {
50           var expdate = new Date ();
51           expdate.setTime(expdate.getTime() +
                                     (24 * 60 * 60 * 1000));
52           SetCookie('DemoName', demoForm.UserName.value,
                                                 expdate);
53           alert('Hey ' + demoForm.UserName.value + ',
                   how is it going? Now all you have to do
                                     is click Enter');
54           return false;
55       } else {
56           alert('You left the Name field blank.');
57           return false;
58       }"></CENTER>
```

Here we have an **onSubmit( )** event handler attached to the form on this page. It responds to a click on Submit Request because the INPUT TYPE is "submit" (line 63). Change the type to "button" and assign the preceding code to its **onClick( )** handler, and this page will function exactly the way it does now.

The opening **if** tests the length of the value in the **UserName** text field. If it's anything but zero, meaning an empty string, the **expdate Date** object is created and assigned a time 24 hours later. It is then passed to **SetCookie( )** as the third argument, which sets the expiry date. The first argument, **DemoName**, becomes the cookie's name and the second—whatever you type in the text field—becomes its value.

This pops open an **Alert** that incorporates your name (or whatever you typed) into the greeting. Otherwise, if you fail to enter a name, the **else** clause launches its own **Alert**, which bluntly reminds you to fill in the form.

```
59   <CENTER></CENTER>
60   <CENTER><FONT SIZE=+1>
             Enter Your Name Here To Request Access: </FONT>
```

```
61   <INPUT TYPE="text" NAME="UserName" SIZE=40></CENTER>
62   <CENTER></CENTER>
63   <CENTER><INPUT TYPE="submit" VALUE="Submit Request">
64   <INPUT TYPE="button" VALUE="Enter"
65       onClick="
66           if(GetCookie('DemoName') == null)
67               alert('Did you submit request?')
68           else
69               window.open('open.htm', '_top')"></FORM></CENTER>
70   </BODY>
71   </HTML>
```

The Enter button starts out checking for the **DemoName** cookie. If it doesn't find one, an **Alert** reminds you that you must first click on Submit Request. If it does, a window opens and loads OPEN.HTM. The **_top** argument to **open( )** ensures that the page appears in the main browser as opposed to a separate window. You can replace that line with

`document.location = "open.htm"`

if you wish, with no adverse effects.

```
1    <HTML>
2    <HEAD>
3    <TITLE></TITLE>
4    </HEAD>
5    <BODY BGCOLOR="ffffff">
6    <H3>Hey ho daddy-o</H3>
7    </BODY>
8    </HTML>
```

As you can see, the code for OPEN.HTM itself is pure HTML and quite simple, so there's really no need to comment on it. It serves as a placeholder for the page(s) of your own making that you want to guard with an "Identify yourself first" routine.

In assessing the value of cookies, don't be misled by their diminutive name. Like the real thing, they can pack a wallop, depending on what you put in them. While it's easy to shrug off 4K as trivial in a world of gigabytes, consider that it's the equivalent of about 750 words. That's roughly a letter-size page, with one-inch margins all around, filled with one long single-spaced paragraph in 12-point Times New Roman. Or it's equivalent to the length of a six-minute speech delivered at a relatively brisk pace of 120 words a minute. Twenty cookies add up to 20 such pages, or a two-hour speech. In other words, you could probably fit an entire movie script into the allotted 82K.

The most important thing to realize in working with cookies is that they are essentially data strings capable of storing information between visits to a site or within the span of a browser session. Your ability to develop cookies depends entirely on your understanding of JavaScript's string-handling functions and your skill in using them.

Last but scarcely least, never forget that, from the standpoint of data integrity, cookies are a totally unreliable medium for storing information between browser sessions, if only because cookie recipients can easily open COOKIES.TXT, scoff at the "Do not edit" instruction, and tamper with the contents at will—or simply delete the file altogether. Cookies are only untouchable within a browser session, while they reside in memory, until they get written to file.

On the other hand, for data that "doesn't really matter" or of the kind that tampering with it has more impact on the user than on you or your organization, cookies can serve as very simple and effective means of giving your client-server interface an attractive personal touch.

Web Servers That Work with Cookies

Here is an incomplete list of servers that support HTTP cookies. The list covers most of the popular web servers, and some are not included simply because we—and no one we know—has tested them.

Apache   This merges header lines onto one line (no redirect and set-cookie at the same time). There is a bug with some versions of Apache that will set a cookie that looks like this:

```
s=09871230948109470192834
```

whenever any other cookie is set. A patch is available from the Apache Project web site. In addition, versions 1.0x and 1.1x can only set one cookie at a time; you can set multiple cookies under version 1.2.

IBM's Internet Connection Server 4.1   This has cookie support, although early versions of their browser did not.

Microsoft Internet Information Server   This merges header lines onto one line (no redirect and set-cookie at the same time).

Netscape Commerce Server 1.12-1.13 for Windows NT, HP, AIX, and SUN   NT versions before 1.13 should be avoided.

O'Reilly's Website 1.1 and Website Professional   You cannot set it to redirect and enforce cookies at the same time.

Other servers that work with cookies include:

◆ Alibaba 2, Windows 95, and NT

◆ EnterpriseWeb IBM Mainframes

- Microsoft FrontPage Server
- NCSA HTTPD 1.5a
- OmniHTTPD for Windows 95
- ORACLE WebServer 2.0 Solaris
- Pictorus Net Servers Mac
- PowerWeb Server++ OS/2
- Purveyor Version 1.2 for NT
- WebServer 4D MacContrib
- WebQuest 2.1 NT
- Webstar 1.2.3 (and up) Macintosh

Search Engines

Don't get your hopes up. It is impractical (at best) to try to produce even a minimally featured webwide search engine using JavaScript. JavaScript simply does not lend itself to interfacing with offline data sources. There are more powerful functions available in CGI (Common Gateway Interface), Java, and other web server-enabled applications that let users find information online.

That said, JavaScript can be used for limited types of data search-related functions that we have grouped under the title "Search Engines." That title is somewhat misleading—for example, you cannot program CGI functions into JavaScript (even a server-side JavaScript application), and therefore cannot create a true Internet search engine such as you might find at Yahoo (**www.yahoo.com**) or AltaVista (**www.altavista.digital.com**). However, you can implement specific Internet search-related features using JavaScript.

This chapter offers scripts in three categories:

◆ *Search agents*   You cannot use JavaScript to create a search engine, but JavaScript can be very useful as a front end to search engines. You may have seen a few of these on the Internet. Users are presented with one or more data entry forms to type in search terms; a drop-down menu gives them the option of choosing from a variety of search engines. This is a helpful tool for users and a nice addition to your web site.

◆ *Site search*   Apropos of our comments leading off this chapter, it is unusual to find a JavaScript that can actually perform a search of the contents at your site. The one we have chosen even uses a type of database; in this case, the database "fields" are hidden HTML files that contain information about your web pages.

◆ *Small database (or array) search and display*   These scripts require that you embed a data source directly into the script, which is then placed on your web page. The data source must be limited in size and scope. If you embed too many data records in your script, then users must wait a corresponding amount of time for the page containing the HTML, script, and embedded data records to download. The examples we provide use a very small set of data records, which is appropriate for this kind of application.

multi1

Online Search Agent 1

[N2 [N2.01 [N2.02+ [N3 [N4 [E3 [E4

The JavaScript search agent—which sends a user's search term to a searchable database, such as Yahoo, and in turn sends the user's browser to a search-results page on that site—is the most common pairing of search functionality and JavaScript. Therefore, we have more examples of that sort of application.

This example presents the search agent functionality at its simplest. Users are presented with an HTML forms interface containing an area to type in their search term and a selection box of search engines (see Figure 6-1). They enter their search term and decide which search engine to use based on choices that you as webmaster make. Then they select a Submit button, leave your web site, and go to the associated search engine's site. The results of their search are then displayed in their browser.

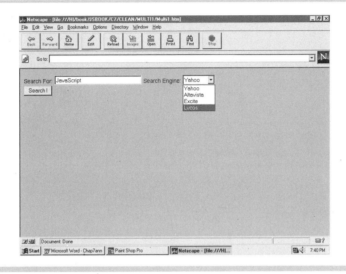

FIGURE 6-1.   Adding functionality to this script is not difficult

Implementing this kind of search agent is very easy. Simply paste the script and form code into an area of your page. Many webmasters reserve a space at the bottom of a page for the offsite search agent. This is because the agent takes the user away from their site. In addition, the upper portion of the web page may contain a sitewide search engine.

To extend a higher level of user friendliness and interactivity to visitors, you may want to place this search agent on its own page. In this way, you can highlight its search features throughout your web site. Most users visit the Web to search for information anyway, and if you can offer them a sort of all-in-one search feature that lets them find that information, you may get them to visit your pages again.

Adding functionality to this script is not difficult, either. You can quickly add more search engine links in the code, and if you are against sending your users away from your site (perhaps to never return), then it may be possible to have the search results open in a separate window or frame.

```
1    <html>
2    <title>
3    </title>
4    <head>
5    <script language="JavaScript">
6    var FirstForm;
7    function StartSearch(){
8        document.forms[FirstForm
             +document.InputForm.SearchSelect.selectedIndex]
                                            .elements[0].value=
                        document.InputForm.SearchWords.value;
9        document.forms[FirstForm
         +document.InputForm.SearchSelect.selectedIndex].submit();
10   }
11   </script>
12   </head>
13   <body>
14   <form Name="InputForm">
15   Search For: <input name="SearchWords" type=text size=30>
16   Search Engine: <select Name="SearchSelect">
17   <option selected>Yahoo
18   <option>AltaVista
19   <option>Excite
20   <option>Lycos
21   </select>
22   <br><input type=button value="Search!"
                                        onClick="StartSearch()">
23   </form>
24   <script language="JavaScript">
                     FirstForm=document.forms.length</script>
25   <form action="http://search.yahoo.com/bin/search"
                                                    method=get>
26   <input type="hidden" size=35 name=p>
27   </form>
28   <form action=
     "http://www.altavista.digital.com/cgi-bin/query" method=get>
29   <input type="hidden" name=q size=35 maxlength=200 value="">
30   <input type="hidden" name=pg value=q>
31   <input type="hidden" name="fmt" value=".">
32   <input type="hidden" name=what value=web>
33   </form>
34   <form action="http://www.excite.com/search.gw" method=post>
35   <input type="hidden" name="search" size=35>
```

```
36   <input type="hidden" name="searchType" value="Keyword">
37   <input type="hidden" name="category"
                                      value="default" checked>
38   <input type="hidden" name="mode" value="relevance">
39   <input type="hidden" name="showqbe" value="1">
40   <input type="hidden" name="display" value="html3,hb">
41   </form>
42   <form action="http://www.lycos.com/cgi-bin/
                      nph-randurl/cgi-bin/largehostpursuit1.html">
43   <input type=hidden size=35 name="query">
44   </form>
45   </body>
46   </HTML>
```

ANNOTATIONS

This script uses a set of four invisible forms—one for each search engine listed—whose hidden fields contain the elements of the appropriate query string for that server. The string is automatically assembled and sent to the search engine by calling on JavaScript's built-in **submit( )** method.

```
1    <html>
2    <title>
3    </title>
4    <head>
5    <script language="JavaScript">
6    var FirstForm;
```

The script begins by declaring an uninitialized variable named **FirstForm**, which in a separate script in line 24 is assigned the value of **document.forms.length**, or the number of forms on the page. The outcome of this assignment depends entirely on its position within the HTML code that creates the form. Up to line 24, there is only one form on the page, so **FirstForm** gets a value of 1. Move the assignment to line 45, and the value of **FirstForm** becomes 5, because four more forms have now been created on the page.

As **FirstForm** serves to align the indexing of the forms array and selection list by compensating for the first user-input form on the page, you could initialize it with

```
                    var FirstForm = 1
```

in line 6 and delete line 24 to eliminate worries about the position of the assignment. Of course, if you have one or more other forms preceding this script on your page, you'll want to assign **FirstForm** the appropriate higher number. In that case, however, you're better off leaving the variable as it is, because line 24 will automatically take care of counting the forms up to that point on the page. Just make sure those other forms are placed either before line 24 or after line 44, so as not to mess up the indexing essential for this script to work properly.

But if this is the only form on your page, you can dispense with the **FirstForm** variable altogether by moving the user-input form (lines 14 through 23) below line 44. The forms array and selection indices will then be aligned, and you can delete "**FirstForm+**" from the index references in lines 8 and 9.

```
7    function StartSearch(){
8       document.forms[FirstForm
             +document.InputForm.SearchSelect.selectedIndex]
                                          .elements[0].value=
                         document.InputForm.SearchWords.value;
9       document.forms[FirstForm
            +document.InputForm.SearchSelect.selectedIndex].submit();
10   }
```

Our script's sole function, **StartSearch( )**, called by the "Search!" button's **onClick** event handler in line 22, makes whatever the user types in the input field the value of the first element in the form associated with the selected search engine. For example, if you were to do an AltaVista search for "cam lock", line 8 would make "cam lock" the value of the hidden element named **q** (line 29) in the AltaVista form (lines 28 through 33). For a Lycos search, it would become the value of the **query** element (line 43) in the Lycos form (lines 42 through 44).

Line 9 then uses the forms array index to submit the form. **submit( )** assembles the form's name=value pairs into a continuous string such as

```
http://altavista.digital.com/cgi-bin/query?
                       q=cam+lock&pg=q&fmt=d&what=web
```

which is sent to the search-engine server for processing.

```
11   </script>
12   </head>
13   <body>
14   <form Name="InputForm">
15   Search For: <input name="SearchWords" type=text size=30>
16   Search Engine: <select Name="SearchSelect">
17   <option selected>Yahoo
18   <option>AltaVista
19   <option>Excite
20   <option>Lycos
21   </select>
22   <br><input type=button value="Search!"
                                    onClick="StartSearch()">
23   </form>
24   <script language="JavaScript">
```

```
                         FirstForm=document.forms.length</script>
25  <form action="http://search.yahoo.com/bin/search"
                                              method=get>
26  <input type="hidden" size=35 name=p>
27  </form>
28  <form action=
     "http://www.altavista.digital.com/cgi-bin/query" method=get>
29  <input type="hidden" name=q size=35 maxlength=200 value="">
30  <input type="hidden" name=pg value=q>
31  <input type="hidden" name="fmt" value=".">
32  <input type="hidden" name=what value=web>
33  </form>
34  <form action="http://www.excite.com/search.gw" method=post>
35  <input type="hidden" name="search" size=35>
36  <input type="hidden" name="searchType" value="Keyword">
37  <input type="hidden" name="category"
                                  value="default" checked>
38  <input type="hidden" name="mode" value="relevance">
39  <input type="hidden" name="showqbe" value="1">
40  <input type="hidden" name="display" value="html3,hb">
41  </form>
42  <form action="http://www.lycos.com/cgi-bin/
                  nph-randurl/cgi-bin/largehostpursuit1.html">
43  <input type=hidden size=35 name="query">
44  </form>
45  </body>
46  </HTML>
```

Apart from the miniscript on line 24 that assigns **FirstForm** its value, the remainder of the page consists of the HTML code for the user-input and hidden search-engine forms.

If you decide to use this type of device on your page, don't forget it means you'll have to keep the name=value pairs in the hidden forms in sync with search-engine server requirements. If any of the servers changes the submit string format, you'll have to make the corresponding adjustments.

To learn about the strings sent to the server, just visit an engine, enter a search item, and the string will be displayed in your browser's location field. From there you can easily copy it to a text file for analysis and storage. The string begins with the engine-server's URL followed by one or more name=value pairs separated by ampersands (&).

You can also adapt these search agents by tinkering with the form elements. Change the value of the AltaVista **what** input (line 32) from "web" to "news," for instance, and the result will be a search of newsgroups instead of web pages. You could even enhance the input form with radio buttons or checkboxes to accommodate search variations or refinements.

multi2

Online Search Agent 2

N2 N2.01 N2.02+ N3 N4 E3 E4

Thoughtful webmasters are always on the lookout for ways to add a bit of interactivity to their pages. Although the previous JavaScript example offers a perfectly usable search agent, the following script takes the same basic coding principles and adds a unique bit of interactive feedback when the user clicks on the Submit button.

There are two HTML pages at work in this example. The first, an entry form, is done in the style of the earlier example—the user is presented with a forms-based text entry field and a choice of search engines to use (see Figure 6-2). A second page, which loads when the Submit button is pressed, lets users know their query has been sent and that the engine will return the search results soon (see Figure 6-3).

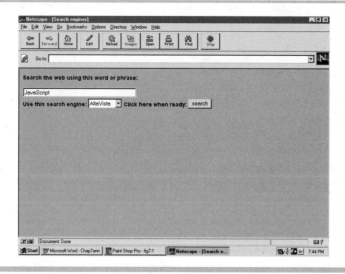

FIGURE 6-2.   The initial search form

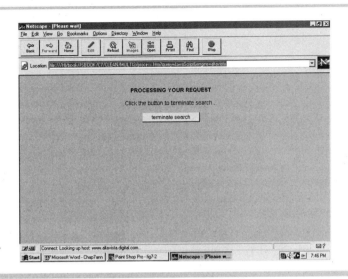

FIGURE 6-3. The search is initiated and offers a bit of feedback

```
1   <HTML>
2   <HEAD>
3   <TITLE>Search engines</TITLE>
4   </HEAD>
5   <BODY>
6   <FORM METHOD="get" ACTION="process.htm">
7   <B><FONT SIZE=3>Search the web using this word or phrase:
8   </B><P>
9   <INPUT TYPE="text" SIZE=40 MAXLENGTH=80
                                    VALUE="" NAME="query">
10  <BR>
11  <B>Use this search engine:</B>
12  <SELECT NAME="engine" ALIGN="right">
13  <OPTION VALUE="altavista" SELECTED>AltaVista
14  <OPTION VALUE="excite">Excite
```

```
15   <OPTION VALUE="infoseek">Infoseek
16   <OPTION VALUE="lycos">Lycos
17   <OPTION VALUE="magellan">Magellan
18   <OPTION VALUE="yahoo">Yahoo
19   </SELECT>
20   <B>Click here when ready: </B>
21   <INPUT TYPE="submit" VALUE="search">
22   </FORM>
23   </BODY>
24   </HTML>
```

This is the JavaScript that initiates the search and takes users to the search engine:

```
1    <HTML>
2    <HEAD>
3    <TITLE>Please wait</TITLE>
4    <SCRIPT LANGUAGE="JavaScript">
5    <!--
6    var prefix = new prefixObject()
7
8    function prefixObject() {
9        this.lycos =
                    "http://www.lycos.com/cgi-bin/pursuit?query="
10       this.altavista =
            "http://www.altavista.digital.com/cgi-bin/query?pg=q&q="
11       this.infoseek =
                        "http://guide-p.infoseek.com//Titles?qt="
12       this.yahoo = "http://av.yahoo.com/bin/search?p="
13       this.magellan =
                "http://searcher.mckinley.com/searcher.cgi?query="
14       this.excite = "http://www.excite.com/search.gw?search="
15   }
16   function callSearch() {
17       var queryArray = location.search.split("=")
18       var query =
            queryArray[1].substring(0, queryArray[1].indexOf("&"))
19       var engine = queryArray[2]
20       location.href = prefix[engine] + query
21   }
22   // -->
23   //SCRIPT>
24   </HEAD>
```

```
25  <BODY onLoad="timerID = setTimeout('callSearch()', 4000)">
26  <CENTER>
27  <BR>
28  <B><FONT SIZE=3>PROCESSING YOUR REQUEST</FONT></B>
29  <P>
30  Click the button to terminate search...
31  <FORM>
32  <INPUT TYPE="button" VALUE="terminate search"
                               onClick="clearTimeout(timerID)">
33  </FORM>
34  </CENTER>
35  </BODY>
36  </HTML>
```

ANNOTATIONS

This script uses the form on the first page to create a location string that loads the
second page, PROCESS.HTM. After a four-second timeout during which the user
can cancel the search, the **callSearch( )** function on the second page pulls the user-
specified query item and search engine from the location string and assembles the
appropriate search string to submit to the engine server.

```
1   <HTML>
2   <HEAD>
3   <TITLE>Search engines</TITLE>
4   </HEAD>
5   <BODY>
6   <FORM METHOD="get" ACTION="process.htm">
7   <B><FONT SIZE=3>Search the web using this word or phrase:
8   </B><P>
9   <INPUT TYPE="text" SIZE=40 MAXLENGTH=80
                                          VALUE="" NAME="query">
10  <BR>
11  <B>Use this search engine:</B>
12  <SELECT NAME="engine" ALIGN="right">
13  <OPTION VALUE="altavista" SELECTED>AltaVista
14  <OPTION VALUE="excite">Excite
15  <OPTION VALUE="infoseek">Infoseek
16  <OPTION VALUE="lycos">Lycos
17  <OPTION VALUE="magellan">Magellan
18  <OPTION VALUE="yahoo">Yahoo
19  </SELECT>
```

```
20  <B>Click here when ready: </B>
21  <INPUT TYPE="submit" VALUE="search">
22  </FORM>
23  </BODY>
24  </HTML>
```

This page uses pure HTML code to create a location string. Clicking on the submit button labeled "search" (line 21) causes the two values in the form—the user-specified query item and search engine—to be read and loads the file PROCESS.HTM assigned to the form's **action** attribute in line 6. Requesting an Excite search for "Hadrosaurus," for example, produces

`process.htm?query=Hadrosaurus&engine=excite`

You can see the string in your browser's location field.

```
1   <HTML>
2   <HEAD>
3   <TITLE>Please wait</TITLE>
4   <SCRIPT LANGUAGE="JavaScript">
5   <!--
6   var prefix = new prefixObject()
7
8   function prefixObject() {
9       this.lycos =
                    "http://www.lycos.com/cgi-bin/pursuit?query="
10      this.altavista =
             "http://www.altavista.digital.com/cgi-bin/query?pg=q&q="
11      this.infoseek =
                        "http://guide-p.infoseek.com//Titles?qt="
12      this.yahoo = "http://av.yahoo.com/bin/search?p="
13      this.magellan =
                "http://searcher.mckinley.com/searcher.cgi?query="
14      this.excite = "http://www.excite.com/search.gw?search="
15  }
```

The script first declares a global variable, **prefix**, as a new instance of the object **prefixObject**, which is then created by lines 8 to 15. Note that JavaScript tolerates a reversal of the logical order of object creation followed by instantiation, so that line 6 does not produce a "**prefixObject** is undefined" JavaScript error message. You cannot, however, do the same with variables. Write

`document.write(firstName);`

`var firstName = "Vanessa";`

and you will get a "**firstName** is undefined" error message.

With the instantiation, **prefix** acquires six properties—**lycos**, **altavista**, **infoseek**, **yahoo**, **magellan**, and **excite**—each consisting of the engine's HTTP address and query string up to the point where the user-entered search item goes. In other words, write

```
document.write(prefix.yahoo)
```

and the output will be

```
http://av.yahoo.com/bin/search?p=
```

Test for the value of **prefixObject.lycos**, however, and the output will be "undefined" because the **this** keyword refers to the calling object—in this case **prefix** or any other instance of **prefixObject** created with the **new** keyword—and not to the **prefixObject( )** function in which it is used.

```
16   function callSearch() {
17       var queryArray = location.search.split("=")
18       var query =
             queryArray[1].substring(0, queryArray[1].indexOf("&"))
19       var engine = queryArray[2]
20       location.href = prefix[engine] + query
21   }
```

The script's main function, **callSearch( )**, is assigned to the <BODY> tag's **onLoad** event handler and starts running after a four-second timeout unless the user cancels the search by clicking on the button labeled "terminate search."

It first creates a new array, **queryArray**, by splitting the **location.search** string at each "=" sign. The **search** property of the **location** object is the portion of the string beginning with the question mark. Using our earlier example, the value of **location.search** would be

```
?query=Hadrosaurus&engine=excite
```

with **split("=")** creating the following array:

```
queryArray[0] = ?query
queryArray[1] = Hadrosaurus&engine
queryArray[2] = excite
```

Line 18 then assigns a new variable, **query**, the substring of **queryArray[1]** extending up to the ampersand. Here it would get the single word "Hadrosaurus." Enter a multiple-word search item in the LOAD-ME.HTM text field, and **query** becomes a string consisting of those words separated by plus signs, for example:

```
Monty+Python's+Flying+Circus
```

The next line assigns **queryArray[2]** to another new variable, **engine**. Then line 20 executes the search by setting the browser window's location to a URL consisting of the specified search-engine address pulled from the **prefix** object with the **query** string attached. In the case of our example, it becomes

```
http://www.excite.com/search.gw?search=Hadrosaurus
```

which the engine-server then processes.

```
22   // -->
23   //SCRIPT>
24   </HEAD>
25   <BODY onLoad="timerID = setTimeout('callSearch()', 4000)">
26   <CENTER>
27   <BR>
28   <B><FONT SIZE=3>PROCESSING YOUR REQUEST</FONT></B>
29   <P>
30   Click the button to terminate search...
31   <FORM>
32   <INPUT TYPE="button" VALUE="terminate search"
                                onClick="clearTimeout(timerID)">
33   </FORM>
34   </CENTER>
35   </BODY>
36   </HTML>
```

Apart from the delayed **onLoad** call to **callSearch( )** in line 25, the body of the page consists of a message that tells the user what is happening and a button whose **onClick** event handler clears the four-second timeout assigned to the **timerID** identifier, thereby canceling the search.

If you don't like the two-page approach used by this script, you can easily adapt the code to a single page. First, copy the entire script from PROCESS.HTM to the head of LOAD-ME.HTM. Then change line 6 of LOAD-ME.HTM from

```
            <FORM METHOD="get" ACTION="process.htm">
```

to

```
            <FORM NAME=searcher>
```

or any other name of your choice. Next, revise **callSearch( )** to read

```
function callSearch() {
    with (document.searcher) {
        var i = engine.selectedIndex;
        var userEng = engine.options[i].value;
        var userQ = query.value.split(" ").join("+");
    }
    location.href = prefix[userEng] + userQ;
}
```

This function uses the **selectedIndex** property to read the **value** property of the option chosen from the **engine** selection list and assigns it to a variable named **userEng**. Then another variable, **userQ**, gets the user-entered query string with any blank spaces replaced by plus signs. Finally, as in the original script, the two variables are used to compile a **location** string with **userEng** indexing the **prefix** object.

Lastly, change the TYPE attribute of the INPUT element on line 21 of LOAD-ME.HTM from "submit" to "button," and assign **callSearch( )** to its **onClick** event handler. Or, if you prefer to keep the timeout/cancel feature, just copy the assignment from the **onLoad** handler in the <BODY> tag of PROCESS.HTM so that your code reads

```
onClick = "timerID = setTimeout('callSearch()', 4000)"
```

Another possible variation on this script is the use of radio buttons instead of a selection list. In that case you could use a **for** loop to scan for the button whose **checked** property is **true** and assign its value to **userEng**. Or you could display each search-engine option as a graphic or text link and make **userEng** the argument to **callSearch( )**:

```
function callSearch(userEng) {
    userQ = document.searcher.query.value.split(" ").join("+");
    location.href = prefix[userEng] + userQ;
}
```

Then call it from each link with the appropriate argument, for example:

```
<a href="javascript:callSearch('lycos')">LYCOS</a>
<a href="javascript:callSearch('excite')">EXCITE</a>
```

and so on. Whatever user-input mechanism you adopt, the important thing is to make sure the value assigned to each choice corresponds to a property of the **prefix** object so that the latter can be properly referenced. You can also easily expand the list of choices with the URL strings for other search engines found throughout this chapter by adding **this** statements to the **prefixObject( )** function. The beauty of this script is that its simple, object-oriented design makes it very easy to maintain, modify, and expand.

boojum

Boojum

N2 **N2.01** **N2.02+** **N3** **N4** **E3** **E4**

If you want to really get your feet wet when it comes to putting a search agent on your web pages, try Boojum. Compared with the two previous examples, it is a more feature-rich implementation of the JavaScript search agent and makes use of HTML frames.

Boojum is a variation on a JavaScript search agent called Snark, which was written by Justin Boyan and should still live at **http://www.cs.cmu.edu/~jab/snark**. Boojum, which was created by John Campbell, is a modification of Boyan's script and in our opinion is a better implementation of comparable code (sorry, Justin).

If you are familiar with the writing of Lewis Carroll, the Snark and Boojum are related. In the 1870s, Lewis Carroll (of *Alice in Wonderland* fame) wrote a humorous poem called *The Hunting of the Snark,* in which a group of travelers search for the elusive and mysterious Snark. The Boojum, a mystical Snark alter-ego, figures prominently in the poem's dénouement, but is never described or illustrated.

The JavaScript Boojum's author, John Campbell, explained after he modified the Snark search engine, that "it is a Boojum"—paraphrasing Carroll. "And," he adds, "if you look at the Boojum page with a non-JavaScript-capable browser, you will see nothing. The Snark in Lewis Carroll's poem was rather like his Cheshire Cat in that it kept vanishing away."

This is Boojum's frameset page:

```
1    <html>
2    <head>
3    <TITLE>Boojum JavaSearch from the Jesus Army</TITLE>
4    </head>
5    <frameset rows=80,*>
6    <frame name="panel" src="boojum1.html" scrolling="no">
7    <frame name="display" src="hunting.html">
8    </frameset>
9    <noframes>
10   <h2 align=center>JavaScript searching</h2>
11   Sorry! For this to work, you need a browser with frames
12   and JavaScript compatibility (such as<a href=
13   "http://home.netscape.com/comprod/mirror/index.html">
14   Netscape v2.0</a> or better).<p>
15   </noframes>
16   </html>
```

This is the top frame that contains the search form:

```
1    <HTML>
2    <head>
3    <TITLE> Hunting the SNARK with JavaScript </TITLE>
4    </head>
5    <body bgcolor="#ffffc0" text="#000080" link="#FF0000"
                              vlink="#800000" alink="#FFFF00">
6    <SCRIPT language="JavaScript">
7    <!-- hide this script
8    // Most code in this script is Copyright(C) 1996,
                              Justin Boyan, jab+j@cs.cmu.edu
9    // For documentation and more info, see:
                              http://www.cs.cmu.edu/~jab/snark/
10   // Modified by John Campbell, john@jesus.org.uk 7 May 1996
```

```
11   // The Snark has changed to a Boojum, you see
12
13   var MAX_ENGINES = 30;
14   var SNARK_STRING = "hunting+the+snark";
15
16   function MakeArray(n) {
17      for (var i = 1; i <= n; i++) {
18        this[i] = 0;
19      }
20      this.maxlen = n;
21      this.len = 0;
22      return this;
23   }
24
25   var engs = new MakeArray(MAX_ENGINES);
26
27   function find_substring(needle, haystack) {
28      var i, needlen = needle.length, haylen = haystack.length;
29      for (i=0; i<=haylen-needlen; i++) {
30         if (needle == haystack.substring(i,i+needlen))
31           return i;
32      }
33      return false;
34   }
35
36   function Engine(name, opts, home, search) {
37      var snark = find_substring(SNARK_STRING, search);
38      this.name = name;
39      this.opts = opts;
40      this.home = home;
41      this.pre_snark = search.substring(0,snark);
42      this.post_snark=search.substring(snark+
                             SNARK_STRING.length, search.length);
43   }
44
45   function Add(name, opts, home, search) {
46      engs.len++;
47      if (engs.len <= engs.maxlen) {
48         engs[engs.len] = new Engine(name, opts, home, search)
49      }
50      else {
51         alert("Better increase MAX_ENGINES: "
```

```
                                              + engs.len + ">" + engs.maxlen)
52      }
53  }
54
55  function DisplayForm() {
56      document.writeln('<CENTER><FORM Name=Snarkform
                    OnSubmit="HandleForm(this); return false">');
57      document.writeln('Look for:
                                    <INPUT size=35 name="query">');
58      document.writeln('In: <SELECT name="service">');
59      for (i=1; i <= engs.len; i++) {
60          document.writeln("<OPTION " + engs[i].opts + "> "
                                            + engs[i].name);
61      }
62      document.writeln('</SELECT>
                        <input type=submit value="Search"><br>');
63      document.writeln('A blank query takes you to the search
                    engine\'s home page.      ');
64      document.writeln('    
                        <a href="boojum_y.html" target="display">
                                    <i>Why Boojum?</i></a>');
65      document.writeln('</FORM> </CENTER>');
66      document.Snarkform.query.focus()
67  }
68
69  function HandleForm(form) {
70      var i, newq="", oldq=form.query.value;
71      for (i=0; i<oldq.length; i++) {
72          var thischar = oldq.charAt(i);
73          if (thischar != ' ')
74              newq += thischar;
75          else if (lastchar != ' ')
76              newq += '+';
77          lastchar = thischar;
78      }
79      var eng = engs[1+form.service.selectedIndex];
80      parent.display.location.href = newq ?
                eng.pre_snark + newq + eng.post_snark : eng.home;
81      document.Snarkform.query.focus()
82  }
83
84  Add("Churches on the Web","",
```

```
 85         "http://www.christianity.net/churchlocator/",
 86         "http://www.christianity.net/cgi/search.cgi?query=
                                        hunting+the+snark");
 87
 88  Add("Church Locator","",
 89        "http://netministries.org/churches.htm",
 90        "http://netministries.org/cgi-bin/nmform02.exe?
                            CHURCHNAME=hunting+the+snark");
 91
 92  Add("CrossSearch","",
 93        "http://www.crosssearch.com/",
 94        "http://www.crosssearch.com/index.html?search=
                                        hunting+the+snark");
 95
 96  Add("Goshen Christian GoSearch", "",
 97        "http://www.goshen.net",
 98        "http://www.goshen.net/gosearch/search2.cgi?words=
                    hunting+the+snark&i=frames&how2=gosearch&bool=
                                AND&s=1&e=10&i=quick&showd=YES");
 99
100  Add("Goshen Christian GoSeek", "",
101        "http://www.goshen.net",
102        "http://www.goshen.net/goseek/goseek.cgi?words=
                        hunting+the+snark&i=frames&s=1&e=10");
103
104  Add("AltaVista", "SELECTED",
105        "http://altavista.digital.com/",
106        "http://altavista.digital.com/cgi-bin/query?pg=
                        q&what=web&fmt=d&q=hunting+the+snark");
107
108  Add("AltaVista (UseNet)", "",
109        "http://altavista.digital.com/",
110        "http://altavista.digital.com/cgi-bin/query?pg=
                        q&what=news&fmt=d&q=hunting+the+snark" );
111
112  Add("DejaNews", "",
113         "http://www.dejanews.com/",
114         "http://search.dejanews.com/nph-dnquery.xp?query=
                                hunting+the+snark&defaultOp=
                            AND&svcclass=dncurrent&maxhits=25");
115
116  Add("Excite", "",
```

```
117        "http://www.excite.com/",
118        "http://www.excite.com/search.gw?search=
                            hunting+the+snark&collection=web");
119
120  Add("Galaxy","",
121        "http://galaxy.einet.net/galaxy.html",
122        "http://galaxy.einet.net/www/www.html?
                                        hunting+the+snark");
123
124  Add("HotBot", "",
125        "http://www.hotbot.com",
126        "http://www.hotbot.com/search.html?MT
                                =hunting+the+snark&DC=25");
127
128  Add("Infoseek UltraSmart", "",
129        "http://www.infoseek.com/Home?pg=Home.html&sv=A2",
130        "http://www.infoseek.com/Titles?qt=
                            hunting+the+snark&col=WW&sv=A2");
131
132  Add("Infoseek (Usenet)", "",
133        "http://www.infoseek.com",
134        "http://www.infoseek.com/Titles?qt=
                            hunting+the+snark&col=NN&sv=A2");
135
136  Add("Lycos", "",
137        "http://www.lycos.com/",
138        "http://www.lycos.com/cgi-bin/pursuit?query=
                            hunting+the+snark&backlink=639");
139
140  Add("Magellan","",
141        "http://www.mckinley.com/",
142        "http://www.mckinley.com/extsearch.cgi?query=
                                        hunting+the+snark");
143
144  Add("MetaCrawler","",
145        "http://www.metacrawler.com/",
146        "http://www.metacrawler.com/crawler?general=
                            hunting+the+snark&method=0&format=1");
147
148  Add("NLightN Universe","",
149        "http://nln5001.nlightn.com/nlndemo/docs/altlogin.htm",
150        "http://nln5001.nlightn.com/cgi-win/cgitest.exe/
```

```
                                     linksearch?FINDSTRING=
                      hunting+the+snark&SQUID=3262XXXXXX0&dbfiles=
                           Universe&search-method=within+field");
151
152 Add("OpenText", "",
153     "http://search.opentext.com",
154     "http://search.opentext.com/omw/simplesearch?SearchFor=
                                   hunting+the+snark&mode=and");
155
156 Add("Reference.com (Newsgroups)","",
157     "http://www.reference.com/",
158     "http://www.reference.com/cgi-bin/pn/go?searchspace=
                        Usenet+%26+Mailing+List+Archive&ranking=
                        by+Relevance&querytext=hunting+the+snark");
159
160 Add("WebCrawler", "",
161     "http://query.webcrawler.com/",
162     "http://query.webcrawler.com/cgi-bin/WebQuery?
                        searchText=hunting+the+snark&maxHits=25");
163
164 Add("Yahoo!", "",
165     "http://www.yahoo.com/",
166     "http://search.yahoo.com/bin/search?p=
                                        hunting+the+snark" );
167
168 DisplayForm();
169 // done hiding from old browsers -->
170 </SCRIPT>
171 <pre>
172 </pre>
173 Do not load this page directly.<p>Please go to the
                            <a href="load-me.html" target="_top">
                                Boojum page</a> instead.<br>
174 </BODY>
175 </html>
```

This is the lower frame containing explanatory information or directions on how to use the search agent:

```
1   <html>
2   <head>
```

```
3    <TITLE>JavaSearch</TITLE>
4    </head>
5    <body bgcolor="#c0FFFF" text="#000000"
                            link="#0000FF" vlink="#800080">
6    <center><h1>JavaScript searching</h1></center>
7    <ul>
8    <li>Enter your search terms and
                select your preferred search engine. You can easily
                            search again with another search engine.
9    <li>To use Boojum, you must have a browser
                        that is capable of frames and JavaScript.
10   <li>You can resize the Boojum search frame
11   </ul><p>
12   </body>
13   </html>
```

ANNOTATIONS

This script uses the string "hunting+the+snark" as a placeholder for the query item in the URL string for each search engine. The **HandleForm( )** function (line 69) called by the input form's **onSubmit** event handler (line 56) then replaces "hunting+the+snark" with the user-entered query and loads the search-engine results into the lower frame. Much of the script's complexity stems from the homemade search-and-replace routine and gives some indication of why JavaScript 1.2's new **search( )** and **replace( )** methods are highly welcome additions to the language.

```
1    <html>
2    <head>
3    <TITLE>Boojum JavaSearch from the Jesus Army</TITLE>
4    </head>
5    <frameset rows=80,*>
6    <frame name="panel" src="boojum1.html" scrolling="no">
7    <frame name="display" src="hunting.html">
8    </frameset>
9    <noframes>
10   <h2 align=center>JavaScript searching</h2>
11   Sorry! For this to work, you need a browser with frames
12   and JavaScript compatibility (such as<a href=
13   "http://home.netscape.com/comprod/mirror/index.html">
14   Netscape v2.0</a> or better).<p>
15   </noframes>
16   </html>
```

The frameset page loads BOOJUM1.HTML into the upper 80-pixel-high frame named **panel**, and HUNTING.HTML into the lower frame called **display** (see Figure 6-4). If the user's browser is incapable of handling frames and JavaScript, the message between the <NOFRAMES> tags with its link to **home.netscape.com** is displayed.

FIGURE 6-4.   A feature-rich implementation of the JavaScript search agent

```
1   <HTML>
2   <head>
3   <TITLE> Hunting the SNARK with JavaScript </TITLE>
4   </head>
5   <body bgcolor="#ffffc0" text="#000080" link="#FF0000"
                              vlink="#800000" alink="#FFFF00">
6   <SCRIPT language="JavaScript">
7   <!-- hide this script
8   // Most code in this script is Copyright(C) 1996,
                              Justin Boyan, jab+j@cs.cmu.edu
9   // For documentation and more info, see:
                              http://www.cs.cmu.edu/~jab/snark/
10  // Modified by John Campbell, john@jesus.org.uk 7 May 1996
11  // The Snark has changed to a Boojum, you see
12
13  var MAX_ENGINES = 30;
14  var SNARK_STRING = "hunting+the+snark";
```

These first two global variables, with their all-uppercase names, are reminiscent of the C convention of using **#define** statements to handle so-called "magic numbers," in other words, numbers whose meaning may not be readily apparent to someone reading a program. For example, a line such as

```
for (i = 0; i <= 52; i++)
```

can leave you wondering, "Why 52?". But create a variable and change the code to

```
for (i = 0; i <= MAX_WEEKS; i++)
```

or

```
for (i = 0; i <= CARDS_IN_DECK; i++)
```

and the answer immediately becomes apparent. Here **MAX_ENGINES** represents the maximum number of search engines this script can handle. It has 21, so you can add nine more before having to increase the value of **MAX_ENGINES**. But you don't really have to worry about counting them, because the author has thoughtfully added an alert in line 51 that tells you the limit has been exceeded.

The second global, **SNARK_STRING**, is assigned the same string that is used as the placeholder for the query item in the search-engine URL strings.

```
16  function MakeArray(n) {
17    for (var i = 1; i <= n; i++) {
18      this[i] = 0;
19    }
20    this.maxlen = n;
21    this.len = 0;
22    return this;
23  }
24
25  var engs = new MakeArray(MAX_ENGINES);
```

Next comes the old-fashioned array constructor that we've seen so often in earlier chapters. It initializes each element with 0 and gives the array two properties: **maxlen** and **len**. The former is assigned **n**, the sole argument to **MakeArray( )**, which when the function is called in line 25 turns out to be the same as **MAX_ENGINES** or 30. **len**, on the other hand, starts out as 0, but ends up holding the number of search engines on the page, in this case 21.

In line 25, the variable **engs** is declared as a new **MakeArray( )**. Here, if you're tempted to update this code by dispensing with **MakeArray( )** and changing line 25 to read

```
var engs = new Array(MAX_ENGINES);
```

remember to give **engs** the two properties it needs for the rest of the script to work properly:

```
engs.maxlen = MAX_ENGINES;   // or engs.length
engs.len = 0;
```

As the argument passed to the **Array( )** constructor is the length of the new array, **engs.maxlen** is the same as **engs.length** (the built-in array property).

```
27   function find_substring(needle, haystack) {
28       var i, needlen = needle.length, haylen = haystack.length;
29       for (i=0; i<=haylen-needlen; i++) {
30           if (needle == haystack.substring(i,i+needlen))
31               return i;
32       }
33       return false;
34   }
```

find_substring( ), called from line 37, takes two arguments, **needle** and **haystack**. The call passes the global variable **SNARK_STRING** (line 14) to **needle**, and **search** to **haystack**. **search**, the fourth property of the **Engine** object created in lines 36 to 43, carries the search engine's URL string with its **SNARK_STRING** placeholder.

The function first declares three local variables, **i**, used to index the position of the **needle** string in the **haystack** string, and **needlen** and **haylen**, assigned the lengths of the two strings. The **for** loop then scans **haystack** for **needle**. This function could also be written as

```
function find_substring(needle, haystack) {
    i = haystack.indexOf(needle);
    if (i != -1) return i;
    else return false;
}
```

to take advantage of JavaScript's built-in **indexOf( )** method, which returns –1 if the search item is not found in the target string. Although strictly speaking the test for **needle**'s existence is unnecessary because all the **haystack** strings contain "hunting+the+snark" as a placeholder, including it just in case is good programming practice.

```
36   function Engine(name, opts, home, search) {
37       var snark = find_substring(SNARK_STRING, search);
38       this.name = name;
39       this.opts = opts;
40       this.home = home;
41       this.pre_snark = search.substring(0,snark);
42       this.post_snark=search.substring(snark+
                         SNARK_STRING.length, search.length);
43   }
```

Next, **Engine( )** creates an object with five properties: **name**, **opts**, **home**, **pre_snark**, and **post_snark**. **name** eventually holds the name of the search engine, and **home**, the web address of its home page. **opts**, which gets either an empty string or "SELECTED," determines which search engine appears by default in the selection list window when the page is first loaded. Lastly, **pre_snark** and **post_snark** serve to hold the portions of the search engine's URL string that come before and after the "hunting+the+snark" or **SNARK_STRING** placeholder. Their values are obtained by use of the **substring( )** method with the local variable **snark** as an index. **snark**'s value is the **i** returned by **find_substring( )**—the starting position of **needle** in **haystack**.

```
45    function Add(name, opts, home, search) {
46        engs.len++;
47        if (engs.len <= engs.maxlen) {
48            engs[engs.len] = new Engine(name, opts, home, search)
49        }
50        else {
51            alert("Better increase MAX_ENGINES: "
                                    + engs.len + ">" + engs.maxlen)
52        }
53    }
```

The **Engine** objects are instantiated by the **Add( )** function, which begins by incrementing **engs.len**, and then tests the resulting value against **engs.maxlen**. If it does not exceed **maxlen**, a new **Engine** indexed by the value of **engs.len** is created by line 48. Its properties are the same as the four arguments passed to **Add( )**. Otherwise, an alert with the warning to increase the value of **MAX_ENGINES** pops open and displays the value of **engs.len** as greater than **engs.maxlen**.

```
55    function DisplayForm() {
56        document.writeln('<CENTER><FORM Name=Snarkform
                    OnSubmit="HandleForm(this); return false">');
57        document.writeln('Look for:
                                    <INPUT size=35 name="query">');
58        document.writeln('In: <SELECT name="service">');
59        for (i=1; i <= engs.len; i++) {
60            document.writeln("<OPTION " + engs[i].opts + "> "
                                    + engs[i].name);
61        }
62        document.writeln('</SELECT>
                        <input type=submit value="Search"><br>');
63        document.writeln('A blank query takes you to the search
                    engine\'s home page.      ');
64        document.writeln('    
                        <a href="boojum_y.html" target="display">
                                    <i>Why Boojum?</i></a>');
```

```
65      document.writeln('</FORM> </CENTER>');
66      document.Snarkform.query.focus()
67   }
```

DisplayForm( ), called from line 168, runs automatically when the page is loaded. It creates the form displayed in the upper frame through a series of calls to **document.writeln**. Line 56 writes the <FORM> tag with **HandleForm( )** assigned to its **onSubmit** event handler, and line 57 constructs the text input field named **query**. Then line 58 followed by the **for** loop in lines 59 through 61 builds the selection list out of the **engs.opts** and **engs.name** properties of each member of the **engs** array. Line 62 creates the submit button labeled "Search," while the next two lines add some instructions as well as a link to an explanatory page. The form is closed by line 65, and line 66 sets the focus on the text input field.

```
69   function HandleForm(form) {
70      var i, newq="", oldq=form.query.value;
71      for (i=0; i<oldq.length; i++) {
72          var thischar = oldq.charAt(i);
73          if (thischar != ' ')
74              newq += thischar;
75          else if (lastchar != ' ')
76              newq += '+';
77          lastchar = thischar;
78      }
79      var eng = engs[1+form.service.selectedIndex];
80      parent.display.location.href = newq ?
                eng.pre_snark + newq + eng.post_snark : eng.home;
81      document.Snarkform.query.focus()
82   }
```

HandleForm( ), this script's main function, is called by the input form's **onSubmit** handler (line 56) when the **submit** button labeled "Search" (line 62) is clicked. It first converts any blank spaces in the user-entered query string into plus signs. To do this, it declares three local variables: **i**, the index used by the **for** loop that handles the conversion; **newq**, initialized as an empty string that ends up holding the result of the process; and **oldq**, which gets the string entered into the form's text field named **query**.

The **for** loop assigns each character in turn to the new local, **thischar**. If **thischar** is not a blank space, it is added to **newq**, the output string, and its value is assigned to yet another variable, **lastchar**. But if **thischar** is a blank space, the **else if** statement takes effect, and if **lastchar** is not a blank space, **newq** is incremented by a plus sign.

You might be tempted to think this is slightly Byzantine logic and try to straighten it out by revising line 75 to read

```
        else if (thischar == ' ')
```

and deleting line 77 because **lastchar** is no longer necessary. In that case, however, if a user enters more than one blank space between words in the **query** field, each is converted into a plus sign. As written, the function ensures that no matter how many blank spaces there are between words, they are replaced by a single plus sign in the output string.

On the other hand, JavaScript 1.2 allows you to reduce the entire conversion process in lines 70 through 78 to one line:

```
var newq =
    form.query.value.split(' ').join('+').replace(/\++/, '+');
```

This assigns **newq** the user-entered string with the blank spaces replaced by plus signs through use of the **split( )** and **join( )** methods, while replacing any occurrences of multiple plus signs in a row with a single one. The first argument to **replace( )** is a so-called "regular expression," or pattern enclosed by two forward slashes. The backslash serves an escape function in indicating that the next character (+) is not special and should be interpreted literally. The second plus sign is special: it is a regular-expression operator that tells **replace( )** any number of plus signs in a row are to be replaced with the second argument, a single plus sign. Or, to take another example:

```
str = "booooooooooooo!"
newstr = str.replace(/o+/, 'oo')
```

makes **newstr** "boo!".

Next, in line 79 a new local variable, **eng**, is assigned the member of the **engs** array indexed by the value of **selectedIndex** plus one. The plus-one is necessary because **engs.len**, the index used in constructing the **engs** array up in line 48, is incremented from its initial value of zero on the first call to **Add( )**, making the first member **engs[1]**. Because the selection list options are indexed starting at zero, this aligns the two arrays.

Then line 80 tests **newq**. If **newq** has a value, meaning that the user has typed something in the **query** field, the location of the lower frame becomes the string sent to the search engine: a compilation of the **pre_snark**, **newq**, and **post_snark** segments. This displays the results of the search. Otherwise, its location becomes the selected search engine's home page.

Finally, line 81 returns the focus back to the **query** input field.

```
84  Add("Churches on the Web","",
85      "http://www.christianity.net/churchlocator/",
86      "http://www.christianity.net/cgi/search.cgi?query=
                                    hunting+the+snark");
```

Lines 84 to 167 create the array of search engines by calling **Add( )** with a succession of arguments representing the site's name, **opts** property, home-page address, and search string with its "hunting+the+snark" placeholder for the query item. The **opts** argument is an empty string except in the case of

```
104  Add("AltaVista", "SELECTED",
105      "http://altavista.digital.com/",
106      "http://altavista.digital.com/cgi-bin/query?pg=
                         q&what=web&fmt=d&q=hunting+the+snark");
```

which makes "AltaVista" appear in the selection-list window when the page loads. Thus if, for instance, you would rather make "Yahoo" the default selection, just change "SELECTED" in line 104 to "" and replace "" in line 164 with "SELECTED".

```
168  DisplayForm();
169  // done hiding from old browsers -->
170  </SCRIPT>
171  <pre>
172  </pre>
173  Do not load this page directly.<p>Please go to the
                         <a href="load-me.html" target="_top">
                         Boojum page</a> instead.<br>
174  </BODY>
175  </html>
```

The script ends with the call to **DisplayForm( )**, which creates the form when the page is loaded, and a link on line 173 that loads the frameset page in case BOOJUM1.HTML has been accessed directly.

```
1    <html>
2    <head>
3    <TITLE>JavaSearch</TITLE>
4    </head>
5    <body bgcolor="#c0FFFF" text="#000000"
                         link="#0000FF" vlink="#800080">
6    <center><h1>JavaScript searching</h1></center>
7    <ul>
8    <li>Enter your search terms and
                 select your preferred search engine. You can easily
                         search again with another search engine.
9    <li>To use Boojum, you must have a browser
                         that is capable of frames and JavaScript.
10   <li>You can resize the Boojum search frame
11   </ul><p>
12   </body>
13   </html>
```

The file HUNTING.HTML loaded into the lower frame contains straightforward HTML code that formats the user instructions as a bulleted list.

The frames structure makes Boojum ideal for using a number of search engines in succession. The search results appear in the lower frame, while the query form with its selection list remains in the upper one. Another advantage not to be overlooked is that the user just has to deal with one simple input form and one set of instructions, as opposed to a variety of layouts, forms, and instructions that can easily become bewildering. Even if you don't make Boojum part of your web site, you can stash the files on your hard drive, bookmark them with your browser, and use them whenever you want to do a one-stop multiengine search.

lyrsrch

Search Using Layers

N2   N2.01   N2.02+   N3   N4   E3   E4

Netscape Communicator 4.0 brings a new set of JavaScript functions to the developer, including Layers. We previously examined Layers in Chapter 1, "External Windows." The Search Using Layers script applies the principles of the JavaScript search agent to this exciting new scripting function.

To recap, Netscape 4.0 Layers allows a web developer to create multiple layers of content on one page. These layers can be used to create complex animations, hide or display content based on what information is selected, and more. To view layers, users must be running version 4.0 of Netscape Navigator, which is better known as Netscape Communicator.

In this search-agent example—in reality a fairly simple implementation of Layers—users pass their mouse over a hypertext link labeled "Search," and a separate window (layer) opens and presents them with a search form (see Figure 6-5).

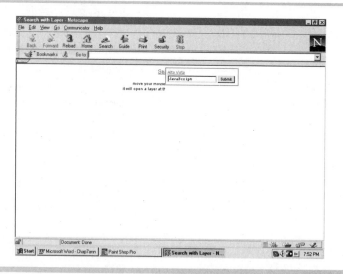

FIGURE 6-5.   A working example of JavaScript 1.2 Layers

```
1   <html>
2   <head>
3   <title>Search with Layer</title>
4   </head>
5   <BODY BGCOLOR="#FFFFFF">
6   <SCRIPT LANGUAGE="JavaScript1.2">
7   <!-- begin
8   function showlayer(e,str) {
9       document.layers[str].left=(e.layerX-13);
10      document.layers[str].top=(e.layerY-13);
11      document.layers[str].visibility="show";
12      return true;
13  }
14  <!-- end -->
15  </SCRIPT>
16  <center>
17  <p>
18  <a href="jv_srch4.html"
            onMouseOver="showlayer(event,'search');return true">
                                            Search</a>
19  <p>
20  <font size=2>
21  Move your mouse cursor over the link<br>
22  it will open a layer at the current mouse position<br>
23  </font>
24  </center>
25  <p>
26  <layer name="search" left="0" top="0" visibility="hide"
                bgcolor="white" onmouseout="visibility='hide'">
27  <body link=#ff0000 vlink=#ff0000>
28  <FORM method=GET action=
                    "http://altavista.digital.com/cgi-bin/query">
29  <table border="1" cellpadding="4" cellspacing="0">
30    <tr><td align="left">
31      <font size="2">
32        <a href="http://www.altavista.com">Alta Vista</a><br>
33        <INPUT TYPE=hidden NAME=pg VALUE=q>
34        <INPUT NAME=q size=20 maxlength=200 VALUE="">
35        <INPUT TYPE=submit VALUE=Submit>
36      </font>
37    </td></tr></table>
38  </FORM>
39  </body>
```

```
40   </layer>
41   </body>
42   </html>
```

ANNOTATIONS

This script consists of a single function, **showlayer( )**, which positions a layer relative to the position of the user's mouse pointer, then displays it by changing the layer's **visibility** property from "hide" to "show." The layer itself contains a search form consisting of an input field and a button which, when clicked, submits the query to AltaVista. Move the mouse pointer off the layer and it vanishes.

The value of this script lies not so much in what it actually does, but rather in its serving as a simple introduction to the kinds of things you can do with layers and events. It also constitutes a neat core that can easily be modified and enhanced in a variety of ways.

```
1    <html>
2    <head>
3    <title>Search with Layer</title>
4    </head>
5    <BODY BGCOLOR="#FFFFFF">
6    <SCRIPT LANGUAGE="JavaScript1.2">
7    <!-- begin
8    function showlayer(e,str) {
9        document.layers[str].left=(e.layerX-13);
10       document.layers[str].top=(e.layerY-13);
11       document.layers[str].visibility="show";
12       return true;
13   }
```

showlayer( ), assigned to the **onMouseOver** event handler of the link on the page, takes two arguments: **e**, which is the event (**onMouseOver** in this case), and **str**, the name of the layer. Lines 9 and 10 set the **left** and **top** properties of the layer, which determine its position from the left and top of the browser window, to 13 pixels up and left from the location of the mouse pointer when it moves into the scope of the link's event handler.

Adjusting the position by 13 pixels ensures that the mouse pointer is well within the layer when it becomes visible. Otherwise, the upper-left corner of the layer coincides exactly with the position of the mouse pointer, and the slightest movement of the mouse up or left would trigger an **onMouseOut** event and hide the layer. Obviously, 13 is an arbitrary number that you might want to adjust, particularly if you're superstitious. Increasing it moves the upper-left corner of the layer farther up and left from the mouse pointer; decreasing it brings that corner closer to the cursor.

layerX and **layerY** are two properties of the **Event** object that specify its horizontal (*X*-axis) and vertical (*Y*-axis) position measured in pixels relative to the layer in which the event occurred. They are respectively synonymous with **x** and **y**, so that in lines 9 and 10 you could write "e.x – 13" and "e.y – 13" and achieve exactly the same effect.

Finally, line 11 sets the **str** layer's **visibility** property to "show," and **showlayer( )** returns **true** to ensure that the link to AltaVista contained within the layer can be followed. As a general rule with events, returning **true** is a signal to Communicator to behave normally (for example, follow a link when clicked, display a character in a text field when a key is pressed, open a pop-up menu in response to a right mouse click, and so on); returning **false** intercepts and halts the default process.

```
14   <!-- end -->
15   </SCRIPT>
16   <center>
17   <p>
18   <a href="jv_srch4.html"
             onMouseOver="showlayer(event,'search');return true">
                                              Search</a>
19   <p>
20   <font size=2>
21   Move your mouse cursor over the link<br>
22   it will open a layer at the current mouse position<br>
23   </font>
24   </center>
25   <p>
```

The most important line in this segment is 18, which sets up the link with its **onMouseOver** event handler that calls **showlayer( )**. The link itself, of course, only works if your hand is quick enough to click on it before the **src** layer pops up as a barrier. (If you're really bored, you can make a game of trying to get your click in first!)

You can expand the page area within which the event is triggered by increasing the size of the word "Search" with HTML text-formatting code, or by using an image for the link. Another simple variation would be to have the layer appear wherever the user clicks on the page. To do this, add the lines

```
window.captureEvents(Event.CLICK);
window.onClick = showlayer;
```

to the script. The first line captures any **Click** event on the page, while the second tells the window what to do when a click occurs. Note that "CLICK" is all uppercase and that there are no brackets after **showlayer** as in a function call. Then delete the **str** argument to **showlayer** in line 8 and replace "str" in lines 9 through 11 with the "search" (or whatever name you give the layer) in either single or double quotation marks.

You could also adapt it to have a double-click show the layer and a single-click hide it with

```
window.captureEvents(Event.CLICK | Event.DBLCLICK);
window.onClick = hidelayer;
window.onDblClick = showlayer;
```

The first line here illustrates the syntax for capturing multiple events: simply separate them by a vertical bar. You also have to create a **hidelayer( )** function:

```
function hidelayer() {
    document.layers['search'].visibility = 'hide';
}
```

Finally, delete the **onMouseOut** event handler from line 26 to keep the layer from disappearing when the mouse pointer moves off it.

While the effect is neat, you'll soon notice a problem when you click on the Submit button, because the window captures that click before it reaches the button. The simplest work-around is to use a double-click event for visibility, and to retain **onMouseOut** or have any other suitable event *except a click* hide the layer.

PROGRAMMER'S TIP   *To get a feel for the x and y coordinates used in positioning layers, add the lines*

```
document.layers['search'].document.forms[0].q.value =
                            'x: ' + e.x + ' - y: ' + e.y;
```

*to the **showlayer( )** function. This displays the coordinates of each click or double-click event in the form's text field.*

```
26  <layer name="search" left="0" top="0" visibility="hide"
                    bgcolor="white" onmouseout="visibility='hide'">
27  <body link=#ff0000 vlink=#ff0000>
28  <FORM method=GET action=
                    "http://altavista.digital.com/cgi-bin/query">
29  <table border="1" cellpadding="4" cellspacing="0">
30    <tr><td align="left">
31      <font size="2">
32        <a href="http://www.altavista.com">Alta Vista</a><br>
33        <INPUT TYPE=hidden NAME=pg VALUE=q>
34        <INPUT NAME=q size=20 maxlength=200 VALUE="">
35        <INPUT TYPE=submit VALUE=Submit>
36      </font>
37    </td></tr></table>
38  </FORM>
39  </body>
40  </layer>
```

```
41   </body>
42   </html>
```

Lines 26 through 40 create the layer containing the input form for an AltaVista search. As in the case of MULTI1.HTM, the first script in this chapter, hidden form fields and the **submit** method are used to compile the string sent to the search-engine server.

Although the NAME attribute in the <LAYERS> tag still works, Netscape now recommends using ID instead, because the latter is also compatible with cascading style sheet (CSS) syntax. Hence you might want to change line 26 to read

<code>ID=search</code>

At least this way you won't have to worry about updating your code should they decide to disable the NAME attribute altogether in this context.

To add more search engines to the layer, you can adapt any of the preceding scripts in this chapter. Or you could delete lines 27 to 39 and add

<code>SRC=multi1.htm</code>

to have the layer load the first script in this chapter with its choice of four search engines. In that case, be sure either to move or copy MULTI1.HTM to the same directory as LYRSRCH.HTM, or to specify the full path in the assignment to SRC.

While you're likely to experience frustration when you first begin working with layers and events, it's well worth getting a solid handle on these new features of the language, because they provide means of creating a much more engaging, controllable, and interactive user-interface than was possible before their introduction with Communicator.

Search Your Web Site

sitesrch

N2 N2.01 N2.02+ N3 N4 E3 E4

The site search is a common web-enabled application that typically uses Perl, C, Java, or some other robust programming language to pass queries and results from browser to web server to a database. The database contains information about a web site's contents. JavaScript is not usually considered a good language for supporting database queries. However, in this example, the script authors added an ersatz database to a frames-based user interface, resulting in a pretty good imitation of a web site search utility.

The database "fields" are hidden HTML files that contain information about your web pages. Using this script, a web site search is best accomplished within a frames document. This permits a single load to memory of the database being searched. If frames are not employed, it means either that you may not give "clickable" links to the search results, or you must reload the entire document, losing some of the bandwidth-conservation benefits of client-side processing. Even though such a search would be accomplished from cache, it still would require a server query and response.

This "amorphous database" structure, as its authors call it, is a computer-friendly approach that is primarily string based as opposed to solely array based. But you can, of course, use whichever approach you prefer. At any rate, the parent frame has to load prior to the other "children" documents.

This is the file containing the frameset tags:

```
1    <HTML>
2    <HEAD><TITLE>JavaScript Site Search</TITLE></HEAD>
3    <!-- This hidden form *must* appear before the HTML specify-
       ing the framesets. This insures that it is loaded prior to
       any of the search documents - important because it contains
       your database for searching. One final note: do not omit
       the asterisk at the end of the "find" value, or the parser
       will miss "seeing" your last record. -->
4    <FORM NAME="searcher">
5    <INPUT TYPE="hidden" NAME="test" VALUE="a">
6    <INPUT TYPE="hidden" NAME="find"
       VALUE='yourfirstfilename.htm~ The title of the first page|
       key topical words used on this page separated by spaces*
       yournextfilename.htm~ The title of the next page|
       keywords in the next page separated by spaces*
       yourthirdfilename.htm~ Its title|its keywords etc. etc.*'>
7    </FORM>
8    <FRAMESET ROWS="*,100">
9      <FRAME SRC="newsrch.htm" SCROLLING="yes" NAME="main">
10     <FRAME SRC="newsrd.htm" SCROLLING="no" NAME="results">
11   </FRAMESET>
12    </HTML>
```

This is the page containing the search form:

```
1    <HTML>
2    <HEAD>
3    <!-- Cut-N-Paste JavaScript from ISN Toolbox
4       Copyright 1996, Infohiway, Inc.  Restricted use is hereby
5       granted (commercial and personal OK) so long as this code
6       is not *directly* sold and the copyright notice is buried
7       somewhere deep in your HTML document.  A link to our site
8       http://www.infohiway.com is always appreciated of course,
9       but is absolutely and positively not necessary. ;-)    -->
```

```
10   <SCRIPT LANGUAGE="JavaScript">
11   <!--Hide JavaScript from Java-Impaired Browsers
12   function doSrch(){
13      parent.document.searcher.test.value="b";
14      parent.results.location.href="newsrd.htm"
15   }
16   // END HIDING CONTENTS -->
17   </SCRIPT>
18   </HEAD>
19   <BODY BGCOLOR="white">
20   <CENTER>
21   <FORM NAME="searcher">
22   <TABLE BORDER=0 WIDTH=486>
23   <TR><TD ALIGN=CENTER>
24   <B>Search Our Site For Topic Words</B>
25   <P>Type Search Word Here: <INPUT TYPE="text" NAME="findword"
                VALUE="" SIZE=20><INPUT TYPE="button" NAME="button"
                  VALUE=" Search " onClick="doSrch();"></TD></TR>
26   </TABLE></FORM>
27   <!-- Put any other content for your page here -->
28   </BODY>
29   </HTML>
```

This is the frame that loads the search results:

```
1    <HTML>
2    <HEAD>
3    <SCRIPT LANGUAGE="JavaScript">
4    <!--Hide JavaScript from Java-Impaired Browsers
5    function initArray(){
6       this.length=initArray.arguments.length;
7       for (var i=0;i<this.length;i++){
8           this[i]=initArray.arguments[i];
9       }
10   }
11   var sr=new initArray("4b","5b","8b","8b");
12   function doSrch(){
13      if (sr[0]=="4b"){
14          parStr();
15      }
16      findw = parent.main.document.searcher.findword.value
17      findw=findw.toLowerCase();
```

```
18      disp = "";
19      document.write('<HTML><BODY BGCOLOR="white">'
20          +'<CENTER><FORM NAME="isn"><TABLE BORDER=0 '
21          +'WIDTH=486><TR><TD VALIGN=TOP><A HREF="you'
22          +'rhomepage.htm" TARGET="_top"><IMG SRC="yo'
23          +'urlogo.gif" BORDER=0 HEIGHT=xx WIDTH=xx A'
24          +'LT="Your Text Description of image"></A><'
25          +'/TD><TD><SELECT NAME="isn1" SIZE=6>');
26      flg=2;
27      for (i=0;i<stp;i++){
28          fold=sr[i].toLowerCase();
29          if (fold.indexOf(findw)>-1){
30              pos=sr[i].indexOf("~");
31              pos1=sr[i].indexOf("|");
32              disp="<OPTION VALUE='"+sr[i].substring(0,pos);
33              if (flg!=3){
34                  disp+="' onClick='' SELECTED>";
35              }
36              else{
37                  disp+="' onClick=''>";
38              }
39          disp+=sr[i].substring(pos+1,pos1);
40          document.write(disp);
41          flg=3;
42          }
43      }
44      if (flg!=2){
45          document.write('</SELECT></TD><TD VALIGN=TOP'
46              +'><INPUT TYPE="button" NAME="button" Value'
47              +'=" Select and Go " onClick="doloc(this.fo'
48              +'rm)">');
49      }
50      document.write('<BR><FONT COLOR="red" SIZE=1><B>');
51      if (flg!=3){
52          document.write('</TD><TD VALIGN=CENTER><FONT '
53              +'COLOR="red"><B>I am sorry.  I found no matches'
54              +'' on "'+findw+'". Feel free to search for an'
55              +'other word!</B></FONT>');
56      }
57      else{
58          document.write('The selection(s) at left w'
59              +'ere found using "'+findw+'".');
60      }
```

```
61    document.write('</B></FONT></TD></TR></TABLE>'
62        +'</FORM></BODY></HTML><P>');
63  }
64
65  function parStr() {
66      srs=parent.document.searcher.find.value;
67      var i=0;
68      while (srs.indexOf("*")>0){
69          pos=srs.indexOf("*");
70          sr[i]=srs.substring(0,pos);
71          srs=srs.substring(pos+1,srs.length);
72          i++;
73          stp=i;
74      }
75  }
76
77  function doloc(){
78      durl=(document.isn.isn1.options
79                      [document.isn.isn1.selectedIndex].value);
79      parent.main.location.href=durl;
80  }
81  // End Hiding -->
82  </SCRIPT>
83  <BODY BGCOLOR="white">
84  <SCRIPT LANGUAGE="JavaScript">
85  <!-- Hide from JavaScript-Impaired Browsers
86  if (parent.document.searcher.test.value != "a"){
87      doSrch();
88  }
89  // End Hiding -->
90  </SCRIPT>
91  </BODY>
92  </HTML>
```

ANNOTATIONS

This script sets up a database consisting of filenames and keywords in the frameset file LOAD-ME.HTM, which creates an upper frame with a search form and a lower one to display the results. If the search item is found, a list of the file titles containing the keyword appears in a selection-list window in the lower frame. Accompanying it is a button which, when clicked, loads the selected file into the upper frame. If the search item is not found among the keywords, a message to that effect appears in the lower frame shown in Figure 6-6.

FIGURE 6-6. A simple site search using JavaScript

To see it work, enter any word from the string assigned to VALUE in line 6. Type "title," for example, and three files will be listed; enter "page" and you'll get two, whereas "topical" will result in only one item appearing in the select list.

```
1   <HTML>
2   <HEAD><TITLE>JavaScript Site Search</TITLE></HEAD>
3   <!-- This hidden form *must* appear before the HTML specify-
       ing the framesets. This insures that it is loaded prior to
       any of the search documents - important because it contains
       your database for searching. One final note: do not omit
       the asterisk at the end of the "find" value, or the parser
       will miss "seeing" your last record. -->
4   <FORM NAME="searcher">
5   <INPUT TYPE="hidden" NAME="test" VALUE="a">
6   <INPUT TYPE="hidden" NAME="find"
       VALUE='yourfirstfilename.htm~ The title of the first page|
       key topical words used on this page separated by spaces*
       yournextfilename.htm~ The title of the next page|
       keywords in the next page separated by spaces*
       yourthirdfilename.htm~ Its title|its keywords etc. etc.*'>
7   </FORM>
```

```
8    <FRAMESET ROWS="*,100">
9      <FRAME SRC="newsrch.htm" SCROLLING="yes" NAME="main">
10     <FRAME SRC="newsrd.htm" SCROLLING="no" NAME="results">
11   </FRAMESET>
12   </HTML>
```

The frameset file contains an invisible form with two hidden elements. The first simply holds the letter "a," which serves as a flag that keeps the lower frame blank until the Search button is first clicked. A click calls **doSrch( )** on line 12, which sets the value of **test** to "b" and reloads NEWSRD.HTM, in which the **if** statement on line 86 controls whether anything is displayed in the frame.

The second input, **find**, is where you have to enter your own filenames, page titles (which appear in the selection list when a search item is found), and keywords. If you would rather use separators other than a tilde (~), vertical bar (|), and asterisk (*), just make the appropriate adjustments to the **indexOf( )** arguments in lines 30–31 and 68–69 of NEWSRD.HTM.

```
1    <HTML>
2    <HEAD>
3    <!-- Cut-N-Paste JavaScript from ISN Toolbox
4       Copyright 1996, Infohiway, Inc.  Restricted use is hereby
5       granted (commercial and personal OK) so long as this code
6       is not *directly* sold and the copyright notice is buried
7       somewhere deep in your HTML document.  A link to our site
8       http://www.infohiway.com is always appreciated of course,
9       but is absolutely and positively not necessary. ;-)   -->
10   <SCRIPT LANGUAGE="JavaScript">
11   <!--Hide JavaScript from Java-Impaired Browsers
12   function doSrch(){
13      parent.document.searcher.test.value="b";
14      parent.results.location.href="newsrd.htm"
15   }
```

This function, assigned to the button labeled "Search," sets the **test** flag's value to "b," and reloads NEWSRD.HTM into the lower frame. This calls the substantially longer **doSrch( )** function in NEWSRD.HTM to display the results of the search.

```
16   // END HIDING CONTENTS -->
17   </SCRIPT>
18   </HEAD>
19   <BODY BGCOLOR="white">
20   <CENTER>
21   <FORM NAME="searcher">
22   <TABLE BORDER=0 WIDTH=486>
23   <TR><TD ALIGN=CENTER>
```

```
24   <B>Search Our Site For Topic Words</B>
25   <P>Type Search Word Here: <INPUT TYPE="text" NAME="findword"
             VALUE="" SIZE=20><INPUT TYPE="button" NAME="button"
                  VALUE=" Search " onClick="doSrch();"></TD></TR>
26   </TABLE></FORM>
27   <!-- Put any other content for your page here -->
28   </BODY>
29   </HTML>
```

The remainder of this file, which is loaded into the upper frame, contains the search input form with its input field named **findword** and the Search button, which calls **doSrch( )** when clicked.

```
1    <HTML>
2    <HEAD>
3    <SCRIPT LANGUAGE="JavaScript">
4    <!--Hide JavaScript from Java-Impaired Browsers
5    function initArray(){
6        this.length=initArray.arguments.length;
7        for (var i=0;i<this.length;i++){
8             this[i]=initArray.arguments[i];
9        }
10   }
11   var sr=new initArray("4b","5b","8b","8b");
```

Here once again we have the standard homemade routine for creating an array with a **length** property, and its instantiation in line 11 with four members. The elements themselves are dummy initialization strings passed as arguments to **initArray( )**. Should you decide to change them to something more meaningful, just be sure to replace the "4b" in line 13 with whatever you substitute in line 11 so that the **if** test succeeds and calls **parStr( )**. The other three members of the array are not used anywhere else in the script, so you don't have to worry about them.

```
12   function doSrch(){
13       if (sr[0]=="4b"){
14           parStr();
15       }
16       findw = parent.main.document.searcher.findword.value
17       findw=findw.toLowerCase();
18       disp = "";
19       document.write('<HTML><BODY BGCOLOR="white">'
20           +'<CENTER><FORM NAME="isn"><TABLE BORDER=0 '
21           +'WIDTH=486><TR><TD VALIGN=TOP><A HREF="you'
22           +'rhomepage.htm" TARGET="_top"><IMG SRC="yo'
23           +'urlogo.gif" BORDER=0 HEIGHT=xx WIDTH=xx A'
```

```
24        +'LT="Your Text Description of image"></A><'
25        +'/TD><TD><SELECT NAME="isn1" SIZE=6>');
26     flg=2;
```

doSrch( ) first checks the value of **sr[0]**, and, if it finds it to be 4b, calls **parStr( )** on line 65, which, as we'll see, loads the string stored in the hidden input named **find** on the frameset page into the **sr** array. The user-entered search item is then assigned to a variable named **findw** which in line 17 is converted to lowercase.

Next a new variable, **disp**, is initialized as an empty string; it will serve to assemble the display of the search results. Then **document.write( )** starts creating the page with a form named **isn**, a table, a linked image, and the beginning of a SELECT named **isn1**. Finally, a variable named **flg**, used in the routine that follows, is set at 2.

```
27     for (i=0;i<stp;i++){
28         fold=sr[i].toLowerCase();
29         if (fold.indexOf(findw)>-1){
30             pos=sr[i].indexOf("~");
31             pos1=sr[i].indexOf("|");
32             disp="<OPTION VALUE='"+sr[i].substring(0,pos);
33             if (flg!=3){
34                 disp+="' onClick='' SELECTED>";
35             }
36             else{
37                 disp+="' onClick=''>";
38             }
39         disp+=sr[i].substring(pos+1,pos1);
40         document.write(disp);
41         flg=3;
42         }
43     }
```

Next comes a **for** loop that produces the selection list. The cycle is controlled by **stp**, a global variable whose value is determined by **parStr( )** through the assignment in line 73. It corresponds to the length of the **sr** array.

The loop assigns each member of **sr** in turn to a variable named **fold**, converts it to lowercase, and uses the **indexOf( )** method to scan the string for **findw**, the user-entered item. If the search string is found, two new variables come into play: **pos**, which is assigned the index of the tilde in that member of **sr**, and **pos1**, which gets the index of the vertical bar.

Next **disp** is assigned the HTML code for an OPTION with the substring of **sr[i]** extending up to the tilde, which contains the filename, as its value. Then, if the value of **flg** is not 3, which it will not be the first time through the loop, line 34 adds the

HTML for making that option SELECTED. Otherwise, the <OPTION> tag is closed with the HTML on line 37.

Line 39 increments **disp** by the substring of **sr[i]** extending from the tilde to the vertical bar—the title of the page that appears in the selection-list window. Then **disp** is written by line 40 and **flg** is set to 3.

```
44    if (flg!=2){
45        document.write('</SELECT></TD><TD VALIGN=TOP'
46            +'><INPUT TYPE="button" NAME="button" Value'
47            +'=" Select and Go " onClick="doloc(this.fo'
48            +'rm)">');
49    }
50    document.write('<BR><FONT COLOR="red" SIZE=1><B>');
```

If the search was successful and the **for** switched the value of **flg** to 3, lines 45 to 48 add a button to the results display with **doloc( )** assigned to its **onClick** event handler. Line 50 then adds some HTML font-formatting code.

```
51    if (flg!=3){
52        document.write('</TD><TD VALIGN=CENTER><FONT '
53            +'COLOR="red"><B>I am sorry.  I found no matches'
54            +' on "'+findw+'". Feel free to search for an'
55            +'other word!</B></FONT>');
56    }
```

On the other hand, if the search was unsuccessful and the value of **flg** is still 2, the message contained in the **document.write( )** extending from line 52 to 55 is displayed.

```
57    else{
58        document.write('The selection(s) at left w'
59            +'ere found using "'+findw+'".');
60    }
61    document.write('</B></FONT></TD></TR></TABLE>'
62        +'</FORM></BODY></HTML><P>');
63    }
```

Otherwise, a successful search message is displayed and the table, form, and page are closed with the appropriate HTML code. Note that both the failure and success messages incorporate the search item by referencing the value of the **findw** variable in lines 54 and 59.

If you decide to use this code, one thing you might want to do is edit the preceding **document.write( )** line breaks to get rid of the split words. This will make the code much easier to read and maintain. Here the splits have been left as-is to show that you can divide lines in this way without affecting the output.

```
65   function parStr() {
66       srs=parent.document.searcher.find.value;
67       var i=0;
68       while (srs.indexOf("*")>0){
69          pos=srs.indexOf("*");
70          sr[i]=srs.substring(0,pos);
71          srs=srs.substring(pos+1,srs.length);
72          i++;
73          stp=i;
74       }
75   }
```

parStr( ), called from line 14 the first time the Search button is clicked when the value of **sr[0]** is 4b, assigns the entire database contained in the **find** hidden input on the frameset page to a new variable, **srs**. It then uses the **indexOf( )** method in a **while** loop to look for the asterisks that separate the database items, each consisting of the filename, page title, and keywords. Each item is in turn assigned to **sr[i]**, and the variable **stp**, used to control the **for** loop in line 27, gets the value of **i**, the index that also represents the current length of the **sr** array.

```
77   function doloc(){
78       durl=(document.isn.isn1.options
                    [document.isn.isn1.selectedIndex].value);
79       parent.main.location.href=durl;
80   }
```

Lastly, **doloc( )**, assigned to the "Select and Go" button that appears in the lower frame alongside the results of a successful search, uses the **selectedIndex** property to pull the value of the chosen title. This value, as we saw in line 32, is the filename associated with the page title in question. It is assigned to a new variable, **durl**, which is then used in line 79 to load that page into the upper frame.

```
81   // End Hiding -->
82   </SCRIPT>
83   <BODY BGCOLOR="white">
84   <SCRIPT LANGUAGE="JavaScript">
85   <!-- Hide from JavaScript-Impaired Browsers
86   if (parent.document.searcher.test.value != "a"){
87       doSrch();
88   }
89   // End Hiding -->
90   </SCRIPT>
91   </BODY>
92   </HTML>
```

The body of the page contains a separate script that looks for "a" in the **test** hidden input on the frameset page. If it does not find an "a," this means that the Search button has been clicked and has called the **doSrch( )** function in NEWSRCH.HTM, which changes the "a" to "b" and reloads NEWSRD.HTM, thereby launching its **doSrch( )** function to display the results. On the other hand, if the value of **test** is "a," it does nothing and the lower frame remains blank.

There are many different ways in which you may wish to tinker with this script. You could use the **Array** object and do away with **initArray( )**, or develop a function that applies **split( )** and **join( )** or even the new JavaScript 1.2 **search( )** method to the database records. You might also want to change the values assigned to **flg** from 2 and 3 to the Boolean literals **true** and **false** to more accurately reflect the variable's on-off function. Numeric flag values are more appropriate when more than two possible states have to be tracked, and even there a meaningful string literal (such as "itemFound" or "noSuchItem") spares you having to add a comment to each number to explain and remember what state it represents.

Yet another possibility is to set up the database records directly as an array in the frameset page. You could make the records an object with three properties:

```
function siteRec(filename, pagetitle, keywords) {
    this.filename = filename;
    this.pagetitle = pagetitle;
    this.keywords = keywords;
}
```

and then write

```
sr[0] = new siteRec("mexfood.htm",
                    "Mexican Food",
                    "enchilada | taco | tamale | tostada")
sr[1] = new siteRec("mexhist.htm",
                    "Mexican History",
                    "Olmec | Mayan | Toltec | Aztec")
```

and so on. This would eliminate parsing because you could then access the records through their properties with, for example,

```
sr[i].pagetitle
```

or

```
sr[i].keywords
```

with **i** as the index variable in a loop. The best place to store the database, of course, is the head of the frameset page to keep it accessible from any page loaded into the frames. With JavaScript 1.2, you could also load it into a hidden layer. And if you have a long list of keywords, you might want to organize them in a form easier to work with than one humongous string. No matter how you set it up, though, a search engine of this kind can be a valuable device for visitors who want to home in on some particular facet of your site.

search2

Simple Data Search

⌐N2⌐ ⌐N2.01⌐ ⌐N2.02+⌐ ⌐N3⌐ ⌐N4⌐ ⌐E3⌐ ⌐E4⌐

Another example of using JavaScript is as a minirepository of data that can be searched. Unlike the previous example, the data set and related HTML code are contained entirely within the <SCRIPT> tags.

The entire data set loads with the code, which under most circumstances means the "database" your users search should be very small. The larger the data set, the longer it takes for your user's browser to load all of the associated data. Keep it simple and small.

This example searches all areas (Date, Name, URL, and Description) for matches and returns a list of hits. The keyword is case sensitive. This script can be easily modified to fit your needs.

```
1    <script language="javascript">
2
3    function makeEntry () {
4        this.Date = "";
5        this.Name="";
6        this.URL = "";
7        this.Desc = "";
8        this.Category = "";
9        return this;
10   }
11
12   function makeArray(n) {
13       this.length = n;
14       for (var k = 1; k <= n; k++) {
15           this[k] = "";
16       }
17       return this;
18   }
19
20   function makeLinks(size) {
21       this.length = size;
22       for (var r=1; r<= size; r++) {
23           this[r] = new makeEntry();
24           this[r].Date = datesArray[r];
25           this[r].Name = namesArray[r];
26           this[r].URL = urlsArray[r];
```

```
27          this[r].Desc = descArray[r];
28      }
29      return this;
30  }
31
32  var linksize=0
33  datesArray = new makeArray(linksize);
34  namesArray = new makeArray(linksize);
35  urlsArray = new makeArray(linksize);
36  descArray = new makeArray(linksize);
37  var arraycount=0
38  arraycount += 1
39  datesArray[arraycount] = "1/1/97 "
40  urlsArray[arraycount] = "http://www.yahoo.com"
41  namesArray[arraycount] = "Yahoo"
42  descArray[arraycount] =
            "An excellent search engine available free on the Web"
43  arraycount += 1
44  datesArray[arraycount] = "1/1/97 "
45  urlsArray[arraycount] = "http://www.lycos.com"
46  namesArray[arraycount] = "Lycos"
47  descArray[arraycount] =
        "An extensive search engine, great alternative to Yahoo"
48  arraycount += 1
49  datesArray[arraycount] = "1/1/97 "
50  urlsArray[arraycount] = "http://www.webcrawler.com"
51  namesArray[arraycount] = "Webcrawler"
52  descArray[arraycount] =
                    "A great search engine from the makers of AOL"
53  arraycount += 1
54  datesArray[arraycount] = "1/1/97 "
55  urlsArray[arraycount] = "http://www.search.com"
56  namesArray[arraycount] = "Search.com"
57  descArray[arraycount] =
        "A collection of hundreds of search engines; from Yahoo
                to a search engine which looks up phone numbers."
58  arraycount += 1
59  datesArray[arraycount] = "1/1/97 "
60  urlsArray[arraycount] = "http://altavista.digital.com"
61  namesArray[arraycount] = "AltaVista"
62  descArray[arraycount] =
                    "This search engine has the largest database
```

```
                    of web sites of all search engines on the Web"
63  linksize = arraycount;
64
65  function showLink (links, index) {
66     document.write("<tr><td>" + links[index].Date +"</td>");
67     document.write("<td><a href=" + links[index].URL +">"
                            + links[index].Name + "</a></td>");
68     document.write("<td>" + links[index].Desc +
                                        "</td></tr>");
69  }
70
71  function searchLinks(links, keyword){
72     document.write("Search results for keyword:"
                                    +keyword +"<br>");
73     document.write("<table border>");
74     for (var q=1; q<=links.length; q++) {
75         if (links[q].URL.indexOf(keyword) != -1){
76             showLink(links,q);
77             continue;
78         }
79         if (links[q].Desc.indexOf(keyword) != -1){
80             showLink(links,q);
81             continue;
82         }
83         if (links[q].Date.indexOf(keyword) != -1) {
84             showLink(links,q);
85             continue;
86         }
87         if (links[q].Name.indexOf(keyword) != -1) {
88             showLink(links,q);
89             continue;
90         }
91     }
92     document.write("</table>");
93  }
94
95  jsi = new makeLinks(linksize);
96  document.write("<title>Search</title><body bgcolor=white>");
97  searchLinks(jsi, prompt("Please enter keywords:) \r
        Search everywhere for :","try typing search engine"));
98  document.write("<hr>");
99  document.write("Click <b>search again</b>
```

```
                                        for another search. <hr>");
100 document.write("<form><input type=button
      onClick='history.go(0)' value='Search Again'></form>");
101 </script>
```

ANNOTATIONS

This script opens a prompt box when the page loads (see Figure 6-7). Typing "search engine," as the author suggests in the prompt, displays all five entries in the database (see Figure 6-8). You can then do searches for words that occur less frequently, and watch it pull only the entries containing them. The URLs are not displayed, but can be viewed in your browser's status bar by running the mouse pointer down the links column. The search includes them, as you can see by typing "digital" or "www," which are found only in the addresses.

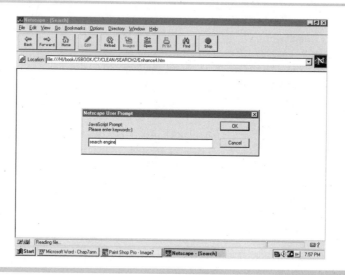

FIGURE 6-7.   The first screen prompts the user for a search string

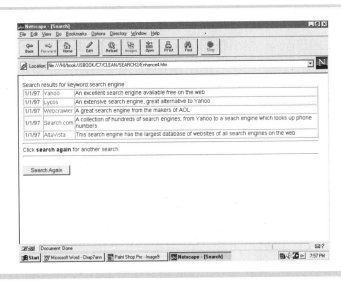

FIGURE 6-8. The results screen formats the output of the search

The data itself is structured as an array of Entry objects named **jsi** whose properties are organized into four subarrays—**datesArray**, **namesArray**, **urlsArray**, and **descArray**. Write

```
document.write(jsi[3].URL)
```

for example, and the output will be "http://www.webcrawler.com." As an array of arrays, **jsi** is a superarray that can be visualized as a box with four drawers, each containing one of the property arrays whose indexing is aligned.

```
1  <script language="javascript">
2
3  function makeEntry (){
4      this.Date = "";
5      this.Name="";
6      this.URL = "";
7      this.Desc = "";
8      this.Category = "";
9      return this;
10 }
```

makeEntry( ), called by **makeLinks( )** in line 23, uses the biblical JavaScript routine to create an Entry object with five properties: **Date**, **Name**, **URL**, **Desc**, and **Category**. The fifth property, **Category**, is not used by the script, but serves as an empty slot that hints at how you might expand the database—create a **catsArray** (unless, of course, you have an allergy).

```
12   function makeArray(n) {
13      this.length = n;
14      for (var k = 1; k <= n; k++) {
15          this[k] = "";
16      }
17      return this;
18   }
```

Next comes our old friend the arraymaker creating the **length** property and setting up an array of **n** empty strings. It is used in lines 33 through 36 to initialize the property arrays.

```
20   function makeLinks(size) {
21      this.length = size;
22      for (var r=1; r<= size; r++) {
23          this[r] = new makeEntry();
24          this[r].Date = datesArray[r];
25          this[r].Name = namesArray[r];
26          this[r].URL = urlsArray[r];
27          this[r].Desc = descArray[r];
28      }
29      return this;
30   }
```

makeLinks( ), called from line 95 when the page is loaded, instantiates the Entry object as an array of **jsis**, and assigns each one its properties from the corresponding property array. As the variable **r** earlier indicates, the indexing begins at 1 and is aligned.

The next code sequence, extending from lines 32 through 63, runs when the page is loaded and constructs the property arrays constituting the database itself.

```
32   var linksize=0
33   datesArray = new makeArray(linksize);
34   namesArray = new makeArray(linksize);
35   urlsArray = new makeArray(linksize);
36   descArray = new makeArray(linksize);
```

The global variable **linksize** declared in line 32 is initialized at zero, and in line 63 ends up getting the value of **arraycount**, the second global declared in 37, which

tracks the number of data entries. Note that, because the value of **linksize** is zero
when passed to **makeArray( )** in lines 33 to 36, the property arrays are initialized
as having zero length and zero member empty strings.

```
37   var arraycount=0
38   arraycount += 1
39   datesArray[arraycount] = "1/1/97 "
40   urlsArray[arraycount] = "http://www.yahoo.com"
41   namesArray[arraycount] = "Yahoo"
42   descArray[arraycount] =
          "An excellent search engine available free on the Web"
```

Next, lines 37 through 62 systematically populate the four property arrays, filling
each with a date, URL, name, and description. Prior to each entry, the value of
arraycount is incremented by one. If you decide to build a larger database by
copying this script, don't forget the increments, or the search function won't
work properly.

```
43   arraycount += 1
44   datesArray[arraycount] = "1/1/97 "
45   urlsArray[arraycount] = "http://www.lycos.com"
46   namesArray[arraycount] = "Lycos"
47   descArray[arraycount] =
          "An extensive search engine, great alternative to Yahoo"
48   arraycount += 1
49   datesArray[arraycount] = "1/1/97 "
50   urlsArray[arraycount] = "http://www.webcrawler.com"
51   namesArray[arraycount] = "Webcrawler"
52   descArray[arraycount] =
                  "A great search engine from the makers of AOL"
53   arraycount += 1
54   datesArray[arraycount] = "1/1/97 "
55   urlsArray[arraycount] = "http://www.search.com"
56   namesArray[arraycount] = "Search.com"
57   descArray[arraycount] =
          "A collection of hundreds of search engines; from Yahoo
              to a search engine which looks up phone numbers."
58   arraycount += 1
59   datesArray[arraycount] = "1/1/97 "
60   urlsArray[arraycount] = "http://altavista.digital.com"
61   namesArray[arraycount] = "AltaVista"
62   descArray[arraycount] =
                  "This search engine has the largest database
                  of web sites of all search engines on the Web"
63   linksize = arraycount;
```

The database construction ends with **arraycount** being assigned to **linksize**, which in line 95 serves as the argument in the call to **makeLinks( )**, where it controls the **jsi** object-instantiation loop.

```
65   function showLink (links, index) {
66       document.write("<tr><td>" + links[index].Date +"</td>");
67       document.write("<td><a href=" + links[index].URL +">"
                                    + links[index].Name + "</a></td>");
68       document.write("<td>" + links[index].Desc +
                                                "</td></tr>");
69   }
```

showLink( ) is the function that displays each of the hits when a search is successful. Called from each of the **if** statements in **searchLinks** that follows, it writes the HTML code for a row of three table cells and fills them with the **Date**, **URL** (inside anchor tags), **Name**, and **Desc** properties of the entries containing the keyword. Its first argument, **links**, carries the entire **jsi** object array passed to it by **searchLinks( )**, which gets it from the call in line 97. The second, **index**, is the entries index picked up from the value of **q** in the **for** loop that follows (lines 74 through 91).

```
71   function searchLinks(links, keyword){
72       document.write("Search results for keyword:"
                                        +keyword +"<br>");
73       document.write("<table border>");
74       for (var q=1; q<=links.length; q++) {
75            if (links[q].URL.indexOf(keyword) != -1){
76                 showLink(links,q);
77                 continue;
78            }
79            if (links[q].Desc.indexOf(keyword) != -1){
80                 showLink(links,q);
81                 continue;
82            }
83            if (links[q].Date.indexOf(keyword) != -1) {
84                 showLink(links,q);
85                 continue;
86            }
87            if (links[q].Name.indexOf(keyword) != -1) {
88                 showLink(links,q);
89                 continue;
90            }
91       }
92       document.write("</table>");
93   }
```

This script's main function, **searchLinks( )**, is called when the page is loaded from line 97. Its first argument, **links**, holds the **jsi** object array; its second, **keyword**, carries whatever string the user types in the prompt box. It first writes an introductory line incorporating the user-entered search item, followed by the opening <TABLE> tag.

It then runs through a **for** loop in which **indexOf( )**, which returns –1 if its argument is not found in the target string, is used to scan the database arrays for **keyword**. Each **if** statement within the loop looks through the data assigned to one of the four properties (**URL**, **Desc**, **Date**, and **Name**). If **keyword** is found, **showLink( )** is called to write the table row containing the entry, and **continue** ensures that when control returns from **showLink( )**, the next **if** test is run so that the entire database is searched. Finally, line 92 writes the HTML code to close the table.

```
95   jsi = new makeLinks(linksize);
96   document.write("<title>Search</title><body bgcolor=white>");
97   searchLinks(jsi, prompt("Please enter keywords:) \r
            Search everywhere for :","try typing search engine"));
98   document.write("<hr>");
99   document.write("Click <b>search again</b>
                                        for another search. <hr>");
100  document.write("<form><input type=button
            onClick='history.go(0)' value='Search Again'></form>");
101  </script>
```

The closing lines of this script, which are run when the page is loaded, create the **jsi** object array making up the database, write the HTML <TITLE> and <BODY> tags, and launch the prompt in line 97. If you enter a search item and click on OK in the dialog box, **searchLinks( )** executes the search. Click Cancel and **keyword** becomes **null**. Either way, once the prompt window closes, lines 98 through 100 execute to write instructions for a new search and create a Search Again button. The JavaScript **history.go( )** method assigned to its **onClick** event handler reloads the page. The argument to **go( )** is the number of entries in the browser's history list to go back; 0 here triggers a page reload. The same effect can be achieved by writing

```
onClick="location.reload()"
```

or using any of various techniques JavaScript provides for loading a specific page.

As mentioned in the general introduction to this script, the snag you run into with JavaScript databases is file size. Moreover, it's highly inefficient to send an entire database through the Web to a client machine when all the user may want is one item within it. One way of dealing with this problem is to create a modular database made up of small HTML files, each containing a unit of the organized information.

For example, a women's wear manufacturer could have separate files for dresses, skirts, suits, slacks, blouses, and so on. The file containing the information about the type of item the visitor is interested in could then be loaded into either a hidden frame or layer from where it could be accessed by the search code. When necessary, the data could even be organized further, for instance, dresses by color and/or style. Nice small files will (barring a web or server traffic jam) ensure users of a snappy response, while at the same time allowing you to build as big a database as you want. The key to building a successful JavaScript database search engine can be summed up in two words: Think small!

local

Local Search

N2 N2.01 N2.02+ N3 N4 **E3** **E4**

Our next script is another variation on the array-based JavaScript search engine, this time providing a more complex results screen, displayed in an HTML forms-based interface. The database, which has only four sample entries, consists of personal information (name, snail- and e-mail address, and phone number).

To search it, you have to select a category such as First Name, Street, City, Telephone Number, and so on—there are seven in all—appearing in a selection list (see Figure 6-9).

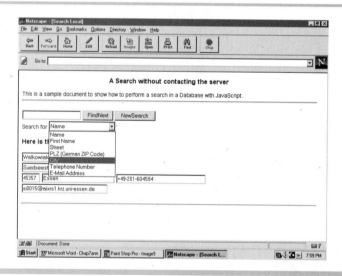

FIGURE 6-9. Choose search criteria from a forms-based selection box

The search, moreover, is limited in scope to the entries for that item. In other words, a name search for "Jefferson," for example, will not pull the entry for someone living on Jefferson Avenue. In addition, the search is case sensitive, but a front-end match is all it takes for a hit. A first-name search for "Sam," for instance, will show the entries for anyone named "Sam," "Samantha," "Samuel," or any other moniker beginning with those three letters. Yet search for "am" and you'll hit a dead end.

The form displays the complete entry for each hit, with each item appearing in a separate text field. Here they are unfortunately unlabeled, but what's what is fairly obvious. Unless you're gifted with highly keen ESP, to make this local search engine return a hit, you'll have to peek at the database in the code that follows to pick a search item. Or just leave the entry field blank and click on the FindNext button to flip through all the records. Do a name search for "Walkowiak" to see how this application handles two hits.

You might also want to add a few more entries of your own with matching features to explore the script's behavior under those circumstances. You can scroll forward through multiple hits by clicking on the FindNext button; when the end of the list is reached, the output fields clear and the next click on FindNext cycles back to the first hit.

```
1    <HTML>
2    <HEAD>
3    <TITLE>Search Local</TITLE>
4    <SCRIPT LANGUAGE = "JavaScript">
5    <!-- By Olaf Walkowiak, Bookmark,
         <si0015@aixrs1.hrz.uni-essen.de>, http://www.bookmark.de

7    function createArray(length)
8    {
9        this.length = length;
10       for(var i = 1; i<= length; i++)
11           this[i] = null;
12       return this;
13   }

15   var Entries = 4;
16   var Separator = ";"
17   var Fields = 7;
18   var iName = 1;
19   var iFirstName = 2;
20   var iStreet = 3;
21   var iPLZ = 4;
22   var iCity = 5;
23   var iPhone = 6;
24   var iEMail = 7;
```

```
25
26   var Data = new createArray(Entries);
27
28   Data[1] = "Walkowiak;Olaf;Suedseestr. 14;45357;Essen;
                    +49-201-604594;si0015@aixrs1.hrz.uni-essen.de";
29   Data[2] = "Muster;Max;Am Hang 13; 12345;Irgendwo;
                        +56-789-123456;max.muster@beispiel.de";
30   Data[3] = "Walkowiak;Kurt;Luebecker Str.65;45145;Essen;
                                    +49-201-xxxxxxxx;";
31   Data[4] = "Broesel;Werner;Boelkstoffstr 12;20123;Saufdorf;
                        +49-xxx-xxxxxxxx;werner@semmel.verlag";
32
33   var LastMatch = 0;
34   function GetField(Entry,number)
35   {
36      var Out = "";
37      var FirstChar;
38      var LastChar;
39
40      FirstChar = 0;
41      LastChar = Entry.indexOf(Separator) ;
42      if (number == 1)
43      {
44         Out += Entry.substring(FirstChar,LastChar);
45         return Out;
46      }
47      if (number == Fields)
48      {
49         Out += Entry.substring(Entry.lastIndexOf(Separator)
                                          + 1,Entry.length)
50         return Out;
51      }
52
53      for(var i =2; i <= number; i++)
54      {
55         FirstChar = LastChar + 1;
56         LastChar = Entry.indexOf(Separator, FirstChar);
57      }
58      Out += Entry.substring(FirstChar,LastChar);
59      return Out;
60   }
61
62   function FindNext(String, number)
```

```
63  {
64     var CompareWith = "";
65     for(var i = LastMatch + 1; i <=Data.length; i++)
66     {
67        var buf = GetField(Data[i],number);
68        var bl = parseInt(buf.length);
69        var sl = parseInt(String.length);
70        if(bl > sl)
71        {
72           CompareWith = buf.substring(0,sl );
73        }
74        else
75        {
76           CompareWith = buf;
77        }
78        if (CompareWith == String)
79        .{
80           LastMatch = i;
81           return i;
82        }
83     }
84     LastMatch = 0;
85      return 0;
86  }
87
88  function ResetSearch()
89  {
90     LastMatch = 0;
91     for(var i = 1; i <=Fields; i++)
92     {
93        document.SearchForm.elements[i+3].value = "";
94     }
95  }
96
97  function TypeNext()
98  {
99     var SearchString = document.SearchForm.Text.value;
100    var index = document.SearchForm.elements[3].
                                     options.selectedIndex + 1;
101    var j = FindNext(SearchString, index);
102    if (j == 0)
103    {
104       alert("End of List reached, Search String not found!
```

```
                              \nPress 'Find Next' again to restart
                                               from top of list!");
105        ResetSearch();
106        return;
107      }
108      var buf = "";
109      for(var i = 1; i <=Fields; i++)
110      {
111         buf = GetField(Data[j],i);
112         document.SearchForm.elements[i+3].value = buf;
113      }
114 }
115 // -->
116 </SCRIPT>
117 </HEAD>
118 <BODY BGCOLOR="#FFFFFF">
119 <CENTER><H3>A Search without contacting the server</H3>
120 </CENTER><P>
121 This is a sample document to show how to perform a search
                              in a Database with JavaScript.<BR>
122 <hr>
123 <FORM NAME="SearchForm" onSubmit="TypeNext();return false">
124 <INPUT NAME="Text" TYPE="TEXT" ROWS=1 COLS=20>
125 <INPUT NAME="FindNext" TYPE="SUBMIT" VALUE="FindNext">
126 <INPUT NAME="NewSearch" TYPE="Reset" VALUE="NewSearch"
                                   onClick ="ResetSearch();"><BR>
127 Search for <SELECT  VALUE="field" SIZE=1>
128 <OPTION>Name
129 <OPTION>First Name
130 <OPTION>Street
131 <OPTION>PLZ (German ZIP Code)
132 <OPTION>City
133 <OPTION>Telephone Number
134 <OPTION>E-Mail Address
135 </SELECT><BR>
136 <H3>Here is the Result:</H3>
137 <INPUT NAME="Result1" TYPE="TEXT" SIZE="15">
138 <INPUT NAME="Result2" TYPE="TEXT" SIZE="15"><BR>
139 <INPUT NAME="Result3" TYPE="TEXT" SIZE="31"><BR>
140 <INPUT NAME="Result4" TYPE="TEXT" SIZE="5">
141 <INPUT NAME="Result5" TYPE="TEXT" SIZE="25">
142 <INPUT NAME="Result6" TYPE="TEXT" SIZE="31"><BR>
143 <INPUT NAME="Result7" TYPE="TEXT" SIZE="30">
```

```
144  </FORM>
145  <HR>
146  </BODY>
147  </HTML>
```

ANNOTATIONS

In this script, each database record is a separate member of the **Data** array. Semicolons are used to separate the seven items comprising each entry. The search process is handled by three core functions: **TypeNext( )**, attached to the form's **onSubmit** handler, runs whenever the FindNext button is clicked and calls on **FindNext( )** to perform the comparisons. **GetField( )** is used by both functions, first to access the records and then to display the hits.

The search function, it should be noted, only pulls one record at a time. Each click on the FindNext button triggers a new search, with the **LastMatch** variable serving as a bookmark.

```
1    <HTML>
2    <HEAD>
3    <TITLE>Search Local</TITLE>
4    <SCRIPT LANGUAGE = "JavaScript">
5    <!-- By Olaf Walkowiak, Bookmark,
         <si0015@aixrs1.hrz.uni-essen.de>, http://www.bookmark.de

6
7    function createArray(length)
8    {
9       this.length = length;
10      for(var i = 1; i<= length; i++)
11          this[i] = null;
12      return this;
13   }
```

Once again, our script begins with an array constructor. The array, initialized with **null**, is instantiated as **Data** by line 26.

```
15   var Entries = 4;
16   var Separator = ";"
17   var Fields = 7;
18   var iName = 1;
19   var iFirstName = 2;
20   var iStreet = 3;
21   var iPLZ = 4;
22   var iCity = 5;
```

```
23   var iPhone = 6;
24   var iEMail = 7;
25
26   var Data = new createArray(Entries);
```

Next comes a series of global variables: **Entries** holds the number of entries; **Fields**, the number of fields; and **Separator**, the character used to separate the items comprising each record or member of the **Data** array. The next seven variables beginning with the letter "i" are not used by the script, but have been kept here because the number assigned to each is the same as the **number** argument used by **GetField( )** and **FindNext( )** to focus the search on that item. The value of **number** in any search is determined by the item chosen from the selection list on the page.

```
28   Data[1] = "Walkowiak;Olaf;Suedseestr. 14;45357;Essen;
                     +49-201-604594;si0015@aixrs1.hrz.uni-essen.de";
29   Data[2] = "Muster;Max;Am Hang 13;12345;Irgendwo;
                     +56-789-123456;max.muster@beispiel.de";
30   Data[3] = "Walkowiak;Kurt;Luebecker Str.65;45145;Essen;
                                   +49-201-xxxxxxxx; ";
31   Data[4] = "Broesel;Werner;Boelkstoffstr 12;20123;Saufdorf;
                     +49-xxx-xxxxxxxx;werner@semmel.verlag";
```

Lines 28 to 31 contain the **Data** array, each a string containing seven information items separated by semicolons. Obviously, if you want to use this script, you'll have to supply your own data and fill it in. Here too the value of making the separator a variable becomes apparent. If, for instance, you prefer having vertical bars as separators, just use them when you construct your database and make line 16 read

```
var Separator = "|";
```

Otherwise, you would have to scour the entire script and revise every occurrence of its use—and hope you don't change your mind!

```
33   var LastMatch = 0;
34   function GetField(Entry,number)
35   {
36      var Out = "";
37      var FirstChar;
38      var LastChar;
39
40      FirstChar = 0;
41      LastChar = Entry.indexOf(Separator) ;
42      if (number == 1)
43      {
44         Out += Entry.substring(FirstChar,LastChar);
45         return Out;
46      }
```

```
47      if (number == Fields)
48      {
49         Out += Entry.substring(Entry.lastIndexOf(Separator)
                                              + 1,Entry.length)
50         return Out;
51      }
52
53      for(var i =2; i <= number; i++)
54      {
55         FirstChar = LastChar + 1;
56         LastChar = Entry.indexOf(Separator, FirstChar);
57      }
58      Out += Entry.substring(FirstChar,LastChar);
59      return Out;
60   }
```

The **LastMatch** variable declared and initialized in line 33 serves, as mentioned, to bookmark the search process in the event of multiple hits.

GetField( )—called by **FindNext( )** in line 67 and **TypeNext( )** in line 111—pulls the data by using JavaScript's **substring( )**, **indexOf( )**, and **lastIndexOf( )** methods. The first of its two arguments, **Entry**, is a member of the **Data** array; the second, **number**, is the search-item index.

The first local variable which **GetField( )** declares and initializes as an empty string, **Out**, will hold the output. The next two are simply declared in lines 37 and 38, then assigned values in 40 and 41. **FirstChar** gets 0 and **LastChar** the index representing the first occurrence of **Separator** (a semicolon) in the **Data** string.

The string is then parsed in one of three ways:

◆ If **number** is 1, **GetField( )** uses the initial values of **FirstChar** and **LastChar** to pull the substring that **Out** then returns to **FindNext( )** for comparison or to **TypeNext( )** for display.

◆ If **number** is 7 (the same value as **Fields**, the number of elements comprising each record), **GetField( )** pulls the substring extending from the index of the last occurrence of a semicolon to the end of the **Data** string.

◆ Otherwise **GetField( )** cycles through the **for** routine in lines 53 to 57 to generate the appropriate **FirstChar** and **LastChar** values for the item specified by **number**, which controls the loop. Each pass through the loop leaps forward one item in the **Data** string, with the final values used to pull the **Out** string this function returns.

As **return** passes control back to the calling function, **GetField( )** terminates on line 45, 50, or 59, depending on the value of **number**.

```
62  function FindNext(String, number)
63  {
64     var CompareWith = "";
65     for(var i = LastMatch + 1; i <=Data.length; i++)
66     {
67        var buf = GetField(Data[i],number);
68        var bl = parseInt(buf.length);
69        var sl = parseInt(String.length);
70        if(bl > sl)
71        {
72           CompareWith = buf.substring(0,sl );
73        }
74        else
75        {
76           CompareWith = buf;
77        }
```

The string comparison itself is done by **FindNext( )**, which is called by **TypeNext( )** in line 101. Its first argument, **String**, holds the user-entered item; the second, **number**, indicates the selected search category (name, address, and so on). The function returns either the index of the next hit or 0 if no match is found.

After declaring and initializing **CompareWith**, a local variable, as an empty string, **FindNext( )** runs a **for** loop. Here the starting value of **i** (**LastMatch** + 1) is what makes the comparison process step through the database from one hit to the next (if any).

The loop first sets up three more local variables: **buf**, which holds the string pulled from the database, and **bl** and **sl**, which get the length of **buf** and **String**, respectively. The use of **parseInt( )** here to force a number is not really necessary, because the JavaScript **length** property is by definition an integer. The length of **bl** and **sl** are then compared in line 70. If **bl** is longer than **sl**, **CompareWith** gets the first **sl** characters of **buf**; otherwise, it gets all of **buf**. This routine is what causes the search engine to display front-end matches as hits—for example, a query for "Frank" will pull not only every "Frank," but also every "Franklin," "Frankfurter," "Frankenstein," and so on.

```
78        if (CompareWith == String)
79        {
80           LastMatch = i;
81           return i;
82        }
83     }
84     LastMatch = 0;
85     return 0;
86  }
```

Line 78 then compares the two strings. If they match, **LastMatch** gets **i** (the **Data** array index of the hit) and **FindNext( )** returns **i**. Otherwise **LastMatch** is reset to 0 and the function returns 0.

```
88   function ResetSearch()
89   {
90      LastMatch = 0;
91      for(var i = 1; i <=Fields; i++)
92      {
93          document.SearchForm.elements[i+3].value = "";
94      }
95   }
```

ResetSearch( ), attached to the NewSearch button in line 126, resets the value of **LastMatch**, the hit index, to 0 and then uses a **for** loop to clear the text fields in the form by making their **value** an empty string. The "+3" in line 93, combined with initializing **i** with 1 in line 91, makes the process skip the first four elements in the form (the entry field, two buttons, and selection list).

```
97   function TypeNext()
98   {
99      var SearchString = document.SearchForm.Text.value;
100     var index = document.SearchForm.elements[3].
                                       options.selectedIndex + 1;
101     var j = FindNext(SearchString, index);
102     if (j == 0)
103     {
104         alert("End of List reached, Search String not found!
                        \nPress 'Find Next' again to restart
                                          from top of list!");
105         ResetSearch();
106         return;
107     }
```

TypeNext( ), the function called by the form's **onSubmit** event handler when the user clicks on the FindNext button, first assigns the user-input contents of the text field to a local variable, **SearchString**. A second local, **index**, gets the index of the search category chosen by the user from the selection list; its value is incremented by one to align the **options** indexing, which begins at zero, with the data-item indexing, which starts at one. The third local, **j**, gets either the value of **i** (the **Data** array index) returned by **FindNext( )** if the search results in a hit, or 0 if no match is found.

If **j** is zero, an alert pops open with a message to the effect that the search has failed and the function dies.

```
108     var buf = "";
109     for(var i = 1; i <=Fields; i++)
```

```
110      {
111          buf = GetField(Data[j],i);
112          document.SearchForm.elements[i+3].value = buf;
113      }
114  }
```

Otherwise a fourth local variable, **buf**, is declared and initialized as an empty string. It is then used in a **for** loop to pull all seven data items comprising the full record for which a match was found from the **Data** array and to display them in the output fields. As in line 93, the "+3" in line 112 is to adjust for the four form elements on the page preceding the search results area. In both cases, the adjustment can be eliminated by giving the form containing the output fields a different name.

```
115  // -->
116  </SCRIPT>
117  </HEAD>
118  <BODY BGCOLOR="#FFFFFF">
119  <CENTER><H3>A Search without contacting the server</H3>
120  </CENTER><P>
121  This is a sample document to show how to perform a search
                                in a Database with JavaScript.<BR>
122  <hr>
123  <FORM NAME="SearchForm" onSubmit="TypeNext();return false">
124  <INPUT NAME="Text" TYPE="TEXT" ROWS=1 COLS=20>
125  <INPUT NAME="FindNext" TYPE="SUBMIT" VALUE="FindNext">
126  <INPUT NAME="NewSearch" TYPE="Reset" VALUE="NewSearch"
                                onClick ="ResetSearch();"><BR>
127  Search for <SELECT  VALUE="field" SIZE=1>
128  <OPTION>Name
129  <OPTION>First Name
130  <OPTION>Street
131  <OPTION>PLZ (German ZIP Code)
132  <OPTION>City
133  <OPTION>Telephone Number
134  <OPTION>E-Mail Address
135  </SELECT><BR>
136  <H3>Here is the Result:</H3>
137  <INPUT NAME="Result1" TYPE="TEXT" SIZE="15">
138  <INPUT NAME="Result2" TYPE="TEXT" SIZE="15"><BR>
139  <INPUT NAME="Result3" TYPE="TEXT" SIZE="31"><BR>
140  <INPUT NAME="Result4" TYPE="TEXT" SIZE="5">
141  <INPUT NAME="Result5" TYPE="TEXT" SIZE="25">
142  <INPUT NAME="Result6" TYPE="TEXT" SIZE="31"><BR>
143  <INPUT NAME="Result7" TYPE="TEXT" SIZE="30">
```

```
144  </FORM>
145  <HR>
146  </BODY>
147  </HTML>
```

The remainder of the page contains the HTML code for the form, with **TypeNext( )** assigned to the form's **onSubmit** handler in line 123 and **ResetSearch( )** assigned to the NewSearch button in line 126. If you prefer, you could assign **TypeNext( )** directly to the FindNext button's **onClick** handler. In that case, be sure to change its TYPE from "Submit" to "Button" in the <INPUT> tag.

This script can serve as a solid foundation for creating a local directory, meaning one for a department, business unit, project team, or the like. At that level, it could become a very useful intranet enhancement. But if your organization has 25,000 employees, forget it—you're better off using a server-side search engine. The optimal size of the database for this type of device probably lies somewhere in the range of 20 to 50 records, with the maximum depending on both the number of entries and the number of data items or fields within each record. The extent to which you dress up the page also comes into play. If you develop lengthy instructions, add all kinds of graphics, and surround the search engine with peripheral information, you'll end up with a very heavy page with little room left for the database.

Another approach you could take is to develop this script into a personal desktop address book accessible with your browser. In that case, database size becomes far less significant, because the file doesn't have to be downloaded. Particularly if there are features of existing address books (such as the one built into Navigator) that you don't like or wish they had, you can build your own custom JavaScript little black book. The drawback, of course, is that the entries may have to be made directly to the script. Because JavaScript doesn't write to disk, you can't just create an input form for new (or the initial) entries as you might with other programming languages. A work-around is to put the data array in a separate file from the functions, but make it accessible to them through a frame or layers arrangement. Entries made via a form could easily be added to the array, which can even be sorted with JavaScript's **sort( )** method. Then have **document.write( )** output the code for the array along with the data it holds to a separate window, and use your browser's File Save function to save the newly written database. Reload the latter and the result should be an updated address book.

directry

Company Directory

{N2 {N2.01 {N2.02+ {N3 {N4 {E3 {E4

This local search engine also operates on an address-book database. It differs from the preceding script in not using search categories but simply using the letters of the alphabet as an index. User control is achieved with radio buttons—a separate one for each letter. When the Find button is clicked, a small window pops open and displays the information on the people whose names begin with the specified letter (see Figure 6-10). Essentially, it's a JavaScript version of address books with a separate tab for each letter of the alphabet.

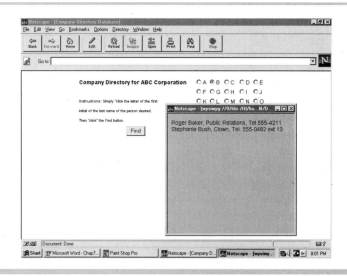

FIGURE 6-10.   Find the data entries by using the alphabet

If you decide to use this script, one of the first enhancements you should make is to add a Close button to the window that displays the results. Otherwise, a second click on the main window (such as to select another letter) sends the child back behind the browser. Although the results of the new search are properly displayed, it's a nuisance having to fetch the child window to see the information. Also, a button is more user friendly in being immediately visible and directly accessible— which the standard **Close** function on the titlebar is not.

```
1   <HTML>
2   <HEAD>
3   <TITLE>Company Directory Database</TITLE>
4   <SCRIPT LANGUAGE="JavaScript">
5   <!-- Hide JavaScript from Java-Impaired Browsers
6   function initArray() {
7      this.length = initArray.arguments.length;
8      for (var i = 0; i < this.length; i++) {
9          this[i] = initArray.arguments[i];
```

```
10      }
11    }
12    var rcrd = new initArray("4b","5b","8b","8b");
13    rcrd[0] = "Randy Alms, Antiques, Tel. 555-8247 "
14           + "       \rShannon Austin, Animation, Tel. 555-0570 "
15           + "       \rJeffrey Asay, Research and Development,
                                          Tel. 555-2520 ";
16    rcrd[1] = "Roger Baker, Public Relations, Tel.555-4211 "
17        + "       \rStephanie Bush, Clown, Tel. 555-0482 ext 13";
18    rcrd[2] = "Carrie Cunnings, Import/Export,
                                          Tel. 555-7192 ext 3";
19    rcrd[3] = "Doug Dougherty, Nanny, Tel. 555-2645  "
20         + "email: markyd@abc.com"
21         + "\rLisa Davids, Secretarial, Tel. 555-5512 ext 11";
22    rcrd[4] = "Tracy Elkin, Media Relations,
                                          Tel. 555-1073 ext 22"
23       + "       \rChris Everet, Financing, Tel. 555-0645 ext 23";
24    rcrd[5] = "Michael Forrest, Tour Guide, Tel. 555-4413 "
25       + "       \rLouise Fillio, Operations, Tel. 555-4990 ext 18";
26    rcrd[6] = "Scott Gisler, Horse Trainer,
                                          Tel. 555-9732 ext 5";
27    rcrd[7] = "Nikki Halesworth, Computers, Tel. 555-8210 ";
28    rcrd[9] = "Bernie Jarvies, Security, Tel. 555-5178 ext 12"
29         + "       \rMichael Jordan, Consultant,
                                          Tel. 555-3092 ext 21";
30    rcrd[10] = "T. Knickerbocker, Insurance, Tel. 555-2338 "
31          + "       \rBoris Kogan, Plumber, Tel. 555-6250 ext 9";
32    rcrd[11] = "Giuseppe Lombardo, Resource, Tel. 555-3812 "
33      + "       \rDana Luxenburg, Mechanic, Tel. 555-8658 ext 11";
34    rcrd[12] = "The Masters, Entertainment, Tel. 555-6622 ext 4"
35          + "       \rDennis Miller, Writer, Tel. 555-7409 ";
36    rcrd[13] = "Christine Nendza, Escort, Tel. 555-9666 ext 22"
37      + "       \rSteve Nigar, Accounts Payable, Tel. 555-8317 ";
38    rcrd[15] = "Carrie Paff, Psychologist, Tel. 555-1776 "
39          + "       \rRichard Petrocelli, Restoration,
                                          Tel. 555-9072 ext 15";
40    rcrd[17] = "David Roth, Photographer, Tel. 555-0844 ext 22"
41          + "       \rStoney Rockwell, Editor, Tel. 555-9582 ";
42    rcrd[18] = "Nora Swallows, Public Relations,
                                          Tel. 555-2651 ext 31"
43          + "       \rKevin Spacey, Designer, Tel. 555-9206 ";
44    rcrd[19] = "Julie Tachiki, Pro Bowler, Tel. 800-555-BOWL "
45          + "       \rEric Towler, Director, Tel. 555-3232 ";
```

```
46  rcrd[21] = "Christopher Vasos, Administration,
                                                    Tel. 555-5718 "
47    + "        \rJona Valentine, Gardener, Tel. 555-3459 ext 7";
48  rcrd[22] = "Josh Wexler, Dentist, Tel. 555-1755 ext 12"
49   + "        \rHenry Winkler, Landscaper, Tel. 555-8307 ext 16";
50  rcrd[24] = "Saivash Yazdi, Chef, Tel. 555-8273 ";
51  rcrd[25] = "Joe Zawicki, Administration, Tel. 555-3526 "
52
53  function dataBase(isnform) {
54     for (var i = 0; i < 26; i++) {
55         if (isnform.alpha[i].checked) {
56             recnum = isnform.alpha[i].value;
57         }
58     }
59     if (rcrd[recnum] != null) {
60         msgWindow=window.open("","displayWindow",
                "toolbar=no,width=325,height=300,directories=no,
                 status=no,scrollbars=yes,resize=no,menubar=no")
61         msgWindow.document.writeln(rcrd[recnum])
62         msgWindow.document.close()
63     }
64     else  alert("Sorry, no listings for that letter");
65  }
66  // End Hiding Script -->
67  </SCRIPT>
68  </HEAD>
69  <BODY BGCOLOR="#FFFFFF">
70  <CENTER>
71  <TABLE BORDER=0 WIDTH=486>
72  <TR><TD><B>Company Directory for ABC Corporation</B></TD>
73  <TD><FORM NAME="isnform">
74  <INPUT TYPE="radio" NAME="alpha" VALUE="0" CHECKED>A</TD>
75  <TD><INPUT TYPE="radio" NAME="alpha" VALUE="1">B</TD>
76  <TD><INPUT TYPE="radio" NAME="alpha" VALUE="2">C</TD>
77  <TD><INPUT TYPE="radio" NAME="alpha" VALUE="3">D</TD>
78  <TD><INPUT TYPE="radio" NAME="alpha" VALUE="4">E</TD></TR>
79  <TR><TD><INPUT TYPE="radio" NAME="alpha" VALUE="5">F</TD>
80  <TD><INPUT TYPE="radio" NAME="alpha" VALUE="6">G</TD>
81  <TD><INPUT TYPE="radio" NAME="alpha" VALUE="7">H</TD>
82  <TD><INPUT TYPE="radio" NAME="alpha" VALUE="8">I</TD>
83  <TD><INPUT TYPE="radio" NAME="alpha" VALUE="9">J</TD></TR>
84  <TR><TD><FONT SIZE=1><B>Instructions: </B> Simply "click
                        the letter of the first</FONT></TD><TD>
```

```
85   <INPUT TYPE="radio" NAME="alpha" VALUE="10">K</TD>
86   <TD><INPUT TYPE="radio" NAME="alpha" VALUE="11">L</TD>
87   <TD><INPUT TYPE="radio" NAME="alpha" VALUE="12">M</TD>
88   <TD><INPUT TYPE="radio" NAME="alpha" VALUE="13">N</TD>
89   <TD><INPUT TYPE="radio" NAME="alpha" VALUE="14">O</TD></TR>
90   <TR><TD><FONT SIZE=1>initial of the last name of the person
                                         desired.</FONT></TD>
91   <TD><INPUT TYPE="radio" NAME="alpha" VALUE="15">P</TD>
92   <TD><INPUT TYPE="radio" NAME="alpha" VALUE="16">Q</TD>
93   <TD><INPUT TYPE="radio" NAME="alpha" VALUE="17">R</TD>
94   <TD><INPUT TYPE="radio" NAME="alpha" VALUE="18">S</TD>
95   <TD><INPUT TYPE="radio" NAME="alpha" VALUE="19">T</TD></TR>
96   <TR><TD><FONT SIZE=1>Then "click" the Find button.
                                         </FONT></TD>
97   <TD><INPUT TYPE="radio" NAME="alpha" VALUE="20">U</TD>
98   <TD><INPUT TYPE="radio" NAME="alpha" VALUE="21">V</TD>
99   <TD><INPUT TYPE="radio" NAME="alpha" VALUE="22">W</TD>
100  <TD><INPUT TYPE="radio" NAME="alpha" VALUE="23">X</TD>
101  <TD><INPUT TYPE="radio" NAME="alpha" VALUE="24">Y</TD></TR>
102  <TR><TD ALIGN=CENTER><INPUT TYPE="button" NAME="but" VALUE="
                  Find " onClick="dataBase(this.form)"></TD>
103  <TD></TD><TD></TD>
104  <TD><INPUT TYPE="radio" NAME="alpha" VALUE="25">Z</TD>
105  </TR></TABLE>
106  </form>
107  </CENTER>
108  </body>
109  </HTML>
```

ANNOTATIONS

This script stores the data in an array, each member of which holds all the entries for a given letter of the alphabet. The main function, **dataBase( )**, determines which radio button has been selected, pulls the corresponding array member, and displays the information in a new window.

```
1   <HTML>
2   <HEAD>
3   <TITLE>Company Directory Database</TITLE>
4   <SCRIPT LANGUAGE="JavaScript">
5   <!-- Hide JavaScript from Java-Impaired Browsers
6   function initArray() {
```

```
7       this.length = initArray.arguments.length;
8       for (var i = 0; i < this.length; i++) {
9            this[i] = initArray.arguments[i];
10      }
11   }
12   var rcrd = new initArray("4b","5b","8b","8b");
```

Like so many others, this script begins with the old way of creating an array with a **length** property. Line 12 instantiates the array as the global variable **rcrd** and initializes it with four dummy members. Then lines 13 through 51 populate **rcrd** with the real data.

```
13   rcrd[0] = "Randy Alms, Antiques, Tel. 555-8247 "
14        + "      \rShannon Austin, Animation, Tel. 555-0570 "
15        + "      \rJeffrey Asay, Research and Development,
                                        Tel. 555-2520 ";
16   rcrd[1] = "Roger Baker, Public Relations, Tel.555-4211 "
17        + "      \rStephanie Bush, Clown, Tel. 555-0482 ext 13";
18   rcrd[2] = "Carrie Cunnings, Import/Export,
                                        Tel. 555-7192 ext 3";
```

The "\r" in front of second and subsequent entries in each record is likely a remnant from initially using a form text area to display the output. To start each entry in the child window on a separate line, you have to use HTML code: just load the file into a text editor, do a search for "\r", and replace with "<br>".

Notice too that the indexing of the **rcrd** array is absolute, with certain numbers skipped to leave room for names beginning with "I," "O," "Q," and a few other letters for which there are presently no entries. This also ensures that the data array is aligned with the radio buttons, which cover all 26 letters of the alphabet.

```
53   function dataBase(isnform) {
54      for (var i = 0; i < 26; i++) {
55         if (isnform.alpha[i].checked) {
56            recnum = isnform.alpha[i].value;
57         }
58      }
```

The main function, **dataBase( )**, is called when the user clicks on the Find button (line 102). Its sole argument, **isnform**, is the form itself. The **for** loop in lines 54 through 58 scans the radio buttons to see which one is checked and assigns its value to the variable **recnum**. The value is simply a number corresponding to the array index. As the array and radio-button indexing are already aligned, you can strip the buttons of their VALUE attribute in lines 74 to 104, and change line 56 to read

```
recnum = i;
```

If nothing else, it'll lighten the page to provide more room for data.

```
59      if (rcrd[recnum] != null) {
60          msgWindow=window.open("","displayWindow",
                "toolbar=no,width=325,height=300,directories=no,
                status=no,scrollbars=yes,resize=no,menubar=no")
61          msgWindow.document.writeln(rcrd[recnum])
62          msgWindow.document.close()
63      }
64      else  alert("Sorry, no listings for that letter");
65  }
```

If **rcrd** has a member indexed by **recnum**, a 325×300-pixel window named **msgWindow** opens and displays the record with **document.writeln( )**. Otherwise the "Sorry, no listings" message appears in an alert box.

```
66  // End Hiding Script -->
67  </SCRIPT>
68  </HEAD>
69  <BODY BGCOLOR="#FFFFFF">
70  <CENTER>
71  <TABLE BORDER=0 WIDTH=486>
72  <TR><TD><B>Company Directory for ABC Corporation</B></TD>
73  <TD><FORM NAME="isnform">
74  <INPUT TYPE="radio" NAME="alpha" VALUE="0" CHECKED>A</TD>
75  <TD><INPUT TYPE="radio" NAME="alpha" VALUE="1">B</TD>
76  <TD><INPUT TYPE="radio" NAME="alpha" VALUE="2">C</TD>
77  <TD><INPUT TYPE="radio" NAME="alpha" VALUE="3">D</TD>
78  <TD><INPUT TYPE="radio" NAME="alpha" VALUE="4">E</TD></TR>
79  <TR><TD><INPUT TYPE="radio" NAME="alpha" VALUE="5">F</TD>
80  <TD><INPUT TYPE="radio" NAME="alpha" VALUE="6">G</TD>
81  <TD><INPUT TYPE="radio" NAME="alpha" VALUE="7">H</TD>
82  <TD><INPUT TYPE="radio" NAME="alpha" VALUE="8">I</TD>
83  <TD><INPUT TYPE="radio" NAME="alpha" VALUE="9">J</TD></TR>
84  <TR><TD><FONT SIZE=1><B>Instructions: </B> Simply "click
                        the letter of the first</FONT></TD><TD>
85  <INPUT TYPE="radio" NAME="alpha" VALUE="10">K</TD>
86  <TD><INPUT TYPE="radio" NAME="alpha" VALUE="11">L</TD>
87  <TD><INPUT TYPE="radio" NAME="alpha" VALUE="12">M</TD>
88  <TD><INPUT TYPE="radio" NAME="alpha" VALUE="13">N</TD>
89  <TD><INPUT TYPE="radio" NAME="alpha" VALUE="14">O</TD></TR>
90  <TR><TD><FONT SIZE=1>initial of the last name of the person
                        desired.</FONT></TD>
91  <TD><INPUT TYPE="radio" NAME="alpha" VALUE="15">P</TD>
92  <TD><INPUT TYPE="radio" NAME="alpha" VALUE="16">Q</TD>
```

```
93    <TD><INPUT TYPE="radio" NAME="alpha" VALUE="17">R</TD>
94    <TD><INPUT TYPE="radio" NAME="alpha" VALUE="18">S</TD>
95    <TD><INPUT TYPE="radio" NAME="alpha" VALUE="19">T</TD></TR>
96    <TR><TD><FONT SIZE=1>Then "click" the Find button.
                                               </FONT></TD>
97    <TD><INPUT TYPE="radio" NAME="alpha" VALUE="20">U</TD>
98    <TD><INPUT TYPE="radio" NAME="alpha" VALUE="21">V</TD>
99    <TD><INPUT TYPE="radio" NAME="alpha" VALUE="22">W</TD>
100   <TD><INPUT TYPE="radio" NAME="alpha" VALUE="23">X</TD>
101   <TD><INPUT TYPE="radio" NAME="alpha" VALUE="24">Y</TD></TR>
102   <TR><TD ALIGN=CENTER><INPUT TYPE="button" NAME="but" VALUE="
                       Find " onClick="dataBase(this.form)"></TD>
103   <TD></TD><TD></TD>
104   <TD><INPUT TYPE="radio" NAME="alpha" VALUE="25">Z</TD>
105   </TR></TABLE>
106   </form>
107   </CENTER>
108   </body>
109   </HTML>
```

The rest of the page contains the standard HTML code for the form named **isnform** with its Find and 26 radio buttons.

In assessing the value of this and similar scripts to your own purposes, don't be misled by the type of data they happen to use. The alphabet-based structure could easily be adapted to a glossary of legal terms or list of travel destinations, for example. Or the radio-button indexing could be applied to product categories, with as few or as many buttons as you need. In the latter case, you would probably be best off creating a separate data array for each category, with the buttons serving to determine which of the arrays is queried.

Another possibility is to merge this approach with the preceding script so that, for example, a click on "M" pulls all the cities whose names begin with that letter, yet the data on each is displayed one-at-a-time so that the user can flip through the hits.

Remember: What a script ostensibly does may just be scratching the surface of what it can really do for you.

swim

Swimming Time Records

[N2] [N2.01] [N2.02+] [N3] [N4] [E3] [E4]

This next script is one you might be inclined to skip, particularly if you have little or no interest in sports, or can't see how swim meet records could possibly have anything to do with your immediate concerns. Well, take a closer look. It shows a very neat and simple way of presenting organized information.

Unlike our previous examples, this script does not use a data array, but instead attaches its database directly to the output form elements. This technique could readily be applied in entirely different circumstances, such as to display product specifications, for example. It's particularly suitable for information that can be presented in a consistent fill-in-the-blanks format (see Figure 6-11).

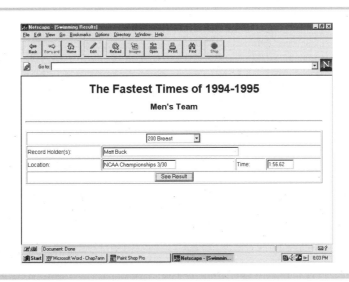

FIGURE 6-11. A powerful script, even if you don't care about swim records

The design makes the database very easy to maintain as well as expand, whether in terms of number of entries, or fields in each record. In either case, however, keep a steady eye on file size, lest you send a cyberwhale bearing down on some innocent surfer who just wants to know the price of bananas this week.

```
1    <html>
2    <head><title>Swimming Results</title>
3    <BODY BGCOLOR="#FFFFFF">
4    <script language="JavaScript">
5    <!--//Hiding code so other browsers won't display it
6    //Code written by Jeff Wood, jeffwood@uga.cc.uga.edu,
                                          I retain all rights
7    //associated with it, whatever that means
8    function clear(form){
9       form.name1.value="";
10      form.location.value="";
11      form.time.value=""}
```

```
12   function recordit(form){
13      clear(form);
14      if(form.selectit[0].selected){
15         alert("You must select an event!")}
16      if(form.selectit[1].selected){
17         form.name1.value="John Stratman";
18         form.location.value="NCAA Championships 3/28";
19         form.time.value="20.43"}
20      if(form.selectit[2].selected){
21         form.name1.value="John Stratman";
22         form.location.value="NCAA Championships 3/30";
23         form.time.value="44.33"}
24      if(form.selectit[3].selected){
25         form.name1.value="Kris Babylon";
26         form.location.value="NCAA Championships 3/29";
27         form.time.value="1:38.74"}
28      if(form.selectit[4].selected){
29         form.name1.value="Dave McLellan";
30         form.location.value="SEC Championships 2/8";
31         form.time.value="4:25.92"}
32      if(form.selectit[5].selected){
33         form.name1.value="Dave McLellan";
34         form.location.value="at North Carolina 10/27";
35         form.time.value="9:12.74"}
36      if(form.selectit[6].selected){
37         form.name1.value="Dave McLellan";
38         form.location.value="SEC Championships 2/10";
39         form.time.value="15:29.91"}
40      if(form.selectit[7].selected){
41         form.name1.value="Heath Edwards";
42         form.location.value="SEC Championships 2/9";
43         form.time.value="49.09"}
44      if(form.selectit[8].selected){
45         form.name1.value="Heath Edwards";
46         form.location.value="NCAA Championships 3/30";
47         form.time.value="1:45.93"}
48      if(form.selectit[9].selected){
49         form.name1.value="Kris Babylon";
50         form.location.value="NCAA Championships 3/28";
51         form.time.value="47.52"}
52      if(form.selectit[10].selected){
53         form.name1.value="Kris Babylon";
54         form.location.value="SEC Championships 2/9";
```

```
55        form.time.value="1:47.88"}
56     if(form.selectit[11].selected){
57        form.name1.value="Matt Buck";
58        form.location.value="NCAA Championships 3/29";
59        form.time.value="53.47"}
60     if(form.selectit[12].selected){
61        form.name1.value="Matt Buck";
62        form.location.value="NCAA Championships 3/30";
63        form.time.value="1:56.62"}
64     if(form.selectit[13].selected){
65        form.name1.value="Kris Babylon";
66        form.location.value="NCAA Championships 3/28";
67        form.time.value="1:47.12"}
68     if(form.selectit[14].selected){
69        form.name1.value="Kris Babylon";
70        form.location.value="NCAA Championships 3/29";
71        form.time.value="3:50.87"}
72     if(form.selectit[15].selected){
73        form.name1.value="Stratman, Wade, Buck, Campbell";
74        form.location.value="SEC Championships 2/7";
75        form.time.value="1:21.93"}
76     if(form.selectit[16].selected){
77        form.name1.value="Stratman, Babylon, Booth, Wade";
78        form.location.value="Tennessee 2/23";
79        form.time.value="2:58.31"}
80     if(form.selectit[17].selected){
81        form.name1.value="Babylon, Edwards, Wade, Booth";
82        form.location.value="NCAA Championships 3/29";
83        form.time.value="6:35.065"}
84     if(form.selectit[18].selected){
85        form.name1.value="Babylon, Buck, Edwards, Stratman";
86        form.location.value="NCAA Championships 3/29";
87        form.time.value="1:29.10"}
88     if(form.selectit[19].selected){
89        form.name1.value="Babylon, Buck, Edwards, Stratman";
90        form.location.value="NCAA Championships 3/28";
91        form.time.value="3:13.97"}
92  }
93  // Done hiding JavaScript from non-compliant browsers-->
94  </script>
95  </head>
96  <center><h1>The Fastest Times of 1994-1995</h1>
97  <h2>Men's Team</h2><hr></center>
```

```
98  <FORM>
99  <table border width="100%">
100 <tr><td colspan=4 align=center>
101 <SELECT NAME="selectit" onChange=clear(form)>
102 <OPTION SELECTED>Select an Event
103 <OPTION>50 Free
104 <OPTION>100 Free
105 <OPTION>200 Free
106 <OPTION>500 Free
107 <OPTION>1,000 Free
108 <OPTION>1,650 Free
109 <OPTION>100 Fly
110 <OPTION>200 Fly
111 <OPTION>100 Back
112 <OPTION>200 Back
113 <OPTION>100 Breast
114 <OPTION>200 Breast
115 <OPTION>200 IM
116 <OPTION>400 IM
117 <OPTION>200 Free Relay
118 <OPTION>400 Free Relay
119 <OPTION>800 Free Relay
120 <OPTION>200 Medley Relay
121 <OPTION>400 Medley Relay
122 </SELECT>
123 </td></tr>
124 <tr><td>Record Holder(s): </td><td colspan=3>
125 <input name="name1" size=48></td></tr>
126 <tr><td>Location: </td><td>
127 <input name="location" size=25></td>
128 <td>Time: </td>
129 <td><input name="time" size=8></td></tr>
130 <tr><td colspan=4 align=center>
131 <INPUT TYPE=BUTTON VALUE="See Result"
                            onClick=recordit(form)></td></tr>
132 </form>
133 </table><p>
134 </body>
135 </HTML>
```

ANNOTATIONS

This script consists of two functions: **clear( )**, which clears the form, and **recordit( )**, which displays the requested information. The data is organized around a selection list of 19 swim-meet events.

```
1    <html>
2    <head><title>Swimming Results</title>
3    <BODY BGCOLOR="#FFFFFF">
4    <script language="JavaScript">
5    <!--//Hiding code so other browsers won't display it
6    //Code written by Jeff Wood, jeffwood@uga.cc.uga.edu,
                                              I retain all rights
7    //associated with it, whatever that means
8    function clear(form){
9        form.name1.value="";
10       form.location.value="";
11       form.time.value=""}
```

clear( ) fills the output form's three text fields (named **name1, location,** and **time**) with empty strings when called by **recordit( )** in line 12, or when the user makes another selection from the list through assignment to the SELECT's **onChange** event handler in line 101.

```
12   function recordit(form){
13       clear(form);
14       if(form.selectit[0].selected){
15           alert("You must select an event!")}
16       if(form.selectit[1].selected){
17           form.name1.value="John Stratman";
18           form.location.value="NCAA Championships 3/28";
19           form.time.value="20.43"}
20       if(form.selectit[2].selected){
21           form.name1.value="John Stratman";
22           form.location.value="NCAA Championships 3/30";
23           form.time.value="44.33"}
24       if(form.selectit[3].selected){
25           form.name1.value="Kris Babylon";
26           form.location.value="NCAA Championships 3/29";
27           form.time.value="1:38.74"}
```

The main function, **recordit( )**, is attached to the form's "See Result Button." It first does some housekeeping with the call to **clear( )** and then uses a series of **if** tests to determine which item in the selection list named **selectit** has been chosen by the user, in which case its **selected** property is "true." The data for that particular entry is then displayed in the form through the assignment to their **value** property.

Meanwhile the zero slot in the selection list contains the default "Select an Event" message, and if the user fails to make a choice, an alert with a reminder pops open.

```
92   }
93   // Done hiding JavaScript from non-compliant browsers-->
94   </script>
95   </head>
96   <center><h1>The Fastest Times of 1994-1995</h1>
97   <h2>Men's Team</h2><hr></center>
98   <FORM>
99   <table border width="100%">
100  <tr><td colspan=4 align=center>
101  <SELECT NAME="selectit" onChange=clear(form)>
102  <OPTION SELECTED>Select an Event
103  <OPTION>50 Free
104  <OPTION>100 Free
105  <OPTION>200 Free
106  <OPTION>500 Free
107  <OPTION>1,000 Free
108  <OPTION>1,650 Free
109  <OPTION>100 Fly
110  <OPTION>200 Fly
111  <OPTION>100 Back
112  <OPTION>200 Back
113  <OPTION>100 Breast
114  <OPTION>200 Breast
115  <OPTION>200 IM
116  <OPTION>400 IM
117  <OPTION>200 Free Relay
118  <OPTION>400 Free Relay
119  <OPTION>800 Free Relay
120  <OPTION>200 Medley Relay
121  <OPTION>400 Medley Relay
122  </SELECT>
123  </td></tr>
124  <tr><td>Record Holder(s): </td><td colspan=3>
125  <input name="name1" size=48></td></tr>
126  <tr><td>Location: </td><td>
127  <input name="location" size=25></td>
```

```
128 <td>Time: </td>
129 <td><input name="time" size=8></td></tr>
130 <tr><td colspan=4 align=center>
131 <INPUT TYPE=BUTTON VALUE="See Result"
                         onClick=recordit(form)></td></tr>
132 </form>
133 </table><p>
134 </body>
135 </HTML>
```

The remainder of the page is standard HTML code that creates the form, names its elements, and assigns the event handlers.

With all of these types of databases, don't forget that you can attach an image to a data record and have it display as part of the output. This simply involves making the graphic filename (and path if necessary) part of each entry, and using the Image object's **src** property to load the file into its slot on the page at the right time.

Also, the database-forms combination can be taken a step further and used to build a shopping-cart-type device. An "Add to order" or "Put in cart" button could call a function that reads the index of the currently displayed item and stores it in a "CustomerOrder" array. The final order form can then be generated by pulling the appropriate fields from the entries in the database by reading the "CustomerOrder" array. Or, the data in the fields required for the order form can be made part of a "CustomerOrder" array from which the order could be written directly.

In the final analysis, the most important thing to bear in mind when working with JavaScript databases is to keep yours small and light. Think modular. That way you can serve up a mountain of data—one swift spoonful at a time!

PART 2

Web Creation Utilities

Menu Systems and Frames   **Server-Side Development**

Menu Systems and Frames

Until the Web is integrated with television or some other medium, its primary use for many users is as a research tool. People want to find information, and no matter how many multimedia doodads and how much fancy page-formatting you add to your web pages, your readers still just want to find information.

This is where menu systems come in, and based on a cursory glance at popular web sites, they are very popular with both readers and web designers. A menu can be as simple as a series of hypertext links stacked together in an unordered HTML list. It can be as complex as a multimedia, full-motion animated, and sound-enabled rotating wheel with different menu selections on each of its 3-D surfaces. Although I do not have the space to provide details about how that 3-D wheel operates, this chapter offers a range of menus for your web pages, which (take my word for it) are significantly less difficult to implement.

There are many potential uses of JavaScript in a menu. For example, you could replace that simple unordered set of hypertext links with a drop-down list—still using simple HTML (in this case, HTML forms)—that contains the title of every page or section on your web site. Apply a few simple JavaScripts to act upon that form, and that simple list becomes a more interactive experience for your readers. There's nothing wrong with adding some fun to your pages.

dropdown

Drop-Down Menu

⌐N2 ⌐N2.01 ⌐N2.02+ ⌐N3 ⌐N4 ⌐E3 ⌐E4

This drop-down menu is a functional example of the menu system that relies on HTML forms. In many cases, it can effectively replace the commonly used and clichéd navigation bar along the left side of the page. Although the left-hand navigation bar is a staple of the Web, it is only so common because a lot of web site designers have run out of ideas, or believe the "left-hand nav" is the closest thing to a user interface that everyone accessing the Web can relate to.

Nonsense.

Try this easy-to-use drop-down menu system (see Figure 7-1). As long as you let your web readers know that they should use your pull-down menu to navigate your site, the need for a left-hand nav goes away, and you can use that left side of the page for other things.

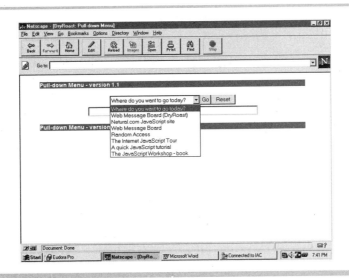

FIGURE 7-1.   A drop-down menu system that relies on HTML forms

```
1    <HTML>
2    <HEAD>
3    <TITLE> DryRoast: Pull-down Menu </TITLE>
4    <SCRIPT LANGUAGE="JavaScript">
5    <!--                                                    -->
6    <!-- Permission to copy, use or plagiarize this script is-->
7    <!-- granted provided you put a link on your page back to-->
8    <!-- here (DryRoast) on your page.                      -->
9    <!--                    Enjoy !                         -->
10   <!--                                                    -->
11   <!-- Written by Richard Dows, Random Access Inc., 5.27.96-->
12   <!--                                                    -->
13   <!-- Revision History:                                 -->
14   <!--                                                    -->
15   <!-- Altered the LookupURL() so that when the confirm is -->
```

```
16   <!-- cancelled it resets the form.                  -->
17   <!--                                                 -->
18   <!-- Version 1.1 - easier and far simpler than before.  -->
19   <!--                                                 -->
20   <!-- Version 1.2 - Thanks to Matt@pg.net! Changed    -->
21   <!-- doMoveBrowser so it uses 'parent' instead of    -->
22   <!-- 'window'.                                        -->
23   <!--                                                 -->
24   <!-- Cloaking Device Enabled --
25   function doMoveBrowser(form) {
26       parent.location.href =
                     form.list.options[getSelectedValue()].value;
27   }
28   function getSelectedValue() {
29       return document.form1.list.selectedIndex
30   }
31   function showURL(form) {
32     form.TextBox.value =
                     form.list.options[getSelectedValue()].value;
33   }
34   // -- end hiding -->
35   </SCRIPT>
36   </HEAD>
37   <BODY BGCOLOR="#FFFFFF"><CENTER>
38   <BASE HREF=
             "http://dryroast.randomc.com/javascript/menu.shtml">
39   </CENTER>
40   <CENTER><TABLE CELLSPACING=0 CELLPADDING=0 WIDTH="90%" >
41   <TR ROWSPAN=1 COLSPAN=1>
42   <TD ALIGN=CENTER VALIGN=top ROWSPAN=1 WIDTH=35 BGCOLOR=red>
43   <FONT FACE="Arial"><FONT COLOR="#FFFFFF"><B>
44   <NOBR>Pull-down Menu - version 1.1</NOBR>
45   </B> </FONT></FONT>
46   </TD></TR>
47   </TABLE></CENTER>
48   <CENTER><FORM NAME="form1">
49   <SELECT NAME="list" onChange="showURL(this.form)">
50   <OPTION SELECTED VALUE="0">
                             Where do you want to go today? 
51   <OPTION VALUE="http://tequila.randomc.com/WB/wwwboard.html">
                             Web Message Board (DryRoast) 
52   <OPTION VALUE="http://www.NETural.com/javascript/">
                             Netural.com JavaScript site 
```

```
53  <OPTION VALUE="http://porthos.phoenixat.com/
        ~warreng/WWWBoard/wwwboard.html">Web Message Board 
54  <OPTION VALUE="http://www.randomc.com">Random Access 
55  <OPTION VALUE="http://www.calweb.com/
        ~dstoflet/tourindx.htm">The Internet JavaScript Tour 
56  <OPTION VALUE="http://www.geocities.com/SiliconValley/6112/
                    resource.htm">A quick JavaScript tutorial 
57  <OPTION VALUE="http://starlingtech.com/books/javascript/">
                    The JavaScript Workshop - book </SELECT>
58  <INPUT type="button" value="Go"
                            onClick="doMoveBrowser(this.form)">
59  <INPUT type="reset" NAME="reset_button" value=" Reset ">
60  </CENTER>
61  <CENTER>
62  <INPUT TYPE="text" NAME="TextBox" SIZE=60></FORM></CENTER>
63  <CENTER><TABLE CELLSPACING=0 CELLPADDING=0 WIDTH="90%" >
64  <TR>
65  <TD ALIGN="CENTER" VALIGN="top" ROWSPAN="1" WIDTH="55"
                                        BGCOLOR="red">
66  <FONT FACE="Arial"><FONT COLOR="#FFFFFF"><B>
67  <NOBR>Pull-down Menu - version 1.1</NOBR></B> </FONT>
68  </FONT></TD></TR>
69  </TABLE></CENTER>
70  <BR>
71  </BODY>
72  </HTML>
```

ANNOTATIONS

This simple script consists of three one-line functions, one of which, **getSelected-Value( )**, is a subroutine of the two others. It clearly shows how sometimes with JavaScript you can mine a mountain of functionality from of a molehill of code.

```
1   <HTML>
2   <HEAD>
3   <TITLE> DryRoast: Pull-down Menu </TITLE>
4   <SCRIPT LANGUAGE="JavaScript">
5   <!--                                                    -->
6   <!-- Permission to copy, use or plagiarize this script is-->
7   <!-- granted provided you put a link on your page back to-->
8   <!-- here (DryRoast) on your page.                        -->
9   <!--                      Enjoy !                         -->
```

```
10   <!--                                                        -->
11   <!-- Written by Richard Dows, Random Access Inc., 5.27.96-->
12   <!--                                                        -->
13   <!-- Revision History:                                      -->
14   <!--                                                        -->
15   <!-- Altered the LookupURL() so that when the confirm is -->
16   <!-- cancelled it resets the form.                          -->
17   <!--                                                        -->
18   <!-- Version 1.1 - easier and far simpler than before.   -->
19   <!--                                                        -->
20   <!-- Version 1.2 - Thanks to Matt@pg.net! Changed          -->
21   <!-- doMoveBrowser so it uses 'parent' instead of         -->
22   <!-- 'window'.                                              -->
23   <!--                                                        -->
24   <!-- Cloaking Device Enabled --
25   function doMoveBrowser(form) {
26      parent.location.href =
                    form.list.options[getSelectedValue()].value;
27   }
28   function getSelectedValue() {
29      return document.form1.list.selectedIndex
30   }
31   function showURL(form) {
32     form.TextBox.value =
                    form.list.options[getSelectedValue()].value;
33   }
```

The first of this script's three simple functions is attached to the Go button's event handler (line 58). When called by a click, **doMoveBrowser( )** assigns the value of the selected option to the **location** property of the main window. As the selection list values are URL strings, this changes the browser's location to the specified address—in other words, it loads that page.

To read the list, **doMoveBrowser( )** calls **getSelectedValue( )**, which returns the selection list's **selectedIndex** property—an integer specifying which item the user has chosen.

getSelectedValue( ) is also used by the third function, **showURL( )**, which displays the value of the selected option, namely its URL, in the form's text field. **showURL( )** is attached to the SELECT's **onChange** event handler, which does not refresh the display automatically—but a click anywhere on the page will do the trick.

Both primary functions take the form itself—passed by use of the standard **this.form**—as argument and make use of the **options** array in accessing the list. **list** in lines 26, 29, and 32 is the name assigned to the SELECT in line 49 and *not* an undocumented JavaScript object.

```
34  // -- end hiding -->
35  </SCRIPT>
36  </HEAD>
37  <BODY BGCOLOR="#FFFFFF"><CENTER>
38  <BASE HREF=
              "http://dryroast.randomc.com/javascript/menu.shtml">
39  </CENTER>
40  <CENTER><TABLE CELLSPACING=0 CELLPADDING=0 WIDTH="90%" >
41  <TR ROWSPAN=1 COLSPAN=1>
42  <TD ALIGN=CENTER VALIGN=top ROWSPAN=1 WIDTH=35 BGCOLOR=red>
43  <FONT FACE="Arial"><FONT COLOR="#FFFFFF"><B>
44  <NOBR>Pull-down Menu - version 1.1</NOBR>
45  </B> </FONT></FONT>
46  </TD></TR>
47  </TABLE></CENTER>
48  <CENTER><FORM NAME="form1">
49  <SELECT NAME="list" onChange="showURL(this.form)">
50  <OPTION SELECTED VALUE="0">
                              Where do you want to go today? 
51  <OPTION VALUE="http://tequila.randomc.com/WB/wwwboard.html">
                              Web Message Board (DryRoast) 
52  <OPTION VALUE="http://www.NETural.com/javascript/">
                              Netural.com JavaScript site 
53  <OPTION VALUE="http://porthos.phoenixat.com/
            ~warreng/WWWBoard/wwwboard.html">Web Message Board 
54  <OPTION VALUE="http://www.randomc.com">Random Access 
55  <OPTION VALUE="http://www.calweb.com/
            ~dstoflet/tourindx.htm">The Internet JavaScript Tour 
56  <OPTION VALUE="http://www.geocities.com/SiliconValley/6112/
                    resource.htm">A quick JavaScript tutorial 
57  <OPTION VALUE="http://starlingtech.com/books/javascript/">
                The JavaScript Workshop - book </SELECT>
58  <INPUT type="button" value="Go"
                          onClick="doMoveBrowser(this.form)">
59  <INPUT type="reset" NAME="reset_button" value=" Reset ">
60  </CENTER>
61  <CENTER>
62  <INPUT TYPE="text" NAME="TextBox" SIZE=60></FORM></CENTER>
63  <CENTER><TABLE CELLSPACING=0 CELLPADDING=0 WIDTH="90%" >
64  <TR>
65  <TD ALIGN="CENTER" VALIGN="top" ROWSPAN="1" WIDTH="55"
                                      BGCOLOR="red">
66  <FONT FACE="Arial"><FONT COLOR="#FFFFFF"><B>
67  <NOBR>Pull-down Menu - version 1.1</NOBR></B> </FONT>
```

```
68  </FONT></TD></TR>
69  </TABLE></CENTER>
70  <BR>
71  </BODY>
72  </HTML>
```

The remainder of the page contains standard HTML code.

While this script is externally oriented in terms of the destinations listed in the menu, you can easily use the same device as an internal guide to areas within your site. All you have to do is revise the HTML SELECT list values and text in lines 50 through 57. The script itself doesn't have to be touched.

menu

Graphical Menu

| N2 | N2.01 | N2.02+ | N3 | N4 | E3 | E4 |

Moving away even more from the simple hypertext menu list, the script mixes several examples of JavaScript functionality to create a kiosk-style menu, of the sort you might see at a museum exhibit that relies on touch screens for user input (see Figure 7-2). In fact, this script is ideal for an organization or individual interested in creating a gallery or theme-based presentation on the Web.

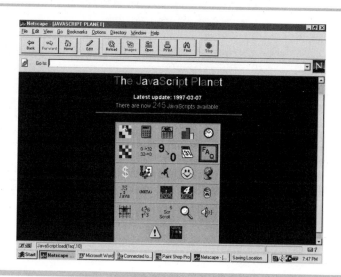

FIGURE 7-2. This menu uses the mouseOver function extensively

As with the museum-style kiosk application, you place a series of images in an easy-to-understand order, preferably centered and in a distinct arrangement that tells users, "this is a way to drill down into the site," without forcing them to wonder what to do next. The images should be easily interpreted by the reader. If you stray too far from the theme of your site, or insert obscure imagery in the menu just to be cute, you risk alienating readers. They will undoubtedly rush out of your site before all the images in your menu can load in their browser.

```
1   <HTML>
2   <HEAD>
3   <TITLE>JAVASCRIPT PLANET</TITLE>
4   <SCRIPT Language="JavaScript1.1">
5
6   <!--hide
7   <!-- IE-Menu -->
8
9   pic = new Array(11)
10  pic[0] = "anim"
11  pic[1] = "calc"
12  pic[2] = "cale"
13  pic[3] = "chart"
14  pic[4] = "cloc"
15  pic[5] = "colo"
16  pic[6] = "conv"
17  pic[7] = "coun"
18  pic[8] = "date"
19  pic[9] = "faq"
20  pic[10] = "fina"
21  pic[11] = "game"
22  pic[12] = "heal"
23  pic[13] = "humo"
24  pic[14] = "inte"
25  pic[15] = "live"
26  pic[16] = "meta"
27  pic[17] = "navi"
28  pic[18] = "nets"
29  pic[19] = "othe"
30  pic[20] = "pass"
31  pic[21] = "rand"
32  pic[22] = "scro"
```

```
33   pic[23] = "sear"
34   pic[24] = "soun"
35   pic[25] = "vali"
36   pic[26] = "vrml"
37   function qOver(imgname, n){
38       if ((navigator.userAgent.indexOf("Mozilla/3.0") != -1) ||
39           (navigator.userAgent.indexOf("Mozilla/4.0") != -1))
40       {
41           imgname.src = pic[n-1]+'u.gif'
42       }
43   }
44   function qOut(imgname, n){
45       if ((navigator.userAgent.indexOf("Mozilla/3.0") != -1) ||
46           (navigator.userAgent.indexOf("Mozilla/4.0") != -1))
47       {
48           imgname.src = pic[n-1]+'g.gif'
49       }
50   }
51   function loadi(ix,n){
52       file = ix + "_i.html"
53       setTimeout("document.location = file",250);
54   }
55   //-->
56   </SCRIPT>
57   </HEAD>
58   <BODY TEXT="#FFFFFF" BGCOLOR="#000000"
                                   LINK="#FFFF00" VLINK="#FF0000">
59   <CENTER><P><BR>
60   <FONT SIZE=+3><FONT COLOR="#FF0000">T</FONT>
61   <FONT COLOR="#FFFF00">h</FONT><FONT COLOR="#FF0000">e</FONT>
62   <FONT COLOR="#FF0000">J</FONT><FONT COLOR="#FFFF00">a</FONT>
63   <FONT COLOR="#FF0000">v</FONT><FONT COLOR="#FFFF00">a</FONT>
64   <FONT COLOR="#FF0000">S</FONT><FONT COLOR="#FFFF00">c</FONT>
65   <FONT COLOR="#FF0000">r</FONT><FONT COLOR="#FFFF00">i</FONT>
66   <FONT COLOR="#FF0000">p</FONT><FONT COLOR="#FFFF00">t</FONT>
67   <FONT COLOR="#FF0000">P</FONT><FONT COLOR="#FFFF00">l</FONT>
68   <FONT COLOR="#FF0000">a</FONT><FONT COLOR="#FFFF00">n</FONT>
69   <FONT COLOR="#FF0000">e</FONT><FONT COLOR="#FFFF00">t</FONT>
70   </P></CENTER>
71   <CENTER><P><B>Latest update: 1997-03-07</B> <BR>
72   There are now <FONT COLOR="#FF0000">
73   <FONT SIZE=+2>245</FONT></FONT> JavaScripts available.
74   <HR width=50%></P></CENTER><CENTER>
```

```
75  <TABLE BORDER=1 CELLSPACING=0 CELLPADDING=0 WIDTH="0"
                                       BGCOLOR="#C0C0C0" >
76  <TR>
77  <TD><A HREF="JavaScript:loadi('anim',1)"
        onMouseOver="qOver(anim, 1)" onMouseOut="qOut(anim, 1)">
78  <IMG SRC="animg.gif" NAME="anim" ALT="Animation"
                            BORDER=0 HEIGHT=45 WIDTH=50></A>
79  <A HREF="JavaScript:loadi('calc',2)"
        onMouseOver="qOver(calc, 2)" onMouseOut="qOut(calc, 2)">
80  <IMG SRC="calcg.gif" NAME="calc" ALT="Calculator"
                            BORDER=0 HEIGHT=45 WIDTH=50></A>
81  <A HREF="JavaScript:loadi('cale',3)"
        onMouseOver="qOver(cale, 3)" onMouseOut="qOut(cale, 3)">
82  <IMG SRC="caleg.gif" NAME="cale" ALT="Calendar"
                            BORDER=0 HEIGHT=45 WIDTH=50></A>
83  <A HREF="JavaScript:loadi('chart',4)"
      onMouseOver="qOver(chart, 4)" onMouseOut="qOut(chart, 4)">
84  <IMG SRC="chartg.gif" NAME="chart" ALT="Charts"
                            BORDER=0 HEIGHT=45 WIDTH=50></A>
85  <A HREF="JavaScript:loadi('cloc',5)"
        onMouseOver="qOver(cloc, 5)" onMouseOut="qOut(cloc, 5)">
86  <IMG SRC="clocg.gif" NAME="cloc" ALT="Clocks"
                            BORDER=0 HEIGHT=45 WIDTH=50></A>
87  </TD>
88  </TR>
89  <TR>
90  <TD><A HREF="JavaScript:loadi('colo',6)"
        onMouseOver="qOver(colo, 6)" onMouseOut="qOut(colo, 6)">
91  <IMG SRC="colog.gif" NAME="colo" ALT="Colors"
                            BORDER=0 HEIGHT=45 WIDTH=50></A>
92  <A HREF="JavaScript:loadi('conv',7)"
        onMouseOver="qOver(conv, 7)" onMouseOut="qOut(conv, 7)">
93  <IMG SRC="convg.gif" NAME="conv" ALT="Conversions"
                            BORDER=0 HEIGHT=45 WIDTH=50></A>
94  <A HREF="JavaScript:loadi('coun',8)"
        onMouseOver="qOver(coun, 8)" onMouseOut="qOut(coun, 8)">
95  <IMG SRC="coung.gif" NAME="coun" ALT="Counters"
                            BORDER=0 HEIGHT=45 WIDTH=50></A>
96  <A HREF="JavaScript:loadi('date',9)"
        onMouseOver="qOver(date, 9)" onMouseOut="qOut(date, 9)">
97  <IMG SRC="dateg.gif" NAME="date" ALT="Dates"
                            BORDER=0 HEIGHT=45 WIDTH=50></A>
98  <A HREF="JavaScript:loadi('faq',10)"
```

```
                onMouseOver="qOver(faq, 10)" onMouseOut="qOut(faq, 10)">
99  <IMG SRC="faqg.gif" NAME="faq" ALT="FAQs"
                                 BORDER=0 HEIGHT=45 WIDTH=50></A>
100 </TD>
101 </TR>
102 <TR>
103 <TD><A HREF="JavaScript:loadi('fina',11)"
        onMouseOver="qOver(fina, 11)" onMouseOut="qOut(fina, 11)">
104 <IMG SRC="finag.gif" NAME="fina" ALT="Finance"
                                 BORDER=0 HEIGHT=45 WIDTH=50></A>
105 <A HREF="JavaScript:loadi('game',12)"
        onMouseOver="qOver(game, 12)" onMouseOut="qOut(game, 12)">
106 <IMG SRC="gameg.gif" NAME="game" ALT="Games"
                                 BORDER=0 HEIGHT=45 WIDTH=50></A>
107 <A HREF="JavaScript:loadi('heal',13)"
        onMouseOver="qOver(heal, 13)" onMouseOut="qOut(heal, 13)">
108 <IMG SRC="healg.gif" NAME="heal" ALT="Health"
                                 BORDER=0 HEIGHT=45 WIDTH=50></A>
109 <A HREF="JavaScript:loadi('humo',14)"
        onMouseOver="qOver(humo, 14)" onMouseOut="qOut(humo, 14)">
110 <IMG SRC="humog.gif" NAME="humo" ALT="Humour"
                                 BORDER=0 HEIGHT=45 WIDTH=50></A>
111 <A HREF="JavaScript:loadi('inte',15)"
        onMouseOver="qOver(inte, 15)" onMouseOut="qOut(inte, 15)">
112 <IMG SRC="integ.gif" NAME="inte" ALT="Internet"
                                 BORDER=0 HEIGHT=45 WIDTH=50></A>
113 </TD>
114 </TR>
115 <TR>
116 <TD><A HREF="JavaScript:loadi('live',16)"
        onMouseOver="qOver(live, 16)" onMouseOut="qOut(live, 16)">
117 <IMG SRC="liveg.gif" NAME="live" ALT="LiveConnect"
                                 BORDER=0 HEIGHT=45 WIDTH=50></A>
118 <A HREF="JavaScript:loadi('meta',17)"
        onMouseOver="qOver(meta, 17)" onMouseOut="qOut(meta, 17)">
119 <IMG SRC="metag.gif" NAME="meta" ALT="META"
                                 BORDER=0 HEIGHT=45 WIDTH=50></A>
120 <A HREF="JavaScript:loadi('navi',18)"
        onMouseOver="qOver(navi, 18)" onMouseOut="qOut(navi, 18)">
121 <IMG SRC="navig.gif" NAME="navi" ALT="Navigation"
                                 BORDER=0 HEIGHT=45 WIDTH=50></A>
122 <A HREF="JavaScript:loadi('nets',19)"
        onMouseOver="qOver(nets, 19)" onMouseOut="qOut(nets, 19)">
```

```
123 <IMG SRC="netsg.gif" NAME="nets" ALT="Netscape 4"
                            BORDER=0 HEIGHT=45 WIDTH=50></A>
124 <A HREF="JavaScript:loadi('othe',20)"
       onMouseOver="qOver(othe, 20)" onMouseOut="qOut(othe, 20)">
125 <IMG SRC="otheg.gif" NAME="othe" ALT="Others"
                            BORDER=0 HEIGHT=45 WIDTH=50></A>
126 </TD>
127 </TR>
128 <TR>
129 <TD><A HREF="JavaScript:loadi('pass',21)"
       onMouseOver="qOver(pass, 21)" onMouseOut="qOut(pass, 21)">
130 <IMG SRC="passg.gif" NAME="pass" ALT="Password"
                            BORDER=0 HEIGHT=45 WIDTH=50></A>
131 <A HREF="JavaScript:loadi('rand',22)"
       onMouseOver="qOver(rand, 22)" onMouseOut="qOut(rand, 22)">
132 <IMG SRC="randg.gif" NAME="rand" ALT="Random"
                            BORDER=0 HEIGHT=45 WIDTH=50></A>
133 <A HREF="JavaScript:loadi('scro',23)"
       onMouseOver="qOver(scro, 23)" onMouseOut="qOut(scro, 23)">
134 <IMG SRC="scrog.gif" NAME="scro" ALT="Scrolls"
                            BORDER=0 HEIGHT=45 WIDTH=50></A>
135 <A HREF="JavaScript:loadi('sear',24)"
       onMouseOver="qOver(sear, 24)" onMouseOut="qOut(sear, 24)">
136 <IMG SRC="searg.gif" NAME="sear" ALT="Search"
                            BORDER=0 HEIGHT=45 WIDTH=50></A>
137 <A HREF="JavaScript:loadi('soun',25)"
       onMouseOver="qOver(soun, 25)" onMouseOut="qOut(soun, 25)">
138 <IMG SRC="soung.gif" NAME="soun" ALT="Sound"
                            BORDER=0 HEIGHT=45 WIDTH=50></A>
139 </TD>
140 </TR>
141 <TR align=center>
142 <TD><A HREF="JavaScript:loadi('vali',26)"
       onMouseOver="qOver(vali, 26)" onMouseOut="qOut(vali, 26)">
143 <IMG SRC="valig.gif" NAME="vali" ALT="Validation"
                            BORDER=0 HEIGHT=45 WIDTH=50></A>
144 <A HREF="JavaScript:loadi('vrml',27)"
       onMouseOver="qOver(vrml, 27)" onMouseOut="qOut(vrml, 27)">
145 <IMG SRC="vrmlg.gif" NAME="vrml" ALT="VRML"
                            BORDER=0 HEIGHT=45 WIDTH=50></A>
146 </TD>
147 </TR>
148 </TABLE></CENTER>
```

```
149   </BODY>
150   </HTML>
```

ANNOTATIONS

This script uses a pair of GIF image files for each menu item. One has a plain gray background, the other, shaded borders to produce a highlight effect. When the user's mouse pointer is over an item, **qOver( )** loads the bordered image; when the pointer moves off, **qOut( )** replaces it with the default gray version. Each image is also a link that calls **loadi( )**, the script's third function, to load the appropriate page after a quarter-of-a-second timeout.

This highlighting only works with Navigator 3.*x* or higher due to the script's use of the Array object introduced with JavaScript 1.1. Lower versions display the default gray-background image files. Also, Navigator 4.*x* automatically displays each image's ALT attribute as "hint" text in fly-out form. This makes the menu much more user friendly, as it is not immediately clear what some of the images mean. For Navigator 3.*x*, you might consider using the status bar to display helpful hints by adding, for example,

```
self.status='Animation'; return true;
```

to the **onMouseOver** assignment in line 77;

```
self.status='Calculator'; return true;
```

to line 79; and so on. In using icons, always bear in mind they can be interpreted to mean different things. Even a symbol as simple as a question mark appearing on a web page can leave you wondering: "Does it mean help in navigating around the site? Information about the organization behind the site? A means of submitting queries?" Adding some form of text label can remove the ambiguity and stave off potential user frustration and annoyance.

```
1    <HTML>
2    <HEAD>
3    <TITLE>JAVASCRIPT PLANET</TITLE>
4    <SCRIPT Language="JavaScript1.1">
5
6    <!--hide
7    <!-- IE-Menu -->
8
9    pic = new Array(11)
10   pic[0] = "anim"
11   pic[1] = "calc"
12   pic[2] = "cale"
13   pic[3] = "chart"
```

```
14  pic[4]  = "cloc"
15  pic[5]  = "colo"
16  pic[6]  = "conv"
17  pic[7]  = "coun"
18  pic[8]  = "date"
19  pic[9]  = "faq"
20  pic[10] = "fina"
21  pic[11] = "game"
22  pic[12] = "heal"
23  pic[13] = "humo"
24  pic[14] = "inte"
25  pic[15] = "live"
26  pic[16] = "meta"
27  pic[17] = "navi"
28  pic[18] = "nets"
29  pic[19] = "othe"
30  pic[20] = "pass"
31  pic[21] = "rand"
32  pic[22] = "scro"
33  pic[23] = "sear"
34  pic[24] = "soun"
35  pic[25] = "vali"
36  pic[26] = "vrml"
```

Line 9 constructs an array named **pic** with a length of 11. The "11" appears to be a leftover from an earlier version of the script, for lines 10 through 36 then proceed to create a 27-member array and fill it with a series of four-letter strings (the one exception is "faq," assigned to **pic[9]**). As this demonstrates, JavaScript arrays are not fixed entities whose length must be determined from the outset, but can be expanded on-the-fly. They can also be destroyed. Add a button to this page with

`onClick="pic=new Array(0)"`

as its event handler. A click will then destroy the original **pic** array by replacing it with a new one of zero length; as a result, **qOver( )** and **qOut( )** will no longer work. Use the more brutal

`pic=null`

as destructor, and **onMouseOver** and **onMouseOut** will trigger JavaScript error messages saying "pic has no properties indexed by...."

This is certainly not to suggest that you should "enhance" this page with a code killer. Rather, JavaScript has object-destruction capabilities which, in the case of a complex application, you might want to use for housekeeping purposes, such as getting rid of an object no longer required by the process. As objects are by definition storage areas, their destruction allows you to free memory space once they have done their job.

Here the strings assigned to the **pic** array are used by the script's three functions to construct the name of the GIF or HTML file they load. In this respect, the array's name is slightly misleading; **pic** is not an array of pictures, but is an array of the first three or four characters in each filename.

```
37   function qOver(imgname, n){
38       if ((navigator.userAgent.indexOf("Mozilla/3.0") != -1) ||
39           (navigator.userAgent.indexOf("Mozilla/4.0") != -1))
40       {
41           imgname.src = pic[n-1]+'u.gif'
42       }
43   }
44   function qOut(imgname, n){
45       if ((navigator.userAgent.indexOf("Mozilla/3.0") != -1) ||
46           (navigator.userAgent.indexOf("Mozilla/4.0") != -1))
47       {
48           imgname.src = pic[n-1]+'g.gif'
49       }
50   }
```

qOver( ) and **qOut( )** are assigned to the **onMouseOver** and **onMouseOut** event handlers of the links comprising the menu. Each takes two arguments, **imgname** and **n**. The **imgname** argument gets the name assigned to each image in the <IMG> tags on lines 78 and following; **n** is an integer used to index the **pic** array. The "–1" in lines 41 and 48 aligns **n** with the **pic** indexing; obviously you can eliminate it by adjusting the function calls so that the value passed to **n** in line 77 is 0 instead of 1, then 1 instead of 2 in line 79, and so on.

As the image names correspond exactly to the members of **pic**, you can dispense with the array altogether. Change line 41 to

```
imgname.src = imgname.name + 'u.gif'
```

and do the same with 48. Note that

```
imgname.src = imgname + 'u.gif'
```

will not work; while **imgname** may look like a string, it really is an Image object whose **name** property holds the actual string.

Both functions are contingent upon the visitor using either Navigator 3.*x* or 4.*x*, which lines 38–39 and 45–46 test for before assembling the filename assigned to the specified image's **src** property.

```
51   function loadi(ix,n){
52       file = ix + "_i.html"
53       setTimeout("document.location = file",250);
54   }
```

loadi( ), assigned to each link's <HREF> tag in lines 77 and following, also takes two arguments. The first, **ix**, gets a string identical to those passed to the preceding two functions; the second, **n**, receives the same index as that used by the event handlers to access the **pic** array. It is not used at all by the function and can be dispensed with. Or, you could make **n** the sole argument and change line 52 to read

`file = pix[n-1] + "_i.html"`

and the calls in 77 and following to

`loadi(1)`

`loadi(2)`

and so on.

loadi( ) first assigns the new variable **file** a string that compiles to the appropriate filename, then with the assignment to **document.location** in line 53 loads the file after a 250-millisecond timeout. The timeout itself is a frill that you can shorten, lengthen, or drop altogether.

```
55  //-->
56  </SCRIPT>
57  </HEAD>
58  <BODY TEXT="#FFFFFF" BGCOLOR="#000000"
                                    LINK="#FFFF00" VLINK="#FF0000">
59  <CENTER><P><BR>
60  <FONT SIZE=+3><FONT COLOR="#FF0000">T</FONT>
61  <FONT COLOR="#FFFF00">h</FONT><FONT COLOR="#FF0000">e</FONT>
62  <FONT COLOR="#FF0000">J</FONT><FONT COLOR="#FFFF00">a</FONT>
63  <FONT COLOR="#FF0000">v</FONT><FONT COLOR="#FFFF00">a</FONT>
64  <FONT COLOR="#FF0000">S</FONT><FONT COLOR="#FFFF00">c</FONT>
65  <FONT COLOR="#FF0000">r</FONT><FONT COLOR="#FFFF00">i</FONT>
66  <FONT COLOR="#FF0000">p</FONT><FONT COLOR="#FFFF00">t</FONT>
67  <FONT COLOR="#FF0000">P</FONT><FONT COLOR="#FFFF00">l</FONT>
68  <FONT COLOR="#FF0000">a</FONT><FONT COLOR="#FFFF00">n</FONT>
69  <FONT COLOR="#FF0000">e</FONT><FONT COLOR="#FFFF00">t</FONT>
70  </P></CENTER>
71  <CENTER><P><B>Latest update: 1997-03-07</B> <BR>
72  There are now <FONT COLOR="#FF0000">
73  <FONT SIZE=+2>245</FONT></FONT> JavaScripts available.
74  <HR width=50%></P></CENTER><CENTER>
75  <TABLE BORDER=1 CELLSPACING=0 CELLPADDING=0 WIDTH="0"
                                    BGCOLOR="#C0C0C0" >
76  <TR>
77  <TD><A HREF="JavaScript:loadi('anim',1)"
        onMouseOver="qOver(anim, 1)" onMouseOut="qOut(anim, 1)">
78  <IMG SRC="animg.gif" NAME="anim" ALT="Animation"
                                    BORDER=0 HEIGHT=45 WIDTH=50></A>
79  <A HREF="JavaScript:loadi('calc',2)"
        onMouseOver="qOver(calc, 2)" onMouseOut="qOut(calc, 2)">
```

```
80    <IMG SRC="calcg.gif" NAME="calc" ALT="Calculator"
                             BORDER=0 HEIGHT=45 WIDTH=50></A>
```

The remainder of the page consists of HTML code, with lines 75 through 148 creating the table in which the menu items are displayed. Each of the 27 links has a JavaScript function call to **loadi( )** assigned to its HREF attribute, and **qOver( )** and **qOut( )** calls attached to its **onMouseOver** and **onMouseOut** event handlers.

```
146   </TD>
147   </TR>
148   </TABLE></CENTER>
149   </BODY>
150   </HTML>
```

This script undoubtedly shows you how to create a simple, attractive, icon-based front page for a site with a large number of subareas. The key to its functionality, of course, is the use of a set of strings to construct the appropriate GIF and HTML filenames for the images and links. This technique of attaching various substrings to a core name is commonly used to process related sets of files and is well worth learning. The place to start is not with the script and its functions. First, devise a (preferably ingenious) file-naming system that readily lends itself to string manipulation. Once that has been properly done, the code should take care of itself.

This is also a technique whose application extends far beyond menus. It can prove useful in just about any context where a batch of related files or data items has to be loaded in response to a user selection. Organize your data and coordinate names—you'll be amazed at how much mileage you can get out of juggling strings!

remote

Remote Menu

| N2 | N2.01 | N2.02+ | N3 | N4 | E3 | E4 |

The "detached" remote control menu is one of the more flexible web inventions. As an exercise in writing JavaScript code, it brings together a variety of functions and elements, including external window control, focus, targeting windows, and (if you feel up to the task) manipulating graphics.

From a reader's point of view, the remote control menu can be a helpful navigation tool. From the web designer's perspective, display-screen real estate is a precious commodity, and whatever it takes to free room on the web page, the better. The reader does not benefit from just any remote menu. There are rules and many web designers either break them or don't bother to learn them.

I'll mention a few rules, for the sake of those who are going to actually read through the code example. However, the web designer who creates the user interface and the JavaScript coder who creates the application are usually two people. In addition, there is some truth to the saying that programmers cannot design good web pages, just as most designers only know how to design and not implement.

It takes a good understanding of user-interface concepts to pull off a good remote control menu. In layperson's terms, a halfway decent one must

◆ Not take up much room on the page

◆ Use color intelligently

◆ Maintain the look and feel of the page or pages that launch the remote

◆ Disappear or somehow go away gracefully

We won't go into detail about the first three bulleted items. If you are a programmer, unless you are qualified as a designer, illustrator, or graphic artist, you should not design the remote. Put your ego aside and allow the artist to design and create graphics, layout, look and feel, and other user interface components.

The fourth item on the list is important for JavaScripters as well as for web users.

Do you want the remote control menu to always be in front of the main browser window (see Figure 7-3)? Under normal circumstances and using script that is compatible with the widest range of JavaScript-enabled web browser software, the external window that contains your remote control will recede behind whatever application or browser window the user makes dominant with a mouse click.

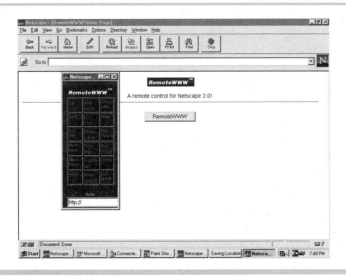

FIGURE 7-3.   The archetypal "floating" remote control—an excellent use of display space

If you wish to write code that works with Netscape Navigator 3.0 or above, you can code the external window to always stay in front of the main browser window. With code that works only under Netscape Communicator 4.0, you can create a window that always sits in front and appears in a predefined X,Y coordinate on the user's display window.

There is a trade-off when you make your JavaScript "provincial"—that is, Netscape only. The JavaScript effect may be supercool and efficient, and conform to some widely held beliefs about the nature of a multimedia user interface, but only a fraction of the browsing population will be able to use your page. One option is to create different versions of your web pages, which are then friendly to whatever web browser is detected (also via JavaScript).

It seems like a lot of extra work (and maintenance), but it's up to you.

Back to the universally browsable remote control window: this initial HTML page contains the script to launch the remote.

LOAD-ME.HTM

```
1   <head>
2   <title>RemoteWWW Home Page</title>
3   <script language="javascript">
4   <!--
5   function startRemote() {
6       remoteWin = window.open("","testRemote",
                          'width=140,height=315,resizable=1');
7       if (remoteWin != null) {
8           remoteWin.opener = self;
9           remoteWin.location = "remote1.htm";
10      }
11  }
12  // -->
13  </script>
14  </head>
15  <body bgcolor="#ffffff">
16  <center>
17  <h2><img src="remote.gif" alt="RemoteWWW"
                          width=120 height=22></h2>
18  A remote control for Netscape 2.0!
19  </center>
20  <hr noshade size=1>
21  <CENTER>
22  <form>
23  <script language="javascript">
24  <!--
```

```
25   document.writeln("<input type=button value=\"RemoteWWW\"
                                    onClick=\"startRemote()\">");
26   //-->
27   </script>
28   </form>
29   </CENTER>
30   </body>
31   </html>
```

Here are the contents of the remote window:

REMOTE1.HTM

```
1    <html>
2    <head>
3    <title>RemoteWWW</title>
4    <script language="javascript">
5
6    function navigate(loc) {
7       opener.location.href = loc;
8       self.blur();
9    }
10   </script>
11   </head>
12   <body bgcolor="#000000" text="#ffffff" link="#ffgg44">
13   <center>
14   <a href="javascript:navigate('')">
15   <img src="remote.gif" border=0 alt="RemoteWWW"
                                    width=120 height=22></a>
16   <table border=1>
17   <tr valign=top>
18   <td width=33%><font size = 2>
19   <a href="javascript:navigate('http://www.yahoo.com/')">
20   Ya-<br>hoo!</a></font></td>
21   <td width=33%><font size = 2>
22   <a href=
         "javascript:navigate('http://altavista.digital.com/')">
23   Alta<br>Vista</a></font></td>
24   <td width=33%><font size = 1>
25   <a href=
         "javascript:navigate('http://www.uroulette.com:8000/')">
```

```
26  URou-<br>Lette</a></font></td>
27  </tr>
28  <tr valign=top>
29  <td width=33%><font size = 2>
30  <a href="javascript:navigate('http://www.sped.ukans.edu/')">
31  SPED</a></font></td>
32  <td width=33%><font size = 2>
33  <a href="javascript:navigate('http://www.lycos.com/')">
34  Ly-<br>cos</a></font></td>
35  <td width=33%><font size = 1>
36  <a href="javascript:navigate('http://www.apple.com/')">
37  Apple</a></font></td>
38  </tr>
39  <tr valign=top>
40  <td width=33%><font size = 1>
41  <a href="javascript:navigate('http://www.pollstar.com/')">
42  Poll-<br>Star</a></font></td>
43  <td width=33%><font size = 2>
44  <a href="javascript:navigate('http://www.blairlake.com/')">
45  Blair-<br>Lake</a></font></td>
46  <td width=33%><font size = 1>
47  <a href="javascript:navigate('http://www.vidgames.com/')">
48  PSX<br>Galleria</a></font></td>
49  </tr>
50  <tr valign=top>
51  <td width=33%><font size = 1>
52  <a href="javascript:navigate('http://www.macintouch.com/')">
53  Macin-<br>touch</a></font></td>
54  <td width=33%><font size = 2>
55  <a href="javascript:navigate(
            'http://hyperarchive.lcs.mit.edu/HyperArchive.html')">
56  Info-<br>Mac</a></font></td>
57  <td width=33%><font size = 2>
58  <a href=
            "javascript:navigate('http://www.ziff.com/~macweek/')">
59  Mac<br>Week</a></font></td>
60  </tr>
61  <tr valign=top>
62  <td width=33%><font size = 1>
63  <a href="javascript:navigate('http://www.macromedia.com/')">
64  Macro-<br>media</a></font></td>
65  <td width=33%><font size = 2>
66  <a href="javascript:navigate('http://www.gamelan.com/')">
```

```
67  Game-<br>lan</a></font></td>
68  <td width=33%><font size = 2>
69  <a href="javascript:navigate('http://cnn.com/')">
70  CNN</a></font></td>
71  </tr>
72  <tr valign=top>
73  <td width=33%><font size = 2>
74  <a href=
        "javascript:navigate('http://espnet.sportszone.com/')">
75  ESPN</a></font></td>
76  <td width=33%><font size = 2>
77  <a href="javascript:navigate('http://www.mapquest.com/')">
78  Map-<br>Quest</a></font></td>
79  <td width=33%><font size = 1>
80  <a href="javascript:navigate(
                        'http://www.majorleaguebaseball.com/')">
81  MLB<br>@BAT</a></font></td>
82  </tr>
83  </table>
84  <form>
85  <font size = 1>Go to:</font><br>
86  <input type="text" name="goUrl"
        onBlur="navigate(this.value)" size=18 value="http://">
87  </form>
88  <form>
89  <nobr>
90  <input type="button" value="&lt;-"
                            onClick="opener.history.back()">
91  <input type="button" value="-&gt;"
                            onClick="opener.history.forward()">
92  <input type="button" value="Off" onClick="self.close()">
93  </nobr> </form> <font size = 1>1996,
94  <a href="javascript:navigate(
                        'http://lark.cc.ukans.edu/~asumner/')">
95  Aaron Sumner</a></font>
96  </center>
97  </body>
98  </html>
```

ANNOTATIONS

This script creates the remote as a new 140×315-pixel window into which it loads REMOTE1.HTM. The remote contains a set of links to various sites and the author's home page, a text field for entering a URL, as well as control buttons with forward, back, and close functions. At its present size, not all of the remote's features are visible when it opens, but the **resizable** option specified in line 6 allows you to stretch the window until they appear. Or, change the **width** value to 160 and **height** to 420 to bring everything into view from the outset.

```
1    <head>
2    <title>RemoteWWW Home Page</title>
3    <script language="javascript">
4    <!--
5    function startRemote() {
6        remoteWin = window.open("","testRemote",
                         'width=140,height=315,resizable=1');
7        if (remoteWin != null) {
8            remoteWin.opener = self;
9            remoteWin.location = "remote1.htm";
10       }
11   }
```

This function, assigned to the "RemoteWWW" button in line 25, opens a child window named **remoteWin**. If creation of the window is successful, **remoteWin** receives an **opener** property defined as the main window (**self**) and used by the **navigate( )** function in REMOTE1.HTM. While **opener** became a built-in Window property with Navigator 3.0, its explicit creation in line 8 ensures that this script works with earlier browser versions. **startRemote( )** then loads REMOTE1.HTM into the child window through the assignment to its **location** property in line 9.

```
12   // -->
13   </script>
14   </head>
15   <body bgcolor="#ffffff">
16   <center>
17   <h2><img src="remote.gif" alt="RemoteWWW"
                             width=120 height=22></h2>
18   A remote control for Netscape 2.0!
19   </center>
20   <hr noshade size=1>
21   <CENTER>
22   <form>
23   <script language="javascript">
24   <!--
```

```
25  document.writeln("<input type=button value=\"RemoteWWW\"
                           onClick=\"startRemote()\">");
26  //-->
27  </script>
28  </form>
29  </CENTER>
30  </body>
31  </html>
```

The body of the page uses a one-line JavaScript function call to **writeln( )** to write the HTML code that creates the button used to open the remote. The backslashes in line 25 are essential to escape the nested double quotation marks; they could be eliminated through the use of single quotes.

REMOTE1.HTM contains a single function, **navigate( )**, which is used by all of the links as well as the text field to load the specified site into the parent window. The remote's three control buttons are assigned built-in JavaScript functions.

```
1  <html>
2  <head>
3  <title>RemoteWWW</title>
4  <script language="javascript">
5
6  function navigate(loc) {
7     opener.location.href = loc;
8     self.blur();
9  }
```

navigate( ) takes a single argument, **loc**, which is the URL string passed to it by the **javascript** call attached to each link in lines 19, 22, and so forth. It uses the **location.href** property to open the target site in the main window. Finally, **blur( )** removes the focus from the remote. In most windowing systems, this sends the remote to the background.

```
10  </script>
11  </head>
12  <body bgcolor="#000000" text="#ffffff" link="#ffgg44">
13  <center>
14  <a href="javascript:navigate('')">
15  <img src="remote.gif" border=0 alt="RemoteWWW"
                              width=120 height=22></a>
16  <table border=1>
17  <tr valign=top>
18  <td width=33%><font size = 2>
19  <a href="javascript:navigate('http://www.yahoo.com/')">
20  Ya-<br>hoo!</a></font></td>
```

```
21   <td width=33%><font size = 2>
22   <a href=
         "javascript:navigate('http://altavista.digital.com/')">
23   Alta<br>Vista</a></font></td>
```

Lines 19, 22, and so on, contain the sequence of calls to **navigate( )**, with the appropriate URL string as the argument assigned to each link's HREF attribute. These are the lines you can change to set up links to your favorite sites or to locations you think might interest your visitors.

For easier maintenance, you might consider making each site an object with two properties, **siteName** and **siteURL**, and making the argument to **navigator( )** an integer that indexes the array. First, create a **webSite** object:

```
function webSite(siteName, siteURL) {
    this.siteName = siteName;
    this.siteURL = siteURL;
}
```

Next instantiate it with

```
remoteSite[0] = new webSite("Ya-<BR>hoo",
                              "http://www.yahoo.com/")
remoteSite[1] = new webSite("Alta<BR>Vista",
                            "http://altavista.digital.com/")
```

and so forth. Then set up **navigate( )**'s new argument and routine:

```
function navigate(i) {
    opener.location = remoteSite[i].siteURL;
}
```

With that you can change the function calls in lines 19, 22, and so on, to

```
javascript:navigate(0)
javascript:navigate(1)
```

and so forth, and use

```
document.write(remoteSite[i].siteName)
```

to display the names in the remote. In addition to putting all the site names and addresses in one place within the code where you can readily change them, this approach makes it easy to create a more complex remote, such as one that allows the user to select different categories of sites. You could make each set of sites a separate array and, if you use a selection list, read its **selectedIndex** property to access the data in the chosen array.

Another enhancement might be to replace the text representing the remote's buttons with graphics. In that case, you could create a **siteImage** property to hold the name of the GIF or JPG file containing the image, and display the site's name in the remote's text field or status bar.

```
83   </table>
84   <form>
```

```
85  <font size = 1>Go to:</font><br>
86  <input type="text" name="goUrl"
            onBlur="navigate(this.value)" size=18 value="http://">
87  </form>
88  <form>
89  <nobr>
90  <input type="button" value="&lt;-"
                                  onClick="opener.history.back()">
91  <input type="button" value="-&gt;"
                                  onClick="opener.history.forward()">
92  <input type="button" value="Off" onClick="self.close()">
93  </nobr> </form> <font size = 1>1996,
94  <a href="javascript:navigate(
                    'http://lark.cc.ukans.edu/~asumner/')">
95  Aaron Sumner</a></font>
96  </center>
97  </body>
98  </html>
```

In line 86, note the assignment of **navigate( )** to the text field's **onBlur** event handler. Its argument, **this.value**, reads the user-entered address and passes it to the function. One problem with the use of **onBlur** in this context is that the user may not know what to do next—even though all it takes to trigger the event-handling process is a click somewhere outside the text field. The simplest way to deal with this is to add a dummy button that forces a user click:

```
<input type=button value=GO>
```

Clicking on the GO button will then automatically launch the **onBlur** event handler by removing the focus from the text field. Because this type of device makes the user click at a specific spot on the page, it also provides a safeguard against an accidental click on a link—for example, causing two calls to **navigate( )** in quick succession. Or you could create an active button by transferring the function call to its event handler with

```
onClick="navigate(document.forms[0].elements[0].value)"
```

(assuming the button appears after the text field in the form).

The two arrow-labeled buttons near the bottom of the remote deploy **history.back( )** and **history.forward( )** so that the user can scroll back and forward through visited pages in the main window. The two methods respectively move the location back and forward one item in the browser's history list. Finally, the Off button in line 92 uses the JavaScript **self.close( )** method to shut the window containing the remote.

This JavaScript remote unfortunately seems to have inherited a property of the real thing: it all too easily vanishes underneath something—in this case, the main window. Changing line 8 to

```
self.focus();
```

is a good way to keep it on top until the user clicks in the main window. This makes the remote easier to use for site hopping. Moreover, once an interesting page has been loaded, this gives the user a chance to position the remote so that it can be brought forward without having to minimize the browser window (unless, of course, the browser is set to fill the screen). By keeping the device in focus, you also won't have some users wondering, "What happened to the remote?"—and thinking it's gone until they close the browser's main window and suddenly realize the little gremlin has been sitting there, hidden, all along. But then object-oriented programming is meant to mirror the real world. Come to think of it, you could simulate a ramshackle home with frames holding area maps of cluttered rooms, have a function hide the remote in a randomly selected spot, and make a JavaScript game of **findRemote( )**—like **resetEClocks( )**, a digital modern life skill well worth teaching youngsters.

Frames and JavaScript

I don't claim to know a lot, but the following are true statements. Some of the best menu systems use frames. Frames are difficult to create, organize, and maintain. A lot of developer confusion surrounds frames.

Here's some more disturbing news: many users do not like frames. In some cases, it is little more than an irrational response to something different. In other cases, the web designer has done such a poor job of implementing frames, users simply cannot figure out how to navigate the web site.

Netscape Navigator and Microsoft Internet Explorer (and a few other browsers, such as Opera) support *frames*, which are separate web pages that can live within a single instance of a web browser and interact with one another. Specifically, they are defined by a document type first implemented by Netscape, a frameset.

With frames, which divide web pages into multiple, scrollable regions, you can present information in a flexible and useful fashion. You can also seriously mess up the look and feel of your web pages. The misuse of frames is the subject of much debate and ridicule on the Internet.

Each region, or frame, has several attributes:

- ◆ It can be given an individual URL, so it can load information independent of the other frames on the page.

- ◆ It can be given a Name, and it can be targeted by other URLs.

- ◆ It can resize dynamically if the user changes the window's size. The resize feature can be disabled, ensuring a constant frame size.

I endorse wholeheartedly some limited applications of frames:

◆ Elements that the user should always see, such as control bars, copyright notices, and title graphics, can be placed in a static, individual frame. As the reader navigates your site, the static frame's contents remain fixed, even if information in adjoining frames changes.

◆ The side-by-side design of frames allows queries to be posed and answered on the same page, with one frame holding the query form and the other presenting the results.

◆ Tables of contents (including menus) become more functional. One frame can contain links that, when clicked, display results in an adjoining frame.

Putting frames-based sites together sounds like a simple task. In the HTML, you need a separate web page that orders and controls the various frames. This is accomplished on the control HTML page by use of the <FRAMESET> tag, which defines the number of frames to be displayed, their layout, and the documents that should be loaded into each frame. Any valid document URL (text, HTML code, images, and so on) can be specified for loading into a Frame.

In addition, the author of a frameset can give each frame a name and then ensure that anchors in one frame use another frame as a target. In essence, the document referenced by the anchor will be loaded in the target frame. This is one of the places where people get confused. In other words, when you click a link in one frame, it makes the document in a different frame change.

With JavaScript, objects defined in one frame can be referenced from another frame, and results produced in one frame can be displayed in another. JavaScript can make reference to any portion of the HTML document or frameset that it is running in. HTML element tags are given a Name attribute, so that every element will have a unique identifier. A JavaScript application can access, modify, or otherwise command just about any part of a document loaded into the browser.

Frames and framesets are no exception. A JavaScript program written as part of a frameset can control all the frames in the frameset. As a result, you can write a JavaScript function that will cause any (or more than one) frame to load a specified URL.

Frames are generated by <FRAMESET> tags, <FRAME> tags, and frame documents. A frame document is structured much as a normal HTML document, except the body container is replaced by a frameset container, which describes the frames that will make up the page. For example:

```
<HTML>
<HEAD>
</HEAD>
<FRAMESET>
</FRAMESET>
</HTML>
```

Compared with HTML tables, frames syntax is similar and can become just as complicated.

The <FRAMESET> tag has two attributes: ROWS and COLS. A frame document has no BODY. No tags that would normally be placed in the BODY can appear before the <FRAMESET> tag, or the <FRAMESET> will be ignored. The <FRAMESET> tag has a matching end tag, and within the <FRAMESET> you can only have other nested <FRAMESET> tags, <FRAME> tags, or the <NOFRAMES> tag.

The ROWS and COLS attributes take as their value a comma-separated list of values. For example:

```
ROWS="row_height_value_list"


COLS="row_height_value_list"
```

These values can be absolute pixel values, percentage values between 1 and 100, or relative scaling values. The number of rows is implicit in the number of elements in the list. As the total height of all the rows must equal the height of the window, row heights might be normalized to achieve this. A missing ROWS or COLS attribute is interpreted as a single row arbitrarily sized to fit.

Here is an example for three rows, the first and the last being smaller than the center row:

```
<FRAMESET ROWS="20%,60%,20%">
```

The <FRAMESET> tag can be nested inside other <FRAMESET> tags. In this case the complete subframe is placed in the space that would be used for the corresponding frame if this had been a <FRAME> tag instead of a nested FRAMESET.

The <FRAME> tag defines a single frame in a frameset. It has seven possible attributes: SRC, NAME, MARGINWIDTH, MARGINHEIGHT, MARGINBORDER, SCROLLING, and NORESIZE. The <FRAME> tag is not a container, so it has no matching end tag.

The SRC attribute takes as its value the URL of the document to be displayed in this particular frame. For instance:

```
SRC="url"
```

Frames without SRC attributes are displayed as a blank space the size the frame would have been.

The NAME attribute is used to assign a name to a frame so it can be targeted by links in other documents. These are usually from other frames in the same document. The NAME attribute is optional; by default all windows are unnamed.

```
NAME="window_name"
```

Names must begin with an alphanumeric character. All other names starting with "_" will be ignored.

MARGINWIDTH and MARGINHEIGHT are optional attributes that can be used when you want some control of the margins for a frame. If specified, the value for MARGINWIDTH is in pixels. Margins cannot be less than one.

```
MARGINWIDTH="value"
MARGINHEIGHT="value"
```

The SCROLLING attribute, also optional, defines a frame with or without a scroll bar.

```
SCROLLING="yes|no|auto"
```

"Yes" results in scroll bars always being visible on that frame. "No" results in scroll bars never being visible. "Auto" instructs the browser to decide whether scroll bars are needed and to place them where necessary. If you do not specify SCROLLING, the attribute defaults to auto.

The NORESIZE attribute has no value. It is a flag that indicates that the frame is not resizable by the user.

The <NOFRAMES> tag is valuable in case you want to create alternative content that is viewable by non-frames-capable clients. A frames-capable Internet client ignores all tags and data between start and end <NOFRAMES> tags; a non-frames-capable client only displays HTML placed between the <NOFRAMES> tags.

Finally, have you ever seen a frames-based web site in which you cannot see any borders between the frames? Although the MARGINBORDER attribute is a bit more obscure than the others, it can make for a very effective use of screen space.

```
MARGINBORDER="value"
```

When **value**=0, frame borders become invisible to users. With a careful mixture of background screen colors, the content of your frames can appear to blend seamlessly. The default value of this attribute—or when there is no MARGINBORDER attribute designated in your FRAME statement—is approximately 1 or whatever the browser can negotiate or is set up to display for border width.

Here is a sample frames-based document. Study it carefully. Although I will not quiz you or check your homework, I advise that you understand the syntax thoroughly before attempting to tackle the script examples that come after. First, assuming you understand HTML tables, here is a sample layout:

```
+-----------------------------------------------------------+
|                      |                   |                 |
|                      |                   |                 |
|                      |                   |                 |
|                      |                   |                 |
|                      |                   |                 |
|                      |                   |                 |
|                      |                   |                 |
|                      |                   |                 |
|                      |                   |                 |
|                      |                   |                 |
|                      | ----------------- |                 |
|                      |                   |                 |
|                      |                   |                 |
```

```
|               |                                |
+----------------------------------------------------- |
|               |                                |
|               |                                |
|               |                                |
|               |                                |
|               |--------------------------------|
|               |                                |
|               |                                |
|               |                                |
|               |                                |
|               |                                |
|               |                                |
|               |                                |
|               |                                |
+-----------------------------------------------+
```

```
<TABLE WIDTH="100%" HEIGHT="100%" BORDER>
    <TR><TD ROWSPAN=2>CELL1</TD><TD>CELL2</TD></TR>
    <TR><TD ROWSPAN=2>CELL3</TD></TR>
    <TR><TD ROWSPAN=2>CELL4</TD></TR>
    <TR><TD>CELL5</TD></TR>
</TABLE>
```

Now let's try that same layout using frames:

```
<FRAMESET COLS="50%,50%">
    <FRAMESET ROWS="50%,50%">
      <FRAME SRC="cell.html">
      <FRAME SRC="cell.html">
    </FRAMESET>
    <FRAMESET ROWS="33%,33%,33%">
      <FRAME SRC="cell.html">
      <FRAME SRC="cell.html">
      <FRAME SRC="cell.html">
    </FRAMESET>
</FRAMESET>
```

Again, here is what the resulting frames-based document will look like:

```
+-----------------------------------------------+
|               |                                |
|               |                                |
|               |                                |
|               |                                |
```

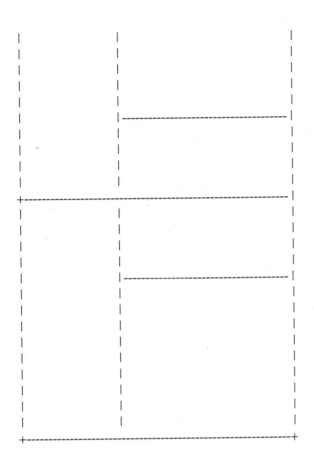

Targeting Windows

This feature gives document writers a little control over where the data appears when a user clicks on a link in their document. It is useful as a stand-alone feature with a document space that can be best viewed with multiple top-level windows (a list-of-subjects window and a window displaying the current subject), but it is most useful in conjunction with Netscape's new frames feature.

Previously when a user clicked on a link, the new document either appeared in the window the user had clicked in, or (under the user's control) it appeared in a new window. Targeting windows allows the document writer to assign names to specific windows, and to target certain documents to always appear in the window bearing the matching name.

A name is assigned to a window in one of three ways:

◆ A document can be sent with the optional HTTP header, as in

```
Window-target: window_name
```

This will force the document to load in the window named **window_name**, or if such a window does not exist, one will be created, and then the document will be loaded in it.

◆ A document can be accessed via a targeted link. In this case there is HTML that assigns a target **window_name** to a link. The document loaded from that link will behave as if it had a Window-target set as in the preceding method.

◆ A window created within a frameset can be named by use of the NAME attribute to the <FRAME> tag.

Targeting within HTML is accomplished by means of the TARGET attribute. This attribute can be added to a variety of HTML tags to target the links referred to by that tag. The attribute is of the form

```
TARGET="window_name"
```

Using a TARGET in an <A> tag is straightforward. The anchor tag normally specifies a link to be loaded when the active item is clicked on. Adding the TARGET attribute to the anchor tag forces that link to be loaded into the targeted window. For example:

```
<A HREF="url" TARGET="window_name">Targeted Anchor</A>
```

When you want all (or most) of the links in a document to be targeted to the same window, you use TARGET in the <BASE> tag. The TARGET attribute establishes a default window_name that all links in this document will be targeted to. This default is overridden by specific instances of the TARGET attribute in individual anchor tags. For example:

```
<BASE TARGET="window_name">
```

When you're using a TARGET in the <AREA> tag, it might be a good idea to be somewhat familiar with what the IETF Internet Draft of Client-Side Image Maps defines as an <AREA> tag. This tag describes a shaped area in a client-side image map and provides the link that should be followed when the user clicks there. Adding the TARGET attribute to the <AREA> tag forces the load of that link into the targeted window. For example:

```
<AREA SHAPE="shape" COORDS="x,y,..." HREF="url"
                                    TARGET="window_name">
```

When you want to place a TARGET in the <FORM> tag, remember that the <FORM> tag normally displays the results of a form submission in the same window the form was submitted from. If the TARGET attribute is added to the <FORM> tag, the result of the form submission is instead loaded into the targeted window. For example:

```
<FORM ACTION="url" TARGET="window_name">
```

Finally, there are "magic" TARGET names. (And you thought there was no such thing as magic!) These names all begin with the underscore character. Recall from earlier examples that you cannot use the underscore character to define any of your named frames.

`TARGET="_blank"`

will cause the link to always be loaded in a new blank window. This window is not named.

`TARGET="_self"`

causes the link to always load in the same window the anchor was clicked in. This is useful for overriding a globally assigned BASE target.

`TARGET="_parent"`

makes the link load in the immediate FRAMESET parent of this document. This defaults to acting like "_self" if the document has no parent.

`TARGET="_top"`

makes the link load in the full body of the window. This defaults to acting like "_self" if the document is already at the top. It is useful for breaking out of an arbitrarily deep FRAME nesting.

Any targeted window name that begins with an underscore but is not one of these names will be ignored.

2in1

Simple Frameset

N2 N2.01 N2.02+ N3 N4 E3 E4

In this example, you click on a link in one frame, triggering a response in another frame. There are three frames: one containing the links and two that are loaded according to the link you click on (see Figure 7-4).

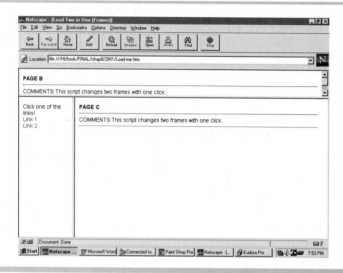

FIGURE 7-4.   Click in one window and the other windows change

The script makes uses of JavaScript as a control for which document loads in which window, according to the targets set up in the script.

Although there may be some practical applications of this type of interframes activity, mostly this script is presented here as an example of how frames work. If you have digested the previous few pages, it should be fairly easy to follow.

The frames are set up by LOAD-ME.HTM.

LOAD-ME.HTM

```
1   <HTML>
2   <HEAD>
3   <TITLE>Load Two in One (Frames)</TITLE>
4   </HEAD>
5   <FRAMESET ROWS="70,*">
6      <FRAME SRC=jv_2i1b.htm NAME="banner">
7      <FRAMESET COLS="150,*">
8         <FRAME SRC=jv_2i1a.htm NAME="nav">
9         <FRAME SRC=jv_2i1c.htm NAME="display">
10     </FRAMESET>
11  </FRAMESET>
12  </HTML>
```

The left frame is set up by JV_2IN1A.HTM.

JV_2IN1A.HTM

```
1   <HTML>
2   <TITLE>Load Two in One (Frames)</TITLE>
3   <HEAD>
4   <SCRIPT>
5   <!--
6   function twoinone(nr){
7       if (nr==1){
8           parent.banner.location.href="jv_2i1c.htm"
9           parent.display.location.href="jv_2i1b.htm"
10      }
11      if (nr==2){
12          parent.banner.location.href="jv_2i1b.htm"
13          parent.display.location.href="jv_2i1c.htm"
14      }
15  }
16  //-->
17  </SCRIPT>
18  </HEAD>
19  <BODY BGCOLOR="#FFFFFF">
20  Click one of the links!<br>
21  <A HREF="JavaScript:twoinone(1)">Link 1</A><BR>
22  <A HREF="JavaScript:twoinone(2)">Link 2</A>
23  </BODY>
24  </HTML>
```

The upper frame is set up by JV_2IN1B.HTM.

JV_2IN1B.HTM

```
1   <HTML>
2   <TITLE>Load Two in One (Frames)</TITLE>
3   <BODY BGCOLOR="#FFFFFF">
4   <b>PAGE B</b><hr>
5   COMMENTS: This script changes two frames with one click.
6   <hr>
7   </BODY>
8   </HTML>
```

The right frame, set up by JV_2IN1C.HTM, is identical to the upper frame.

JV_2IN1C.HTM

```
1   <HTML>
2   <TITLE>Load Two in One (Frames)</TITLE>
3   <BODY BGCOLOR="#FFFFFF">
4   <b>PAGE C</b><hr>
5   COMMENTS: This script changes two frames with one click.
6   <hr>
7   </BODY>
8   </HTML>
```

ANNOTATIONS

Here the only file of interest is JV_2IN1A.HTM, which contains the page-loading JavaScript. The other three are passive pages consisting solely of standard HTML formatting code. The dual pageload is accomplished by a single function, **twoinone( )**. Its **nr** argument is a flag whose value determines which page gets loaded into which frame.

```
1    <HTML>
2    <TITLE>Load Two in One (Frames)</TITLE>
3    <HEAD>
4    <SCRIPT>
5    <!--
6    function twoinone(nr){
7        if (nr==1){
8            parent.banner.location.href="jv_2i1c.htm"
9            parent.display.location.href="jv_2i1b.htm"
10       }
11       if (nr==2){
12           parent.banner.location.href="jv_2i1b.htm"
13           parent.display.location.href="jv_2i1c.htm"
14       }
15   }
```

Called by clicks on the links in lines 21 and 22, **twoinone( )** uses the value of **nr** to determine which of two routines to follow: load JV_2I1C.HTM into the frame named **banner** and JV_2I1B.HTM into **display**, or vice versa, by setting their **location.href** property.

Because only two files are used, this function may give the impression of being a not particularly useful page-swapping routine. Use four different files, however, and you'll get a much clearer picture of what it does. Moreover, you can easily add more links and create file-loading routines for higher values of **nr**.

Don't forget that any of the files loaded by **twoinone( )** can be a frameset file, enabling you to nest various frame-structured designs within these top-level frames.

```
16   //-->
17   </SCRIPT>
18   </HEAD>
19   <BODY BGCOLOR="#FFFFFF">
20   Click one of the links!<br>
21   <A HREF="JavaScript:twoinone(1)">Link 1</A><BR>
22   <A HREF="JavaScript:twoinone(2)">Link 2</A>
23   </BODY>
24   </HTML>
```

When first working with frames, JavaScript programmers often run into referencing problems. The basic rule, however, is simple. To reference items in one frame from another, spell out the entire object chain, starting from the top. For example, if the **twoinone( )** function were moved to JV_2I1C.HTM, the file loaded into the frame named **display**, it could be called from the link in the **nav** frame (JV_2I1A.HTM) with

```
javascript:parent.display.twoinone()
```

or

```
javascript:top.display.twoinone()
```

Scripts in a parent frame can refer to a child frame directly by name (without prepending **self**). A script in LOAD-ME.HTM, for instance, need simply say

```
display.twoinone()
```

or

```
banner.twoinone()
```

to call the function from the files loaded into those two frames. Move **twoinone( )** to the top frameset file and

```
parent.twoinone()
```

will run it. The same applies to objects and properties, as well as variables, all of which belong to the frame (and not to the document in it). For example, if you created an object named **Brontozilla** with a **mood** property, you might write

```
top.display.Brontozilla.mood = seeBarney
```

and call a method with

```
top.display.Brontozilla.stompStompSTOMP(mood)
```

which might include

```
for (var stomp = 0; stomp < mood; stomp++)
        top.display.Brontozilla.clout *= 10
```

to magnify **clout** tenfold with each pass. An Image object belongs to **document**, so it would have to be referred to as

```
top.display.document.bgPic.src = "grapesplotch.jpg"
```

Similarly, form elements belong to **document**, so that you would have to spell out

```
top.display.document.outForm.outField.value = "The End"
```

to reference the hypothetical text area named **outField** in **outForm**.

    Another option is to use the built-in Frames array. In this script, **banner** is **frames[0]**, **display** is **frames[1]**, and **nav** is **frames[2]** based on the order of their creation in the frameset file. Yet another technique is to write

```
top.frames['display'].twoinone()
```

which combines name and array referencing. Bear in mind that JavaScript error messages can send you down the wrong track. "Brontozilla has no property named clout," for instance, does not necessarily mean that you mangled the creation of **Brontozilla** and left your Humongousaur without **clout**. It could just be that you're not referencing **Brontozilla** accurately.

rollover

Illustrated Menu with Mouseover

| N2 | N2.01 | N2.02+ | N3 | N4 | E3 | E4 |

This script uses frames and an unusual menu metaphor for adding a bit of magic to a page. Users see a link on a page, and in this case it beckons them to send an e-mail message. They pass their mouse over the "Mail Me" link, and suddenly a graphic appears (see Figure 7-5). If they pass the mouse over the link again, the graphic disappears.

FIGURE 7-5. The mail icon appears during a mouseOver event

From the users' point of view, the unexpected is often the most fun they can have on the Web, and once they get over the surprise, the mail link still functions as a "mailto" link—except that in my script the mail link has been disarmed. To activate it, just change the HREF assignment in line 6 of JV_REQ1A.HTM from the dummy hash mark (#) to a valid "mailto:" URL.

Here is the file that contains the frameset commands:

LOAD-ME.HTM

```
1   <HTML>
2   <HEAD>
3   <TITLE>Rollover Link Example</TITLE>
```

```
4    </HEAD>
5    <FRAMESET COLS="80%, 20%" frameborder="no" border=0
                             framespacing=0 framecolor="ffffff">
6       <FRAME SRC="jv_req1d.html"
                      marginwidth=1 marginheight=1 name="info">
7       <FRAMESET ROWS="50%, 50%">
8          <FRAME SRC="jv_req1a.html"
                      marginwidth=1 marginheight=1 name="upper">
9          <FRAME SRC="jv_req1b.html" marginwidth=1
                      marginheight=1 name="lower" scrolling=no>
10      </FRAMESET>
11   </FRAMESET>
12   </HTML>
```

Here is the large frame that fills most of the screen and sits against the left margin. This is where you will want to place the bulk of your content.

JV_REQ1D.HTM

```
1    <HTML>
2    <HEAD>
3    <TITLE>UPPER</TITLE>
4    </HEAD>
5    <BODY BGCOLOR="FFFFFF">
6    <hr>
7    COMMENTS: Move the mouse over the link in the "Mail Me"-link
                             and the picture will change.
8    <hr>
9    </body>
10   </HTML>
```

To the right of this frame, you want to place the HTML link that controls the lower frame:

JV_REQ1A.HTM

```
1    <HTML>
2    <HEAD>
3    <TITLE>UPPER</TITLE>
```

```
4    </HEAD>
5    <BODY BGCOLOR="FFFFFF">
6    <a href="#" onmouseover=
        "parent.lower.location.href='jv_req1c.html'; return true"
         onmouseout="parent.lower.location.href='jv_req1b.html'">
7    Mail Icon</a>
8    </body>
9    </HTML
```

Finally, the frame that sits in the lower right, which appears to perform all the magic that the user sees, is just an empty HTML page with a white background color.

JV_REQ1B.HTM

```
1    <HTML>
2    <HEAD>
3    <TITLE>LOWER</TITLE>
4    </HEAD>
5    <BODY BGCOLOR="FFFFFF">
6    </BODY>
7    </HTML>
```

ANNOTATIONS

Here again, the JavaScript is all in one file: JV_REQ1A.HTM. Moreover, the entire script is contained in the assignments to **onMouseOver** and **onMouseOut**.

```
1    <HTML>
2    <HEAD>
3    <TITLE>UPPER</TITLE>
4    </HEAD>
5    <BODY BGCOLOR="FFFFFF">
6    <a href="#" onmouseover=
        "parent.lower.location.href='jv_req1c.html'; return true"
         onmouseout="parent.lower.location.href='jv_req1b.html'">
7    Mail Icon</a>
8    </body>
9    </HTML
```

The two event handlers in line 6 switch the file in the frame named **lower** back and forth between JV_REQ1C.HTML, which contains the image of the clipboard, and JV_REQ1B.HTML, a blank page, through the assignments to its **location.href** property.

Layers, because their position and size can be specified to the pixel, allow you to create the same now-you-see-it-now-you-don't effect anywhere on the page simply by toggling their **visibility** property between **show** and **hide**. To appreciate the difference between frames and layers, think of *frames* as multiple screens you can create in a variety of geometric patterns within the browser window. A *layer*, on the other hand, more closely resembles a television picture-within-a-picture that can be positioned anywhere within the main window and given a specific size.

To create a 100×100 pixel area 150 pixels in from both the top and left of the browser window with frames, you have to carve out three full rows and divide the middle one into three columns. Worse yet, you would have to split up the content of the rest of the page among the surrounding four (or more) frames. With layers you simply specify size and position, and display or hide content by toggling the layer's **visibility** property.

fancy

Fancy Frames-Based Menu

| N2 | N2.01 | N2.02+ | N3 | N4 | E3 | E4 |

It's time for the classic use of frames on web pages: the menu system uses a navigation bar on the left, in one frame; the content appears on the right side of the screen, in a second frame. The user clicks on a menu entry on the left, and the appropriate web page is loaded in the right frame (see Figure 7-6). With some variations, this is the most common (and probably most effective) use of minimal JavaScript and frames.

FIGURE 7-6. The icons on the left frame control the content to the right

The only real JavaScript in this example is the "rollover" menu icons, which change their appearance when users move their mouse over them.

LOAD-ME.HTM

```
1   <html>
2   <head>
3   <title>frames by javascript</title>
```

```
4   </head>
5   <frameset cols="23%,*">
6   <frame src="buttons.htm" noresize name="buttons"
                                            scrolling=no>
7   <frame src="cover.htm" noresize name="main" scrolling=auto>
8   </frameset>
9   </frameset>
10  <no frames>
11  <body bgcolor="#ffffff">
12  <center><h1>Javascript: The eZine!</h1></center>
13  <hr>
14  Since this is an eZine about Javascript,
            you really ought to get a browser that supports it.
15  Why not check out <a href="http://home.netscape.com/">
                                Netscape Navigator 3.0</a>?
16  <hr>
17  </body>
18  </noframes>
19  </html>
```

As the users pass their mouse cursor over the menu choices, there is a rollover effect.

BUTTONS.HTM

```
1   <html>
2   <head>
3   <title>3D Visualization</title>
4   <script language="JavaScript">
5   var img1 = new Image();
6   var img2 = new Image();
7   var img3 = new Image();
8   var img4 = new Image();
9   var img5 = new Image();
10  var img6 = new Image();
11  var img7 = new Image();
12  var img8 = new Image();
13  var img9 = new Image();
14
15  function init() {
16      img1.src = "a2.gif";
17      img2.src = "b2.gif";
```

```
18      img3.src = "c2.gif";
19      img4.src = "d2.gif";
20      img5.src = "e2.gif";
21      img6.src = "f2.gif";
22      img7.src = "g2.gif";
23      img8.src = "h2.gif";
24      img9.src = "i2.gif";
25   }
26
27   function highlight(img) {
28      document[img].src = img + "2.gif";
29   }
30
31   function unhighlight(img) {
32      document[img].src = img + "1.gif";
33   }
34   </script>
35   </head>
36   <body bgcolor="fff5ee">
37   <center>
38   <hr size=4>
39   <p>
40   <a href="mktng.htm" target="main"
                                    onMouseOver="highlight('a');"
                                    onMouseOut="unhighlight('a');">
41   <IMG NAME="a" SRC="a1.gif" BORDER=0></A>
42   <br>
43   <a href="wsd.htm"  target="main"
                                    onMouseOver="highlight('b');"
                                    onMouseOut="unhighlight('b');">
44   <IMG NAME="b" SRC="b1.gif" BORDER=0></A>
45   <br>
46   <a href="3dvisi.htm" target="main"
                                    onMouseOver="highlight('c');"
                                    onMouseOut="unhighlight('c');">
47   <IMG NAME="c" SRC="c1.gif" BORDER=0></A>
48   <br>
49   <a href="folio.htm" target="main"
                                    onMouseOver="highlight('d');"
                                    onMouseOut="unhighlight('d');">
50   <IMG NAME="d" SRC="d1.gif" BORDER=0></A>
51   <br>
52   <a href="ref.htm" target="main"
```

```
                                  onMouseOver="highlight('e');"
                                  onMouseOut="unhighlight('e');">
53    <IMG NAME="e" SRC="e1.gif" BORDER=0></A>
54    <br>
55    <a href="links.htm" target="main"
                                  onMouseOver="highlight('f');"
                                  onMouseOut="unhighlight('f');">
56    <IMG NAME="f" SRC="f1.gif" BORDER=0></A>
57    <br>
58    <a href="enquiry.htm" target="main"
                                  onMouseOver="highlight('h');"
                                  onMouseOut="unhighlight('h');">
59    <IMG NAME="h" SRC="h1.gif" BORDER=0></A>
60    <br>
61    <a href="../index.htm" target="_top"
                                  onMouseOver="highlight('i');"
                                  onMouseOut="unhighlight('i');">
62    <IMG NAME="i" SRC="i1.gif" BORDER=0 ></A>
63    <br>
64    <p>
65    <hr size=4>
66    <p>
67    <a href="mailto: info@visitune.nl">
68    <img src="pictures/mail2.gif"  border="0"></A>
69    <br>
70    <p>
71    <hr size=4>
72    <font size=1>
73    <strong>LAST MODIFIED</strong>
74    <font size=>
75    <script language="JavaScript">
76    <!--Hide from non-Javascript browsers
77    function DisplayDate(dateString)
78    {
79       d = new Date(dateString);
80          return" " + (d.getMonth() + 1) + "/"
                                  + d.getDate() + "/" + d.getYear();
81    }
82    document.write("<font size=2>");
83    document.write("<B>" +
                      DisplayDate(document.lastModified) + "</B>");
84    document.write("<P><font size=>");
85    //-->
```

```
86   </script>
87   </body>
88   </html>
```

COVER.HTM

```
1    <html>
2    <head>
3    <title>Internet marketing</title>
4    </head>
5    <body background="backgr3.jpg">
6    <table width=100%>
7    <tr>
8    <td><img src="logo.gif" align=left  border="0"></td>
9    <td align=right valign=bottom>
10   <img src="mktng.gif" border="0"></center></td>
11   </tr>
12   <tr>
13   <td colspan=2><hr size=4></td>
14   </tr>
15   </table>
16   <p>
17   <table width=100%>
18   <tr>
19   <td><font size="-1">Hoe bereik ik mijn potentiële klanten...
     niet alleen die naast de deur, maar ook diegene die een land
     of werelddeel van mij verwijderd zijn. Hoe breng ik een zo
     duidelijk mogelijk beeld van onze onderneming naar buiten...
     onze specialiteit, produkten..onze service.<br>
20   Op welke wijze kan ik zo effectief mogelijk communiceren met
     personen in ondernemingen en organisaties, die in mijn
     produkten geïnteresseerd zijn.<br>
21   <p>
22   Vragen, waar de traditionele marketingmethoden, elk voor
     zich slechts een beperkt antwoord op kunnen geven. Meestal
     is het éénrichtingsverkeer van traditionele reclame en
     commercieel drukwerk. De inter-communicatieve middelen,
     zoals telemarketing, inzet van buitendienst-medewerkers en
     de deelname aan beurzen, kunnen gezien de kosten slechts
     selectief worden ingezet.<br>
23   Uw lange termijn strategie, gericht op groei van uw
```

```
       marktaandeel en het aanboren van nieuwe markten
       (globalisering), vraagt een nieuw arsenaal van marketing
       communicatie instrumenten.<br>
24     Aanwezigheid op het Internet met een goed gedocumenteerde
       inter-aktieve Website, verschaft u een krachtig en relatief
       goedkoop instrument voor de realisatie van uw lange termijn
       doelstellingen.<br>
25     <p>
26     </font></td>
27     </tr>
28     </table>
29     </body>
30     </html>
```

ANNOTATIONS

The script in BUTTONS.HTM highlights each menu selection when the mouse pointer is over it by replacing the default GIF file in which the text is green with one containing exactly the same image, except that the text is now red. When the mouse pointer moves off the menu item, the green-text image file is reloaded.

The effect does not work with the bottom two menu items, "antwoord formulier" and "index," because the H1.GIF and I1.GIF image files loaded by the page contain red instead of green text, as do the H2.GIF and I2.GIF files with which **onMouseOver** replaces them.

The script also contains a handy function that automatically displays the date on which the page was last modified.

```
1     <html>
2     <head>
3     <title>3D Visualization</title>
4     <script language="JavaScript">
5     var img1 = new Image();
6     var img2 = new Image();
7     var img3 = new Image();
8     var img4 = new Image();
9     var img5 = new Image();
10    var img6 = new Image();
11    var img7 = new Image();
12    var img8 = new Image();
13    var img9 = new Image();
14
15    function init() {
```

```
16      img1.src = "a2.gif";
17      img2.src = "b2.gif";
18      img3.src = "c2.gif";
19      img4.src = "d2.gif";
20      img5.src = "e2.gif";
21      img6.src = "f2.gif";
22      img7.src = "g2.gif";
23      img8.src = "h2.gif";
24      img9.src = "i2.gif";
25   }
```

First, the script creates a set of Image objects named **img1** through **img9**. Next the **init( )** function assigns a GIF file to the **src** property of each of the nine new images. These files, whose names end in "2," are those with the red text. The purpose of creating the Image objects and specifying the source files is to have the browser get the red-text GIF files immediately and store them in the cache. This makes the **onMouseOver** highlight effect more instantaneous.

Unfortunately, this does not happen in this case because **init( )** is not called. To have the function do its job, just add the call

```
init();
```

after line 25. You may also notice that the **img7** slot is really empty: there are no G1.GIF and G2.GIF files, and there are only eight, not nine, menu items.

```
27   function highlight(img) {
28      document[img].src = img + "2.gif";
29   }
30
31   function unhighlight(img) {
32      document[img].src = img + "1.gif";
33   }
```

highlight( ) and **unhighlight( )**, the two simple functions that switch the images back and forth, both take the same argument, **img**, which is a single letter that represents the name given to the image in the <IMG> tag as well as the letter used to name its GIF file (with "1" appended for green and "2" for red text). The string passed to **img** serves both to reference the specific image and to construct the filename assigned to the image's **src** property.

The syntax used to refer to the image here is unorthodox. Strictly speaking, according to JavaScript documentation, it should be

```
document.images[img].src
```

But presumably because images are a property of **document**, the abbreviated reference is sufficient to identify the **document** element bearing the name passed to

img. Similarly, if you had a form named "orderForm" with a field called "totOrder," you could refer to it with

```
document['orderForm'].totOrder.value
```

instead of the more common

```
document.orderForm.totOrder.value
```

This type of object array referencing by name is especially useful in combination with a variable or a function argument, as in this script. If you test the value of **document['orderForm']** or **document['d']** (one of the names passed to **img**), the output will be "object Form" and "object Image," respectively.

```
34   </script>
35   </head>
36   <body bgcolor="fff5ee">
37   <center>
38   <hr size=4>
39   <p>
40   <a href="mktng.htm" target="main"
                             onMouseOver="highlight('a');"
                             onMouseOut="unhighlight('a');">
41   <IMG NAME="a" SRC="a1.gif" BORDER=0></A>
42   <br>
43   <a href="wsd.htm"  target="main"
                             onMouseOver="highlight('b');"
                             onMouseOut="unhighlight('b');">
44   <IMG NAME="b" SRC="b1.gif" BORDER=0></A>
```

Lines 40 to 62 contain the HTML code for the eight links, each with its **onMouseOver** call to **highlight( )** and **onMouseOut** call to **unhighlight( )**. In each case, the argument passed to the twin functions is the same as the single-letter name assigned to the image used to display the link.

```
63   <br>
64   <p>
65   <hr size=4>
66   <p>
67   <a href="mailto: info@visitune.nl">
68   <img src="pictures/mail2.gif"  border="0"></A>
69   <br>
70   <p>
71   <hr size=4>
72   <font size=1>
73   <strong>LAST MODIFIED</strong>
74   <font size=>
75   <script language="JavaScript">
```

```
76   <!--Hide from non-Javascript browsers
77   function DisplayDate(dateString)
78   {
79      d = new Date(dateString);
80         return" " + (d.getMonth() + 1) + "/"
                              + d.getDate() + "/" + d.getYear();
81   }
82   document.write("<font size=2>");
83   document.write("<B>" +
                     DisplayDate(document.lastModified) + "</B>");
84   document.write("<P><font size=>");
85   //-->
86   </script>
87   </body>
88   </html>
```

DisplayDate( ), a separate function that displays the date the document was last modified, receives the JavaScript **document.lastModified** property as its argument, creates a new Date named **d** with it, and then uses **d**'s properties to format the date for display. The "1" added to the integer returned by **d.getMonth( )** compensates for the month count beginning at zero.

As **document.lastModified** returns a string in the form MM/DD/YY HH:MM:SS, the formatting done by **DisplayDate( )** could be achieved by putting

document.lastModified.substring(0,8)

between the plus signs in line 83 and dispensing with the function altogether.

This script is yet another example of the fact that it does not necessarily take reams of JavaScript to create an attractive, professional-looking effect. A few lines can sometimes achieve a lot. In a context such as this, the JavaScript code is really only one of many elements creating the page's overall appeal. It probably took considerably more effort to make sure the GIFs with the different-colored lettering matched perfectly; to get the colors, fonts, and layout just right; to select a background image that didn't overwhelm the text; and to do all the other work that went into this page, than to produce the script. As this shows, JavaScript doesn't necessarily have to be the star of your site—it can also turn in an outstanding performance as an extra that makes its impact without stealing the show.

hierarc

Hierarchical Menu System

⌐N2 ⌐N2.01 ⌐N2.02+ ⌐N3 ⌐N4 ⌐E3 ⌐E4

Of the numerous "exploding" menuing systems on the Web, this one, by Marcelino Martins, is one of the best and most attractive. The hierarchical, exploding menu system acts much like an outline. Each top-level menu topic has a series of child (subordinate) topics. The difference between a traditional outline and this example is in the JavaScript—it is an interactive menu, one that expands and collapses on cue (see Figure 7-7).

FIGURE 7-7.   This menu expands and contracts in hierarchical outline fashion

For web designers, there are surprisingly few practical applications of this menu type. If you want to place a manual or some documentation online, this system may work for you. In the example next, the application is a series of hot links. In other words, Martins re-created a list of favorite links in a hierarchical format.

Let's start with the "frames-maker" document:

LOAD-ME.HTM

```
1    <!--
2    You are free to copy the "Folder-Tree" script
                        as long as you keep this copyright notice:
3    *
4    * Script found in:
                    http://www.geocities.com/Paris/LeftBank/2178/
5    *
6    * Author: Marcelino Alves Martins (martins@hks.com)
7    *
8    Version control:  Creation: January '97.
```

```
9                        Last changes: June '97
10
11  For other information refer to
12  http://www.geocities.com/Paris/LeftBank/2178/foldertree.html
13  -->
14  <HTML>
15  <HEAD>
16  <title>Marcelino Martins' Home Page</title>
17  <script LANGUAGE="JavaScript">
18  <!-- to hide script contents from old browsers
19
20  function generateTree()
21  {
22     var aux1, aux2, aux3
23     foldersTree = folderNode("Start folder")
24     aux1 = appendChild(foldersTree, folderNode("Local docs"))
25     aux2 = appendChild(aux1, leafNode("Profile"))
26     appendChild(aux2,
27        generateDocEntry(0, "Personal info", "ident.html", ""))
28     appendChild(aux2,
                generateDocEntry(0, "Resume", "resume.html", ""))
28     aux2 = appendChild(aux1, leafNode("Likes"))
29     appendChild(aux2,
             generateDocEntry(0, "Portugal", "portugal.html", ""))
30     appendChild(aux2,
                generateDocEntry(0, "Music", "musica.htm", ""))
31     appendChild(aux2,
           generateDocEntry(0, "Books & Movies", "arts.html", ""))
32     aux1 = appendChild(foldersTree,
                                  folderNode("Web favorites"))
33     aux2 = appendChild(aux1, leafNode("Friends with sites"))
34     appendChild(aux2,generateDocEntry(1,
           "Ana Maria", "wwwAlu.ci.uminho.pt:8888/~si8900/", ""))
35     appendChild(aux2,generateDocEntry(1,
              "Ant&oacute;nio Almeida", "lemac18.lemac.ist.utl.pt/
                                  ~aalmeida/myhomepage.html", ""))
36     appendChild(aux2,generateDocEntry(1,
                                      "Ant&oacute;nio Figueiredo",
                          "www.cfn.ist.utl.pt/~antonio/", ""))
37     appendChild(aux2,generateDocEntry(1,
           "Ant&oacute;nio Sargento", "www.ip.pt/~ip101065/", ""))
38     appendChild(aux2,generateDocEntry(1, "Francisco Rosa",
                        "albertina.inesc.pt/people/fjar", ""))
```

```
39   appendChild(aux2,generateDocEntry(1, "Humberto Fernando",
                        "www.cfn.ist.utl.pt/~fernando/", ""))
40   appendChild(aux2,generateDocEntry(1, "Jo&atilde;o Cruz",
                        "www.geocities.com/Paris/3853/", ""))
41   appendChild(aux2,generateDocEntry(1, "Nabil M. Lawandy",
          "www.chem.brown.edu/brochure/people/nml/nml.html", ""))
42   appendChild(aux2,generateDocEntry(1, "Nuno Marques",
                        "www-ia.di.fct.unl.pt/~nmm", ""))
43   appendChild(aux2,generateDocEntry(1,
                                "Teresa Gon&ccedil;alves",
                        "albertina.inesc.pt/people/tsg", ""))
44   aux2 = appendChild(aux1, folderNode("Readings"))
45   aux3 = appendChild(aux2, leafNode("News"))
46   appendChild(aux3, generateDocEntry(1,
                        "CNN", "www.cnn.com/", ""))
47   appendChild(aux3, generateDocEntry(1,
             "PUBLICO", "www.publico.pt/publico/hoje", ""))
48   appendChild(aux3, generateDocEntry(1,
                        "Di&aacute;rio de Noticias",
                        "www.dn.pt/homepage/home.htm", ""))
49   appendChild(aux3, generateDocEntry(1, "Portuguese
       Soccer Championship", "www.dn.pt/des/primeira.htm", ""))
50   aux3 = appendChild(aux2, leafNode("Cartoons"))
51   appendChild(aux3, generateDocEntry(1, "The Dilbert Zone",
                "www.unitedmedia.com/comics/dilbert/", ""))
52   appendChild(aux3, generateDocEntry(1, "Randy Glasbergen",
                        "www.borg.com/~rjgtoons/toon.html", ""))
53   aux3 = appendChild(aux2, leafNode("Science"))
54   appendChild(aux3, generateDocEntry(1,
                                "Discover Magazine",
          "www.enews.com/magazines/discover/page1a.html", ""))
55   appendChild(aux3, generateDocEntry(1,
             "Scientific American", "www.sciam.com/", ""))
56   aux3 = appendChild(aux2, leafNode("Reference"))
57   appendChild(aux3, generateDocEntry(1,
             "Internet Movie Database", "us.imdb.com/", ""))
58   appendChild(aux3, generateDocEntry(1, "MapQuest!
          Interactive Atlas Welcome!", "www.mapquest.com/cgi-
                        bin/mqatlas?screen=wm_register&link=
                        wm_main&uid=104adz16d09jizx", ""))
59   appendChild(aux3, generateDocEntry(1, "BigYellow",
                        "s8.bigyellow.com/", ""))
60   appendChild(aux3, generateDocEntry(1, "HomeArts Recipe
```

```
           Finder", "homearts.com/waisform/recipe.htm", ""))
61   aux3 = appendChild(aux2, leafNode("Computers"))
62   appendChild(aux3,generateDocEntry(1, "Byte",
                                       "www.byte.com/", ""))
63   appendChild(aux3,generateDocEntry(1, "Python",
                                       "www.python.org/", ""))
64   appendChild(aux3,generateDocEntry(1, "ZDNet",
                                       "www.zdnet.com", ""))
65   aux3 = appendChild(aux2, leafNode("Other"))
66   appendChild(aux3, generateDocEntry(1, "Motorcyle",
                                       "www.motorcycle.com", ""))
67   appendChild(aux3, generateDocEntry(1, "Agenda Cultural
                 de Lisboa", "marte.consiste.pt/agenda", ""))
68   aux2 = appendChild(aux1, leafNode("Searches"))
69   appendChild(aux2, generateDocEntry(1, "Excite",
                                       "www.excite.com", ""))
70   appendChild(aux2, generateDocEntry(1, "Altavista",
                                       "altavista.digital.com", ""))
71   appendChild(aux2, generateDocEntry(1, "SAPO
                       (portuguese sites)", "sapo.ua.pt", ""))
72   appendChild(aux2, generateDocEntry(1, "Point's Top 5%",
                                       "www.pointcom.com/", ""))
73   appendChild(aux2, generateDocEntry(1, "Top 5% Portugal",
                       "www.ip.pt/top5portugal/main.html", ""))
74   aux2 = appendChild(aux1, folderNode("Sights & Sounds"))
75   aux3 = appendChild(aux2, leafNode("Radios"))
76   appendChild(aux3, generateDocEntry(1,
                         "R&aacute;dio Comercial On-line",
                 "www.radiocomercial.pt/audio/audio.html", ""))
77   appendChild(aux3, generateDocEntry(1,
         "TSF- A R&aacute;dio em Directo", "www.tsf.pt/", ""))
78   aux3 = appendChild(aux2, leafNode("Cameras"))
79   appendChild(aux3, generateDocEntry(1, "Lisboa/Amoreiras",
                                "expotelecom.telepac.pt/e_futuro/
                                rc/transito/amoreiras.jpg", ""))
80   appendChild(aux3, generateDocEntry(1,
                         "Lisboa/Pra&ccedil;a de Espanha",
                                "expotelecom.telepac.pt/e_futuro/
                                rc/transito/pespanha.jpg", ""))
81   appendChild(aux3, generateDocEntry(1, "Lisboa/Ponte",
                                "expotelecom.telepac.pt/e_futuro/
                                rc/transito/ponte.jpg", ""))
82   appendChild(aux3, generateDocEntry(1, "Downtown
```

```
                        Providence", "rhodeisland.com/webcam.jpg", ""))
83     appendChild(aux3, generateDocEntry(1, "Home of WORLD
                        NETCAMS", "trendy.net/sites/netcams/", ""))
84     aux2 = appendChild(aux1, folderNode("Downloads"))
85     aux3 = appendChild(aux2, leafNode("Shareware"))
86     appendChild(aux3, generateDocEntry(1, "Windows95.com",
                                "www.windows95.com/apps", ""))
87     appendChild(aux3, generateDocEntry(1, "shareware.com",
                                "www.shareware.com", ""))
88     aux3 = appendChild(aux2, leafNode("Firmware"))
89     appendChild(aux3, generateDocEntry(1, "Iomega zip",
                        "www.iomega.com/product/zip/index.html", ""))
90     appendChild(aux3, generateDocEntry(1, "USRobotics",
                        "www.usrobotics.com/home/20411.02.html", ""))
91     appendChild(aux3, generateDocEntry(1, "Matrox Mystique",
                        "www.matrox.com/mgaweb/3dgaming.htm", ""))
92     appendChild(aux3, generateDocEntry(1, "Radio Track",
                                "www.aimslab.com/", ""))
93     aux2 = appendChild(aux1, folderNode("Shopping"))
94     aux3 = appendChild(aux2, leafNode("Books"))
95     appendChild(aux3, generateDocEntry(1, "Amazon.com Books",
                                "www.amazon.com/", ""))
96     aux3 = appendChild(aux2, leafNode("Hardware & Software"))
97     appendChild(aux3, generateDocEntry(1, "ISN -
            Internet Shopping Network", "www.internet.net/", ""))
98     appendChild(aux3, generateDocEntry(1, "Computer Express",
                                "www.cexpress.com/", ""))
99     aux3 = appendChild(aux2, leafNode("Shopping Center"))
100    appendChild(aux3, generateDocEntry(1, "IMALL Homepage",
                                "www.imall.com/", ""))
101    appendChild(aux3, generateDocEntry(1, "BizWeb",
                                "www.bizweb.com/", ""))
102    aux3 = appendChild(aux2, leafNode("Other"))
103    appendChild(aux3, generateDocEntry(1, "Edmund's
            Automobile Buyer's Guides", "www.edmunds.com/", ""))
104 }
105
106 function folderNode(name)
107 {
108    var arrayAux
109    arrayAux = new Array
110    arrayAux[0] = 0
111    arrayAux[1] = 0
```

```
112     arrayAux[2] = 0
113     arrayAux[3] = name
114     return arrayAux
115 }
116
117 function leafNode(name)
118 {
119     var arrayAux
120     arrayAux = new Array
121     arrayAux[0] = 0
122     arrayAux[1] = 0
123     arrayAux[2] = 1
124     arrayAux[3] = name
125     return arrayAux
126 }
127
128 function appendChild(parent, child)
129 {
130     parent[parent.length] = child
131     return child
132 }
133
134 function generateDocEntry(icon, docDescription, link)
135 {
136     var retString =""
137     if (icon==0)
138         retString = "<A href='"+link+"' target=folderFrame>
                        <img src='doc.gif' alt='Opens in right frame'"
139     else
140         retString = "<A href='http://"+link+"' target=_blank>
                        <img src='link.gif' alt='Opens in new window'"
141     retString = retString + " border=0></a><td nowrap>
                            <font size=-1 face='Arial, Helvetica'>"
                                + docDescription + "</font>"
142     return retString
143 }
144
145 function redrawTree()
146 {
147     var doc = top.treeFrame.window.document
148     doc.clear()
149     doc.write("<body bgcolor='white'>")
150     redrawNode(foldersTree, doc, 0, 1, "")
```

```
151    doc.close()
152 }
153
154 function redrawNode(foldersNode, doc, level,
                                           lastNode, leftSide)
155 {
156    var i=0
157    doc.write("<table border=0 cellspacing=0 cellpadding=0>")
158    doc.write("<tr><td valign = middle nowrap>")
159    doc.write(leftSide)
160    if (level>0)
161        if (lastNode)
162        {
163            doc.write("<img src='lastnode.gif'
                                     width=16 height=22>")
164            leftSide = leftSide + "<img src='blank.gif'
                                     width=16 height=22>"
165        }
166        else
167        {
168            doc.write("<img src='node.gif'
                                     width=16 height=22>")
169            leftSide = leftSide + "<img src='vertline.gif'
                                     width=16 height=22>"
170        }
171    displayIconAndLabel(foldersNode, doc)
172    doc.write("</table>")
173    if (foldersNode.length > 4 && foldersNode[0])
174    {
175        if (!foldersNode[2])
176        {
177            level=level+1
178            for (i=4; i<foldersNode.length;i++)
179                if (i==foldersNode.length-1)
180                    redrawNode(foldersNode[i],
                                     doc, level, 1, leftSide)
181                else
182                    redrawNode(foldersNode[i],
                                     doc, level, 0, leftSide)
183        }
184        else
185        {
```

```
186              for (i=4; i<foldersNode.length;i++)
187              {
188                  doc.write("<table border=0 cellspacing=0
                                    cellpadding=0 valign=center>")
189                  doc.write("<tr><td nowrap>")
190                  doc.write(leftSide)
191                  if (i==foldersNode.length - 1)
192                      doc.write("<img src='lastnode.gif'
                                            width=16 height=22>")
193                  else
194                      doc.write("<img src='node.gif'
                                            width=16 height=22>")
195                  doc.write(foldersNode[i])
196                  doc.write("</table>")
197              }
198          }
199      }
200 }
201
202 function displayIconAndLabel(foldersNode, doc)
203 {
204    doc.write("<A href='javascript:
                    top.openBranch(\"" + foldersNode[3] + "\")'")
205    if (foldersNode[1])
206    {
207        doc.write("onMouseOver='window.status=
                    \"Close folder\"; return true'><img src=")
208        doc.write("opfolder.gif width=24 height=22
                                        border=noborder></a>")
209    }
210    else
211    {
212        doc.write("onMouseOver='window.status=
                    \"Open folder\"; return true'><img src=")
213        doc.write("clfolder.gif width=24 height=22
                                        border=noborder></a>")
214    }
215    doc.write("<td valign=middle align=left nowrap>")
216    doc.write("<font size=-1 face='Arial, Helvetica'>"
                                    +foldersNode[3]+"</font>")
217 }
218
219 function closeFolders(foldersNode)
```

```
220  {
221     var i=0
222     if (!foldersNode[2])
223     {
224         for (i=4; i< foldersNode.length; i++)
225             closeFolders(foldersNode[i])
226     }
227     foldersNode[0] = 0
228     foldersNode[1] = 0
229  }
230
231  function clickOnFolderRec(foldersNode, folderName)
232  {
233     var i=0
234     if (foldersNode[3] == folderName)
235     {
236         if (foldersNode[0])
237             closeFolders(foldersNode)
238         else
239         {
240             foldersNode[0] = 1
241             foldersNode[1] = 1
242         }
243     }
244     else
245     {
246         if (!foldersNode[2])
247             for (i=4; i< foldersNode.length; i++)
248                 clickOnFolderRec(foldersNode[i], folderName)
249     }
250  }
251
252  function openBranch(branchName)
253  {
254     clickOnFolderRec(foldersTree, branchName)
255     if (branchName=="Start folder" && foldersTree[0]==0)
256         top.folderFrame.location="basefldr.htm"
257     timeOutId = setTimeout("redrawTree()",100)
258  }
259
260  function initializeTree()
261  {
262     generateTree()
```

```
263    redrawTree()
264 }
265 var foldersTree = 0
266 var timeOutId = 0
267 generateTree()
268 // end hiding contents from old browsers   -->
269 </script>
270 </HEAD>
271 <FRAMESET cols="200,*"  onLoad='initializeTree()'>
272    <FRAME src="basetree.htm" name="treeFrame">
273    <FRAME SRC="basefldr.htm" name="folderFrame">
274 </FRAMESET>
275 </HTML>
```

Here is the frame that holds the hierarchical menu system. The initial screen that the users see, a straight HTML page, is reproduced next. When all of the images and data have been loaded by the script contained in INDEX.HTM, this initial HTML page is overwritten.

BASETREE.HTM

```
1  <HTML>
2  <BODY bgColor=white>
3  <center>
4  <h3>This site runs JavaScript&#174;. </h3>
5  <p>
6  You should not stop your browser while loading this page,
                a tree structure will be built in this left frame
                                        in a few seconds. <br>
7  (If not, click <a href="compatib.htm">here</a>.)
8  <br>
9  <font size=-1>Loading auxiliary bitmaps:<br>
10 <img src='clfolder.gif'><img src='opfolder.gif'>
11 <img src='node.gif'><img src='lastnode.gif'>
12 <img src='vertline.gif'><img src='blank.gif'>
13 <img src='doc.gif'><img src='link.gif'>
14 <br>
15 </center>
16 </BODY>
17 </HTML>
```

Here is the code that makes up the initial target frame, the frame that will hold all of the content that is called by the hierarchical menu:

BASEFLDR.HTM

```
1   <HTML>
2   <head>
3   <title>Welcome to Marcelino's Home Page</title>
4   </head>
5   <body bgcolor=white>
6   <center>
7   <br>
8   <img src="hptitle.gif" height=100 width=284>
9   <hr noshade size=3 color='black'>
10  <table>
11  <tr><td width=50><td>
12  Welcome. <br><br>
13  Hope you find whatever you're looking for. Here you have
    links to local documents with information about myself and
    some of the things I enjoy, as well as a very restrictive
    set of links to other places on the Web that I find useful
    and where I go back again and again. <br><br>
14  Browse this site using the <A HREF="fldrtree.html" target =
    "_top"><i>Folder-Tree</i></a> on the left side frame. Click
    a folder to display more folders; click a local document to
    display its contents on the right frame; click on a link to
    open a new window with the chosen site; close the Start
    Folder to see this page again.<br><br>
15  Questions, comments, suggestions? Please
    <A HREF="mailto:martins@hks.com">mail</a> me.<br>
16  Have fun!<br>
17  </table>
18  <hr noshade size=3 color='black'>
19  </center>
20  </BODY>
21  </HTML>
```

ANNOTATIONS

While this last script undoubtedly falls into the category of "Advanced JavaScript," if you've come this far, there is nothing in it that you should not be able to understand.

The script that creates the folder tree is found in the head of the frameset file, LOAD-ME.HTM.

The tree is displayed by means of eight tiny GIF files containing images of an open and closed folder, the document and link icons, the three line shapes (vertical branch, bottom-node corner, and vertical with right branch) that delineate the tree, and a blank used where there are no lines. These files appear briefly at the bottom of the text in the left frame before being almost immediately overwritten by the "Start folder" display. For a closer look at them, just click on your browser's Back button.

Each component of the tree is enclosed in a two-cell table: the left holds one or more of the GIFs, and the right the accompanying text derived from the strings in **generateTree( )**. To view the table setup, you can temporarily change the **border** settings in lines 157 and 188 from 0 to 1.

The data displayed in the tree is stored in a four-dimensional array. There are three keys to understanding this intricately designed script: **generateTree( )**, which builds the data array; **redrawTree( )**, which displays the data; and **openBranch( )**, which is called when the user clicks on a folder.

```
1    <!--
2    You are free to copy the "Folder-Tree" script
                        as long as you keep this copyright notice:
3    *
4    * Script found in:
                   http://www.geocities.com/Paris/LeftBank/2178/
5    *
6    * Author: Marcelino Alves Martins (martins@hks.com)
7    *
8    Version control:  Creation: January '97.
9                      Last changes: June '97
10
11   For other information refer to
12   http://www.geocities.com/Paris/LeftBank/2178/foldertree.html
13   -->
14   <HTML>
15   <HEAD>
16   <title>Marcelino Martins' Home Page</title>
17   <script LANGUAGE="JavaScript">
18   <!-- to hide script contents from old browsers
19
20   function generateTree()
21   {
22      var aux1, aux2, aux3
23      foldersTree = folderNode("Start folder")
```

generateTree( ) first declares three local variables that represent the three levels of folders within the tree. The easiest way to see the three levels is to open the entire tree. The first is represented by "Local docs" and "Web favorites"; the second, by "Profile," "Likes," "Friends with sites," "Readings," and so on; and the third, by the folders within the second, such as "Radios" and "Cameras" in "Sights & Sounds."

These variables are used in constructing **foldersTree**, the four-dimensional array containing the data. **foldersTree** is first assigned a call to **folderNode( )** (line 106), which creates and returns a four-member array. The first three are flags that we'll take a closer look at later; the fourth gets the folder's name from the argument passed to **folderNode( )**, in this case **"Start folder."** In other words, line 23 is the equivalent of writing

```
foldersTree[0] = 0
foldersTree[1] = 0
foldersTree[2] = 0
foldersTree[3] = "Start folder"
```

Next the variables come into play:

```
24    aux1 = appendChild(foldersTree, folderNode("Local docs"))
```

aux1 gets a call to **appendChild( )** (line 128) with **foldersTree** as its first argument and a new call to **folderNode( )** as its second. This attaches the new array returned by the call to **folderNode( )** to the end of **foldersTree**, so that

```
foldersTree[4][0] = 0
foldersTree[4][1] = 0
foldersTree[4][2] = 0
foldersTree[4][3] = "Local docs"
```

foldersTree is now a two-dimensional array.

```
25    aux2 = appendChild(aux1, leafNode("Profile"))
26    appendChild(aux2,
        generateDocEntry(0, "Personal info", "ident.html", ""))
27    appendChild(aux2,
            generateDocEntry(0, "Resume", "resume.html", ""))
```

These next three lines now add a third dimension to the array. **aux2** gets a call to **appendChild( )** with **aux1** as the first argument (the appendee) and a call to **leafNode( )** which, like **folderNode( )**, returns a four-member array (the appended). The only difference is that **leafNode( )** sets the third flag to "1" instead of "0" to indicate that this is a folder with no subfolders (a *leaf node* in the language of tree structures). In effect, this expands **foldersTree** with

```
foldersTree[4][4][0] = 0
foldersTree[4][4][1] = 0
foldersTree[4][4][2] = 1
foldersTree[4][4][3] = "Profile"
```

```
        foldersTree[4][4][4] = "[GIFlink] Personal info"
        foldersTree[4][4][5] = "[GIFlink] Resume"
```

The fourth and fifth members of the array are the strings returned by the calls to **generateDocEntry( )** in lines 26 and 27. The first argument indicates which of the two image files to use: "0" for DOC.GIF (material at the author's site) and "1" for LINK.GIF (links to other sites). The second argument is the name of the item, and the third, the HTML file associated with the link. The fourth argument, an empty string, is not used by the function.

generateDocEntry( ) (line 134) takes these three elements and returns a string consisting of an HTML anchor tag containing the image and link, followed by the item's name. **[GIFlink]** refers to the linked-image portion of the string.

```
28      aux2 = appendChild(aux1, leafNode("Likes"))
29      appendChild(aux2,
            generateDocEntry(0, "Portugal", "portugal.html", ""))
30      appendChild(aux2,
                generateDocEntry(0, "Music", "musica.htm", ""))
31      appendChild(aux2,
          generateDocEntry(0, "Books & Movies", "arts.html", ""))
```

Similarly, lines 28 through 31 generate **treeFolders[4][5][0]** through **treeFolders[4][5][6]**.

```
32      aux1 = appendChild(foldersTree,
                            folderNode("Web favorites"))
```

Next the new assignment to **aux1** in line 32 starts populating **treeFolders[5]** so that

```
        foldersTree[5][0] = 0
        foldersTree[5][1] = 0
        foldersTree[5][2] = 0
        foldersTree[5][3] = "Web favorites"
```

lines 33 to 43 then start filling the third dimension of **foldersTree[5]** in exactly the same way as we saw with **folders[4]**. The fourth dimension comes with the assignment to **aux3** in line 45.

```
45      aux3 = appendChild(aux2, leafNode("News"))
46      appendChild(aux3, generateDocEntry(1,
                                "CNN", "www.cnn.com/", ""))
47      appendChild(aux3, generateDocEntry(1,
                "PUBLICO", "www.publico.pt/publico/hoje", ""))
48      appendChild(aux3, generateDocEntry(1,
                                "Di&aacute;rio de Noticias",
                    "www.dn.pt/homepage/home.htm", ""))
49      appendChild(aux3, generateDocEntry(1, "Portuguese
        Soccer Championship", "www.dn.pt/des/primeira.htm", ""))
```

Those five lines result in

```
foldersTree[5][5][4][0] = 0
foldersTree[5][5][4][1] = 0
foldersTree[5][5][4][2] = 1
foldersTree[5][5][4][3] = "News"
foldersTree[5][5][4][4] = "[GIFlink] CNN"
foldersTree[5][5][4][5] = "[GIFlink] PUBLICO"
foldersTree[5][5][4][6] = "[GIFlink] Diário de Noticias"
foldersTree[5][5][4][7] =
                 "[GIFlink] Portuguese Soccer Championship"
```

This routine continues until line 103 generates the final member of the array, equivalent to

```
foldersTree[5][9][7][4] =
                 "[GIFlink] Edmund's Automobile Buyer's Guides"
```

You can read the array indexing directly from the tree. Each of the four levels nested in "Start folder" is a dimension, and the count at each folder starts at 4 (remember, the first three positions are always filled by flags). For example, backtracking from right to left, "The Dilbert Zone" is the first item [4] in "Cartoons," which is the second entry [5] in "Readings," itself the second [5] in "Web favorites," which is the second [5] under "Start folder," making it **foldersTree[5][5][5][4]**. Similarly, you can determine that "Motorcycle" is **foldersTree[5][5][9][4]**, "Downtown Providence" is **foldersTree[5][7][5][7]**, and so on.

Adding

```
top.folderFrame.document.write(foldersTree + '<br>')
```

after line 103 at the end of **generateTree( )** will display the entire **foldersTree** array as one long string in the main window. In the same way, you can use **document.write** to probe what's where in the array. Thus, the output from

```
top.folderFrame.document.write(foldersTree[5][8][4][5] + '<br>')
```

will be LINK.GIF with a link to **http://www.shareware.com** (look at the status bar when your mouse pointer is over it) and with the descriptive tag **shareware.com**. It's well worth exploring the array in this way to get a clear picture of exactly how and where the data is stored in **treeFolders**, and to see its leaves with their three components: image file, link, and text.

generateTree( ) is called from line 262 by **initializeTree( )**, which is assigned to the frameset's **onLoad** handler in line 271. There is also a second call in line 267 because, according to the author's comment, "sometimes when the user reloads the document Netscape 3.01 does not trigger the onLoad event."

```
106  function folderNode(name)
107  {
108      var arrayAux
109      arrayAux = new Array
110      arrayAux[0] = 0
```

```
111     arrayAux[1] = 0
112     arrayAux[2] = 0
113     arrayAux[3] = name
114     return arrayAux
115 }
116
117 function leafNode(name)
118 {
119     var arrayAux
120     arrayAux = new Array
121     arrayAux[0] = 0
122     arrayAux[1] = 0
123     arrayAux[2] = 1
124     arrayAux[3] = name
125     return arrayAux
126 }
```

Lines 106 through 126 contain the two array-makers, **folderNode( )** and **leafNode( )**, used by **generateTree( )**. They declare **arrayAux** as a **new Array**, then assign the Boolean flags to its first three members and their argument, **name**, to its fourth.

The first and second flags respectively keep track of whether each node and each folder is closed (0) or open (1). The third flag signals whether the node is a branch (0) or leaf (1), in other words, whether it contains subfolders or documents (leaves). This leaf setting is the only difference between **folderNode( )** and **leafNode( )**.

The two functions could be combined into one by adding a second argument that sets the third flag through assignment to **arrayAux[2]**, for instance:

```
function makeNode(name, flag) {
    [...]
    arrayAux[2] = flag;
    [...]
}
```

with the remainder of the function as is.

If you use **document.write( )** to examine the contents of **foldersTree**, you can watch the first two flag values change as different folders and subfolders are opened and closed.

```
128 function appendChild(parent, child)
129 {
130     parent[parent.length] = child
131     return child
132 }
```

The next subroutine used by **generateTree( )**, **appendChild( )**, receives the **foldersTree** array up to that point as its first argument, and the next member— whatever is returned by **folderNode( )**, **leafNode( )**, or **generateDocEntry( )**—as its second. Line 130 attaches that object to the end of **foldersTree** through the reference to **parent.length**, which indexes the next empty slot in the array. (Because array indexing begins with zero, the index of the last member of an array is **length** – 1.)

```
134  function generateDocEntry(icon, docDescription, link)
135  {
136     var retString =""
137     if (icon==0)
138        retString = "<A href='"+link+"' target=folderFrame>
                       <img src='doc.gif' alt='Opens in right frame'"
139     else
140        retString = "<A href='http://"+link+"' target=_blank>
                       <img src='link.gif' alt='Opens in new window'"
141     retString = retString + " border=0></a><td nowrap>
                              <font size=-1 face='Arial, Helvetica'>"
                                     + docDescription + "</font>"
142     return retString
143  }
```

The last of the subroutines used by **generateTree( )**, **generateDocEntry( )**, creates the linked-image and description strings stored in the leaves of the tree. The **icon** argument, whose value it tests, determines whether DOC.GIF or LINK.GIF is used as the image file. Moreover, in the former case, the **link** is to a page within the author's site, so a simple filename is used. In the latter, the links are to other sites, so the "http://" prefix is attached by line 140. Lines 138 and 140 assemble the HTML code for the graphic link, and then line 141 appends the closing anchor tag along with the font-formatted descriptive text.

```
145  function redrawTree()
146  {
147     var doc = top.treeFrame.window.document
148     doc.clear()
149     doc.write("<body bgcolor='white'>")
150     redrawNode(foldersTree, doc, 0, 1, "")
151     doc.close()
152  }
```

redrawTree( ), the second function called by **initializeTree( )** when the page is first loaded, is the main tree-display function. First, it declares **doc** as a local variable and assigns it **top.treeFrame.window.document**—the output area. This saves having to use the long reference in every statement.

Line 148 is puzzling because JavaScript has no documented **clear( )** method, yet it does not produce the expected "Window.Document.clear is not a function" error message. Attach **document.clear( )** to a button, and a click will make the document (whether in the same window or another frame) flash similar to a screen refresh. It does not clear the window or frame in the sense of deleting its contents to start out with a blank page.

Then after a line of HTML formatting, the call to **redrawNode( )** in line 150 produces the display.

```
154  function redrawNode(foldersNode, doc, level,
                                       lastNode, leftSide)
155  {
156      var i=0
157      doc.write("<table border=0 cellspacing=0 cellpadding=0>")
158      doc.write("<tr><td valign = middle nowrap>")
159      doc.write(leftSide)
```

redrawNode( )'s first argument, **foldersNode**, gets the entire **foldersTree** object. Its second argument, **doc**, gets the abbreviated reference from line 147. **level** starts out at 0 and is incremented in line 177 for folders containing subfolders. **LastNode** is a Boolean flag set to "1" for the last node on a branch (in other words, the last subfolder within a folder), otherwise its value is 0. Finally, **leftSide**, which starts out as an empty string, ends up getting the HTML code for the line or blank GIFs loaded into the left side of the two-cell tables used to display the file tree.

After declaring the loop-control variable, **i**, in line 156, **redrawNode( )** begins writing the table with the three calls to **doc.write( )**.

```
160      if (level>0)
161          if (lastNode)
162          {
163              doc.write("<img src='lastnode.gif'
                                         width=16 height=22>")
164              leftSide = leftSide + "<img src='blank.gif'
                                         width=16 height=22"
165          }
166          else
167          {
168              doc.write("<img src='node.gif'
                                         width=16 height=22>")
169              leftSide = leftSide + "<img src='vertline.gif'
                                         width=16 height=22"
170          }
```

Next the **if** in line 160 tests the value of **level**. If it is greater than zero, the **if** in 161 checks whether **lastNode** is set to zero or one. If it is 1 (true), LASTNODE.GIF is displayed and BLANK.GIF is added to **leftSide**. Otherwise the image file becomes NODE.GIF, and VERTLINE.GIF is tagged on to **leftSide**.

```
171     displayIconAndLabel(foldersNode, doc)
172     doc.write("</table>")
```

Then the call to **displayIconAndLabel( )** displays the image of the open or closed folder along with its descriptive text and the table is closed. The next **if** sequence, which spans the remainder of **redrawNode( )** from lines 173 to 199, handles open nodes that contain subnodes. A **length** greater than 4 indicates subnodes, and if **foldersNode[0]** is true, the first flag is set at "1," meaning the node is open.

```
173     if (foldersNode.length > 4 && foldersNode[0])
174     {
175         if (!foldersNode[2])
176         {
177             level=level+1
178             for (i=4; i<foldersNode.length;i++)
179                 if (i==foldersNode.length-1)
180                     redrawNode(foldersNode[i],
                                        doc, level, 1, leftSide)
181                 else
182                     redrawNode(foldersNode[i],
                                        doc, level, 0, leftSide)
183         }
```

Line 175 next checks the setting of the third flag. If it is 0, the item is not a leaf (document). In that case, **level** is incremented and the **for** loop displays the remainder of **foldersNode[i]** through recursive calls to **redrawNode( )**. For the last node (**length** – 1), the **lastNode** argument in the call is set to "1"; otherwise it remains 0.

```
184         else
185         {
186             for (i=4; i<foldersNode.length;i++)
187             {
188                 doc.write("<table border=0 cellspacing=0
                                    cellpadding=0 valign=center>")
189                 doc.write("<tr><td nowrap>")
190                 doc.write(leftSide)
191                 if (i==foldersNode.length - 1)
192                     doc.write("<img src='lastnode.gif'
                                            width=16 height=22>")
193                 else
194                     doc.write("<img src='node.gif'
                                            width=16 height=22>")
```

```
195             doc.write(foldersNode[i])
196             doc.write("</table>")
197         }
198     }
199   }
200 }
```

Lastly, the **else** routine extending from lines 184 to 198 processes folders that contain documents rather than subfolders. Again, **foldersNode.length** is used as the control in a **for** loop, and the **if** test in line 191 handles the final item within the folder by displaying LASTNODE.GIF instead of NODE.GIF. Then line 195 pulls the contents of **foldersNode[i]**, and line 196 closes the table.

```
202 function displayIconAndLabel(foldersNode, doc)
203 {
204   doc.write("<A href='javascript:
                  top.openBranch(\"" + foldersNode[3] + "\")'")
205   if (foldersNode[1])
206   {
207       doc.write("onMouseOver='window.status=
                  \"Close folder\"; return true'><img src=")
208       doc.write("opfolder.gif width=24 height=22
                                    border=noborder></a>")
209   }
210   else
211   {
212       doc.write("onMouseOver='window.status=
                  \"Open folder\"; return true'><img src=")
213       doc.write("clfolder.gif width=24 height=22
                                    border=noborder></a>")
214   }
215   doc.write("<td valign=middle align=left nowrap>")
216   doc.write("<font size=-1 face='Arial, Helvetica'>"
                                  +foldersNode[3]+"</font>")
217 }
```

The **displayIconAndLabel( )** subroutine is called by **redrawNode( )** in line 171. First it writes the HTML code for a **javascript** link that calls **openBranch( )** with the fourth member of **foldersNode**, the folder's name, as an argument. Then, if **foldersNode[1]** is set to "1," meaning the folder is open, it writes the code for a "Close folder" **onMouseOver** status-bar message and displays OPFOLDER.GIF, the open-folder icon. Otherwise it sets up an "Open Folder" help message and uses the closed-folder icon. Then lines 215 and 216 create the right-side table cell and fill it with the folder's name.

```
219 function closeFolders(foldersNode)
220 {
221     var i=0
222     if (!foldersNode[2])
223     {
224         for (i=4; i< foldersNode.length; i++)
225             closeFolders(foldersNode[i])
226     }
227     foldersNode[0] = 0
228     foldersNode[1] = 0
229 }
```

   closeFolders( ), called by **clickOnFolderRec( )** in line 237, sets the **foldersNode[0]** and **foldersNode[1]** flags to "0" to signal that the node and folder are closed, with the recursive call in the **for** loop on line 225 taking care of all the subfolders along a branch.

```
231 function clickOnFolderRec(foldersNode, folderName)
232 {
233     var i=0
234     if (foldersNode[3] == folderName)
235     {
236         if (foldersNode[0])
237             closeFolders(foldersNode)
238         else
239         {
240             foldersNode[0] = 1
241             foldersNode[1] = 1
242         }
243     }
244     else
245     {
246         if (!foldersNode[2])
247             for (i=4; i< foldersNode.length; i++)
248                 clickOnFolderRec(foldersNode[i], folderName)
249     }
250 }
```

   clickOnFolderRec( ) is called by **openBranch( )**, the function triggered by a user click on either a closed or open folder. Its first argument receives **foldersTree**, its second holds the name of the folder obtained from the argument to **openBranch( )**. If **folderName** matches **foldersNode[3]** (the array member that holds the name), the folder is either closed if it is open, or opened by setting the first two flags to "1." Otherwise, the recursive call in line 248 processes the rest of the branch.

```
252  function openBranch(branchName)
253  {
254      clickOnFolderRec(foldersTree, branchName)
255      if (branchName=="Start folder" && foldersTree[0]==0)
256          top.folderFrame.location="basefldr.htm"
257      timeOutId = setTimeout("redrawTree()",100)
258  }
```

openBranch( ) calls **clickOnFolderRec( )**, and if "Start folder" is closed, meaning the entire tree is closed, BASEFLDR.HTM is loaded into the main frame. Then **redrawTree( )** is called after a tenth-of-a-second timeout.

```
260  function initializeTree()
261  {
262      generateTree()
263      redrawTree()
264  }
265  var foldersTree = 0
266  var timeOutId = 0
267  generateTree()
```

As mentioned, **initializeTree( )** is assigned to the frameset's **onLoad** event handler so as to run when the page is loaded. It calls the two main functions that respectively create and display the file tree. Finally, the script ends by declaring **foldersTree** and **timeOutId** as global variables and initializing them with 0. The call to **generateTree( )** in line 267, as noted earlier, is to handle buggy behavior by Navigator 3.01 when the page is reloaded.

```
268  // end hiding contents from old browsers   -->
269  </script>
270  </HEAD>
271  <FRAMESET cols="200,*"  onLoad='initializeTree()'>
272      <FRAME src="basetree.htm" name="treeFrame">
273      <FRAME SRC="basefldr.htm" name="folderFrame">
274  </FRAMESET>
275  </HTML>
```

As you can see, this entire script is contained in the head of the frameset file—the ideal aerie for JavaScript code, because it can sit up there and create or be accessed by multiple pages without getting annihilated by a simple **document.write( )** or pageload. In working with layers, you also have the option of loading your page or pages of code into hidden layers. Only script written between the <LAYER> tags is local in scope; code contained in pages loaded into a layer can be referenced by other layers.

This complex, elegant script is undoubtedly an example of JavaScript at its finest. It performs a useful function. It creates a simple, friendly, and engaging user interface. And it makes full use of JavaScript's ability to construct complex data structures, as well as to accommodate relatively sophisticated algorithms and programming techniques.

The convergence of the Web with home/office information/communication/ multimedia/ entertainment systems is transforming web sites from passive collections of HTML text and graphic files into the dynamic interface that today's keyboard, mouse, and push-button users expect. JavaScript is one factor contributing to that change, and while its scope is limited to the browser, that stage is room enough to put on an impressive performance.

At the same time, as stressed throughout these pages, you can also use JavaScript to excess, concocting pages that spark reactions ranging from a wince to a groan to rage. No one really wants to see flashing titles, bouncing balls, and scrolling text in a scientific paper discussing muon-catalyzed cold fusion. Leave the gimmicks for the neon jungles and used-car dealers of cyberspace.

Yet as we have seen, JavaScript can do a lot more than dress up a page with jazzy, dazzling glitter. It already possesses substantial data-processing capacity, and its capabilities are enhanced with each new release. Moreover, as the next chapter reveals, it also has a lesser-known but valuable server-side face.

The power and beauty of a programming language are inevitably rooted in the building blocks it provides in the form of elements (keywords, statements, objects, properties, and methods) and grammar. But their expression, intensity, and creation depend entirely on you—the JavaScript programmer.

Server-Side Development

Contact Manager (manager)

U p to now, we have focused exclusively on JavaScript for the web client. Indeed, client-side JavaScript is very commonly used, but what about server-side scripting? Entire books about server-side JavaScript have been written. Netscape Communications, the creators of JavaScript, adapted the language for server-side functions and called it LiveWire.

Server-Side JavaScript

LiveWire is also the name of a product that you can buy with your Netscape web server. It includes tools for developing server-side JavaScript. Once you have mastered LiveWire, you can create numerous applications, from simple contact managers to complex web site management systems. LiveWire can be a good tool for creating rich, interactive content. If you want to create web applications that interact with Oracle, Sybase, or Informix databases, an enhanced version of Live-Wire, LiveWire Pro, ships with Netscape's Enterprise web server.

With LiveWire, you can create dynamic HTML pages that change based on changing data and user actions. Here is the basic procedure to create and run a LiveWire application:

- ◆ Create the source files (JavaScript embedded in HTML or JavaScript only).

- ◆ Compile the source files with the LiveWire compiler, to create the bytecode executable (WEB file).

- ◆ Install the application with Application Manager, to enable the LiveWire server extension to run the application.

- ◆ Run the application by accessing it with the Navigator; the LiveWire server extension generates dynamic HTML, which the client displays.

Programming with LiveWire Pro is not well documented, even by its creators, and database programmers will in particular run up against this. In the spirit of the Internet, developers exchange tips and tricks about LiveWire programming via Usenet newsgroups, web-based discussion forums, and the like. Still, any serious application tool requires extensive documentation.

It is far beyond the scope of this book to elaborate in detail about LiveWire. It is central to the Netscape web server architecture and can be used to develop full-featured database back-ends to the Netscape server environment. Author Dewayne McNair's server-side JavaScript example is intended as an introduction to LiveWire and as an overview of how server-side JavaScripts are constructed.

LiveWire comes with four main components, and all interaction with the server is handled through a web browser interface. The components are discussed next.

SiteManager   SiteManager has a two-pane interface. The left pane is a file manager, and you organize your site using this tool. The right pane, the property pane, displays attributes related to whatever object is selected in the left pane.

Navigator Gold or Netscape Composer   The Gold version of Netscape Navigator is the HTML-authoring interface for LiveWire. Even Netscape Composer—which ships with Netscape Communicator 4.0—is not a superior authoring environment, but it will do. It is required if you intend to author JavaScript using Netscape Visual JavaScript development software. Visual JavaScript (see Appendix A) is intended for those who are dying for a halfway decent authoring tool under LiveWire; Navigator Gold never supported creating and manipulating either frames or JavaScript.

The LiveWire Compiler   The LiveWire compiler compiles server-side JavaScript and runs it on the Netscape web server. Server-side JavaScript resides directly on HTML pages, between the <SERVER> and </SERVER> tags. You can also use the backquote or tick (`) character if you need to insert short JavaScript statements inside other HTML tags. The LiveWire package comes with a compiler that precompiles the JavaScript into run-time WEB files.

Server Extension and Application Manager   The LiveWire server extension includes Application Manager, a forms-based utility that lets you install and control server-side JavaScript applications.

As web clients attach to the server, the LiveWire extension creates a variety of objects. Your server-side JavaScript has access to the server's file system.

THE NETSCAPE SERVER-SIDE OBJECT MODEL

Server-side script is embedded in an HTML page. The web client request is directed to a URL that appears at first glance to be an ordinary web page. However, the request can be accompanied by query information (such as that generated by an HTML form), which runs a process or processes on the web server. LiveWire processes the contents of an HTTP request, such as URL, query string, headers, cookies, and any **Post** data, and creates a set of objects for the server-side scripts. These objects are data structures used to organize information.

For example, the **request** object holds information about an HTTP request. Netscape has a relatively simple **request** object that holds the kind of information exchanged all the time between client and server, such as the type of browser and IP address of the client.

The **client** object provides server-side scripts with a place to store information between user requests. It provides the necessary source of continuity, so a sequence of pages can behave in a programmed, predictable fashion despite the more or less stateless nature of the HTTP protocol. A script can save any data under any variable name in the client object. The client browser is sent a cookie that acts as a key to locate the data when the next request is sent to the same page or another page in the same server directory.

The **project** object provides server-side scripts with a set of common **data** objects shared by all the pages and related to all the clients of a common application program. Under this arrangement, a server-side application is the set of pages in a common subdirectory. This object can also be "locked." In this way, sensitive information or other resources will be used only one request at a time.

A **server** object represents features that are global to all applications hosted by the same server. In addition, it can be locked and can hold global user data.

Under nearly every other web-based exchange of data between the web client and a back-end process or database, the answer to the above-mentioned server-side, object-oriented exchange is usually CGI. An exception to this is the Microsoft Internet Information Server, which uses an object-based system that closely resembles the Netscape architecture.

LiveWire systems manage this normally problematic CGI-type data exchange automatically; the process is built in, so the programmer does not have to reinvent basic infrastructure.

NETSCAPE SCRIPT PROGRAMMING SERVICES

Although Netscape servers provide server-side scripts that can read or write disk files and provide access to databases, this database support is poorly documented. Netscape has made some improvement in this area since version 1.0 of its web server suite was released, but the manuals and even the online references are almost unusable for complex programming.

There are many unpleasant surprises for database programmers who desire to understand how objects work under the LiveWire system. Though LiveWire shows much potential in the database-application area, it needs to grow up. Its creators need to first provide better documentation for this language.

SERVER-SIDE SCRIPT SYNTAX

There are two ways to embed a JavaScript statement in HTML:

◆ With the SERVER tag, you precede JavaScript statements with <SERVER> and follow them with </SERVER>. The tags can enclose a single statement or several statements. Do not use a SERVER tag inside another HTML tag.

◆ With a backquote character, you can enclose JavaScript expressions inside HTML tags. This is done to generate HTML attributes or attribute values based on JavaScript values.

Using the SERVER tag, you can generate HTML with the **write** function, or simply execute a JavaScript statement.

The **write** function causes LiveWire to generate HTML. When the client accesses an application, it receives HTML from the server. The client does not recognize that the HTML came from a LiveWire application. A JavaScript statement that does not include a **write** function simply performs the statement and does not generate HTML.

The following excerpt from the Hello World sample application illustrates these two ways of using JavaScript:

```
<P>This time you are
<SERVER>
write(request.newname)
client.oldname = request.newname
</SERVER>
```

The first line generates HTML based on the value of **request.newname**. If **request.newname** is "Mr. Jones," it will generate this HTML:

```
<P>This time you are Mr. Jones.
```

The second line in the excerpt simply performs a JavaScript statement, assigning the value of **request.newname** to **client.oldname**. It does not generate any HTML.

When you use backquotes (\Q), you can enclose JavaScript expressions as substitutes for HTML attribute names or values. JavaScript embedded in HTML with backquotes automatically generates HTML; you do not need to use **write**.

For example, consider the following line:

```
<IMG SRC=\Q"images/hang" + client.num_misses + ".gif"\Q>
```

This line dynamically generates the name of the image to use based on the value of **client.num_misses**. The backquotes enclose a JavaScript expression that concatenates the string "images/hang" with the integer value of **client.num_misses** and ".gif". The result is a string such as "images/hang0.gif" or "images/hang1.gif". JavaScript automatically converts the integer value to a string. The result is HTML in the manner of

```
<IMG SRC="images/hang0.gif">
```

The order of the quotation marks is important. The backquote comes first, indicating what follows is a JavaScript expression consisting of a string ("images/hang"), concatenated with an integer (**client.num_misses**), concatenated with another string (".gif"). JavaScript converts the entire expression to a string, and LiveWire adds the necessary quotation marks around the attribute value. You cannot put a JavaScript expression for an attribute value inside double quotation marks, as it would be interpreted as the literal attribute value.

LiveWire automatically adds quotation marks around an attribute value when you enclose a JavaScript expression in backquotes. Do not provide them yourself, except for string literals, as in the preceding example.

For example, an anchor tag has HREF and may have NAME attributes, among others. HREF makes the tag a hyperlink, and NAME makes it a named anchor. The following script could create either a hyperlink or a target, depending on the value of the **attrib** and **val** properties of **client**:

```
<A \Qclient.attrib\Q = \Qclient.val\Q> Netscape Communications </A>
```

You could use the following code before the preceding statement to set the properties according to a request variable:

```
<SERVER>
if (request.choice == "link") {
   client.attrib = "HREF"
   client.val = "http://www.poopdeck.com"
}
if (request.choice == "target") {
   client.attrib = "NAME"
   client.val = "NetHead"
}
</SERVER>
```

If **request.choice** is "link," the result would be

```
<A HREF="http://home.poopdeck.com"> Poopdeck Inc. </A>
```

If **request.choice** is "target," the result would be

```
<A NAME="NetHead"> Poopdeck Inc.</A>
```

In either case, LiveWire adds the quotation marks around the attribute values produced in HTML.

manager

Contact Manager

| N2 | N2.01 | N2.02+ | N3 | N4 | E3 | E4 |

Written by Dewayne McNair, this server-side JavaScript application is a good example of the construction and implementation of LiveWire. It provides a simple name and address database; the interface provided in the example is intended for an administrator of the list. Although there is no administrator's login, it would be fairly easy to add that function.

Users can browse, add, and delete names in the list. The application presents a series of frames, with an HTML form that loads and displays names, addresses, phone numbers, and other information (see Figure 8-1).

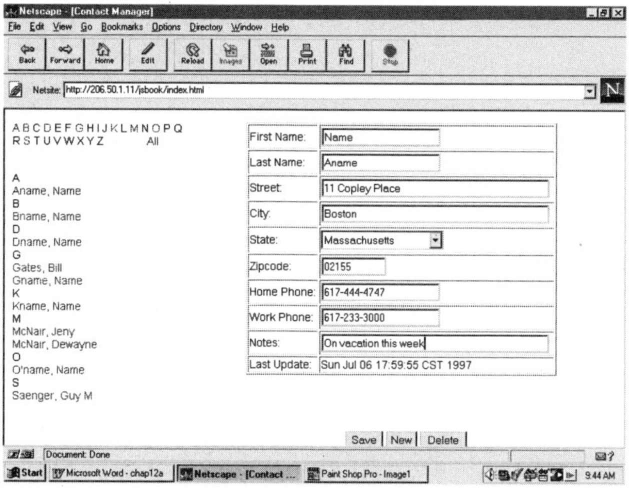

FIGURE 8-1. Users can browse, add, and delete names in the list

A precise search feature is not included. Users can view a list of all names in the list, or view only those names that start with a specific letter of the alphabet. The result of any operation is reflected.

The LiveWire application is intended for use at a company's web site, to replace the printed phone list that takes time to photocopy and distribute on a regular basis.

START.HTML

One of the optional configuration parameters for a LiveWire application is the *initial page.* This value is the name of the initial file that LiveWire serves when an application is first run and is generally used to initialize the application. This file, START.HTML, serves as the application's initial page.

```
1   <html>
2   <head>
3   <title>Contact Manager Start Page</title>
4   </head>
5   <server>
6     appInit ();
7     dbConnect ();
8   </server>
9   </html>
```

ANNOTATIONS

```
1    <html>
2    <head>
3    <title>Contact Manager Start Page</title>
4    </head>
5    <server>
6      appInit ();
7      dbConnect ();
8    </server>
9    </html>
```

Similar to other HTML constructs, LiveWire JavaScript code is enclosed in an opening tag <SERVER> and close tag </SERVER>. The function call to **appInit** on line 6 takes care of initializing several variables that will be used later in the application. On line 7, the call to **dbConnect** establishes a database connection that will be used throughout the application.

INDEX.HTML

This file defines the physical layout of the application by defining a series of framesets.

```
1    <html>
2    <head>
3    <title>Contact Manager</title>
4    </head>
5    <frameset cols="30%,*" border=0 borderwidth=0>
6    <frameset rows="15%,*">
7    <frame name="frame1" src="frame1.html" target=
     "frame2" scrolling=no>
8    <frame name="frame2" src="frame2.html" target=
     "frame3">
9    </frameset>
10   <frameset rows="92%,*">
11   <server>
12   write ('<frame name="frame3" src="frame3.html?
     id=' + request.id + '">')
13   </server>
14   <frame name="frame4" src="frame4.html" scrolling=no>
15   </frameset>
```

```
16    </frameset>
17    </html>
```

ANNOTATIONS

```
1     <html>
2     <head>
3     <title>Contact Manager</title>
4     </head>
5     <frameset cols="30%,*" border=0 borderwidth=0>
6     <frameset rows="15%,*">
7     <frame name="frame1" src="frame1.html" target=
      "frame2" scrolling=no>
8     <frame name="frame2" src="frame2.html" target=
      "frame3">
9     </frameset>
10    <frameset rows="92%,*">
11    <server>
12    write ('<frame name="frame3" src="frame3.html?
      id=' + request.id + '">')
13    </server>
```

Lines 11–13 define one of the frames by dynamically generating the HTML needed to pass a required parameter to the third frame.

```
14    <frame name="frame4" src="frame4.html" scrolling=no>
15    </frameset>
16    </frameset>
17    </html>
```

FRAME1.HTML

The scripts and contents of this file create an index of the existing contacts in the database. The alphabet is shown with each letter as a link to the corresponding section of frame 2. For instance, the letter *B* is a link to the section of frame 2 containing all of the contacts with a last name starting with *B*. If there are no contacts with a last name starting with *B*, the letter *B* is still shown, but there isn't a link. As will be shown later, this page is reloaded every time an addition or deletion occurs, so the index is guaranteed to stay in sync with the frame it is referencing—that is, frame 2 (see Figure 8-2).

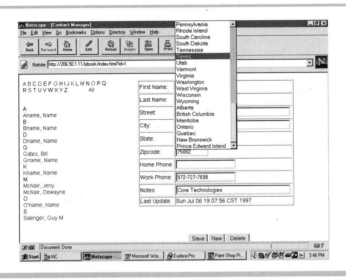

FIGURE 8-2.   A forms-based interface

```
1    <html>
2    <head>
3    <title></title>
4    <base target="frame2">
5    </head>
6    <body bgcolor="#ffffff">
7    <server>
8    var abc = "ABCDEFGHIJKLMNOPQRSTUVWXYZ"
9    function indexObject ()
10   {
11     for (var i = 0; i < abc.length; i++)
12     {
13       this[abc.charAt (i)] = 0
14     }
15     return (this)
16   }
17
18   var contact_idx = new indexObject ()
19   var sql = "select lname[1] from contact order
     by lname"
20   var cursor = database.cursor (sql)
21   while (cursor.next ())
22   {
```

```
23    var idx = cursor.lname.toUpperCase ()
24    contact_idx[idx]++;
25  }
26  cursor.close ()
27
28  for (var i = 0; i < abc.length; i++)
29  {
30    if (contact_idx[abc.charAt (i)] == 0)
31      write (abc.charAt (i) + ' ')
32    else
33      write ('<a href="frame2.html#' + abc.
         charAt (i) + '">' +
34            abc.charAt (i) + '</a> ')
35  }
36  write ('         
        ');
37  write ('<a href="showall.html" target="_top">
     All</a>');
38  </server>
39  </body>
40  </html>
```

ANNOTATIONS

```
1    <html>
2    <head>
3    <title></title>
4    <base target="frame2">
5    </head>
```

Setting the target value in the BASE tag ensures that all actions in this frame will be directed to the frame indicated. The **target** parameter could just as easily have been added to each individual link instead of being placed in the HEAD section— this just saves some typing.

```
6    <body bgcolor="#ffffff">
7    <server>
8    var abc = "ABCDEFGHIJKLMNOPQRSTUVWXYZ"
9    function indexObject ()
10   {
11     for (var i = 0; i < abc.length; i++)
12     {
13       this[abc.charAt (i)] = 0
```

```
14      }
15    return (this)
16  }
17
18  var contact_idx = new indexObject ()
```

The first function of this file, **indexObject**, creates an array consisting of the letters of the alphabet. Using the string **abc** defined earlier, lines 11–13 initialize the key's values to be zero. This associative array provides a convenient way to determine if an item has been previously seen. Line 18 initializes storage for the new array and assigns it to **contact_idx**.

```
19  var sql = "select lname[1] from contact order
    by lname"
20  var cursor = database.cursor (sql)
```

Line 19 defines an SQL query to pull the first character of the last name of each entry in the contact table. Furthermore, the result set will be ordered by the last name field, guaranteeing that all of the *A*'s will be grouped together, all of the *B*'s, and so on.

```
21  while (cursor.next ())
22  {
23      var idx = cursor.lname.toUpperCase ()
24      contact_idx[idx]++;
25  }
```

In looping through the result set, the associative array defined earlier is used to keep track of how many times each letter is seen. If the contact table contains five contacts with last name starting with *A*, two starting with *B*, 20 starting with *C*, and zero starting with *D*, the resulting structure of **contact_idx** will be

```
contact_idx['A'] = 5
contact_idx['B'] = 2
contact_idx['C'] = 20
contact_idx['D'] = 0
```

The value of each item is of little significance. It is only important that the application knows whether entries exist for a given letter. As you may have guessed, this will be used to decide whether a link needs to be created for each letter.

```
26  cursor.close ()
27
```

Nothing magical here—close the cursor and move on.

```
28  for (var i = 0; i < abc.length; i++)
29  {
```

```
30    if (contact_idx[abc.charAt (i)] == 0)
31       write (abc.charAt (i) + ' ')
32    else
33       write ('<a href="frame2.html#' + abc.
         charAt (i) + '">' +
34             abc.charAt (i) + '</a> ')
35    }
```

Lines 28–35 make up the bulk of the work done by this page. Again, looping through each character in the string, line 30 uses the previously gathered information to determine if there are any entries for the current character. If not, the letter is simply printed. If so, a link to the appropriate section of frame 2 is generated.

```
36    write ('         
            ');
37    write ('<a href="showall.html" target="_top">
         All</a>');
38    </server>
```

Finally, a link is shown to another page that will display all of the contacts in a printable format. Notice again in line 37 the mixed use of single and double quotes. When generating HTML, it is often easier to use single quotes to delimit string literals, as most HTML tags can contain one or more sets of double quotes marking their parameters and values. On the other hand, double quotes are often easier to use when you're dynamically building SQL queries.

```
39    </body>
40    </html>
```

FRAME2.HTML

The scripts and contents of this file print a list of the contacts sorted by last name. Each contact is a link that, when clicked, shows all of the detail information for that person in frame 3.

```
1    <html>
2    <head>
3    <title></title>
4    <base target="frame3">
5    </head>
6    <body bgcolor="#ffffff">
7    <server>
8    var current_char = ""
```

```
9    var sql = "select * from contact order by lname"
10   var cursor = database.cursor (sql)
11   while (cursor.next ())
12   {
13     if (current_char != cursor.lname.charAt (0))
14     {
15       current_char = cursor.lname.charAt (0);
16       writeln ('<a name="' + current_char +'">
         </a>' +
17             current_char + '<br>')
18     }
19     writeln ('<a href="frame3.html?id=' + cursor.
       id + '">' +
20             trim (cursor.lname) + ', ' + trim (cursor.
             fname) + '</A><br>')
21   }
22   cursor.close ()
23   </server>
24   </body>
25   </html>
```

ANNOTATIONS

```
1    <html>
2    <head>
3    <title></title>
4    <base target="frame3">
5    </head>
```

As in FRAME2.HTML, the target of all actions in this frame is set to be a different frame—frame 3 in this case.

```
6    <body bgcolor="#ffffff">
7    <server>
8    var current_char = ""
9    var sql = "select * from contact order by lname"
10   var cursor = database.cursor (sql)
```

Line 7 defines a variable that will be used to keep track of the first letter of the last name of the contact currently being printed. Lines 9–10 create a cursor pulling all contacts from the database ordered by last name.

```
11  while (cursor.next ())
12  {
13    if (current_char != cursor.lname.charAt (0))
14    {
15      current_char = cursor.lname.charAt (0);
16      writeln ('<a name="' + current_char +'">
      </a>' +
17              current_char + '<br>')
18    }
```

In looping through the result set of the query, a check is made to determine if the first character of the last name of the entry being printed is different from that of the previous entry. If so, a heading needs to be printed, and the value of **current_char** updated.

```
19    writeln ('<a href="frame3.html?id=' + cursor.
      id + '">' +
20            trim (cursor.lname) + ', ' + trim (cursor.
              fname) + '</A><br>')
21  }
```

Each entry is then printed with a link being created around the last name, first name pair. Before being printed, however, the values for last name and first name are sent to a function that trims (that is, deletes) any trailing white space.

```
22  cursor.close ()
23  </server>
24  </body>
25  </html>
```

FRAME3.HTML

The scripts and contents of this file display the detail information on each contact. By use of a form, the data is presented such that it may be updated or changed at the same time as it is viewed. The contact to display is determined by the value of **id** passed in via a **Post** or **Get**. This frame and page also serve as the method for entering new contacts by passing a value of zero for **id** (see Figure 8-3).

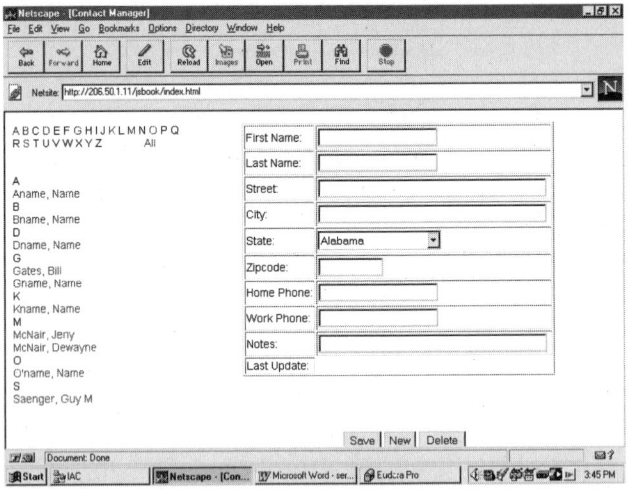

FIGURE 8-3.   Enter new names using an HTML form

```
1   <html>
2   <head>
3   <title></title>
4   </head>
5   <server>
6   function copyContact (obj)
7   {
8     this.id      = (isNum (obj.id) ? obj.
      id      + "" : "0")
9     this.fname   = (obj.fname   ? obj.
      fname   + "" : "");
10    this.lname   = (obj.lname   ? obj.
      lname   + "" : "");
11    this.street  = (obj.street  ? obj.
      street  + "" : "");
12    this.city    = (obj.city    ? obj.
      city    + "" : "");
13    this.state   = (obj.state   ? obj.
      state   + "" : "");
14    this.zipcode = (obj.zipcode ? obj.
      zipcode + "" : "");
15    this.homephone = (obj.homephone ? obj.
      homephone + "" : "");
```

```
16   this.workphone  = (obj.workphone ? obj.
     workphone + "" : "");
17   this.notes      = (obj.notes     ? obj.
     notes     + "" : "");
18   this.lastupdate = (obj.lastupdate ? obj.
     lastupdate + "" : "");
19   return (this);
20 }
21 </server>
22 <body bgcolor="#ffffff">
23 <server>
24 var sql = "select * from contact where id=
   '" + request.id + "'";
25 var cursor = database.cursor (sql);
26 cursor.next ();
27 var contact = new copyContact (cursor);
28 cursor.close ();
29 for (var i in contact)
30 {
31   contact[i] = trim (contact[i]);
32 }
33 </server>
34 <form name="form" action="contact.html">
35 <input type="hidden" name="id" value=
   `contact.id`>
36 <input type="hidden" name="op" value="">
37 <center>
38 <table border=1>
39 <tr>
40   <td>First Name:</td>
41   <td>
42     <input type="text" name="fname" value=
       `contact.fname`
43           size=20 maxlength=20>
44   </td>
45 </tr>
46 <tr>
47   <td>Last Name:</td>
48   <td>
49     <input type="text" name="lname" value=
       `contact.lname`
50           size=20 maxlength=20>
51   </td>
```

```
52  </tr>
53  <tr>
54    <td>Street:</td>
55    <td>
56      <input type="text" name="street" value=
      `contact.street`
57            size=40 maxlength=80>
58    </td>
59  </tr>
60  <tr>
61    <td>City:</td>
62    <td>
63      <input type="text" name="city" value=`
      contact.city`
64            size=40 maxlength=40>
65    </td>
66  </tr>
67  <tr>
68    <td>State:</td>
69    <td>
70      <server>
71        sql = "select code, value from
        lookup where type='STATE'";
72        dbShowSelect ("state", contact.
        state, sql);
73      </server>
74    </td>
75  </tr>
76  <tr>
77    <td>Zipcode:</td>
78    <td>
79      <input type="text" name="zipcode" value=
      `contact.zipcode`
80            size=10 maxlength=10>
81    </td>
82  </tr>
83  <tr>
84    <td>Home Phone:</td>
85    <td>
86      <input type="text" name="homephone" value=
      `contact.homephone`
87            size=20 maxlength=20>
88    </td>
```

```
89   </tr>
90   <tr>
91     <td>Work Phone:</td>
92     <td>
93       <input type="text" name="workphone" value=
          `contact.workphone`
94               size=20 maxlength=20>
95     </td>
96   </tr>
97   <tr>
98     <td>Notes:</td>
99     <td>
100     <textarea name="notes" rows=5 cols=40>
        <server>write (contact.notes)</server></textarea>
101    </td>
102  </tr>
103  <tr>
104    <td>Last Update:</td>
105    <td>
106    <server>
107       writeln (contact.lastupdate);
108    </server>
109    </td>
110  </tr>
111  </table>
112  </center>
113  </form>
114  </body>
115  </html>
```

ANNOTATIONS

```
1    <html>
2    <head>
3    <title></title>
4    </head>
5    <server>
6    function copyContact (obj)
7    {
8      this.id        = (isNum (obj.id) ? obj.
       id        + "" : "0")
9      this.fname     = (obj.fname     ? obj.
```

```
       fname        + "" : "");
10     this.lname       = (obj.lname      ? obj.
       lname        + "" : "");
11     this.street      = (obj.street     ? obj.
       street       + "" : "");
12     this.city        = (obj.city       ? obj.
       city         + "" : "");
13     this.state       = (obj.state      ? obj.
       state        + "" : "");
14     this.zipcode     = (obj.zipcode    ? obj.
       zipcode      + "" : "");
15     this.homephone   = (obj.homephone  ? obj.
       homephone    + "" : "");
16     this.workphone   = (obj.workphone  ? obj.
       workphone    + "" : "");
17     this.notes       = (obj.notes      ? obj.
       notes        + "" : "");
18     this.lastupdate = (obj.lastupdate ? obj.
       lastupdate + "" : "");
19     return (this);
20   }
```

In LiveWire, trying to access a variable that doesn't exist or has a **null** value often causes unpredictable results. In the design of the database for this application, we specified that most fields could contain **null** values. To deal with the possible problems from this, the **copyContact** function is employed to create a new **contact** object based on values from a **cursor** object. The new **contact** object has the same fields as the cursor, but checks are made to make sure the properties are either the same value as the cursor or empty (not **null**).

```
21   </server>
22   <body bgcolor="#ffffff">
23   <server>
24   var sql = "select * from contact where id=
     '" + request.id + "'";
25   var cursor = database.cursor (sql);
26   cursor.next ();
27   var contact = new copyContact (cursor);
28   cursor.close ();
```

The SQL query defined on line 24 selects all of the information for the specific contact identified by **request.id**. A "safe" copy of the contact information in the cursor is made and the cursor is closed.

```
29   for (var i in contact)
30   {
```

```
31    contact[i] = trim (contact[i]);
32  }
```

Lines 29–32 show how it is possible to programmatically loop through all of the attributes of an object. Here, each item is trimmed of any trailing white space and saved to its original position.

```
33  </server>
34  <form name="form" action="contact.html">
35  <input type="hidden" name="id" value=
    `contact.id`>
```

Line 35 shows a method of referencing LiveWire variables outside of the normal <SERVER></SERVER> constructs. Valid only in HTML form elements of type **input**, this syntax allows LiveWire to fill in the value of the variable **contact.id** as the page is parsed and delivered to the client. Surrounding quotes are added for the value, so that multiple word values do not cause problems. If **contact.id** had a value of 10, the resulting line would be

```
<input type="hidden" name="id" value="10">
```

```
36  <input type="hidden" name="op" value="">
```

A hidden variable **op** is created, which will be used to signal later functions, the type of operation the user wants to perform. Its value will be dynamically set before the submission of this page to be the action selected by the user.

```
37  <center>
38  <table border=1>
39  <tr>
40    <td>First Name:</td>
41    <td>
42      <input type="text" name="fname" value=
        `contact.fname`
43            size=20 maxlength=20>
44    </td>
45  </tr>
46  <tr>
47    <td>Last Name:</td>
48    <td>
49      <input type="text" name="lname" value=
        `contact.lname`
50            size=20 maxlength=20>
51    </td>
52  </tr>
53  <tr>
54    <td>Street:</td>
55    <td>
```

```
56        <input type="text" name="street" value=
          `contact.street`
57                size=40 maxlength=80>
58    </td>
59  </tr>
60  <tr>
61    <td>City:</td>
62    <td>
63        <input type="text" name="city" value=
          `contact.city`
64                size=40 maxlength=40>
65    </td>
66  </tr>
```

Lines 39–66 use basic HTML to create the form elements for displaying the contact's first and last name, street address, and city. The LiveWire variables containing the values needed are again referenced by use of the `variable` construct. Using this method makes the code much more readable and thus easier to maintain.

```
67  <tr>
68    <td>State:</td>
69    <td>
70        <server>
71            sql = "select code, value from
              lookup where type='STATE'";
72            dbShowSelect ("state", contact.
              state, sql);
73        </server>
74    </td>
75  </tr>
```

To display a list of states and their two-letter codes, the function **dbShowSelect** is called. **DbShowSelect** is a generic function defined as

DbShowSelect (arg1, arg2, arg3)

where **arg1** is the name to give to the selected item, **arg2** is the default value, and **arg3** is an SQL statement that generates a result set of name and value pairs. The name and value will be used to create an option item for each row in the result set.

```
76  <tr>
77    <td>Zipcode:</td>
78    <td>
79        <input type="text" name="zipcode" value=
          `contact.zipcode`
80                size=10 maxlength=10>
81    </td>
```

```
82  </tr>
83  <tr>
84    <td>Home Phone:</td>
85    <td>
86       <input type="text" name="homephone" value=
         `contact.homephone`
87                size=20 maxlength=20>
88    </td>
89  </tr>
90  <tr>
91    <td>Work Phone:</td>
92    <td>
93       <input type="text" name="workphone" value=
         `contact.workphone`
94                size=20 maxlength=20>
95    </td>
96  </tr>
```

As before, lines 76–96 use basic HTML to create form elements for displaying the ZIP code, home phone, and work phone.

```
97  <tr>
98    <td>Notes:</td>
99    <td>
100      <textarea name="notes" rows=5 cols=40>
         <server>write (contact.notes)</server></textarea>
101    </td>
102 </tr>
```

As stated earlier, the `variable` construct only works with form elements of type **input**. To display the value for a **textarea** element, the value must be written by use of the <SERVER></SERVER> tags. The function **write** is used instead of **writeln**, to avoid having an extraneous blank line displayed in the **textarea** box.

```
103 <tr>
104    <td>Last Update:</td>
105    <td>
106    <server>
107       writeln (contact.lastupdate);
108    </server>
109    </td>
110 </tr>
```

Shown only as informational and not editable, the time this record was last updated is displayed to the user.

```
111  </table>
112  </center>
113  </form>
114  </body>
115  </html>
```

FRAME4.HTML

The scripts and contents of this file display a series of buttons that allows users to add a new contact, save any edits they've made on the current contact, or delete the current contact. Each of the buttons has an associated **onClick** method that performs action-specific checks and then invokes the **submit** method of the form declared in frame 3. These functions provide an example of cross-frame communication as well as examples of client-to-server communication.

```
1   <html>
2   <head>
3   <title></title>
4   <script>
5   function properName (obj)
6   {
7     var first = obj.value.charAt (0);
8     var rest  = obj.value.substring (1, obj.value.length);
9     obj.value = first.toUpperCase () + rest;
10  }
11
12  function emptyValue (value, fieldname)
13  {
14    if (value == null || value == "")
15    {
16      alert (fieldname + " cannot be empty.")
17        return (true)
18    }
19    return (false)
20  }
21
22  function validateData ()
23  {
24    properName (top.frame3.document.form.fname);
25    properName (top.frame3.document.form.lname);
26    if (emptyValue (top.frame3.document.form.
      fname.value, "First Name"))
27        return (false);
```

```
28    if (emptyValue (top.frame3.document.form.
      lname.value, "Last Name"))
29       return (false);
30    return (true);
31  }
32
33  function doSave ()
34  {
35    if (! validateData ())
36       return (false);
37    top.frame3.document.form.op.value = "SAVE";
38    top.frame3.document.form.submit ();
39    return (true);
40  }
41
42  function doNew ()
43  {
44    top.frame3.location = "frame3.html?id=0";
45    return (true)
46  }
47
48  function doDelete ()
49  {
50    if (! confirm ("Are you sure you want
      to delete this item?"))
51      return (false);
52    top.frame3.document.form.op.value = "DELETE";
53    top.frame3.document.form.submit ();
54    return (true);
55  }
56  </script>
57  </head>
58
59  <body bgcolor="#ffffff">
60  <form name="form" method="POST">
61  <center>
62  <input type="button" name="save"
63                     value="Save" onClick=
                       "return (doSave ())">
64  <input type="button" name="add"
65                     value="New" onClick=
                       "return (doNew ())">
66  <input type="button" name="del"
```

```
67                      value="Delete" onClick=
   "return (doDelete ())">
68   </center>
69   </form>
70   </body>
71   </html>
```

ANNOTATIONS

```
1    <html>
2    <head>
3    <title></title>
4    <script>
5    function properName (obj)
6    {
7      var first = obj.value.charAt (0);
8      var rest  = obj.value.substring (1, obj.value.length);
9      obj.value = first.toUpperCase () + rest;
10   }
```

This function is a simplistic example of massaging data on the client side before it is sent to the server. The first character of the supplied string is forced to uppercase, and the resulting string is returned.

```
11
12   function emptyValue (value, fieldname)
13   {
14     if (value == null || value == "")
15       {
```

The passed in value is checked against the preceding two conditions to determine if it is indeed empty. Another case that might be added to the conditions is if the value contained only spaces or tabs.

```
16       alert (fieldname + " cannot be empty.")
17       return (true)
```

Now that the supplied string has been deemed empty, a warning needs to be shown to the user so that the problem can be corrected. Passing in the field name makes this function generic enough to work for the different form elements, and at the same time gives the user specific information about which field contained an error.

```
18     }
19     return (false)
20   }
```

If the supplied string was not empty, **false** is returned.

```
21
22    function validateData ()
23    {
24       properName (top.frame3.document.form.fname);
25       properName (top.frame3.document.form.lname);
26       if (emptyValue (top.frame3.document.form.
      fname.value, "First Name"))
27            return (false);
28       if (emptyValue (top.frame3.document.form.
      lname.value, "Last Name"))
29            return (false);
30      return (true);
31    }
```

The first task of this function is to verify that the user has supplied data for the required fields—**fname** and **lname**. The **emptyValue** function is used to check a value and display a label. If the first argument to **emptyValue** is either **null** or empty, an alert box will be displayed informing the user that the field identified by the second argument cannot be empty, and a value of **true** is returned. If the first argument is non**null** or nonempty, the function returns **false**. If **emptyValue** returns **true**, the data supplied by the user is not valid and a value of **false** is returned to the caller.

```
32
33   function doSave ()
34   {
35     if (! validateData ())
36         return (false);
```

The user has selected the option to save changes, but before the request is processed, the data the user supplied should be checked for validity. The function **validateData( )** does this, returning **true** if the data checks out, **false** otherwise.

```
37     top.frame3.document.form.op.value = "SAVE";
38     top.frame3.document.form.submit ();
39     return (true);
40   }
```

Line 37 sets a variable that will be used on the server side to determine what action to take. In this case, "op" stands for "Operation." Line 38 calls the submit action for the form, and line 39 exits the function.

```
41
42   function doNew ()
43   {
44     top.frame3.location = "frame3.html?id=0";
```

```
45    return (true)
46  }
```

The user has selected the option to create a new record. To process this request, the location value of frame 3 is replaced. A value of 0 is used for the **id** to indicate a new record is to be created.

```
47
48  function doDelete ()
49  {
50    if (! confirm ("Are you sure you want
      to delete this item?"))
51      return (false);
```

The user has selected the option to delete the current record. However, deleting a record is usually a drastic act, so the user is asked to confirm the actions. The **confirm** function displays a message to users allowing them to either press OK or Cancel. If the user presses Cancel, **false** is returned and this function ends. The function continues if the user presses "OK"—in other words, if **true** is returned (see Figure 8-4).

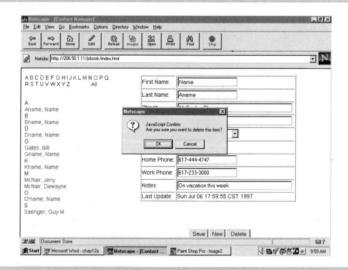

FIGURE 8-4. Record deletions must be confirmed

```
52    top.frame3.document.form.op.value = "DELETE";
53    top.frame3.document.form.submit ();
54    return (true);
55  }
```

Line 52 sets a variable that will be used on the server side to determine what action to take. Line 53 calls the submit action for the form, and line 54 exits the function.

```
56  </script>
57  </head>
58
59  <body bgcolor="#ffffff">
60  <form name="form" method="POST">
61  <center>
62  <input type="button" name="save"
63                      value="Save" onClick=
    "return (doSave ())">
64  <input type="button" name="add"
65                      value="New" onClick=
                        "return (doNew ())">
66  <input type="button" name="del"
67                      value="Delete" onClick=
    "return (doDelete ())">
68  </center>
69  </form>
```

Lines 60–69 define the action buttons and their associated **onClick** values. The functions **doSave**, **doNew**, and **doDelete** ultimately return **false** so that no action is actually taken by the browser.

```
70  </body>
71  </html>
```

CONTACT.HTML

The scripts and contents of this file are as follows:

```
1   <html>
2   <head>
3   <title></title>
4   </head>
5   <server>
6   function saveContact ()
7   {
8     var id = 0;
9     var code = 0;
10    var sql = "select * from contact where id=
      '" + request.id + "'";
11    if (recordExists (sql))
```

```
12    {
13        sql = "update contact set " +
14        "fname=" + checkForNull (replace
          Char (request.fname, "'", "''")) +
15        "lname=" + checkForNull (replace
          Char (request.lname, "'", "''")) +
16        "street=" + checkForNull (replace
          Char (request.street, "'", "''"))+
17        "city=" + checkForNull (replace
          Char (request.city, "'", "''"))+
18        "state=" + checkForNull (replace
          Char (request.state, "'", "''"))+
19        "zipcode=" + checkForNull(replace
          Char(request.zipcode,"'","''")) +
20        "homephone="+checkForNull(replace
          Char(request.homephone,"'","''"))+
21        "workphone="+checkForNull(replace
          Char(request.workphone,"'","''"))+
22        "notes=" + checkForNull (replace
          Char (request.notes, "'", "''"))+
23       "lastupdate=" + "'" + getTodays
         TimeStamp() + "'" +
24        " where id='" + request.id + "'";
25        code = database.execute (sql);
26        checkDBCode (code);
27        id = request.id;
28    }
29    else
30    {
31        sql = "insert into contact (" +
32              "fname, lname, street, city,
              state, zipcode," +
33              "homephone, workphone, notes,
              lastupdate) values (" +
34              checkForNull (replace
               Char (request.fname, "'", "''")) +
35              checkForNull (replace
               Char (request.lname, "'", "''")) +
36              checkForNull (replace
               Char (request.street, "'", "''")) +
37              checkForNull (replace
               Char (request.city, "'", "''")) +
38              checkForNull (replace
```

```
              Char (request.state, "'", "''")) +
39            checkForNull (replace
              Char (request.zipcode, "'", "''")) +
40            checkForNull (replace
              Char (request.homephone, "'", "''")) +
41            checkForNull (replace
              Char (request.workphone, "'", "''")) +
42            checkForNull (replace
              Char (request.notes, "'", "''")) +
43            "'" + getTodays
              TimeStamp() + "')";
44      id = getSerialFromInsert (sql);
45    }
46
47    return (id);
48  }
49
50  function deleteContact ()
51  {
52    var sql = "delete from contact where id=
      '" + request.id + "'";
53    var code = database.execute (sql);
54    checkDBCode (code);
55    return (0);
56  }
57
58  var id = 0;
59  if (request.op == "SAVE")
60    id = saveContact ();
61  else if (request.op == "DELETE")
62    id = deleteContact ();
63  writeln ('<script>')
64  writeln ('<!--- Hide script from old browsers.')
65  writeln ('top.location = "index.html?id=
      ' + id + '"')
66  writeln ('// End the hiding here. -->')
67  writeln ('</script>')
68  </server>
69
70  <body bgcolor="#ffffff">
71  </body>
72  </html>
```

ANNOTATIONS

```
1    <html>
2    <head>
3    <title></title>
4    </head>
5    <server>
6    function saveContact ()
7    {
8      var id = 0;
9      var code = 0;
10     var sql = "select * from contact where id=
       '" + request.id + "'";
11     if (recordExists (sql))
```

Although it may not seem like it, **saveContact** is a relatively simple function. A check is made on line 11 to determine if an update or insert is needed, should a record already exist with the current **id**. The caller of this function expects to receive a value to be used as the **id** of the record to be displayed in frame 3.

```
12       {
13         sql = "update contact set " +
14         "fname=" + checkForNull (replace
           Char (request.fname, "'", "''")) +
15         "lname=" + checkForNull (replace
           Char (request.lname, "'", "''")) +
16         "street=" + checkForNull (replace
           Char (request.street, "'", "''"))+
17         "city=" + checkForNull (replace
           Char (request.city, "'", "''"))+
18         "state=" + checkForNull (replace
           Char (request.state, "'", "''"))+
19         "zipcode=" + checkForNull(replace
           Char(request.zipcode,"'","''")) +
20         "homephone="+checkForNull(replace
           Char(request.homephone,"'","''"))+
21         "workphone="+checkForNull(replace
           Char(request.workphone,"'","''"))+
22         "notes=" + checkForNull (replace
           Char (request.notes, "'", "''"))+
23         "lastupdate=" + "'" + getTodays
           TimeStamp() + "'" +
24         " where id='" + request.id + "'";
```

Lines 13–24 build the SQL statement used to perform the update. Line 25 uses the **database** object to execute the query. Line 26 checks the return code from the function. Lastly, line 27 sets the value of the **id** to return to the caller to be the same as was passed in.

```
25        code = database.execute (sql);
26        checkDBCode (code);
27        id = request.id;
28     }
29     else
30     {
31        sql = "insert into contact (" +
32               "fname, lname, street, city,
               state, zipcode," +
33               "homephone, workphone, notes,
               lastupdate) values (" +
34               checkForNull (replace
               Char (request.fname, "'", "''")) +
35               checkForNull (replace
               Char (request.lname, "'", "''")) +
36               checkForNull (replace
               Char (request.street, "'", "''")) +
37               checkForNull (replace
               Char (request.city, "'", "''")) +
38               checkForNull (replace
               Char (request.state, "'", "''")) +
39               checkForNull (replace
               Char (request.zipcode, "'", "''")) +
40               checkForNull (replace
               Char (request.homephone, "'", "''")) +
41               checkForNull (replace
               Char (request.workphone, "'", "''")) +
42               checkForNull (replace
               Char (request.notes, "'", "''")) +
43               "'" + getTodays
               TimeStamp () + "')";
44        id = getSerialFromInsert (sql);
45     }
46
47     return (id);
48  }
49
```

Lines 31–43 build the SQL statement used to perform an insert. Line 44 calls a specialized function that performs the insert and returns the value assigned to the serial field **id**. This serial field is maintained by the database engine and is used as a unique identifier for each contact. Line 47 exits the function by returning to the caller the value of the updated contact **id**.

```
50   function deleteContact ()
51   {
52     var sql = "delete from contact where id=
       '" + request.id + "'";
53     var code = database.execute (sql);
54     checkDBCode (code);
55     return (0);
56   }
```

In **deleteContact( )**, a pass-through SQL query is utilized to perform the deletion of the specified contact. The **execute** method of the **database** object is used when no answer set will be returned. The database return code is checked to make sure the delete was successful, and a value of zero is returned. The caller uses the value returned as the new contact to display, and as stated earlier, a value of zero forces a blank or new contact.

```
57
58   var id = 0;
59   if (request.op == "SAVE")
60     id = saveContact ();
61   else if (request.op == "DELETE")
62     id = deleteContact ();
63   writeln ('<script>')
64   writeln ('<!--- Hide script from old browsers.')
65   writeln ('top.location = "index.html?id=
       ' + id + '"')
66   writeln ('// End the hiding here. -->')
67   writeln ('</script>')
68   </server>
69
70   <body bgcolor="#ffffff">
71   </body>
72   </html>
```

SHOWALL.HTML

The scripts and contents of this file provide a mechanism for dumping the contents of the contacts table into a report. The report is laid out in a column format utilizing HTML PRE tags—preformatted text—to maintain control over spacing (see Figure 8-5).

FIGURE 8-5. Viewing all name and address entries

```
1    <html>
2    <head>
3    <title>Contact Manager - Show All Entries</title>
4    </head>
5    <body bgcolor="#ffffff">
6    <center>
7    <font size="+2">Contact Manager</font>
8    </center>
9    <pre>
10   <server>
11
12   var sql = "";
13   var width = 0;
14   var lines = "";
15   sql = "select count (*) from contact";
16   writeln ('Total Entries : ' + countRows (sql));
17   var fname_len = getMaxLen ("contact", "fname", 10);
18   var lname_len = getMaxLen ("contact", "lname", 10);
19   var city_len  = getMaxLen ("contact", "city", 10);
20   var phone_len = getMaxLen ("contact", "homephone", 12);
```

```
21  var view_len  = 7;
22  width = view_len + fname_len + lname_len + city_
    len + phone_len + 2 + 12;
23
24  for (var i = 0; i < width; i++)
25    lines += "-";
26
27  writeln (lines);
28  write ('|'); write (pad ('', view_len));
29  write ('|'); write (pad ('FIRST', fname_len));
30  write ('|'); write (pad ('LAST', lname_len));
31  write ('|'); write (pad ('CITY', city_len));
32  write ('|'); write (pad ('ST', 2));
33  write ('|'); write (pad ('HOME PHONE', phone_len));
34  write ('|'); writeln ('');
35  writeln (lines);
36
37  sql = "select * from contact";
38  var cursor = database.cursor (sql);
39  while (cursor.next ())
40  {
41    link = '<a href="/jsbook/index.html?
     id=' + cursor.id + '">View</a>'
42    write ('|'); write (pad ('  ' + link + '  '
     , view_len));
43    write ('|'); write (pad (cursor.fname, fname_len));
44    write ('|'); write (pad (cursor.lname, lname_len));
45    write ('|'); write (pad (cursor.city,  city_len));
46    write ('|'); write (pad (cursor.state, 2));
47    write ('|'); write (pad (cursor.homephone, phone_len));
48    write ('|');
49    write ('\n');
50  }
51  cursor.close ();
52  writeln (lines);
53  </server>
54  </pre>
55  </body>
56  </html>
```

ANNOTATIONS

```
1    <html>
2    <head>
3    <title>Contact Manager - Show All Entries</title>
4    </head>
5    <body bgcolor="#ffffff">
6    <center>
7    <font size="+2">Contact Manager</font>
8    </center>
9    <pre>
10   <server>
11
12   var sql = "";
13   var width = 0;
14   var lines = "";
```

First, variables to be used later in the script are initialized: **sql** will be used for several SQL statements, **width** will hold the total width of all the columns, and **lines** will hold a series of dashes used as a field separator.

```
15   sql = "select count (*) from contact";
16   writeln ('Total Entries : ' + countRows (sql));
```

By use of the function **countRows**, the total number of contacts in the database is displayed to the user.

```
17   var fname_len = getMaxLen ("contact", "fname", 10);
18   var lname_len = getMaxLen ("contact", "lname", 10);
19   var city_len  = getMaxLen ("contact", "city", 10);
20   var phone_len = getMaxLen ("contact", "homephone", 12);
21   var view_len  = 7;
22   width = view_len + fname_len + lname_len + city_
     len + phone_len + 2 + 12;
23
```

Next, the function **getMaxLen** is used to obtain the maximum length of the items in a specified table. The values calculated on lines 17–21 are used on line 22 to determine the overall width of the reporting table.

```
24   for (var i = 0; i < width; i++)
25     lines += "-";
26
```

Using the calculated width of the table, a line of dashes is created. This line will be used for creating table headings.

```
27  writeln (lines);
28  write ('|'); write (pad ('', view_len));
29  write ('|'); write (pad ('FIRST', fname_len));
30  write ('|'); write (pad ('LAST', lname_len));
31  write ('|'); write (pad ('CITY', city_len));
32  write ('|'); write (pad ('ST', 2));
33  write ('|'); write (pad ('HOME PHONE', phone_len));
34  write ('|'); writeln ('');
35  writeln (lines);
36
```

Every report should have a heading row, and lines 27–36 provide just that. The **pad** function, which takes a string and an integer as an argument, adds white space to the end of the string to extend its length to that of the second argument. For each of the columns, the maximum length calculated earlier is passed to the function **pad** as the minimum length value.

```
37  sql = "select * from contact";
38  var cursor = database.cursor (sql);
```

Lines 37 and 38 create a result set containing every contact in the database. Although no ordering is specified, the SQL query could have easily been written as

```
    sql = "select * from contact order by lname";
```

```
39  while (cursor.next ())
40  {
41     link = '<a href="/jsbook/index.html?
           id=' + cursor.id + '">View</a>'
42     write ('|'); write (pad ('  ' + link + '  ', view_len));
43     write ('|'); write (pad (cursor.fname, fname_len));
44     write ('|'); write (pad (cursor.lname, lname_len));
45     write ('|'); write (pad (cursor.city,  city_len));
46     write ('|'); write (pad (cursor.state, 2));
47     write ('|'); write (pad (cursor.homephone, phone_len));
48     write ('|');
49     write ('\n');
50  }
```

Lines 39–50 print a summary of the information for each contact. In addition, a **View** link is created for each record that allows the user to view all the information for a particular entry. As when the headings are created, the **pad** function is used to force the entries for each column to be the correct width.

```
51  cursor.close ();
52  writeln (lines);
53  </server>
```

Finally, the database cursor is closed, and the footer of the table is printed.

```
54   </pre>
55   </body>
56   </html>
```

APPERR.HTML

The scripts and contents of this file provide the framework for informing the user that a catastrophic error has occurred in the application. The most likely causes for arriving here would be the failure to establish a connection with the database or a failure of some type when trying to read the application's INI file during startup.

```
1    <html>
2    <head>
3    <title>Application Error</title>
4    </head>
5    <body bgcolor="#ffffff">
6    <server>
7    var msg = "Your request could not be processed
     because " +
8                " an application error occurred.\\n\\n";
9
10   if (client.app_err && client.app_err != "null")
11   {
12     msg += replaceChar (client.app_err, "\n", "\\n");
13   }
14   msg += " Please contact the administrator for
     assistance.";
15   msg = replaceChar (msg, "'", "'''");
16
17   client.app_err = null;
18
19   writeln ('<script>');
20   writeln ('   alert ("' + msg + '")');
21   writeln ('</script>');
22
23   dbRelease ();
24   </server>
25   </body>
26   </html>
```

ANNOTATIONS

```
1    <html>
2    <head>
3    <title>Application Error</title>
4    </head>
5    <body bgcolor="#ffffff">
6    <server>
7    var msg = "Your request could not be processed
     because " +
8               " an application error occurred.\\n\\n";
9
10   if (client.app_err && client.app_err != "null")
11   {
12     msg += replaceChar (client.app_err, "\n", "\\n");
13   }
14   msg += " Please contact the administrator for
     assistance.";
15   msg = replaceChar (msg, "'", "''");
```

The first section of this file defines the message that will be shown to the user. Line 10 determines if a specific error message was set by the caller and if so, appends the text onto the previous contents of the message. The function **replaceChar** performs a check on the passed in string and substitutes all occurrences of the second parameter with the third parameter.

```
16
17   client.app_err = null;
```

As the **client** object was used to pass information between the last page and this one, it would be a good idea to clear this property so that successive redirects to this page will function properly. Notice that **client.app_err** does not have to be set by the calling function or page.

```
18
19   writeln ('<script>');
20   writeln ('   alert ("' + msg + '")');
21   writeln ('</script>');
22
23   dbRelease ();
24   </server>
25   </body>
26   </html>
```

DBASE.JS

This file contains various functions for dealing with the **database** object. By maintaining similar functions in a JS file, you can easily reuse the code in other projects.

```
1    function dbConnect ()
2    {
3      if (!database.connected ())
4         database.connect ("INFORMIX", project.
          db_connect, project.db_user,
5                          project.db_pass, project.db_name);
6
7      if (! database.connected ())
8         redirect ("apperr.html");
9    }
10
11   function dbRelease ()
12   {
13     if (database.connected ())
14        database.disconnect ();
15   }
16
17   function checkDBError (msg)
18   {
19     if (database.majorErrorCode() != 0)
20     {
21        client.app_err = (msg ? msg + "\n\n" : "")     +
22                         database.majorErrorCode()     + ":" +
23                         database.majorErrorMessage()
24        redirect ("apperr.html");
25     }
26   }
27
28   function countRows (sql)
29   {
30     var cursor = database.cursor (sql);
31     cursor.next();
32     var count = cursor[0];
33     cursor.close();
34     return (count)
35   }
```

```
36
37   function recordExists (sql)
38   {
39     var cursor = database.cursor (sql);
40     cursor.next();
41     var count = cursor[0];
42     cursor.close();
43     return (count == 0 ? false : true)
44   }
45
46   function dbShowSelect (name, def, sql)
47   {
48     var cursor = database.cursor (sql);
49     writeln ('<select name="' + name + '">');
50     while (cursor.next())
51     {
52        write ('<option value="' + cursor[0] + '"');
53        write (cursor[0] == def ? " selected" : "");
54        writeln ('>' + cursor[1]);
55     }
56     writeln ('</select>');
57     cursor.close();
58   }
59
60   function checkDBCode (code)
61   {
62     if (code == 0)
63        return;
64
65     writeln ('<script>');
66     writeln ('<!--- Hide script from old browsers.');
67     writeln ('var msg="An error occurred while
       saving your information!'+
68             '\\n\\n' +
69             database.majorErrorCode () + ' : ' +
70             chop (database.majorErrorMessage ()) + '"');
71
72     writeln ('alert (msg)');
73     writeln ('// End the hiding here. -->');
74     writeln ('</script>');
75   }
76
77   function checkForNull (str)
```

```
 78  {
 79    if (str == "")
 80       return ('null,')
 81    else
 82       return ("'" + str + "',")
 83  }
 84
 85  function getMaxLen (table, field, min)
 86  {
 87    var sql = "select max (length (" + field + "
       )) len from " + table;
 88    var cursor = database.cursor (sql);
 89    cursor.next ();
 90    var len = cursor.len;
 91    cursor.close ();
 92    return (len > min ? len : min);
 93  }
 94
 95  function getSerialFromInsert (sql)
 96  {
 97    project.lock ();
 98
 99    database.execute (sql);
100     checkDBError (sql);
101
102     sql = "select dbinfo('sqlca.sqlerrd1') from
        systables where tabid=1"
103     var cursor = database.cursor (sql);
104     cursor.next ();
105     var id = cursor[0] + "";
106     cursor.close ();
107     project.unlock ();
108     return (id);
109  }
```

ANNOTATIONS

```
 1    function dbConnect ()
 2    {
```

This function performs the basic task of connecting the application to a database. The function takes no arguments and returns no information. Before this function is called, the project variables containing the database login information must have been initialized.

```
3     if (!database.connected ())
4         database.connect ("INFORMIX", project.
          db_connect, project.db_user,
5                             project.db_pass, project.db_name);
6
```

Lines 3–6 determine if the application is already connected to the database. If not, a connection is created.

```
7     if (! database.connected ())
8         redirect ("apperr.html");
9     }
```

At this point, there should be a valid database connection—either one already existed before this function call, or one was created earlier. If **database.connected** returns **false**, the user needs to be notified that a connection could not be established. In the application presented here, this is a fatal error and the application must end. The client browser is redirected to a page that displays a message notifying the user that a database error has occurred. The contents of APPERR.HTML are shown later in this section.

```
10
11    function dbRelease ()
12    {
13      if (database.connected ())
14          database.disconnect ();
15    }
```

This is a very simple function that determines if the application is connected to a database and if so, releases that connection. No arguments are needed and no value is returned.

```
16
17    function checkDBError (msg)
18    {
19      if (database.majorErrorCode() != 0)
20      {
21        client.app_err = (msg ? msg + "\n\n" : "")      +
22                             database.majorErrorCode()      + ":" +
23                             database.majorErrorMessage()
24          redirect ("apperr.html");
25      }
26    }
```

The **checkDBError** function demonstrates another method of handling errors that may occur when dealing with a database. As in **checkDBCode( )**, the error code returned from the database is checked to determine if it is zero. If it is, the function simply exits. If not, an error has occurred, and once again the user is notified. Unlike **checkDBCode**, in which the application displays an error message and then continues, this function halts the flow of the application by redirecting the client browser to another page. The **client** object is used to pass a message to the next page, APPERR.HTML, where it will be displayed to the user.

```
27
28   function countRows (sql)
29   {
30     var cursor = database.cursor (sql);
31     cursor.next();
32     var count = cursor[0];
33     cursor.close();
34     return (count)
35   }
36
37   function recordExists (sql)
38   {
39     var cursor = database.cursor (sql);
40     cursor.next();
41     var count = cursor[0];
42     cursor.close();
43     return (count == 0 ? false : true)
44   }
```

recordExists is a utility function used to determine if a specific record currently exists in the database. The function takes as its single parameter an SQL statement of the form

```
select count(*) from tablename where condition;
```

Line 41 pulls the count returned from the database and stores it in a temporary variable. After the cursor is closed, the return value is determined by the ternary operator. If the count returned by the query is 0, the record doesn't exist and a value of **false** is returned. If the count returned is not 0, the record must exist and a value of **true** is returned.

```
45
46   function dbShowSelect (name, def, sql)
47   {
48     var cursor = database.cursor (sql);
49     writeln ('<select name="' + name + '">');
```

```
50    while (cursor.next())
51    {
52        write ('<option value="' + cursor[0] + '"');
53        write (cursor[0] == def ? " selected" : "");
54        writeln ('>' + cursor[1]);
55    }
56    writeln ('</select>');
57    cursor.close();
58  }
59
60  function checkDBCode (code)
61  {
62    if (code == 0)
63        return;
```

The first step in this function is to determine if the passed in value, a return code from a database operation, is equal to zero. If this is the case, the function exits. If this is not the case, the application needs to inform the user that a database error has occurred.

```
64
65    writeln ('<script>');
66    writeln ('<!--- Hide script from old browsers.');
67    writeln ('var msg="An error occurred while
      saving your information!'+
68              '\\n\\n' +
69              database.majorErrorCode () + ' : ' +
70              chop (database.majorErrorMessage ()) + '"');
71
72    writeln ('alert (msg)');
73    writeln ('// End the hiding here. -->');
74    writeln ('</script>');
75  }
```

The remainder of this function writes client-side JavaScript that, when executed, will create an alert window with an informational message. The **majorErrorCode( )** and **majorErrorMessage( )** methods of the **database** object return vendor-specific information about the error that occurred.

```
76
77  function checkForNull (str)
78  {
79    if (str == "")
80        return ('null,')
81    else
```

```
82        return ("'" + str + "',")
83   }
```

checkForNull is a utility function that checks the passed in string to see if it is empty. The function is used in building an SQL query where the value being added may be empty or **null**. In either case, an actual "null" is entered into the field instead of the JavaScript empty or **null**. In most databases, a value of **null** is treated differently than a value of empty.

```
84
85   function getMaxLen (table, field, min)
86   {
87     var sql = "select max (length (" + field + "
       )) len from " + table;
88     var cursor = database.cursor (sql);
89     cursor.next ();
90     var len = cursor.len;
91     cursor.close ();
92     return (len > min ? len : min);
93   }
```

In **getMaxLen( )**, the two aggregate functions **max** and **length** are combined to determine the length of the longest item in a field of a database table. When the value is obtained, it is compared against the minimum value supplied and the larger of the two is returned.

```
94
95   function getSerialFromInsert (sql)
96   {
97     project.lock ();
98
99     database.execute (sql);
100    checkDBError (sql);
```

The first task of the **getSerialFromInsert( )** function is to perform a lock on the project so that only one client is accessing this code at a time. Once the lock has been established, the passed in SQL statement is executed and the database error codes are checked.

```
101
102    sql = "select dbinfo('sqlca.sqlerrd1') from
       systables where tabid=1"
103    var cursor = database.cursor (sql);
104    cursor.next ();
105    var id = cursor[0] + "";
106    cursor.close ();
```

After the initial insert has been accomplished, the value of the serial field of the record just inserted is retrieved from the system tables. This code is Informix specific and will need to be changed if another type of database is used.

```
107    project.unlock ();
108    return (id);
109  }
```

The final task is to unlock the project and return the **id** retrieved from the system tables.

MISC.JS

This file contains miscellaneous functions used throughout the application. The functions are placed here instead of in an HTML file so that they may be easily transported to other applications. As in the file DBASE.JS, the functions contained here were written to be generic and not to contain application-specific information.

```
1    function appInit ()
2    {
3      var ini_file = new File ("/home/mcnair/
       livewire/contact/contact.ini");
4      project.lock();
5      if (! ini_file.open ("r"))
6      {
7        client.app_err = "Cannot open .ini file!";
8        redirect ("apperr.html");
9      }
10     else
11     {
12       while (! ini_file.eof())
13       {
14         var line = ini_file.readln();
15         if (line.charAt (0) == "#" || line =
           = "" || line == null)
16           continue
17         var vals = new split (line, "=", 2);
18         var prop = vals[0].toLowerCase();
19         var val  = (vals[1] != null ? vals[1] : "")
20         project[prop] = val;
21       }
22       ini_file.close();
23     }
24     project.unlock();
```

```
25  }
26
27  function writeln (text)
28  {
29    write (text + '\n');
30  }
31
32  function chop (str)
33  {
34    return (str.substring (0, str.length - 1))
35  }
36
37  function trim (str)
38  {
39    if (str == "") return (str);
40
41    for (var i = str.length - 1; i >= 0; i--)
42      if (str.charAt (i) != " ")
43        return (str.substring (0, i + 1));
44    return (str);
45  }
46
47  function split (str, ch, n)
48  {
49    var i     = 0;
50    var idx   = 0;
51    var start = 0;
52    n = (isNum (n) ? n : 999999)
53    while (start < str.length)
54    {
55      idx = str.indexOf (ch, start);
56      if (idx == -1) break;
57      if (i == n) break;
58      this[i++] = str.substring (start, idx);
59      start = idx + 1;
60    }
61    if (str.substring (start, str.length) != "")
62      this[i++] = str.substring (start, str.length);
63    this.length = i;
64    return (this);
65  }
66
67  function clientAlert (msg)
```

```
68  {
69    writeln ('<script>');
70    writeln ('alert (\'' + msg + '\')');
71    writeln ('</script>');
72  }
73
74  function replaceChar (str, ch1, ch2)
75  {
76    var c;
77    var tstr = "";
78    if (str == "" || str.indexOf(ch1) < 0)
79       return (str);
80    for (var i = 0; i < str.length; i++)
81    {
82       c = str.charAt(i);
83       if (c != ch1)
84          tstr += c;
85       else
86          tstr += ch2;
87    }
88    return (tstr);
89  }
90
91  function isNum (num)
92  {
93   if ((parseInt (num) + "") == "NaN")
94       return (false);
95    return (true);
96  }
97
98  function pad (str, len)
99  {
100     if (str == null) str = "";
101     while (str.length <= len)
102     {
103        str += " ";
104     }
105     return (str);
106 }
107
108 function getTodaysTimeStamp ()
109 {
110     var d = new Date ();
```

```
111    var date = d.getYear()+"-" +(d.getMonth()+1)
       +"-" + d.getDate() + " ";
112    date += d.getHours() + ":" + d.getMinutes()
       + ":" + d.getSeconds();
113    return (date);
114 }
```

ANNOTATIONS

```
1   function appInit ()
2   {
```

This function contains the code necessary to properly initialize our application with data that will be used throughout the life span of the program. The function takes no arguments and returns no information.

```
3   var ini_file = new File ("/home/mcnair/
    livewire/contact/contact.ini");
```

The **appInit** function first initiates an object that points to a file containing our application information. Global data, such as database logins and passwords, will be stored here, as well as any other information that might change. An alternative to this approach is to hard-code the information within the application itself. However, by utilizing the approach presented here, you'll make it easier for your application to work in a different environment without having to actually recompile it. This is especially helpful when development is done on one platform and then moved to another for production.

The INI file contains multiple lines with a single name=value pair on each line. Blank lines are ignored, as are lines beginning with a "#" character. This allows for organization and comments of our data within the file.

```
4   project.lock();
```

As we are modifying data on a global scale, we need to make sure this section of code is executed by only one thread at a time. To accomplish this, we use the special **lock** function of the **project** object. This function guarantees that other requests for this section of code will have to wait until we explicitly do an unlock via the **project.unlock** method, or until the current request is completed, at which time the project will automatically be unlocked.

```
5   if (! ini_file.open ("r"))
6   {
7       client.app_err = "Cannot open .ini file!";
8       redirect ("apperr.html");
```

```
9        }
10    else
11      {
```

Next, the INI file is opened for reading. If the open fails, the application won't be properly initialized, so there's no point in allowing the request to continue to be processed. To this end, we use the top-level LiveWire function redirect. It takes one argument—the location to which you want to redirect the client. In our case, we want to notify the user that a critical error has occurred.

```
12        while (! ini_file.eof())
13          {
```

If the INI file was successfully opened for reading, the name=value pairs can be read in and used to initialize the application.

The first step is to create a loop that continues until the end of the file is reached.

```
14          var line = ini_file.readln();
15          if (line.charAt (0) == "#" || line =
            = "" || line == null)
16            continue
```

After reading in a line, we want to make sure it has valid data. If any of the test conditions is **true**, the **continue** statement is executed. This ends the current iteration of the loop, causing the current line to be ignored. Execution resumes at line 12 and the loop continues.

```
17          var vals = new split (line, "=", 2);
```

Line 17 calls a function **split** that takes a string and splits it into multiple items based on a delimiter. While the code for **split** will be presented later, based on the arguments listed on line 17, you can see that the line just read in will be split based on the "=" character. This result of the **split** function call is a *two-element array*. The first element, **vals[0]**, is the name part of our name=value pair. The second, **vals[1]**, is the value part.

```
18          var prop = vals[0].toLowerCase();
19          var val  = (vals[1] != null ? vals[1] : "")
```

Now that the input line has been parsed, the individual items are formatted into their final state. Line 18 converts the name part to all lowercase. This is not necessary, of course, but it allows the programmer a consistent interface to the data. Line 19 makes sure that the value returned by split is not **null**. Here, JavaScript's ternary operator is used to perform a condensed **if-then-else** clause. Line 19 could have been written as

```
    var val = ""
    if (vals[1] != null)
       val = vals[1]
```

using three lines of code instead of one.

```
20          project[prop] = val;
21       }
```

Now that the values read in have been validated, they can be applied to the application. The **project** variable is simply another JavaScript object to which properties can be added. Line 20 shows an assignment being made that adds a property to the **project** object and assigns it the value associated with the name=value pair read in from the INI file. For instance, if the INI file contained the line

```
DB_CONNECT=ifmx_online
```

line 20 would evaluate to

```
project[db_connect] = "ifmx_online"
```

```
22          ini_file.close();
23       }
24    project.unlock();
25 }
```

The final steps of this function are to close the input file and to unlock the project. At this point, the application variables have been initialized and stored in the global **project** variable.

```
26
27 function writeln (text)
28 {
29    write (text + '\n');
30 }
31
32 function chop (str)
33 {
34    return (str.substring (0, str.length - 1))
35 }
36
37 function trim (str)
38 {
39    if (str == "") return (str);
40
41    for (var i = str.length - 1; i >= 0; i--)
42       if (str.charAt (i) != " ")
43          return (str.substring (0, i + 1));
44    return (str);
45 }
```

```
46
47  function split (str, ch, n)
48  {
```

This function creates an array of items by breaking the string **str** into parts at a specified character **ch**. Optionally, the caller may specify the maximum number of items **n** to be returned.

```
49      var i     = 0;
50      var idx   = 0;
51      var start = 0;
52      n = (isNum (n) ? n : 999999)
```

Lines 49–52 initialize the local variables that will be used in this function. Line 52 uses the ternary operator to determine if the caller has specified a maximum number of elements to return.

isNum is a simple function that returns **true** if the passed in value is a number and **false** if not. If the caller did not specify **n**, it will be **null** (**isNum** will return **false**) and the maximum number of elements to return is set to an extremely large number.

```
53      while (start < str.length)
54      {
55          idx = str.indexOf (ch, start);
```

While looping through the entire string, the index of the delimiter character is found starting from the previous position. The starting position will be zero for the first pass, as initialized earlier.

```
56          if (idx == -1) break;
57          if (i == n) break;
```

If **indexOf** returns –1, there are no more occurrences of the delimiter in the string and it is time to quit looping. Furthermore, if the maximum number of items to return has been reached, it is time to quit. Using the **break** statement signals JavaScript to stop execution of the current loop and to continue to execute after the end of the loop block.

```
58          this[i++] = str.substring (start, idx);
59          start = idx + 1;
```

At this point, the part of the string from the starting point to the location of the delimiter is added to the array being built. The starting point is updated to be the next character position from the location of the delimiter.

```
60      }
61      if (str.substring (start, str.length) != "")
62          this[i++] = str.substring (start, str.length);
```

Now that the loop is finished, a check is made to determine if any data still remains in the string that hasn't been parsed. If so, it is simply added as the last element in the array.

```
63      this.length = i;
64      return (this);
65  }
```

The final steps of this function are to set the length of the array and to return it. The caller must take care to allocate space for the **array** object via the new function call, as shown in the example next:

```
var items =  new split ("name=value", "=")
```

```
66
67  function clientAlert (msg)
68  {
69    writeln ('<script>');
70    writeln ('alert (\'' + msg + '\')');
71    writeln ('</script>');
72  }
73
74  function replaceChar (str, ch1, ch2)
75  {
76    var c;
77    var tstr = "";
78    if (str == "" || str.indexOf(ch1) < 0)
79        return (str);
```

The first section of this function determines if this string really needs to be processed. If the string is empty or there are no occurrences of the character to replace, the original string is passed back to the caller.

```
80      for (var i = 0; i < str.length; i++)
81      {
82          c = str.charAt(i);
83          if (c != ch1)
84              tstr += c;
85          else
86              tstr += ch2;
87      }
```

The bulk of the work for this function is performed in lines 80–87. A loop is formed to iterate through the string. Each character is examined. If it doesn't match the character to be replaced, it is added to the string being built. If it does match, the substitute character is added instead.

```
88     return (tstr);
89  }
```

Finally, the string with the replaced characters is returned to the caller.

```
90
91  function isNum (num)
92  {
93     if ((parseInt (num) + "") == "NaN")
94          return (false);
95      return (true);
96  }
97
98  function pad (str, len)
99  {
100    if (str == null) str = "";
101    while (str.length <= len)
102    {
103       str += " ";
104    }
105    return (str);
106 }
```

This is a utility function used to pad the passed in string with spaces. If the passed in string is **null**, it is initialized to an empty string. A **while** loop is then set up to add spaces to the end of the string until its length is that of the second parameter.

```
107
108 function getTodaysTimeStamp ()
109 {
110    var d = new Date ();
111    var date = d.getYear()+"-" +(d.getMonth()+1)
       +"-" + d.getDate()+" ";
112    date += d.getHours() + ":" + d.getMinutes()
       + ":" + d.getSeconds();
113    return (date);
114 }
```

getTodaysTimeStamp is a utility function that returns a string containing the current time and date in the format

```
YYYY-MM-DD HH:MM:SS
```

This function provides the same functionality as the **toLocaleString** method of a **date** object. However, different locales return the date information in different formats, so the preceding function provides the application with a portable way to obtain the date/time information.

CONTACT.INI

This file contains information read during the application startup phase and is used to initialize the server variables.

```
1   DB_CONNECT=ifmx_online
2   DB_USER=
3   DB_PASS=
4   DB_NAME=jsbook
```

ANNOTATIONS

```
1   DB_CONNECT=ifmx_online
2   DB_USER=
3   DB_PASS=
4   DB_NAME=jsbook
```

No annotations are necessary; the file contents are self-explanatory.

Appendixes

JavaScript Programming Tools   JavaScript-Enabled Web Sites

APPENDIX A

JavaScript Programming Tools

In addition to JavaScript's popularity as a client-side scripting language for the Web, programmers have been demanding software to help them manage JavaScript code and to easily program their dynamic content. Compared with other scripting languages and Java, JavaScript is simpler to learn and need not be compiled beforehand. A web browser interprets the JavaScript code when the page loads, increasing the speed of the applications, unlike Java.

"Dynamic content" means presenting web readers with information based on user preferences rather than strictly static HTML pages. In other words, dynamic content is HTML-based content that is created by the server on-the-fly, via functions that interact between server and a database that houses the web site's content. JavaScript can play a large role in delivering dynamic web content, and in this case programmers need to create JavaScript that can be compiled and run on a server.

Two products, Netscape Communications Corp.'s Visual JavaScript and Borland International Corp.'s IntraBuilder Client/Server, facilitate this web-to-database process. The latter is a best buy in this product category, with excellent code-management and editing features and surprisingly easy-to-use functions for connecting databases to the Web via JavaScript.

Visual JavaScript, on the other hand, is a Java-based integrated development environment (IDE) that pays off if you are willing to spend a lot of time understanding its peculiar interface and methods. The Java-based user interface is just different enough to be annoying, and as with most of Netscape's products, Visual JavaScript has been available for public use during its alpha and beta development phases. It is, then, a good buy for any developer who has "grown up" using the Netscape web server suite of products.

Even if you do not want to create server-based dynamic web pages, and manage your client-side JavaScript projects, you have probably been wondering when a few useful tools would appear. Acadia Inc.'s Infuse is a stand-alone integrated development environment for JavaScript, with many features that will appeal to programmers.

One of the most popular HTML editors, Sausage Software Inc.'s Hot Dog Professional, now comes with an optional JavaScript Editor. Unlike the other products reviewed here, it is for people who just want to whip up some fast JavaScript code and place it on HTML pages. As such, it is an extremely easy-to-use tool that will appeal to nonprogrammers.

Visual JavaScript 1.0 PR3

Netscape Communications Corp.
http://www.netscape.com
One of the most popular web servers, Netscape's Enterprise Server, comes with an extensive tool set for creating dynamic content, including a server-side version of

the scripting language called LiveWire. If you have invested in Netscape's web server offerings, it was good to hear early in 1997 that the vendor was answering your prayers with an IDE for JavaScript creation, called Visual JavaScript.

At press time, Netscape was still testing Visual JavaScript publicly—we looked at PR3 (Preview Release 3), which was about 80 percent functional and quite buggy. As such, we will not look at it in the same light as the other products, which are relatively stable, finished products.

We recommend Visual JavaScript only to those who have chosen the Netscape server product line as a tool for managing their web site content. As those people are really the only audience for this product, they are more likely to put up with the oddball user interface and program glitches, as well as Netscape's singular approach to making web sites work dynamically. If you use any other web server solution, jump to the next product.

Visual JavaScript is more correctly a Java-based rapid application development (RAD) tool. It requires Netscape's Communicator 4.0 web browser and SuiteSpot 3.0 server products to build JavaScript-enabled dynamic web applications.

The visual JavaScript code builder is the product's best feature, although the Java-based GUI takes some getting used to. If you are familiar with application development using Visual Basic, this product's interface will throw you for a loop, as it behaves in the manner of X-Windows rather than Microsoft Windows (see Figure A-1).

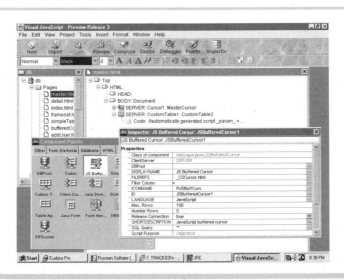

FIGURE A-1. Netscape's Visual JavaScript PR3

As we had a limited amount of time to work with this product, all we attempted was to deploy one of the database samples that comes with Visual JavaScript. Once past the steep learning curve, we still were unable to successfully deploy the sample application because this version does not yet support full deployment of applications. Some features will not be available until the 1.0 version is released, reportedly in late 1997. Until then, the reviewed beta version is free.

Enterprise programmers will find the product gets easier with use, and building multiplatform client-side and server-side applications becomes a fast process of reusing components and code. Although the product will support multiple component types—including HTML, JavaBeans, Java applets, CORBA (Common Object Request Broker Architecture) objects, and JavaScript components—we focused on JavaScript.

Though Visual Basic users will not be swayed to use this product, it eases what have been difficult processes using LiveWire. The drag-and-drop interface lets us build our sample application by using bits of code left over from our experiments with IntraBuilder. The Component Palette lets us add HTML, JavaScript, and JavaBeans elements to form the basic HTML pages in our application; an Inspector and Connections Builder enable us to set properties and make connections between these elements.

We wanted to incorporate data stored on an ODBC-driven Access database, but there are incompatibilities between Visual JavaScript and Access. We were, however, able to connect to a SQL Server database without difficulty. The well-written documentation answered all of our questions about how the various functions worked.

Last but not least, Visual JavaScript needs a very fast computer to work well. As it was written in Java, expect a long loading time. Our 166MHz Pentium Pro seemed barely adequate for the task. It works well, but you must have a lot of patience. Even if you have a Pentium Pro with 64MB of RAM, it's dog slow.

IntraBuilder Client/Server 1.5

Borland International Inc.
http://www.borland.com

A light-year's leap beyond the competition, Borland International's IntraBuilder Client/Server is a significant advancement in web-based database application development. It relies heavily on JavaScript to deploy its dynamic web applications and includes useful graphical web design tools, server-side processing, distributed server technology, and native access to all major server databases.

Unfortunately, unlike Visual JavaScript and a Java-oriented competitor, NetDynamics Inc.'s NetDynamics, IntraBuilder does not work with UNIX-based web servers; instead, it is compatible with any Windows NT web server.

IntraBuilder lets even nonprogrammers create and manage web sites. It also prepares complex reports and database-oriented small web applications, and connects natively to databases and web servers. The JavaScript support is superb, and the visual development environment was a big time-saver during our development effort. Nonprogrammers may have to spend a lot of time with the documentation, which is well-organized and generally easy to understand.

IntraBuilder's preprocessor software module sits on your web server, intercepting data to and from the client browser. The HTML content that flows between client and server is generated dynamically from scripts you develop in IntraBuilder's visual design environment.

We set up IntraBuilder with Netscape's FastTrack 2.0 server and created a database application that was similar to the test application we used with Visual JavaScript. Although we were not limited to using only server-side JavaScript code in the application—you can drop client-side JavaScript methods, Java applets, and ActiveX controls—we decided to play with IntraBuilder's server-side JavaScript support. IntraBuilder's version of server-side JavaScript goes beyond the Netscape standard, adding database support, inheritance, code blocks, and exception handling.

IntraBuilder's visual design module manages web server and database connections using Borland's Database Engine and server agents. The connections support Netscape's NSAPI Web server API, Microsoft's ISAPI Web server API, and CGI. The agents create dynamic HTML from JavaScript forms and reports. During tests, the visual designer automatically created the appropriate JavaScript language statements and specified the content and appearance of our web pages (see Figure A-2).

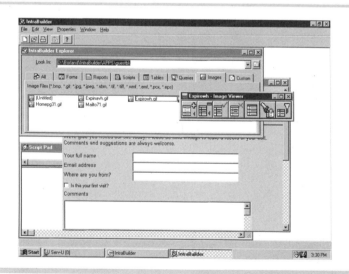

FIGURE A-2. Borland International's IntraBuilder Client/Server 1.5

In developing our test application—using Microsoft Access—the simplest web page is as easy as dropping a table you have selected in the Database Explorer window onto the visual design window. As our application used only server-side JavaScript, it could be viewed using any client browser that supports HTML tables and forms.

To specify the JavaScript-enabled queries to our database, we used IntraBuilder's visual query tool. It quickly assembled the resulting SQL statements in a window on our desktop. IntraBuilder works with ODBC or native RDBMS connections, such as DB2, Oracle, Sybase, Informix, InterBase, and SQL Server. You can run agents on your web server, but they also can run on a separate machine. Each agent can use up to 10MB of RAM, so this distributed capability makes the product scalable.

If the $1,995 IntraBuilder Client/Server is too powerful for your use, there are less robust variations you can try. The $99 IntraBuilder Standard is limited to Borland's web server and provides local database access only. The $499 IntraBuilder Professional supports third-party web servers and multiple agents, but has limited database access and no distributed abilities.

Acadia Infuse 1.01/2.0

Acadia Software Inc.
http://www.acadians.com
Acadia's Infuse 1.01 is an excellent tool for anyone reasonably familiar with creating client-side JavaScript. Unlike Visual JavaScript and IntraBuilder, Infuse is a programmer's editor only. Its IDE components are designed to help users create client-side JavaScript easily, and to help them keep track of code for easy reuse. Its editor features are especially useful for newcomers, while the code-management features are more suited to experienced programmers.

Infuse was one of the first authoring tools built explicitly for creating JavaScript-enhanced web pages. It comes with the expected features of HTML editors, such as quick-keys and drag-and-drop code, and Acadia has extended these features to include JavaScript. We were able to drag and drop different functions and methods, and to create simple JavaScript applications with the click of a button.

With Infuse's extremely easy-to-use user interface, we were able to begin immediately, with very little prior checking with the overall good documentation. Along with quick-keys for coding simple HTML and JavaScript, there is a complete list of HTML tags and JavaScript functions located in a resizable window. We could double-click or drag and drop any of these into the current document.

The list of JavaScript functions is convenient for programmers who have recently become acquainted with the language. Absolute novices should spend some time with a beginner's tutorial, such as the materials available at Netscape's web site.

Infuse contains references to all JavaScript objects and methods, so remembering exactly which method goes with which object is not essential. For example, if you would like to create a button that leads to the previous page, you may only remember that you need something with "back." Using Infuse, you can locate "window," then within that object, the method "history," and then "back()"; selecting "back()" will give you "window.history.back()." In Infuse 2.0, the next version of the product that should have been released when you read this, the reference list is searchable, speeding up such a process.

Infuse's JavaScript repository includes another convenience, language functionality elements, such as if-else and loops. Dragging "if..else" onto the current document results in the addition of an if-else template containing the word "expression" where the if-expression goes and "// Enter code here" where the result-code goes. This eliminates the confusion of sticky syntax details.

Though Infuse is an excellent tool for those becoming acquainted with JavaScript, its purpose is not to teach JavaScript. The user definitely needs some familiarity with the language to provide an adequate knowledge base. With this, the tool is exceptionally useful as a reference and exploration tool.

Anyone who started coding in HTML before the revolution of editors probably still does the majority of coding manually, avoiding timely use of the mouse. Similarly, JavaScript-savvy programmers may prefer to type rather than drag and drop. In this sense, Infuse's editor features are not always useful. However, Infuse's code-management features are especially helpful when creating complex client-side JavaScript projects. Infuse supports LiveWire, or server-side, script creation as well. Again, if you understand how to program in LiveWire, this product will be a good addition to your tool arsenal (see Figure A-3).

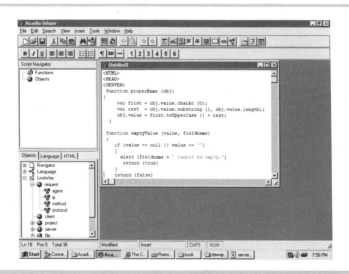

FIGURE A-3. Acadia's Infuse 1.01

The Script Navigator, located in a resizable window at the side of the screen, contains a list of the functions and objects in the current document. Clicking any of these sends the cursor to the location of that portion of the code. Another excellent tool is the aptly named "frequent scripts," which provide the JavaScript code for a variety of frequently used scripts. Also, we could add our own scripts to this section, allowing easy reuse of code.

There were a few problems with Infuse 1.01 that seem to be fixed in version 2.0. For example, the HTML-editor part of version 1.01 lacks a few features of a top-notch HTML editor. There is no visual way to create tables, and no way to preview pages in the editor itself. In addition, Infuse 2.0 will support JScript and VBScript, which offer "scripting wizards" that allow the user to create simple customized scripts without coding.

A single-user license for Infuse 1.01 is $129.95. A three-user license package sells for $279.95, a five-user license package, for $349.95.

Hot Dog Professional 4:
JavaScript Editor and JavaScript Tools

Sausage Software Inc.
http://www.sausage.com

Sausage Software's Hot Dog Professional HTML editor is one of the top web page editors. Version 4.x, which shipped in June 1997 and has been upgraded gradually throughout the year, includes external editor's "helpers" called Supertoolz. One of these Supertoolz, matter-of-factly titled JavaScript Editor, is a handy utility that lets you create scripts using drop-down menus.

JavaScript Editor does little more than help web developers construct client-side JavaScripts on-the-fly. It is not really a tool for writing JavaScript, in that it lets you choose JavaScript objects from a series of drop-down menus (see Figure A-4). If there are JavaScript objects already on your web page, you can add events to objects.

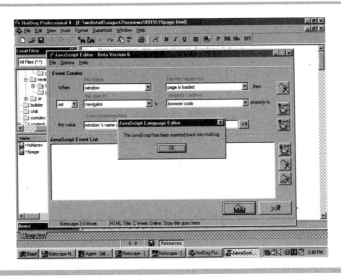

FIGURE A-4. Sausage Software's Hot Dog Professional 4 JavaScript Editor

Even though this Supertoolz editor is still in public beta, we were impressed by its ease of use. We were able to create JavaScript examples very quickly.

For example, it was quite simple to turn an image that is a link into a picture that changes when the mouse is moved over the image. In addition, we created a script that loads two external windows. To make the external windows interact, we had to go back over the JavaScript code.

We had to place text and graphics on our HTML pages before editing the JavaScript. When the JavaScript Editor translates the drop-down and English instructions into JavaScript and inserts them into the page, it does not always respect the positions of the images.

However, using this tool successfully presupposes that you already understand the ins and outs of JavaScript. It really is not for the beginner. Another of Hot Dog Professional's Supertoolz, called JavaScript Tools, comes with prefabricated scripts that you can drop into pages. Both products cost $49.95 each, above the cost of the HTML editor, which is $129.95.

As the JavaScript Editor is in beta, it crashes every once in awhile. It's a simple matter to end the program using the Windows 95 task-management function, but annoying nonetheless. In addition, we noticed OLE communications between Hot Dog Professional and the JavaScript Editor did not always take place successfully. We could not pinpoint the trouble, as Hot Dog Professional is a tad buggy, as well.

JavaScript-Enabled Web Sites

For those who want to know more about JavaScript, the best place to look is on the Web. What follows is a partial listing of web sites devoted to the language. It is the listing that we used in preparing this book. Any of the examples in this book were first discovered at these sites, and all of the sites contain worthwhile examples of JavaScript.

A note of warning, though. The Web is a volatile place, and as with many of the sites you might bookmark in your browser any day of the week, some of these sites may not work anymore. They worked as we went to press, however. So enjoy.

Web pages are denoted with a URL that begins "http://", and Usenet news resources begin with "news:".

24-Hour JavaScripts   This is a terrific site with an attitude and hundreds of free scripts to choose from. (**http://www.javascripts.com**)

Ad/Vantage Pawluk   This site offers tips, tricks, and sample code, arranged neatly and easily followed. (**http://www.pawluk.com/pages/javatech/javascr.htm**)

Adrenalin Labs   This site includes an outstanding scrolling frame example, among other things. (**http://www.calweb.com/~dstoflet/js_exmpl.htm**)

Andrew's JavaScript Homepage   This site is a nicely designed JavaScript repository and contains some scripts that no one else seems to have. (**http://www.alarmix.net/ freeweb/pfaff/english/java**)

Beginner's Guide to JavaScript   You'll find basic scripting functions presented in a clear manner that will appeal to those with some understanding of programming. (**http://www.geocities.com/SiliconValley/Park/2554/index.html**)

Cameron's JavaScript Stuff   This site offers a small but potent selection of script examples. (**http://www.bloke.com/javascript**)

Cookies and JavaScript   This site has a working example of a fill-in form that uses cookies to recall user data—such as browser type, I.P. address, etc.—from session to session. (**http://www.envmed.rochester.edu/www/javascriptfordata**)

Coolnerds Electronic JavaScript Reference   This site is a convenient online reference that covers all JavaScript functions, methods, and so on. (**http://www.coolnerds.com/refs/javaref.htm**)

Cut'n'Paste JavaScript   One of the longest-running script example sites, this has numerous examples from simple to complex. (**http://www.infohiway.com/javascript/indexf.htm**)

Danny Goodman's JavaScript Pages   This site provides script samples taken from the book *JavaScript Bible*. (**http://www.dannyg.com/javascript/index.html**)

DryRoast   This site is a bit disorganized, but contains a wealth of excellent links to good script examples. (**http://dryroast.randomc.com**)

Hotsyte   This site offers an index of current JavaScript sites, as well as a healthy collection of public domain scripts, including the awesome Tim Wildman collection. (**http://www.serve.com/hotsyte**)

Hiway Technologies' Java and JavaScript Forum   Another helpful discussion area, this site uses a web-based interface. (**http://www.hway.net/webforum/java/index.html**)

Hunting the SNARK with JavaScript   This is a good JavaScript-based search interface. (**http://www.cs.cmu.edu/~jab/snark**)

JAS's International JavaScript Resources   One of the most useful index sites, this includes a healthy number of international web sites experimenting with JavaScript. (**http://www.ios.com/~jas/jas.htm**)

JavaScript 411   This site hasn't been updated in some time, but there are still many useful scripts and tutorials housed here. (**http://www.freqgrafx.com/411/index.html**)

The JavaScript Archive   This is a long-running script repository—one of the best (see Figure B-1). (**http://planetx.bloomu.edu/~mpscho/jsarchive**)

FIGURE B-1.   The JavaScript Archive

JavaScript Examples   This site has a large assortment of script examples taken from the recent book by Michael Moncur. (**http://starlingtech.com/books/ javascript/examples**)

JavaScript for the Total Non-Programmer   This online tutorial takes you step-by-step through the fundamentals of JavaScript. (**http://www.webteacher.com/ javatour.htm**)

JavaScript Games Realm   This site makes interesting use of VRML, JavaScript, and MIDI sound, and contains a collection of JavaScript games. (**http://members.tripod.com/~jsgamerealm/bmjsgr.htm**)

JavaScript Graphics Plotting   This site has examples of creating and using both one- and two-dimensional arrays. (**http://www.nicholson.com/rhn/plot.js.html**)

JavaScript Guide   Netscape's online documentation covers JavaScript 1.1 and 1.2, but does not contain enough useful code examples for beginners. (**http://developer.netscape.com/library/documentation/communicator/jsguide4/ index.htm**)

JavaScript Planet   This site has hundreds of useful scripts—the best of its kind. (**http://www.geocities.com/SiliconValley/7116**)

JavaScript Sourcebook   This site is Gordon McComb's support site for his book; Gordon is a lot more active on the various JavaScript Usenet newsgroups. (**http://gmccomb.com/javascript**)

JavaScript Webring   Here you can investigate many sites that use or demonstrate JavaScript. (**http://www.webring.org/cgi-bin/ webring?ring=javascriptring&id=94&next5**)

JS Resources A 2 Z   This site is Reaz Hoque's outstanding documentation page—it includes good JavaScript examples. (**http://www.ibic.com/java**)

JScript   This site is the home page for the Microsoft alternative to JavaScript. (**http://www.microsoft.com/jscript/**)

Just Another JavaScript Related Homepage   This is a small site with a few very useful script examples. (**http://perso.wanadoo.fr/glacon.sismique**)

Live Software   The home of two valuable Usenet newsgroups, this site also contains some script examples.

- **http://www.livesoftware.com/jrc**
- **news://news.livesoftware.com/livesoftware.javascript.developer**
- **news://news.livesoftware.com/livesoftware.javascript.examples**

Netscape DevEdge Newsgroups   These sites are moderated discussion forums devoted to JavaScript, LiveWire, the Netscape JavaScript developer products, and so on. They are invaluable, but they cost money to use. (**news:secnews.netscape.com**)

NetscapeWorld   Not affiliated with Netscape, this tech-heavy magazine has some of the best links to JavaScript resources.

- **http://www.netscapeworld.com**
- **http://www.netscapeworld.com/netscapeworld/common/ nw.jumps.html#javascript**

Nick Heinle's Scripts   These two sites feature the excellent script examples from the 17-year-old JavaScript guru (see Figure B-2 for a look at the Web Coder site).

- **http://webreference.com/javascript**
- **http://www.webcoder.com/index_real.html**

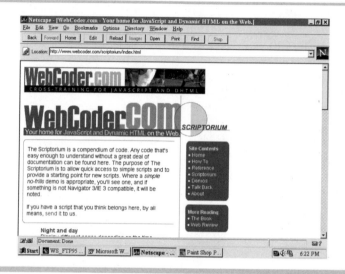

FIGURE B-2. Webcoder.com

Random Image Link   This site is a random graphical banner that is controlled via the Reload function on the browser. (**http://hjs.geol.uib.no/TechCorner/ Random_Image_URL.html-ssi**)

Ron's JavaScript Resources   This site has a good metaindex of links and resources, updated on a reliable basis. (**http://w3.one.net/~ronlwzz/JavaScript.htm**)

Usenet News Group   This is an excellent forum for questions and answers. (**news:comp.lang.javascript**)

Voodoo's Introduction to JavaScript   The granddaddy of JavaScript tutorials, this site is still valid and useful. (**http://rummelplatz.uni-mannheim.de/~skoch/js/ index.htm**)

Index

ABOUT THE CD

Each JavaScript example from the book is represented on the accompanying CD-ROM. To access and browse the CD-ROM, you must load the file INDEX.HTM into your Web browser. This CD-ROM is ISO-9660 compatible, meaning that it will work on practically all CD-ROM drives. Although the files were created under Windows 95, you should have no difficulty reading the CD-ROM with Windows 3.1 or Unix-based Web browsers. If you use a Macintosh, the CD-ROM will work on your computer, but you will have to deal with files that do not have data forks.

Once you access the CD-ROM, you will see all the scripts arranged by chapter number and script example, as organized in the book.

Chapter 1
Function
More
Parent
Pop1
Pop2
Replace
Riddle
Select
Simp1
Simp2
Simp3
Window
Winopts

Chapter 2
Alert1
Alert2
Alert3
Confirm
Mouseovr
Name
Onload1
Reverse
Status
Timer
Usermsgs
Various
Ysjs

Chapter 3
1letter
Banner
Banner2
Barclock
Barfill
Bounce
Controls
Flash
Statusbt
Timer
Typewrit

Chapter 4
Advanced
Banner1
Banner2
Button
Button2
Feeder
Led
Messages
Random
Rotate
Teletype

Chapter 5
Calendar
Count+
Counter
Dortch
Duncooky

Persform
Validate
Visit

Chapter 6
Boojum
Directry
Local
Lyrsrch
Multi1
Multi2
Search2
Sitesrch
Swim

Chapter 7
2in1
Dropdown
Fancy
Hierarc
Menu
Remote
Rollover

Chapter 8
The scripts in Chapter 8 are intended for use on a Netscape server that is set up to run server-side scripts. You cannot run them on a Web browser.

WARNING: BEFORE OPENING THE DISC PACKAGE, CAREFULLY READ THE TERMS AND CONDITIONS OF THE FOLLOWING COPYRIGHT STATEMENT AND LIMITED CD-ROM WARRANTY.

Copyright Statement

This software is protected by both United States copyright law and international copyright treaty provision. Except as noted in the contents of the CD-ROM, you must treat this software just like a book. However, you may copy it into a computer to be used and you may make archival copies of the software for the sole purpose of backing up the software and protecting your investment from loss. By saying, "just like a book," The McGraw-Hill Companies, Inc. ("Osborne/McGraw-Hill") means, for example, that this software may be used by any number of people and may be freely moved from one computer location to another, so long as there is no possibility of its being used at one location or on one computer while it is being used at another. Just as a book cannot be read by two different people in two different places at the same time, neither can the software be used by two different people in two different places at the same time.

Limited Warranty

Osborne/McGraw-Hill warrants the physical compact disc enclosed herein to be free of defects in materials and workmanship for a period of sixty days from the purchase date. If the CD included in your book has defects in materials or workmanship, please call McGraw-Hill at 1-800-217-0059, 9am to 5pm, Monday through Friday, Eastern Standard Time, and McGraw-Hill will replace the defective disc.

The entire and exclusive liability and remedy for breach of this Limited Warranty shall be limited to replacement of the defective disc, and shall not include or extend to any claim for or right to cover any other damages, including but not limited to, loss of profit, data, or use of the software, or special incidental, or consequential damages or other similar claims, even if Osborne/McGraw-Hill has been specifically advised of the possibility of such damages. In no event will Osborne/McGraw-Hill's liability for any damages to you or any other person ever exceed the lower of the suggested list price or actual price paid for the license to use the software, regardless of any form of the claim.

OSBORNE/McGRAW-HILL SPECIFICALLY DISCLAIMS ALL OTHER WARRANTIES, EXPRESS OR IMPLIED, INCLUDING BUT NOT LIMITED TO, ANY IMPLIED WARRANTY OF MERCHANTABILITY OR FITNESS FOR A PARTICULAR PURPOSE. Specifically, Osborne/McGraw-Hill makes no representation or warranty that the software is fit for any particular purpose, and any implied warranty of merchantability is limited to the sixty-day duration of the Limited Warranty covering the physical disc only (and not the software), and is otherwise expressly and specifically disclaimed.

This limited warranty gives you specific legal rights; you may have others which may vary from state to state. Some states do not allow the exclusion of incidental or consequential damages, or the limitation on how long an implied warranty lasts, so some of the above may not apply to you.

This agreement constitutes the entire agreement between the parties relating to use of the Product. The terms of any purchase order shall have no effect on the terms of this Agreement. Failure of Osborne/McGraw-Hill to insist at any time on strict compliance with this Agreement shall not constitute a waiver of any rights under this Agreement. This Agreement shall be construed and governed in accordance with the laws of New York. If any provision of this Agreement is held to be contrary to law, that provision will be enforced to the maximum extent permissible, and the remaining provisions will remain in force and effect.

NO TECHNICAL SUPPORT IS PROVIDED WITH THIS CD-ROM.